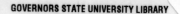

SUBSTANCE ABUSE

Pharmacologic, Developmental, and Clinical Perspectives

SUBSTANCE ABUSE

Pharmacologic, Developmental, and Clinical Perspectives

Second Edition

Edited by

Gerald Bennett, Ph.D., R.N.
Associate Professor and Chairman
Department of Mental Health Psychiatric Nursing
School of Nursing
Medical College of Georgia
Augusta, Georgia

Donna S. Woolf, Pharm.D., R. Ph.
Clinical Pharmacist
Peachford Hospital
Atlanta, Georgia

Delmar Publishers Inc.

NOTICE TO THE RE RC 564 .S836 1991

Cover illustration: Ron Young
Cover design: Nancy Gworek

Delmar Staff:
Executive Editor: Barbara E. Norwitz
Developmental Editor: Marjorie A. Bruce
Managing Editor: Susan Simpfenderfer
Project Editor: Mary P. Robinson
Production Coordinator: Sandra Woods
Design Supervisor: Susan C. Mathews
Design Coordinator: Karen Kunz Kemp

For information, write:
Delmar Publishers, Inc.
2 Computer Drive West, Box 15-015
Albany, NY 12212

Printed in the United States of America
Published simultaneously in Canada
by Nelson Canada
A Division of The Thomson Corporation

10 9 8 7 6 5 4 3 2 1

Library of Congress Cataloging-in-Publication Data

Substance abuse: pharmacologic, developmental, and clinical
    perspectives / edited by Gerald Bennett, Donna S. Woolf. — 2nd ed.
      p. cm.
    Includes bibliographical references.
    Includes index.
    ISBN 0-8273-4205-5
    1. Substance abuse. 2. Alcoholism. I. Bennett, Gerald, 1951-
      II. Woolf, Donna S.
    [DNLM: 1. Substance Abuse. WM 270 S9413]
RC564.S836   1991
616.86—dc20
DNLM/DLC
for Library of Congress   90-3985
                                            CIP

CONTRIBUTORS

James R. Allen, M.D., M.P.H.
Director, National AIDS Program Office
Office of the Assistant Secretary for Health
Department of Health and Human Services
Washington, DC

Gerald Bennett, Ph.D., R.N.
Associate Professor
Department of Mental Health-Psychiatric Nursing
School of Nursing
Medical College of Georgia
Augusta, Georgia

Mary Boyd, M.N., R.N.
Doctoral Student
School of Nursing
University of Virginia
Charlottesville, Virginia

Claudia Crenshaw, M.N., R.N., C.S.
Private Practice
Decatur, Georgia

Mary Ann Walsh Eells, Ed.D., R.N., C.S.
Associate Professor
School of Nursing
University of Maryland
Baltimore, Maryland

John M. Holbrook, Ph.D.
Professor
Department of Pharmaceutical Sciences
Mercer University School of Pharmacy
Atlanta, Georgia

Janet H. Lee, M.S.N., R.N.
Clinical Instructor
York Technical College
Ft. Mill, South Carolina

H. Horton McCurdy, Ph.D.
Research Toxicologist
Division of Forensic Sciences
Georgia Bureau of Investigation
Decatur, Georgia

Susan R. McKay, Ph.D., R.N.
Psychologist, Health Education and
Psychological Services
Laramie, Wyoming

Dennis F. Moore, Pharm.D., R.Ph.
Assistant Administrator, Woodhill
Asheville, North Carolina

MaryLou Scavnicky-Mylant, Ph.D., C.A.R.N./P.N.P.
Associate Professor
School of Nursing
University of Wyoming
Laramie, Wyoming

Ann Solari-Twadell, M.P.A., R.N.
Director of Congregational Health Partnership
Director of National Parish Nurse Resource Center
Park Ridge, Illinois

Eleanor Sullivan, Ph.D., R.N.
Dean, School of Nursing
University of Kansas
Kansas City, Kansas

Ann D. Sumners, Ph.D., R.N.
Associate Professor
University of North Carolina-Charlotte
Charlotte, North Carolina

Donna S. Woolf, Pharm.D., R.Ph.
Clinical Pharmacist
Peachford Hospital
Atlanta, Georgia

DEDICATION

To Sharon.

G.B.

To the Emory University Health Science Library and Bill,
for their unceasing support.

D.S.W.

FOREWORD

Although the abuse of alcohol and other drugs has existed for centuries, in recent years the magnitude of substance-related problems and addictive processes, as well as their health implications, have emerged as major social and health issues. Research of the past twenty years offers new insights into the nature of addiction and challenges our beliefs and practices in the therapeutic use of drugs as well as their potential to compromise mental health and the well-being of society. This volume, therefore, is a timely and significant contribution to the literature on mental health and the addictions.

The editors and contributing authors provide a broad scientific base of pharmacologic knowledge about common drugs of abuse, including nicotine. The dynamics of drug use, abuse, and addiction for the individual, family, and community are explored in a life cycle context, and patterns of dependence among special populations such as health professionals and the aged are presented. Although nursing actions are specifically highlighted, interventions by other health disciplines can be derived readily from theoretically sound principles. Prevention and immediate and long-term interventions have applicability for team approaches as well as care delivery by the individual practitioner. In fact, the importance and advantages of interdisciplinary collaboration in addressing the complexities of drug dependency are emphasized throughout.

Nurse contributors lend support to current efforts toward clear definitions of emerging roles for nurse generalists and specialists in relation to drug abuse and dependence. The imperative need for all practicing nurses to be aware of the scope and nature of drug and alcohol problems and prepared to identify these major public health concerns is demonstrated in approaches within the frames of maternal-child health, adult health, and gerontology. These chapters offer guidance for the beginning practitioner. In addition, described assessment techniques and strategies consistent with comprehensive nursing care extend intervention beyond health teaching and referral, toward the identification of more specialized, in-depth nursing skills central to effective treatment and long-term recovery. Efforts to formulate the specialty of addictions nursing are of particular relevance to national trends in prevention and treatment of the addictions and professional nursing.

Substance Abuse: Pharmacologic, Developmental, and Clinical Perspectives provides a new and comprehensive resource for the understanding of drugs of abuse, their action, patterns of use, and implications of their use for the health of the client throughout the life span. It calls our attention to an aspect of health care poorly understood and long neglected. Through the provision of new knowledge and the expansion and application of basic nursing skills to previously ill-defined approaches to client care, it will stimulate the beginning practitioner as well as the practicing nurse. For those seeking to specialize in addictions nursing, the book raises important questions and outlines the challenges ahead. Readers and the recipients of nursing care will benefit from the content, clinical expertise, and broad perspectives the authors and editors present in this volume.

Madeline A. Naegle, Ph.D., F.A.A.N.
Associate Professor, Division of Nursing
SEHNAP, New York University

PREFACE

We were pleased that nurses and other health professionals found the First Edition to be an engaging introduction to the substance abuse field and applicable to clinical practice. Substance abuse continues to have an enormous impact on society and health. The emergence of new issues as well as advances in research demanded a revision of the text. The Second Edition represents an effort to retain the format of the original book while updating and expanding into other critical areas such as AIDS, drug screening, children of alcoholics, addictive eating patterns, and the emerging speciality of addictions nursing.

We have chosen to emphasize pharmacology, developmental theory, and clinical practice. These perspectives promote a biopsychosocial view of substance abuse. The theme that runs throughout the book is that nurses and other health professionals need to be knowledgeable about the substances of abuse and be prepared to consider substance abuse a potential or existing health problem among all age groups and in all clinical settings.

We believe that alcohol and other drug abuse is best viewed in a broad sense and have used the term *substance abuse* to make this point. This term avoids the redundancy of "alcohol and drug abuse" and the common misinterpretation of "drug abuse" as referring to substances other than alcohol. Clearly, the widespread abuse of alcohol in our society is our largest substance abuse problem. Thus, the book devotes more emphasis to alcohol-related problems than to those related to other drugs.

We define *substance abuse* as a pattern of psychoactive substance use that involves hazards to health. Inherent in the term *abuse* are at least two values we recognize and accept. First, we believe it is possible to establish that consumption of certain substances, in sufficient quantities, poses hazards to health. Second, we hold that nurses and other health professionals have a responsibility to recognize these hazards despite social norms that may encourage psychoactive substance consumption.

The book is organized into three parts, each with a special perspective on substance abuse as a health problem. Part One focuses on what is known about the various substances of abuse. Part Two provides a review of substance abuse in society within the context of the human life span and developmental theory. Part Three turns to the recognition and treatment of substance abuse in general practice and within the substance abuse treatment setting.

Our aim is to present detailed findings about substance abuse to a broad audience, including nurses in practice, nursing students, nurse educators, and other health professionals in various stages of their careers. The study of substance abuse is an interdisciplinary field. Editorial collaboration and the selection of contributors for this volume were in part guided by our belief in the interdisciplinary approach to substance abuse prevention and treatment.

In addition, communication gaps among educators, clinicians who specialize in substance abuse, and practitioners in other specialities who often encounter substance abuse need to be bridged. We have selected contributors from these various backgrounds and propose that the combination of topics covered offers the reader a broad survey of substance abuse issues, with implications for practice in many clinical situations.

We thank all those who participated in writing and preparing the book for publication. We are grateful to the contributors for their willingness to review and edit their chapters a number of times so that a well-organized and consistent text could be developed. We acknowledge Cathy Pirtle's significant role as the revision coordinator and primary typist for the project. We also wish to thank Patty Dyches for typing several chapters. Lynette Jack reviewed some chapters, and we found her comments very helpful. Finally, we are thankful to our families and friends, without whose support this book could not have been written.

G.B.
D.S.W.

ACKNOWLEDGMENTS

Appreciation is expressed to the following professionals whose thorough reviews helped refine the final draft of the text.

Nellie F. Nelson, M.S.N., C.A.R.N.
Chair, Addictions Nursing Certification Board, and
National Nurses Society on Addictions, and
Nursing Faculty
Scottsdale Community College
Scottsdale, Arizona

Martha L. Kuhns, M.S.N., R.N., C.S.
School of Nursing
Duquesne University
Pittsburgh, Pennsylvania

Sandra H. Tweed, M.S., R.N.
Doctoral Candidate
University of Wisconsin–Madison
Madison, Wisconsin

CONTENTS

PART THREE
CLINICAL PRACTICE IN SUBSTANCE ABUSE TREATMENT

INDEX OF TABLES

PART ONE | SUBSTANCES OF ABUSE

THE AUTONOMIC AND CENTRAL NERVOUS SYSTEMS

John M. Holbrook

All chemical substances that have a potential for abuse produce their desirable (and often undesirable) effects by mechanisms involving the nervous system. To understand how abused substances produce their sought-after effects and why various modalities are used to treat their toxic manifestations, a basic knowledge of the structure and function of the nervous system is necessary. The following overview presents the major components of the nervous system and their functions. This information is not intended as a comprehensive review of neuroanatomy, but rather as a basis for understanding the drug-related material to be presented in later chapters in this text. Additional information may be obtained from the references and selected readings listed at the end of this chapter.

Anatomically, the nervous system is divided into two major components: the *central nervous system (CNS)* and the *peripheral nervous system.* The CNS, composed of the brain and spinal cord, is responsible for integrative functions related to both conscious and subconscious activities of the body. It is also ultimately responsible for the interpretation of, and reaction to, all information that the body receives from the environment. The peripheral nervous system is made up of nerve fibers that conduct information toward the CNS *(afferent fibers)* and nerve fibers that conduct directives from the CNS to all body areas *(efferent fibers).* Before undertaking a general discussion of the nervous system, a brief review of the basic unit of the nervous system, the *neuron,* and the mechanisms by which information is transferred throughout the nervous system is in order.

THE NEURON

The *neuron,* or *nerve cell,* is the base of all activities of the nervous system. Neurons differ from other body cells in two respects: *(1)* they can conduct information in the form of electrical impulses over long distances;

and *(2)* they relate to other nerve cells and innervated tissue in a highly specialized manner. The neuron consists of a cell body, an *axon,* which carries information away from the cell body, and one or more *dendrites,* which carry information toward the cell body. Some axons are surrounded by a layer of fatty tissue called a *myelin sheath,* which develops within the nervous system over a period of years and serves as a protective coating.

The ability of the neuron to transmit information from one site to another is a function of its electrical transmission capability and its capacity to synthesize, store, and release highly specific chemicals *(neurotransmitters)* from nerve endings. The site where two nerve endings meet or where a nerve meets the tissue that it innervates is a small gap that is termed the *synapse,* or *synaptic cleft.* For electrical impulses to cross a synapse, a neurotransmitter is released from one nerve ending to travel across the synapse and stimulate receptors on an adjacent nerve or tissue (see Fig. 1.1).

THE PERIPHERAL NERVOUS SYSTEM

The *peripheral nervous system* consists of all the nerve fibers that conduct information to and from the CNS and that lie outside the brain and spinal cord. Peripheral afferent fibers are involved with sensations such as pain, temperature, and touch, whereas peripheral efferent fibers are involved with the control of specific body functions. Efferent fibers are divided into two categories: *(1) somatic fibers,* which control the function of skeletal muscle, and *(2) autonomic fibers,* which control the activities of smooth muscle, cardiac muscle, and glands of excretion.

Somatic nerve fibers leave the spinal cord at various levels, depending on the location of the innervated skeletal muscle, and continue as an uninterrupted unit from their site of origin *(motor neuron)* to skeletal

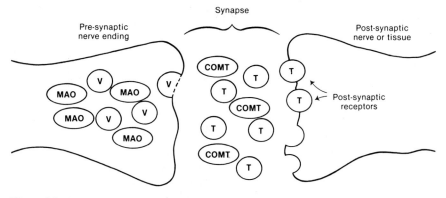

Figure 1.1
*Schematic of the proposed relationship between the nerve ending and a second nerve fiber or innervated tissue. **V** = storage vesicles for neurotransmitters; **MAO** = monoamine oxidase; **COMT** = catechol-o-methyltransferase; **T** = neurotransmitter*

muscle tissue. The site at which the somatic fiber meets the skeletal muscle is termed the *neuromuscular junction (NMJ)*. The neurotransmitter at the NMJ is acetylcholine (Ach).

Autonomic efferent fibers control the automatic or subconscious functioning of smooth and cardiac muscle and exocrine glands. These fibers are responsible for activities such as the maintenance of tone in the gastrointestinal tract and blood vessels, regulation of heart rate, and release of substances such as saliva, respiratory secretions, and gastric acid. Autonomic fiber tracts actually consist of two separate fibers. The first fiber *(presynaptic fiber)* originates inside the spinal cord and terminates at a synapse somewhere in the periphery. The second fiber *(postsynaptic fiber)* originates at the synapse and terminates at the innervated tissue. In most instances, the synapses of a number of fibers are grouped together and termed a *ganglion*. In such cases, the presynaptic and postsynaptic fibers are referred to as *preganglionic* and *postganglionic fibers,* respectively. The site at which the postganglionic fiber synapses with the innervated tissue is termed the *neuroeffector junction (NEJ)*.

Autonomic fibers are categorized by two methods. The first and older method of classification is based on the sites at which preganglionic fibers leave the CNS. Nerves that exit from the thoracic and lumbar levels of the spinal cord are termed *sympathetic,* whereas those that exit from the sacral level of the spinal cord and cranium are termed *parasympathetic.*

The second method of classification is based on the neurotransmitter released at the NEJ by the nerve fiber. Nerves that release Ach are termed *cholinergic,* whereas those that release norepinephrine (NE) are termed *adrenergic.* In general, the term *sympathetic* is interchangeable with adrenergic and the term *parasympathetic* is interchangeable with cholinergic. Cholinergic and adrenergic are usually the preferred terms when discussing drug effects on autonomic function because they designate the specific neurotransmitters affected by the drugs.

Within the *autonomic nervous system (ANS),* receptor sites for Ach and NE have a very specific nomenclature based on their location and function. Cholinergic receptor sites are found in the ganglionic synapses of both the sympathetic and parasympathetic nervous system. They are also found at the NEJ of parasympathetic fibers. Cholinergic receptor sites are categorized as being either *muscarinic* or *nicotinic,* based on whether they respond to the alkaloids muscarine or nicotine, respectively. Muscarinic receptors are found at the parasympathetic NEJ. Nicotinic receptors are found at all autonomic ganglia and at the somatic NMJ.

Adrenergic receptor sites in the ANS are found only at the sympathetic NEJ. Adrenergic receptors are divided into three categories: *alpha, beta$_1$,* and *beta$_2$.* In general, stimulation of the alpha-adrenergic receptor site causes an increase in activity of the innervated tissue. Alpha receptors are found primarily in arterioles and therefore are important in the maintenance of blood pressure. Stimulation of alpha receptors by NE leads to arteriolar constriction, which increases blood pressure. Beta$_1$ receptors are found only in cardiac tissue. Stimulation of these receptors leads to an increase in heart rate. Beta$_2$ receptors are found at various sites such as in bronchial smooth muscle and in blood vessels of skeletal muscle. Stimulation of beta$_2$ receptors leads to relaxation of the innervated tissue, that is, stimulation of beta$_2$ receptors in bronchial smooth muscle produces relaxation and increases the ability to inhale air.

The *parasympathetic nervous system* controls subconscious activity during periods of relaxation. Under parasympathetic control, heart rate is decreased as are most other body functions; however, gastrointestinal activity is increased to facilitate the digestion of food. The sympathetic nervous system controls the body during periods of activity. Following stimulation of adrenergic receptors, heart rate and blood pressure increase, blood flow to skeletal muscle is increased, air intake is facilitated, and parasympathetic functions are depressed. Activation of sympathetic functions has been termed the *fight or flight mechanism* because it prepares the body for a high level of activity. *Epinephrine,* another neurotransmitter, plays a key role in the stimulation of adrenergic receptors for vigorous activity. Epinephrine is released during periods of stress from the adrenal gland and is transported by the circulatory system throughout the body (including the CNS) to increase adrenergic activity.

THE CENTRAL NERVOUS SYSTEM

The CNS serves as the control center for all body functions at both the conscious and subconscious levels. Thus, all information perceived by the body is ultimately transmitted to the CNS for interpretation, all body functions are integrated within the CNS, and all activities of the body are controlled from the CNS.

The CNS consists of the *spinal cord* and the *brain.* The spinal cord is a collection of afferent and efferent fibers that are surrounded and protected by the spine. Within the spinal cord, nerves with similar functions or nerves that originate or terminate in the same sites are found in tracts. The spinal cord also contains *nuclei,* which are functionally the same as autonomic ganglia. The human brain is the site of control of body function; it also has the capability to think, reason, originate and display emotion, and interact with a constantly chang-

ing environment. The brain is composed of a number of discrete areas, some of which function relatively independently *(structures)* and some of which function in an integrated fashion with other brain areas *(systems).* For the purposes of this overview, the brain structures will be discussed first, followed by a brief review of the systems.

Brain Structures

The primary structures of the brain include the *cerebral cortex, thalamus, hypothalamus, medulla,* and *pons.* The primary systems are the *limbic system, extrapyramidal system,* and *reticular activating system.* Some functional overlap exists between the brain structures and the brain systems. This overlap will be considered in the discussion of the systems.

The cerebral cortex is a thin layer of cells covering the outside of the brain hemispheres. The cortex is considered to be the seat of conscious activity and behavior control. It is involved with the ability to think, reason, learn, and remember, and serves as the highest level of integration for all body functions. The cortex is also involved with the primary control of skeletal muscle function and the interpretation of sensations. It is divided into four areas or *lobes,* each of which is involved in specific functions. The *frontal lobe* is involved in pyramidal skeletal muscle control, abstract thought, and some emotional responding. The *temporal lobe* is involved in the interpretation of auditory stimulation and some emotional responses. The *occipital lobe* is involved in visual interpretation, and the *parietal lobe* is involved in interpretations of sensations, orientation to time and space, and language discrimination. The primary neurotransmitter of the cortex appears to be NE, which will be discussed more fully in a later section of this chapter.

The cortex is the area of the brain most sensitive to the actions of many drugs. Nonspecific depressants such as the barbiturates produce sedation, ataxia, and slurred speech because of their cortical effects. Stimulants such as amphetamine and cocaine produce arousal by affecting cortical function either by a direct action on cortical neurons or by stimulation of fiber tracts that affect cortical function.

Located within the cerebral hemispheres are a number of structures involved with many diverse functions. Figure 1.2 illustrates these structures and their spatial arrangement.

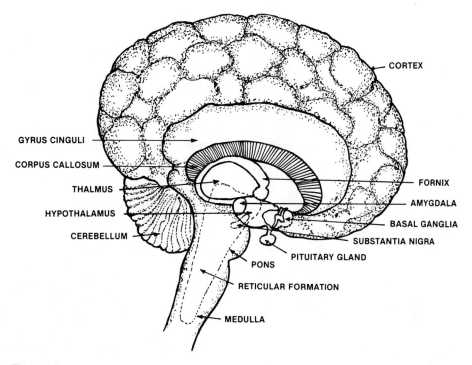

Figure 1.2
Schematic of the relationship among structures of the brain.

The thalamus, epithalamus, subthalamus, and hypothalamus are located in the area termed the *midbrain.* The thalamus is composed of a number of nuclei that act as relay stations for information passing between the cortex and other brain areas and peripheral sites. The epithalamus contains some nuclei involved with olfactory sensations and the *pineal gland,* which is involved with biochemical responses to light, circadian rhythms, and hormonal control of sexual development. The subthalamus is associated with the integration of some extrapyramidal system functions and contains fiber tracts connecting other areas of the midbrain. Although many drugs may affect the function of these structures nonspecifically, the opioid analgesics appear to produce at least part of their analgesic activity by blocking the transmission of pain impulses between the thalamus and the sensory cortex.

The hypothalamus is made up of a large mass of nuclei and serves a number of diverse functions. It is the highest level of integration for the ANS and serves as the output system for emotion generated by the limbic system. It regulates endocrine gland function by producing releasing factors that control the release of hormones from the pituitary gland, thus maintaining various homeostatic processes such as fluid volume, body temperature, and blood pressure. It is also involved in transmitting to the thalamus impulses concerned with cortical arousal.

Drugs that depress hypothalamic function usually do so nonspecifically and in a dose-dependent fashion. Such drugs include neuroleptic agents such as Thorazine and Mellaril, barbiturates, and opioid analgesics.

The medulla and pons are structures lying below the midbrain in the area termed the *brain stem.* The medulla is an extension of the spinal cord and resembles the cord in that it is composed primarily of fiber tracts. In addition, the medulla plays a very important role in the control of automatic functions. The medulla is chiefly responsible for the regulation of respiration *(respiratory center),* blood vessel tone *(vasomotor center),* heart rate, and gastrointestinal motility and tone. It also contains the *chemoreceptor trigger zone (CTZ)*, which elicits vomiting when stimulated by many chemicals.

The pons lies above the medulla and also serves a regulatory function. The *raphe nuclei* of the pons are involved in sleep patterns, especially slow-wave, or nondream, sleep (SWS). Many of the fiber tracts that pass through the medulla also pass through the pons.

Generally, the brain stem structures are least sensitive to the effects of drugs; however, in overdose situations, drugs that depress nervous system function can depress brain stem function and produce death due to respiratory depression or cardiovascular collapse.

Brain Systems

Brain systems are groups of structures that function interdependently to provide or control specialized activities. These systems make use of the structures previously mentioned as well as other, smaller structures whose functions are not as well understood.

The limbic system, often considered the seat of emotion (Swonger & Constantine, 1983), is composed of a number of structures and interconnecting fiber tracts. This system is also termed the *rhinencephalon,* or *"nose brain,"* because of its relationship with olfaction. Some of the structures of the limbic system are the *amygdaloid complex, hippocampus, septal area, limbic midbrain,* and a number of *fiber tracts* connecting these structures to each other and to other sites such as the hypothalamus, anterior thalamus, mamillary bodies, and frontal cortex. Together, these structures form a system that has the ability to originate emotion and display that emotion, primarily through the ANS (Akert & Hummel, 1968).

The amygdaloid complex and hippocampus are nuclear masses in the lower tip of the temporal lobes of the cortex. The amygdaloid complex is associated with the sense of smell and with behaviors such as fear, aggressiveness, learning, and discrimination. The hippocampus is associated with behavioral arousal. It has been proposed that the hippocampus serves to regulate response inhibition *(discrimination)* and is involved in both short- and long-term memory (Swonger & Constantine, 1983).

The septal area has been called the "pleasure area of the brain" because its stimulation in humans or animals is very rewarding. It is connected to other limbic association sites such as the hypothalamus, hippocampus, amygdala, reticular formation, and thalamus. The septal area controls some emotional behaviors such as aggressiveness and "startle" responses.

The limbic midbrain is an area near the hypothalamus connected by fiber tracts to other limbic structures and to the reticular formation. It is apparently involved with short-term memory and the ability to respond emotionally to certain stimuli. The limbic structures are interconnected by fiber tracts such as the *fornix* and *medial forebrain bundle (MFB)*. The fornix originates in the hippocampus and transmits information to the hypothalamus and brain stem.

The MFB is considered the major pathway associated with reward (pleasure). It is an ascending pathway that uses NE as its neurotransmitter. Nerve tracts that use serotonin are found adjacent to the MFB and terminate in many areas of the limbic system and other structures. The serotonin-containing fibers balance the inhibitory activity of the limbic system with the excitatory activity of the reticular formation.

The neurotransmitters involved with the limbic system are *dopamine (DA), Ach, NE,* and *serotonin*. Although the roles of these neurotransmitters in normal emotional functioning has not been completely elucidated, decreased levels of both NE and serotonin have been associated with the occurrence of endogenous depression (Maas, 1975). An increased sensitivity of DA receptors or excessive synthesis or release of DA has been associated with the occurrence of schizophrenia (Van Kammen, 1977). Ach has been proposed as the neurotransmitter that mediates punishment (Stein, 1971). It is probable that a precise balance among these neurotransmitters throughout the limbic system rather than precise concentrations of any one of them accounts for normal emotional functioning.

The extrapyramidal system is a complex, highly interconnected system, which, along with the *pyramidal system,* is responsible for the control of skeletal muscle function. The pyramidal system is a fiber tract originating in the motor cortex, descending through the midbrain and brain stem, and terminating at motor neurons in the spinal cord. A second nerve originates at the motor neuron and continues (as a somatic efferent fiber) to the NMJ. As the pyramidal fibers descend through the brain, they give off collateral fibers that relay information to various extrapyramidal structures that modify and refine skeletal muscle movements.

The primary structures associated with extrapyramidal function are the *corpus striatum, substantia nigra, red nucleus, vestibular system,* and *cerebellum.*

In addition to these structures, a diffuse group of nuclei, the *brain stem reticular formation,* is involved in the flow of impulses from the extrapyramidal system into the spinal cord.

The corpus striatum, substantia nigra, and red nucleus act in an integrated fashion to regulate muscle tone for discrete muscle movement and to control body position so that such movement can occur. The primary neurotransmitters involved with these structures are DA, found in high concentration in the substantia nigra, and Ach, which is found primarily in the corpus striatum. Alteration of the levels of either of these neurotransmitters results in deficits of normal muscle function. For example, blockade of DA receptors in the substantia nigra by neuroleptics results in a syndrome characterized by increased skeletal muscle tone (rigidity), tremor, and loss of associated movements.

The two other functional components of the extrapyramidal system are the *vestibular system* and the *cerebellum.* The vestibular system (inner ear) is included in the extrapryamidal system because of its effects on posture and reflexes associated with balance. The vestibular system contains receptors that can detect position of the head, acceleration, and pull of gravity. The output of the vestibular system goes to the spinal cord where it aids in maintaining body posture and muscle tone of sufficient strength to offset the pull of gravity and to the cerebellum where its information is integrated with information from other brain areas.

The cerebellum, which is located at the base of the brain behind the pons, is involved with the control of muscle tone and in servomechanistic activities requiring hand-to-eye coordination. The cerebellum receives input from the motor cortex, corpus striatum, reticular formation, and vestibular system and, peripherally, from receptors in skeletal muscle and tendons that gauge tone. The output of the cerebellum goes either to the motor cortex or to the reticular formation. The cerebellum thus serves as a modulator of intentional and subconscious motor activity. Simply stated, the cerebellum receives the input from the motor cortex (which indicates the muscle function to be performed) and the input from other extrapyramidal areas (which indicates the current position and condition of muscle), and makes whatever changes are necessary so that the intended function can be performed. This activity obviously occurs very rapidly since there is time for the cerebellum to affect both motor cortex and skeletal muscle peripherally.

The *reticular activating system (RAS)* is another brain system whose function can be significantly altered by substance abuse. The RAS is a portion of a larger system, the *reticular formation (RF),* a diffuse collection of nuclei scattered from the lower medulla to midthalamus. Although the function of all of the RF nuclei is not known, some of them, as previously mentioned, are involved in relaying information from the extrapyramidal system to the spinal cord. Other nuclei, some of which comprise the RAS, are involved with sensory functions.

Nuclei that comprise the RAS are found in two areas, the *mesencephalon* and the *thalamus.* The mesencephalic or ascending RAS is believed to be responsible for the normal waking state of the brain and for generalized activation of the cortex. The *thalamic RAS,* or *diffuse thalamic system (DTS),* also alerts the cortex but is more discrete and can activate specific cortical areas rather than the entire cortex.

In addition to cortical stimulation, the RAS also acts as a filtering system to decrease the influence of extraneous cortical stimuli and increase the ability to concentrate. The mechanism by which this filtering process is accomplished is unknown, but it is probable that the DTS is involved since this portion of the RAS has the ability to discretely stimulate cortical sites.

Two clinical syndromes are associated with malfunction of the RAS. *Narcolepsy,* characterized by an inability to stay awake, occurs due to a decreased ability of the RAS to stimulate the cortex. The second syndrome, *hyperkinesis,* is seen in children and is characterized by a short attention span, hyperactivity, and inability to concentrate. Hyperkinesis occurs due to a decrease in the function of the filtering portion of the RAS. Interestingly, both narcolepsy and hyperkinesis in children respond to treatment with CNS stimulants.

Another important function of the RAS involves the control of the *sleep-wake cycle.* At one time it was thought that sleeping was simply a passive process made possible by a lack of stimulation of the cortex by the RAS. It is now known that sleep can be induced by stimulation of specific brain areas and that destruction of these areas produces insomnia. Thus, the sleep-wake cycle may be considered an active process regulated by specific brain areas.

The time spent in sleep is divided into two states, based on electroencephalographic (EEG) patterns of brain electrical activity. These states are termed *desynchronized* and *synchronized (slow-wave)*. Synchronized sleep is further subdivided into four stages.

Most sleep time (75%–80%) is spent in SWS (deep sleep) characterized by slow, synchronized EEG waves. The amount of time spent in SWS is increased following physical exertion, and it is probable that this sleep state is essential for overcoming fatigue. Increasing brain serotonin levels will produce an increase in SWS time.

The remainder of sleep time (20%–25%) is spent in a desynchronized sleep state characterized by rapid changes in the EEG pattern. Desynchronized sleep is also termed *rapid eye movement (REM) sleep* because while in this state the eyes dart back and forth as if following a rapidly moving object. REM sleep is also characterized by skeletal muscle relaxation and is considered essential for maintenance of a normal emotional state. When REM sleep is decreased due to the action of drugs such as barbiturates and antidepressants, or loss of total sleep time, abnormal behavior and irregular emotional states may occur. Symptoms of REM sleep deprivation may include irritability, aggression, shortened attention span, hallucinations, and psychotic episodes.

When levels of NE, the neurotransmitter probably involved with REM sleep, are increased, REM sleep time is decreased, and vice versa. Thus, it appears that when NE levels are low and cortical activation is minimal, REM sleep can occur. Drugs that increase NE levels, such as amphetamine, decrease REM sleep time. Chronic use of such agents could result in significant REM sleep deprivation and serious behavioral changes. Drugs that increase serotonin levels, such as antidepressants, could possibly decrease REM sleep time by increasing the total amount of SWS.

NEUROTRANSMITTERS

Within the nervous system, information is transferred from one site to another by the combined activities of *electrical impulses (action potentials)* and *neurotransmitters*. Action potentials are generated following the combining of a neurotransmitter with a specific receptor site. Once generated, the action potential is capable of transmitting information over long segments of nerve fibers as well as causing the release of neurotransmitters. Neurotransmitters are endogenously synthesized chemicals serving as messengers between two or more

nerve fibers or between a nerve fiber and the tissue innervated by that nerve fiber. Figure 1.1 diagrammatically represents the relationship between the nerve terminal and an innervated tissue. When an action potential reaches the nerve terminal, a neurotransmitter is released into the synapse. The neurotransmitter then moves across the synapse to combine chemically with specific receptor sites. The result of the reaction between the neurotransmitter and its receptors may be either *(1)* stimulation or inhibition of a specific function such as smooth muscle movement or salivation or *(2)* propagation of the action potential along a second nerve fiber. Once the function of the neurotransmitter has been completed, the transmitter's activity is terminated by enzymatic destruction or by reuptake into the nerve terminal from which it was released or both.

The endogenous substances currently categorized as neurotransmitters are Ach, DA, serotonin, NE, epinephrine, gamma-aminobutyric acid (GABA), glycine, and glutamic acid. It is certain that other endogenous substances will be included within this category as research continues.

Most drugs that affect the nervous system produce their actions by modification of the functions of neurotransmitters. Drugs may act by stimulating or inhibiting the synthesis or release of neurotransmitters, by accelerating or decreasing the rate at which the action of the neurotransmitter is terminated, by mimicking the action of the neurotransmitter at its receptor site, or by preventing the combining of the neurotransmitter with its receptor site. Virtually all abused substances produce their actions by altering neurotransmitter function within the CNS. The following information deals with current views concerning the location and functions of neurotransmitters within the nervous system.

Acetylcholine

Ach is considered to be the most widely distributed neurotransmitter, being found in both the peripheral and central nervous systems. It is synthesized from acetyl coenzyme A and choline by the enzyme choline acetylase and is stored in vesicles in the nerve terminal until released into the synapse. Once in the synapse, Ach chemically combines with receptors to produce the desired reaction and is subsequently destroyed by the enzyme acetylcholinesterase. The destruction of Ach results in the liberation of choline, which is taken back into the nerve ending by an active uptake process and is reused in the synthesis of new Ach.

Ach is found in the peripheral nervous system as the transmitter in autonomic ganglia, the parasympathetic NEJ, and the somatic NMJ. In the CNS, Ach is found in a number of sites in the brain stem, midbrain, cortical areas, and in the spinal cord.

In the brain stem, Ach is found in the RF where it is involved in control of the level of cortical arousal. In one area Ach appears to depress the ascending RAS, whereas in another area it appears to increase arousal. Ach is also thought to be the transmitter for some cells of the respiratory center of the medulla.

In the midbrain, Ach is found in the thalamus in sensory relay nuclei and the nuclei of the DTS. Ach is also found in the hypothalamus, where it is involved in the release of antidiuretic hormone (ADH) and adrenocorticotropic hormone (ACTH) and in the control of body temperature. In addition, it is found in the limbic system where it plays a role in the elaboration of emotion and in the corpus striatum where it is involved in the control of fine skeletal muscle movement. In the cortex, Ach serves as the neurotransmitter in the ascending cortical arousal mechanism.

The behavioral effects of Ach have been determined by using drugs, such as atropine, that prevent Ach from combining with its receptor sites in the CNS. When cholinergic receptor sites are blocked, the behavioral effects elicited include memory impairment, slurred speech, drowsiness, hallucinations, and confused behavior. These central effects are often collectively termed *atropine psychosis.*

Norepinephrine

NE is also found in both the peripheral and central nervous systems. NE is synthesized in a three-step reaction that uses the amino acid L-tyrosine as the starting chemical, L-tyrosine is converted to dihydroxyphenylalanine (DOPA) by the enzyme tyrosine hydroxylase. DOPA is converted to DA by the enzyme 1-aromatic acid decarboxylase (DOPA decarboxylase) and DA is then converted to NE by the enzyme dopamine-β-hydroxylase.

The release of NE stored in nerve terminals depends on the occurrence of an action potential and the movement of calcium ions into the nerve ending when the action potential arrives at the nerve terminal.

NE activity is terminated by two mechanisms, enzymatic degradation and reuptake into the nerve terminal from which it was released. Of these two mechanisms, reuptake is primarily responsible for the termination of NE effects.

Two enzymes, *monoamine oxidase (MAO)* and *catechol-O-methyl transferase (COMT),* are involved in the destruction of NE. MAO is a nonspecific enzyme found within the nerve terminal, whereas COMT is a more specific enzyme found in the synapse.

The reuptake of NE into the nerve terminal occurs due to an active transport process that will also transport compounds with structures similar to NE, such as DA and serotonin.

NE is found in the peripheral nervous system only at the adrenergic NEJ of the ANS. In the CNS, NE is found in localized sites, such as a number of ascending pathways which originate in the brain stem, and travels upward to the cortex and cerebellum. NE is also found in cells within the RF and in fiber tracts descending from the brain stem into the spinal cord.

Functionally, NE is involved in the control of mood, in cortical arousal, and in the perception of pleasurable emotions.

Dopamine

DA has been thought of as a transmitter for only the past 20 years. As a precursor of NE, its synthesis is the same as that previously described. Its storage, release, and termination of action are also closely related to those described for NE.

DA is found in the peripheral nervous system in renal vascular beds where its action results in vasodilatation. In the CNS, DA is found in a pathway linking the substantia nigra with the corpus striatium *(nigrostriatal pathway).* At this site, DA is involved in the control of fine skeletal muscle movement. It is also the transmitter in a fiber tract connecting the hypothalamus with the pituitary gland and is involved in the secretion of the posterior pituitary hormones. A third site at which DA is a neurotransmitter is the limbic system where it is associated with the control of emotions.

In one aspect, dopaminergic neuronal pathways appear unique. They are apparently associated with a compensatory mechanism activated only when the normal functioning of the pathway is altered. When the DA receptor is blocked by a drug, an increase in the release of DA from the nerve terminal occurs. This mechanism is thought by some to be related to the development of physical dependence on opioid analgesics.

DA is also one of the neurotransmitters involved in the regulation of aggressive behavior. When DA receptors are excessively stimulated, behaviors such as aggression, stereotypy, and decreased physical activity occur.

Serotonin

Serotonin (5-hydroxytryptamine; 5-HT) is a neurotransmitter in humans; it is also found widely in nature. Fruits such as the pineapple and banana contain large amounts of 5-HT. In the human, 98%–99% of the 5-HT is found outside the nervous system (in the gastrointestinal tract and platelets) and only 1%–2% in the CNS.

5-HT is synthesized in a two-step process. The starting product is the essential amino acid tryptophan. Tryptophan is converted to 5-hydroxytryptophan by the enzyme tryptophan-5-hydroxylase. 5-hydroxytryptophan is then converted to 5-HT by the enzyme 1-aromatic amino acid decarboxylase.

The storage, release, and termination of action of 5-HT is the same as described for NE and DA with the exception that 5-HT is metabolized only by MAO. The reuptake process for 5-HT appears to be identical to that of DA and NE and of equal importance in its termination of action.

In the CNS, 5-HT is found in a small number of discrete pathways originating in the area of the limbic system. Some of these fiber tracts carry information to other areas of the limbic system, such as the hippocampus and amygdala. Other tracts ascend to the cortex or descend into the spinal cord.

The behavioral effects of 5-HT are not as yet clearly defined. When brain levels of 5-HT are increased, sedation and lethargy occur. When 5-HT levels are decreased, insomnia occurs. There is now considerable evidence that 5-HT is also involved in the control of mood, especially in the prevention of depression. Several of the antidepressant agents currently in use appear to produce their antidepressant effects by increasing brain 5-HT levels (Maas, 1975).

GABA, Glutamic Acid, Glycine, and Aspartate

GABA, glutamic acid, glycine, and *aspartate* are amino acids that appear to play neurotransmitter roles in the CNS. It has been more difficult to qualify these agents as neurotransmitters than some of the previously mentioned endogenous substances because they are found throughout the nervous system as precursors for protein synthesis. A growing body of evidence, however, indicates that these amino acids play a significant role in neurotransmitters within the CNS.

GABA is considered the most important inhibitory transmitter in the CNS. It is found throughout the brain and spinal cord. Glutamic acid and aspartate are found in high concentrations in the brain and have powerful excitatory effects on nerves throughout the CNS. Glycine serves as an inhibitory transmitter in the spinal cord, lower brain stem, and possibly the retina.

Of these four amino acids, the neurotransmitter functions of GABA have received the most scrutiny. Although GABA does not appear to play a major role in the control of emotional behavior, its actions have been linked to the control of skeletal muscle functions mediated through the cerebellum. GABA also mediates local neuronal inhibition in both lower brain areas, the cortex and spinal cord.

The effects of benzodiazepines and barbiturates as sedative-hypnotics are thought to be mediated by GABA-ergic mechanisms. Both benzodiazepines and barbiturates facilitate the inhibitory actions of GABA but by different mechanisms. Specific benzodiazepine receptors have been found throughout the CNS, always directly associated with GABA receptors. Benzodiazepines intensify the inhibitory effects of GABA without directly affecting GABA receptors or associated chloride channels. Barbiturates also enhance the effects of GABA, but do so by prolonging rather than intensifying the action of GABA (Trevor & Way, 1987).

Both glutamic acid and aspartate act as excitatory neurotransmitters when applied directly to most neurons in the CNS. Although in most systems studied their actions appear to be nonspecific, these two amino acids have highly selective reuptake systems, which makes them likely neurotransmitters (Cooper, Bloom, & Roth, 1986).

Glycine, an apparent inhibitory neurotransmitter, has been found in spinal cord neurons in high concentrations. It is found in nerve endings distinct from those in which GABA is found. When glycine is applied to spinal cord nerve endings, it decreases the excitability of motor neurons and interneurons; however, when applied to cortical neurons, it does not decrease their excitability. It has yet to be shown conclusively that glycine serves as a discrete inhibitory transmitter because there is no direct confirmation that glycine is the main substance contained in the nerve terminals of interneurons connected to motor neurons in the spinal cord.

Other Neurotransmitters

One of the most exciting areas of research today involves the search for new neurotransmitters and the determination of the effects of drugs on the actions of these substances. Among the newer proposed transmitters are the *cyclic nucleotides, prostaglandins, histamine,* and *substance P.*

The cyclic nucleotides such as cyclic AMP (adenosine 3'-5'-monophosphate) have been established as the mediators of a number of peripheral hormonal effects. They are often termed *second messengers* because they appear to ''translate'' the presence of hormones into specific cellular effects.

The role of cyclic AMP has been studied more extensively than that of cyclic guanosine monophosphate (GMP). Although several neurotransmitters such as DA, NE, 5-HT, and histamine affect cyclic AMP levels, only Ach increases levels of cyclic GMP.

Cyclic AMP is found in large concentrations in the CNS and is a likely neurotransmitter. It is produced from adenosine triphosphate by the enzyme adenyl cyclase and is inactivated by the enzyme phosphodiesterase. The activity of adenyl cyclase is increased by several neurotransmitters including NE, DA, 5-HT, and histamine. This stimulation of adenyl cyclase results in an increase in levels of cyclic AMP. The levels of cyclic AMP can also be increased by blocking its inactivation by phosphodiesterase. The inactivation of cyclic AMP can be blocked by drugs such as caffeine.

The role of cyclic AMP as a second messenger has been studied in the cortex, midbrain, cerebellum, and cervical ganglion. In the cortex, NE, DA, 5-HT, and histamine all elevate cyclic AMP levels by stimulation of adenyl cyclase. In the midbrain (caudate nucleus) and superior cervical ganglion, DA elevates cyclic AMP levels. In the cerebellum, cyclic AMP appears to

mediate the inhibitory effects of NE on pathways involved in skeletal muscle coordination.

It appears likely that many of the effects attributed to drugs are a function of their actions on cyclic AMP. For example, the hallucinatory drugs such as lysergic acid diethylamide (LSD) produce increased cyclic AMP levels; antianxiety drugs increase cyclic AMP levels by antagonizing phosphodiesterase activity; and lithium inhibits the activity of adenyl cyclase, thus decreasing levels of cyclic AMP.

Prostaglandins are long-chain fatty acids (lipids) derived from prostanoic acid. They are found throughout the nervous system and in almost all other areas of the body. They modulate activity of the sympathetic nervous system by altering both the release of NE and the sensitivity of the adrenergic receptor site. The CNS is capable of synthesizing some prostaglandins but appears to store them only to a limited extent.

Prostaglandins do not appear to perform as typical neurotransmitters of the CNS. Their role is thought to be related to their actions on cyclic AMP synthesis and metabolism. In various brain sites, the prostaglandins may either stimulate or inhibit the synthesis or the metabolism of cyclic AMP. In the CNS, it is possible that the prostaglandins act as inhibitors to the increase in cyclic AMP levels produced by NE, thus serving as modulators of NE activity in key CNS neuronal pathways.

Documentation of histamine as a neurotransmitter in the CNS has been difficult since it is found in abundance in mast cells. Some evidence indicates that it is found in certain nuclei in the hypothalamus and in selected nerve terminals in high concentrations. At present, no specific CNS histamine receptors have been characterized, and no specific reuptake mechanism has been determined.

Histamine is found in high concentration in the hypothalamus and RF. In neurons at these sites, histamine increases cyclic AMP levels by stimulation of adenyl cyclase. The effects of histamine at these sites appears to be inhibitory.

The peptide known as substance P was first detected almost 50 years ago, but little is known about this potential neurotransmitter. It is found in the gastrointestinal tract and the nervous system in all peripheral nerves and ganglia that have been studied. In the CNS, the highest concentration of substance P is found in the substantia nigra, with smaller concentrations in the thalamus, hypothalamus, and caudate nucleus.

Research concerning the role of substance P as a neurotransmitter has been greatly hampered due to problems with purification; however, recently the amino acid sequence has been determined, and the compound has been synthesized and studied in various brain areas. Although it has been determined that this substance is extremely potent in depolarizing cell membranes, further research is needed to determine the precise role of this endogenous substance in CNS neurotransmission.

SUMMARY

Although the peripheral nervous system actions of some drugs of abuse are important as side effects, most desired and undesired actions of the drugs of abuse are a result of the drugs' actions on the CNS. An understanding of the functions of brain structures and systems is essential if the complex array of symptoms seen in the substance abuser is to be unraveled. Because this subject is highly technical, the reader is referred not only to a reference list, but to an additional readings list for selected overviews of certain subjects.

REFERENCES

Akert, K., & Hummel, P. (1968). *The limbic system anatomy and physiology.* Nutley, NJ: Roche Laboratories.

Cooper, J.R., Bloom, F.E., & Roth, R.H. (1986). *The biochemical basis of neuropharmacology* (pp. 124–172). New York: Oxford University Press.

Maas, J. W. (1975). Biogenic amines and depression. *Archives of General Psychiatry, 32,* 1357–1361.

Stein, L. (1971). Neurochemistry of reward and punishment: Some implications for the etiology of schizophrenia. *Journal of Psychiatric Research, 8,* 345–361.

Swonger, A. K., & Constantine, L. L. (1983). *Drugs and therapy* (pp. 239–251). Boston: Little, Brown.

Trevor, A. J., & Way, W. L. (1987). Sedative-Hypnotics. In B. G. Katzung (Ed.), *Basic and clinical pharmacology* (pp. 241–253). Norwalk, CT: Appleton & Lange.

Van Kammen, D. P. (1977). Gamma-aminobutyric acid (GABA) and the dopamine hypothesis of schizophrenia. *American Journal of Psychiatry, 134,* 138–143.

ADDITIONAL READINGS

Chusid, J. G. (1985). *Correlative neuroanatomy and functional neurology.* Los Altos, CA: Lange.

Gilman, S., & Winans-Newman, S. (1986). *Manter and Gantz's essentials of clinical neuroanatomy and neurophysiology.* Philadelphia: Davis Co.

Goldberg, S. (1986). *Clinical neuroanatomy made ridiculously simple.* Miami: MedMaster.

Guyton, A. C. (1986). *Textbook of medical physiology.* Philadelphia: W. B. Saunders.

House, E. L., & Pansky, B. A. (1967). *Functional approach to neuroanatomy.* New York: McGraw-Hill.

Robison, G. A., Butcher, R. W., & Sutherland, E. W. (1971). *Cyclic AMP.* New York: Academic Press.

CHAPTER 2 | CNS DEPRESSANTS: ALCOHOL

Donna S. Woolf

Alcohol has existed since the beginning of time. The use and abuse of alcohol has been recorded by historians for centuries, and alcohol as a beverage has fulfilled special functions in our society (Keller, 1979). It is drunk as a part of ritualistic celebrations, such as birth and marriage, as well as a salve for the emotional pain of rejection, despair, and grief. Alcoholic beverages are also served as liquids to accompany meals.

The exact time at which the human discovered alcohol's inebriating properties and learned to produce natural alcoholic products is unknown. The distillation process was not discovered until the twelfth century, and production of grain alcohol on a large scale did not occur until the seventeenth century. With the ability to produce beverages of high alcohol content, such as gin, rum, and whiskey, came the opportunity to consume higher concentrations of alcohol than was possible with beer and wine. By the early 1800s, Benjamin Rush, a renowned physician, had begun to call the excessive, chronic drinking of alcohol a disease and addiction (Keller, 1979).

As America grew and spread westward, so did the use and abuse of alcohol. Even the temperance movement, associated with powerful political machines, could not enforce or legislate sobriety, and it became clear that the use of alcohol in this country was here to stay.

Since legislating the use of alcohol had not eradicated the disease of alcoholism, a small group of people began to think that science might be able to prevent or treat the ravages of alcoholism (Keller, 1979). Many research and training organizations were established to attempt to find the cause and thus the "cure" for alcoholism. More important to the addicts, their families, and health professionals was the establishment of the Alcoholics Anonymous (AA) mode of treatment. This organization of self-help groups, which was founded in the 1930s, appealed to people who wanted to learn how to live with the problem of addiction rather than to focus on why they had the disease.

Research continues to the present day to determine the causes of alcohol addiction and to learn why alcohol causes specific diseases. The remainder of this chapter will present some of the knowledge that scientists have painfully extracted from years of research.

TYPES OF ALCOHOL CONSUMED

Alcohol (ethanol) is available in many forms. Table 2.1 presents approximate amounts of alcohol present in the most common forms of alcoholic beverages (Leake & Silverman, 1971). The equivalent "doses" of each form are given to help the practitioner properly evaluate the amount of alcohol that has been ingested. It should be remembered that the alcoholic content of the beverage causes the pharmacologic effect. Drinking "only" beer does not ensure that a person will not become addicted to alcohol. Although the beer drinker may consume larger amounts of liquid than the bourbon drinker, the amount of alcohol consumed may be the same.

Other products that contain alcohol may be abused. Alcohol has been used as a solvent in the preparation of medicinal compounds for many years. It is sometimes added to medicinal preparations for its central nervous system (CNS) depressant qualities. As unpleasant as it may sound, cough and cold elixirs, shaving lotions, and extract of vanilla are occasionally drunk by desperate people when other forms of alcohol are unavailable.

Table 2.1

Alcohol Content and Equivalent "Doses" of Alcoholic Beverages

Beverage	≈ % Alcohol	Equivalent "Dose"
Beer	4	can + (15 oz)
Wine	14	glass (4 oz)
Dessert wine	20	small glass (3 oz)
Distilled liquor	40	jigger (1 ½ oz)
Liqueurs	40	jigger (1 ½ oz)

ROUTE OF ADMINISTRATION

Alcohol is exclusively abused by oral ingestion, although other routes of administration have limited use in medical practice. It is possible to absorb alcohol by inhalation, but this manner of ingestion is not practical for the addict (Ritchie, 1985). The intravenous and topical use of alcohol in practice will not be discussed here; the reader is referred to a general pharmacology text.

ABSORPTION

After ingestion, alcohol is rapidly absorbed from the stomach and the small intestine and is then uniformly distributed throughout body tissue and fluids. The absorption of alcohol from the stomach increases as the gastric alcohol concentration increases. As alcohol concentrations rise, the rate of absorption slows as the astringent actions of alcohol restrict the blood supply to the stomach. Absorption of alcohol from the stomach can be slowed by the ingestion of food or milk. Absorption can also be affected by the time over which the beverage is drunk and the type and volume of the beverage consumed. These facts are generally known among drinkers, and the addict may become skillful at modifying the rapidity of intoxication by manipulating food intake and the type of alcohol ingested.

Factors such as the presence of food or the concentration of alcohol in the beverage do not generally affect the absorption of alcohol from the small intestine, although Broitman, Gottlieb, and Vitale (1976) report that carbohydrates may enhance alcohol absorption by the intestines. The complete absorption of alcohol usually takes 2–6 hours (Ritchie, 1985).

METABOLISM

The body metabolizes (oxidizes) 90%–98% of ingested alcohol. The small amount that is not oxidized is excreted in the urine by the kidney and exhaled by the lungs. The amount of alcohol oxidized reaches 10% only when an excessively large amount of alcohol has been consumed. Alcohol is metabolized according to the rules of *zero-order kinetics* (Ritchie, 1985). This means that the amount of alcohol metabolized is unaffected by the amount of alcohol drunk at one time. How fast metabolism of alcohol occurs in any one person also depends on the weight and the tolerance of the drinker. When more alcohol is consumed than can be metabolized, the alcohol accumulates, and the drinker becomes intoxicated.

Routes of Alcohol Metabolism

Alcohol Dehydrogenase Oxidation

Most ingested alcohol is metabolized in the liver, especially in the *cytosol,* which is the cell sap. There, alcohol is oxidized to acetaldehyde with the help of a zinc-containing enzyme, *alcohol dehydrogenase* (see Fig. 2.1). Eventually, the acetaldehyde is further oxidized, and products of the reaction are used in the citric acid cycle. For the initial alcohol oxidation to take place, *nicotinamide adenine dinucleotide (NAD)* must also be present to act as a cofactor (Ritchie, 1985). The availability of NAD for use as a cofactor is the limiting factor in the metabolism of alcohol (Theorell & Bonnichsen, 1951). As the NAD is reduced to NADH (see Fig. 2.1), extra hydrogen ions are available and participate in vital body reactions. The NADH is reoxidized to NAD by the respiratory chain in the liver mitochondria (Kircka & Clark, 1979). The NAD is once again available to participate in alcohol oxidation. Biochemical changes, which are caused by the excess production of NADH and hydrogen, will be discussed in a subsequent section.

Other Methods of Alcohol Metabolism

When alcohol is present in high concentrations, another system, the *microsomal ethanol oxidizing system (MEOS),* has been identified as able to metabolize alcohol to acetaldehyde (Teschke, Matsuzaki, Ohnishi, Hasumura, & Lieber, 1977). This system of alcohol metabolism has been proposed as the basis for many alcohol–drug interactions (Rubin & Lieber, 1968). Since the MEOS is known to metabolize many drugs, it has been suggested that an increase in MEOS enzymes induced by chronic alcohol intake may accelerate the metabolism and clearance of other drugs (Lieber, Rubin, & DeCarli, 1971) (see Fig. 2.1). It may also partially explain the increase in tolerance to alcohol in alcoholics who have been chronically drinking alcohol.

TOLERANCE

After alcohol has been repeatedly ingested, the amount of alcohol taken must be increased to achieve the same

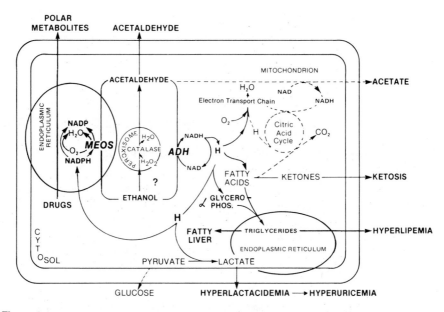

Figure 2.1

Metabolic effects of alcohol on the liver. Metabolism of alcohol in the hepatocyte and schematic representation of its link to fatty liver, hyperlipemia, hyperuricemia, hyperlactacidemia, ketosis, and hypoglycemia. **ADH** *= alcohol dehydrogenase;* **MEOS** *= microsomal ethanol-oxidizing system;* **NAD** *= nicotinamide adenine dinucleotide;* **NADH** *= nicotinamide adenine dinucleotide, reduced form;* **NADP** *= nicotinamide adenine dinucleotide phosphate;* **NADPH** *= nicotinamide adenine dinucleotide phosphate, reduced form. Pathways decreased by alcohol are represented by dashed lines. From "Metabolic effects of alcohol on the liver," by C. S. Lieber and L. M. DeCarli, in* Metabolic aspects of alcoholism, *edited by C. S. Lieber. © 1977. Reproduced with permission from MTP Press Limited.*

effects. This effect is called *tolerance* and occurs with several other drugs in addition to alcohol. Although tolerance does not always indicate the presence of an addictive process, it is a commonly seen phenomenon in the alcoholic and is frequently used as one criterion to evaluate addiction. It should be noted that although tolerance to the effects of alcohol occurs, there is little change in the alcohol concentration required to produce death from overdose (Jaffe, 1985).

Several factors are involved in the development of tolerance. Tolerance represents the adaptation of metabolism, cells, and behavior to the chronic presence of a drug. Although these types of tolerance have been identified, the biochemical basis for tolerance is unclear.

Metabolic Tolerance

The chronic ingestion of alcohol and certain other drugs may affect the rate at which the metabolism of these chemicals occurs. The liver attempts to adapt to the challenge to detoxify large quantities of alcohol by increasing the hepatic enzyme activity. This adaptation results in an increased metabolism of alcohol in both alcoholics and nonalcoholics. This type of tolerance will decline after several weeks of abstinence. Tolerance of this type is also called *pharmacokinetic* or *dispositional tolerance* (Jaffe, 1985).

Cellular Adaptation

Since differences in the metabolism of alcohol cannot account for the degree of tolerance to alcohol that occurs in the addict, it has been suggested that CNS cells adapt to the presence of chronic alcohol levels (Mendelson, 1971). This phenomenon is called *cellular adaptation* or *functional tolerance*. How these cells might adapt to account for cellular tolerance is unclear. Alcohol-induced changes in neurotransmitters, CNS receptors, and acetaldehyde condensation products are all areas of current study. Research also continues into how alcohol-induced adaptive changes in the lipid composition of the CNS may contribute to the development of tolerance and dependence (Tabakoff & Hoffman, 1983).

Behavioral Tolerance

With practice and considerable effort, substance abusers may adapt their behavior so that they can keep functioning at work, school, or home while grossly intoxicated. This phenomenon is termed *behavioral tolerance*. Animals in research studies also exhibit behavioral tolerance to adapt drug-induced behavior so rewards can still be earned and punishment avoided (Jaffe, 1985).

Cross-Tolerance

Cross-tolerance between alcohol and other CNS depressants does occur (Jaffe, 1985). This means that if a person shows tolerance to alcohol, tolerance may also be shown to other drugs, particularly the sedative-hypnotic drugs. The cross-tolerance exhibited between alcohol and anesthetics or other sedative-hypnotics probably represents a combination of cellular and metabolic tolerance. It should be noted that alcoholics with measurable blood alcohol levels will still show the additive effects of two CNS depressants if another drug is given simultaneously. Cross-tolerant addicts whose blood alcohol levels are high can still be dangerously depressed by combinations of alcohol and anesthesics or withdrawal treatments.

Tolerance Fluctuation

Tolerance to alcohol does decrease with time, although persistent changes in the CNS induced by chronic alcohol ingestion can be shown (Tabakoff & Hoffman, 1983). Investigators have reported that it takes much less time to produce tolerance on a second spree of drinking than it did on the first. It appears that both tolerance and dependence on alcohol decrease slowly and may persist for months or years.

Alcoholics occasionally report a "drop in tolerance" when the disease has progressed to a chronic state. They report that whereas they could previously drink large amounts of alcohol without intoxication, now one or two drinks make them "very sick." This may be due to the development of a severely scarred liver that cannot metabolize alcohol. Such a condition may also be affected by head injuries, which change the ability of the person to maintain behavioral tolerance (Williams & Salamy, 1972).

PHARMACOLOGIC ACTIONS

Effect on CNS

Alcohol, like other hypnotic or sedative drugs, produces a general dose-dependent depression of the CNS. Because alcohol in low doses depresses areas of the brain that are normally inhibitory, alcohol has been mistakenly described as a "stimulant." The effects of alcohol on the CNS follow the clinical view that the depressant's actions extend down the neuraxis (Himwich & Callison, 1972). Many of the initial behavioral changes due to the effects of alcohol involve the *reticular formation (RF)*. The RF, which extends through the middle portion of the brain stem upward to the thalamus, initiates diffuse activation of the cortex. The *cortex,* which is the brain area involved in the most highly integrated thinking processes and the voluntary control of behavior, is thus susceptible to alcohol's depressant effects. With increasing doses, the depressant effect of alcohol progresses down the brain stem and will finally depress the medulla oblongata, resulting in respiratory arrest (Himwich & Callison, 1972; Ritchie, 1985).

Anesthetic and Analgesic Actions

Regardless of all the alcohol that was used as an anesthetic during bullet removal surgery in old-time western movies, alcohol fails to qualify as a safe anesthetic. A safe general anesthetic is a short-acting drug with a wide margin between the dose inducing anesthesia and the dose severely depressing respiration. Since alcohol must be metabolized before excretion, its actions are too long for use as an anesthetic. More importantly, the anesthetic dose of alcohol is quite close to the lethal dose (Ritchie, 1985).

The ingestion of approximately 3 jiggers (4.7 oz) of distilled liquor can raise the pain threshold 35%–40% above normal (Wikler, Goodell, & Wolff, 1945). Intoxicated persons have been known to sustain painful injuries without complaint until the alcohol level subsides. Alcohol causes euphoria, which could cause the intoxicated person to ignore the pain.

Alcohol does not increase, and usually decreases, the ability to perform tasks requiring mental or motor ability. The person may believe that ability is increased due to the cortical effects of alcohol on judgment (Ritchie, 1985). An intoxicated person often staggers because of loss of motor control. While intoxicated, the person may become talkative, vivacious, and exhibit mood swings ranging from crying to extreme jolliness.

Alcohol's Effects on Neurotransmitters

Research studies demonstrating the effect of alcohol on biologically active chemicals are complex and often contradictory. Studies have been done on the effect on neurotransmitters of chronic alcohol use, sporadic alcohol use, and alcohol use by the nonaddict. With few exceptions, these studies have not involved actual sampling of tissue or fluid in the human CNS because of ethical and technical barriers.

Peripheral studies suggest that alcohol increases blood levels of norepinephrine (NE) and epinephrine in normal nonalcoholics (Gitlow, Dziedzic, Dziedzic, & Wong, 1976). This may be explained by a decrease in plasma clearance of catecholamines due to the inhibition of reuptake into the neuron (Eisenhofer, Lambie, & Johnson, 1983). Alcoholics have been shown to have increased urinary levels of catecholamines during ingestion and withdrawal (Ogata, Mendelson, Mello, & Majchrowicz, 1971). Although numerous changes in NE, epinephrine, and 5-hydroxytryptamine (5-HT) occur when alcohol is ingested, how these changes might relate to CNS changes remains unclear.

One theory of how alcohol is involved in an addictive process has been widely debated by experts. This theory suggests that alkaloidlike substances are formed when alcohol is consumed. It is proposed that these products, called *tetrahydroisoquinolines (TIQ),* are formed by the reaction of biologically active amines with products of alcohol metabolism, such as acetaldehyde. Tetrahydropapaveroline (THP) is often mentioned as a product of this reaction. It is suggested that these chemicals may act as morphinelike substances, thereby producing addiction. Several criticisms of this theory have been set forth. Among these are the recognized differences in the clinical symptoms of alcohol and alkaloid (opioid) withdrawal and dependence (Seevers, 1970). Researchers have not yet been able to show the presence of TIQ in the brain during or after alcohol administration (Tabakoff & Hoffman, 1983).

There appear to be some similarities in the mechanisms of actions of opioids and alcohol since naloxone can reverse alcoholic coma (Lyon & Anthony, 1982).

Miscellaneous CNS Effects

Aside from the direct depressant action of alcohol on various brain structures, many of the consequences of alcohol abuse, such as withdrawal, involve the CNS. Some diseases due to nutritional deficiencies secondary to alcoholism involve the CNS.

Another effect of alcohol on the CNS is its ability to produce changes in brain sleep patterns. Because alcohol is a CNS depressant, excessive periods of sleep can occur during intoxication. Hypersomnic episodes also occur during binges. In this case, the alcoholic elects to abstain for one day of the binge and usually sleeps for most of the 24 hours (Mello & Mendelson, 1970). Alcohol reduces the percentage of rapid eye movement (REM) sleep during drinking periods. REM sleep increases (rebounds) dramatically during withdrawal (Gross & Hastey, 1976), resulting in withdrawal insomnia.

Alcoholic Blackouts

An alcohol-induced *blackout* is a period of transient amnesia occurring during a drinking period. During the blackout, which may last for hours or days, the person appears fully conscious. There is some debate as to the diagnostic utility of the occurrence of blackouts in identifying the presence or progression of alcohol addiction. Although some researchers claim that blackouts do occur in persons who never become addicted (Victor & Laureno, 1978), many clinicians find that the occurrence of blackout episodes is a useful indicator of abuse.

Two types of memory loss during intoxication have been described (Goodwin, 1971). Fuguelike episodes of irreversible amnesia consist of total classic amnesia for the blackout period. A second type of memory loss is the fragmentary blackout period which may be partially remembered when the person is told of the event. Either type of blackout can occur in the same person.

Few specific answers have been found to explain the blackout. Blackouts and the chronic effects of alcohol on memory appear closely related. The frequency of blackouts increases with the frequency of intoxication and with drinking large amounts over short periods of time (Poikolainen, 1982). Serotonergic pathways may be involved in the development of blackouts, since tryptophan levels have been found to be depressed in alcoholics with histories of blackouts (Branchey, Branchey, Zucker, Shaw, & Lieber, 1985).

Alcohol Intoxication

Most states have set legal limits for alcohol intoxication. These limits are defined by blood alcohol levels and usually range from 80 mg to 100 mg alcohol/100 ml blood. Most nontolerant drinkers will exhibit behavioral signs of intoxication at levels of 100–150 mg alcohol/100 ml blood. Blood levels above 200 mg alcohol/100 ml blood would usually result in gross intoxication, and levels above 300 mg alcohol/100 ml blood usually result in a coma or stupor. As metabolic, cellular, and behavioral tolerances develop, these figures are no longer accurate. Addicts may have blood levels of 200–300 mg alcohol/100 ml of blood and still retain some semblance of control over motor functions, thought processes, and memory (Mendelson & Mello, 1985). Clinically, this becomes important since the addict's behavioral impairment by alcohol may be more subtle due to tolerance.

NAD: NADH-RELATED DISEASES

Several diseases and syndromes seen in the alcoholic have been directly linked to biochemical changes induced by the metabolism of large amounts of alcohol. Blood glucose fluctuations, ketoacidosis, hyperlipemia, fatty liver, hyperuricemia, and gout may all be linked to biochemical derangements in the liver.

The role of NAD in the first step of the metabolism of alcohol is important. The function of the cofactor NAD is to accept the hydrogen ion, which was liberated by the oxidation of the alcohol (ethanol) molecule (see Fig. 2.1). Under normal conditions, there is a specific ratio between the amount of NAD and NADH present. When large amounts of alcohol must be continuously metabolized, excessive NADH is produced. NADH builds up because energy is required for NADH to be reconverted to NAD.

Excessive NADH affects other biochemical reactions in the liver since several important reactions require either NAD or NADH as cofactors. Blood chemistry alterations and several diseases may be induced by the altered ratio of NAD and NADH.

Alcoholic Hypoglycemia and Hyperglycemia

Many reasons have been cited for alcohol-induced alterations in the blood glucose levels, although the cause of these disorders is uncertain (Lieber, 1972). In persons whose glycogen stores are depleted, as in the malnourished alcoholic, a decrease in the availability of precursors used to synthesize glucose in the liver can cause a precipitous fall in the blood glucose levels (Kircka & Clark, 1979).

There are several reasons for this decrease in gluconeogenesis, most of which are indirectly related to the altered NAD:NADH ratio. The citric acid cycle's function is slowed by the excess NADH directly influencing glucose synthesis. The amino acids that must be converted to pyruvate before being utilized in gluconeogenesis are not readily utilized since the diversion of pyruvate to lactate decreases the available amount of pyruvate (Freinkel et al., 1965; Kircka & Clark, 1979; Lieber, 1972) (see Fig. 2.1).

Symptoms of alcohol withdrawal may resemble those of alcoholic hypoglycemia. Both conditions may cause a stuporous state, as well as tremulousness, anxiety, profuse sweating, and fainting (Cohen, 1980). Alcoholic hypoglycemia may be related to such diseases as alcoholic hepatitis, cirrhosis, and alcoholic pancreatitis. Alcohol-induced hyperglycemia has been reported occasionally, although the mechanisms by which this occurs are even less understood than those by which alcoholic hypoglycemia occurs (Lieber, 1972).

Alcoholic Ketoacidosis

Even when food intake is adequate, alcoholics may produce excess ketone bodies, resulting in ketoacidosis (Lefevre, Adler, & Lieber, 1970). The formation of excess ketones, acetoacetate, β-hydroxybutyrate, and acetone is one mechanism by which the liver can dispose of excess fatty acids formed because of alcohol's metabolism (see Fig. 2.1). Confusion, paroxysmal dyspnea, and dehydration may occur as consequences of alcohol-induced ketoacidosis. Abdominal pain and dehydration due to nausea and vomiting may occur as consequences of alcohol-induced ketoacidoses (Cooperman, Davidoff, Spark, & Pallotta, 1974).

Alcohol and Hyperlipemia, Fatty Liver

The increased NADH:NAD ratio in the liver has several known effects on lipid compounds in humans. The deposition of fatty acids in the liver is generally viewed as a fully reversible disorder on the discontinuation of alcohol abuse; however, the subsequent development of alcoholic hepatitis and cirrhosis is associated with a greater risk of permanent liver damage or death.

The mechanisms by which some alcohol abusers develop hyperlipemia and fatty liver, whereas others do not, is not fully understood. Several theories concerning alcohol's role in the pathogenesis of fatty liver have been suggested (Kudzma & Schonfeld, 1971; Lieber & DeCarli, 1977; Walker & Gordon, 1970). Excess NADH in the liver slows the reactions of the citric acid cycle, which uses NAD as a cofactor. This means that hydrogen equivalents from alcohol's oxidation are more likely to be used as fuel for mitochondrial reactions than those generated by the citric acid cycle. Since fatty acids usually serve as a source for two carbon fragments in the citric acid cycle (see Fig. 2.1), they are no longer needed and accumulate. Other excess NADH is used by the liver to increase lipid synthesis, decrease the breakdown of dietary fatty acids, and increase triglyceride production, all of which result in the deposition of lipids in the liver (Lieber & DeCarli, 1977). In the presence of large amounts of alcohol, adipose tissue is broken down to fatty acids that may be deposited in the liver (Lieber & DeCarli, 1977). Excess NADH raises the concentration of alpha-glycerophosphate (Nikkila & Ojala, 1963), which encourages the trapping of fatty acids (see Fig. 2.1). Alcohol may also increase the hepatic synthesis of precursors to beta-lipoproteins (Kudzma & Schonfeld, 1971). All of these changes continue, despite adequate nutrition in the alcoholic (Bendersky, 1975; Lieber & DeCarli, 1977).

Hyperlactacidemia, Hyperuricemia, and Gout

The elevated NADH:NAD ratio in the liver favors the conversion of pyruvate to lactate and results in excessive lactic acid blood levels (Mays, 1979). Lactate and urate compete for excretion by the renal tubules, resulting in the favored excretion of lactate and the retention of urate (Bendersky, 1975). Gouty attacks, as well as asymptomatic hyperuricemia, are commonly seen in the heavy drinker (Newcombe, 1972). Alcohol-induced turnover of adenosine triphosphate (ATP) may contribute to increased urate synthesis and hyperuricemia (Faller & Fox, 1982).

Alcohol and the Liver

The infamous medical consequences of alcohol abuse on the liver are widely known. Three distinct diseases of the liver are recognized as caused by chronic alcoholic abuse. These diseases are *fatty liver* (Lieber & DeCarli, 1977), a reversible disease; *alcoholic hepatitis,* an acute disease with a mortality rate of 10%–30% (Lieber, 1976); and *cirrhosis,* the most severe of the three diseases. Once the scar tissue of cirrhosis has developed, the liver cell will not function again. The severely damaged cells present in cirrhosis represent an irreversible consequence of alcohol abuse. Several life-threatening complications of cirrhosis may develop. Ascites, gastric or esophageal varices, functional renal failure, and encephalopathy all contribute to the lethal reputation of cirrhosis.

There is some debate as to whether the disease leading to cirrhosis must proceed stepwise from fatty liver to hepatitis to cirrhosis, but there is no debate that each disease state occurs in response to alcohol abuse. Cirrhosis commonly develops without hepatitis in some populations (Lieber, 1984). It has now been proven that, although malnutrition can contribute to the development of alcoholic liver disease, alcohol is a direct hepatotoxic substance capable of causing injury even when the diet is sufficient (Lieber, 1976; Lieber, DeCarli, & Rubin, 1975).

Alcohol and the Gastrointestinal Tract

Esophagus, Stomach, and Intestines

High concentrations of alcohol have been shown to damage the lining of the stomach and esophagus, irritate the mucosa, and cause inflammation. Alcohol consumption so effectively promotes the secretion of gastric acid that the administration of alcohol has been used as a test of the ability of the gastric glands to secrete hydrochloric acid (Ritchie, 1985). The combination of other stomach irritants, such as aspirin, with alcohol can result in enhanced irritation and bleeding. Although acute gastritis after alcohol intake has been known since the 1800s, the frequency of chronic gastritis in the alcoholic is debated in the literature. The amount of alcohol ingested by the alcoholic is capable of producing alterations in the stomach and duodenum that can be seen on microscopic examination, and alcohol consumption is implicated as a causative factor in the development of duodenitis (Gottfried, Korsten, & Lieber, 1978). Complaints of gastric pain, vomiting, and diarrhea are common in the alcoholic. Gastritis is often the first complaint that will send the alcoholic to a physician.

Alcohol and the Pancreas

Alcoholics clearly have a higher risk of developing pancreatitis than the abstainer (Little, 1987). Research studies estimate that 40%-95% of patients who develop pancreatitis are chronic and heavy users of alcohol (Webster, 1975). Alcohol-induced pancreatitis does not appear to take as long to develop as alcoholic cirrhosis (Kraft & Saletta, 1976). Symptoms of pancreatitis may develop in five years from the onset of heavy drinking, resulting in the possibility of the occurrence of pancreatitis in young abusers.

As with several other alcohol-related diseases, the means by which alcohol causes pancreatitis is multifaceted (Sarles, 1984). Pancreatitis occurs more frequently in the alcoholic than in the abstainer because alcohol modifies pancreatic secretions. Increases in pancreatic protein secretion, mainly enzymes, may be influenced by cholinergic mechanisms. This makes the fluid more viscous (Little, 1987). Bicarbonate secretion is decreased, leading to a decrease in pH and possibly to the formation of stones. Decreased secretions of citrate and secretory trypsin inhibitors are seen.

Regardless of the mechanism by which alcohol promotes pancreatitis, its clinical importance lies in the possibility that the alcoholic will develop a fulminating illness that can result in death (Kraft & Saletta, 1976). Recovery is possible in mild or moderately severe cases of pancreatitis, but the disease may recur with continued abuse (Webster, 1975).

Alcohol and Cancer

Alcohol consumption plays a role in the development of several types of cancer, particularly cancers of the head and neck. Cancers of the mouth, larynx, tongue, esophagus, liver, and lung occur significantly more frequently in alcoholics than in the general population (Lieber, Garro, Leo, Mak, & Worner, 1986). The risk of cancer due to the excessive use of alcohol is increased by about a third in the 20% of the population

who drink most heavily (Rothman, 1975). One complicating factor involved in studies to determine alcohol's role as a carcinogen is that many addicts also smoke. One study found that 75%–90% of the alcoholic subjects smoked (Kissin, Kaley, Su, & Lerner, 1973). Cigarette use alone is known to increase the risk of cancer in some of the same body areas, making separation of the two factors difficult.

The mechanisms of the carcinogenic action of alcohol are unclear. Several theories have been proposed as areas for research (Lieber et al., 1986). Besides the possibility that alcohol itself causes the cancer, alcohol might act as a solvent for the cancer causing agent (Lowenfels, 1975; McCoy & Wynder, 1979). By increasing the metabolizing enzymes in the liver, alcohol might speed the conversion of noncarcinogens to carcinogens (Lieber, Seitz, Garro, & Worner, 1979; McCoy & Wynder, 1979). There may be a relationship between nutritional deficiencies in the alcoholic and the development of cancer (Lieber et al., 1979; Lowenfels, 1975; McCoy & Wynder, 1979). Perhaps, in the cirrhotic patient, the liver is no longer functioning well enough to detoxify carcinogens, such as tobacco, that are taken into the body (McCoy & Wynder, 1979). Alcohol may cause cellular injury, resulting in cellular metabolic changes (Lieber et al., 1979; Lowenfels, 1975; McCoy & Wynder, 1979). Many other possibilities exist that have not yet been researched. The knowledge of the increased risk of developing cancer caused by heavy alcohol consumption may be of some value as a deterrent to alcohol abuse.

Alcohol and Hypothalamic-Pituitary-Gonadal Function

Although a relationship between liver disease, alcohol intake, hypogonadism, and hyperestrogenization had been observed during the early 1900s, it was not until the 1930s that it was recognized that retained estrogenic substances caused feminization of alcoholic cirrhotic males (Van Thiel & Lester, 1976). With developing expertise in the laboratory techniques to measure steroids, interest was renewed in finding the causes of the relationship of alcohol to abnormal sexual changes.

Sexual changes of hypogonadism and hyperestrogenism in the alcoholic occur in both chronic alcoholics with evidence of liver dysfunction and in those without significant liver disease. Since liver disease is not always present in the alcoholic, it must be assumed that some part of the sexual changes in the alcoholic are caused by the alcohol itself and not by its effects on the liver alone (Van Thiel & Lester, 1976).

Hypogonadism

Moderate, sporadic doses of alcohol can depress testosterone levels (Gordon, Altman, Southren, Rubin, & Lieber, 1976; Mendelson, Mello, & Ellingboe, 1977). Hypoandrogenization may lead to symptoms of decreased beard growth, prostatic atrophy, reduced libido, and impotence (Mendelson et al., 1977). This occurs independently of cirrhosis or nutritional factors. These changes are probably due to the direct metabolic effects of alcohol.

Acetaldehyde produced by alcohol oxidation is more toxic to the testosterone-producing Leydig cells, located in the testes, than alcohol. It binds to Leydig cell membranes, causing injury and leading to the production of testicular autoantibodies which can perpetuate injury after alcohol has stopped (Van Thiel & Gavaler, 1986).

Alcohol metabolism in the testes can affect vitamin metabolism and the production of sperm in males. The metabolism of alcohol is thought to reduce the activity of key enzymes in testicular steroid metabolism because of the increased NADH:NAD ratio (see NAD- and NADH-Related Diseases section).

Hyperestrogenization

As alcohol abuse continues, liver changes begin to play a role in the body estrogen levels. In male chronic alcoholics, plasma estrogen levels are maintained at normal to increased levels, even in the presence of androgen deficiency. Estradiol receptors in the liver and testes are increased as alcohol abuse continues (Eagon, Porter, & Van Thiel, 1983). Alcohol abuse causes both liver disease with subsequent portal-systemic shunting and the induction of aromatase enzymes. These two events result in an increased conversion of androgens to estrogens by nonhepatic and nongonadal tissue. It has been suggested that tissues of the alcoholic male may have an increased response to normal estrogen levels, resulting in feminization (Van Thiel & Gavaler, 1986). Alcohol-induced feminization includes symptoms of testicular atrophy, the development of breasts in males, and changes in body hair and fat distribution (Van Thiel & Lester, 1976).

Alcohol and Female Sex Hormones

Research investigating alcohol's effects on endocrine function in women is sparse and conflicting. Alcoholic women complain of infertility, menstrual irregularity, and loss of libido (Borhanmanesh & Haghighi, 1970). Other investigations of alcoholic women with chronic pancreatitis or cirrhosis of the liver reveal that 67% had amenorrhea and 84% of these women of reproductive age had evidence of hypothalamic disorders (Hughes et al., 1980). More research is needed in this area.

Alcohol and Infectious Disease

Alcoholics have a poor resistance to infection. Reasons for this phenomenon are obscure, but a depression of the movement of white blood cells into inflamed areas may partially account for this tendency (Eichner, 1973; Ritchie, 1985). Pneumonoccal sepsis and its high mortality has been shown to be related to leukopenia and alcoholism (Perlino & Rimland, 1985). Studies show that the combination of alcoholism and tuberculosis is relatively frequent (Hudolin, 1975; Proust, 1977). This is of interest in clinic settings where large numbers of alcoholic clients are treated, since routine screening for tuberculosis is advisable. Clients who resume drinking may not be compliant with the lengthy drug treatment required to cure pulmonary tuberculosis, resulting in treatment failure or tuberculosis relapse.

Alcohol and Skeletal Muscle

Large doses of alcohol are toxic to both skeletal and cardiac muscle. A wide variety of acute and chronic myopathies are common in the alcoholic client. These toxic effects appear to be dose dependent (Urbano-Marquez et al., 1989).

Alcohol and the Cardiovascular System

Alcohol is known to affect the cardiovascular system in several ways. In moderate doses, alcohol causes vasodilatation due to central effects, producing a characteristic flushed skin. This enhanced cutaneous blood flow causes a rapid heat loss (Ritchie, 1985). Although drinking alcohol may cause one to ''feel'' warmer, the core body temperature may drop to a dangerous level. Alcohol is not a good coronary vasodilator and is of no value in the treatment of angina (Ritchie, 1985).

The relationship of alcohol consumption to alterations in blood pressure is one of great debate (Maheswaran, Potter, & Beevers, 1986). One epidemiologic study, involving 83,947 subjects, suggested that regularly consuming more than three drinks per day is a risk factor for the development of hypertension (Klatsky, Friedman, Siegelaub, & Gerard, 1977). This area is difficult to investigate because stress might increase alcohol consumption as well as blood pressure.

The diagnosis and treatment of essential hypertension in the alcoholic client may be difficult, because the client may try to decrease the amount of alcohol consumed or abstain before keeping the appointment for the treatment of other illnesses. Evaluation by health professionals then reveals mild to moderate hypertension, sometimes caused by early stages of withdrawal. Separating clients requiring chronic therapy for essential hypertension from those who exhibit sporatic hypertension during withdrawal can be challenging.

We do know that the ingestion of intoxicating doses of alcohol causes a decrease in blood pressure. Low to moderate doses of alcohol do not significantly change the blood pressure (Ritchie, 1985).

There is evidence that chronic alcohol use will cause myocardial damage (Bing, 1982). Prolonged, heavy alcohol use both decreases the ability of the heart muscle to contract and affects cellular metabolism, especially in the mitochondria (Bing, Tillmanns, & Ikeda, 1975). Symptoms of alcoholic cardiomyopathy include cardiomegaly and signs of congestive heart failure, such as shortness of breath and edema (Reagin & Ettinger, 1979; Ritchie, 1985; Talbott, 1975; U. S. Department of Health, Education and Welfare, 1978).

Irregularities in cardiac rhythm have been reported during severe intoxication and during withdrawal (Reagin & Ettinger, 1979; Talbott, 1975; U. S. Department of Health, Education and Welfare, 1978). Commonly reported arrhythmias include atrial fibrillation, supraventricular tachycardia, isolated premature ventricular contractions, and nodal rhythms. Atrial fibrillation is so frequently observed that it has been named the *holiday heart syndrome* (Reagin & Ettinger, 1979, p. 41). Its name was derived from the frequent occurrence of atrial fibrillation during or at the end of a holiday period associated with high alcohol intake.

Studies of the relationship of alcohol intake to coronary artery disease and myocardial infarction have stirred debate among the members of the medical community, as well as among alcoholics who wished a reason to drink. These studies have indicated that nondrinkers were at slightly greater risk to die from coronary disease (Klatsky, Friedman, & Siegelaub, 1981; National Heart Institute, 1968; Yano, Rhoads, & Kagan, 1977). The protective effects of small amounts

of alcohol seem to occur since alcohol decreases low-density lipoproteins and increases high-density lipoproteins (Ritchie, 1985). Heavy alcohol use has been reported as a risk factor in the development of stroke in men (Gill, Zezulka, Shipley, Gill, & Beevers, 1986). It should be noted that the alcohol intake that seemed to be "protective" against coronary disease was low, and higher levels of alcohol consumption may be detrimental.

Other cardiovascular diseases may be associated with nutritional deficiencies that are commonly found in the alcoholic. Thiamine (vitamin B_1) deficiencies can produce beriberi, which has prominent cardiovascular symptoms (Guyton, 1986; Marcus & Coulston, 1985).

Alcohol and Vitamin and Mineral Deficiencies

Alcohol is of no nutritional value although a few alcoholic beverages do contain small amounts of essential nutrients (Vitale & Coffey, 1971). The ingestion of large amounts of alcohol often results in limited or sporadic food ingestion, resulting in vitamin deficiencies. An alcoholic may obtain more than one-half the daily caloric requirements from the alcohol alone since alcohol provides 7 kcal/g energy (Ritchie, 1985). Secondary deficiencies may develop, due to alcohol-related defects in absorption and storage of vitamins (Vitale & Coffey, 1971). These alcohol-related defects may involve gastrointestinal damage, which impairs absorption or the liver, which is the primary organ involved in vitamin storage and in the conversion of precursor forms of vitamins to their active metabolites.

Deficiencies of the B vitamins are known to occur in the alcoholic. Vitamin B_1 deficiency can occur in the alcoholic in the absence of dietary deficiencies or malabsorption by the intestines (Thomson, Baker, & Leevy, 1970). Vitamin B_1 deficiencies may result in cardiovascular symptoms, alcoholic neuritis, Wernick's syndrome, and Korsakoff's psychosis. Pyridoxine (vitamin B_6) deficiencies also occur in the alcoholic and may result in sideroblastic anemias (Hines, 1975). Studies of vitamin B_{12} levels in the alcoholic have produced varied results. Some studies cite normal serum levels of vitamin B_{12} and others show low levels due to impaired vitamin absorption (Lindenbaum & Lieber, 1969, 1975; Pezzimenti & Lindenbaum, 1972).

Deficiencies of vitamins D, K, and A have been reported in alcoholics. Dietary deficiencies and malabsorption secondary to steatorrhea contribute to decreased levels of these vitamins in the alcoholic (Avioli & Haddad, 1973; Roberts & Cederbaum, 1972). Vitamin A deficiency in the alcoholic may occur because both the breakdown of alcohol and the conversion of inactive vitamin A to active vitamin A require the enzyme alcohol dehydrogenase. This competition results in a decreased level of active vitamin A, a high incidence of night blindness, and azoospermia (Van Thiel, Gavaler, & Lester, 1974). Alcoholics with fatty liver or hepatitis have an 80%–90% decrease in hepatic vitamin A levels (Lieber, 1984). The combination of impaired vitamin D metabolism, chronic intake of aluminum-containing antacids, and increased parathyroid hormone and corticosteroid levels may result in an increased incidence of osteoporosis in alcoholic women and men (Spencer et al., 1986).

The metabolism of iron is altered by alcohol (Herbert & Tisman, 1975). Even when an alcoholic is well nourished and has no anemia, abnormalities in iron metabolism exist, which will convert to normal when sobriety is achieved (Eichner, 1973). Alcohol may depress marrow utilization of iron (Waters, Morley, & Rankin, 1966). The interference in iron metabolism caused by chronic drinking is significant in producing an iron overload in the alcoholic (Charlton, Jacobs, Seftel, & Bothwell, 1964). It is important that the diagnosis of idiopathic hemochromatosis be made only after complete review of the case. A reversal of the overload may be achieved by B vitamin administration and discontinuance of alcohol consumption (Herbert & Tisman, 1975).

Magnesium

Magnesium deficiency does occur in many chronic alcoholics (Jones, Shane, Jacobs, & Flink, 1969; Mendelson, Ogata, & Mello, 1969; Wolfe & Victor, 1969). It is not clear why this is true although magnesium loss in the urine is increased with alcohol intake (Vitale & Coffey, 1971).

The relationship of a deficiency of magnesium to symptoms of alcohol withdrawal has been studied by several research groups. One study found that those alcoholic clients who had seizures in response to a stroboscopic light stimulus also had low magnesium levels. These seizures were abolished by the administration of enough magnesium to raise the level to normal (Wolfe & Victor, 1969). Some symptoms of alcohol

withdrawal are similar to those of magnesium deficiency (Flink, 1986). The role of magnesium in the production of delirium tremens (DTs) has been studied to a limited extent, but no definitive causal relationship has been shown. More carefully timed studies of the relationship of magnesium levels to DTs need to be performed.

Alcohol and the Kidney

Alcoholic beverages have a reputation for increasing the frequency and volume of urination. Although it is true that the consumption of large amounts of fluid in the beverage should increase the volume of urine formed, alcohol itself is a diuretic. While the blood alcohol level is rising, the secretion of the antidiuretic hormone (ADH) from the posterior pituitary is suppressed, resulting in diuresis (Ritchie, 1985). This effect does not occur while the blood alcohol level is constant or falling (Haggard, Greenberg, & Carroll, 1941) and, in fact, the chronic alcoholic may retain fluid.

Alcohol Withdrawal

The ability of chronic alcohol intake to cause physical dependence is dramatically demonstrated by the emergence of a withdrawal syndrome upon a decrease in the blood alcohol concentration of the abuser. Symptoms may emerge in the morning after an "overnight" abstinence. In the heavy drinker, symptoms may emerge when daily intake is decreased from a quart to a pint of alcoholic beverages.

Physical dependence on alcohol does not occur suddenly. The disease is a progressive illness that often begins with intermittent drinking of small amounts of alcohol, increasing over a period of years to the consumption of large amounts of alcohol for extended periods of time.

How long drinking has occurred and how much alcohol is consistently consumed are important factors in how severe the withdrawal symptoms will become (Mello & Mendelson, 1976). One study on the length of alcohol abuse reported that 68% of the clients who had abused alcohol for 3–5 years developed symptoms of tremors and autonomic hyperactivity (Ballenger & Post, 1978). More severe withdrawal reactions, such as seizures, occurred in clients who had abused alcohol for 6 years or longer. Of severe withdrawal reactions, such as DTs, 80% occurred in persons who had abused

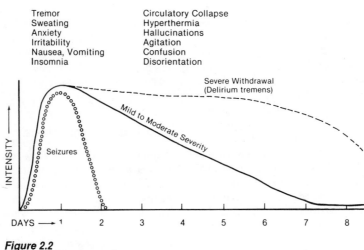

Figure 2.2
Alcohol withdrawal patterns.

alcohol for 10 years or longer (Ballenger & Post, 1978). The consumption of a fifth of whiskey daily will usually precipitate more severe withdrawal syndromes than the consumption of a pint per day (French, 1972).

The alcohol withdrawal syndrome is usually complete in 5–7 days if complications, such as DTs or death, do not develop (Jaffe, 1985) (see Fig. 2.2.). Persons with mild or moderate withdrawal symptoms show substantial improvement in 3–4 days. Although alcohol-induced seizures occur during the first 2 days of withdrawal, some severe withdrawal symptoms (DTs) do not develop until 2–4 days after drinking has stopped. Those clients who develop these withdrawal symptoms may require close medical supervision for a week or longer.

The therapeutic problems involved in the treatment of withdrawal syndrome lie in the unpredictability of the progression and severity of each person's withdrawal. Schemes of alcohol withdrawal symptoms that dictate exactly when or if a client will exhibit any one symptom are not accurate and may be misleading to the inexperienced. There is considerable overlapping of withdrawal stages in any classification scheme (Johnson, 1961) although there is usually a stepwise progression of symptoms.

Victor and Adams (1953) proposed a classification of withdrawal symptoms in "states," which was important since it was the first such proposal. This classification lacked flexibility, however, and research has continued to develop a useful measure of the progression of withdrawal symptoms. Variations on the classification of Victor and Adams (1953) have produced the four "stages" of withdrawal (tremor, hallucinations, seizures, DTs) often used by treatment programs.

The onset of alcohol withdrawal symptoms is usually within 6–12 hours after drinking has stopped (Johnson, 1961). Symptoms of anxiety, agitation, and irritability begin during that time. A coarse tremor is common and may be related to increases in blood epinephrine and NE levels during withdrawal (Ogata, et al., 1971). Sometimes the client may not appear to shake but may report "shaking inside."

Other symptoms that may also be related to increase sympathetic activity in the autonomic nervous system (ANS) are diaphoresis and tachycardia. Systolic hypertension is common during withdrawal and is an easily monitored warning sign (Clark & Friedman, 1985). Respirations may or may not increase during withdrawal. Increases are particularly likely if anxiety is severe, and hyperventilation may then become a secondary problem. Temperature elevations may be due to withdrawal processes, but fevers of 101° F or above are commonly associated with infection (Gross, Lewis, & Hastey, 1974).

Gastrointestinal disturbances are often seen in the early stages of withdrawal and may include nausea, vomiting, diarrhea, and anorexia. The alcoholic may complain of insomnia or vivid dreams. Although the addict may begin to sleep at night by the end of the withdrawal period, some alcoholics take weeks or months to reestablish the pattern that is "normal" for them.

Alcohol-induced seizures occur within the first 48 hours after abstinence (Victor & Brausch, 1967). Grand mal seizures may occur singly, in bursts, or, in rare cases, continuously. These seizures usually represent a progression of the withdrawal process but precede the development of DTs. Although the majority of seizures that occur during withdrawal are due to the withdrawal process itself, one must always consider other etiologies for seizures. Blackouts and stupor may prevent these clients' awareness of the occurrence of head injuries. Alcoholic epileptics may have recurrent seizures due to the lowered seizure threshold during withdrawal, as well as to sporadic compliance with drug regimens used to treat epilepsy.

As the syndrome progresses, other symptoms emerge. Some early symptoms, such as tremor, sweating, anxiety, and tachycardia, increase. Other symptoms, such as disorientation, the clouding of sensorium, and hallucinations or delusions, develop.

Hallucinations may be auditory, visual, olfactory, or tactile. Hallucinations, often of a persecutory nature, when seen in a patient with a relatively clear sensorium are usually labeled *alcoholic hallucinosis*. This may be considered a variant of DTs and may become chronic if drinking continues. During alcoholic hallucinosis, the client may act in response to the "voices" and may remember the hallucinations after withdrawal is complete. Visual hallucinations occur five times more often in alcohol withdrawal than either auditory hallucinations or mixed hallucinations (Victor & Adams, 1953).

Delirium tremens (DTs) is a term used to describe the most advanced progression of the alcohol withdrawal syndrome. Estimates of mortality due to DTs are up to 15%. This mortality rate can be lowered to approximately 1% with early recognition of the syndrome, aggressive pharmacotherapy, and improved therapy for the physical complications of alcohol withdrawal (Sellers & Kalant, 1976; Victor & Laureno, 1978).

Symptoms of DTs develop 2–3 days after drinking has stopped (see Fig. 2.2). Psychiatric symptoms of DTs include disorientation, delirium, and agitation. Physical symptoms of severe diaphoresis, tachycardia, cardiovascular collapse, and fever are complicated by associated medical consequences of chronic alcohol abuse, such as pneumonia, congestive heart failure, pan-

creatitis, or hepatic failure. If alcohol abuse continues, the symptoms of subsequent withdrawal episodes generally worsen (Ballenger & Post, 1978; Gross et al., 1974) and a history of DTs should warn of the possibility of DTs in future withdrawals.

Although DTs is a syndrome familiar to professionals as a medical emergency, alcoholics or lay persons may label any symptom of alcohol withdrawal "the DTs." It is better to inquire about specific symptoms when taking an alcohol history than to ask if DTs have ever occurred.

SUMMARY

Alcohol is our most socially acceptable, widely used drug. Yet, it is quite likely that alcohol would not be approved by the Food and Drug Administration for use as a sedative or hypnotic drug since its risks on long-term use outweigh its benefits.

Alcohol abuse is more physically destructive than the abuse of almost any other popular drug. Alcohol causes changes, often debilitating, in the heart, the pancreas, the liver, the stomach, esophagus, intestines, and the skeletal muscle. Metabolic changes induced by alcohol consumption can cause variations in blood glucose levels, increases in uric acid levels, and deposition of fat in the liver.

Not only is alcohol abuse physically debilitating, but the withdrawal from alcohol is potentially life-threatening. The withdrawal syndrome includes symptoms of anxiety, hypertension, sweating, hallucinations, disorientation, and grand mal seizures.

REFERENCES

Avioli, L. U., & Haddad, J. G. (1973). Vitamin D: Current concepts. *Metabolism, 22*(3), 507–531.

Ballenger, J. C., & Post, R. M. (1978). Kindling as a model for alcohol withdrawal syndromes. *British Journal of Psychiatry, 133,* 1–14.

Bendersky, G. (1975). Etiology of hyperuricemia. *Annals of Clinical Laboratory Science, 5,* 456–467.

Bing, R. J. (1982). Effect of alcohol on the heart and cardiac metabolism. *Federation Proceedings, 41*(8), 2443–2446.

Bing, R. J., Tillmanns, H., & Ikeda, S. (1975). Metabolic effects of alcohol on the heart. *Annals of the New York Academy of Sciences, 252,* 243–249.

Borhanmanesh, F., & Haghighi, P. (1970). Pregnancy in patients with cirrhosis of the liver. *Obstetrics and Gynaecology, 36,* 315–324.

Branchey, L., Branchey, M., Zucker, D., Shaw, S., & Lieber, C. S. (1985). Association between low plasma tryptophan and blackouts in male alcoholic patients. *Alcoholism: Clinical and Experimental Research, 9*(5), 393–395.

Broitman, S. A., Gottlieb, L. S., & Vitale, J. J. (1976). Augmentation of ethanol absorption by mono- and disaccharides. *Gastroenterology, 70,* 1101–1107.

Charlton, R. W., Jacobs, P., Seftel, H., & Bothwell, T. H. (1964). Effect of alcohol on iron absorption. *British Medical Journal, 2,* 1427–1429.

Clark, L. T., & Friedman, H. S. (1985). Hypertension associated with alcohol withdrawal: Assessment of mechanisms and complications. *Alcoholism: Clinical and Experimental Research, 9*(2), 125–130.

Cohen S. (1980). Alcoholic hypoglycemia. *Drug Abuse and Alcoholism Newsletter, 9*(2).

Cooperman, M.T., Davidoff, F., Spark, R., & Pallotta, J. (1974). Clinical studies of alcoholic ketoacidosis. *Diabetes, 23,* 433–439.

Eagon, P. K., Porter, L. E., Van Thiel, D. H. (1983). The role of estrogens and androgens in the feminization of the chronic alcoholic male. *Alcoholism: Clinical and Experimental Research, 7,* 140–143.

Eichner, E. R. (1973). The hematologic disorders of alcoholism. *American Journal of Medicine, 54,* 621–630.

Eisenhofer, G., Lambie, D. G., & Johnson, R. H. (1983). Effects of ethanol on plasma catecholamines and norepinephrine clearance. *Clinical Pharmacology and Therapeutics, 34,* 143–147.

Faller, J., & Fox, I. H. (1982). Ethanol-induced hyperuricemia: Evidence for increased urate production by activation of adenine nucleotide turnover. *New England Journal of Medicine, 307,* 1598–1602.

Flink, E. B. (1986). Magnesium deficiency in alcoholism. *Alcoholism: Clinical and Experimental Research, 10*(6), 590–594.

Freinkel, N., Arky, R. A., Singer, D. L., Cohen, A. K., Bleicher, S. J., Anderson, J. B., Silbert, C. K., & Foster, A. E. (1965). Alcohol hypoglycemia. 4. Current concepts of its pathogenesis. *Diabetes, 14,* 350.

French, S. W. (1972). Acute and chronic toxicity of alcohol. In B. Kissin & H. Begleiter (Eds.), *The biology of alcoholism: Biochemistry* (Vol. 1) (pp. 437–511). New York: Plenum Press.

Gill, J. S., Zezulka, A. V., Shipley, M. J., Gill, S. K., & Beevers, D. G. (1986). Stroke and alcohol consumption. *New England Journal of Medicine, 315*(17), 1041–1046.

Gitlow, S. E., Dziedzic, L. M., Dziedzic, S. W., & Wong, B. L. (1976). Influence of ethanol on human catecholamine metabolism. *Annals of the New York Academy of Sciences, 273,* 263–279.

Goodwin, D. W. (1971). Two species of alcoholic "blackouts." *American Journal of Psychiatry, 127*(2), 1665–1670.

Gordon, G. G., Altman, K., Southren, A. L., Rubin, E., & Lieber, C. S. (1976). Effect of alcohol (ethanol) administration on sex-hormone metabolism in normal men. *New England Journal of Medicine, 295*(15), 793–797.

Gottfried, E. B., Korsten, M. A., & Lieber, C. S. (1978). Alcohol-induced gastric and duodenal lesions in man. *American Journal of Gastroenterology, 70,* 587–592.

Gross, M. M., & Hastey, J. M. (1976). Sleep disturbances in alcoholism. In R. E. Tarter & A. A. Sugerman (Eds.), *Alcoholism: Interdisciplinary approaches to an enduring problem* (pp. 257–307). Reading, MA: Addison-Wesley.

Gross, M. M., Lewis, E., & Hastey, J. M. (1974). Acute alcohol withdrawal syndrome. In B. Kissin & H. Begleiter (Eds.), *The biology of alcoholism: Clinical pathology* (Vol. 3) (pp. 191–263). New York: Plenum Press.

Guyton, A. C. (1986). *Textbook of medical physiology* (7th ed.). Philadelphia: W. B. Saunders.

Haggard, H. W., Greenberg, L. A., & Carroll, R. P. (1941). Studies in the absorption, distribution, and elimination of alcohol. 8. The diuresis from alcohol and its influence on the elimination of alcohol in the urine. *Journal of Pharmacological and Experimental Therapies, 71,* 349–357.

Herbert, V., & Tisman, G. (1975). Hematologic effects of alcohol. *Annals of the New York Academy of Sciences, 252,* 307–315.

Himwich, H. E., & Callison, D. A. (1972). The effect of alcohol on evoked potentials of various parts of the central nervous system of the cat. In B. Kissin & H. Begleiter (Eds.), *The biology of alcoholism: Physiology and behavior* (Vol. 2) (pp. 67–84). New York: Plenum Press.

Hines, J. D. (1975). Hematologic abnormalities involving vitamin B_6 and folate metabolism in alcoholic subjects. *Annals of the New York Academy of Sciences, 252,* 316–327.

Hudolin, V. (1975). Tuberculosis and alcoholism. *Annals of the New York Academy of Sciences, 252,* 353–363.

Hughes, J. N., Coste, T., Perret, G., Jayle, M. F., Sebaoun, J., & Modigliani, E., (1980). Hypothalamo-pituitary ovarian function in thirty-one women with chronic alcoholism. *Clinical Endocrinology, 12,* 543–551.

Jaffe, J. H. (1985). Drug addiction and drug abuse. In A. G. Gilman, L. S. Goodman, T. W. Rall, & F. Murad (Eds.), *Goodman and Gilman's the pharmacological basis of therapeutics* (pp. 532–581). New York: Macmillan.

Johnson, R. B. (1961). The alcohol withdrawal syndromes. *Quarterly Journal of Studies in Alcohol,* Suppl. No. 1, 66–76.

Jones, J. E., Shane, S. R., Jacobs, W. H., & Flink, E. B. (1969). Magnesium balance studies in chronic alcoholism. *Annals of the New York Academy of Sciences, 162,* 934–946.

Keller, M. (1979). A historical overview of alcohol and alcoholism. *Cancer Research, 39,* 2822–2829.

Kircka, L. J. & Clark, P. M. S. (1979). *Biochemistry of alcohol and alcoholism.* New York: John Wiley & Sons.

Kissin, B., Kaley, M., Su, W. H., & Lerner, R. (1973). Head and neck cancer in alcoholics. *Journal of the American Medical Association, 224*(8), 1174–1175.

Klatsky, A. L., Friedman, G. D., & Siegelaub, A. B. (1981). Alcohol and mortality. A ten-year Kaiser-Permanente experience. *Annals of Internal Medicine, 95,* 139–145.

Klatsky, A. L., Friedman, G. D., Siegelaub, A. B., & Gerard, M. J. (1977). Alcohol consumption and blood pressure. *New England Journal of Medicine, 296,* 1194–1200.

Kraft, A. R., & Saletta, J. D. (1976). Acute alcoholic pancreatitis: Current concepts and controversies. *Surgery Annual, 8,* 145–171.

Kudzma, D. J., & Schonfeld, G. (1971). Alcoholic hyperlipidemia: Induction by ethanol but not by carbohydrate. *Journal of Laboratory and Clinical Medicine, 77*(3), 384–395.

Leake, C. D., & Silverman, M. (1971). The chemistry of alcoholic beverages. In B. Kissin & H. Begleiter (Eds.), *The biology of alcoholism: Biochemistry* (Vol. 1) (pp. 575–612). New York: Plenum Press.

Lefevre, A. F., Adler, H. M., & Lieber, C. S. (1970). Effect of ethanol on ketone metabolism. *Journal of Clinical Investigation, 49,* 1775–1782.

Lieber, C. S. (1972). Alcohol. In S. J. Mulé & H. Brill (Eds.), *Chemical and biological aspects of drug dependence* (pp. 135–162). Cleveland: CRC Press.

Lieber, C. S. (1976). Liver disease and alcohol: Fatty liver, alcoholic hepatitis, cirrhosis and their interrelationships. *Annals of the New York Academy of Sciences, 283,* 63–84.

Lieber, C. S. (1984). Alcohol and the liver: 1984 update. *Hepatology, 4*(6), 1243–1260.

Lieber, C. S., & DeCarli, L. M. (1977). Metabolic effects of alcohol on the liver. In C. S. Lieber (Ed.), *Metabolic aspects of alcoholism* (pp. 31–79). Lancaster, England: MTP Press.

Lieber, C. S., DeCarli, L. M., & Rubin, E. (1975). Sequential production of fatty liver, hepatitis and cirrhosis in subhuman primates fed ethanol with adequate diets. *Proceedings of the National Academy of Sciences of the United States of America, 72*(2), 437–441.

Lieber, C. S., Garro, A., Leo, M. A., Mak, K. M., & Worner, T. (1986). Alcohol and cancer. *Hepatology, 6*(5), 1005–1019.

Lieber, C. S., Rubin, E., & DeCarli, L. M. (1971). Effects of ethanol on lipid, uric acid, intermediary and drug metabolism including the pathogenesis of the alcoholic fatty liver. In B. Kissin & H. Begleiter (Eds.), *The biology of alcoholism: Biochemistry* (Vol. 1) (pp. 263–305). New York: Plenum Press.

Lieber, C. S., Seitz, H. K., Garro, A. J., & Worner, T. M. (1979). Alcohol-related diseases and carcinogenesis. *Cancer Research, 39,* 2863–2886.

Lindenbaum, J., & Lieber, C. S. (1969). Alcohol-induced malabsorption of vitamin B_{12} in man. *Nature, 224,* 806.

Lindenbaum, J., & Lieber, C. S. (1975). Effects of chronic ethanol administration on intestinal absorption in man in the absence of nutritional deficiency. *Annals of the New York Academy of Sciences, 252,* 228–234.

Little, J. M. (1987). Alcohol abuse and chronic pancreatitis. *Surgery, 101*(3), 357–360.

Lowenfels, A. B. (1975). Alcoholism and the risk of cancer. *Annals of the New York Academy of Sciences, 252,* 365–374.

Lyon, L. J., & Anthony, J. (1982). Reversal of alcoholic coma by naloxone. *Annals of Internal Medicine, 96,* 464–465.

Maheswaran, R., Potter, J. F., & Beevers, D. G. (1986). The role of alcohol in hypertension. *Journal of Clinical Hypertension, 2,* 172–178.

Marcus, R., & Coulston, A. M. (1985). Water-soluble vitamins: The vitamin B complex and ascorbic acid. In A. G. Gilman, L. S. Goodman, T. W. Rall, & F. Murad (Eds.), *Goodman and Gilman's the pharmacologic basis of therapeutics* (pp. 1551–1572). New York: Macmillan.

Mays, P. A. (1979). Metabolism of lipids. 2. Role of tissues. In H. A. Harper, V. W. Rodwell, & P. A. Mays (Eds.), *Review of physiological chemistry* (pp. 14–23). Los Altos, CA: Lange.

McCoy, G. D., & Wynder, E. L. (1979). Etiological and preventive implications in alcohol carcinogenesis. *Cancer Research, 39,* 2844–2850.

Mello, N. K., & Mendelson, J. H. (1970). Experimentally induced intoxication in alcoholics: A comparison between programmed and spontaneous drinking. *The Journal of Pharmacological and Experimental Therapeutics, 173*(1), 101–116.

Mello, N. K., & Mendelson, J. H. (1976). The development of alcohol dependence: A clinical study. *McLean Hospital Journal, 1,* 64–84.

Mendelson, J. H. (1971). Biochemical mechanisms of alcohol addiction. In B. Kissin & H. Begleiter (Eds.), *The biology of alcoholism: Biochemistry* (Vol. 1) (pp. 513–544). New York: Plenum Press.

Mendelson, J. H., & Mello, N. K. (1985). Diagnostic criteria for alcoholism and alcohol abuse. In J. H. Mendelson & N. K. Mello (Eds.), *The diagnosis and treatment of alcoholism* (pp. 1–20). New York: McGraw-Hill.

Mendelson, J. H., Mello, N. K., & Ellingboe, J. (1977). Effects of acute alcohol intake on pituitary-gonadal hormones in normal human males. *The Journal of Pharmacological and Experimental Therapeutics, 202,* 676–682.

Mendelson, J. H., Ogata, M., & Mello, N. K. (1969). Effects of alcohol ingestion and withdrawal on magnesium states of alcoholics: Clinical and experimental findings. *Annals of the New York Academy of Sciences, 162,* 918–933.

National Heart Institute (1968). *The Framingham heart study: Habits and coronary heart disease* (Public Health Service Publication No. 1515). Washington, DC: U. S. Government Printing Office.

Newcombe, D. S. (1972). Ethanol metabolism and uric acid. *Metabolism, 21*(12), 1193–1203.

Nikkila, E. A., & Ojala, K. (1963). Role of hepatic L-α-glycerophosphate and triglyceride synthesis in the production of fatty liver by ethanol. *Proceedings of the Society of Experimental and Biological Medicine, 113,* 814–817.

Ogata, M., Mendelson, J. H., Mello, N. K., & Majchrowicz, E. (1971). Adrenal function and alcoholism. 2. Catecholamines. *Psychosomatic Medicine, 33,* 159–180.

Perlino, C. A., & Rimland, D. (1985). Alcoholism, leukopenia, and pneumococcal sepsis. *American Review of Respiratory Disease, 132*(4), 757–760.

Pezzimenti, J. F., & Lindenbaum, J. (1972). Megaloblastic anaemia associated with erythroid hypoplasia. *American Journal of Medicine. 53,* 748–754.

Poikolainen, K (1982). Blackouts increase with age, social class and the frequency of intoxication. *Acta Neurologica Scandinavica, 66,* 555–560.

Proust, A. J. (1977). High risk groups in tuberculosis. *New England Medical Journal, 86,* 27–29.

Reagin, T. J., & Ettinger, P. O. (1979). Varied cardiac abnormalities in alcoholics. *Alcoholism: Clinical and Experimental Research, 3*(1), 40–45.

Ritchie, J. M. (1985). The aliphatic alcohols. In A. G. Gilman, L. S. Goodman, T. W. Rall, & F. Murad (Eds.), *Goodman and Gilman's the pharmacological basis of therapeutics* (pp. 372–386). New York: Macmillan.

Roberts, H. R., & Cederbaum, A. I. (1972). The liver and blood coagulation: Physiology and pathology. *Gastroenterology, 63*(2): 297–320.

Rothman, K. (1975). Alcohol. In J. Fraumeni (Ed.), *Persons at high risk of cancer* (pp. 139–150). New York: Academic Press.

Rubin, E., & Lieber, C. S. (1968). Hepatic microsomal enzymes in man and rat: Induction and inhibition by ethanol. *Science, 162,* 690–691.

Sarles, H. (1984). Alcohol and the pancreas. *Acta Medica Scandinavica* (Supplement), *703,* 235–249.

Seevers, M. H. (1970). Morphine and ethanol physical dependence: A critique of a hypothesis. *Science, 170,* 1113–1114.

Sellers, E. M., & Kalant, H. (1976). Alcohol intoxication and withdrawal. *New England Journal of Medicine, 294*(4), 757–762.

Spencer, H., Rubio, N., Rubio, E., Indreika, M., & Seitam, A. (1986). Chronic alcoholism: Frequently overlooked cause of osteoporosis in men. *American Journal of Medicine, 80*(3), 393–397.

Tabakoff, B., & Hoffman, P. L. (1983). Neurochemical aspects of tolerance to and physical dependence on alcohol. In B. Kissin & H. Begleiter (Eds.), *The biology of alcoholism: The pathogenesis of alcoholism* (Vol. 7) (pp. 199–252). New York: Plenum Press.

Talbott, D. G. (1975). Primary alcoholic heart disease. *Annals of the New York Academy of Sciences, 252,* 237–241.

Teschke, R., Matsuzaki, S., Ohnishi, K., Hasumura, Y., & Lieber, C. S. (1977). Metabolism of alcohol at high concentrations: Role and biochemical nature of the hepatic microsomal oxidizing system. *Advances in Experimental Medicine and Biology, 85A,* 257–280.

Theorell, H., & Bonnichsen, R. (1951). Studies on liver alcohol dehydrogenase. 1. Equilibria and initial reaction velocities. *Acta Chemica Scandinavica Series B. Organic Chemistry and Biochemistry, 5,* 1105–1126.

Thomson, A. D., Baker, H., & Leevy, C. M. (1970). Patterns of ^{35}S-thiamine hydrochloride absorption in the malnourished alcoholic patient. *Journal of Laboratory and Clinical Medicine, 76*(1), 34–45.

U. S. Department of Health, Education and Welfare (1978). *Third special report to the Congress on alcohol and health* (DHEW Publication No. ADM 78–569). Washington, DC: U. S. Government Printing Office.

Urbano-Marquez, A., Estruch, R., Navarro-Lopez, F., Grau, J. M., Mont, L., & Rubin, E. (1989). The effects of alcoholism on skeletal and cardiac muscle. *New England Journal of Medicine, 320* (7), 409–415.

Van Thiel, D. H., & Gavaler, J. S. (1986). Hypothalamic-pituitary-gonadal function in liver disease with particular attention to the endocrine effects of chronic alcohol abuse. In H. Popper & F. Schaffner (Eds.), *Progress in Liver Disease (Vol. III)* (pp. 273–282). New York: Grune & Stratton.

Van Thiel, D. H., Gavaler, J., & Lester, R. (1974). Ethanol inhibition of vitamin A metabolism in the testes: Possible mechanism for sterility in alcoholics. *Science, 186,* 941–942.

Van Thiel, D. H., & Lester, R. (1976). Alcoholism: Its effects on hypothalamic pituitary gonadal function. *Gastroenterology, 71,* 318–327.

Victor, M., & Adams, R. D. (1953). The effects of alcohol on the nervous system. *Research Publications of the Association for Research in Nervous & Mental Disease, 32,* 526–573.

Victor, M., & Brausch, J. (1967). The role of abstinence in the genesis of alcoholic epilepsy. *Epilepsy, 8,* 1–20.

Victor, M., & Laureno, R. (1978). Neurologic complications of alcohol abuse: Epidemiologic aspects. In B. S. Schoenberg (Ed.), *Advances in neurology* (19) (pp. 603–617). New York: Raven Press.

Vitale, J. J., & Coffey, J. (1971). Alcohol and vitamin metabolism. In B. Kissin & H. Begleiter (Eds.), *The biology of alcoholism: Biochemistry* (Vol. 1) (pp. 327–352). New York: Plenum Press.

Walker, J. E. C., & Gordon, E. K. (1970). Biochemical aspects associated with an ethanol induced fatty liver. *Biochemical Journal, 119,* 511–516.

Waters, A. H., Morley, A. A., & Rankin, J. G. (1966). Effect of alcohol on haemopoiesis. *British Medical Journal, 2,* 1565–1568.

Webster, P. D. (1975). Secretory and metabolic effects of alcohol on the pancreas. *Annals of the New York Academy of Sciences, 252,* 183–186.

Wikler, A., Goodell, H., & Wolff, H. G. (1945). Studies on pain: The effect of analgesic agents on sensations other than pain. *Journal of Pharmacological and Experimental Therapeutics, 83,* 294–299.

Williams, H. L., & Salamy, A. (1972). Alcohol and sleep. In B. Kissin & H. Begleiter (Eds.), *The biology of alcoholism: Physiology and behavior* (Vol. 2) (pp. 435–483). New York: Plenum Press.

Wolfe, S. M., & Victor, M. (1969). The relationship of hypomagnesmia and alkalosis to alcohol withdrawal symptoms. *Annals of the New York Academy of Sciences, 162,* 973–984.

Yano, L., Rhoads, G. G., & Kagan, A. (1977). Coffee, alcohol and risk of coronary heart disease among Japanese men living in Hawaii. *New England Journal of Medicine, 297,* 405–409.

CNS DEPRESSANTS: OTHER SEDATIVE-HYPNOTICS

Donna S. Woolf

Of all the drugs used in clinical practice, the sedative-hypnotic-antianxiety drugs are the most widely prescribed (Harvey, 1985). When a group of drugs is this widely prescribed and can act on the central nervous system (CNS) to produce euphoria, the potential for abuse exists.

Sedative is an old, somewhat vague term that is applied to drugs that calm anxiety and decrease wakefulness. *Hypnotics* produce drowsiness or induce a sleeplike state from which the person can be aroused. Older CNS depressant drugs, such as the barbiturates, act as sedatives when given in low doses, produce hypnotic effects when given in higher doses, and can produce anesthesia if the dose is high enough. The *antianxiety drugs,* specifically the benzodiazepine group, allay anxiety but are more specific as to which brain neurons are depressed. They are not used as anesthetics, even in high doses.

GENERAL PHARMACOLOGY OF SEDATIVES, HYPNOTICS, AND ANTIANXIETY DRUGS

Before 1900, only a few drugs were specifically used as sedatives or hypnotics. Among the few were the bromides, chloral hydrate, paraldehyde, and alcohol. Alcohol's pharmacology is addressed in Chapter 2. The bromides are now obsolete drugs because of their slow onset of action and high toxicity (Harvey, 1985) and will not be covered in this text.

In 1903, the first barbiturate, barbital, was introduced, and a new era of sedative and hypnotic drugs began (Harvey, 1985). A few other drugs in this general class were marketed, but none could displace the barbiturates' hold on the prescribing market. In 1961, the introduction of chlordiazepoxide (Librium) provided the prescriber with a clinically "superior" product, and the benzodiazepine agents overtook the barbiturate market. It is likely that the future prescribing of barbiturates as sedative or hypnotic drugs will continue to fall behind the benzodiazepine drug group.

The pharmacology of each of the diverse CNS depressant drugs will be presented in individual sections. The withdrawal patterns of these drugs are similar in symptoms and have been termed the *general depressant withdrawal syndrome* (Jaffe, 1985, p. 547). The withdrawal patterns are presented in a separate, comparative section following the general pharmacology.

It should be noted that when any of the drugs in this section are combined with other CNS depressants, additive, if not synergistic, depressant effects occur (see Chapter 8). This principle becomes important when the issue of acute intoxication with CNS depressants is faced. Overdosages of benzodiazepine drugs alone are usually survived. Combinations of benzodiazepines with depressants such as alcohol are sometimes fatal (Greenblatt, Allen, Noel, & Shader, 1977).

Barbiturates

The barbiturate drugs have a long and successful history. Clinically, the barbiturates are used as sedatives, hypnotics, anesthetics, and anticonvulsants. Only the abuse of and physical dependence on barbiturates as sedatives or hypnotics will be considered here. For specific information about the use of barbiturates to induce anesthesia or to treat epilepsy, the reader is referred to a general pharmacology text.

Many studies have been done to elucidate exactly how the barbiturates produce their varied effects on each CNS structure. For more information on this technical aspect of barbiturate pharmacology, the reader is referred to Harvey (1975) for an overview of the subject. Recent developments in elucidating the mechanisms of actions of the barbiturates have linked the anticonvulsant actions of these drugs to the inhibition of gamma-aminobutyric acid (GABA) complexes (Olsen & Leeb-Lundberg, 1981). These developments are interesting since they are showing some common links between the actions of benzodiazepine and barbiturate drugs.

Forms of Barbiturates

The classification of the barbiturates has become vague over the last few years as the pharmacokinetic knowledge about these drugs has been refined. The classical delineations of the drugs divided them into long-acting barbiturates, short-to-intermediate-acting barbiturates, and ultra-short-acting barbiturates (Harvey, 1975). Problems arose when it was found that the length of

time that the drug action persisted did not parallel the time it took to eliminate half the dose of the drug (the *elimination half-life*). Although the old classification is not used, nothing has been devised to replace it—so confusion remains. Included in Table 3.1 are the half-lives (t1/2) of the commonly used and abused barbiturates. The t1/2 represents the time it takes for the body to eliminate one-half the ingested drug dose. Table 3.1 is important since it determines the likelihood that the drug will accumulate and how long one can expect some residual drug effects. It also helps the clinician to predict the length of the withdrawal syndrome since the

Table 3.1
Routes of Abuse and Half-Lives of Barbiturates and Miscellaneous Sedatives and Hypnotics

Generic	Trade Name	Slang	Routes of Abuse[a]	Half-Life (in hours)
Barbiturates:				
Amobarbital	Amytal	Blue velvet, bluebirds, blue devils, blue heavens, blues	PO, IV, IM	8–42
Secobarbital	Seconal	Reds, redbirds, red devils, seggy	PO, IV, IM	15–40
Pentobarbital	Nembutal	Nembies, yellows, yellow jackets	PO, IV, IM	15–48
Phenobarbital	Luminal and others		PO, IV, IM	80–120
Butabarbital	Butisol		PO	34–42
Secobarbital/ amobarbital	Tuinal	Rainbows, reds and blues, tooies, double trouble	PO, IV, IM	15–40
Others:				
Ethchlorvynol	Placidyl		PO, IV	10–25
Chloral hydrate	Noctec and others	Mickey Finn	PO	4–9.5[b]
Glutethimide	Doriden		PO	5–22
Meprobamate	Equanil, Miltown		PO	6–17
Methaqualone	No longer on market	Ludes, Sopors quads	PO	10–40
Methyprylon	Noludar		PO	3–6
Paraldehyde	Generic		PO	3.4–9.8

Note: The data in column 5 are from Harvey, 1985; Olin, 1987.
[a] PO = oral
   IM = intramuscular
   IV = intravenous
[b] Includes half-life of major metabolite

longer acting drugs tend to have prolonged withdrawals. Street or slang names of some of the sedative and hypnotic drugs are listed in Table 3.1. The barbiturates have so many slang names that a listing of all of them would be impossible.

Although the oral ingestion of barbiturates for abuse purposes is more common than injection, intravenous and intramuscular routes have been used. Some people abuse barbiturates to produce sleep, but more probably abuse them for the euphoria they cause. McClane and Martin (1976) have compared barbiturates' euphoriant effects to those of morphine. It is not uncommon for barbiturates and amphetamines to be abused at the same time (see Chapter 4). Abusers claim that this combination produces more elation than either drug alone. The barbiturates are sometimes used by the abuser to "take the edge off" (to reduce the anxiety caused by high doses of amphetamines).

Physiologic Effects of Barbiturates

The CNS is the main site of action of the barbiturate drugs. Although the barbiturates depress all structures in the CNS, some areas of the CNS are affected selectively, according to the dosage. The CNS is especially sensitive to the effects of the barbiturates, so even anesthetic doses of the drug are unlikely to cause depression of cardiac, skeletal, or smooth muscle. Toxicities to these systems occur only after overdosage.

Certain barbiturates, particularly phenobarbital, are selective anticonvulsants and can offer protection against seizures at dosages that do not sedate the client. Barbiturates *do not* reduce pain. They may actually increase sensitivity to pain (Harvey, 1985). If the client is in pain when the barbiturate is taken, excitement instead of sedation may occur.

Barbiturates alter the stages of sleep, particularly when taken in large doses. Rebound of these stages occurs when the drugs are discontinued (Harvey, 1985).

Barbiturates depress respiration since these drugs depress the respiratory neurogenic drive. When barbiturates are given orally in therapeutic doses, the respiratory depression is not clinically significant. Clients who have overdosed or who suffer diseases of insufficient pulmonary function should be carefully monitored for excess respiratory depression. The injectable administration of barbiturates, as seen when they are used as general anesthetics, increases the drugs' propensity to produce respiratory depression.

The liver enzyme systems are profoundly affected by the barbiturates. The microsomal enzyme system, which metabolizes the barbiturates, is stimulated. This affects the metabolism of many other drugs, which are also metabolized by this system. This accounts for several of the known drug interactions of the barbiturates. The barbiturates actually stimulate their own metabolism. Clients with acute intermittent porphyria should *never* be given barbiturates. The barbiturates accelerate the existing problem of the synthesis of porphyrins, leading to severe attacks of the disease, including death or paralysis (Harvey, 1975).

Side Effects of Barbiturates

The side effects of barbiturate drug therapy include drowsiness, particularly hangover drowsiness. After hypnotic doses are given, residual effects on motor skills are thought to occur. Some clients may experience paradoxical excitement, irritability, or delirium when barbiturates are given. These effects occur in the elderly and debilitated. Excitatory hangovers are more likely to be due to the continued presence of other chemical forms of the drugs (excitatory enantiomers) or withdrawal symptoms (Harvey, 1985).

Tolerance, Abuse, and Physical Dependence on Barbiturates

The chronic use or abuse of barbiturate drugs leads to tolerance development and physical dependence. This single statement accounts for the decrease in clinical use of the barbiturates.

Tolerance to the barbiturates develops quickly. Types of tolerance are discussed in Chapter 2. *Dispositional tolerance,* which results from changes in the organism (such as changes in drug metabolism), can be shown in animals after administering only a few doses of barbiturates. *Pharmacodynamic tolerance* to the barbiturates develops over a period of weeks. Although the dosage required to give the same effects may be higher, the lethal dose of the barbiturates does not continue to increase. Therefore, the addict may continue to increase the dose of the barbiturates until the body can no longer compensate with tolerance mechanisms. At that point, overdosage occurs. Barbiturate overdosage will be discussed in a subsequent section.

Physical dependence on the barbiturates is evidenced by a *severe* withdrawal syndrome. Clients who have chronically abused barbiturates, particularly barbiturates with short-to-intermediate action, can die during untreated barbiturate withdrawal (Fraser, Shaver, Maxwell, & Isbell, 1953).

Barbiturate Overdosage

Overdosage of barbiturates occurs through attempts to commit suicide, miscalculations by drug abusers, and accidents such as might occur in children. Death occurs in 0.5%–12% of barbiturate overdose cases (Harvey, 1985). Symptoms of overdosage of the sedative, hypnotic, and antianxiety drugs are often compared to symptoms of barbiturate poisoning so the symptoms of barbiturate overdosage will be described here.

The fatal dose of barbiturates with intermediate or short half-lives is usually lower than the fatal dose of drugs with longer half-lives. For example, to induce severe poisoning, it takes less pentobarbital than phenobarbital when they are compared on a milligram-to-milligram basis.

Since the barbiturates depress the CNS, symptoms of barbiturate overdosage will invariably be severe inebriation or coma, if the dosage was sufficient. The pupils usually constrict early in poisoning but may dilate if hypoxia ensues. Respirations are depressed and mechanical support may be required. Pneumonia or pulmonary edema are common complications and cause some of the deaths from barbiturate overdosage. Blood pressure falls and shock may result. Temperature often drops. Renal failure due to circulatory collapse may occur.

In many cases of severe poisoning, particularly when renal failure occurs, hemodialysis or hemoperfusion is used as an effective way of removing the barbiturate. Supportive care of the client suffering from barbiturate poisoning is essential. For further information concerning complications of barbiturate poisoning and its treatment, see Gary and Tresnewsky (1983).

Chloral Hydrate

Chloral hydrate is a general CNS depressant, available in capsules and liquid for oral use. Its most famous nickname is the "Mickey Finn," which is a name applied to the mixture of alcohol and chloral hydrate. The combination is a favorite in movie or book schemes that use "knockout drops." Since alcohol and chloral hydrate are both depressants, a synergistic effect could be predicted from the combination (see Chapter 8). Alcohol accelerates the breakdown of chloral hydrate to trichloroethanol. Chloral hydrate slows the enzyme that

breaks down alcohol, resulting in higher blood alcohol concentrations (Sellers, Carr, Bernstein, Sellers, & Koch-Weser, 1972). Chloral hydrate is not as popular on the street as other hypnotics. Its abuse is generally seen in those who obtain it with a legal prescription for use as a hypnotic.

Chloral hydrate is a relatively short-acting chemical. The t1/2 of trichloroethanol, the metabolite responsible for the majority of the drug's actions, is 4–12 hours (Harvey, 1985). One of the drug's minor metabolites, trichloroacetic acid, has a t1/2 of 4 days, and accumulation of this metabolite can occur with chronic administration (Breimer, 1977). Chloral hydrate is metabolized by the enzyme alcohol dehydrogenase. The hypnotic dose of chloral hydrate ranges from 500 mg to as high as 2 g in some persons.

Chloral hydrate does not reduce pain; and if pain is present when it is given, delirium or excitement may result (Harvey, 1985). Chloral hydrate is a gastric irritant and has an offensive taste. A similar chloral compound, triclofos (Triclos), has a less disagreeable taste. Hangover occurs with chloral hydrate but less often than with other CNS depressants.

Poisoning by chloral hydrate resembles barbiturate overdosage. Vomiting, pinpoint pupils, and hepatic and renal irritation may occur (Harvey, 1985). Toxic doses of chloral hydrate cause cardiac arrhythmias.

The chronic abuse of chloral hydrate causes physical dependence and tolerance. A drop in tolerance after habitual abuse has been reported. This decrease in tolerance may result in overdosage. Chronic abuse often results in gastritis, hepatic and renal damage, and dermatitis (Harvey, 1985).

Paraldehyde

Paraldehyde is a general CNS depressant, available only as a liquid. It is usually administered orally, but it can be given in an oil retention enema. Due to the extreme irritability of the drug on intramuscular or intravenous administration, these routes of administration have been discontinued.

The most impressive quality of parldehyde is its putrid odor and taste. Once smelled or tasted, it will not be soon forgotten by staff or clients. The odor of paraldehyde makes the client who has taken the drug readily identifiable.

Paraldehyde gained some of its use in the treatment of alcohol withdrawal because it had the reputation of being excreted by the lungs. This statement is misleading since 70%–80% of the drug is metabolized in the liver, leaving less than 30% of the drug to be excreted through the lungs. When liver function is impaired, more of the drug may be expired through the lungs (Harvey, 1985).

Paraldehyde's sedative effects begin about 20 minutes after oral ingestion. The t1/2 of paraldehyde averages 3.4–9.8 hours (Olin, 1987). Other than sedation and gastric irritation, paraldehyde has few side effects in normal doses. Respirations and blood pressure are usually not affected by normal doses. In large doses, hypotension and respiratory depression may occur. The usual hypnotic dose of paraldehyde is 4–8 ml although higher doses may be required in the treatment of alcohol withdrawal (Olin, 1987).

Paraldehyde gives problems both to those professionals who administer and to those who dispense it. The drug is chemically unstable. After paraldehyde has been exposed to air, it rapidly decomposes to acetic acid. Open bottles must be discarded after 24 hours since administering acetic acid can be harmful to the client. Paraldehyde is incompatible with plastic and must be measured and administered in glass containers.

Those who have smelled or tasted paraldehyde may find it incredible that paraldehyde is occasionally abused. Some who abuse paraldehyde were introduced to the drug as a treatment for alcohol withdrawal. Paraldehyde tolerance, dependence, and withdrawal closely resemble alcohol tolerance, dependence, and withdrawal (see Chapter 2).

Glutethimide

Glutethimide (Doriden) is a general CNS depressant prescribed as a hypnotic. Its use as a hypnotic is hard to justify, because acute and chronic abuse are difficult to treat, and other safer hypnotics are available.

Glutethimide is highly fat soluble (i.e., after ingestion, it is quickly distributed into the body's fat stores from the bloodstream). Glutethimide is metabolized by the liver and accelerates the activity of the microsomal enzyme system, which metabolizes many drugs. For this reason, glutethimide increases the metabolism of the barbiturates. Glutethimide has a t1/2 of 5–22 hours, but in overdosages the t1/2 may rise to as much as 100 hours (Harvey, 1985).

Glutethimide is highly anticholinergic and produces dry mouth, pupillary dilation, and slowed intestinal motility. Osteomalacia may occur when the drug is used chronically (Harvey, 1985).

As few as 10 glutethimide tablets (500 mg) can cause severe intoxication. Glutethimide poisoning may cause the level of consciousness of the client to rise and fall as the drug moves from its fatty tissue storage compartment. This is sometimes called *waxing and waning* (Myers & Stockard, 1975). Symptoms of overdosage are similar to those seen in barbiturate intoxication although respiratory depression may be somewhat less severe (Harvey, 1985).

The chronic use of glutethimide produces physical dependence and tolerance similar to that seen with barbiturate dependence. Symptoms of withdrawal have been reported not only in chronic abusers who abstain from the drug, but also in those taking regular, moderate doses (500–3000 mg daily) who abstain from the drug. Acute intoxication without chronic use can also produce some withdrawal symptoms (Good, 1976). Catatonic reactions have been reported when glutethimide was withdrawn (Good, 1976). Symptoms of withdrawal include nausea, abdominal cramps, disorientation, sweating, headaches, tremors, seizures, insomnia, and anxiety (Good, 1976).

Methyprylon

Methyprylon (Noludar) is a general CNS depressant introduced in 1955 for use as a hypnotic. The drug is similar in chemical structure to glutethimide. Side effects of methyprylon include rash, stomach upset, nausea, vomiting, diarrhea, and headache.

After oral administration, the drug is metabolized by the microsomal enzyme system of the liver. Although the plasma t1/2 is 4 hours (Harvey, 1985), higher dosages, as may be seen in acute overdosage, result in much longer half-lives (Pancorbo, Palagi, Piecoro, & Wilson, 1977). Overdosage may result in a coma lasting up to 5 days (Harvey, 1985). Acute overdosage symptoms resemble those of barbiturate poisoning.

As with glutethimide and barbiturates, physical dependence on and tolerance to methyprylon do occur. Withdrawal symptoms are similar to those of barbiturate withdrawal, including seizures (Harvey, 1985).

Ethchlorvynol

Ethchlorvynol (Placidyl) is a highly fat-soluble chemical clinically used as a hypnotic because of its CNS depressant actions. Although the drug is available only in a soft capsule form, to be taken orally, intravenous abuse of the contents of the capsule has been reported (Glauser, et al., 1976). This is achieved by withdrawing the semiliquid contents of the capsule with a needle and syringe and injecting it. The usual adult dose of ethchlorvynol as a hypnotic is 500 mg although 4000 mg may be used daily by the addict (Harvey, 1985).

Side effects of ethchlorvynol include positional nystagmus, diplopia, hangover, hypotension, nausea, and vomiting. A mintlike taste is usually reported after oral and intravenous use. Both large oral doses and intravenous abuse can produce pulmonary edema (Glauser, et al., 1976).

The t1/2 of ethchlorvynol can only be explained on a two-compartmental kinetic basis. One to three hours after administration, about one-half of the dose will disappear from the bloodstream. The drug then is moved into the fat-soluble areas of the body, and 10–25 hours are required to eliminate half of this dose (Cummins, Martin, & Scherfling, 1971). For this reason, overdosages may result in a slow elimination of the drug, and the length of coma from excessive doses may depend on how much drug was taken. Respiratory depression, bradycardia, and hypothermia may occur with acute intoxication (Harvey, 1985).

Physical dependence and tolerance occur when ethchlorvynol is abused, and withdrawal resembles that of short-to-intermediate-acting barbiturates. Schizophreniclike reactions may occur during withdrawal (Harvey, 1985).

Meprobamate

Meprobamate (Miltown, Equanil) was introduced in 1955 as an antianxiety drug. It has also been widely used as a muscle relaxant although there is doubt as to the drug's efficacy for this indication. In fact, meprobamate had immediate marketing success without well-substantiated literature support for its effectiveness as an antianxiety drug (Greenblatt & Shader, 1971).

In contrast to some other drugs discussed in this chapter, meprobamate cannot be used to induce anesthesia and is somewhat selective in the CNS areas it depresses (Harvey, 1985). The drug is known to depress the hypothalamus and the limbic system, areas usually affected by selective antianxiety drugs (Harvey, 1985). Meprobamate is occasionally used as a hypnotic.

Meprobamate's main site of metabolism is the liver's microsomal enzyme system. Chronic use of the

drug can increase the usual t1/2 of 5–17 hours to 24–48 hours. The main side effects of meprobamate are ataxia and drowsiness.

Meprobamate was first marketed as having a low potential for abuse. Soon after widespread prescribing began, widespread abuse also began. Physical dependence and tolerance occur with chronic use of meprobamate. Doses of 2.4 g/d (six of the 400-mg tablets) for a period of approximately a month can produce withdrawal symptoms if the drug is abruptly discontinued. About 10% of these untreated cases will have grand mal seizures during withdrawal (Harvey, 1985). The symptoms of meprobamate withdrawal resemble those of most sedative or hypnotic drugs.

Methaqualone

Methaqualone is a nonbarbiturate CNS depressant which has been withdrawn from the United States market. It is still widely abused from illegal sources. Former trade names include Quaalude and Sopor. Methaqualone has sedative and hypnotic properties, as well as some anticonvulsant and antitussive actions.

Slang terms for methaqualone, other than the trade names are listed in Table 3.1. Sometimes, the act of taking methaqualone, either singly or in combination with alcohol, is called "luding out."

It is interesting that methaqualone was initially marketed in the United States as having a low potential for abuse since prior experiences in Japan had proven the potential for abuse. The rapid upsurge of methaqualone abuse, which began in the early 1970s, was accelerated by the rumor among abusers that the drug had aphrodisiac properties. The usual desired drug dosage was one that will produce a "buzz" without producing sleep. The street dose of the drug was widely variant, with some nontolerant users taking 75 mg and some experienced users taking 2000 mg (Harvey, 1985).

Methaqualone is most commonly abused by oral administration. The t1/2 of the drug is 10–40 hours; however, when high doses (2–3 g) are taken over 6–8 hours, methaqualone serum levels may be detected for up to 3 days (Delong, Smyth, Polk, Nayak, & Reavey-Cantwell, 1976). The drug is metabolized in the liver by the hepatic microsomal system (Brown & Goenechea, 1973).

Frequently, methaqualone produces side effects of fatigue and dizziness. Other side effects of methaqualone use are headache, loss of appetite, nausea, abdominal cramps, and epistaxis (Inaba, Gay, Newmeyer, &

Whitehead, 1973). High doses of methaqualone may produce a transient tingling, prickling, or numbness of the extremities (Inaba, et al., 1973). The abuser sometimes perceives this effect as pleasant. In some cases, paresthesia has lasted for 3 or 4 days after the methaqualone was stopped (Hoaken, 1975). Intoxication from methaqualone can produce symptoms of a thick, dry tongue, dry mouth, constipation, and feelings of depersonalization (Inaba, et al., 1973). Hangover is frequent with methaqualone use.

Symptoms of methaqualone overdosage are much like those of barbiturate overdosage; however, paradoxical excitement with delirium and seizures may be seen (Harvey, 1985). Deaths due to concomitant methaqualone and alcohol ingestion have occurred.

Chronic methaqualone use produces physical dependence and tolerance. Withdrawal is "as dangerous as that seen from the short-acting barbiturates and can produce death" (Wesson & Smith, 1978, p. 128). Symptoms of methaqualone withdrawal resemble those of the short-to-intermediate-acting barbiturates.

Antihistamines

Prescription and nonprescription antihistamine drugs are occasionally prescribed as "hypnotics" or "sleep-aids." The use of these drugs in facilitating sleepiness is possible, because drowsiness is a side effect of many antihistamines. Tolerance often occurs to these drowsiness side effects, and antihistamines do not produce a true hypnosis. One reason that these drugs are used is to avoid the use of other effective sedative or hypnotic drugs that may accumulate in the body and have tolerance or physical dependence liabilities. Sedating antihistamines are frequently prescribed as sleep-aids for geriatric clients. They are widely promoted by the media to encourage "safe and restful sleep" in all adults. The use and overuse of these antihistamines is covered in Chapter 7.

Benzodiazepines

The benzodiazepines (see Table 3.2) have become famous among health professionals who treat substance abuse. There are several reasons for their notoriety.

1. They are widely prescribed and, hence, readily available for abuse.
2. Some clinicians still deny that addiction to benzodiazepines occurs.
3. The timing of the benzodiazepine withdrawal syndrome is delayed, and the symptoms may be subtle.

Table 3.2
Routes of Abuse and Half-Lives of Benzodiazepines

Generic	Trade Name	Routes of Abuse[a]	Half-Life (in hours)
Chlordiazepoxide	Librium and others	PO, IM, IV	5–15
Diazepam	Valium and others	PO, IM, IV	30–60
Lorazepam	Ativan	PO, IM, IV	10–20
Oxazepam	Serax	PO	5–10
Prazepam	Centrax	PO	24–200[b]
Flurazepam	Dalmane	PO	50–100[b]
Chlorazepate	Tranxene, Azene	PO	50–80[b]
Tenazepam	Restoril	PO	10–17
Clonazepam	Klonopin	PO	18–50
Alprazolam	Xanax	PO	12–15
Halazepam	Paxipam	PO	14
Triazolam	Halcion	PO	1.5–5.4

Note: The data in column 4 are from Harvey, 1985; Olin, 1987.
[a] PO = oral
   IM = intramuscular
   IV = intravenous
[b] Includes half-life of major metabolite

The benzodiazepines are used in clinical practice primarily as antianxiety agents and hypnotics. Some members of this drug group also possess muscle-relaxant and anticonvulsant properties (Harvey, 1985).

Mechanism of Action

The exact method by which the benzodiazepines decrease anxiety, relax muscles, or stop the spread of seizure is undergoing an explosive amount of research at this time. The current main area of interest centers on the discovery of a *CNS benzodiazepine-specific receptor* (Haefely, Kyburz, Gerecke, & Möhler, 1985). It has been found that the benzodiazepine drugs, as well as other minor tranquilizers and anticonvulsant and convulsant drugs, produce at least part of their pharmacologic effects by affecting one or more regulatory sites on a benzodiazepine receptor complex (Haefely et al., 1985; Olsen & Leeb-Lundburg, 1981). This complex is thought to consist of a benzodiazepine receptor that is functionally coupled to a GABA receptor and an associated chloride channel. It should be remembered that GABA is a major inhibitory neurotransmitter in the CNS (see Chapter 1). Activation of this neurotransmitter would result in neuronal depression in the neurons mediated by GABA. The highest densities of benzodiazepine binding sites are found in the cerebral cortex, structures of the limbic system, and the cerebellar cortex (Haefely et al., 1985).

Researchers are actively searching for a naturally occurring substance that might act on these benzodiazepine receptors. Some compounds, such as beta-carbolines, were initially thought to be such substances, but were later found to be methodologic artifacts. Research with these compounds continues. Certain congeners of the benzodiazepines have been found which can inhibit the action and binding of the benzodiazepines to their receptors.

CNS Actions. The benzodiazepines do not depress all neurons in the CNS to the same extent. Low doses of the benzodiazepines produce drowsiness or sedation. As the dosage is increased, sleep ensues, then stupor. Surgical anesthesia cannot be induced with the benzodiazepines although a benzodiazepine is sometimes administered before anesthesia since the drug can impair recent memory (Harvey, 1985).

The benzodiazepines shorten stage 4 sleep (see Chapter 1). Since night terrors and somnambulism occur in this stage, certain benzodiazepines are used to treat these specific sleep disorders. The time spent in rapid eye movement (REM) sleep is unusually shortened by benzodiazepines. Although stage 4 and REM sleep are shortened, total sleep time is usually increased when benzodiazepines are taken (Harvey, 1985).

Antianxiety and anticonvulsant pharmacologic effects of the benzodiazepines have been linked to the limbic system, particularly the hippocampus and amygdala (see Chapter 1). Sleep induction and muscle relaxation have been linked to the reticular formation (RF) and the spinal cord (Robertson, 1980).

Respiration

In normal persons, respirations are rarely depressed by the benzodiazepines. When chronic obstructive pulmonary disease is present, the respiratory depressant effects of diazepam and other benzodiazepines may be pronounced (Rao, Sherbaniuk, Prasad, Lee, & Sproule, 1973). Most respiratory depression caused by the benzodiazepines has been reported in clients who have been given or who have taken more than one depressant. When diazepam is combined with opioids or with general anesthetics, occasional apnea can occur (Harvey, 1985).

Cardiovascular Effects

The benzodiazepines have little effect on the cardiovascular system, except when large doses are taken. Overdosage or extremely large dosages may result in a decrease in systolic blood pressure and a reflex increase in heart rate (Rao et al., 1973).

Absorption. The speed by which a benzodiazepine enters the blood determines how quickly it acts, because all the benzodiazepines are highly lipid soluble and quickly enter brain tissue. Diazepam and clorazepate are absorbed rapidly and reach peak plasma concentrations in less than 1.2 hours. Clorazepate's absorption, however, depends on its conversion to desmethyldiazepam in stomach acid. Triazolam, alprazolam, and lorazepam and intermediate in absorption, requiring 1.2–2.0 hours to peak concentration after oral doses. Oxazepam, temazepam and prazepam are slower in onset, taking 2–3 hours or more for peak concentrations (Greenblatt, Divoll, Abernethy, Ochs, & Shader, 1983). Benzodiazepines are erratically absorbed for all the available injectable benzodiazepines, with the exception of lorazepam.

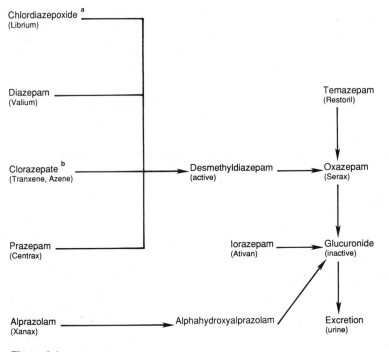

Figure 3.1
Major metabolic pathways of antianxiety benzodiazepines. [a]Chlordiazepoxide has several active metabolites. [b]Chlorazepate is converted to metabolite by stomach acid. Data are from Greenblatt, Knowles, et al., 1977; Greenblatt, Shader, & Koch-Weser, 1975a; Greenblatt, Shader, & Koch-Weser, 1975b.

Metabolism and Pharmacokinetics

Most of the benzodiazepine compounds undergo metabolism in the liver. Many are metabolized to active metabolites (see Fig. 3.1). How these compounds are metabolized indicates which benzodiazepine compounds are likely to accumulate. The long action of the active metabolites of these compounds may greatly add to the time it takes for the body to rid itself of an active drug. For example, from Figure 3.1, one could predict that diazepam (Valium), or the active metabolite, might remain in the body for a longer period of time than oxazepam (Serax) or lorazepam (Ativan). This scheme may also explain the similarities in drug actions of different benzodiazepines since many of the marketed compounds have common active metabolites.

Since the liver is the site of benzodiazepine metabolism, clients with liver impairment, such as alcoholics, may accumulate benzodiazepines (Klotz, Avant, Hoyumpa, Schenker, & Wilkinson, 1975). It should be noted, however, that alcoholics in the withdrawal phase may show lower blood levels of benzodiazepines than would be predicted following oral administration. Poor gastric absorption of the drug as well as liver abnormalities may explain part of this phenomenon (Sellman, Pekkarinen, Kangas, & Raijola, 1975).

The half-lives of benzodiazepines do not accurately predict the duration of action (Greenblatt & Shader, 1985). The action of benzodiazepines may be terminated by receptor adaptation to the drug's presence (cellular tolerance) or by the drug leaving the receptor site. The drug may either leave the receptor by moving to a storage area, fat tissue in this case, or by moving to the liver where it is metabolized and prepared for clearance. Data suggest that the extent to which a benzodiazepine is distributed in lipid or fat is more important than metabolism in predicting how long a single dose will act.

During repeated doses, benzodiazepine accumulation depends on the elimination half-life. Benzodiazepines with long half-lives will accumulate extensively; those with short half-lives will accumulate little, reach consistent, steady, blood levels (steady state) quickly, and will wash out quickly after repeated dosing.

These data are essential to the understanding of varied withdrawal patterns among the benzodiazepine drugs (see Withdrawal from CNS Depressants).

The half-lives of some benzodiazepines are prolonged in the elderly (Greenblatt et al., 1983). Benzodiazepines that have long half-lives, or have active metabolites, should be used with great caution in geriatric clients. In the elderly, a four- to fivefold increase in the half-life of diazepam (Valium) has been reported (Klotz et al., 1975). If benzodiazepines are used at all in elderly clients, accumulation effects could be minimized by administering a drug that has a relatively short half-life and few, if any, active metabolites, such as oxazepam (Serax) or lorazepam (Ativan).

Side Effects

As might be predicted from the pharmacologic actions of the benzodiazepines, drowsiness, motor incoordination, and ataxia are common side effects. In some alcoholic circles, these side effects account for the benzodiazepines' nickname—*solid alcohol*. Some clients experience increased hostility or rage while taking benzodiazepines (Harvey, 1985). Confusion may occur with hypnotic doses, in sensitive persons, or in the elderly. A metallic-like aftertaste, dry mouth, blurred vision, and headaches occur in some persons who take benzodiazepines.

Overdosage

Benzodiazepines are frequently prescribed in large quantities and are easily available. They are, therefore, prime agents for use in suicide attempts. Surprisingly few deaths due to benzodiazepine poisoning have occurred. Overdosage with benzodiazepines rarely requires ventilatory assistance unless the overdosage is the result of benzodiazepines plus other CNS depressants (Greenblatt, Allen, et al., 1977). "Treatment for overdosage is purely supportive of respiratory and cardiovascular function" (Baldessarini, 1985, p. 436.) One benzodiazepine antagonist (Ro 15-1788) is being investigated for use in the treatment of overdosage (Harvey, 1985).

Tolerance and Physical Dependence

Tolerance to the benzodiazepines and cross-tolerance to other CNS depressants occurs when benzodiazepine drugs are chronically used (Harvey, 1985). Physical

dependence as evidenced by withdrawal symptoms has also been shown after low-dose and high-dose use (Busto et al., 1986; Smith & Wesson, 1985).

When high doses of benzodiazepines are taken for a month or longer, there is little debate that a withdrawal syndrome and dependency similar to other sedative-hypnotics occurs, including seizures, psychosis, anxiety, tremor, and nightmares. The dependence debate has occurred when therapeutic doses of benzodiazepines are taken for months to years. Researchers have debated whether the symptoms that emerge after discontinuing therapeutic doses are the result of the reemergence of symptoms that were present before drug therapy, a progression of the anxiety disorder which was previously masked, the expectations of the individual who has heard the widespread publicity about this drug group, or a true withdrawal syndrome (Smith & Wesson, 1985).

WITHDRAWAL FROM CNS DEPRESSANTS

There are many similarities in the withdrawal symptoms of drugs in the CNS depressant class. These similarities have led to the development of the terms *general depressant withdrawal syndrome* (Jaffe, 1985, p. 547).

As with alcohol withdrawal, the occurrence and severity of the general depressant withdrawal syndrome differs with the individual client, how long the drug has been abused, and at what dose it has been taken (see Chapter 2). There are no clear-cut rules. Mild withdrawal symptoms may be misdiagnosed as anxiety and more drug prescribed. Nausea, vomiting, and diarrhea may be attributed to gastritis. In this way, milder symptoms of withdrawal may be overlooked or denied by clients and, sometimes, by their health care providers.

The timing of withdrawal symptoms varies considerably with the particular chemical abused. In general, the intensity of withdrawal symptoms and the duration of the withdrawal syndrome can be correlated with the half-life of the abused drug. Withdrawal from short-acting drugs, such as paraldehyde, alcohol, or chloral hydrate, produces intense withdrawal syndromes, lasting approximately 5–7 days. Withdrawal from long-acting drugs, such as phenobarbital or diazepam, produces syndromes that may begin several days after the drug is discontinued; these syndromes may be somewhat less intense than syndromes of withdrawal from short-acting drugs, but may be prolonged.

Pregnant women who are physically dependent on barbiturates or other CNS depressants will give birth to babies who show signs of the general depressant withdrawal syndrome. The symptoms of withdrawal are similar to those seen in infants born to heroin addicts (Desmond, Schwanecke, Wilson, Yasunaga, & Burgdorff, 1972).

Withdrawal from Short-Acting CNS Depressants

Short-acting depressants, such as chloral hydrate, paraldehyde, and methyprylon (Noludar), have withdrawal syndromes that are clinically similar in timing and symptoms to the alcohol withdrawal syndrome presented in Chapter 2. Methyprylon (Noludar) can, with high doses, exhibit a greatly increased half-life (Pancorbo et al., 1977) so that in some clients the duration of the withdrawal syndrome may lie somewhere between that of alcohol withdrawal and that of short-to-intermediate-acting barbiturate withdrawal.

Withdrawal from Short-to-Intermediate-Acting CNS Depressants

Withdrawal from the barbiturates classically designated *short-to-intermediate-acting* (secobarbital, pentobarbital, and amobarbital) and withdrawal from other CNS depressents with moderately long half-lives (see Table 3.1) are remarkably similar (see Fig. 3.2). As with alcohol withdrawal, these withdrawal symptoms are severe, and death during withdrawal has been reported (Fraser et al., 1953). It usually takes 8–12 hours for the abuser

to stop showing signs of intoxication. For a short time, the client may actually look improved. As the drug begins to leave the body, withdrawal symptoms appear with increasing severity. Symptoms of anxiety, panic, weakness, orthostatic hypotension with tachycardia, fasciculations, sweating, insomnia, nausea, vomiting or diarrhea, and anorexia appear to be most severe during the first 2–3 days of withdrawal but may last for 2 weeks (Fraser, Wikler, Essig, & Isbell, 1958; Good, 1976; Inaba et al., 1973; Jaffe, 1985). Grand mal-type seizures are a *common* feature of barbiturate and other CNS depressants' withdrawal syndromes. It is the fear of seizures that sometimes nudges the barbiturate abuser to seek help. The seizures generally occur on the second or third day of withdrawal (Jaffe, 1985) although without treatment, the possibility of seizures occurring for up to a week should be considered (see Fig. 3.2). If the syndrome is not treated effectively (see Chapter 17), a delirium may develop. This delirium, or psychosis, may be acute or chronic and is similar in symptoms to alcoholic delirium (see Chapter 2). The client may be disoriented, confused, and may experience auditory or visual hallucinations. As with the alcoholic's delirium, once the delirium from barbiturate withdrawal has developed, it is difficult to stop its progression, even by administering barbiturates (Jaffe, 1985).

The widespread use of short-acting benzodiazepines in the treatment of panic disorders and triazolam in the treatment of insomnia have resulted in numerous reports of withdrawal syndromes. Reactions appear around the time of the symptoms seen from withdrawal of the short-to-intermediate-acting barbiturates. There have been reports of more severe withdrawal reactions

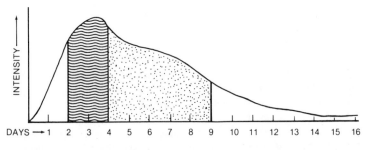

Figure 3.2
Withdrawal syndrome from the short-to-intermediate-acting CNS depressants. Peak of seizure activity is represented by wavy lines; onset of psychosis or delirium is represented by dotted area.

requiring carefully tapered withdrawal regimens with these shorter-acting benzodiazepines, particularly alprazolam (Xanax) (Fyer, et al., 1987; Noyes, et al., 1986).

Withdrawal, including psychosis and delirium, have followed the discontinuance of higher doses of triazolam (Halcion). Another short-acting benzodiazepine, lorazepam (Ativan), includes seizures in its withdrawal pattern (Howe, 1980).

Withdrawal from Long-Acting CNS Depressants

Symptoms of withdrawal from long-acting CNS depressants are similar in nature, although less intense than those of the short-to-intermediate-acting CNS depressants. Although withdrawal symptoms may include anorexia, nausea, vomiting, sweating, and twitching (Hollister, Motzenbecker, & Degan, 1961), prominent features of long-acting benzodiazepine withdrawal include attacks of panic, depression, severe agitation, insomnia, paresthesias, headache, inability to concentrate, and anxiety (Hanna, 1972; Jaffe, 1985; Fox, Note 1). It has been suggested by Vernelle Fox (Note 1) that withdrawal from benzodiazepine drugs occurs in waves of symptoms, particularly waves of panic, rather than as a peak of severe symptoms followed by a smooth decline (see Fig. 3.3). Smith and Wesson (1985) state that the waves of symptoms may represent an important difference between low-dose benzodiazepine withdrawal and the reemergence of anxiety symptoms present before drug therapy. Symptoms of withdrawal from the long-acting CNS depressant drugs may last 2–3 weeks. Withdrawal syndromes from long-acting CNS depres-

sants may take 4–8 days to develop, and grand mal seizures have been reported on the seventh to eighth day (Hollister et al., 1961). Figure 3.3 illustrates the timing of symptoms of higher doses of long-acting CNS depressants.

Withdrawal from High-Dose Versus Low-Dose Benzodiazepines

A general discussion of withdrawal from sedative-hypnotic drugs deserves a short differentiation between high-dose and low-dose benzodiazepine withdrawal patterns. The abuse of high doses of benzodiazepines for 1–6 months usually produces withdrawal patterns as illustrated in Figures 3.2 and 3.3. Patterns of shorter-acting benzodiazepines, such as oxazepam, lorazepam, alprazolam, triazolam, and temazepam, may more closely resemble Figure 3.2. The use of low dosages of benzodiazepines for more than 6 months is more likely to result in a waxing and waning of more subtle symptoms as anxiety, insomnia, muscle spasms, sweating, difficulty concentrating, paresthesias, tremor, fear, and fatigue, lasting for weeks to months (Smith & Wesson, 1985). Abusers of higher doses of benzodiazepines for longer than 6 months could then expect to experience the acute pattern, immediately followed by low-dose patterns of withdrawal.

SUMMARY

The CNS depressant drugs are a widely used, widely abused group of drugs. Tolerance and physical depend-

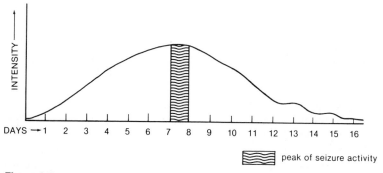

Figure 3.3
Withdrawal syndrome from the long-acting CNS depressants.

ence occur with most of the drugs used to produce sedation, to induce sleep, and to allay anxiety.

The withdrawal symptoms of many of these syndromes are so similar that they are often called the *general depressant withdrawal syndrome* (Jaffe, 1985, p. 547). Differences in the withdrawal syndromes mainly occur in the time at which the syndrome begins after drug intake is abruptly stopped. These timing differences can be correlated with how long it takes the drug, or its active metabolites, to leave the body. The withdrawal syndromes from the CNS depressants can be life-threatening and require close professional supervision.

REFERENCES

Baldessarini, R. J. (1985). Drugs and the treatment of psychiatric disorders. In A. G. Gilman, L. S. Goodman, T. W. Rall, & F. Murad (Eds.), *Goodman and Gilman's the pharmacological basis of therapeutics* (pp. 387–445). New York: Macmillan.

Breimer, D. D. (1977). Clinical pharmacokinetics of hypnotics. *Clinical Pharmacokinetics, 2,* 93–109.

Brown, S. S., & Goenechea, S. (1973). Methaqualone: Metabolic, kinetic, and clinical pharmacologic observations. *Clinical Pharmacology and Therapeutics, 14*(3), 314–324.

Busto, U., Sellars, E. M., Naranjo, C. A., Cappell, H., Sanchez-Craig, M., & Skyora, K. (1986). Withdrawal reaction after long-term therapeutic use of benzodiazepines. *The New England Journal of Medicine, 315*(14), 854–859.

Cummins, L. M., Martin, Y. C., & Scherfling, E. E. (1971). Serum and urine levels of ethchlorvynol in man. *Journal of Pharmaceutical Sciences, 60*(2), 261–263.

Delong, A. F., Smyth, R. D., Polk, A., Nayak, R. K., & Reavey-Cantwell, N. H. (1976). Blood levels of methaqualone in man following chronic therapeutic doses. *Archives Internationales Pharmacodynamie et de Therapie, 222,* 322–331.

Desmond, M. M., Schwanecke, R. P., Wilson, G. S., Yasunaga, S., & Burgdorff, I. (1972). Maternal barbiturate utilization and neonatal withdrawal symptomatology. *Journal of Pediatrics, 80*(2), 190–197.

Fraser, H. F., Shaver, M. R., Maxwell, E. S., & Isbell, H. (1953). Deaths due to withdrawal of barbiturates. *Annals of Internal Medicine, 38,* 1319–1325.

Fraser, H. F., Wilker, A., Essig, C. F., & Isbell, H. (1958). Degree of physical dependence induced by secobarbital or phenobarbital. *Journal of the American Medical Association, 166,* 126–129.

Fyer, A. J., Liebowitz, M. R., Gorman, J. M., Campeas, R., Levin, A., Davies, S. O., Goetz, D., & Klein, D. F., (1987). Discontinuation of alprazolam treatment in panic patients. *American Journal of Psychiatry, 144*(3), 303–308.

Gary, N. E., & Tresnewsky, O. (1983). Clinical aspects of drug intoxication: Barbiturates and a potpourri of other sedatives, hypnotics and tranquilizers. *Heart & Lung, 12,* 122–127.

Glauser, F. L., Smith, W. R., Caldwell, A., Hoshiko, M., Dolan, G. S., Baer, H., & Olsher, N. (1976). Ethchlorvynol (Placidyl)-induced pulmonary edema. *Annals of Internal Medicine, 84,* 46–48.

Good, M. I. (1976). Catatonia-like symptomatology and withdrawal dyskinesias. *American Journal of Psychiatry, 133*(12), 1454–1456.

Greenblatt, D. J., Allen, M. D., Noel, B. J., & Shader, R. I. (1977). Acute overdosage with benzodiazepine derivatives. *Clinical Pharmacology and Therapeutics, 21*(4), 497–514.

Greenblatt, D. J., Divoll, M., Abernethy, D. R., Ochs, H. R., & Shader, R. I. (1983). Benzodiazepine kinetics: Implications for therapeutics and pharmacogeriatrics. *Drug Metabolism Review, 14*(2), 251–292.

Greenblatt, D. J., Knowles, J. A., Comer, W. H., Shader, R. I., Harmatz, J. S., & Ruelius, H. W. (1977). Clinical pharmacokinetics of lorazepam. IV. Long-term oral administration. *Journal of Clinical Pharmacology, 17*(8 & 9), 495–500.

Greenblatt, D. J., & Shader, R. I. (1971). Meprobamate: A study of irrational drug use. *American Journal of Psychiatry, 127*(10), 1297–1303.

Greenblatt, D. J., & Shader, R. I. (1985). Clinical pharmacokinetics of the benzodiazepines. In D. E. Smith & D. R. Wesson (Eds.), *The benzodiazepines: Current standards for medical practice* (pp. 43–58). Hingham, MA: MTP Press.

Greenblatt, D. J., Shader, R. I., & Koch-Weser, J. (1975a). Flurazepam hydrochloride, a benzodiazepine hypnotic. *Annals of Internal Medicine, 83*(2), 237–241.

Greenblatt, D. J., Shader, R. I., & Koch-Weser, J. (1975b). Pharmacokinetics in clinical medicine: Oxazepam versus other benzodiazepines. *Diseases of the Nervous System, 36*(5), 6–13.

Haefely, W., Kyburz, E., Gerecke, M., & Möhler, H. (1985). Recent advances in the molecular pharmacology of benzodiazepine receptors and in the structure-activity relationships of their agonists and antagonists. *Advances in Drug Research, 14,* 165–322.

Hanna, S. M. (1972). A case of oxazepam (Serenid D) dependence. *British Journal of Psychiatry, 120,* 443–445.

Harvey, S. C. (1985). Hypnotics and sedatives. In A. G. Gilman, L. S. Goodman, T. W. Rall, & F. Murad (Eds.), *Goodman and Gilman's the pharmacological basis of therapeutics* (pp. 339–371). New York: Macmillan.

Harvey, S. M. (1975). Hypnotics and sedatives: The barbiturtes. In L. S. Goodman & A. Gilman (Eds.), *Goodman and Gilman's the pharmacological basis of therapeutics* (pp. 102–136). New York: Macmillan.

Hoaken, P. C. S. (1975). Adverse effect of methaqualone. *Canadian Medical Association Journal, 112,* 685.

Hollister, L. E., Motzenbecker, F. P., & Degan, R. O. (1961). Withdrawal reactions from chlordiazepoxide (Librium). *Psychopharmacologia, 2,* 63–68.

Howe, J. G. (1980). Lorazepam withdrawal seizures. *British Medical Journal, 280,* 1163–1164.

Inaba, D. S., Gay, G. R., Newmeyer, J. A., & Whitehead, C. (1973). Methaqualone abuse: Luding out. *Journal of American Medical Association, 224*(11), 1505–1509.

Jaffe, J. H. (1985). Drug addiction and drug abuse. In A. G. Gilman, L. S. Goodman, T. W. Rall, & F. Murad (Eds.), *Goodman and Gilman's the pharmacological basis of therapeutics* (pp. 532–581). New York: Macmillan.

Klotz, U., Avant, G. R., Hoyumpa, A., Schenker, S., & Wilkinson, G. R. (1975). The effects of age and liver disease on the disposition and elimination of diazepam in adult man. *The Journal of Clinical Investigation, 55,* 347–359.

McClane, T. K., & Martin, W. R. (1976). Subjective and physiologic effects of morphine, pentobarbital, and meprobamate. *Clinical Pharmacology and Therapeutics, 20*(2), 192–198.

Myers, R. R., & Stockard, J. J. (1975). Neurologic and electroencephalographic correlates in glutethimide intoxication. *Clinical Pharmacology and Therapeutics, 17*(2), 212–220.

Noyes, R., Perry, P. J., Crowe, R. R., Coryell, W. H., Clancy, J., Yamada, T., & Gabel, J. (1986). Seizures following the withdrawal of alprazolam. *Journal of Nervous and Mental Disease, 174*(1), 50–52.

Olin, B. R., (Ed.). (1987). *Facts and comparisons.* St. Louis: Facts and Comparisons, Inc.

Olsen, R. W., & Leeb-Lundberg, F. (1981). Convulsant and anticonvulsant drug-binding sites related to GABA-regulated chloride ion channels. *Advances in Biochemical Psychopharmacology, 26,* 93–102.

Pancorbo, A. S., Palagi, P. A., Piecoro, J. J., & Wilson, H. D. (1977). Hemodialysis in methyprylon overdose. Some pharmacokinetic considerations. *Journal of American Medical Association, 237,* 470–471.

Rao, S., Sherbaniuk, R. W., Prasad, K., Lee, S. J. K., & Sproule, B. J. (1973). Cardiopulmonary effects of diazepam. *Clinical Pharmacology and Therapeutics, 14*(2), 182–189.

Robertson, H. A. (1980). The benzodiazepine receptor: The pharmacology of emotion. *Le Journal Canadien des Sciences Neurologiques, 7*(3), 243–245.

Sellers, E. M., Carr, G., Bernstein, J. G., Sellers, S., & Koch-Weser, J. (1972). Interaction of chloral hydrate and ethanol in man. II. Hemodynamics and performance. *Clinical Pharmacology and Therapeutics, 13*(1), 50–58.

Sellman, R., Pekkarinen, A., Kangas, L., & Raijola, E. (1975). Reduced concentrations of plasma diazepam in chronic alcoholic patients following an oral administration of diazepam. *Acta Pharmacologica et Toxicologica, 36,* 25–32.

Smith, D. E., & Wesson, D. R. (1985). Benzodiazepine dependency syndromes. In D. E. Smith & D. R. Wesson (Eds.). *The benzodiazepines: Current standards for medical practice* (pp. 235–248). Hingham, MA: MTP Press.

Wesson, D. R., & Smith, D. E. (1978). Barbiturates and other sedative-hypnotics. In A. Schecter (Ed.), *Treatment aspects of drug dependence* (pp. 117–129). West Palm Beach, FL: CRC Press.

REFERENCE NOTE

1. Fox, V. *Recognizing multiple simultaneous drug withdrawal syndromes.* Paper presented at the National Council on Alcoholism/American Medical Society on Alcoholism Medical-Scientific Conference, Washington, D.C., May 6-8, 1976.

CHAPTER 4

CNS STIMULANTS

John M. Holbrook

Central nervous system (CNS) stimulants are pharmacologic agents that have the ability to increase cortical alertness and electrical activity throughout the brain and spinal cord. They appear both to mimic the action and increase synaptic levels of the neurotransmitters dopamine and norepinephrine (NE) in specific brain areas such as the cortex and reticular activating system (RAS). Included in the category of CNS stimulants are the amphetamines, cocaine, synthetic amphetaminelike anorectics, caffeine, and nicotine (see Table 4.1). These agents have in common the ability to activate the cortex either directly or via the RAS, produce an alerting response, decrease fatigue, and elevate mood.

In toxic doses, CNS stimulants produce anxiety, a psychotic state, convulsions, and death. Drugs within this category, with the exception of nicotine, differ primarily in their relative potencies and duration of action. Their mechanisms of action appear to be the same, and their toxic effects are extensions of their therapeutic actions.

Stimulant use and misuse has been known in almost every culture, from the use of cocaine by the Incas to combat fatigue and elevate mood to the use of caffeine in coffee, tea, or cola beverages by every strata of the American population as a pick-me-up to offset fatigue. Few, if any, drugs have a greater appeal for abuse than do the CNS stimulants, or "uppers." Their primary sought-after effect appears to be their cortical stimulant action, which has been equated to a feeling resembling sexual orgasm. The result of cortical stimulation is manifested as an increased level of behavioral activity, for example, hyperverbalization, increased motor activity, and an increased sensitivity to sensory input. These actions are highly sought-after by the "drug-abusing" population, including the inveterate coffee drinker.

Stimulants are abused and misused in different ways by various segments of the population. Truck drivers, pilots, housewives, and students may occasionally use stimulants to add a few hours to the day or to combat fatigue when the day has already become too long. A cup of coffee or tea, both of which contain caffeine, may be used for the same purpose and provide the same level of cortical stimulation. At the other end of the spectrum of stimulant abuse is the methamphetamine, or

Table 4.1
CNS Stimulants (Excluding Amphetaminelike Anorectics)

Generic Name	Trade Name	Street Name(s)
Cocaine HCl	None	Dope, coke, snow, lady, gold dust
Cocaine freebase	None	Crack
Racemic amphetamine	Benzedrine	Uppers, bennies, peaches
Dextroamphetamine	Dexedrine	Dexies, oranges, hearts
Methamphetamine	Desoxyn	Speed, meth, crystal, whites
Methamphetamine freebase	None	Ice
Amphetamine complex	Biphetamine	Black beauty, RJS
Caffeine	NoDoz, Stim Tabs, S-250	None
Methylphenidate	Ritalin	Unknown

"speed," user whose goal-directed behavior involves the procurement and self-injection of this potentially toxic substance. During a "run," the speed user may inject as much as 10 g/d for 3–4 days before "crashing" in a stupor. Between these extremes are found the occasional abusers, or "recreational users," as they tend to call themselves, who may snort cocaine or "pop a pill" in a social setting.

Although the stimulant drugs have some therapeutic value, their potential for abuse often overshadows their efficacy. In fact, their level of abuse has increased so greatly in recent years that strict federal regulations have been instituted to deter their street use. Their high level of abuse has also resulted in reevaluation of their therapeutic efficacy and consequent curtailment of their clinical use. Even with more strict control of these drugs, their abuse at times seems severe enough to warrant their removal from the legal drug market.

AMPHETAMINE

Amphetamine is a generic term that applies to a group of synthetic compounds derived from ephedrine. Included in this group are racemic amphetamine, dextroamphetamine, and methamphetamine. A number of other compounds with amphetaminelike actions have also been synthesized and will be discussed later in this chapter.

The amphetamines were synthesized in the early 1930s as substitutes for ephedrine. Over a period of about 10 years, it was found that these compounds were useful as bronchial dilators and in the treatment of narcolepsy, hyperkinesis, and obesity. During this time, it was also found that these drugs were potent CNS stimulants, capable of decreasing fatigue and producing behavioral arousal. Almost from their initial usage, their abuse potential was generally acknowledged although little effort was made to control their illicit use.

The first amphetamine compound marketed was racemic amphetamine in the Benzedrine inhaler used to alleviate nasal congestion. Between 1932 and 1946, the abuse of Benzedrine became widespread because of its accessibility as a nonprescription drug, even though it was as potent as any amphetamine compound requiring a prescription. Benzedrine abuse was common enough to inspire popular tunes such as "Who Put the Benzedrine in Mrs. Murphy's Ovaltine" (Ray & Ksir, 1987). The abuse of the Benzedrine inhaler finally ended in

1949 when the manufacturer changed the compound in the inhaler from Benzedrine to Benzedrex, a decongestant with little CNS stimulant properties. In 1959, the Food and Drug Administration banned the use of amphetamines in inhalers.

The use and abuse of amphetamines was greatly potentiated by World War (WW) II, during which time the amphetamines were widely used to decrease fatigue and increase the alertness of military personnel. It has been reported that during WWII the United States and Great Britain together used almost 150 million doses of amphetamine to aid in the war effort (Bloomquist, 1970). Following WW II, amphetamine abuse increased worldwide. In Japan, methamphetamine was sold without a prescription, which led to a high level of abuse. In addition, opinions as to the potential for abuse of amphetamines differed radically in different areas of the world. While legislation was being enacted in Sweden to provide greater legal control over amphetamines, in Great Britain, amphetamines were considered to be relatively safe from abuse and nontoxic (Bloomquist, 1970).

Amphetamine abuse may range from college students and truck drivers who use amphetamines to increase alertness and ward off sleep, to the heavy abuser who injects methamphetamine intravenously in "runs" that may last as long as several days. Although the behavioral effects of amphetamine are similar to those of cocaine, they differ in that amphetamine has a much longer duration of action than cocaine and is also orally active. Thus, there is a greater potential for adverse reactions and severe toxicity with the amphetamines than with cocaine.

The amphetamines in current use are listed in Table 4.1 with their trade and street names. All of these agents have the same general clinical indications, including treatment of narcolepsy and hyperkinesis and as adjunctive, short-term therapy for obesity. They all mimic the actions of the CNS neurotransmitters NE and dopamine and can be administered orally or intravenously. They are slowly metabolized by hepatic enzymes but are often found in significant amounts unmetabolized in the urine. Acidification of the urine enhances amphetamine excretion and significantly shortens its half-life (Morgan, 1978).

Several theories have been proposed to explain the mechanisms by which the amphetamines produce their pharmacologic actions. They have been reported to produce a direct stimulation of the adrenergic receptor and to indirectly increase NE levels at the synapse by inhibiting the monoamine oxidase enzyme system and by inhibiting NE reuptake into nerve endings. It is probable that a combination of these effects is involved in the actions of amphetamine.

A number of adverse physiologic effects are associated with the use of amphetamines. Their toxic manifestations appear to be an extension of these effects. In the peripheral nervous system, amphetamine stimulates both alpha and beta adrenergic receptor sites. In therapeutic doses, the usual effects include an increase in blood pressure, a reflexive decrease in heart rate, relaxation of bronchial smooth muscle, stimulation of the bladder sphincter (which makes urination difficult), and a decrease in gastrointestinal tract motility usually producing constipation.

Alterations in metabolic processes are commonly seen with the use of amphetamines. These alterations include an increase in the general rate of cellular metabolism, an increase in oxygen consumption, and an increase in body temperature. There is also a general increase in plasma free fatty acid levels, as would be expected, but no significant change in plasma glucose concentrations (Haefely, Bartholini, & Pletscher, 1976).

Amphetamines stimulate the CNS in a dose-related manner. Therapeutic doses increase alertness and decrease fatigue, elevate mood and frequently produce euphoria. Motor activity is increased and physical performance of simple tasks is improved (Weiss & Laites, 1967). Due to the prolonged increase in alertness, sleep patterns are disturbed and total sleep time is decreased leading to a decrease in rapid eye movement (REM) sleep. When amphetamine use is discontinued, a characteristic REM sleep rebound usually occurs.

In high abuse doses, the amphetamines produce both autonomic and central mediated symptoms. The primary peripheral toxic symptoms are related to cardiovascular function and include tachycardia, headache, and, when the amphetamines are taken in sufficiently high doses, arrhythmias that may be life-threatening. Hypertension may initially occur, followed by hypotension as cardiovascular integrity becomes compromised. Gastrointestinal function may be altered, and nausea, vomiting, diarrhea, and cramping may occur. In some toxic cases, excessive sweating may occur, whereas in others, hyperthermia may develop and produce death. Death may also ensue from increased cardiovascular function leading to stroke.

The psychologic effects of high-dose amphetamine abuse have been well-documented in the literature and are collectively termed *amphetamine psychosis*. Amphetamine psychosis closely resembles a true paranoid schizophrenia, and in the clinical setting, it is almost impossible to distinguish between the two illnesses.

The major symptoms of amphetamine psychosis include paranoid ideation with well-formed delusions, stereotyped compulsive behaviors, visual and auditory hallucinations, tactile and olfactory hallucinations, and increased sexuality. The paranoid features of amphetamine psychosis include increased awareness, increased curiosity, and seemingly overwhelming fear (Ellenwood, 1967). Stereotyped compulsive behaviors such as pacing back and forth, facial grimacing, and repeatedly taking an object apart and putting it back together may be seen.

Auditory, visual, tactile, and olfactory hallucinations have all been reported as components of amphetamine psychosis. Auditory and visual hallucinations have an equally frequent incidence. Auditory hallucinations seem to be well-correlated with psychosis developing with chronic abuse, whereas visual hallucinations are more frequently seen in clients who develop acute amphetamine intoxication (Connell, 1958). Tactile hallucinations take the form of delusions of insects or worms crawling on the skin, whereas olfactory hallucinations may be unspecified.

Although some clients may experience a decrease in sexuality, the majority experience heightened sexual activity or desire. This powerful aphrodisiac effect may be one reason for relapse into amphetamine abuse after periods of abstinence from the drug.

Although the clinical picture of amphetamine psychosis closely resembles that of paranoid schizophrenia and other drug-related toxic states, some differential symptoms are beneficial in the diagnosis of this condition. Auditory hallucinations, occurring in schizophrenia and amphetamine psychosis, consist of vague noises and voices. Other drugs, such as the hallucinogens, almost always produce hallucinations of a visual nature. The tactile and olfactory hallucinations occurring in amphetamine psychosis are almost never seen in schizophrenia, but may be seen as part of the withdrawal syndrome associated with CNS depressants such as alcohol. A striking difference between the schizophrenic client and the client in amphetamine psychosis is the retention of clear consciousness and correct orientation by the amphetamine abuser. The amphetamine abuser's memory of the toxic stimulant episode is usually acute in contrast to the schizophrenic who usually has no memory of any events during a psychotic episode. Also in contrast to the schizophrenic, the toxic amphetamine abuser usually does not have a distinct thought disorder and his or her mood leans more toward anxiety rather than being flat.

The amphetamines are considered to have a high abuse liability. Although no physical withdrawal syndrome occurs following the abrupt discontinuation of their use, psychologic changes that may last for several months are usually prominent. These changes include apathy, long periods of sleep, irritability, depression, and disorientation. The paranoid state usually disappears within 7–10 days, but some delusions may persist, making it difficult for the patient to function normally in society for a year or longer.

Chronic use of the amphetamines leads to the development of tolerance to the stimulant effects and to the appetite-suppressant effects, even when they are administered in low therapeutic doses. High-dose, chronic abuse leads to a substantial degree of tolerance. Some abusers may use as much as 1 g/d. Different patterns of abuse greatly influence the rate at which tolerance develops. The oral administration of racemic or dextroamphetamine in oral therapeutic doses of 5–30 mg/dose will produce tolerance more slowly than intravenous administration. The highest reported tolerance development occurs with the use of methamphetamine, or *speed*. Although the number of methamphetamine users is considered to be relatively small, their style of abuse relegates them almost into a cult category. Typical use begins with intravenous doses of about 15–30 mg. Injections are repeated in a speed "binge," or run, that may last for 3–4 days. During this run, tolerance develops rapidly and doses as large as 500–1000 mg may be taken in a single injection. Each injection results in a "flash," or "rush," that has been described as a full-body orgasm. Between injections, which may occur as frequently as 10 times a day, euphoria is present.

The newest chemical form of methamphetamine to become available on the illicit drug market is methamphetamine freebase, which is known on the streets as "ice." It is similar to cocaine freebase in that it can be smoked, is rapidly absorbed by the lungs, and reaches the brain and produces intense stimulation in a matter of seconds. Little information concerning the toxicology of ice is currently available; however, it is anticipated that this new form may be even more toxic than the methamphetamine salt forms because of its route of administration.

The growing popularity of ice can be attributed, at least partially, to the increasing success of law enforcement agencies in decreasing the importation of cocaine. Unfortunately, as the availability of cocaine freebase and crack decreases, other drugs are being sought as alternatives for illicit sale on the street. In the near future, ice may prove to be the replacement for crack because it is easily synthesized and self-administered by smoking.

The rush produced by the amphetamines contrasts sharply with the at-ease, drifting feeling produced by opioid analgesics such as heroin. Some persons prefer the combination of the effects of stimulants and narcotics and inject speedballs of either cocaine or amphetamines with heroin. With either combination, the result is a brief, intense "orgasmic" high, followed by a prolonged euphoria.

In the modern drug culture, toxicity associated with the use of amphetamines has increased in frequency and is occurring in young abusers. Actual statistics of mortality directly related to amphetamine overdose are sketchy. Lethality has been reported to occur after the intravenous injection of as little as 120 mg but nontolerant users have survived doses of as much as 500 mg (Morgan, 1978).

COCAINE

When the Spaniards conquered the Incas of Peru, they found natives who appeared contented and thriving under the hardships of their high-altitude mountain life. Upon investigation, they found a direct connection between the general good spirits and endurance of the natives and the balls of leaves that were always kept tucked in their cheeks. These leaves, which were also used as money in their economic system, were obtained from the plant *Erythroxylon coca,* which grew wild and was also cultivated in small patches throughout the mountains of Peru and Bolivia. Much later, it was learned that the leaves contained the alkaloid cocaine—"dope," "coke," "snow," "gold dust," "lady"—which had been reputed since as early as A.D. 500 to lift the spirits, produce freedom from fatigue and provide a general feeling of well-being. The leaves the natives chewed would indeed lift the spirits, since they could contain as much as 2% cocaine!

Cocaine reached Europe in the mid-1800s when a French chemist, Angelo Mariani, began to import large quantities of coca leaves. Mariani extracted cocaine from them and used the extract in the manufacture of lozenges, tea, and the Mariani Coca Wine that eventually made him both rich and famous (Ray & Ksir, 1987). The medicinal use of cocaine was expanded by Sigmund Freud who advocated its use in the treatment of clients undergoing narcotic withdrawal. Freud soon realized the abuse potential of cocaine, but by the time he did, it had already been incorporated into a number of patent medicines including Coca-Cola. It remained in preparations of this type until the Pure Food and Drug Act became law in 1906.

Because of the unique cortical stimulant effects of cocaine, it is prized among drug abusers. In the United States, cocaine has always been a favored social and recreational drug, but due to its cost, its social use is usually limited to the middle and upper socioeconomic classes. The use of cocaine may be associated with criminal activity necessary to procure enough funds to obtain an adequate drug supply. For some, cocaine is *the* drug, and no risk or effort is too great if the result is the procurement of more cocaine.

Cocaine is self-administered by almost any route, but in the social setting the preferred method is "snorting," or inhalation, for absorption through the nasal mucosa. Cocaine is also well-absorbed through the buccal membranes—the preferred route of the Incas—and may be injected intravenously. Cocaine is also ingested by the oral route, but this method is probably less favored because of the slower onset of stimulant effect seen in most people.

In comparison to other CNS stimulants, cocaine has a very short half-life. After intranasal or buccal absorption, the effects normally last 5–15 minutes although some users will claim that the subjective effects may last as long as 1 hour. Once in the bloodstream, most of the cocaine is rapidly metabolized to benzoylecgonine and excreted as such although some cocaine may be excreted unchanged. To maintain CNS stimulation over long periods of time, it must be inhaled or injected every 15–30 minutes.

The medical use of cocaine is limited because of its high abuse potential and because of the availability of other compounds with a similar pharmacologic profile but less abuse liability. Cocaine was the first widely used local anesthetic and today is still used in some areas for eye surgery and to facilitate throat examinations. It is thought to produce its local anesthetic action by preventing the generation and conduction of the nerve cell action potential. This is a relatively nonspecific ef-

fect and is similar to the local anesthetic effect produced by barbiturates and alcohol. As a local anesthetic, cocaine has one major advantage: whereas other local anesthetics must be used in combination with a vasoconstrictor such as epinephrine to control their absorption into the systemic circulation, cocaine itself is a potent vasoconstrictor and can be used alone. For the cocaine abuser, this is a very undesirable effect since the vasoconstriction can lead to considerable damage to the nasal or buccal mucosa when cocaine is frequently used.

Cocaine is also found as a component of Brompton's cocktail or mixture, an oral narcotic combination used for chronic severe pain and to elevate mood in terminally ill clients. The original formula for this preparation included heroin or morphine (10 mg), cocaine (10 mg), alcohol, chloroform, water, and simple syrup. It was administered on a regular schedule rather than on an "as needed" basis. Currently, the term Brompton's mixture denotes any alcoholic solution containing morphine and either cocaine or a phenothiazine; however, cocaine apparently does not add to the mixture's effectiveness since a single-entity narcotic solution may be as effective as the drug combination (Olin, 1987).

The mechanism(s) by which cocaine produces its mood elevation or euphoria has not been clearly elucidated. Its effects have been linked both to a direct effect on cortical cells or the ascending RAS and to an alteration of central catecholamine levels. Cocaine is known to inhibit the reuptake of NE at adrenergic synapses, which may account for some of its central and peripheral effects, but its euphoric action appears to be related to its ability to alter central dopamine levels. The euphoria produced by cocaine, as well as by other CNS stimulants, can be blocked, at least partially, by neuroleptic drugs that block dopamine receptor sites (Ellenwood, 1979).

The CNS stimulation produced by cocaine is dose related. Low doses of cocaine produce cortical stimulation evidenced by an increase in motor activity and obvious behavioral arousal. Moderate doses produce stimulation of respiratory centers of the medulla and, peripherally, increase heart rate and blood pressure. Toxic doses of cocaine produce spinal convulsions, coma, and death. Death due to cocaine overdosage may be related either to depression of the medullary respiratory centers following convulsions or to cardiac arrhythmias and subsequent cardiovascular collapse.

The abuse potential of cocaine is apparently limited only by its availability and cost. Subjectively, cocaine produces a "high" not encountered with any other drug. The high has been compared to orgasm and is of a short enough duration to make it desirable as a recreational drug. Most cocaine users have a very limited intake, and thus whether or not cocaine produces physical dependence as evidenced by a distinct abstinence syndrome is still highly debatable. With most social use of cocaine, physical dependence probably does not occur because of limited intake and its rapid metabolism. Tolerance to the cardiac stimulant and convulsant effects of cocaine has been reported (Matsuzaki, 1978), but it appears that sensitivity to the CNS stimulant effects of cocaine develops when it is used chronically (Castellani, Ellenwood, & Kilbey, 1978).

Aside from those who use cocaine casually and on a very limited basis is a population of abusers who use the drug chronically and in fairly large quantities. Under circumstances of chronic, high-dose use, the behavioral parameters of cocaine differ significantly. In such users, the abrupt withdrawal of cocaine produces an abstinence syndrome characterized by a strong craving for the drug, prolonged sleep, fatigue, increased hunger, and behavioral depression (Post, Kotin, & Goodwin, 1974). High doses of cocaine may also produce a syndrome termed *cocaine psychosis,* which does not significantly differ from the classical symptoms of schizophrenia or the paranoid delusional state.

A relatively new occurrence in the use of cocaine is that of purification of street-quality cocaine before its use. The process is termed *free-basing* and is performed to remove water-soluble adulterants, to produce a substance more palatable for smoking, and to increase lipid solubility of the cocaine for better absorption.

Cocaine freebase is an intermediate compound in the production of cocaine hydrochloride salt. During the past decade, users have reobtained the freebase from its salt by dissolving the cocaine hydrochloride in an alkaline, aqueous solution, then separating the cocaine from the aqueous solution with an organic solvent. Cocaine freebase is then obtained as a white, talclike powder by evaporation of the organic solvent (Woodford, Note 1). Since late in 1985, cocaine freebase has been produced in large volumes by drug dealers as "crack," so called because of the cracking sound it makes when smoked. Crack is produced by "cooking" street-grade cocaine in an aqueous solution of ammonia or baking soda. The resulting product resembles shavings from a bar of soap and is often packaged in small Pyrex tubes in which the crack can be smoked. The process by which the crack is made is much less dangerous than that involving the evaporation of highly flammable organic solvents, and the purity of the cocaine freebase may reach as high as 90% (Rusche, 1986).

Cocaine freebase may be sprinkled on a tobacco or marihuana cigarette and smoked or may be vaporized and smoked through a glass pipe.

The free-basing processes remove only the water-soluble adulterants used as cutting agents from the street-grade cocaine. They will not remove other salts such as procaine hydrochloride or substances already in the freebase state such as lidocaine freebase; thus these substances can remain as adulterants (Woodford, Note 1).

The habitual cocaine user has often been erroneously labeled a "sex-crazed dope fiend," but this phrase is usually quite contrary to the actual clinical behavioral picture. The cocaine user who "runs" cocaine for a period of hours or even days usually withdraws into a world apart and is rarely dangerous when under the influence of cocaine unless a toxic psychosis develops.

The occurrence of toxic psychosis depends on the amount and frequency of cocaine use and, with the availability of highly pure crack, such behavioral reactions are expected to be seen more frequently. The immediate after-effects of crack use, such as agitation and depression, may also result in highly unstable behaviors. Newman and Anderson (1986) have also reported the use of crack in combination with phencylidine (referred to as "space-basing") which results in intense out-of-control behaviors.

AMPHETAMINELIKE CNS STIMULANTS

When the full implications of the abuse potential of CNS stimulants such as the amphetamines and cocaine were realized, research was undertaken throughout the world to find drugs that could be utilized for the treatment of hyperkinesis, narcolepsy, and obesity. The primary goal of this research was to produce a synthetic agent that would stimulate specific brain areas to treat these syndromes but that would have little or no potential for abuse. Unfortunately, no drug has yet been produced to provide the desired therapeutic effect without some abuse potential. Table 4.2 lists the amphetaminelike stimulants that are primarily utilized for the short-term treatment of obesity. With their pharmacologic profile and potential for abuse, it is very difficult to

Table 4.2
Amphetaminelike CNS Stimulants (Anorectics)

Generic Name	Trade Name	Therapeutic Doses (mg/d)
Benzphetamine	Didrex	25–50
Phenmetrazine	Preludin	50–75
Phentermine	Ionamin, Fastin, Tora	15–37.5
Phendimetrazine	Delcozine	35
Diethylproprion	Tenuate, Tepanil	25–75
Mazindol	Sanorex	1–3

rationalize their clinical use under most circumstances. The possible exception to this statement is methylphenidate (Ritalin), which will be discussed later.

Clinical data related to the amphetaminelike CNS stimulants indicate that the majority of these agents differ from amphetamines primarily in potency. They are used only by the oral route and produce dose-related CNS stimulation. In abuse doses, which may be as high as 10 times the usual therapeutic dose, their effects are the same as those of amphetamine. Their misuse and abuse by the general population is thought to be greater than that of the amphetamines because of their relative ease of attainment through legal channels. If they have any advantage at all on the street, it is that they are legally manufactured and therefore cannot be as easily adulterated with other toxic compounds as is sometimes the case with amphetamines and cocaine.

These agents produce psychologic dependence of the same magnitude as the amphetamines. Following chronic, high-dose intake, a characteristic withdrawal syndrome is observed. This syndrome includes hyperirritability, drowsiness, fatigue, and lethargy. Tolerance develops to the CNS effects of these stimulants and often the abuser will stop using these drugs, or "crash," purposely, so that after a few drug-free days, the tolerance has disappeared, and drug intake can be resumed at a greatly reduced dose. During the crash period, CNS depressants may be used to decrease the withdrawal effects. Chronic, high-dose use produces the same toxic psychosis previously described for amphetamines.

The only agent in this category with a therapeutic use other than the short-term treatment of obesity is

methylphenidate (Ritalin), which is the drug of choice for the treatment of hyperkinesis. The potency of methylphenidate has been reported to lie between that of the amphetamines and caffeine (Ray & Ksir, 1987). Its abuse potential is probably as high as that of amphetamine, and it is as readily available on the street.

CAFFEINE

Of the CNS stimulants, the one best known, most frequently used, misused, and abused is caffeine, which is found in a variety of beverages such as coffee, tea, cocoa, cola beverages, and nonprescription drugs. A selected list of such caffeine sources is found in Table 4.3.

Caffeine has been used therapeutically as a respiratory stimulant but has been replaced by more specific agents. In humans, caffeine is well-absorbed after oral administration with peak plasma levels occurring within an hour after its ingestion. About 90% of absorbed caffeine is metabolized before being excreted.

Caffeine is pharmacologically categorized as a mild CNS stimulant with moderate diuretic properties. When ingested orally, the stimulant effects of caffeine are apparent within 30 minutes and may last for 3–5 hours. Tolerance develops to the stimulant effects of caffeine, and loss of tolerance requires up to 2 months of abstinence. The level of tolerance development to caffeine is not great, and tolerance can usually be overcome by increasing the intake.

Although caffeine is not noted for its toxic effects, it does produce a definite syndrome of adverse effects and, in sufficiently high doses, can produce convulsions, due to CNS stimulation, followed by coma and death. Oral doses of 200 mg caffeine (2 cups of coffee) will produce CNS stimulation and definite cortical arousal possibly due to direct stimulation of cortical cells. This dose will also elevate mood, produce insomnia, and, in susceptible people, increase irritability and anxiety.

Caffeine doses of 500 mg will produce autonomic effects such as tachycardia and respiratory stimulation. This dose also causes dilatation of peripheral blood vessels and constriction of blood vessels in the CNS. There is also some indication that caffeine increases plasma glucose and lipid levels.

Lethality related to caffeine is extremely rare although one death has been reported to occur at an intravenous dose of 3.2 g. Although the estimated oral lethal dose is 10 g, there have been no reports of death following high oral doses of caffeine.

Because of widespread social use, it is difficult to distinguish between the appropriate use and the misuse of caffeine. Is drinking a morning cup of coffee or tea to enhance the awakening process or the afternoon cola drink as a pick-me-up truly abuse? What about the coffee drinker who averages 10–15 cups daily? Is this just heavy use or is it abuse for the CNS-stimulant properties of caffeine? It is probably most appropriate to consider caffeine abuse in light of the development of tolerance and dependence with an ensuing abstinence syndrome when intake is abruptly halted.

As mentioned previously, tolerance to the effects of caffeine develops slowly and can be overcome by increasing intake. Physical dependence (as well as psychologic dependence) on caffeine also develops. The abstinence syndrome is characterized by nausea, lethargy, and headache (Goldstein & Kaiser, 1969) and is usually seen when the intake is greater than 5 cups of coffee or tea a day.

Behaviorally, caffeine appears to improve performance by decreasing boredom and increasing attention. It also decreases fatigue and appears to increase the ability to process sensory information; however, in increased doses, the CNS-stimulant effects may tend to decrease the performance of complex functions (Weiss & Laites, 1967).

Overall, caffeine seems to be the safest and mildest of the CNS stimulants. Although its abuse potential cannot be overlooked, it presently does not appear to produce a great threat in the drug culture. A possible exception to this statement concerns the pregnant female. For further information concerning the effects of caffeine during pregnancy, see Chapter 10.

Table 4.3

Caffeine Content of Certain Beverages, Foods, and Drugs

Source	Approximate Amount of Caffeine per Unit (mg)
Beverages	
Coffee (5 oz)	
Brewed or instant	30–180
Decaffeinated	1–5
Tea (5 oz)	
Brewed, domestic or imported	20–110
Instant	25–50
Iced, (12 oz)	67–76
Cocoa beverage (5 oz)	2–20
Chocolate milk beverage (8 oz)	2–7
Soft Drinks (12 oz; selected)	
Sugar Free Mr. Pibb	58.8
Tab, Coca-Cola, Diet Coke	45.6–46.8
Dr. Pepper	39.6
Pepsi Cola	38.4
Canada Dry Diet Cola	1.2
Foods (1 oz)	
Milk chocolate	1–15
Dark, semisweet chocolate	5–35
Baker's chocolate	26
Chocolate-flavored syrup	4
Drugs	
Analgesics	
Anacin, Bromo-Seltzer, Midol, Cope, Vanquish	32-33
Excedrin	65
Stimulants	
No Doz	100
Vivarin	200
Caffedrine	250
Many cold preparations	32

Source: Adapted from O. S. Ray and C. Ksir, *Drugs, Society and Human Behavior* (4th ed.). St. Louis: Times Mirror/Mosby College Publishing, 1987.

NICOTINE

Like caffeine, nicotine is a mild CNS stimulant whose abuse is known throughout the world. Nicotine differs from caffeine in that it has no therapeutic value and is an exceedingly toxic chemical. Nicotine is found in nature as a constituent of the tobacco plant. Many health hazards have been associated with the use of tobacco, some of which appear related to nicotine, whereas others appear to be related to the smoking process itself and to contaminents found in smoke. With respect to abuse of nicotine-containing products, the associated psychologic and physical dependence are entirely related to the effects of nicotine.

Over the past four or five centuries, the use of tobacco products has alternately been favored and found in disfavor both as a medicinal agent and as a socially acceptable abuse substance. One of the earliest reports of tobacco smoking, or "drinking," was in the late 1500s in Europe, when such tobacco use was punishable by imprisonment. Within 30 years, however, tobacco was being used medicinally to treat a wide variety of conditions, including chronic cough. In the 1600s tobacco smoking fell somewhat from favor, but its use was quickly continued as powdered tobacco, or "snuff," which was inhaled through the nose. "Snuffing" as a fad did not last long in Europe, and by the early 1700s, tobacco smoking was again in vogue (although the use of snuff is still found worldwide today). The availability of tobacco to the common person increased during the early 1700s, partially because a strain of tobacco plant was found which grew very well on the newly settled North American continent. Tobacco growing soon became a very profitable business, and the export of American tobacco reached the international markets. During the 1800s and early 1900s, a method was perfected for partially drying tobacco and forming a plug that could be stored for long periods of time. This plug of tobacco was chewed rather than smoked, and use by this method has continued to the present.

This century has seen the greatest degree of nicotine abuse by smoking, chewing, and snuffing. The reasons for this increased level of abuse are many. First, the technologic age made possible the mass production of cigarettes, cigars, plugs, snuff, and pipe tobacco, efficiently and in great quantities. Second, mass advertising campaigns made cigarette smoking the "in" thing, even though the medical media has made quite clear the health hazards associated with tobacco use. Third, the psychologic dependence produced by nicotine appears to be as difficult to alter as that associated with most of the other highly abused substances available today.

As previously mentioned, many of the health hazards associated with the use of tobacco are clearly related to the method of abuse seen most frequently—smoking. For nicotine to be released from tobacco, the tobacco must be burned. The nicotine thus released is inhaled as a component of smoke along with a number of other toxic compounds including carbon monoxide and tar, the small particles of incompletely burned waste products of tobacco. Several of the components of the tar portion of tobacco smoke have been reported to be carcinogenic in animals and in humans (Surgeon General, 1979).

Nicotine itself produces a number of well-documented effects on the nervous system, aside from the obvious physical and psychologic dependence. The pharmacologic effects of nicotine on the autonomic nervous system have been extensively studied. The effects on other body systems and the CNS have also been studied to some extent, but since nicotine has no therapeutic use, there have been few in-depth studies in areas other than those directly related to its abuse via tobacco smoking; therefore, the following information is presented with reference to the effects of nicotine that are related to its use by smoking.

Nicotine is well absorbed from the vasculature of the lungs, and when inhaled reaches the CNS almost as rapidly as when injected intravenously. It is 80%–90% metabolized by the liver. With chronic use, nicotine stimulates hepatic microsomal enzymes and thus increases its own rate of metabolism as well as that of drugs detoxified by the liver. The increased rate of metabolism of nicotine accounts, in part, for the development of tolerance to its effects and to its increased use. Nicotine intake is thought to be related to the maintenance of an optimal plasma level in most chronic tobacco users so that as tolerance develops, the daily intake must be increased to continue the desired effect. Although only about 10% of nicotine is excreted unchanged by the kidney, this portion may become significant in the maintenance of pleasurable plasma levels by the chronic user since nicotine stimulates the release of antidiuretic hormone, which tends to decrease the overall rate of excretion.

Nicotine produces discernible effects on both the peripheral and central nervous systems in quantities obtained while smoking. About 10% of the nicotine contained in tobacco is absorbed through smoking; therefore, a cigar containing 60 mg nicotine will yield 6 mg if completely smoked. The only reason that nicotine lethalities do not usually occur is that the nicotine absorption does not all occur at once, but is spaced evenly over a period of time.

In the peripheral nervous system, nicotine stimulates at low doses and produces depolarization blockade at higher doses at both the autonomic ganglia and the somatic neuromuscular junction. Inhaled nicotine usually produces only ganglionic stimulation, but some chronic users report some relaxation of skeletal muscle (Domino, 1973). Since nicotine mimics the actions of acetylcholine, these effects would be expected to occur, but some of the other effects of nicotine are not related to cholinergic mechanisms. Nicotine stimulates the release of epinephrine from the adrenal gland, therefore producing a widespread adrenergic response resulting in effects such as constriction of peripheral blood vessels, decreased body temperature, and increased blood pressure. Nicotine inhibits contractions of gastric smooth muscle associated with hunger and therefore produces a mild anorectic effect. It also decreases the sensitivity of some sensory receptor sites (pain, heat, taste buds). The reason for this decreased sensitivity is unknown, although the effects of heated smoke on the taste buds probably accounts for part of their decreased sensitivity.

The CNS effects of nicotine are characterized by cortical stimulation and an arousal response. The cortical effect may be due to direct stimulation of cortical neurons. Nicotine produces both psychologic and physical dependence, and the nature of the psychologic effects is due, at least in some users, to these CNS stimulant effects. The initial stimulation produced by nicotine is followed by CNS depression, and it may be reasoned that in some people with a high level of anxiety CNS depression is the desired effect rather than CNS stimulation.

The withdrawal syndrome characterizing nicotine physical dependence usually begins within 1–2 hours after nicotine intake is abruptly halted. The symptoms of withdrawal include a characteristic "craving," restlessness, decreased ability to concentrate, and hyperirritability. These symptoms may last from a few days to several weeks or months (Surgeon General, 1979). There may also be some withdrawal changes related to autonomic activity, such as decreased heart rate and decreased blood pressure. Such effects may simply be related to a return to normal levels of functioning.

It has been noted that appetite increases during the early period of withdrawal, and some people continue to use nicotine as a method to prevent weight gain. It is most probable that appetite does improve, due both to the decreased effects of nicotine on gastric contractions and taste buds and to the decrease in the release of epinephrine from the adrenal gland, which would result in a decreased stimulation of the basal metabolism rate. In reality, weight gain should be no problem when smoking is discontinued if normal dietary controls are followed and eating does not become a substitute for the nicotine habit.

SUMMARY

The misuse and abuse of stimulant drugs is a major problem in the United States today. Their ability to stimulate the cortex and alleviate fatigue makes them ideal candidates for casual as well as hard-core abuse patterns. In sufficient doses, stimulants have the ability to produce behavior patterns resembling psychosis and paranoid states. In toxic doses, they may produce death due to cardiovascular collapse or CNS depression. With the exception of nicotine, they have not been shown to produce a significant level of physical dependence but will produce an extremely high level of psychologic dependence.

REFERENCES

Bloomquist, E. R. (1970). The use and abuse of stimulants. In W. G. Clark & J. del Giudice (Eds.), *Principles of psychopharmacology* (pp. 477–488). New York: Academic Press.

Castellani, S., Ellenwood, E. H., Jr., & Kilbey, M. M. (1978). Behavioral analysis of chronic cocaine intoxication in the cat. *Biological Psychiatry, 13,* 203–206.

Connell, P. H. (1958). *Amphetamine psychosis.* Maudsley Monograph, No. 5. London: Oxford University Press.

Domino, E. F. (1973). Neuropsychopharmacology of nicotine and tobacco smoking. In W. L. Dunn, Jr. (Ed.), *Smoking behavior: Motives and incentives* (pp. 5–31). Washington, DC: V. H. Winston & Sons.

Ellenwood, E. H., Jr. (1967). Amphetamine psychosis I: Description of the individuals and process. *Journal of Nervous and Mental Disease, 144,* 273–283.

Ellenwood, E. H., Jr. (1979). Amphetamines/anoretics, In. R. I. DuPont, A. Goldstein, & J. O'Donnell (Eds.), *Handbook on drug abuse* (pp. 213–221). Washington, DC: U. S. Government Printing Office.

Goldstein, A., & Kaiser, S. (1969). Psychotropic effects of caffeine in man. III. A questionnaire survey of coffee drinking and its effects in a group of housewives. *Clinical Pharmacology and Therapeutics, 10*(4), 477–488.

Haefely, W., Bartholini, G., & Pletscher, A. (1976). Monoaminergic drugs: General pharmacology. *Pharmacology and Therapeutics, 3,* 185–218.

Matsuzaki, M. (1978). Alteration in pattern of EEG activities and convulsant effect of cocaine following chronic administration in the resus monkey. *Electroencephalography and Clinical Neurophysiology, 45,* 1–15.

Morgan, J. P. (1978). The clinical pharmacology of amphetamine. In D. E. Smith (Ed.), *Amphetamine, use, misuse and abuse* (pp. 3–10). Boston: G. K. Hall.

Newman, S. & Anderson, B. (1986). *Cocaine* (Available from the drug Education Center, Inc., 1416 E. Morehead St., Charlotte, NC 28204)

Olin, B. R. (Ed.) (1987). *Facts and comparisons* (p. 242f). St. Louis: Facts and Comparisons, Inc.

Post, R. M., Kotin, J., & Goodwin, K. F. (1974). The effects of cocaine on depressed patients. *American Journal of Psychiatry, 131,* 511–517.

Ray, O. S., & Ksir, C. (1987). *Drugs, society and human behavior* (pp. 99–124). St. Louis: Times Mirror/Mosby College Publishing.

Rusche, S. (1986 September). *Crack Update.* (Available from Families in Action National Drug Information Center, 3845 N. Druid Hills Rd., Decatur, GA 30033)

Surgeon General (1979). *Smoking and health* (pp. 5:54–57). (U. S. Public Health Service Publication No. 79-50066). Washington, DC: U. S. Government Printing Office.

Weiss, B. & Laites, V. (1967). Enhancement of human performance by caffeine and the amphetamines. *Pharmacological Review, 14,* 1–36.

REFERENCE NOTE

1. Woodford, J. Personal communication, January 4, 1982.

CHAPTER 5

OPIOIDS

Donna S. Woolf

The opioid drugs are undisputed champions in their ability to relieve pain. Despite the addictive qualities of all the drugs in this group, opioids are widely prescribed and administered because of their effectiveness. The term *opioid* is used in this text to encompass natural drugs from the opium poppy, as well as synthetic drugs possessing distinct chemical structures but pharmacologically similar to the natural opium products. The text is limited to drugs used or abused by addicts and includes the group of drugs often called *narcotics* by addicts and professionals.

THE HISTORY OF OPIOIDS

Opium has been used through history for a wide variety of illnesses. Literature from Greece, Rome, and Egypt all give accounts of the use of the *Papaver somniferum,* better known as the opium poppy. The magical resin from the ripe poppy has been used to treat dysentery, to allay pain, to suppress cough, to "cure" anxiety and mental disorders, as well as to give pleasure and euphoria.

After years of using crude opium extracts, it was discovered that opium contained several drugs. "Pure" morphine and codeine became popular substitutes for crude opium.

During the 1800s, Chinese immigrants brought opium smoking to the United States (Criswell & Levitt, 1975). Patent medicines, which contained opium and alcohol, became popular, and Civil War soldiers were given morphine freely as an analgesic. However, the enactment of the Harrison Narcotic Act in 1914 curtailed the free sale of opioids without a doctor's order, and the addict was forced to seek new, illegal sources for the drug.

An upsurge of opioid abuse during the 1960s and 1970s produced a dramatic increase in the number of young opioid addicts. In 1969, more teenagers in New York City died as a result of heroin use than from all other causes (Criswell & Levitt, 1975). The end of the Vietnam War brought addicted soldiers home from that

opium-rich area. In 1982, 1.2% of persons aged 18–25 reported having at least a single use of heroin (Jaffe & Martin, 1985). Chemically dependent health professionals frequently report opioid abuse (DaDalt, 1986; Sullivan, 1987). The development of other analgesic drugs, patterned after the naturally occurring opioids, gave drug abuse treatment centers new drugs to add to the lists of abused chemicals.

The value of opioids as analgesics is undisputed in treating both acute pain and the prolonged pain of diseases such as terminal cancer. Our society, however, is oriented toward the use of chemicals to get instant relief from every ill. With this attitude prevailing and with the opioids' propensity for producing physical dependence, the abuse of and addiction to these drugs should not come as a surprise.

CLASSIFICATION OF OPIOIDS

Many different terms have been used to describe opioid drugs. Since the term *narcotic* is commonly used by the addict, it is also commonly used by addiction professionals to describe morphine-type drugs. The term narcotic implies that the drug was derived from opium. New drugs possessing pharmacologic actions similar to morphine's may be synthetic or semisynthetic. Some drugs now included in this classification not only act like morphine but may also block the effects of morphine. No classification scheme accurately divides all the abused analgesics, so three divisions have been used to provide structure for this chapter. The section concerning naturally occurring opioids will include discussions of the abused alkaloids of opium. A section on synthetic or semi-synthetic opioids will describe the pharmacology of opioids such as heroin, meperidine (Demerol), methadone, and oxycodone (in Percodan). A final section will discuss drugs that act like morphine at some drug receptor sites, yet block morphinelike actions at others. This group will include drugs such as pentazocine (Talwin).

Another way to classify opioid drugs is being developed, based on a drug's actions on opioid receptors. In 1973 several groups of researchers described specific binding sites for opioids. The existence of as many as eight types of opioid receptors has been suggested (Jaffe & Martin, 1985). Substantial evidence abounds for four types of opioid receptors called mu, kappa, delta, and sigma. The mu receptor is thought to regulate physical dependence and the withdrawal syndrome, respiratory depression, euphoria, and supraspinal analgesia. Kappa receptors mediate sedation, miosis, and spinal analgesia. Hallucinations, dysphoria, and respiratory and vasomotor stimulation are thought to be caused by action on the sigma receptor. Specific effects of compounds on the delta receptor have not been adequately defined, but they may be involved in alterations of affective behavior. Actions of the currently available opioid drugs are interpreted at the mu, kappa, and sigma receptors. Attachment of a drug at one of these opioid receptors would produce a different response from that seen with attachment at a different opioid receptor.

GENERAL OPIOID PHARMACOLOGY

Although the opioids have subtle differences in duration of effects, severity of side effects, withdrawal patterns, and absorption, several general pharmacologic characteristics can be described for the group as a whole.

Central Nervous System Effects

All of the drugs of the opioid type affect the central nervous system (CNS). They cause mood changes and mental clouding. Euphoria, rather than mental clouding, is often described by addicts (Jaffe & Martin, 1985). The reduction of pain and the production of drowsiness are common, although these two symptoms do not have to coexist. Mental changes, drowsiness, and analgesia are all increased as the dose is increased.

It has been generally accepted that most drugs that we use mimic or block substances normally present in the body. Since our miraculous bodies do not have receptor sites merely awaiting the discovery and ingestion of a particular drug, there must be a natural function for the receptor sites to which the opioid drugs bind. In 1975, Hughes and Kosterlitz, and their co-workers, isolated a peptidelike substance with morphinelike activity. Three families of endogenous peptides, the enkeph-

alins, the dynorphins, and the endorphins, have been identified. Generally called the opiopeptins, each family has a distinct physiologic precursor and is distributed in identifiable body areas (Jaffe & Martin, 1985). Opiopeptins function as neurotransmitters or neurohormones, but much remains unclear as to how they function within the body. These substances may have actions not only related to pain regulation, but also to the regulation of mood, respiration, temperature, cardiovascular changes, intestinal activity, drinking behavior, and endocrine effects (Way, 1986).

The pain-relieving properties of opioids are probably produced by the drug's ability to react with the neuron and alter the release of natural body chemicals called neurotransmitters (Jaffe & Martin, 1985). These neurotransmitters, acetylcholine, norepinephrine, substance P, and dopamine, are affected by opioid drugs, resulting in the decreased response to painful stimuli. How opioid drugs mimic naturally occurring opiopeptins is not clear. The two most popular hypotheses explaining the events surrounding transmitter release and the inhibition of neuronal firing are related to calcium ion disposition or to cyclic adenosine monophosphate (Way, 1986).

Four other effects of opioids are a result of the drug's actions on the brain. Pupillary constriction occurs as a result of the stimulation of the oculomotor nerve (Lee & Wang, 1975). This is one side effect to which the opioid addict does not develop tolerance and which is difficult for the addict to hide. It is, therefore, used as a diagnostic tool to recognize opioid intoxication. Respiratory depression induced by opioid drugs is the result of a decrease in function of the brain stem respiratory centers, as well as of a depression of the medulla (Flórez, McCarthy, & Borison, 1968; Jaffe & Martin, 1985). The opioids, particularly codeine, have been used for years as antitussive agents. This effect is at least partially due to a suppression of part of the medullary cough center (Chakravarty, Matallana, Jensen, & Borison, 1956). Opioids stimulate the chemoreceptor trigger zone in the medulla causing the nausea and vomiting often associated with their clinical use.

Gastrointestinal Effects

Other prominent effects of the opioids include their effect on the bowel. In humans, morphine increases stomach tone, decreases propulsive waves in the small and large intestines, and increases the tone of the anal sphincter (Jaffe & Martin, 1985). The sum of these effects produces constipation. Little tolerance develops to the constipating effects of the opioids (Hug, 1972). Prolonged drug use may result in fecal impaction.

Cardiovascular Effects

Opioid drugs dilate peripheral blood vessels. Although when the client is lying down, few blood pressure changes are seen, when the client taking opioids stands, orthostatic hypotension frequently occurs. The blood pressure is not usually significantly depressed until severe intoxication occurs. Hypotension can be partially caused by opioid-induced histamine release (Jaffe & Martin, 1985). Opioids such as morphine do not significantly change the cardiac work and, in fact, may decrease the work of the heart (Alderman, Barry, Graham, & Harrison, 1972). Morphine and other opioids are fre-

quently used to treat severe pain associated with myocardial infarction.

Methods of Administration and Absorption

Opioid drugs can be absorbed into the body in many ways. Opioids have been snorted, injected under the skin *("skin popping"),* injected intravenously, smoked, and swallowed (Baden, 1975). Which method of administration is used depends on the user, the drug, the ratio of effectiveness of the swallowed drug to the injected drug, and the frequency with which side effects occur with a particular method of administration. Differences in absorption by different methods of administration will be discussed in subsequent sections. Table 5.1 lists the usual abused methods of administration for opioids.

Table 5.1
Comparison of the Pharmacologic Properties of Abused Opioids

Generic (Trade) Name	Administration Methods[a]	Physical Dependence Liability	Withdrawal Symptoms
Opium (in paregoric)	PO, SN, S	High	Like morphine
Heroin (h, junk, smack, horse, Persian brown)	I, S, SN	High	Like morphine
Morphine	I, PO	High	See text
Oxymorphone (Numorphan)	I	High	Like morphine
Oxycodone (in Percodan)	PO, I	High	Close to morphine
Hydromorphone (Dilaudid)	PO, I	High	Like Morphine
Diphenoxylate (in Lomotil)	PO	Low to moderate	Less than Morphine
Meperidine (Demerol)	PO, I	High	See text
Anileridine (Leritine)	I	High	Like meperidine
Alphaprodine (Nisentil)	I	High	Like meperidine
Hydrocodone (in Hycodan)	PO, I	Moderate to high	Between morphine and codeine
Codeine (alone and in combinations)	PO, I	Low to moderate	See text
Propoxyphene (Darvon)	PO, I	Low to moderate	Close to codeine
Methadone (Dolophine)	PO, I	High	See text
Pentazocine (Talwin)	PO, I	Moderate	See text
Butorphanol (Stadol)	I	Low to moderate	Like pentazocine
Nalbuphine (Nubain)	I	Low to moderate	Like pentazocine

Source: Data in column 4 from "Opioid analgesics and antagonists" by J. H. Jaffe and W. R. Martin, in A. G. Gilman, L. S. Goodman, & A. Gilman (Eds.), *Goodman and Gilman's the pharmacological basis of therapeutics.* Copyright 1985 by Macmillan. Reprinted by permission. Data in columns 2 and 3 are from *Drugs of Abuse,* 1979.
[a] PO = oral, SN = snorted, S = smoked, I = injected

The intravenous method of administration produces intense effects as well as rapid addiction. These intense feelings experienced on injection of an opioid drug are often called a *"rush"* or *"kick"* and are usually compared to a sexual orgasm. The rush usually lasts less than a minute but is pleasurable enough to encourage continued drug use despite the nausea and vomiting that sometimes accompany opioid use. The ability to achieve high blood levels of the drug, frequent administration, and length of time used contribute to the rapid development of physical dependence. It is possible for an abuser to use opioids sporadically and thus to avoid physical dependence as evidenced by withdrawal symptoms. The intravenous method of administration has the distinction of being the most dangerous of all methods of abuse because of the likelihood of overdosage and serious medical complications that accompany the injection of unsterile, foreign particles. The exchange of blood that accompanies the sharing of needles puts one at risk for sharing diseases as well (see Chapter 24).

Skin popping, another common method of administration, does not give the user a rush of the same intensity or speed as the intravenous injection, but it also does not require the user to locate a vein in which to inject the drug. Skin popping does not carry the risk of producing a foreign-body embolus although it is associated with serious dermatological infections.

Swallowing a tablet is a socially acceptable method of taking drugs. Taking chemicals orally produces less intense feelings than those obtained by injecting the drug, but the user does not have to use needles or prepare the drug.

Opium and heroin have been smoked and snorted as a method of abuse. Research has not given us much information concerning the amount of heroin that is absorbed through the nose after snorting, but it is assumed that most of the drug that enters the nose is absorbed (Ream, Robinson, Richter, Hegge, & Holloway, 1975). Only about one-fifth of smoked heroin is absorbed (Mo & Way, 1966).

Adverse Effects

The usual pharmacologic effects of opioids cause many side effects commonly listed in drug profiles. These include drowsiness, constipation, nausea, vomiting, and orthostatic hypotension. Allergies to the opioids are rarely seen, although rashes have occurred. The occasional client may become delirious, necessitating discontinuance of therapy. Anaphylactic shock may rarely occur after intravenous administration and may be more common in the addict than we can prove.

The abuse of an opioid drug is not associated with the induction of physical disease as is seen with the abuse of alcohol. Opioids do not induce cirrhosis, pancreatitis, or cardiomyopathies when used in a sterile fashion. The recognition of intravenous drug abuse as a risk factor in contracting acquired immune deficiency syndrome (AIDS), however, negates any advantage the abuse of opioid drugs might have over alcohol in inducing physical damage.

Many of the established physiologic consequences of opioid abuse are related to the form of the drug taken, the method of administration, the conditions under which it is taken, and the method by which the drug must be obtained.

Drug Interactions with Opioids

Many drugs have additive effects when given with opioids. Alcohol and opioids are a dangerous combination that may produce marked sedation and respiratory depression. Other combinations, such as phenothiazines, monoamine oxidase inhibitors, and tricyclic antidepressants produce supra-additive effects, inducing a dangerous depression (Hansten, 1985). Sometimes, the additive effects of these combinations are put to use by combining drugs, such as hydroxyzine (Vistaril) and promethazine (Phenergan), with the opioid. The required dose of the opioid can then be decreased.

Tolerance and Addiction Potential

With the opioid drugs, tolerance may develop to one of their effects but not to others. The morphine addict will continue to have pinpoint pupils even though the euphoric effects are not experienced. In contrast to the experiences of the alcoholic, the tolerance of the addict drops dramatically after the withdrawal period (Jaffe & Martin, 1985). "Street" users have been known to purposefully abstain for short periods of time to allow the tolerance to decrease to a level that can again be afforded as well as enjoyed. As tolerance increases, the lethal dose of the drug also increases, although there is always a lethal dose for any person. Daily doses of over 3 g meperidine have been taken by tolerant people (Jaffe & Martin, 1985). Inaccurately guessing the new dose of the drug when tolerance has dropped may result in an overdose in the street user.

The addict who is tolerant to one opioid will usually show tolerance to other opioid drugs. Likewise, the addict who is physically dependent on one opioid and exhibits signs and symptoms of withdrawal when the drug is stopped, can suppress those symptoms by switching to another opioid. When the substituted drug is stopped, withdrawal will be characteristic of the substitute drug (Ream et al., 1975). This phenomenon is the basis for using another opioid in place of the drug of abuse to detoxify the opioid addict.

All of the drugs discussed in this chapter can be abused and are physically addicting. All produce withdrawal patterns, and individual differences in these patterns will be discussed under each category. Table 5.1 compares the liability for abuse of the opioid drugs. Although all of the opioids can be abused, some are more rapidly addicting and have a higher liability for abuse than others (Jaffe & Martin, 1985).

NATURALLY OCCURRING OPIOIDS

Raw opium, a resin obtained from the poppy, contains several chemical compounds, some of which are pain-killers (Criswell & Levitt, 1975). Only one-fourth of raw opium contains its physiologically active chemicals called *alkaloids*. Morphine, which constitutes about 10% of the alkaloids, and codeine, which constitutes about 0.5% of the alkaloids (Jaffe & Martin, 1985), are the only two clinically used, natural analgesics present in the poppy. Another alkaloid, thebaine, which is not used as an analgesic, is used to prepare other drugs, such as oxycodone, contained in Percodan. Although it is possible to synthesize morphine in the laboratory, the world still relies on the ancient, but efficient, methods of obtaining morphine from the opium poppy.

Morphine Properties

Morphine is the drug to which most opioids are compared. It acts primarily as an agonist at the mu receptor, although it does bind to kappa receptors as well. The section on general pharmacologic properties of opioids was based primarily on the actions of morphine.

The way morphine is introduced into the body affects the effectiveness of the dose. When taken orally, morphine gives low levels of the drug in the plasma despite the fact that it is absorbed from the gastrointestinal tract. This is due to the metabolism of significant amounts of the drug in its first pass through the liver. Some metabolism of morphine also takes place in the mucosal cells of the small intestine (Brunk & Delle, 1974). For these reasons, the abuser prefers taking morphine by the injectable method.

Most morphine is excreted from the body by the kidney. Urine morphine is largely in the metabolite form, although small amounts of free morphine can be detected. About 90% of morphine is excreted from the body during a 24-hour period (Jaffe & Martin, 1985). Some morphine is excreted in the feces.

The effects of morphine taken orally or injected subcutaneously last for 4–5 hours. Intravenous injections may last for a shorter period of time.

Morphine Withdrawal

Abrupt abstinence from morphine and closely related drugs, such as Dilaudid, Numorphan, and heroin, produces a well-recognized pattern of signs and symptoms as illustrated in Figure 5.1. Withdrawal generally begins within 8–12 hours after the last opioid dose and the syndrome becomes most intense by 36–48 hours (Himmelsbach, 1941; Jaffe, 1985; Ream et al., 1975). Shortly after the earliest signs of withdrawal emerge, the addict may fall into a fretful period of sleep. After sleeping for several hours, the addict usually wakens with worsened symptoms (Jaffe, 1985). Gooseflesh creates skin that looks similar to that of a plucked turkey (Jaffe, 1985, p. 544) and has inspired the use of the phrase *"cold turkey."* As Figure 5.1 illustrates, the acute phase of opioid withdrawal is over in around 10–14 days. However, a chronic opioid withdrawal with prolonged symptoms of irritability, inability to handle minor problems, anxiety, and multiple physical complaints is often connected with the conscious or unconscious desire to obtain drugs.

Codeine Properties

When pure, codeine is a white crystalline powder. Although it does occur naturally in the opium poppy, it is present only in small quantities. Most commercially available codeine is chemically produced from natural morphine (Soine & Willette, 1971).

Codeine is usually abused by swallowing because it is almost as effective when taken orally as when

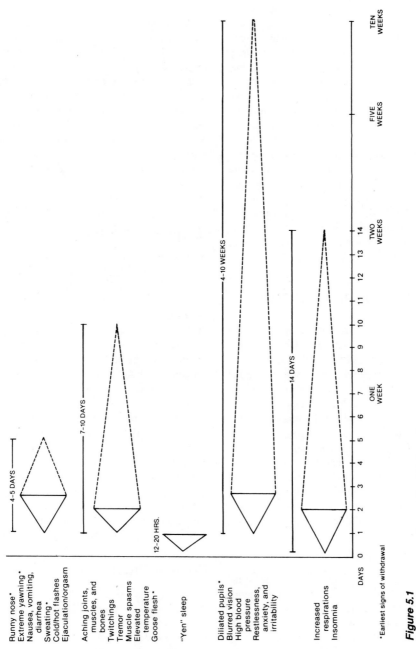

Figure 5.1
Signs and symptoms of morphine withdrawal.

injected. Although codeine is metabolized in the liver, all of the dose is not broken down in the first pass through the liver. Codeine is metabolized to several inactive compounds, and 10% is converted to morphine. The metabolized drug is then excreted by the kidney. Codeine's effects last about 4–6 hours when taken orally (Jaffe & Martin, 1985). Abused codeine is often obtained in the form of combination analgesic tablets, cough syrups, or elixirs. Codeine appears to be less rapidly addicting than morphine, although dependency is possible.

Codeine Withdrawal

Codeine withdrawal symptoms are similar to, but less severe than, those seen in the client withdrawing from morphine (Jaffe, 1985). Severe symptoms of withdrawal are seen only when the codeine is abused injectably or when huge amounts are taken orally. As with other opioids, it may take several weeks before the milder, prolonged abstinence syndrome is over. Since these products are rather freely prescribed for outpatients with pain, these clients may focus on pain during the protracted abstinence syndrome. Although the pain may certainly be real and present, the withdrawal syndrome may combine with physical pain to make it difficult for the addict to remain drug free.

SEMISYNTHETIC AND SYNTHETIC OPIOIDS

When scientists realized that small modifications of the naturally occurring opioids could create new analgesic drugs, many new opioid compounds were created and evaluated. The basic pharmacologic profile for morphine applies to most of these opioids, although subtle differences in side effects and actions will be seen.

Morphinelike Synthetic Opioids

One technically easy way that the morphine molecule could be changed in the laboratory was through conversion to herion (Fishman & Hahn, 1975). Other derivatives, such as hydromorphone (Dilaudid), oxymorphone (Numorphan), oxycodone (in Percodan), and hydrocodone (in Hycodan), were also synthesized.

Heroin Properties

Pure heroin is a white powder, but street varieties may be brown from impurities. A dose of heroin in the United States is called a "bag" and generally contains

1–5 mg heroin (Cushman, 1973). In the bloodstream, heroin is rapidly converted to morphine, and most of the actions of heroin are produced by morphine. Martin and Fraser (1961) report that with intravenous administration, 1 mg heroin is approximately equal to 2 mg morphine. Heroin is "absorbed" into lipids more readily than morphine. Heroin, therefore, crosses the lipid blood–brain barrier more easily than does morphine and acts more quickly (Oldendorf, Hyman, Braun, & Oldendorf, 1972). Once in the brain, heroin is converted to morphine. Heroin in this way "carries morphine" to the CNS, and intravenous heroin can be differentiated from morphine by the addict for this reason.

Heroin Withdrawal

Since heroin is converted to morphine in the body, it is logical that heroin withdrawal is almost identical to morphine withdrawal, as illustrated in Figure 5.1. Heroin withdrawal may begin slightly earlier than morphine withdrawal (Isbell & White, 1953). The severity of most withdrawal patterns partially depends on the dose of the drug taken. Since the method by which the drug was introduced into the body affects the amount of drug that reaches the receptor site, withdrawal may be more severe in a person who has used intravenous heroin than in one who has smoked it, partly because the dose received from smoking heroin is smaller than that received by intravenous use (Ream et al., 1975).

The source of an illicit drug may also give predictions as to withdrawal severity. Vietnam War veterans were able to purchase heroin of over 90% purity (Holloway, 1974). The ingested doses of this heroin were high, and severe withdrawal patterns could be predicted from the high-dose exposure.

Other Derivates of Morphine and Codeine

Hydromorphone (Dilaudid), oxymorphone (Numorphan), oxycodone (in Percodan), and hydrocodone (in Hycodan) are all semisynthetic derivatives of the morphine or codeine molecule. Withdrawal patterns are very similar to that of morphine (see Fig. 5.1). Dilaudid withdrawal may commence slightly earlier than morphine withdrawal (Isbell & White, 1953). Percodan and Hycodan, like codeine, are quite effective when taken orally and are often abused by this route.

Meperidinelike Synthetic Opioids

Meperidine, a synthetic opioid, is chemically unlike morphine, although it is as widely used as an analgesic as is morphine. Meperidinelike synthetics bind as agonists more strongly with kappa opioid receptors than morphine (Jaffe & Martin, 1985). Nisentil, Leritine, Sublimaze and diphenoxylate (in Lomotil) are all included in this group.

Meperidine Properties

Meperidine shares several common properties with morphine. It is commonly used in practice as an analgesic, and it binds to the same opioid receptor as morphine. Meperidine, like morphine, depresses respiration, is less effective when taken orally than when injected, and is rapidly addicting.

Meperidine does have a few different pharmacologic properties from those of morphine. About 80–100 mg meperidine is equivalent to 10 mg morphine. Meperidine's effects are produced more rapidly than morphine's although the duration of the drug's actions is shorter (Jaffe & Martin, 1985). Since meperidine is chiefly metabolized in the liver, it should be noted that in addicts who have cirrhosis from alcohol abuse, meperidine's duration may be prolonged (Klotz, McHorse, Wilkinson, & Schenker, 1974). Meperidine is not as constipating as morphine, although it can reduce gastrointestinal spasm as does morphine.

Toxic doses of meperidine, in contrast to morphine, can cause CNS excitement, including convulsions (Jaffe & Martin, 1985). Meperidine has significant atropinelike actions to which even the tolerant client may react. This means that when high doses of meperidine are taken by some meperidine addicts, dilated pupils rather than pinpoint pupils may be present (Jaffe, 1985). Addicts report that meperidine causes more dizziness and elation than morphine (Isbell & White, 1953). Both Nisentil and Leritine are chemicals that were derived from meperidine. Their pharmacologic properties are very close to those of meperidine.

Fentanyl (Sublimaze), a synthetic opioid, is 80 times as potent as morphine as an analgesic. Its primary medical use is as an adjunct to other agents in the induction of general anesthesia. A substance known as "China white" on the street is alpha-methyl fentanyl. Some drugs sold as "China white" may actually be heroin.

Diphenoxylate, which is the active ingredient in Lomotil, is chemically similar to meperidine. Its prominent effects on the gastrointestinal tract are responsible for its primary use in the treatment of diarrhea. The drug was found to produce little euphoria when therapeutic doses were given for short periods of time.

Large doses of the drug produce effects that are typical of other opioid drugs. The inclusion of atropine sulfate in the marketed product does decrease the likelihood of abuse, since atropine's side effects are uncomfortable. Addicts do abuse Lomotil, despite the atropine, and its use in addicts should be severely restricted. Diphenoxylate is water insoluble, which limits its abuse to oral administration (Jaffe, 1985).

Meperidine Withdrawal

Meperidine withdrawal is similar to morphine withdrawal in that the same general symptoms occur (see Fig. 5.1). The timing and severity of the occurrence of these symptoms is, however, different. Usually, addicting drugs that have shorter durations of action produce more severe, but shorter, withdrawal syndromes (Jaffe, 1985). The meperidine addict begins to show signs of withdrawal within about 3 hours after the last dose of the drug (Isbell & White, 1953). The peak of intensity of meperidine withdrawal is usually more severe than that of morphine and occurs 8–12 hours after the last dose (Isbell & White, 1953). Muscular twitching and nervousness are often more intense in meperidine withdrawal than in morphine withdrawal, although nausea and vomiting are less severe (Jaffe, 1985). Meperidine withdrawal is usually shorter than morphine withdrawal, although a protracted syndrome may be seen with meperidine. The withdrawal from Nisentil and Leritine is similar to that from meperidine.

Methadonelike Opioids

Another group of synthetic opioids that are chemically similar includes methadone and propoxyphene (Darvon). This group of opioids act primarily as mu agonists.

Methadone Properties

Methadone is an effective pain reliever as well as a cough suppressant. In the United States, methadone is chiefly used as an analgesic and detoxification drug. This opioid is extremely addicting when used intravenously, so methadone is usually administered orally. Methadone is about one-half as potent when given orally as it is when given by injection (Martin et al., 1973). Methadone's effects last so long that administration more often than once a day is rarely required during methadone maintenance. Methadone exhibits the same basic pharmacologic effects as morphine. Methadone's effects are due to the parent molecule, and the primary site of metabolism is the liver. When methadone is given in high doses, as is seen in methadone maintenance therapy, cross-tolerance develops to other opioids, such as heroin. The abuse of heroin while the client is on ''methadone maintenance'' results in no euphoria—which discourages heroin use (Verebely, Volavka, Mulé, & Resnick, 1975). Other drugs used as opioid detoxification agents are covered in Chapter 17.

The use of methadone for extended periods of time, as may be observed in methadone maintenance regimens, is associated with several side effects directly due to the methadone. Most of these effects are those that can be predicted when one reviews the usual pharmacologic effects of opioids. Among these effects are constipation and increased sweating. Other adverse effects reported by clients include libido and orgasm alterations, menstrual irregularities, insomnia, and changes in appetite (Kreek, 1978).

Methadone Withdrawal

A person who chronically ingests methadone will become physically dependent on it. The withdrawal from methadone has symptoms similar to morphine's (see Fig. 5.1) except that the syndrome is slower to develop and prolonged. Symptoms may not occur for 1–2 days after the drug is stopped. As with morphine, an early, acute withdrawal occurs, which is at its worst on the third day of abstinence and continues for 2–3 weeks. Acute symptoms may then begin to decrease but are not gone until 1.5 months after abstinence has begun. Many addicts find it difficult to cope with an acute phase lasting for such a long time. A protracted withdrawal is seen with methadone, with symptoms of fatigue, sluggishness, irritability, and numerous vague physical complaints. These symptoms may last for as long as 6 months (Martin et al., 1973). Methadone withdrawal is particularly severe when precipitated by the administration of an antagonist such as Narcan.

Propoxyphene Properties

Propoxyphene, marketed as Darvon, is chemically related to methadone. It is often marketed in combination with aspirin or acetaminophen and is used in medical practice to treat mild to moderate pain. Large doses of propoxyphene produce euphoria and intoxication. Propoxyphene is abused, but its addiction liability is lower than that of morphine or methadone. Table 5.1 shows a comparison of the opioids' addiction liability.

The abuse of large amounts of propoxyphene can cause gastrointestinal upsets and dizziness, as well as toxic psychosis (Jaffe, 1985). The hydrochloride salt of propoxyphene has been abused by the injectable route, but the drug is very irritating and causes severe tissue damage when used in this manner. The napsylate salt, such as Darvon-N, is not easily dissolved and is, therefore, harder to abuse by the injectable route.

Propoxyphene Withdrawal

Physical withdrawal from propoxyphene is considerably milder than from morphine or methadone. Withdrawal has been reported after chronic use of up to 800 mg/d (Jaffe, 1985). One should expect milder symptoms of morphine withdrawal patterns to occur. Some physical complications of withdrawal can be attributed to the ingestion of large amounts of aspirin or acetaminophen.

AGONIST–ANTAGONIST OPIOIDS

The agonist–antagonist opioids are a class of drugs used to relieve pain. They produce euphoria and, for that reason, are abused. The most commonly abused drug in this class is pentazocine (Talwin).

Opioids and other drugs are thought to produce a response in a client by attaching or binding to a specific place called a *receptor site* (see Fig. 5.2). When a drug is the correct shape to fit this receptor, it may attach and produce a response. This drug, which is called an *agonist,* may produce the desired drug effects as well as undesired ones. Morphine is a good example of an opioid agonist. Some drugs, such as naloxone (Narcan), are able to bind to the receptor site but do not produce any response. If the drug binds strongly enough, other opioid drugs cannot then get to the receptor to produce a response. Drugs such as naloxone (Narcan) are used to keep morphine from staying bound to the receptor site when an overdose has been administered or taken, thereby immediately stopping the agonistic effects of morphine.

Not all opioid drugs fall exclusively into one category. To understand some opioid drugs, one must be familiar with how a drug acts on a receptor.

Opioids are thought to produce a response by attaching to the aforementioned receptors. When a drug is correct to fit a certain receptor, it may attach and produce a response. This drug, called an *agonist,* then produces a pharmacologic effect. Morphine is a good

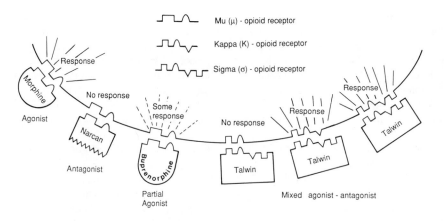

Figure 5.2
Agonist and agonist–antagonist opioid responses.

example of an agonist at the mu and kappa opioid receptors, producing analgesia, euphoria, respiratory depression, physical dependence, sedation, and miosis. Drugs which bind to a receptor, producing no action at all and preventing other drugs from binding to that site are called *antagonists*. Naloxone (Narcan) is an opioid antagonist used to keep opioids from occupying the mu and the kappa receptors, thereby immediately stopping the strong agonist actions in overdose situations. Another group of drugs can have mixed actions at opioid receptors. This group of drugs, called *agonist–antagonists*, can be of two types. One group binds to the receptor, but does not elicit maximal responses. These drugs, *partial agonists*, such as buprenorphine and propiram, are not presently marketed for use in the United States. Another *mixed agonist–antagonist* group, acts as agonist at one receptor but antagonist at another. The prototype drug of this group is pentazocine.

Pentazocine Properties

Pentazocine, which is marketed as Talwin, is a mixed agonist-antagonist opioid drug. It has antagonist action at the mu receptor and agonist action at the kappa and sigma receptors. When given to a morphine-dependent person, large doses of Talwin can actually precipitate withdrawal symptoms (Jasinski, Martin, & Hoeldtke, 1970), because the morphine is blocked from reaching the dependent receptor. It acts in the CNS as well as on

the intestinal tract in a manner that is similar to morphinelike opioids. The analgesia provided by pentazocine is probably the result of its action on kappa receptors. Actions on the sigma receptors may be responsible for the dysphoria and hallucinations caused by pentazocine.

Pentazocine is abused for the euphoria that it produces. Sedation, respiratory depression, dizziness, nausea, pinpoint pupils, and constipation are all symptoms seen in the pentazocine abuser (Jaffe & Martin, 1985; Jasinski et al., 1970). The cardiovascular response to pentazocine differs from that seen with morphine administration. High doses of pentazocine cause the pulse and blood pressure to rise (Jaffe & Martin, 1985) and can also cause an increase in cardiac work.

The chronic abuse of pentazocine produces some dysphoric symptoms. These effects are of two types. One set of symptoms resembles the complaints of tranquilizer abusers. These complaints include lethargy, weakness, and sleepiness. The other types of symptoms described by abusers resemble side effects of the hallucinogenic drugs (Jasinski et al., 1970). Strange dreams, nightmares, hallucinations, visual distortions, uncontrollable thoughts, anxiety, and irritability are some of these complaints. These disturbing psychotomimetic effects have been known to persist for longer than 12 hours (Jasinski et al., 1970). These psychotomimetic effects are occasionally experienced as adverse reactions by the nonaddicted client who receives the drug as an analgesic.

Pentazocine is abused by the oral method of administration, but higher blood levels and more rapid dependence are achieved by injectable use. Pentazocine is about one-fourth as potent when taken orally as when injected. The injection of pentazocine is very irritating to tissue, and pain on injection is a common complaint of the addict and the nonaddict. Repeated injection may cause fibrosis of the injection site.

Pentazocine is occasionally combined with tripelennamine in street abuse and used intravenously. This combination is occasionally used as a heroin substitute and is called "Ts and blues."

Nalbuphine Properties

Nalbuphine (Nubain) is a mixed agonist–antagonist which produces its analgesic effects by acting on kappa opioid receptors. It has more potent antagonistic actions at mu receptors than pentazocine. It is available in injectable form only.

Intramuscular doses of nalbuphine cause analgesic effects similar to morphine. Respirations may be depressed by nalbuphine up to dosages around 30 mg, where no further depression occurs (Jaffe & Martin, 1985). Sedation, headache, and sweating are the most common side effects. Blood pressure is usually not altered with nalbuphine administration (Jasinski & Mansky, 1972). The gastrointestinal effects of nalbuphine are similar to those of pentazocine. Nalbuphine's effects on sigma opioid receptors can result in psychotomimetic symptoms, although less frequently than with pentazocine. Dosages above 70 mg produce dysphoria and racing thoughts more frequently than lower dosages.

In persons not dependent on mu opioid agonist drugs as morphine or heroin, nalbuphine's potential for abuse is similar to that seen with injectable pentazocine. A person who is dependent on mu-agonists, as heroin, will choose nalbuphine infrequently as a substitute, since its strong mu-antagonist actions can precipitate withdrawal symptoms (Jaffe & Martin, 1985). It is not presently listed in any schedule of the Controlled Substance Act.

Butorphanol Properties

Butorphanol (Stadol) is a mixed agonist–antagonist drug which produces analgesic effects by action on kappa opioid receptors. Therapeutic doses of butorphanol cause an increase in cardiac work and a slight decrease in arterial pressure (Jaffe & Martin, 1985). Butorphanol is available only as an injectable product. Side effects include sedation, weakness and nausea. Dysphoric reactions, as floating feelings, occur with a frequency less than that of pentazocine and more than that of nalbuphine. These reactions are probably the result of actions on sigma opioid receptors. Butorphanol is thought to be neither an agonist nor antagonist on mu opioid receptors (Jaffe & Martin, 1985). It is not presently listed in any schedule of the Controlled Substance Act.

Pentazocine, Nalbuphine, and Butorphanol Withdrawal

The chronic abuse of pentazocine causes physical dependence, as evidenced by a withdrawal syndrome appearing 6–8 hours after the cessation of an injectable habit. Although the withdrawal is milder than the withdrawal from morphine, many of the symptoms are the same. The syndrome usually peaks by the end of the second day of abstinence, and the acute syndrome has usually passed in 8 days. Morphine withdrawal symptoms, such as insomnia, restlessness, low-grade fever, hyperpnea, anorexia with weight loss, and "drug-seeking behavior" (Jasinski et al., 1970, p. 399) are present. Blood pressure does not usually increase during this type of withdrawal (Jasinski et al., 1970). Butorphanol and nalbuphine have withdrawal patterns similar to those of pentazocine.

SUMMARY

The opioid drugs, despite their addictive qualities, are the most effective drugs available to treat pain. This drug group includes naturally occurring chemicals, such as morphine and codeine; synthetic and semisynthetic compounds, such as heroin and meperidine; and mixed agonist–antagonist drugs, such as pentazocine. Morphine is the prototype of the opioid drugs, to which all opioid drugs are compared and contrasted.

The discovery of several types of opioid receptors has enabled us to understand more fully both effects and side effects of the available opioid drugs. Mu, sigma, and kappa opioid receptor theory can be used to both classify and explain seemingly contradictory drug actions.

Although the opioids do have subtle differences in action, all affect the CNS to produce mood changes, drowsiness, respiratory depression, and analgesia. The gastrointestinal tract and the cardiovascular system are also affected by the opioids.

Tolerance and addiction occur when opioids are used repeatedly. An addict's abrupt abstinence from opioid drugs produces a recognizable pattern of signs and symptoms including nausea, vomiting, twitching, aching, runny nose, dilated pupils, anxiety, and goose-flesh. Although the acute withdrawal phase of opioid withdrawal is over in approximately 2 weeks, a protracted withdrawal syndrome may last for 2 months.

Naturally occurring opioidlike compounds in the CNS, called opiopeptins, have been discussed. These compounds offer exciting areas for research in the development of new pain-relieving drugs as well as in the exploration of the etiology of addictive diseases.

REFERENCES

Alderman, E. L., Barry, W. H., Graham, A. F., & Harrison, D. C. (1972). Hemodynamic effects of morphine and pentazocine differ in cardiac patients. *New England Journal of Medicine, 287*(13), 623–627.

Baden, M. M. (1975). Pathology of the addictive states. In R. W. Richter (Ed.), *Medical aspects of drug abuse* (pp. 189–211). Hagerstown, MD: Harper & Row.

Brunk, S. F., & Delle, M. (1974). Morphine metabolism in man. *Clinical Pharmacology and Therapeutics, 16*(1), 51–57.

Chakravarty, N. K., Matallana, A., Jensen, R., & Borison, H. L. (1956). Central effects of antitussive drugs on cough and respiration. *Journal of Pharmacological and Experimental Therapeutics, 117,* 127–135.

Criswell, H. E., & Levitt, R. A. (1975). The narcotic analgesics. In R. A. Levitt (Ed.), *Psychopharmacology: A biological approach* (pp. 187–230). New York: John Wiley & Sons.

Cushman, P. (1973). Street heroin in Washington, D.C. *New England Journal of Medicine, 289*(21), 1151.

DaDalt, R. A. (1986). Changing patterns of drug diversion. *American Journal of Nursing, 86*(7), 792–794.

Drugs of abuse (1979) [Reprinted from *Drug Enforcement, 6*(2), Stock No. 620–056/3]. Washington, DC: U. S. Government Printing Office.

Fishman, J., & Hahn, E. F. (1975). The opiates. In R. W. Richter (Ed.), *Medical aspects of drug abuse* (pp. 37–64). Hagerstown, MD: Harper & Row.

Flórez, J., McCarthy, L. E., & Borison, H. L. (1968). A comparative study in the cat of the respiratory effects of morphine injected intravenously and into the cerebrospinal fluid. *Journal of Pharmacological and Experimental Therapeutics, 163,* 448–455.

Hansten, P. D. (1985). *Drug interactions* (5th ed.). Philadelphia: Lea & Febiger.

Himmelsbach, C. K. (1941). The morphine abstinence syndrome, its nature and treatment. *Annals of Internal Medicine, 15,* 829–839.

Holloway, H. C. (1974). Epidemiology of herion dependency among soldiers in Vietnam. *Military Medicine, 139,* 108–113.

Hug, C. C. (1972). Characteristics and theories related to acute and chronic tolerance development. In S. J. Mulé & H. Brill (Eds.), *Chemical and biological aspects of drug dependence* (pp. 307–358). Cleveland: CRC Press.

Hughes, J., Smith, T. W., Kosterlitz, H. W., Fothergill, L. A., Morgan, B. A., & Morris, H. R. (1975). Identification of two related pentapeptides from the brain with potent opiate agonist activity. *Nature, 258,* 577–579.

Isbell, H., & White, W. M. (1953). Clinical characteristics of addictions. *American Journal of Medicine, 14,* 558–565.

Jaffe, J. H. (1985). Drug addiction and drug abuse. In A. G. Gilman, L. S. Goodman, T. W. Rall, & F. Murad (Eds.), *Goodman and Gilman's the pharmacological basis of therapeutics* (pp. 532–581). New York: Macmillan.

Jaffe, J. H., & Martin, W. R. (1985). Opioid analgesics and antagonists. In A. G. Gilman, L. S. Goodman, T. W. Rall, & F. Murad (Eds.), *Goodman and Gilman's the pharmacological basis of therapeutics* (pp. 491–531). New York: Macmillan.

Jasinski, D. R., & Mansky, P. A. (1972). Evaluation of nalbuphine for abuse potential. *Clinical Pharmacology and Therapeutics, 13*(1), 78–90.

Jasinski, D. R., Martin, W. R., & Hoeldtke, R. D. (1970). Effects of short- and long-term administration of pentazocine in man. *Clinical Pharmacology and Therapeutics, 11,* 385–403.

Klotz, U., McHorse, T. S., Wilkinson, G. R., & Schenker, S. (1974). The effect of cirrhosis on the disposition and elimination of meperidine in man. *Clinical Pharmacology and Therapeutics, 16,* 667–675.

Kreek, M. H. (1978). Medical complications in methadone patients. *Annals of the New York Academy of Sciences, 311,* 110–132.

Lee, H. K., & Wang, S. C. (1975). Mechanism of morphine-induced miosis in the dog. *Journal of Pharmacological and Experimental Therapeutics, 192*(2), 415–431.

Martin, W. R., & Fraser, H. F. (1961). A comparative study of physiological and subjective effects of heroin and morphine administered intravenously in post-addicts. *Journal of Pharmacological and Experimental Therapeutics, 133,* 388–399.

Martin, W. R., Jasinski, D. R., Haertzen, C. A., Kay, D. C., Jones, B. E., Mansky, P. A., & Carpenter, R. W. (1973). Methadone—a re-evaluation. *Archives of General Psychiatry, 28,* 286–295.

Mo, B. P., & Way, E. L. (1966). An assessment of inhalation as a mode of administration of heroin by addicts. *Journal of Pharmacological and Experimental Therapeutics, 154,* 142–151.

Oldendorf, W. H., Hyman, S., Braun, L., & Oldendorf, S. Z. (1972). Blood–brain barrier: Penetration of morphine, codeine, heroin, and methadone after carotid injection. *Science, 178,* 984–986.

Ream, N. W., Robinson, M. G., Richter, R. W., Hegge, F. W., & Holloway, H. C. (1975). Opiate dependence and acute abstinence. In R. W. Richter (Ed.), *Medical aspects of drug abuse* (pp. 81–123). Hagerstown, MD: Harper & Row.

Soine, T. O., & Willette, R. E. (1971). Analgesic agents. In C. O. Wilson, O. Gisvold, & R. F. Doerge (Eds.), *Textbook of organic, medicinal and pharmaceutical chemistry* (pp. 699–753). Philadelphia: J. B. Lippincott.

Sullivan, E. J. (1987). Comparison of chemically dependent and nondependent nurses on familial, personal and professional characteristics. *Journal of Studies on Alcohol, 48*(6), 563–568.

Verebely, K., Volavka, J., Mulé, S., & Resnick, R. (1975). Methadone in man: Pharmacokinetic and excretion studies in acute and chronic treatment. *Clinical Pharmacology and Therapeutics, 18*(2), 180–190.

Way, E. L. (1986). Sites and mechanisms of basic narcotic receptor function based on current research. *Annals of Emergency Medicine, 15*(9), 1021–1035.

CHAPTER 6

HALLUCINOGENS

John M. Holbrook

Naturally occurring chemicals that distort the perception of reality have been used for centuries in some cultures to provide religious experiences. These chemicals, such as mescaline and psilocybin, have been somewhat replaced in the modern drug culture by more potent and usually, more toxic, synthetic agents that produce essentially the same "mind-altering" effects. In the past two decades, the use of both the natural and synthetic agents has increased dramatically even though the inherent dangers of such use have been well publicized. The popularity of these agents is a phenomenon difficult to rationalize because their effects are unpredictable, yet their use continues to increase worldwide.

Chemicals that alter or distort reality have been given a number of descriptive titles including *hallucinogens, psychotogens, psychotomimetics, phantasticants, mind-benders,* and *psychedelics.* Although none of these titles is sufficiently broad or accurate enough to encompass the entire category, the term *hallucinogen* will be used here because the occurrence of hallucinations appears to be one effect common to the majority of these agents at some dose.

Hallucinogens alter the normal functioning of both the peripheral nervous system and central nervous system (CNS). They excite the CNS, increase blood pressure and body temperature, and produce mydriasis. They produce conceptual distortions of time and distance, impair rational judgment, and may produce either euphoria or depression. In susceptible people or at high doses, they produce delusions and visual hallucinations. The much publicized psychedelic experience has components such as hallucinations and perceptual alterations, that is, "seeing sounds and hearing colors" occurring along with some autonomic changes. Some users, especially the novice, may experience an adverse reaction consisting of anxiety, agitation, and insomnia that may lead to behavior harmful to the user or to others.

The perceptual distortions produced by the hallucinogenic agents have often been compared to the clinical manifestations of chronic schizophrenia and the acute psychotic break. Some hallucinogens, such as lysergic acid diethylamide (LSD), have been used to produce an experimental schizophrenialike state for research purposes; however, although the condition produced by the hallucinogens resembles schizophrenia to some degree, there are enough differences between them to make them clinically distinguishable. For example, the psychotic client in an active schizophrenic state has little or no concept of reality and later, no memory of the psychotic episode. This is in sharp contrast to the person undergoing a psychedelic experience who is in touch with reality, but has perceptual distortions and who retains a vivid memory of the entire experience. In addition, hallucinations associated with psychosis are predominantly auditory, whereas those associated with hallucinogens are usually visual.

Reports of perceptual distortions related to the use of hallucinogens include an increased sensitivity to sensory input and a sense of *depersonalization* (of observing oneself having the experience and of participating in the experience at the same time). Although some users describe the feeling as one of being at peace with self and the universe, others describe the experience as spiritual in nature. Such experiences often lead the user to repeat the "trip" in an attempt to further explore and expand the inner self.

The majority of the hallucinogenic agents used today are potent synthetic compounds chemically related to the naturally occurring agents psilocybin and mescaline. In the following discussion, the hallucinogens will be grouped according to their chemical composition (see Table 6.1) rather than being grouped as naturally occurring or synthetic. Group I contains agents having an indole nucleus and producing effects similar to those of psilocybin. Group II contains agents that are chemically phenethylamines or related structures and that have activities similar to mescaline. Group III contains two agents, cannabis and phencyclidine, that are not structurally related to the compounds in group I or group II or to each other.

Group I hallucinogens produce similar subjective effects and differ primarily in their duration and intensity

Table 6.1
Hallucinogens

Group	Agents
Indole amines or substituted indole alkylamines	Lysergic acid diethylamide (LSD)
	Psilocin
	Psilocybin
	Dimethyltryptamine (DMT)
	Diethyltryptamine (DET)
Beta-phenethylamines or substituted phenyl alkylamines	Mescaline
	2,5 Dimethyl-4-ethylamphetamine (STP, DOM)
	Methoxyamphetamine (MDA)
	Methoxymethylene-dioxyamphetamine (MMDA)
	Methylene–dioxyamphetamine (MDMA, see page 73)
	Methylene–dioxyethamphetamine (MDEA, see page 73)
	Paramethoxy-amphetamine (PMA)
Miscellaneous	Cannabis (marihuana, THC)
	Phencyclidine (PCP)

of action. They all contain an indole nucleus that is also the basic structural component of the neurotransmitter serotonin. Their mechanism of action in producing hallucinations is thought to be related to interference with the functioning of nerve fibers using serotonin as their transmitter.

INDOLAMINES OR SUBSTITUTED INDOLE ALKYLAMINES

Lysergic Acid Diethylamide

Of the potent hallucinogenic agents that have found a wide sphere of use in recent years, none has been so widely acclaimed as LSD. At various times, it has been used as a psychotherapeutic agent, as an adjunct in the treatment of opiate and alcohol withdrawal syndromes, and in the production of a tranquil state to reduce the need for narcotic analgesics in terminally ill patients. In each case its use has been discontinued because it was found to be ineffective or because the risks of its use were too great. In the drug culture, however, LSD has become the forerunner of a number of synthetic compounds used to "expand the mind" or produce psychedelic experiences.

LSD was first synthesized in 1938 by Dr. Albert Hoffman from lysergic acid, a compound derived from the ergot alkaloids. Hoffman accidentally ingested some of the LSD several years after its synthesis (1943) and made the first LSD "trip"! He later reported the details of his experience (Hoffman, 1968) and the details of his report vary little from more recent reports of the LSD experience. His description of the experience included vertigo, visual disturbances, confusion alternating with clarity of thought, paresis, heaviness of the limbs, agitation, dry mouth, and a feeling of choking.

The reports of Hoffman's initial experiences with LSD and his early research with human subjects led to the hypothesis that LSD produces a reversible psychotic state not unlike that seen in the schizophrenic patient, and within a short time LSD was being used in research to investigate the biochemical etiology of schizophrenia. Unfortunately, LSD soon reached the illicit drug market and its abuse began to overshadow its use as a clinical research tool. During the 1960s, its abuse became so widespread that the manufacturer refused to continue supplying it for legitimate research. LSD's

Table 6.2
Hallucinogens: Selected Street Names

Hallucinogen	Street Name(s)
Cannabis (marihuana)	Acapulco gold, ace, ashes, baby, bhang, bomber, broccoli, butter, gage, ganja, grass, hemp, jive, joint, Mary Jane, pot, tea, THC, weed
DMT	AMT, businessman's trip, DMT
Hash, hashish	Black hash (hashish containing opium), black Russian (potent, dark hashish), gram, keif
LSD	Acid, barrels (tablet), battery acid, Berkeley blood, big D, blotter acid, blue acid, blue microdot, chief, contact lens (on round gelatin flake), HCP, sugar, sunshine, window pane, Zen
MDA	Love drug
Mescaline	Bad seed, big chief, cactus, chief, peyote, pink wedge, white light
PCP	Angel dust, flying saucers, hair, hog, horse tranq., mist, peace pill
Psilocybin	Exotic mushroom, God's flesh
MDMA	XTC, ecstacy, Adam
MDEA	Eve

illicit use peaked in the 1960s and waned during the early and mid-1970s; however, it appears to be returning as a favored abuse substance of the 1980s.

LSD has many street names (see Table 6.2), some of which are indicative of the "dosage forms" in which it is available. LSD is a clear liquid and is usually placed on some material for oral ingestion. For example, *blotter acid* is LSD on a small square of blotter paper or decal; *window panes* are thin gelatin squares containing LSD.

LSD is extremely potent, with the usual hallucinogenic dose being 30–50 μg of the pure substance. On the street, where LSD is often adulterated, the dose may be several times this amount. It is usually administered orally, but some users prefer to inject it intravenously (Materson & Barrett-Conner, 1967). It is rapidly absorbed from the stomach and appears to concentrate centrally in the visual cortex, limbic system, and reticular formation. It has a half-life of about 3 hours and is totally inactivated in the liver. The inactive LSD metabolite, 2-oxy-LSD, is excreted via the kidney.

The mechanism by which LSD produces its hallucinogenic effect is still largely unknown. It apparently stimulates the same cells in the reticular formation that are stimulated by amphetamine and also disrupts the functioning of fiber tracts utilizing serotonin as their neurotransmitter. The stimulant effect of LSD increases the transfer of sensory information to the cortex, whereas the effect on serotonergic pathways results in a decreased ability to select what input reaches the cortex.

LSD produces definite effects on the autonomic nervous system (ANS) including dizziness, hot and cold flashes, dry mouth, dilated pupils, elevated body temperature, and increased blood pressure. At times, excessive salivation rather than dry mouth may be noted. The CNS effects of LSD usually include altered sensations, perception, and mood, abnormality of color, time, and space perception, and visual hallucinations. In addition, LSD produces alterations in reasoning and may lead the user to feel all-powerful or capable of insights into himself or others that were never before possible.

Although many LSD users describe "trips" only in positive terms, in many instances the use of LSD produces adverse effects that may be life-threatening to the user as well as to others. Three types of adverse reactions to LSD have been documented. These are the *panic reaction,* the *overt psychosis,* and the *flashback.* Although the first two types of reactions are considered to be totally undesirable, the flashback may, at times, be viewed as desirable, and attempts have been made by users to stimulate the occurrence of these phenomena.

The *panic reaction* is an extreme anxiety attack thought to occur due to altered perception or the fear that the person will not "return" from the trip. The user becomes hyperactive, the mood is labile, and reasoning is illogical. The fear may be severe enough to cause the person to attempt totally illogical feats such as jumping from one building to another to escape the adverse situation. The panic reaction may last 24–48 hours but does not leave residual effects.

The *overt psychosis* produced by LSD occurs as a true loss of touch with reality and the return to normal mental functioning may occur very slowly. It is thought that the overt psychosis occurs in people who are prepsychotic in their drug-free state. The clinical manifestations of such a reaction closely resemble the acute psychotic break. People undergoing this adverse reaction may become dangerous, and medically supervised detoxification is usually mandatory.

One of the most frightening of the LSD adverse effects is the occurrence of the *flashback,* the recurrence of the "trip" weeks or months after the LSD has last been ingested. The occurrence and frequency of flashbacks are variable and unpredictable. They seem to occur most frequently just before going to sleep, while driving, and during periods of high stress (Schick & Smith, 1970). The occurrence of flashbacks decreases with time if there is no further use of hallucinogenic drugs; however, the occurrence of such a phenomenon

certainly points to the possibility that some permanent damage may occur if LSD is used chronically by a susceptible person.

There have been reports of chromosome damage and teratogenic effects related to LSD use. These reported effects have not been well documented, and there is much contradictory data in the scientific literature (Gilmour, Bloom, Lele, Robbins, & Maximilian, 1971). Although there is not much proof that LSD is capable of altering the chromosomes of a healthy person, there is also no real proof that LSD will not do some permanent damage. The ultimate proof of the effects of LSD may come in the next two generations, at which time it will certainly be too late for corrective measures.

The use of LSD does not lead to the development of either physical or psychologic dependence. Tolerance does develop to a high degree and very rapidly. Repeated daily doses of LSD for 3–4 days produce complete tolerance. Recovery from the tolerance occurs rapidly so that a chronic user can get the desired effect from the same dose week after week. Cross-tolerance develops between LSD, mescaline, and psilocybin, but not between these and other hallucinogens.

Psilocybin and Psilocin

Psilocybin and psilocin are naturally occurring hallucinogens found in several varities of mushrooms indigenous to the United States and Mexico. Psilocybin is found in the greatest concentration (0.2%–0.5%) in the *Psilocybe mexicana* mushroom, which also contains traces of the more potent psilocin.

The *Psilocybe* mushroom has been used for its hallucinogenic effects by the natives of southern Mexico for centuries. Historically, its use was primarily limited to religious occasions and some social events, but in the past 25–30 years the psychedelic properties of psilocybin have come under the scrutiny of the research world and have been exploited by the street drug culture.

Psilocybin was isolated from its natural source by Dr. Albert Hoffman (of LSD fame) in the late 1950s and synthesized in his laboratory in 1961. Hoffman, who was familiar with the hallucinogenic effects of LSD, ingested 32 dried *Psilocybe* mushrooms to determine the effects of psilocybin. He found that the effects produced were very similar to his initial LSD experience. The experience was shorter than that which occurred with LSD, lasting only about 6 hours, and the peak of the intoxication occurred approximately 1.5

hours following ingestion of the mushrooms. Subjectively, however, the perceptual distortions had the same qualities as those produced by LSD.

Psilocybin is abused primarily by oral ingestion of either the fresh or dried mushroom, which is often incorporated into food. Although it is well absorbed from the gastrointestinal tract, it often produces violent nausea and vomiting so that much of the ingested mushrooms are lost. Part of the absorbed psilocybin is metabolized to an inactive form in the liver, but a greater portion is excreted unchanged by the kidney. The inactive metabolites of psilocybin have been reported to remain in the body for several days (Kalberer, Kreis, & Rutschmann, 1962).

The hallucinations and perceptual distortions produced by psilocybin are thought to occur due to its actions on serotonergic fiber tracts, although it has both central serotonergic and adrenergic effects. An average 4-mg dose of psilocybin produces a pleasant experience characterized by physical and mental relaxation and slight perceptual distortions. As the dose is increased, perceptual distortions are enhanced and hallucinations may occur. Autonomic effects are minimal and usually include mydriasis, increased blood pressure, and increased heart rate (Diagnosis and management of reactions to drug abuse, 1977). In some cases, nausea, photosensitivity, muscle weakness, and vertigo may also occur.

The toxic syndrome seen with psilocybin is very similar to that seen with LSD and is characterized by elevated body temperature, flushing, convulsions (rarely), euphoria, anxiety or panic, paranoid thought disorder (although the sensorium remains clear), and depersonalization (Diagnosis and management, 1977).

Neither physical nor psychologic dependence has been reported to occur with the use of psilocybin. Tolerance does not appear to develop to the hallucinogenic effects, but this could be because psilocybin is not used on a regular basis as are some of the other hallucinogens.

Dimethyltryptamine and Diethyltryptamine

Both dimethyltryptamine (DMT) and diethyltryptamine (DET) are chemical analogues of tryptamine, a substance found widely scattered in natural resources. DMT also occurs in nature, but a plant source for DET has not yet been discovered.

DMT was first synthesized in 1931 but was not widely acclaimed as a hallucinogen until 1956. Plants containing DMT have been used for centuries in tropical countries as hallucinogens. The leaves and seeds of such plants are dried and powdered into a snuff that, when inhaled, produces a short, intense hallucinatory experience.

At one point in its history, DMT was proposed as a possible etiologic link with schizophrenia. Both tryptamine and the enzyme that converts tryptamine to DMT are found in humans, but there is presently no evidence that DMT is formed in the body by this enzyme. DMT has, however, been found in trace amounts in the blood of both normal and schizophrenic clients although its origin and function is unknown (Shulgin, 1976).

DMT and DET are not orally active and are administered by injection and by inhalation. They are frequently added to tobacco or marihuana and smoked or sniffed. When injected intramuscularly, the peak plasma levels and euphoric effect of DMT occur after 10 minutes and the half-life is approximately 15 minutes.

A DMT dose of 30 mg by inhalation or 75 mg by intramuscular injection is sufficient to produce a psychedelic experience. Five minutes after the intramuscular injection of DMT, autonomic effects such as mydriasis, tachycardia, and hypertension are evident. Within 15 minutes, hallucinations occur, accompanied by difficulty in concentrating and euphoria. When DMT is inhaled, the entire experience lasts only about 10 minutes and, since it can be used during a lunch hour, has been termed a *businessman's trip* (Szara, 1970).

As with LSD and psilocybin, some users develop an acute anxiety attack or panic reaction; they are rarely candidates for medical detoxification because of the short duration of the effect. The symptoms of this toxic reaction are essentially the same as those listed previously for psilocybin.

Repeated use of DMT (and probably DET) does not lead to the development of either physical or psychologic dependence. If tolerance develops, its occurrence is very gradual, probably due to the short duration of effect.

BETA-PHENETHYLAMINES OR SUBSTITUTED PHENYL ALKYLAMINES

Mescaline

Mescaline, like psilocybin, is a naturally occurring hallucinogen used for centuries in religious rites performed by Mexican natives. In the late 1800s, its use for religious purposes was incorporated into ceremonies performed by North American tribes. Today it is the only hallucinogenic compound used legally for religious purposes by members of the Native American Church of the United States.

Mescaline is the primary active ingredient of the peyote cactus, a small plant found in the southwestern United States and in Mexico. Most of the peyote plant grows underground, with only a small pin-cushion top or crown being visible above ground. The peyote crown is sliced into discs, which are sun-dried and termed *mescal buttons*. When the buttons are used in religious rites, they are held in the mouth until soft and then swallowed. The dried buttons may also be powdered, and the powder may be ingested. Mescaline is also produced synthetically, but the majority of this substance used today comes from the natural source.

Mescaline is self-administered by the oral route and is well absorbed from the gastrointestinal tract. Maximum brain levels are reached in 1–2 hours after ingestion. The therapeutic half-life of mescaline is approximately 6 hours, although it may remain in the brain for up to 9–10 hours.

A dose of 3 mg/kg produces euphoria, whereas 5 mg/kg will produce a full-blown hallucinatory experience with a duration of 5–12 hours. Mescaline apparently undergoes little or no hepatic metabolism, and the majority of a single dose is excreted unchanged by the kidney. The lack of a hepatic metabolic pathway for mescaline probably accounts for its long duration of action.

Mescaline produces discernible effects on both the peripheral and central nervous systems. A dose of 350-500 mg will produce mydriasis, increased heart rate and blood pressure, and elevated body temperature due to actions on peripheral adrenergic nerve fibers. Toxic doses may produce convulsions and death due to respiratory depression (Ray & Ksir, 1987).

Although mescaline is chemically related to the catecholamine neurotransmitters, its hallucinatory effects closely resemble those agents possessing an indole nucleus. In addition, mescaline produces cross-tolerance to both LSD and psilocybin and, therefore, it is thought that the hallucinations produced by mescaline are due to an effect on serotonergic nerve fibers rather than on adrenergic nerve fibers.

The psychologic effects produced by mescaline are very similar to those produced by LSD, which were previously described. A toxic psychotic reaction does occur with high doses of mescaline and is characterized by delusions, paranoid thought patterns, and possible panic. The very low potency of mescaline as compared with other hallucinogens makes the occurrence of toxic overdosage a rare phenomenon.

Neither physical nor psychologic dependence has been reported to occur with the use of mescaline although tolerance does develop slowly with repeated use.

Amphetaminelike Hallucinogens: DOM (STP), MDA, MMDA, PMA, MDMA, and MDEA

Among the very potent hallucinogens of the current drug culture are found the derivatives of amphetamine such as 2,5 dimethyl-4-ethylamphetamine (STP, DOM), methoxy-amphetamine (MDA), methoxymethylene-dioxyamphetamine (MMDA), paramethoxy-amphetamine (PMA), methylene-dioxyamphetamine (MDMA), and methylene-dioxyethamphetamine (MDEA).

The effects of these agents closely resemble those of amphetamine, but they have the added capability of producing hallucinations. Chemically, they are related to both amphetamine and mescaline. They differ primarily in their speed of onset, duration of action, potency, and capacity to modify mood with or without producing hallucinations. In general, lower doses produce euphoria, whereas higher doses produce hallucinations.

They are usually taken orally, but sometimes they are inhaled or injected intravenously. Their metabolic fate is apparently similar to that which has been described for amphetamine.

The best known and most frequently used of the amphetaminelike hallucinogens is DOM, which was synthesized in 1963 and entered the drug scene in 1967. On the street, DOM was first called STP, after a motor-oil additive, but STP was soon interpreted as "Serenity, Tranquility, and Peace."

A dose of 1–3 mg DOM produces a pleasant euphoria, whereas a dose of 3–5 mg will produce hallucinations lasting 6–8 hours. It has been reported that DOM produces a very long hallucinatory experience and that the effects are different from those produced by other hallucinogens. The reasons for the apparent excessive length and unusual experiences produced by DOM are twofold: first, doses of DOM often sold on the street are larger than the amount required to produce hallucinations (up to 10 mg), and second, since DOM is manufactured illicitly, it is usually impure and the concentration may vary greatly from one batch to the next. Under controlled studies, it has been found that the effects of DOM are similar to those of other hallucinogens (Snyder, Faillace, & Hollister, 1967).

DOM often appears to produce a combination of the effects of amphetamine and LSD, with amphetaminelike effects appearing at lower doses and LSD-like effects, including hallucinations, occurring only at higher doses. During its early years in street use, DOM produced a much higher incidence of acute and chronic toxicity than did the other frequently used hallucinogens such as LSD.

Peripherally, the adrenergic effects of DOM result in mydriasis, increased heart rate and blood pressure, and possibly elevated body temperature. Because of the potent amphetaminelike effect, the risk of cardiovascular collapse and hypertensive crisis are much greater than with hallucinogens such as mescaline or LSD. The CNS effects appear initially as mood elevation and euphoria, followed by vivid hallucinations if the dose is sufficiently large. Stimulation of the CNS may be sufficient to produce convulsions that are life-threatening and a state resembling amphetamine psychosis. As with the other hallucinogens, it is possible to produce acute anxiety or a panic reaction with DOM in sufficiently high doses.

The effects of MDA, MMDA, and PMA are similar to those reported for DOM. MDA differs from the other two compounds in that it does not produce either auditory or visual hallucinations. With these compounds the amphetaminelike stimulation persists longer than the hallucinogenic effect so that the "crash" may be characterized by extended euphoria rather than the depression frequently seen with LSD (Dimijian, 1976).

A major problem noted with the abuse of these compounds stems from their excessive toxicity at higher doses. Since this toxicity is related to CNS stimulation, the expected effect would be increased adrenergic activity with possible convulsions and death due to respiratory depression.

MDMA and MDEA are structurally related to MDA and have been categorized as "designer drugs." However, both MDA and MDMA were first synthesized in the early 1900s and have only more recently been *rediscovered* (Climko, Roehrich, Sweeny, & Al-Razi, 1986–87). MDEA has been available as a recreational drug since the mid-1980s. Its increase in popularity has coincided with the emergency classification of MDMA as a Schedule I drug by the Drug Enforcement Agency in 1985.

MDMA has originally developed as an appetite suppressant but was never marketed (Dowling, McDonough, & Bost, 1987). Greer and Strassman (1985) have reported the use of MDMA in the early 1970s by a limited number of psychiatrists as an adjunct to psychotherapy; but since 1983, its use has been primarily recreational. MDEA appears to produce effects similar to those of MDMA, but of a lower magnitude (Dowling et al., 1987).

Davis, Hatoum, and Waters (1987) have reported that currently available animal data relating to MDMA tend to predict a significant human toxicity with symptomatology similar to that reported for MDA. In a 1987 reported by Dowling and coworkers, five deaths related to MDMA or MDEA were reviewed. It was found that, in three cases, the drugs may have contributed to death by the induction of arrhythmias in individuals with underlying natural disease while in another patient, MDMA induced behavior that resulted in accidental death. In the fifth death, MDMA was considered to be the immediate cause due to cardiac arrhythmia.

Although deaths related to the use of MDMA and MDEA are rare, they do occur, and preexisting cardiovascular disease may be a predisposing factor. It is unlikely that the potential psychotherapeutic value of these compounds will outweigh the risk factors associated with their recreational use.

MISCELLANEOUS HALLUCINOGENS: PHENCYCLIDINE AND MARIHUANA

The miscellaneous category of hallucinogens contains two compounds, phencyclidine (PCP) and marihuana. Neither of these abuse substances conforms to the general characteristics of the other agents discussed in this chapter, yet each does produce some hallucinatory effects at some doses.

Phencyclidine

PCP was first synthesized in 1957 for use as an anesthetic-analgesic agent. However, during initial clinical trials PCP produced adverse reactions, which sometimes included hallucinations, as its effects wore off. In 1965, PCP was withdrawn from clinical trials and limited to veterinary use. By 1978, its abuse had reached such proportions that its legal manufacture was halted.

PCP first appeared on the drug scene in 1965, but was not well received because of the high frequency of adverse effects that the users experienced. During the mid-1970s, for unexplainable reasons, its use began to increase, and it currently remains one of the most frequently abused substances.

When PCP first became available as a street drug it was obtained through illegal diversion of the drug from legal sources and was of constant purity and concentration. Today, PCP is no longer legally manufactured, but it can be produced without technical skills from widely available chemicals. Thus, there is a wide variation in the degree of purity and dosage forms of PCP manufactured in clandestine laboratories. When PCP is pure, it is a white granular powder (angel dust), but on the street its purity ranges from 5% to 30% and its color ranges from tan to brown.

PCP has many street names (see Table 6.2). It is often sold on the street as powdered mescaline (which it closely resembles physically), LSD, or synthetic tetrahydrocannabinol (THC). Its dosage forms include capsules, tablets, liquids, and powders. The liquid or powder may be added to a leafy material such as parsley, mint, oregano, or marihuana and smoked. The common combination of PCP and marihuana is referred to on the street as *crystal T*. People who abuse PCP on parsley often are termed *parsley monsters*. People high on PCP are said to be *crystalized*.

PCP is self-administered orally, by inhalation, and at times by intravenous injection. It is sometimes administered in combination with other abused substances such as amphetamine, cocaine, methaqualone, LSD, mescaline, and procaine. When PCP is administered alone, it is well absorbed following all modes of administration. An oral dose of 2-10 mg produces a CNS effect within 1 hour with the maximum effect being delayed for up to 5 hours (Ray & Ksir, 1987). The duration of effect may be up to 12 hours. PCP is metabolized in the liver with only a small fraction being excreted unchanged via the kidney.

It is difficult to comprehend why PCP has attained such popularity as an abused substance when it produces such a myriad of effects, many of which are perceived as undesirable even in the chronic user. Pharmacologically, PCP could be categorized as a *nonspecific CNS depressant* (similar to barbiturates or alcohol), as an *anticholinergic* (similar to atropine), as an *anesthetic, tranquilizer,* or *psychedelic*. Its proposed mechanisms of action are as diverse as its effects, and it is highly likely that PCP's actions are related to effects on more than one transmitter. Structurally, PCP is similar to both norepinephrine (NE) and serotonin. It has been proposed that PCP inhibits NE reuptake (O'Donnell & Wanstall, 1968) and has monoamine oxidase inhibitor activity (Usdin & Usdin, 1961). PCP in large doses has also been shown to increase brain acetylcholine levels by inhibition of acetylcholinesterase (Domino & Wilson, 1972) as well as to have antimuscarinic activity (Paster, Maoyani, Weinstein, & Sokolovsky, 1974). Either of these effects on neurotransmitters could be responsible for the behavioral effects elicited by PCP.

The behavioral effects associated with PCP use are variable, and often they depend on both the person and the environment. Clinical investigations have found four phases of the PCP abuse syndrome that may appear in successive stages. The first phase is termed *acute PCP toxicity* and is characterized by combativeness, catatonia, convulsions, and coma, all of which are dose-related. Phase I toxicity may be accompanied by a fatal hypertensive crisis, but this is a rare occurrence. Visual disturbances are common, with distortions in the size and shape of objects and in distance perception being most common. Occasionally, auditory hallucinations may occur. Sufficiently high PCP doses will produce grand mal seizures, coma, and death due to respiratory depression or cardiovascular collapse. Phase I may last for up to 72 hours and after that period of time the sensorium clears. Some clients may progress from phase I to phase II—*toxic psychosis*.

PCP toxic psychosis is not clearly dose related and does not inevitably follow phase I. It does appear to occur most frequently in the chronic abuser. Toxic psychosis is characterized by both visual and auditory hallucinations, agitation, paranoid delusions, and disturbed judgment ability. The user may become hostile and combative and may become dangerous to others as well as himself. Phase II may last up to 7 days or longer.

Phase III of the PCP syndrome is characterized by *psychotic episodes,* which appear much like schizophrenia and may last for a month or more. A number of reports have indicated that PCP ingestion can produce a state similar to schizophrenia in certain people, most of whom have psychotic or prepsychotic personalities. This type of episode may occur after a single PCP ingestion and is considered to be an adverse reaction to an underlying psychologic condition. The symptoms of this phase include thought disorders that come and go, paranoid ideation, and disorders of affect.

The fourth phase of the PCP behavioral syndrome is *PCP-induced depression,* which may follow any of the three phases mentioned, although probably it occurs more frequently following phase III. Phase IV is especially serious because the user has a higher potential for suicide or may turn to the use of other street drugs to alleviate the depression. The depression is accompanied by prolonged mental dysfunction that may continue for several months following the last PCP dose.

Unlike most of the other hallucinogenic drugs, a number of deaths have been directly attributed to the use of PCP, and, in addition, numerous accidental deaths have occurred due to overdose and to the behavioral changes the drug precipitated. Burns and Lerner (1978) indicated that of 19 reported PCP deaths, 11 were from drowning—one while in the shower. The PCP users apparently lost their orientation while swimming and could not reach the surface of the water. In this same study, three deaths occurred due to suicide, and one death resulted from threatening behavior leading to the user being shot.

The behavior of the person under the influence of PCP is highly unpredictable and may lead to life-threatening situations. The PCP psychosis previously mentioned is sometimes also characterized by delusions of superhuman strength, persecution, and grandiosity. The user may alternate between states of suspicion, anger, and terror, and may be cooperative at one time and assaultive at another. Some users develop paranoid delusions to the point that they use lethal weapons to defend themselves from their imagined enemies.

PCP has not been reported to produce physical dependence even with chronic use. Psychologic dependence characterized by "craving" has been frequently reported in chronic users, as has the slow development of tolerance. The development of tolerance apparently occurs only with frequent use such as on a daily basis. Users have reported daily intake of PCP (by smoking) ranging from 80 mg (1–2 street joints) up to 1 g.

In recent years, methods for quantitating plasma and urine levels of PCP have been perfected, and these assays are frequently used to confirm suspected PCP toxicities. Statistical evaluations of reported blood levels indicate that plasma concentrations as low as 100 μg/ml are associated with distinct behavioral effects. Plasma levels of 1.0 mg/ml are associated with coma and possible death, whereas levels of 2.0–2.5 mg/ml are always lethal, producing seizures and death due to respiratory depression. Although PCP plasma and urine levels are useful in cases of acute intoxication, the user who enters the acute psychotic state will usually show no plasma or urine levels of PCP.

Marihuana, Hashish, and Hash(ish) Oil

Although marihuana is included in the category of hallucinogens, it differs from the agents previously mentioned in that it produces hallucinations only in very high doses that can rarely be obtained by its usual routes of self-administration. It does, however, produce many behavioral effects similar to those seen with alcohol, including an initial stimulation that may be perceived as anxiety, followed by a pleasant euphoria. During the euphoric period, the user is relaxed and frequently introspective. Perceptual distortions also occur, especially with respect to time and distance, but the overall experience is usually perceived as pleasant and is more so following chronic use.

Marihuana use has been reported as early as 2737 B.C. in China. In the United States, its use dates back to the early 1900s when it was used as a psychologic tool. In the late 1920s, an association between marihuana and criminal activity was reported. By 1936, every state had laws that regulated the use, possession, and sale of marihuana; and in 1937, the federal government passed the Marihuana Tax Act that made it almost impossible to buy or sell marihuana, but did not outlaw its use. Following the Marihuana Tax Act, the Bureau of Narcotics formulated a uniform marihuana law that made the possession of one specific marihuana plant, *Cannabis sativa,* illegal.

It was not until the 1950s and 1960s that marihuana reached the level of prominence in drug abuse circles that it still enjoys and became the symbol of the "antiestablishment" generation. Although medical and sociologic reports in the 1930s and 1940s were primarily negative toward marihuana, in the 1960s the emergence of literature favoring the use of marihuana and advocating its decriminalization began. In the past 20 years, the marihuana controversy has continued to escalate, due both to its possible use as a therapeutic agent and to the apparent lack of legal forces to prevent its widespread use.

The primary psychoactive constituent of the marihuana plant is delta-9-tetrahydrocannabinol (THC), which is concentrated in the resin found in the flowering tops and leaves. The potency of any marihuana preparation depends on the amount of resin it contains and the potency of the resin. Three types of cannabis preparations are found in use on the street. Marihuana is the most prevalent type, composed of the dried leaves, stems, and flowers of the plant; it is smoked or added to food items. Hash or hashish is a potent concentrate of the resin derived from the flowering tops of the plant. Hash oil is a very concentrated THC made by boiling hashish in a solvent and filtering out the solid matter. The THC content of commonly available marihuana has increased in recent years and may now be as high as 5%–6%. The THC content in hashish may be as high as 10%, whereas the THC content in hash oil may reach 63% (Ray & Ksir, 1987). A drop of hash oil on a tobacco cigarette is probably equivalent in potency to a regular marihuana cigarette or "joint."

Marihuana is usually self-administered either by the oral route or by inhalation (smoking). The drug that is taken into the body by the oral route is metabolized in the liver, whereas that taken in by smoking is metabolized to some extent in the lungs. Since different enzyme systems are involved at these sites, a number of different THC metabolites are possible. Several of these metabolites are known to be psychoactive and others may have different types of biologic activity.

The THC that is absorbed into the systemic circulation leaves the bloodstream very rapidly due to its high degree of fat solubility and rapid metabolism. An initial plasma concentration of 100 ng/ml will decrease within 1 hour to a concentration of 5–10 ng/ml even though the behavioral effects may persist for 2–3 hours (Jones, 1980). A portion of the plasma THC is hydroxylated in the liver to another psychoactive compound, 11-hydroxy-THC, as well as to at least 20 other compounds (Lemberger & Rubin, 1978).

From plasma, THC is rapidly moved into various body compartments with highest concentrations occurring in fatty tissues. From the fatty tissues, THC is slowly released back into the systemic circulation. Measurable levels of THC in the blood of chronic users can be detected for up to 6 days following the last marihuana cigarette. The plasma half-life of marihuana has recently been reported to be about 19 hours in frequent users (Hunt & Jones, 1980) but is probably much longer in the inexperienced user. Such slow THC clearance from the body suggests the possibility of cumulative behavior toxicity as is seen with other psychoactive compounds.

The metabolites of THC are eliminated through the feces and, in small amounts, through the urine. These metabolites may be found for weeks following the last drug use.

The mechanisms by which THC and its metabolites produce their behavioral and physiologic effects are currently not well understood although our knowledge in these areas is rapidly increasing. It is known that these compounds affect brain amine levels (Johnson & Dewey, 1978), produce ultrastructural changes in some neurons (Myers & Heath, 1979), and cross biologic membranes (Schou, Prockop, Dalhstrom & Rohde, 1977).

The variety and intensity of the behavioral and physiologic effects produced by marihuana have been long debated. There is, however, little doubt that the chronic intake of marihuana in large doses is detrimental to normal functioning. The effects of casual, infrequent use of small amounts of marihuana is much more debatable at the present time.

A variety of adverse effects have been attributed to marihuana in recent years. Such effects have been reported to involve the cardiovascular, respiratory, neuroendocrine, and nervous systems. As research continues, still other effects, as well as the mechanisms by which they occur, will become evident.

The effects on the cardiovascular system include tachycardia and orthostatic (postural) hypotension, with no other effect on cardiac muscle contractility. Since blood pressure is decreased, myocardial oxygen supply is decreased, and oxygen demand is increased due to tachycardia. This may produce problems in clients with already compromised coronary circulation. With chronic use, orthostatic hypotension may disappear due to an expansion in plasma volume (Benowitz & Jones, 1975).

Effects on the respiratory system are due in part to the direct effects of marihuana but also to the consequences of inhalation of combustible products. Marihuana is commonly smoked and greater than 70% of the particulate matter in smoke is retained in the lungs to form the residue termed *tar*. Marihuana produces more tar than an equivalent weight of tobacco, and the smoke is held in the lungs for longer time periods, thus facilitating tar deposits.

Although marihuana ingestion initially produces bronchodilatation and improved respiratory function, chronic use results in obstructive airway disorders. In addition, macrophages that are useful in clearing debris from alveoli have their bacteria-inactivating activity impaired when exposed to marihuana smoke. Chronic exposure to marihuana smoke appears to impair pulmonary defense mechanisms and to produce cellular changes in lung tissue that may be precancerous (Leuchtenberger, Leuchtenberger, Zbinden, & Schleh, 1976). Marihuana smokers often have laryngitis, bronchitis, cough, hoarseness, and other related symptoms after periods of frequent use.

The neuroendocrine effects of marihuana are related to effects on hypothalamic-pituitary function, possibly on neurotransmitters involved with endocrine function. Chronic use of marihuana has been reported to produce alterations in reproductive hormones (Smith, Ruppert, & Beoch, 1979), spermatogenesis (Harclerode, 1980), and ovulation (Smith et al., 1979). Single doses of THC will inhibit pituitary gonadotropin secretion, which will last for 12–24 hours depending on the dosage. Asch, Fernandez, Smith, and Pauerotein (1979) have shown that the suppression of ovulation in rabbits can be reversed by the administration of hypothalamic-releasing factors, indicating that the site of action of THC is hypothalamic rather than at the level of the pituitary gland.

Some of the neurologic effects of marihuana are clearly evident following a single acute dose, whereas others are evident only after chronic use. Changes in perception, mood, behavior, memory, and cognition are effects sought by the marihuana user and are presumed by at least some researchers to be evidence of at least temporary neurologic damage. An important consideration is whether these temporary changes can become permanent with chronic use. These neurologic effects are clearly dose related.

Acute intoxication with marihuana results in a feeling of relaxation, euphoria, and sensory alterations. In common with other hallucinogens, marihuana impairs judgment of time and distance, recent memory and learning ability, and decreases physical coordination. As doses of marihuana are increased, tremors, muscle rigidity, and myoclonus may occur, and with sufficiently high doses, organic toxicity may be seen.

High on the list of neurologic effects produced by marihuana is a syndrome termed *amotivation,* which is characterized by apathy, a lack of concern for the future, and a loss of motivation. Although this syndrome has been reported to occur in the marihuana user, it has been difficult to study under controlled clinical situations. Most of the reports of the occurrence of amotivation have come from chronic use studies in countries where marihuana is freely available and have shown decreased work output and initiative in chronic users (Sharma, 1975).

Several types of psychiatric disorders have been reported to occur with the use of marihuana, but whether or not they result from a specific pathology has not yet been proven. It is probable that psychopathology may already be present in some marihuana users, and the drug simply accentuates the symptomatology.

The most commonly reported adverse psychologic reaction to marihuana is the acute anxiety attack that may range in intensity from mild anxiety with restlessness to a panic reaction accompanied by paranoid delusions. Some sensitive people may experience a toxic psychosis characterized by loss of reality testing, delusions, hallucinations, and inappropriate behavior. Such reactions appear to occur most frequently in the inexperienced user and those users who are under stress, depressed, or schizophrenic.

Mild and moderate adverse symptoms usually disappear within a few hours, especially if the person is maintained in quiet, supportive surroundings. Marihuana psychosis may last for 1–6 weeks or longer and, in contrast to paranoid schizophrenia, is characterized by more abnormal behavior, more violence and panic, and lack of overt thought disorders.

Marihuana flashbacks have been reported to occur, but their etiology has not been explained, nor has there been evidence to link such flashbacks with chronicity of use or dose.

Both tolerance and physical dependence have been reported to develop with the chronic use of marihuana. As with other psychotropic drugs, the development of tolerance depends on the dose and chronicity of use as well as on the drug effect being measured. Effects such as euphoria and tachycardia tend to disappear rapidly in the chronic user even when the dosage level is low. Tolerance to these effects also tends to be lost rapidly so that tolerance may never be evident in the casual or infrequent user. As definite tolerance to marihuana develops, mild physical dependence also occurs. In physically dependent people, a mild withdrawal syndrome appears within hours of the last dose and is characterized by irritability, restlessness, anorexia, insomnia, sweating, nausea, vomiting, and diarrhea (Jones, Benowitz, & Bachman, 1976). Such symptoms of withdrawal were noted only after high-dose, chronic intake; however, less intense symptoms were evident in users who smoked an average of five marihuana cigarettes over a 64-day period (Nowlan & Cohen, 1977).

Since the withdrawal syndrome is mild, there is little evidence to correlate impending withdrawal with drug-seeking behavior. Certainly, there is little reason to believe that fear of such withdrawal would lead to criminal actions related to procurement of more drugs. However, psychologic factors related to the individual user and a profound degree of psychologic dependence that could develop in susceptible users might tend to greatly increase drug-seeking behavior and thus increase the tendency toward criminal activity.

SUMMARY

The hallucinogens are a diverse group of chemicals, both synthetic and naturally occurring, which have in common the ability to alter reality and judgment and to produce delusions and hallucinations. In normally used doses, they are capable of producing effects closely resembling the clinical symptoms of psychosis. These compounds are considered to be highly toxic. The reactions they produce are highly unpredictable, especially in the novice user, and may result in physical harm to the user as well as to others.

REFERENCES

Asch, R. H., Fernandez, E. O., Smith, C. G., & Pauerotein, C. J. (1979). Blockage of the ovulatory reflex in the rabbit with delta-9-tetrahydrocannabinol. *Fertility and Sterility, 31,* 331.

Benowitz, N. L., & Jones, R. T. (1975). Cardiovascular effects of prolonged delta-9-tetrahydrocannabinol ingestion. *Clinical Pharmacology and Therapeutics, 18*(13), 287–297.

Burns, R. S., & Lerner, S. E. (1978). The cause of phencyclidine-related deaths. *Clinical Toxicology, 12*(4), 463–481.

Climko, R. P., Roehrich, H., Sweeney, D. R., & Al-Razi, J. (1986–87). Ecstasy: Review of MDMA and MDA. *International Journal of Psychiatry in Medicine, 16*(4), 359–371.

Davis, W. M., Hatoum, H. T., & Waters, I. W. (1987). Toxicity of MDA (3,4-methylenedioxyamphetamine) considered for relevance to hazards of MDMA (Ecstasy) abuse. *Alcohol and Drug Research, 7,* 123–134.

Diagnosis and management of reactions to drug abuse (1977). *The Medical letter, 19*(3), 13–16.

Dimijian, G. C. (1976). Contemporary drug abuse. In A. Goth (Ed.), *Medical pharmacology principles and concepts* (pp. 297–329). St. Louis: C. V. Mosby.

Domino, E. F., & Wilson, A. E. (1972). Psychotropic drug influences on brain acetylcholine utilization. *Psychopharmacologia, 25,* 291–298.

Dowling, G. P., McDonough, E. T., & Bost, R. O. (1987). 'Eve' and 'Ecstasy': A report of five deaths associated with the use of MDEA and MDMA. *Journal of the American Medical Association, 257,* 1615–1617.

Gilmour, D. G., Bloom, A. D., Lele, K. P., Robbins, E. S., & Maximilian, C. (1971). Chromosomal aberrations in users of psychoactive drugs. *Archives of General Psychiatry, 24,* 268–272.

Greer, G., & Strassman, R. J. (1985). Information on 'Ecstasy'. *American Journal of Psychiatry, 142,* 1391.

Harclerode, J. (1980). The effects of marijuana on reproduction and development. In R. C. Peterson (Ed.), *Marijuana Research Findings: 1980* (pp. 137–166). Washington, DC: National Institute on Drug Abuse.

Hoffman, A. (1968). Psychotomimetic agents. In A. Burger (Ed.), *Drugs affecting the central nervous system* (Vol. 2) (pp. 169–226). New York: Marcel Dekker.

Hunt, C. A., & Jones, R. T. (1980). Tolerance and disposition of tetrahydrocannabinol in man. *Journal of Pharmacology and Experimental Therapeutics, 215,* 35–44.

Johnson, K. M., & Dewey, W. C. (1978). The effect of delta-9-tetrahydrocannabinol on the conversion of [^{3}H] tryptophan to 5-[^{3}H]-hydroxytriptamine in the mouse brain. *Journal of Pharmacology and Experimental Therapeutics, 207,* 140–150.

Jones, R. T. (1980). Human effects: An overview. In R. C. Peterson (Ed.), *Marijuana research findings: 1980.* National Institute on Drug Abuse (NIDA Research Monograph 31, pp. 54–76). Washington, DC: U. S. Government Printing Office.

Jones, R. T., Benowitz, N., & Bachman, J. (1976). Clinical studies of cannabis tolerance and dependence. *Annals of the New York Academy of Sciences, 282,* 221–239.

Kalberer, F., Kreis, W., & Rutschmann, J. (1962, April-May). The fate of psilocin in the rat. *Biochemical Pharmacology, 11,* 261–269.

Lemberger, L., & Rubin, A. (1978). Cannabis: The role of metabolism in the development of tolerance. *Drug Metabolism Review, 8*(1), 59–68.

Leuchtenberger, C., Leuchtenberger, R., Zbinden, J., & Schleh, E. (1976). Cytological and cytochemical effects of whole smoke and of the gas vapor phase from marijuana cigarettes on growth and DNA metabolism of cultured mammalian cells. In G. G. Nahas (Ed.), *Marihuana: Chemistry, biochemistry and cellular effects* (pp. 243–256). New York: Springer Verlag.

Materson, B. J., & Barrett-Conner, E. (1967). LSD "mainlining": A new hazard to health. *Journal of the American Medical Assoication, 200*(12), 1126–1127.

Myers, W. A., III, & Heath, R. G. (1979). *Cannabis sativa:* Ultrastructural changes in organelles of neurons in brain septal region of monkeys. *Journal of the Neurological Sciences, 4,* 9–17.

Nowlan, R., & Cohen, S. (1977). Tolerance to marijuana. Heart rate and subjective "high." *Clinical Pharmacology and Therapeutics, 22*(5), 550–556.

O'Donnell, S. R., & Wanstall, J. C. (1968, February). Actions of phencyclidine on the perfused rabbit ear. *Journal of Pharmacy and Pharmacology, 20,* 125–131.

Paster, Z., Maoyani, S., Weinstein, H., & Sokolovsky, M. (1974). Cholinolytic action of phencyclidine derivatives. *European Journal of Pharmacology, 25,* 270–274.

Ray, O. S., & Ksir, C. (1987). *Drugs, society and human behavior* (pp. 273–299). St. Louis: Times Mirror/Mosby College Publishing.

Schick, J. F. E., & Smith, D. E. (1970). Analysis of the LSD flashback. *Journal of Psychedelic Drugs, 3*(1), 13–19.

Schou, J., Prockop, L. D., Dalhstrom, G., & Rohde, C. (1977). Penetration of delta-9-tetrahydrocannabinol and 11-OH-delta-9-tetrahydrocannabinol through the blood brain barrier. *Acta Pharmacologia et Toxicologia, 41,* 33–38.

Sharma, B. R. (1975). Cannabis and its users in Nepal. *British Journal of Psychiatry, 127,* 550–552.

Shulgin, A. T. (1976, April/June). Profiles of psychedelic drugs. *Journal of Psychedelic Drugs, 8*(2), 167–168.

Smith, C. G., Ruppert, M. J., & Beoch, N. F. (1979). Comparison of the effects of marijuana extract and delta-9-tetrahydrocannabinol on gonadotropin levels in the rhesus monkey. *Pharmacologist, 21,* 203.

Snyder, S. H., Faillace, L., & Hollister, L. (1967). 2,5 Dimethoxy-4-methylamphetamine (STP): A new hallucinogenic drug. *Science, 158,* 669–670.

Szara, S. (1970). DMT (N,N-dimethyltryptamine) and homologues: Clinical and pharmacological consideration. In D. H. Efron (Ed.), *Psychotomimetic drugs.* New York: Raven Press.

Usdin, E., & Usdin, V. R. (1961). Effects of psychotropic compounds on enzyme system II: In vitro inhibition of monoamine oxidase. *Proceedings of the Society for Experimental Biology and Medicine, 108,* 461–463.

OVER-THE-COUNTER DRUGS

Donna S. Woolf
Dennis F. Moore

Over-the-counter (OTC) drugs are those available without prescription, intended for the treatment of minor ailments that are believed to be self-limiting. But since all drugs have their toxicities and not all seemingly minor illnesses are self-limiting, potential problems exist with their large-scale usage. A plethora of these drugs exists for the treatment of various disorders.

Any drug can be abused regardless of its pharmacology. Laxatives and certain analgesics are prime examples of drugs of abuse even though they possess few, if any, psychoactive properties. Their abuse is generally secondary to misinformation regarding the drug or the condition being treated. Yet, mind-altering drugs are abused because of their ability to act as reinforcers by producing desirable effects on one's mood. Currently available OTC psychoactive drugs seem to be poor reinforcers of their own consumption, thus accounting for their low abuse potential. One seldom sees these drugs identified as a client's "primary drug of abuse." The use of these drugs in sizable quantities is usually seen when the abuser's drug of choice is unavailable or when some preexisting psychopathology exists and attempts are being made at self-medication.

A poorly researched but valid concern is the use of these drugs for legitimate illnesses in those clients having a history of drug abuse or addiction. Anecdotal accounts exist as to how addicted people relapse after exposure to these drugs and that they should avoid the consumption of "mood-altering drugs." Due to uncertainties about the concept of *cross-addiction,* as well as about altered electrophysiologic states in the nervous system of addicted people, abstinence from these drugs may be indicated. If they alter the addicted person's ability to self-assess drug consumption, the potential exists for relapse after innocent attempts at self-medication for the conditions for which they are indicated.

Self-medication is a part of our existence in the industrially developed nations. The growing orientation to a "natural health" philosophy, development of home health services, and our increasing intolerance to pain and discomfort (Illich, 1974) are factors forcing our evaluation of drugs used outside the traditional "physician–patient" relationship. Additionally, the young generation appears to have a liberal attitude toward drug usage. We are encouraged daily by advertising that "a pill" is the answer to our problems. If we do not believe there is a problem worthy of treatment, a multimedia campaign will convince us that such a disease exists.

No attempt will be made in this chapter to cover all the OTC drugs available. Rather, we will concentrate on the four clinical classes that have been identified in the past as producing the most psychoactive properties. They are sedatives, cough and cold products, appetite suppressants, and analgesics. Ipecac syrup and laxatives are abused by clients with eating disorders (see Chapter 23).

SEDATIVES

It has been estimated that 35% of adults experience insomnia in any 1-year period. One-half of these persons report the problem as serious (Mellinger, Balter, & Uhlenhuth, 1985). Slightly over 3% of these adults have used OTC sleep-aids. Because insomnia is a frequent complaint of the client who is withdrawing or abusing, the use of OTC sedatives is common among substance abusers. This is a source of concern because of the apparent ineffectiveness of these drugs as well as their potential for adverse effects.

The scientific exploration of sleep is beginning to change our approach to sleep and its treatment. Sleep requirements differ from person to person and change in each person over a lifetime. Yet, many feel compelled to induce 8 hours of sleep regardless of their body's requirements. Apparently, no sedatives produce a "natural" sleep. All sedative products alter the normal sleep patterns, the effects of which are unknown at this time. Few drugs, whether prescription or OTC, are effective for longer than a few nights.

OTC sedatives have obtained a bad reputation during the past few years, especially in mental health circles. Before 1979, these drugs contained scopolamine, a potential cause of "atropinic psychosis." Users, especially the elderly and those with preexisting psychiatric disorders, frequently developed central nervous system (CNS) toxicity.

Pharmacology

The presently marketed OTC sedatives depend on the presence of either pyrilamine, diphenhydramine, or doxylamine for their sedative properties (see Table 7.1). Sedation is a side effect of the drug. Most chemically similar drugs are marketed as antihistamines, not as sedatives. After taking the recommended doses of these drugs, most clients will develop some sedation. Other side effects are most often a reflection of their anticholinergic effects and include dry mouth, tremors, and diplopia. Additionally, side effects such as paradoxical insomnia or a feeling of heaviness and weakness may develop. No long-term studies evaluating the effectiveness and safety of these drugs have been performed. These drugs are not particularly effective in treating the insomnia produced by withdrawal.

Toxicity

Toxicities of these new formulations have yet to be reported. However, one would not expect the degree of toxicity once seen with those combinations that included scopolamine. But since diphenhydramine, pyrilamine, and doxylamine have anticholinergic properties, one should expect that large doses would produce confusion and memory impairment.

Table 7.1
Selected Over-the-Counter Sedatives

Trade Name	Ingredients
Compoze	Diphenhydramine, 50 mg
Nervine	Diphenhydramine, 25 mg
Nytol	Diphenhydramine, 25 mg
Quiet World	Pyrilamine maleate, 25 mg Acetaminophen 162.5 mg or Aspirin, 227.5 mg
Sleep-Eze-3	Diphenhydramine, 25 mg
Sominex-2	Diphenhydramine, 25 mg
Unisom	Doxylamine succinate, 25 mg

The acute toxicity of large doses would be similar to that of other antihistamines. This would include fixed and dilated pupils, fever, excitement, and hallucinations. Treatment should be supportive, with measures taken to prevent absorption, such as lavage or emesis.

APPETITE SUPPRESSANTS

The common factor in all obesity is the consumption of more energy than is being used by the body. One method of attacking the problem is to decrease the amount of energy consumed. An attractive way to accomplish this is to take a drug that reduces appetite. Practically all drugs that produce this effect are CNS stimulants. Few drugs that reduce appetite fail to produce CNS stimulation. Due to this stimulant effect, they cannot be given in late afternoon because of their ability to interfere with sleep. Yet, late in the day is when most people have difficulty adhering to a diet. Thus, there are legitimate questions as to how effective stimulant therapy is in producing meaningful weight reduction.

Pharmacology

OTC diet preparations primarily contain phenylpropanolamine in short-acting 25-mg doses or 75-mg long-acting forms. Phenylpropanolamine is a stimulant of the sympathetic nervous system with actions similar to ephedrine; however, it lacks the same degree of central effects. Its primary usage is as a decongestant in OTC cold preparations in combination with an antihistamine. In high doses it can have significant CNS stimulant properties that probably contribute to its anorexic effects. As would be expected, high doses will elevate mood and increase confidence and initiative. Some users develop headaches, irritability, apprehension, and psychosis. Instances of hypertension have also been reported following the consumption of these agents. Those users with a prior history of mental illness run a greater risk of having hallucinations.

Although caffeine is no longer included in most OTC diet-aids, information concerning its use is included due to its continued inclusion in many street or mail-order "look-alike" products. Caffeine belongs to the class of chemicals known as *xanthines*. It is probably one of the most widely used drugs in our society due to its presence in tea, cola drinks, and coffee. It has diuretic as well as CNS stimulant properties; the latter apparently account for its use as an anorexic. Although its effectiveness as a diuretic decreases with prolonged administration, tolerance apparently does not develop to its stimulant properties. It will produce an increase in motor activity through its ability to stimulate all levels of the CNS.

Toxicity

The CNS toxicity of phenylpropanolamine is manifested by anxiety, insomnia, agitation, apprehension, and psychosis (Schaffer & Pauli, 1980). Cardiovascular effects such as flushing, palpitations, hypertension (Horowitz, McNeil, Sweet, Mendelson, & Louis, 1979), and cardiac arrhythmias may occur in especially sensitive people or those taking toxic doses. Some patients experience depression after stopping high doses. Dietz (1981) reported data on seven clients who experienced symptoms ranging from tremor and restlessness to agitation and hallucinations after ingesting phenylpropanolamine. Glick, Hoying, Cerullo, and Perlman (1987) have reported a case of phenylpropanolamine-induced CNS vasculitis and intracerebral hemorrhage.

The toxicity of caffeine is similar to that of phenylpropanolamine. The amount present in the various "look-alike" preparations is not alarming. However, when taken along with one's normal daily intake of caffeine or with phenylpropanolamine, the amounts could become significant. In many people the consumption of caffeine in amounts in excess of 1000 mg/d may produce behavioral symptoms mimicking anxiety neurosis, including nervousness, irritability, and agitation. Acute caffeine toxicity is rare. The fatal dose in the human is about 10 g (see Chapter 4).

The toxicity of phenylpropanolamine may become more evident with the recent marketing of the higher dose products. Also, phenylpropanolamine is appearing in the analysis of street drugs (Cohen, 1980), with the drug paraphernalia shops selling it under names such as "Pseudocaine," "Coco Snow," and "Rock Crystal." It is also being packaged in capsules that look like the more popular amphetamines and being sold as such on the street. This could result in severe problems if a person accustomed to taking these weaker "look-alikes" obtained the real product and took a comparable quantity of the drug. Additional regulatory controls over phenylpropanolamine will probably be forthcoming.

COUGH AND COLD PRODUCTS

The diverse, minor discomforts of upper respiratory illnesses are commonly treated by use of OTC cough and cold products. Viral infections probably account for the majority of symptoms that are suppressed by these products. However, they are also used for conditions such as allergies, sinusitis, pneumonia, and coughs due to smoking. They constitute a market that exceeds $600 million annually.

The abuse potential of these OTC cough and cold products is difficult to evaluate. There have been anecdotal reports of the misuse of some alcohol-containing products to produce mood alteration. The potential exists for psychophysiologic reactions due to the variety and concentrations of products they contain. Almost everyone who has taken an antihistamine or decongestant has felt some alteration in mental function, whether it be sedation or stimulation.

Few of these products contain a single ingredient. Most have multiple ingredients intended to manage a variety of symptoms. Table 7.2 contains a sampling of OTC cough and cold products that contain many ingredients in combination with alcohol. No attempt will be made to list all products and their contents. Rather, the various classes of individual ingredients will be discussed with the representatives of each class.

Pharmacology

Antihistamines are present in most OTC cough and cold products. The most common examples are chlorpheniramine and pyrilamine. However, the rationale for their inclusion is anything but clear. The role of histamine in symptom formation is not conclusive. Most antihistamines possess anticholinergic properties that may account for a decrease in mucous secretion and less rhinorrhea.

Decongestants such as phenylephrine, pseudoephedrine, and phenylpropanolamine are present in many OTC cough and cold products. They are designed to decrease client discomfort through decreasing edema and swelling of mucous membranes. This is accomplished through stimulation of adrenergic receptors in the vascular smooth muscle. Because they are sympathomimetics, the sympathetic system is sometimes overstimulated with these agents and accounts for most side effects seen.

Antitussives, exemplified by codeine and dextromethorphan, are present in OTC cough and cold

Table 7.2
Contents of Selected Over-the-Counter Cough and Cold Mixtures

Name	Antihistamine[a]	Antitussive[a]	Decongestant[a]	Alcohol	Other
Romilar CR	—	Dextromethorphan 15 mg	—	20%	–
Nyquil Liquid	Doxylamine succinate	Dextromethorphan 15 mg	Pseudoephedrine	25%	+
Cheracol	—	Codeine, 10 mg	—	4.75%	+
Formula 44 Cough Mixture	Chlorpheniramine	Dextromethorphan	—	10%	–
Terpin Hydrate & Codeine Elix.	—	Codeine, 10 mg	—	41%	+

[a] Contents are expressed in amounts per 5 ml.

preparations. They act by depressing the centers in the brain responsible for the cough reflex. Codeine is probably the most effective. Dextromethorphan, an isomer of codeine, is the most widely used antitussive. It produces fewer adverse effects than codeine, such as respiratory depression, constipation, and euphoria. Some states still allow the OTC sale of codeine-containing cough products; this probably makes little sense considering their abuse potential.

The amount of alcohol in some of these OTC cough and cold preparations adds significantly to their effects. When the alcohol content approaches 25%, even prescribed doses will produce CNS effects whether or not those effects are sought by the client. These preparations can be a source of alcohol for addicts when beverage alcohol is unavailable. Additionally, health practitioners should realize that the alcohol content of these products is more than adequate to trigger a reaction in someone taking disulfiram (Antabuse).

Toxicity

Because of the variety of ingredients found in these OTC cough and cold products, the symptoms of toxicity may vary accordingly. Many of these products will produce anticholinergic symptoms. Those with sympathomimetics may produce symptoms of agitation, nervousness, palpitations, and hypertension. The majority of OTC antihistamines cause drowsiness. Those that contain products in combination with alcohol may produce an additive drug interaction resulting in increased sedation. The treatment should be symptomatic. In the case of respiratory depression due to excessive cough suppressants, treatment may resemble that for opioid overdose.

ANALGESICS

The extent to which OTC analgesics are consumed in this country is nothing short of phenomenal. Although they are seldom consumed for their mood-altering effects, they are used to alleviate a variety of aches and pains. The extent of their misuse is nebulous, but it is difficult to imagine that there exists bona fide needs for the massive amounts consumed. Companies advertise these products using ads that are somewhat misleading and frankly embarrassing to those who advocate judicious drug therapy. Additionally, TV ads for these products sometimes target the symptoms of intemperate alcohol consumption as being the indications for their usage. They commonly contain salicylates, ibuprofen, or acetaminophen singularly or in combination with other products. In addition to the indications for which nonaddicted persons use analgesics, addicted clients frequently use analgesics to treat aches and pains related to withdrawal or injuries sustained while inebriated.

Pharmacology

Aspirin, ibuprofen, and acetaminophen produce similar analgesic and antipyretic effects. They probably act through both central and peripheral mechanisms. Acetaminophen lacks the antiinflammatory effects of aspirin and ibuprofen due to its lessened ability to block prostaglandin synthesis in the periphery. As analgesics they are best used for diffuse aches and pains, symptoms that normally accompany minor drug withdrawal states. Ibuprofen and similar prescription-only drugs are effective in treating dysmenorrhea, probably due to the inhibition of prostaglandins (Owen, 1984).

Toxicity

Although serious reactions can occur after the ingestion of aspirin, acetaminophen, and ibuprofen, these reactions are deemed rare enough to allow for safe self-administration and OTC status. These chemicals do not produce physical dependency.

Salicylates have long been known to produce both acute and chronic toxicity. Acute toxicity may result in several physical complications, especially disturbances of acid–base balance, gastrointestinal symptoms, hemorrhage, and encephalopathy. Mental disturbances have been observed that simulate alcoholic inebriation (Woodbury & Fingl, 1975). However, the experience is seldom pleasurable. The chronic self-administration of salicylates, in an effort to alleviate withdrawal symptoms, may result in these metabolic disturbances.

Acetaminophen was once thought to be safer than aspirin as an analgesic and antipyretic. However, it is now recognized that fatal hepatic necrosis may result from acute overdosage (Flower, Moncada, & Vane, 1985). It also appears that chronic moderate dosage may also produce liver damage. Heavy users of alcohol are especially vulnerable to acetaminophen-induced liver damage. The image portrayed by advertising that ''extra-strength'' products are superior may result in increased toxicity through unnecessary drug exposures.

The primary toxicities seen with ibuprofen involve the gastrointestinal tract. Heartburn and epigastric pain are experienced by about 5%–15% of those taking the drug (Flower, et al., 1985). These effects are similar to those of aspirin. Clients with aspirin allergy or hypersensitivity should avoid ibuprofen since cross-sensitivity reactions have been reported. Other less frequently seen side effects of ibuprofen include dizziness, blurred vision, fluid retention, and rashes. Although ibuprofen overdosage may be less frequently fatal than acetaminophen or aspirin overdosage, serious reactions such as renal failure may occur (Veltri & Rollins, 1988).

SUMMARY

There are few reasons to deny a society the possibility of self-medication with certain OTC products. However, these are far from innocuous drugs when used inappropriately or to excess. Certain OTC sedatives, cough and cold products, appetite suppressants, and analgesics have mood-altering properties; many are frequently misused. The extent of their usage dictates that health care practitioners must become more influential in educating clients in appropriate self-medication as well as recognize abuse when it occurs.

REFERENCES

Cohen, S. (1980). Over-the-counter medicines. Psychophysiologic reactions. *Drug Abuse and Alcoholism Newsletter, 9*(7).

Dietz, J. (1981). Amphetamine-like reactions to phenylpropanolamine. *Journal of the American Medical Association, 245,* 601–602.

Flower, R. J., Moncada, S., & Vane, J. R. (1985). Analgesics—Antipyretics and anti-inflammatory agents; drugs employed in the treatment of gout. In A. G. Gillman, L. S. Goodman, T. W. Rall, & F. Murad (Eds.), *Goodman and Gilman's the pharmacological basis of therapeutics* (pp. 674–715). New York: Macmillan.

Glick, R., Hoying, J., Cerullo, L., & Perlman, S. (1987). Phenylpropanolamine: An over-the-counter drug causing central nervous system vasculitis and intracerebral hemorrhage. *Neurosurgery, 20*(6), 969–974.

Horowitz, J. D., McNeil, J. J., Sweet, B., Mendelsohn, F. A., & Louis, J. (1979). Hypertension and postural hypotension induced by phenylpropanolamine (Trimolets). *Medical Journal of Australia, 1,* 175–176.

Illich, I. (1974). Medical nemesis. *Lancet, 1,* 918–921.

Mellinger, G., Balter, M. B., & Uhlenhuth, I. (1985). Insomnia and its treatment. Prevalence and correlates. *Archives of General Psychiatry, 42,* 225–232.

Owen, P. (1984). Prostaglandin synthetase inhibitors in the treatment of primary dysmenorrhea. *American Journal of Obstetrics and Gynecology, 148*(1), 96–103.

Schaffer, C. B., & Pauli, M. W. (1980). Psychotic reaction caused by proprietary oral diet agents. *American Journal of Psychiatry, 137*(10), 1256–1257.

Veltri, J. C., & Rollins, D. E. (1988). A comparison of the frequency and severity of poisoning cases for ingestion of acetaminophen, aspirin, and ibuprofen. *American Journal of Emergency Medicine, 6*(2), 104–107.

Woodbury, D. M., & Fingl, E. (1975). Analgesics—antipyretics, anti–inflammatory agents; drugs, employed in the therapy of gout. In L. S. Goodman & A. Gilman (Eds.), *Goodman and Gilman's the pharmacological basis of therapeutics* (pp. 325–358). New York: Macmillan.

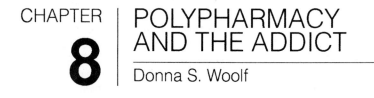

CHAPTER 8 | POLYPHARMACY AND THE ADDICT
Donna S. Woolf

When an addict comes to a treatment center or a medical facility for help, therapeutic questions concerning the use of "physical health" medications invariably arise. Many addicts have physical problems that are directly attributable to the prolonged abuse of drugs or related to the loss of the desire or the ability to take care of their bodies.

Weighty books have been devoted to some of these problems, as well as to the possible interactions between prescribed drugs and abused drugs. This chapter will present some frequently encountered drug interactions and physical changes that may result from drug abuse. There is no doubt that some interactions and problems will be omitted, so the professional is urged to consult drug specialists when any therapeutic questions arise. The drug interactions that will be addressed are those influenced by the act of chemical abuse. They should be viewed as *additions* to the drug interactions that are possible in any client. The reader is referred to a current drug interactions text for general nonabuse-related reactions.

PRINCIPLES OF DRUG INTERACTIONS

Whenever two or more drugs are present in the body at the same time, the potential for an interaction exists. Since polydrug abusers, by definition, use more than one chemical, there is an ever-present possibility that the combination of drugs may add to the complexity of symptoms that this client describes. Factors that may influence the response of an addict to medications administered for a concomitant disease will be briefly discussed in this section.

The Pharmacologic Outcome of Drug Interactions

The terminology of drug interactions is quite confusing to both professionals and clients. Three terms commonly used to describe the possible responses to drug combinations are *addition, potentiation,* and *antagonism* (Fingl & Woodbury, 1975; Martin, 1978).

Addition

Additive effects may occur when two or more drugs producing the same effects by the same mechanism of action are combined (Martin, 1978). The effects produced are greater than would be expected for one drug alone but do not exceed the effects that would be expected from the simple addition of the drug responses. Unless the dose of a drug is so high that undesirable side effects are produced, two drugs with the same therapeutic effects would rarely be prescribed concurrently. Two drugs with the same action may, however, be inadvertently prescribed to a client when more than one physician is consulted or when the drugs are self-prescribed by the client. Clients might receive diazepam from one physician and oxazepam from another, resulting in predicted oversedation.

Potentiation

When two drugs are given together, it is possible for one of the drugs to enhance or potentiate the effects of the other drug (Martin, 1978). There are several mechanisms by which this may occur. The metabolism, absorption, or excretion of one drug may be altered by that of another drug, resulting in enhanced therapeutic effects. For example, this occurs when probenecid is administered with ampicillin. The probenecid decreases the excretion of the ampicillin by the kidney tubules. The ampicillin is then excreted slowly, and blood levels remain high: its effects are potentiated.

Synergism is a type of potentiation that is particularly important in evaluating drug reactions in the abuser. The combination of two drugs may result in much greater drug actions than would be obtained by simple addition. Combinations of central nervous system (CNS) depressants are frequently given as examples of synergism. Profound CNS depression, resulting in death, has occurred when alcohol has been combined with barbiturates, benzodiazepines, or opioids.

Even combinations of sedating antihistamines and moderate amounts of alcohol can act synergistically to produce somnolence in a person who functions well with equal doses of one of the individual drugs.

The concept of synergism is important in the treatment of the drug abuser who enters a treatment facility for detoxification. Heavily medicating a client with CNS depressant drugs, such as chlordiazepoxide (Librium) or phenobarbital, while the blood alcohol level is still high carries the same risk as giving the client alcohol and a CNS depressant concomitantly. Any client who has been given medications for withdrawal should be carefully evaluated when it becomes necessary to administer adjunctive medications such as antiemetics or antihistamines. The client should be monitored for signs of synergism, such as decreases in blood pressure, depression of respirations, staggering, excessive sedation, or slurred speech.

Antagonism

When two drugs are combined, one of the drugs may lessen or completely reverse the effects of the other drug (Martin, 1978). The blood levels and the effectiveness of tetracycline are decreased when this drug is given with milk or an antacid. In this example, the effects of tetracycline are reduced but not completely blocked.

Some drugs in combination can antagonize or cancel each other's effects. This type of inhibition, called *antagonism,* is usually seen with the combination of two drugs with opposite pharmacologic activity. Addicts may not know the theories underlying antagonism but frequently use this principle. Alcohol or barbiturates may be combined with stimulants, such as amphetamines, to "take the edge off" or reduce the anxiety caused by the amphetamines. Caffeine, in the form of black coffee, is a drug that is commonly administered by an inebriate's friends in an attempt to counteract the depressant effects of alcohol. Opioid antagonists, such as Narcan, are used in emergency treatment facilities to counteract the respiratory depression caused by opioid drugs. Few examples of antagonism act as effectively as Narcan, and even the experienced addict finds it difficult to completely cancel one drug's effects with another.

FACTORS THAT AFFECT DRUG RESPONSE IN THE ADDICT

The actions of a drug can be augmented or diminished by altering the drug's absorption, metabolism, or excre-

tion. These increases or decreases in drug action caused by alterations in absorption, metabolism, or excretion are called *pharmacokinetic interactions.* Some of these alterations are directly related to drug abuse by the addict. *Pharmacodynamic interactions* are those that have to do with alterations in the actual mechanisms by which a drug acts. These interactions frequently involve effects at the drug receptor, as the blockage of an agonist by an antagonist drug molecule. Once a drug has reached the site where it acts, another drug may change the pharmacologic effect by competing for the receptor, changing the receptor, changing other cell components at that site, or acting on another body system which performs similar or opposite effects (Shinn & Shrewsbury, 1985). The blockade of heroin by an opioid-receptor-antagonist, Narcan, is a good example of this type of interaction.

Absorption

For a drug to exert an action, it must somehow enter the body. It may be swallowed, injected, inhaled, or inserted rectally or vaginally. The chronic use of certain drugs of abuse may alter how well a drug prescribed for physical disease will be absorbed. When the drug of abuse has been taken by injection, wide areas of muscle and skin scarring may make it difficult to find a suitable injection site for insulin or other drugs requiring injection. Injection of many drugs into hard, scarred areas results in erratic absorption. The intravenous method of administration may be difficult in the addict, since most accessible veins have been damaged by the addict's administration of irritating, impure drugs. The chronic use of alcohol can affect the stomach lining and the motility of the gastrointestinal tract. Irritating drugs may not be tolerated by the client, and vomiting and diarrhea may greatly affect the absorption of administered drugs.

Metabolism

The metabolism of drugs can occur in several organs of the body, but the liver is the most common site of drug detoxification. Liver damage may greatly affect the body's ability to detoxify drugs needed by the addict to treat physical disease. Chronic alcohol abuse is associated with alcoholic hepatitis and cirrhosis, which may result in a decrease in liver function. The injectable abuse of drugs is associated with hepatitis of viral origin, which also decreases the ability of the liver to function properly. In these clients, drug dosages may have to be decreased, depending on the excretion patterns and kinetics of the individual drugs.

The breakdown of many drugs by the liver involves enzyme systems that catalyze chemical reactions. Two entirely different situations face the prescriber as a result of these systems. When the abuser is inebriated, the available enzyme systems are nearly saturated by the abused drug. If those same systems are required to metabolize another drug that is given to the client, this will result in rapidly rising blood levels of the administered drug, since no enzymes are now available for its degradation. These clients may be very sensitive to small drug doses until the abused drug is cleared by the system. In contrast, sedative, opioid, and alcohol abusers develop increased enzyme activity in the liver to try to rid the body rapidly of the foreign chemicals. The user who is not acutely intoxicated or who is already in withdrawal may exhibit a need for larger doses of drugs that are metabolized by these same enzyme systems. Larger than usual doses of general anesthetics may be required to anesthetize the addict for surgery.

Drugs other than the drugs preferred by the addict may affect, to some extent, the blood levels of prescribed drugs. Smoking tobacco can induce enzymes that metabolize drugs. The clinical effects of pentazocine (Talwin) and propoxyphene (Darvon) are reduced in heavy tobacco users (Boston Collaborative Drug Surveillance Program, 1973; Kerri-Szanto & Pomeroy, 1971).

Excretion

Renal changes in the addict are usually the result of emboli damage or the body's response to the injection of foreign particles. Kilcoyne (1975) has described a nephrotic syndrome that may occur in abusers of heroin. This may result in a decrease in renal function in these patients. Although kidney damage is not as commonly seen as liver damage in the addict, any decrease in kidney function affects, to some degree, the excretion of an administered drug.

GUIDELINES FOR MONITORING OR PRESCRIBING FOR THE ABSTINENT ADDICT

Several questions should be asked any time a medication is prescribed for an addict. What is the abuse po-

tential of the drug that is to be prescribed? What are the consequences if the addict returns to drug use or abuse while taking the prescribed drug? What physical changes induced by the drug that was abused will affect the actions of the prescribed drug? Are there any ingredients in the pharmaceutic preparation, such as alcohol, that might sabotage the addict's effort to remain drug-free? How will the drug that is to be prescribed interact with other medications that the addict may currently take? Although the addict who is in treatment strives for *complete* drug freedom, medications for infections and chronic physical diseases may at times prove lifesaving.

Abuse Potential

One of the primary considerations in monitoring or prescribing medication for the addict is the evaluation of the potential of that drug for abuse. Does the drug contain chemicals that are known to cause dependence in humans?

It is easy to put a blanket "veto" over all the drugs in the opioid, stimulant, antianxiety, and sedative drug groups for use by the addict. Problems with this theory, however admirable it is, arise when the addict must undergo surgery or suffers severe injury. It is unrealistic for the abstinent addict to believe that most surgery will occur without the use of a sedating anesthetic drug. Medication may be required to relieve the addict's pain after surgery, but a plan should be formulated to taper and discontinue the medication before the addict is discharged. Nonaddicting pain relievers, such as acetaminophen and aspirin, or newer nonaddicting, nonsteroidal antiinflammatory analgesics, such as ibuprofen (Motrin), should be used if the client still experiences pain at the time of discharge.

Most of the drugs in the opioid, antianxiety, and sedative groups are physically addicting. Although the addict may not be dependent on a particular drug in these groups, the behavioral pattern is established, and taking a pill(s) to solve a problem is a way of life. It is difficult for the outpatient addict to avoid overusing the amount of medication that is often dispensed. Only small amounts of an abusable drug should be dispensed at one time. The medication should be stopped at a specified date and reviewed daily. These guidelines apply to chemicals with "low" abuse potential as well as to the more obvious opioids, benzodiazepines, or hypnotics. Combination products should have each ingredient and the vehicle, if any, reviewed to determine if the contents have abuse liability.

Other alternatives to the use of sleep-aids, anxiety reducers, and painkillers should be taught. For some clients, this may include referral to clinics that specialize in the treatment of pain. It may also involve teaching the addict relaxation techniques or biofeedback methods.

Resumed Drug Abuse

Since addiction is a disease often involving relapses, or "slips," the professional should always evaluate the consequences that may result from the combination of prescribed drugs and the primary drug of abuse of the client. To consider all these possibilities is impossible, but a few common problems will be addressed.

Antihypertensive Drugs

Hypertension is a symptom usually requiring drug therapy. Although some addicts may have been falsely labeled as having hypertension when the blood pressure elevation was caused by withdrawal, the majority of addicts who take these drugs need them consistently. When antihypertensive drugs are combined with excessive amounts of alcohol, opioids, or barbiturates, severe orthostatic hypotension and fainting may occur. The client may discontinue the antihypertensive drug to avoid these effects. Antihypertensive drugs, such as guanethidine (Ismelin), reserpine, methyldopa (Aldomet), propranolol (Inderal), as well as the thiazide diuretics, may all exhibit an additive lowering effect on the blood pressure. Clonidine, another antihypertensive drug, has been reported to produce a rebound hypertension when it is abruptly discontinued. This should be considered when prescribing this drug to a client whose compliance is unreliable.

Antidiabetic Drugs

The combination of insulin-dependent diabetes and addiction to alcohol is a life-threatening one. Alcohol potentiates the hypoglycemic effects of insulin, yet can decrease the half-life of oral antidiabetic drugs by increasing metabolism (Ritchie, 1985). Excessive drinking by the diabetic can lead to coma and death, and blood sugar levels may be erratic and difficult to stabilize. Some of the oral antidiabetic drugs have other drug interactions with alcohol resulting from their ability to block alcohol's metabolism. The interaction of acetohexamide (Dymelor), tolbutamide (Orinase), and tolazamide (Tolinase) with alcohol results in symptoms that mimic the alcohol-disulfiram (Antabuse) reaction (Dolger, 1957). Symptoms of nausea, flushing, and headaches have also occurred when alcohol is combined with chlorpropamide (Diabinese), although enzyme inhibition is probably not the cause (Signorelli, 1959). Not all clients on these drugs experience this reaction, but it is recommended that clients on oral antidiabetic drugs avoid alcohol. If alcohol has been abused chronically, the oral antidiabetic drugs may be rapidly metabolized by the liver enzymes (Griffin & D'Arcy, 1979; Olin, 1987). This can result in a decreased action of the antidiabetic drug to reduce the blood glucose.

Bronchodilator Drugs

Many drugs used to treat diseases such as asthma contain theophylline or related drugs and can cause CNS stimulation. These actions are usually interpreted by the client as anxiety rather than as a "high." Since antianxiety drugs, such as phenobarbital, may be included in some asthma preparations to treat the drug-induced anxiety, these formulations should be carefully screened for abusable chemicals before they are prescribed. Alcohol is also a common ingredient in the liquid preparations of theophylline and aminophylline. Careful dosage regulation may be necessary to minimize side effects of anxiety and nausea, or the drug abuser may attempt to "treat" the anxiety by using more drugs.

Disulfiramlike Drugs

Most professionals in the field of addiction are familiar with the symptoms of the alcohol-disulfiram (Antabuse) drug reaction. The flushing, dizziness, nausea, vomiting, and headaches produced by this drug combination may be seen when several other drugs are combined with alcohol. Besides the previously discussed oral antidiabetic drugs, certain monoamine oxidase-inhibiting drugs, such as Furoxone, Parnate, Matulane, certain cephalosporins as Moxam, Mandol, and Cefobid, and metronidazole (Flagyl), can cause the reaction when these drugs are combined with alcohol. The reaction is not as predictable as the alcohol-disulfiram reaction.

Antihistamine Drugs

Whether or not the antihistamines should be used by the addict is a matter of some controversy. Although these drugs are not physically addicting, they are occasionally abused by the addict who wants to achieve some sedation. Addicts who abuse other CNS depressants may experience additive sedation when the drug of abuse is combined with an antihistamine. Since these drugs do cause sedation, they should be avoided by the addict whenever possible. Limited use of these chemicals can bring relief from symptoms of allergies or colds.

Antituberculosis Drugs

Since tuberculosis is found in the alcoholic and in other abusers, it is important to be aware of the possible complications of drug therapy used in tuberculosis treatment. Isoniazid (INH), which is a primary drug used to treat this disease, will cause peripheral neuritis in 10%–20% of clients who are not also given vitamin B_6 (Mandell & Sande, 1985). This is especially noteworthy in the alcoholic client, since B vitamin deficiencies may already exist. INH-induced vitamin B_6 deficiency, manifested by peripheral neuropathy, occurs in these patients because vitamin B_6 excretion is increased by INH. INH is capable of causing severe liver injury. INH-induced hepatitis may occur after at least 2 months of therapy and is more common in middle-aged and elderly clients (Mandell & Sande, 1985; Thompson, 1976). INH can decrease the body's ability to metabolize diphenylhydantoin (Dilantin) which may result in Dilantin toxicity. INH should be given to clients requiring Dilantin only with careful monitoring of Dilantin blood levels. Rifampin, another drug used to treat tuberculosis, is also known to cause liver damage. Alcoholism seems to predispose the client to developing hepatic disease caused by rifampin (Thompson, 1976).

DRUG INTERACTIONS WITH MAINTENANCE MEDICATIONS

Two commonly encountered maintenance medications given to addicts are disulfiram and methadone. Several drug interactions between disulfiram or methadone and other medications are known to occur (Martin, 1978; Shinn & Shrewsbury, 1985).

Disulfiram can inhibit the breakdown of several drugs other than alcohol and causes significant increases in the blood levels of these drugs. Dangerous increases in the blood levels of anticonvulsants, such as Dilantin, and anticoagulants, such as Coumadin, may be

seen when either drug is given with disulfiram (Kiorboe, 1966; O'Reilly, 1971). Drugs producing reactions similar to those of the alcohol–disulfiram combination have been discussed previously.

A client who is taking methadone as a maintenance drug should be warned of the synergistic depressant effects, such as drowsiness, that may occur when methadone is combined with alcohol, antihistamines, barbiturates, or benzodiazepines. Opioid antagonists, such as Narcan, will produce immediate and severe withdrawal symptoms when given to the methadone-dependent client. Agonist–antagonist drugs, such as Talwin, may also precipitate withdrawal. The administration of rifampin to treat tuberculosis may induce opioid withdrawal in the client maintained on methadone by inducing enzymes that speed the breakdown of methadone (Kreek, Garfield, Gutjahr, & Giusti, 1976). When methadone-dependent clients require surgery, higher doses and more frequent administration of opioids for analgesia will usually be required (Kreek, 1975).

Naltrexone (Trexan), a pure opioid antagonist is less frequently prescribed as a maintenance deterent to opioid abuse. Its interactions are extensions of its intended actions. Persons requiring opioid analgesia, cough preparations, and antidiarrheal drugs may not receive benefit from these drugs while taking naltrexone.

SUMMARY

The presence of an addictive disease should affect the selection of medications to treat physical illness. Drug interactions of addition, potentiation, and antagonism may be experienced by the polydrug abuser as well as the client in treatment who receives more than one drug for detoxification. Drug responses in the addict may be altered by changes in drug absorption, metabolism, and excretion induced by the physiologic changes occurring with long-term substance abuse.

Certain therapeutic questions should be considered every time a drug is prescribed for a substance abuser. The potential for abuse of the prescribed drug, the consequences of a drug interaction between the prescribed drug and an abused substance, and drug interactions between a prescribed drug and maintenance medications such as disulfiram (Antabuse) or methadone must be carefully reviewed.

REFERENCES

Boston Collaborative Drug Surveillance Program (1973). Decreased clinical efficacy of propoxyphene in cigarette smokers. *Clinical Pharmacology and Therapeutics, 14,* 259–263.

Dolger, H. (1957). Experience with the tolbutamide treatment of five hundred cases of diabetes on an ambulatory basis. *Annals of the New York Academy of Sciences, 71,* 275–290.

Fingl, E., & Woodbury, D. M. (1975). General principles. In L. S. Goodman & A. Gilman (Eds.), *Goodman and Gilman's the pharmacological basis of therapeutics* (pp. 1–46). New York: Macmillan.

Griffin, J. P., & D'Arcy, P. F. (1979). *A manual of adverse drug interactions* (p. 172). London: Wright & Sons.

Kerri-Szanto, M., & Pomeroy, J. R. (1971). Atmospheric pollution and pentazocine metabolism. *Lancet, 1,* 947–949.

Kilcoyne, M. M. (1975). Heroin-related nephrotic syndrome. In R. W. Richter (Ed.), *Medical aspects of drug abuse* (pp. 243–250). Hagerstown, MD: Harper & Row.

Kiorboe, E. (1966). Phenytoin intoxication during treatment with Antabuse. *Epilepsia, 7,* 246–249.

Kreek, M. J. (1975). Methadone maintenance treatment for chronic opiate addiction. In R. W. Richter (Ed.), *Medical aspects of drug abuse* (pp. 167–185). Hagerstown, MD: Harper & Row.

Kreek, M. J., Garfield, J. W., Gutjahr, C. L., & Giusti, L. M. (1976). Rifampin-induced methadone withdrawal. *New England Journal of Medicine, 294,* 1104–1106.

Mandell, G. L., & Sande, M. A. (1985). Antimicrobial agents: Drugs used in the chemotherapy of tuberculosis and leprosy. In A. G. Gilman, L. S. Goodman, T. W. Rall, & F. Murad (Eds.), *Goodman and Gilman's the pharmacological basis of therapeutics* (pp. 1199–1218). New York: Macmillan.

Martin, E. W. (1978). *Hazards of medication* (2d ed.) (pp. 351–393). Philadelphia: J. B. Lippincott.

Olin, B. R. (Ed.) (1987). *Facts and comparisons* (p. 130H). St. Louis: Facts and Comparisons, Inc.

O'Reilly, R. A. (1971). Potentiation of anticoagulant effect by disulfiram. *Clinical Research, 19,* 180.

Ritchie, J. M. (1985). The aliphatic alcohols. In A. G. Gilman, L. S. Goodman, T. W. Rall, & F. Murad (Eds.), *Goodman and Gilman's the pharmacological basis of therapeutics* (pp. 372–386). New York: Macmillan.

Shinn, A. F., & Shrewsbury, R. P. (1985). *Evaluations of drug interactions* (3d ed.) (pp. 22–23, 48, 249, 381). St. Louis: C. V. Mosby.

Signorelli, S. (1959). Tolerance for alcohol in patients on chlorpropamide. *Annals of the New York Academy of Sciences, 74,* 900–903.

Thompson, J. E. (1976). The effect of rifampicin on liver morphology in tuberculous alcoholics. *Australian and New Zealand Journal of Medicine, 6,* 111–116.

CHAPTER 9 | DRUG SCREENING

John M. Holbrook
H. Horton McCurdy

The illicit use of drugs and the abuse of alcohol impinge on all areas of our lives, including the home, schools, community, and the workplace. According to a National Institute on Drug Abuse survey, the highest drug-using population today is the young working adult. The results of this survey indicated that 29% of employed adults 20–40 years of age used an illicit drug at least once within the year prior to the survey, and 19% reported use within the preceding month (Backer, 1987). It is therefore not surprising that management is placing an increased emphasis on methods to ensure that the workplace is maintained as a safe and healthy environment.

One method that is increasingly being used in an attempt to deter illicit drug use in the adult work force and to identify abusers of these drugs involves screening employees for the presence of illicit drugs in biologic samples. Such screening procedures involve testing for the presence of drugs in blood or urine or both. During the past 5–10 years, urine drug screens have become common in the workplace and more recently, the use of drug screening as a standard practice before employment has come into vogue. Drug screening is also used with armed forces personnel and workers in transportation, for paroled criminals and, more recently, for role models such as athletes. The driving force most likely related to the increased use of drug screening procedures in all walks of life is the increasing awareness of the impact of drug use on public safety and the loss to society of the individual's productivity.

The concept of drug screening is not new. In current terminology, drug testing implies the identification and the quantitation of drugs and chemicals in biologic fluids, primarily blood and urine. Since the development of the first procedures for drug identification over 100 years ago, the scope of such testing has grown dramatically and today encompasses both medical and legal aspects. In the clinical/medical context, quantification of plasma or serum drug levels may be essential in the management of patients being treated with drugs having marginal therapeutic indices as well as in the identification of unknown intoxicants. Quantification of drug levels may also be valuable in assessing kinetically related drug interactions and in estimating appropriate drug dosing schedules in patients with physiologic abnormalities.

In the legal context, quantification and identification of substances in biologic specimens including blood, urine, gastric contents, and various body tissues such as brain and liver are used in cases of intoxication, whether accidental or intentional. For many legal purposes, determination of blood levels of abused substances serves as the basis for prosecution. This is possible because of our increasing understanding of the correlation between blood levels of many abused substances and the occurrence of intoxication. In forensic cases, biologic samples are usually subjected to an initial screening process that detects the presence of a wide variety of substances. Both blood and urine samples may be used for screening. If a substance is detected, the amount of the substance in a specific quantity of blood may be determined.

Screening procedures increasingly are being used to detect illicit drug use in the general population. This type of screening was first used in the mid-1960s in connection with methadone treatment programs. Patients enrolled in these programs are subjected to periodic urine drug screening procedures to determine if they are complying with their prescribed methadone dosing schedule as well as to determine if they are using any illicit drugs.

The advances in drug screening methods have also made it possible to use drug screening techniques routinely in many areas of clinical practice, such as in the emergency room and in many of the major treatment settings.

Today, urine drug screening is being used more frequently in the employment process and in the testing of athletes. The use of urine drug screening has become a topic of heated debate for legal and ethical reasons, and its future in these areas is subject to serious consideration.

The information presented here is not intended to be an exhaustive discourse on all facets of drug screening under scrutiny today. It does present some of the major topics of interest within the area of drug screening with emphasis on applications to urine screening.

BIOLOGIC SAMPLES

The two most frequently used biologic samples for drug screening are urine and blood, although in drug-related deaths, drug levels may be obtained from other tissues such as liver and brain. Urine is usually the preferred biologic sample for rapidly determining whether a drug or other substance is present in the system because it is easily obtained and manipulated for testing procedures. The major limitation of the use of urine for detection purposes is that it is not possible to quantitate the amount of the substance in the urine and correlate that quantity to any effects produced by the substance.

For employment purposes, where the major concern is whether or not illicit drug use has occurred recently, urine is the preferred specimen because it can be obtained noninvasively and in relatively large quantities. In addition, most drugs and drug metabolites can usually be found for longer periods of time and at higher concentrations in urine than in the blood (days as compared to hours). Table 9.1 lists some drugs commonly found in urine with respect to length of detection time.

Because of the legal ramifications related to positive drug urine screens, employees or potential employees may attempt to alter the results of a screen by adulterating the sample or by substituting a ''clean'' sample in place of the employee's own sample. Table 9.2 lists some common methods to ensure the validity of the urine sample under consideration.

In the future, other easily obtained biologic specimens, such as saliva, hair, and breath samples, may be used more frequently in screening procedures. Currently, breath specimens are used in the quantitation of blood ethanol concentrations, and it is feasible that saliva and hair samples may be used to document drug use history. The analysis of saliva can demonstrate usage of drugs, particularly marihuana, in the immediate past. The active ingredient of marihuana can be found in saliva for a few hours after the drug is smoked (Mason & McBay, 1985), and this information could be used as a tool for determining impairment. The analysis of hair samples holds the possibility of demonstrating the use of drugs weeks and perhaps months and years previously (Baumgartner, Jones, & Black, 1981).

Table 9.1

Duration of Detection of Drugs Commonly Encountered in Urine Drug Screens

Drugs Normally Detected in Urine < 4 Days after Use	
Drug Class	**Examples**
Stimulants	Dextroamphetamine, cocaine
Sedative-hypnotics	Amytal, Tuinal, Alurate, Butisol, Butalbital, Nembutal, Seconal, Lotusate
Narcotic analgesics	Codeine, heroin, morphine, oxycodone, hydrocodone, Levo-Dromoran, oxymorphone
Hallucinogens	Phencyclidine (PCP)

Drugs Normally Detected in Urine > 4 Days after Use	
Drug Class	**Examples**
Sedative-hypnotics	Phenobarbital
Antianxiety	Librium, Valium, Tranxene, Dalmane, Ativan, oxazepam, Paxipam
Hallucinogens	Marihuana, hashish

Source: From *Employee Testing and the Law* (pp. 1–8) by D. L. Black, 1988, Chapel Hill, NC: Vanguard Information Publishing. Copyright 1988 by Vanguard Information Publishing. Adapted by permission.

Analytical techniques of this type are still in the formative stages, but demonstrate the possibility of future technical advances.

BASICS OF DRUG TESTING

With the increased emphasis on drug screening and the potential profitability of performing such tests, many laboratories, especially hospital-based clinical laboratories, are considering the undertaking of such procedures on a commercial basis. Prior to undertaking such a venture, many factors must be examined, not the least of which is the principal caveat of the forensic testing laboratory: *no errors are permitted.*

Table 9.2
Checks to Help Verify Urine Specimen is Unadulterated

Many employers mandate that an employee (upon request of a supervisor based on his observation of "different" behavior) produce a urine under observation within 3 hours of the request. Even with a time window for urination, it may not be possible to collect the specimen. The following is a list of laboratory checks that can be made to help certify that a urine specimen is indeed unadulterated.

1. Do a urinary creatinine—average for urine 2 mg/ml.
2. Do a refractive index (Rf)—a urinary Rf should be 1.005 to 1.030. A low Rf may indicate dilution of the specimen; a high Rf may suggest the addition of foreign substances.
3. Look for a precipitate or solids in the urine. This may suggest the addition of a solid material that may interfere with selected methodologies.
4. Look at the urine color. A very light yellow color may suggest dilution, while other non-yellow colors may suggest the addition of other liquids, eg, apple juice.
5. Note the temperature of the urine collection container when received in your hand. A container holding freshly voided undiluted urine will feel warm (about 37°C).
6. Note the odor. A nonurine smell may be consistent with adulteration from "fruity liquids," perfumes, or a detergent.
7. Have a urinary dip stick available for testing. A "healthy" individual produces a urine that is negative for glucose and ketone bodies and has a pH between 6 and 8. A 6-pad dip stick should be negative when used for testing fresh urine specimens from "healthy" individuals.

Note: Successful adulteration of a urine specimen submitted for drug analysis is method dependent. However, dilution of the specimen with water from the toilet may be the single best method to produce a false-negative result.

Individuals whose specimens are being analyzed have the right to challenge any and all results, and these challenges may result in legal complications. Consequently, assurances must be made in the laboratory that the results reported are true and accurate. Since many clinical laboratories are not equipped to deal with all of the necessary legal and analytical requirements, screening for illicit drugs is often best performed in laboratories whose functions are related specifically to this type of testing. The reporting of a positive drug screen may result in serious ramifications for the individual, including loss of job, position, and social standing and even incarceration should legal prosecution occur.

SCREENING METHODS

Large-scale urine drug screening has resulted in the need to quickly and accurately distinguish between drug-positive and drug-negative samples. The ideal drug screening procedure should lend itself to automation, be reasonably simple to perform, and possess a precision not adversely influenced by operator technique. The earliest technical approaches to drug screening were based on the technique of *thin-layer chromatography* (TLC). This technique involves the application of known and unknown compounds to an absorbent material such as silica gel affixed to a glass plate. This TLC plate is then placed in just enough solvent (mobile phase) to cover the bottom of the plate. The ascending movement of the mobile phase on the plate causes the compounds to separate, and the substances can be visualized by spraying the plate with various reagents which produce characteristic colors. The particular compounds are identified by comparing the distances that the compounds move up the plate with known drug standards.

The use of TLC has the advantages of low cost, rapidity of analysis, and to some extent, automation. Its disadvantages include lack of specificity and sensitivity, dependency on the operator's expertise, and false positive results due to interference by other substances.

The growing demand for assay methods with greater sensitivity and specificity with freedom from false positive results has led to the development of procedures termed "immunoassay" techniques. These techniques include *enzyme immunoassay (EMIT), radioimmunoassay (RIA)*, and *fluorescence polarization immunoassay (FPIA)*. All three of these techniques are popular because they are suitable for urine drug screening, but they can also be readily applied toward the analysis of drugs in other biologic specimens, particularly blood, with only minor modifications to the procedures.

The basis for the immunoassay techniques is the competition between labeled and unlabeled drugs or drug metabolites for a specific number of binding sites on a specially prepared antibody. The drug being assayed is attached (labeled) to an enzyme capable of producing a quantifiable chemical reaction. In EMIT, the urine sample is mixed with a reagent containing glucose-6-phosphate (substrate) and antibodies to the drug, as well as a second reagent containing a drug derivative labeled with the enzyme glucose-6-phosphate dehydrogenase. When the enzyme–drug complex is attached to an antibody site, it is incapable of interacting with the substrate. If the limited numbers of binding sites on the antibody are all used up by unlabeled drug, the enzyme–drug complex is then free to react with the substrate, and this increased enzyme activity is proportional to the concentration of drug in the urine. This method is also termed homogenous enzyme immunoassay (EIA).

RIA uses known amounts of radioactive-labeled drug (usually iodine 125) added to a biologic sample together with a known amount of antibody to a drug or its metabolite. This mixture is incubated for a period of time to allow the radioactive-labeled drug to compete with unlabeled drug for antibody-binding sites. The radioactive drug–antibody complex is then separated from the mixture, and radioactivity of the complex is determined and compared to controls prepared in the same manner. A schematic of the RIA technique is presented in Figure 9.1.

FPIA uses a fluorescein-labeled drug that competes with the drug or metabolite being assayed for attachment to the antibody-binding sites.

All of the immunoassays are capable of detecting very small concentrations of drug, have good sensitivity and selectivity, require a minimal amount of sample preparation, and do not require exceptional technical skills for their performance. In addition, the instrumentation requirements for these assays is modest. For many applications, immunoassays are an excellent means for separating drug-positive biologic samples from negative ones.

Although immunoassays are generally considered to be the first testing procedures for the detection of drugs in biologic samples, a second test or confirmation test must be used to ensure the accuracy of the results. Confirmation requires the use of an independent chemical or physical method to confirm the results of the initial screening test. Thus, it would not be appropriate to

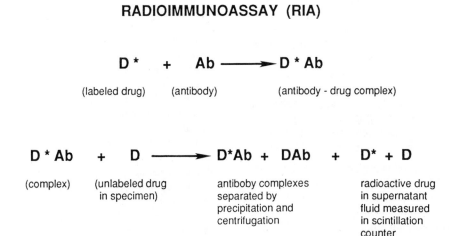

RADIOIMMUNOASSAY (RIA)

$$D* \ + \ Ab \longrightarrow D*Ab$$

(labeled drug)   (antibody)   (antibody - drug complex)

$$D*Ab \ + \ D \longrightarrow D*Ab \ + \ DAb \ + \ D* \ + \ D$$

(complex)   (unlabeled drug   antiboby complexes   radioactive drug
            in specimen)   separated by   in supernatant
                             precipitation and   fluid measured
                             centrifugation   in scintillation
                                                   counter

Figure 9.1
Schematic of the RIA (radioimmunoassay) technique. From Courtroom Toxicology *(p. 30-35) by M. Houts, R. C. Baselt, & R. H. Cravey, 1988, New York, NY: Matthew Bender, Inc. Copyright 1988 by Matthew Bender & Co., and reprinted with permission from* Courtroom Toxicology.

confirm an RIA result with an EMIT procedure since both are immunoassays.

One of the most common confirmation techniques uses *gas chromatography (GC)*. This technique is also used for initial identification of drugs. It has a tremendous capacity for separating complex mixtures of drugs into individual components. The procedure uses an inert gas, usually helium, as the moving phase to transport a vaporized sample through a heated glass column containing a stationary liquid phase (solvent). The interaction between the vaporized sample containing the drug and the solvent as it travels through the heated column results in the separation of the mixture into its individual components. The separated compounds emerge from the column after characteristic periods of time (termed retention times) and enter a detector for identification. One of the most sensitive detectors is the mass spectrophotometer (MS). The use of GC with mass spectrophotometry is referred to as GC/MS and is considered to be the ultimate means of drug identification in biologic fluids because of its specificity, sensitivity, and reliability. Its disadvantages include high cost of instrumentation and requirement of a high level of technical skill on the part of the operator.

ANALYSIS OF SOME DRUGS OF INTEREST

Ethanol

Ethanol is by far the most commonly encountered chemical in drug analyses following accidents and arrests, accounting for 70%–80% of those arrested in driving under the influence (DUI) cases. Ethanol has been implicated in many traffic mishaps resulting in fatal or disabling injuries (*Accident Facts,* 1980).

To successfully prosecute the DUI offender, the quantity of ethanol in the blood must be measured accurately and the results equated with the expected effects of ethanol at the determined level. For purposes of legal prosecution, most states have legislated *per se* standards, meaning that if a blood ethanol concentration exceeds a specified level (usually 0.1g/100 ml blood), intoxication is presumed automatically.

A number of analytical methods for ethanol are available including *enzymatic oxidation, breathalyzer analysis,* and *headspace GC*. Enzymatic oxidation, though suitable for the clinical laboratory, is usually not appropriate for forensic and clinical purposes because it is not particularly selective for ethanol. The procedure may be contaminated by alcohol from room air, and the results are linear only up to a certain point.

Both breathalyzer analysis and headspace GC analysis are acceptable analytical methods for forensic and clinical purposes. Breathalyzer analysis involves the use of an autoanalyzer, termed an intoximeter, which determines the ethanol content of a breath sample. This methodology is often preferred in the forensic area because of the ease of obtaining the sample for analysis; however, breath sample analysis tends to be somewhat less accurate in the estimation of the blood alcohol level.

The intoximeter functions on the principle that 2100 cc alveolar air contains the same amount of alcohol as 1 ml blood. In actuality, the 2100:1 ratio is only an approximation for the general population in which extremes do exist. Some individuals may have a ratio as low as 1100:1, whereas others may have a ratio as high as 3400:1 (Dubowski & O'Neill, 1979). For most of the population, the ratio is 2100:1 or *higher* which could actually underestimate the blood alcohol level, favoring many of the individuals being tested.

The analysis of the alcohol content by the intoximeter involves measuring the energy absorbed from an infrared beam set at a 3.45 μ band width. The amount of energy absorbed is directly proportional to the number of alcohol molecules in the chamber, which is then related to the blood alcohol content.

The GC method of analysis for alcohol involves the use of a specific quantity of blood and an appropriate internal standard. The internal standard is a compound similar to alcohol that can be assayed along with the alcohol in the GC.

The blood specimen and internal standard are placed in a sealed vial, which is heated to approximately 60°C for 30 minutes, during which time all of the alcohol and internal standard (e.g., n-propanol) are volatilized and collect above the liquid in the vial in the "headspace." A portion of this gaseous phase is sampled into the GC for analysis and comparison to known standards.

The result of a GC alcohol analysis is usually not confirmed by another analytical method because it is impractical. GC procedures for alcohol analysis are specific, and there are few, if any, known interferences. Potentially interfering substances such as methanol, acetone, and isopropanol are easily separated from ethanol by the GC techniques used.

Cocaine and Marihuana

The analysis of cocaine and marihuana will be considered together because detection of these compounds is based on the presence of their metabolites rather than the parent compounds. This is because both cocaine and marihuana are rapidly metabolized in the blood to metabolites detectable in blood and especially in urine for much longer periods of time. The primary metabolite of marihuana (delta-9-tetrahydrocannabinol or THC) is 11-nor-delta-9-THC-9-carboxylic acid or THC-COOH. The primary metabolite of cocaine is benzoylecgonine. Both compounds are detected in urine. The immunoassays for cocaine and marihuana use antibodies generated specifically to the metabolites rather than the parent compounds.

Opiates

The opiate family of drugs includes morphine, codeine, and various semisynthetic and synthetic compounds (opioids). The presence of these compounds in biologic samples is determined by immunoassays that readily detect some, but not all, of the compounds in this group.

Heroin is a semisynthetic (diacetyl) derivative of morphine. In the body, it is metabolized first to 6-monoacetylmorphine (6-MAM) and then to morphine. Heroin is not detected in biologic samples, but 6-MAM can be detected, and its presence may be indicative of heroin use.

Morphine may also be detected after codeine ingestion because morphine is one of the principal metabolites of codeine. Thus, the detection of both morphine and codeine in a biologic sample is consistent with the use of only codeine. The converse is not true because codeine is not a metabolite of morphine.

Codeine, morphine, and morphine-3-glucuronide (the principal urinary metabolite of morphine) are readily detected in urine by immunoassay procedures. However, most of these procedures cannot distinguish between these drugs so that any or all may produce a positive result. GC/MS procedures are used to determine which drug is actually present.

Poppy seeds contain enough morphine and codeine to produce a urine-positive immunoassay result for up to 60 hours after their ingestion and this positive result is confirmable by GC/MS. The detection of 6-MAM in urine by GC/MS may be used to distinguish between an opiate-positive result related to heroin use as opposed to poppy seed ingestion (Mulé & Casella, 1988).

Amphetamines

Amphetamines and related drugs such as methamphetamine and phentermine are detected in biologic samples by immunoassays that vary widely in their selectivity. For example, RIA methods detect only amphetamine, FPIA methods detect both methamphetamine and amphetamine, and EMIT methods detect a wide range of amphetamines and amphetaminelike compounds including phenylpropanolamine and ephedrine. Because amphetamine is a principle metabolite of methamphetamine, the two may be detected when only the methamphetamine has been ingested. Great caution must be exercised in choosing the appropriate analytical technique for amphetamine analysis and confirmation to ensure accurate results.

Barbiturates and Benzodiazepines

The chemical nature of the barbiturates determines the length of time during which they are detectable in urine, but in general they are easily detected and confirmed. Long-acting, water-soluble barbiturates such as phenobarbital are excreted slowly into the urine and are detectable for a number of days, whereas the short-acting agents such as amobarbital, secobarbital, and butalbital are detectable in urine for only 2–3 days.

The long-acting benzodiazepines such as diazepam, chlordiazepoxide, and clorazepate and their metabolites may be excreted into the urine and detected for weeks and even months when their use has been chronic for months or years. The high-potency, low-dose benzodiazepines such as lorazepam and triazolam produce such small blood and urine levels that their detection and confirmation is difficult by currently available methods.

OTHER CONCEPTS IN DRUG SCREENING

Cross-Reactivity in Immunoassays

Some antibodies are very specific in their reactions and there are few, if any, interfering or cross-reacting substances. Such antibodies respond only to specific analytes. Other antibodies are not as specific and respond in varying degrees to closely related analytes.

For example, marihuana is excreted in urine primarily as THC-COOH, but a number of other chemically similar marihuana metabolites are also excreted in urine. The marihuana antibodies do not differentiate between these closely related metabolites and react more or less positively to all of them. Thus, marihuana immunoassay reports indicate the presence of "total cannabinoids" rather than just THC-COOH, the primary metabolite. Confirmation for the presence of THC-COOH may be performed using an MS/GC technique.

Similarly, the EMIT barbiturate antibody is made against the barbiturate secobarbital, but is produced in a manner such that it reacts well with other barbiturates. The antibody is said to have good "cross-reactivity" with the whole family of barbiturates and is fairly nonspecific for the entire class of drugs. This antibody would not, however, react with other nonbarbiturate drugs.

Some antibodies are extremely specific and react only with specific analytes. The antibody to morphine will not respond in the presence of codeine, and the antibody for amphetamine will not cross-react with methamphetamine. In most cases, an antibody that has good cross-reactivity within a class of drugs is useful for screening purposes.

Detection Limits

For every analytical procedure, there exists some level at which the concentration of the drug in the biologic sample can no longer be reliably determined as positive. This level is the lower detection limit and is often termed the *"cut-off"* point. The cut-off point is used to establish realistic limits between samples that can be accurately deemed positive and those which should be reported as negative. The cut-off point for an assay is established by the analysis of urine samples containing known quantities of the drug in question. Any sample giving a reading at or above the cut-off point is considered to be positive, and any value below the cut-off is considered negative. The cut-off point varies with the assay method, with more sensitive assays having a lower cut-off point.

False Negative and False Positive Results

Inaccurate test results are of two types: false negative results in which the sample contains drugs not detected and false positive results in which the sample is actually drug free. Several years ago much discussion regarding the reliability of the results of urine screening for drugs followed the publication of a study by the Centers for Disease Control which found high error rates in laboratories serving methadone treatment facilities (Hansen, Caudill, & Boone, 1985).

Laboratories with appropriate quality control programs use ongoing checks and balances to detect such errors before they are reported. A false positive report is more undesirable than a false negative one because it can result in unjustified actions (sometimes legal) against the individual. The possibility of a false positive result being reported is greatly reduced in laboratories that use appropriate confirmation procedures.

Some false results may be beyond the control of the laboratory. For example, samples may be switched at the collection point or deliberately contaminated. A well-identified and controlled chain of custody from the collection site to the analytical laboratory is essential to avoid such occurrences.

The media and others (Morgan, 1984) have also expressed concern regarding the false positive rate of some immunoassays, stating that some tests have a 1-in-20 rate of false positives. By implication, the false positive rate is therefore 5%. Although this may be true under some unusual circumstances, in reality such a rate is acceptable because a screening procedure is used only for screening. There is no intention for such procedures to provide definitive, legally defensible results. Following the initial screening procedures, positive samples undergo further screening by other methods to ensure the result is accurate. As previously mentioned, chemically similar compounds can and do cross-react with certain antibodies, resulting in false positive results. For example, phenylpropanolamine in a urine sample will result in a false positive for amphetamine with some amphetamine antibodies. However, when the results are confirmed by an alternate method, the phenylpropanolamine would be discovered. The use of appropriate confirming methods virtually eliminates false positive results and the reported results become legally defensible. Therefore, although an individual may attempt to build a legal defense by attacking the analytical procedures, in reality there is little likelihood of a false positive report when appropriate safeguards are used.

Passive Inhalation

Recently, a great deal of concern has been leveled toward the "passive" inhalation of marihuana, related to exposure at parties or in closed automobiles. There is little, if any, validity to such concerns since controlled laboratory studies have shown that only in the most extreme cases does passive inhalation of marihuana smoke exceed an immunoassay cutoff for total cannabinoids above 20 ng/ml (Parez-Reyes, Di Guiseppi, Mason, & Davis, 1983). It is generally accepted that passive inhalation cannot occur beyond an immunoassay cutoff of 50 ng/ml (Baselt, 1984). Since most laboratories screen for marihuana in urine using a cutoff of 100 ng/ml, passive inhalation cannot be used as an issue when positive results are reported.

SUMMARY

Routine screening of biologic samples for forensic purposes has developed into an exacting science in recent years because of the continuing increase in illicit drug use throughout all strata of society and because of the rapid advances in analytical techniques used for such procedures. However, the appropriateness of random, routine screening for illicit drug use in the workplace is still subject to debate and will likely continue to be for the forseeable future. The increasing use of drug screening for employment, in athletics, in the armed services, and in clinical settings as well as in the forensic area has led to the development of new sensitive and highly accurate techniques for analysis. The growing awareness of the need for quality control in laboratories and the use of confirmation methods has greatly reduced the potential for inaccurate results, especially false positives. Although great concern exists with regard to the ethical issues surrounding the use of drug screening, the careful application of available screening procedures ensures that the results will accurately reflect drug use of the individuals who are evaluated.

REFERENCES

Accident Facts. (1980). Available from National Safety Council, 444 North Michigan Avenue, Chicago, IL 60611.

Backer, T. E. (1987). *Strategic planning for workplace drug abuse programs*. National Institute on Drug Abuse (DHHS Publication No. ADM 87-1538). Washington, DC: U. S. Government Printing Office.

Baselt, R. C. (1984). The analysis of delta-9-tetrahydrocannabinol and its metabolites by immunoassay. In R. C. Baselt (Ed.), *Advances in analytical toxicology* (Vol. 1) (pp. 81–123). Foster City, CA: Biomedical Publications.

Baumgartner, W. A., Jones, P. F., & Black, C. T. (1981). Detection of phencyclidine in hair. *Journal of Forensic Sciences, 26,* 576–581.

Dubowski, K. M., & O'Neill, B. (1979). The blood/breath ratio of alcohol. *Clinical Chemistry, 25,* 1144.

Hansen, H. J., Caudill, S. P., & Boone, J. (1985). Crisis in drug testing. Results of CDC blind study. *Journal of the American Medical Association, 253*(16), 2382–2387.

Mason, A. P., & McBay, A. J. (1985). Cannabis: Pharmacology and interpretation of effects. *Journal of Forensic Sciences, 30,* 615–631.

Morgan, J. P. (1984). Problems of mass urine screening for misused drugs. *Journal of Psychoactive Drugs, 16*(4), 305–317.

Mulé S. J., & Casella, G. A. (1988). Rendering the poppyseed defense defenseless: Identification of 6-monoacetylmorphine in urine by gas-chromatography/mass spectrometry. *Clinical Chemistry, 34,* 1427–1430.

Parez-Reyes, M., Di Guiseppi, S., Mason, A. P., & Davis, K. H. (1983). Passive inhalation of marijuana smoke and urinary excretion of cannabinoids. *Clinical Pharmacology and Therapeutics, 34,* 36–41.

PART TWO

SUBSTANCE ABUSE PROBLEMS THROUGHOUT THE LIFE SPAN

SUBSTANCE ABUSE DURING THE CHILDBEARING YEAR

Susan R. McKay
MaryLou Scavnicky-Mylant

The childbearing year is one of tremendous change and growth for parents and for the developing child. During no other period in life does a woman's body make so many dramatic physical adjustments. Simultaneously, the baby is growing at a phenomenal rate, never again to be equaled.

EMBRYONIC AND FETAL DEVELOPMENT

The *embryonic stage of development* (the first 8 weeks after conception) is characterized by continuous changes of cell division, cell migration, and cell differentiation (Tuchmann-Duplessis, 1980). Embryo implantation occurs during the first 2 weeks after conception, and the developing embryo extracts its nutritional supplies from the uterine lining until the placenta is fully functioning at the end of the first trimester. Although organ systems are rapidly developing, specific organ functions do not characterize the embryonic period.

From 15–25 days after conception the central nervous system (CNS) is differentiating. By 20–30 days of life the precursors to the axial skeleton, limb buds, and musculature are apparent. During the period from 24–40 days, major differentiation of the eyes, heart, and lower limbs occurs. By 60 days, organ differentiation is well underway and is complete by 90 days. For the remainder of pregnancy, maturation is the main growth activity (O'Brien & McManus, 1977).

Vulnerability to *teratogenic effects* (the production of physical defects) is maximum during the period of organ differentiation (Tuchmann-Duplessis, 1980) and ranges from practically no measurable effects to toxicity so marked that the embryo is aborted. In the middle range of effects, gross anatomic defects or permanent but perhaps subtle metabolic and functional defects (Gullekson & Temple, 1978) may occur. Some organ systems such as the external genitalia, teeth, and CNS

continue to undergo important changes throughout the pregnancy and remain vulnerable to factors that may interfere with their development. The CNS, for example, may be affected during the entire prenatal period.

SUBSTANCE ABUSE DURING THE CHILDBEARING YEAR

When a pregnant or lactating woman ingests any substance into her body whether through her digestive, respiratory, or circulatory system, the potential for danger to the fetus or infant exists. Taken in its broadest sense, poor nutritional habits may be considered a form of substance abuse because of long-term effects that can occur in both mother and child. In any form, the developing child is usually most devastated by maternal substance abuse because of extreme vulnerability in a period of rapid development.

Pregnant and lactating women are part of a larger drug-oriented culture using drugs not only for therapeutic purposes but for pleasure, relaxation, and social participation (Cooper, 1978). Drug intake often continues during the childbearing year for a variety of reasons. The woman may not know she is pregnant, or she may continue taking drugs because of habituation. Other women simply are unaware of the dangerous effects of drugs on their growing child. Thus, pregnant or soon-to-be pregnant women need to be asked specifically about every drug from heroin to aspirin and caffeine.

Accurate statistics concerning maternal drug consumption during the childbearing year are difficult to obtain. Statistics concerning maternal drug use are often based on retrospective recall of pregnant women during or after pregnancy (Schnoll, 1986). Women's reports of current drug use during the first trimester (most vulnerable time for the fetus) have been identified as particularly inaccurate. A more accurate response is given when women are asked about the past, such as a prior-to-pregnancy rate, or told that their response will be verified through urinalysis (Day, Wagener, & Taylor, 1985). Few studies, however, have systematically verified their results with urine toxicology (Schnoll, 1986). On the other hand, prospective studies in which inquiries begin at the time of conception and are superior scientifically to retrospective studies demand hundreds of thousands of subjects and may not include the women at highest risk since only a small number of these women receive prenatal care (Abel, 1985).

Even harder to demonstrate is the relationship between drug intake and teratogenic effects. Retrospective studies, besides being incomplete, contain inevitable bias in their search for a teratogenic agent (Abel, 1985; O'Brien & McManus, 1977). Many women take a variety of over-the-counter (OTC) drugs and never consider them drugs. In fact, the vast majority of drugs used during pregnancy are self-prescribed by pregnant women (Finnegan, 1976). It ''. . .has been reported that as many as 60% of pregnant women use some medication during their pregnancy. The drugs used are primarily over-the-counter analgesics, antinauseants, and sleep medication'' (Schnoll, 1986, p. 7).

Recent findings by Chasnoff (Eleven percent of gravidas, 1988), which were validated with urine testings, found that at least 11% of women from urban, suburban, and rural areas had used illegal drugs during their pregnancy. The overall rate varied not by population served, but by the drug history protocols used by each of the 40 hospitals surveyed. The survey also dealt only with illegal drug use and not alcohol, which experts consider to be an even greater problem during pregnancy.

Chasnoff (1990) further reports of a more recent study, which involved 100% of all public and 70% of all private first prenatal visits in a specific southeastern county of the United States. At this first visit, blind urine toxicology tests were done for cocaine, marihuana, alcohol, and opiates. Positive results for one or more of these substances were identified among 16.3% of the public versus 13.1% of the private and 14.1% of the black versus 15.4% of the white clients. Alcohol use was again poorly assessed in this study, because urine toxicology for alcohol is essentially worthless.

Mechanism of Drug Effects

Drugs can affect the developing embryo or fetus through a variety of mechanisms (Sullivan, 1976). The drug may be directly toxic to the embryo or fetus, and metabolites of the drug produced by the mother or in the embryo or fetus may also be toxic. The mere presence of a drug, however, does not mean a toxic effect will result, because the embryo has multiple lines of defense and the ability to repair itself (Hutchings, 1985).

Drugs may also interact synergistically along with other biologic and environmental factors or form a final common pathway versus having drug-specific teratogenic effects. For example, the correlation between fetal alcohol syndrome (FAS) and alcohol may occur simply because alcohol is the most common teratogen humans expose themselves to. Features compatible with FAS have been found among infants of women with PKU (phenylketonuria) and women who smoked marihuana during their pregnancy (Hingson et al., 1982; Lipson, Yu, O'Halloran, & Williams, 1981; Zuckerman, 1985). Abnormalities in children exposed to benzodiazepines in utero also resemble FAS (Laegreid, Olegard, Wahlstrom, & Conradi, 1987).

To produce teratogenic effects, the drug must be given at an appropriate dosage and must act at a very precise moment of morphogenesis in the embryo. The amount of the drug transferred to the fetus from the mother depends on the concentration delivered to the fetus per unit time (Tuchmann-Duplessis, 1980). For example, drugs taken orally may undergo significant first-pass metabolism in the liver, reducing their ability to cross the placenta, as compared with drugs taken intravenously or by inhalation, which do not undergo this first step and more readily cross the placenta.

The time that a drug is taken during pregnancy is extremely critical, with the first 8 weeks being the most important in terms of embryonic development. In fact, drugs severely affecting the embryo during this time usually cause a spontaneous abortion (Schnoll, 1986). A small dose of a drug in early pregnancy may have a far more profound effect than several large doses late in pregnancy (Tuchmann-Duplessis, 1980). For example, Chasnoff (1990) has identified that infants of mothers who used cocaine during the first trimester did not do any better behaviorally or neurologically than infants of mothers who used cocaine throughout their pregnancy.

Thus, the developmental outcome of any drug exposure is the result of a complex interaction of events (Zuckerman, 1985). Schnoll (1986) believes that to ''. . .understand the effects of drug use during pregnancy, it is necessary to look at the maternal-placental-fetal unit'' (p. 7).

Maternal Factors

Age, hormonal balance, and maternal diet can alter susceptibility of the embryo to drug effects. The nutritional condition of the mother may affect the expression of the genes and enhance the harmful effects of drugs. Chronic and metabolic maternal diseases such as diabetes, obesity, hypertension, toxemia, and liver dysfunction can enhance the noxious action of drugs and increase fetal damage. The drugs themselves may also influence the oxygen-carrying capacity of maternal blood flow, affect maternal blood glucose levels, or reduce the availability of essential vitamins, hormones, amino acids, and trace elements, thus, potentiating their effect on the fetus (Tuchmann-Duplessis, 1980).

Pregnancy itself can further alter a woman's response to certain drugs by either increasing or decreasing the amount of drug reaching the fetus (Schnoll, 1986). For example, changes in absorption for many drugs may result due to decreased gastrointestinal motility, alterations in gastric pH and buffer capacity, and increased mucous secretions occurring during pregnancy (Schnoll, 1986). As pregnancy advances, the glomerular filtration rate and drug excretion increases, venous pressure is altered, and absorption of intramuscularly administered drugs is reduced. Increased progesterone levels increase hepatic metabolism of drugs, plasma proteins decrease, and so does protein binding, making more free drug available. Increases in total body water and fat also alter drug disposition during pregnancy (Rebond, Groulade, & Groslambert, 1963; Schnoll, 1986).

Placental Factors

Although once assumed to be a barrier against harmful substances, the placenta is an organ of transfer, and equilibration of drugs between maternal and fetal circulation is extremely rapid (Horning, Butler, Hill, & Nowlin, 1975). Almost any substance administered to the mother can penetrate the placenta—at least to some extent—unless it is destroyed or altered during passage. For example, drugs bound to plasma proteins, often in an ionized state, will not cross the placenta at all, or not as easily, due to the size of the drug–protein complex (Mirkin & Singh, 1976). Schnoll (1986) describes a simple rule of thumb as any drug which crosses the blood–brain barrier and has an effect on the CNS of the mother will also cross the placenta.

Schnoll (1986) describes the placenta as an active versus passive organ, however, and reports recent studies that identify its metabolic functions in oxidation, reduction, hydrolysis, and conjugation of drugs. Placenta transfer also does not appear to be the main determinant of teratogenic effects. Tuchmann-Duplessis (1980) states that the toxicity of a drug is regulated by the pharmacologic and physiochemical nature of the drug compounds or of their metabolites and by the possibility of sufficient accumulation in a genetically susceptible embryo.

Fetal Factors

For teratogenic effects to occur, a given drug must achieve its specific threshold level by a sufficient dose and over a sufficient duration of time. The fetus must also be genetically susceptible, because not all embryos and fetuses exposed to a drug develop problems (Schnoll, 1986).

Although little is known about the functions of the human fetus in relation to drugs (Schnoll, 1986), current knowledge indicates that the fetus and placenta can metabolize drugs at a low rate. Glucuronyl transferase activity, however, seems to be especially low and results in failure to terminate the biologic effects of drugs (Juchau, 1985; Schnoll, 1986). Although the capacity of the placenta to metabolize drugs increases as term approaches (Yaffe, 1979), drug effects are still far from innocuous.

In addition to the dysmorphic teratology, behavioral teratology resulting from the maternal-placental-fetal factors discussed earlier and the parenting unit must be considered (Schnoll, 1986). Thus, the developmental outcome of any drug exposure is the result of a complex interaction of events (Zuckerman, 1985). A transactional model of perinatal risk (Sameroff & Chandler, 1975) involving an ongoing interaction of biologic and environmental factors, such as the caretaking environment, may be most appropriate when assessing the developmental consequences of prenatal drug exposure (Zuckerman, 1985). This model will be applied to the discussion of each drug of abuse identified in this chapter.

Lactation and Drug Transfer

Drug exposure of offspring may also occur postnatally through breast-feeding, since most drugs ingested by a mother during lactation are passed through her breast milk. The concentration of the drug in the breast milk, however, depends on the solubility, protein binding, and pH of the drug, as well as the time of ingestion by the mother, age of the baby, and cumulative effects over time (Wilton, 1988).

Thus, although breast-feeding is advantageous, especially for the chemically dependent mother, the infant is at a much higher risk if the mother is still abusing substances. Wilton (1988) identifies that besides the advantages of easier digestibility and available antibodies for the infant, and rapidity of uterine involution for the mother, the ". . .calming effect that prolactin has on the brain during suckling may help" the chemically dependent ". . .mother deal with a baby who may be jittery" (p. 149). Most of the latest findings on the commonly abused drugs, however, indicate that breast-feeding by a drug-abusing mother can be harmful to the baby.

For example, although most narcotic analgesics in therapeutic doses pose no problem in breast-fed infants, with regular use they can cause symptoms of dependence and withdrawal, especially with heroin (Wilton, 1988). Neonatal depression has been observed with codeine; failure to thrive and drowsiness with Darvon and Percodan; drowsiness and poor feeding with Demerol; and depression and symptoms of failure to thrive with methadone when being used regularly in the lactating mother (Lauwers & Woessner, 1983). Thus, drugs that are contraindicated in lactation include heroin, phencyclidine (PCP), cocaine, Haldol, lithium, meprobamate, Librium, diazepam (Valium), and marihuana (Wilton, 1988).

The effects on lactation of many of the other drugs have not been studied or have been negligible except in higher dosages and so are often used with caution. For example, the Perinatal Center of Chemical Dependence at Northwestern Memorial Hospital advises lactating mothers to pump and discard their breast milk for 24 hours after ingesting large amounts of alcohol. Alcohol was the second most common drug of choice used postnatally by 7% of 41 mothers studied who were attending this clinic. Breast-feeding is recommended only if the mother has been drug free for 3 months during her pregnancy, substantiated by urine toxicology, is in treatment and consistent with her appointments, is human immunodeficiency virus (HIV) negative, and is compliant with prenatal recommendations (Wilton, 1988).

The risks versus benefits of breast-feeding should be assessed with all new mothers whether they have been identified as chemically dependent or not. If 60% of women in the United States breast-feed at hospital discharge (Martinez & Krieger, 1985) and have used some type of medication during their pregnancy (Schnoll, 1986) with at least 11% of pregnant women having used an illegal drug (Chasnoff, 1988, 1990), the chances of the risk:benefit ratio being almost equal for some women can be very high.

CAFFEINE, SMOKING, AND ALCOHOL

Of significant concern because they may produce teratogenic and growth defects as well as birth complications are drugs that are abundantly used during pregnancy, often with little understanding of potential fetal effects. Because these forms of substance abuse occur so frequently and in an interrelated fashion, it is difficult to separate out the effects of each variable in producing fetal and maternal damage. The woman who smokes often drinks coffee while she smokes (Haworth, Ellestad-Sayed, Dilling, & King, 1980); the pregnant drinker is more likely than her nondrinking counterpart to smoke. In a recent survey of 308 women at their first prenatal visit, 40% reported smoking, 13% acknowledged regular alcohol consumption (83% of whom also smoked), and the mean caffeine consumption was 51–84 mg. This was below the reported average daily caffeine intake (Brooten et al., 1987). Johnson, McCarter, and Ferencz (1987) also report that of 1336 mothers of infants, 21% used alcohol only, 14% cigarettes only, and 10% used a combination of both during their pregnancy. Habits are often so ingrained that a woman does not realize she is drinking or smoking to the extent that she is. Because of the frequency and seeming social acceptability of these behaviors, maternal smoking and alcohol and caffeine use are all a significant concern if fetal outcome is to be improved.

Caffeine

Caffeine is found in soft drinks, chocolate, cocoa, and a large number of OTC and prescription drugs. It is readily absorbed from the gastrointestinal tract and crosses the placenta (Mirkin & Singh, 1976). In pregnant women the plasma half-life has been known to increase from two- to four-fold the time identified in healthy adults (Knutti, Rothweiler, & Schlatter, 1982). Also, the newborn infant, whether full-term or premature, metabolizes caffeine poorly because the newborn infant lacks the enzymes needed to metabolize caffeine until several days after birth. The plasma half-life is, therefore, increased 32–149 hours (Horning et al., 1973).

Caffeine is a strong drug that stimulates the CNS and, if consumed in large amounts, causes symptoms such as nervousness, irritability, insomnia, anxiety, and disturbances in heart rate and rhythm. If maternal caffeine intake continues during lactation, the baby may respond by being restless or wakeful, especially after large amounts of caffeine have been ingested by the mother.

Information about the possible adverse effects of caffeine on fetal development is often incomplete and conflicting. Caffeine may possibly interfere with cell growth and chromosomal structure by increasing adenosine-3':5'-cyclic monophosphate in cells. It may also act directly on nucleic acids, because it is structurally similar to adenine and guanine (Srisuphan & Bracken, 1986; Weathersbee & Lodge, 1977). Caffeine also increases catecholamines (Anton, 1979), which may cause fetal hypoxia due to vasoconstriction of uteroplacental circulation (Srisuphan & Bracken, 1986).

A study by Weathersbee, Olsen, and Lodge (1977) reported a higher rate of spontaneous abortions among women whose caffeine intake was very high (>600 mg). Srisuphan and Bracken (1986) attempted to validate this finding through a prospective cohort study of 3135 women and identified that women who consumed moderate-to-heavy amounts of caffeine (>150 mg) were significantly more likely to experience late first or second trimester spontaneous abortions. Cigarette smoking, alcohol, and drug use were unrelated to spontaneous abortions in the first or second trimester. Epidemiologic studies, however, have indicated no teratogenic effects in women who are heavy coffee drinkers during pregnancy despite malformations and mutagenicity produced in rats, mice, and bacteria exposed to high doses of caffeine. However, the synergistic effect of caffeine with other agents to produce such abnormalities has not been investigated extensively (Abbott, 1986). For example, smoking stimulates the elimination of caffeine (Kaplan, 1981). Srisuphan and Bracken (1986) also hypothesize that a component of coffee other than caffeine may be the compound associated with spontaneous abortions.

Smoking

Caffeine ingestion and smoking habits have been identified as being correlated (Toubas et al., 1986) and constituting a higher risk for the developing fetus. Doses of 300 mg or more of caffeine daily accentuated the decrease in birth weight caused by smoking (Beaulac-Baillargeon & Desrosiers, 1987).

Smoking during the childbearing year has long been recognized as producing harmful fetal and neonatal consequences; however, 70% of the women who give birth in this country are aged 18–30 and among these women aged 20–24, the prevalence of smoking has increased from 33% in 1980 to 38% in 1983 (Koop, 1986). Although smoking in the United States has declined among adults from 42% in 1964 (U. S. Department of Health and Human Services, 1982) to 30% in 1985 (National Center for Health Statistics, 1985), smoking among women has not (Pinney, 1987). In samples of pregnant women, the percentage of smokers ranges from 23% (Hill, Craig, Chaney, Tennyson, & McCulley, 1977) to 54% (Niswander & Gordon, 1972).

Recent reports of the increased risks from smoking during pregnancy identify the risk of having a spontaneous abortion to be 1.7; preterm birth, 1.36; low-birth-weight (LBW) infant, 1.98; and perinatal death, 1.25 (Koop, 1986). According to one authority, 50,000 fetal deaths and 4000 infant deaths every year result from smoking during pregnancy (Ravenholt, 1987). The Centers for Disease Control (CDC) also estimate that smoking accounts for 25% of LBW infants in the United States (Hogue & Sappenfield, 1987).

This almost twofold risk of having a LBW infant is independent of the risks posed by other factors (Hogue & Sappenfield, 1987). There is also a symmetrical decrease in birth length (Persson, Grennert, Gennser, & Kullander, 1978). In fact, smoking may actually be the most important risk factor for fetal growth—so much so that the name "fetal tobacco syndrome" (FTS) has been coined for infants under 2500 g and over 37 weeks' gestation born to mothers who smoke at least five cigarettes daily and for whom no other reason for growth retardation is obvious (Nieburg, Marks, McLaren, & Remington, 1985).

Hogue and Sappenfield (1987) believe that even though the concept of FTS focuses attention on the adverse effects of smoking on infant outcome, it underemphasizes the many other effects described earlier. Of even greater importance may be the possible maiming effects of smoking on surviving infants. For example, Ravenholt (1987) examined data from earlier studies done in Seattle and identified an increase in childhood leukemia among offspring of mothers who smoked heavily during pregnancy.

Physiologic Effects of Nicotine*

A number of factors contribute to the pathophysiologic changes in the fetus and placenta due to smoking (see Fig. 10.1). Cigarette smoke contains over 1000 drugs (Kline, Stein, Susser, & Warburton, 1977). The mechanisms of action leading to growth retardation are mainly nicotine-caused vasoconstriction, carbon monoxide poisoning, inhibition of carbonic anhydrase necessary for oxygenation, and the formation of thiocynate, leading to hypoxia. Nicotine appears to act on sympathetic ganglia and the adrenal medulla to cause a release of acetylcholine, epinephrine, and norepinephrine, resulting in increased heart rate and cardiac output, vasoconstriction of the peripheral vessels, a rise in blood pressure, changes in carbohydrate and fat metabolism, an increased tendency toward thrombophlebitis, and the release of antidiuretic hormone (Pirani, 1978). Smoking only two cigarettes abruptly raises a pregnant woman's blood levels of epinephrine and norepinephrine; simultaneously, the fetal heart rate accelerates markedly—indicating possible oxygen deprivation due to decreased blood supply (Quigley, Sheehan, Wilkes, & Yen, 1979). Stopping smoking has been shown to increase the amount of available oxygen within a period of 48 hours (Davies, Latto, Jones, Veale, & Wardrop, 1979).

Experiments with rhesus monkeys found that when the mother was injected with pharmacologic doses of nicotine, marked cardiovascular disturbances occurred in both mother and fetus (Suzuki et al., 1971). Subsequent monkey studies showed that nicotine crosses the placenta rapidly and remains in higher concentration in the fetal than in the maternal circulation (Suzuki et al., 1974). Significant reduction in uterine arterial blood flow resulted when the pregnant monkey was infused with nicotine, the implication being that oxygen transfer was considerably reduced—a factor that must be significant in producing hypoxia and mixed respiratory and metabolic acidosis (Suzuki, Johnson, & Minei, 1980). Besides the potential hypoxic effect of nicotine, cadmium, another toxic element of cigarette smoke, is released. Cadmium, and its interference with fetal zinc

*Adapted from "Smoking during the childbearing year," by Susan McKay. *The American Journal of Maternal Child Nursing*, 1980, *5*, 46–50. Copyright 1980, American Journal of Nursing Company. Reproduced with permission from *MCN, The American Journal of Maternal Child Nursing*, January/February 1980, Vol. 5, No. 1.

uptake, may be related to the decrease in birth weight of infants whose mothers smoked prenatally (Kuhnert et al., 1987).

Placentas of smokers are thinner and rounder than those of nonsmokers. Calcification, primarily of the maternal surface, is much more prevalent in smokers than in nonsmokers; and patchy subchorionic fibrin deposits occur with greater relative frequency in placentas of smokers—changes associated with shorter gestations among smokers (Christianson, 1979). Severe vascular changes have been found in the umbilical arteries and veins and in the vessels of the placental villi in pregnant women who smoke, suggesting that the vessels of the newborn child may exhibit similar changes (Asmussen, 1978). Newborn babies of smokers show an elevation in red cell volume as if they were oxygen deprived (Pirani, 1978).

Increased carbon monoxide concentration also occurs in both mother and fetus as a result of maternal smoking. The level is related to the number of cigarettes smoked daily. There appears to be a negative correlation between the birth weight of babies and the mean values of maternal carboxyhemoglobin levels. Cyanide plasma levels in the maternal and cord blood of women who smoke are significantly higher than such levels in the blood of women who don't smoke. As with carbon monoxide, the effect of cyanide on the tissues is *cellular anoxia* (Pirani, 1978).

A potential abnormal development of infant breathing regulation may result due to fetal hypoxia or the direct action of nicotine. Infants with apnea have been identified as having significantly greater rates of central apnea when their mothers smoked prenatally. These mothers were also ingesting approximately 610 mg caffeine daily, which was also significantly correlated with central apnea in their infants (Toubas et al., 1986). Smoking habits of mothers during the infancy of their offspring also showed a strong positive relationship to the incidence of obstructive apnea in their infants. Active exposure prenatally as well as passive exposure of infants to smoking is associated not only with an increase in upper respiratory tract infections, but also with chronic middle ear effusion (Kraemer et al., 1983; Taylor & Wadsworth, 1987). The latter may be indicative of a possible congenital effect of smoking during pregnancy. An association between oral clefts and smoking has been identified (Andrews & McGarry, 1972; Ericson, Kallen, & Westerholm, 1979; Khoury et al., 1987; Saxen, 1974). No increase in the overall level

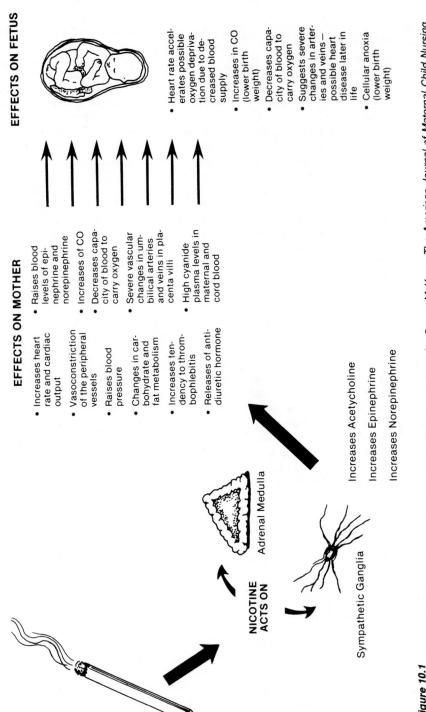

EFFECTS ON FETUS

- Heart rate accelerates possible oxygen deprivation due to decreased blood supply
- Increases in CO (lower birth weight)
- Decreases capacity of blood to carry oxygen
- Suggests severe changes in arteries and veins — possible heart disease later in life
- Cellular anoxia (lower birth weight)

EFFECTS ON MOTHER

- Increases heart rate and cardiac output
- Vasoconstriction of the peripheral vessels
- Raises blood pressure
- Changes in carbohydrate and fat metabolism
- Increases tendency to thrombophlebitis
- Releases of anti-diuretic hormone
- Raises blood levels of epinephrine and norepinephrine
- Increases of CO
- Decreases capacity of blood to carry oxygen
- Severe vascular changes in umbilical arteries and veins in placenta villi
- High cyanide plasma levels in maternal and cord blood

NICOTINE ACTS ON

Adrenal Medulla

Sympathetic Ganglia

Increases Acetycholine

Increases Epinephrine

Increases Norepinephrine

Figure 10.1
Effects of maternal smoking. From "Smoking during the childbearing year," by Susan McKay. *The American Journal of Maternal Child Nursing,* 1980, 5, 48. Copyright 1980 by the American Journal of Nursing Company. Reproduced with permission from *MCN, The American Journal of Maternal Child Nursing,* January/February, Vol. 5, No. 1.

of congenital malformations, however, has been found, although smokers may miscarry a malformed fetus more often than nonsmokers (Shiono cited in Lincoln, 1986).

Breast-feeding and Smoking

Besides passive exposure to smoking, infants can also be exposed to nicotine through the milk of smoking mothers, although, smoking heavily (20–30 cigarettes daily) while breast-feeding can result in decreased milk production (Hervada, Feit, & Sagraves, 1978). The dose of nicotine infants receive varies greatly depending on the degree of passive smoking and breast-feeding they are exposed to. For example, newborn infants nursed by smoking mothers and unexposed to passive smoking had a median ratio (ng nicotine/ mg creatinine) of 14 versus a median ratio of 35 among older and non-breast-fed infants exposed only to passive smoking (Luck & Nau, 1985).

Breast-fed infants of smokers may exhibit symptoms of nausea, vomiting, abdominal cramping, and diarrhea (Vorherr, 1974). Nicotine has also been implicated in apneic attacks and overexcitability in breast-fed infants (Luck & Nau, 1985). Because of these potential effects, the lactating woman is advised to stop smoking.

Alcohol

The association between maternal alcohol ingestion and fetal outcome has been widely recognized in the United States only since 1973 when aberrant morphogenesis in offspring was observed in eight unrelated children born to chronic alcoholics (Jones, Smith, Streissguth, & Ulleland, 1973). Extensive evidence to support alcohol's teratogenic effects has been documented through strong and consistent associations, dose–response relationships, and biologic plausibility (Cooper, 1987).

FAS is thought to be one of three leading causes of birth defects—the other two being spina bifida and Down's syndrome. The incidence of FAS, depending on the population studied and criteria used (Cooper, 1987), ranges from 0.4–3.1/1000 births in the general population (Abel, 1984; Rosett & Weiner, 1985) to 690/1000 among children of alcoholic women (Abel, 1984; Streissguth, Landesman-Dwyer, Martin, & Smith, 1980).

Behaviorally, these infants show motor signs such as being tremulous, jittery, irritable, and nonalert, and they demonstrate a weak sucking reflex—all indications of possible permanent CNS damage (Streissguth,

1978). In some infants, failure to thrive has been associated with a weak sucking reflex. Sleep disturbances have also been reported (Sander et al., 1977).

In 1980, the Fetal Alcohol Study Group of the Research Society on Alcoholism recommended that for a diagnosis of fetal alcohol syndrome to be present, a child must have signs in each of the following three categories (Cooper, 1987):

1. *Prenatal and/or postnatal growth retardation:* weight, length, or head circumference below the 10th percentile when corrected for gestational age. Maternal alcohol use has been shown to produce growth deficiencies in babies even when controlling for variables such as smoking, parity, and gestational age (Streissguth et al., 1980). Women who drink heavily, or at least 1.6 oz alcohol per day, have infants who are significantly lighter than abstainers (Rosett & Weiner, 1985).

These babies seldom ''catch up'' with their peers even when put in optimal environments (Erb & Andresen, 1978) and remain small or more than two standard deviations below the mean for height and weight (Clarren & Smith, 1978). Catch-up growth has only been identified among children with milder forms of FAS (Weiner & Morse, 1988). Maternal alcohol abuse before conception is also associated with intrauterine growth retardation—even if abstinence is reportedly maintained during pregnancy (Little, Barr, Herman, & Streissguth, 1980).

2. *CNS involvement:* signs of neurologic abnormality, developmental delay, or intellectual impairment. Mental retardation is the most serious of the defects and is probably the most sensitive manifestation of maternal alcohol abuse (Mulvihill & Yeager, 1976). Evidence points to a prenatal origin of mental retardation rather than postnatal exposure to alcoholic parents (Clarren & Smith, 1978). The average IQ of FAS victims is 68, or in the mildly retarded range (Little & Streissguth, 1981). Some children may be of average intelligence, but demonstrate CNS impairment through attentional deficits (Shaywitz, Cohen & Shaywitz, 1980).

Both microcephaly and mental deficiency are thought to be caused by deficient brain growth in babies of alcoholic mothers (Clarren, Alvord, Smith, Streissguth, & Sumi, 1978). Severity of the structural damage to the brain appears related to dosage and gestational timing as well as individual fetus response. Streissguth, Clarren, and Jones (1985) also identified a relationship between the degree of mental deficiency and extent of craniofacial abnormalities.

3. *Characteristic facial dysmorphology* with at least two of the following three signs:

    a. Microcephaly or head circumference below the 3rd percentile

    b. Microopthalmia or short palpebral fissures or both

    c. Poorly developed philtrum, thin upper lip, or flattening of the maxillary area

Because of the subtle nature of some of these manifestations, those untrained in observation of the specific features of FAS may simply label these children as abnormal looking. A standardized evaluation guide for the assessment of FAS features should be used (Graham, Phillips, Herman, & Little, 1982). These facial features may not be as unique as once thought, however. A recent report demonstrated a similarity between FAS facial characteristics and the faces of children of mothers with PKU (Lipson et al., 1981) and women who smoked marihuana during their pregnancy (Hingson et al., 1982).

Many other abnormalities may also be seen alone or with FAS, which tends to further complicate diagnosis. These include eye and ear defects, genitourinary problems such as undescended testicles and renal anomalies, hemangiomas, cardiac malformations, joint and limb anomalies such as fetal clubfoot, fingerprint and palmar crease abnormalities, cleft palate, benign tumors, and hernias (National Institute on Alcohol Abuse and Alcoholism [NIAAA], 1984; Qazi et al., 1979; Streissguth, 1977). For example, in a recent study of 14 children with FAS by Church and Gerkin ("Fetal Alcohol Syndrome," 1988), 13 or 93% had recurrent otitis media and receptive/expressive language delays and 29% had a sensorineural hearing loss.

Partial Teratologic Effects

If only one of these three major characteristics is present and the mother is suspected of abusing alcohol prenatally, the diagnosis of fetal alcohol effects is made (Abel, 1984). Fetal alcohol effects account for a far greater number of affected babies than does the full-blown syndrome. For every child with FAS, 10 others may be born with its partial effects (National Clearinghouse for Alcohol Information [NCALI], 1985).

Whereas the full FAS represents the extreme end of a dose–response curve and does not appear to be extremely common (El-Guebaly & Offord, 1977), there is probably a positive slope beginning at a far lower level of alcohol abuse (Fielding & Yankauer, 1978). The extent to which infants show the FAS is related to the dose and length of exposure to alcohol in utero (Erb & Andresen, 1978), the genetic background of the fetus, gestational age, and individual susceptibility. Girls, for instance, have been found to display FAS at significantly higher rates than boys (Erb & Andresen, 1978). Another example is the report that twins (monozygotic and dizygotic) born to alcoholic mothers have slightly different fetal alcohol characteristics—apparently due to differences in susceptibility to the dysmorphogenic influence of alcohol (Christoffell & Salafsky, 1975; Palmer, Leightman, Ouellette, & Warner, 1974).

Clarren and Smith (1978), however, believe that the partial expression of FAS can only be referred to as *suspected fetal alcohol effects,* since the compatible features associated with the complete FAS may not be specific to alcohol. For example, women who abuse marihuana prenatally are five times more likely than nonusers and women who gain less than 5 lb are two times more likely to deliver a child with fetal alcohol effects (Hingson et al., 1982).

Physiologic Mechanism of Alcohol's Effects

Intervening variables such as caffeine, nicotine, drug and nutritional intake, maternal metabolism, socioeconomic factors, genetic background, and regularity of medical care all make difficult the precise identification of the mechanisms by which alcohol or its breakdown products produce their effects on the embryo and fetus. Each of these factors has been hypothesized as potentiating the action of the primary teratogen alcohol. Abel and Dintcheff (1978), however, conclude that altered maternal nutrition is not responsible for the growth deficiencies, malformations, and stillbirths but that the culprit is prenatal exposure to alcohol of the developing fetus.

Animal studies have shown the effects of alcohol to be directly related to the level of maternal blood alcohol rather than to the amount of alcohol ingested (Erb & Andresen, 1978). Alcohol rapidly crosses the placental and blood–brain barriers of the fetus and reaches approximately the same levels of concentration as those found in the mother; the fetus, however, is unable to clear the alcohol from its system with the same efficiency as the mother, apparently because of a decreased level of hepatic dehydrogenase activity that does not reach the adult level until approximately 5 years of age (Zervoudakis, Fuchs, & Krauss, 1980). Although alcohol can be metabolized by the near-term fetus, more than 12 hours are required to clear the drug when the mother's blood alcohol level is 100 mg/dl or more (Weathersbee & Lodge, 1979).

Alcohol, caffeine, and nicotine are alike in that their use dramatically increases circulating levels of catecholamines, which are all thought to alter placental blood flow patterns and oxygenation through their vasoconstrictive effects. Studies have shown that the vascular bed of the pregnant uterus is extremely sensitive to injections of catecholamines, even in physiologic rather than pharmacologic doses; thus catecholamine release may be of special significance in the pathologic changes accompanying alcohol, caffeine, and nicotine use during pregnancy (Weathersbee & Lodge, 1979).

Alcohol use also leads to increased lactate levels in the circulating blood, a change that is readily reflected in both maternal and fetal blood supplies. The accumulation of lactate along with its accompanying acidosis alters uterine perfusion, fetal growth, and CNS functioning. Additionally, hypoglycemia can occur because alcohol inhibits gluconeogenesis (Weathersbee & Lodge, 1979). Alcohol may also interfere with the passage of amino acids across the placenta; thus, protein synthesis and growth are inhibited (Henderson et al., 1981). Besides an overall decrease in brain growth, anatomic abnormalities in the hippocampus, the center for learning/memory performance and controlling inhibiting behavior, have been noted in animals (Barnes & Walker, 1981; Davies & Smith, 1981; West, Hodges, & Black, 1981).

Alcohol's Effects According to Stage of Pregnancy

Early pregnancy seems to be the most critical period for adverse fetal effects—especially in the month preceding recognition of the pregnancy, which includes the first few weeks after conception (Hanson, Smith, & Streissguth, 1978). A recent study of Ernhart, Morrow-Tlucak, Sokol, Ager, and Martier (Find moderate alcohol, 1988), however, found that moderate alcohol intake in the early stages of pregnancy did not appear to increase the risk of birth defects significantly. The threshold for increased risk was at three drinks a day in early pregnancy. Ernhart believes this finding should serve as a reassurance to patients who drank alcohol before realizing they were pregnant, but is not a signal that drinking is acceptable for pregnant women.

The middle trimester of pregnancy appears to be a period when the fetus is least susceptible to alcohol's effect. However, evidence now supports an association between alcohol consumption and spontaneous abortions during this time. Heavy alcohol consumption near term may exert its most profound effect on fetal nutrition and size, including brain growth (National Clearinghouse for Alcohol Information, 1985; Ouellette, Rosett, Rosman, & Weiner, 1977). A prospective study of the association between moderate maternal alcohol consumption and infant birth weight concluded that a significant relationship existed between the ingestion of 1 oz absolute alcohol daily before pregnancy and an average decrease in birth weight of 91 g; the same amount of alcohol ingested in late pregnancy was associated with a decrease of 160 g (Little, 1977).

A retrospective study of the 7-year period from 1970 to 1977 reviewed the effects on newborn infants of maternal treatment with alcohol to arrest premature labor. Results indicated that maternal intravenous administration of alcohol carries a significant risk to the immature fetus (<2000 g) if birth takes place less than 12 hours after the infusion is completed. Apgar scores were significantly lower, and a higher incidence of respiratory distress occurred in these infants (Zervoudakis et al., 1980). Bills (1980) observed that if a depressant medication is given in addition to the alcohol infusion and premature labor is not suppressed, the resulting infant may be born with a profound CNS depression. One can surmise from these reports that the use of alcohol to curtail premature labor may be quite hazardous due to extreme toxic effects on the fetus and newborn.

Changes Related to Alcohol Consumption During Pregnancy

Reports from the University of Washington School of Medicine (Little, 1977; Little & Streissguth, 1978) describe changes in women's drinking habits that accompany pregnancy. Alcohol consumption decreased dramatically and spontaneously after conception, the amount of decrease being directly proportionate to the level of prepregnancy drinking; that is, the heaviest drinkers before pregnancy tended to be the heaviest drinkers after conception. Binge drinking, however, increased during pregnancy at the same time that the amount of modal drinking decreased. The amount consumed during binge drinking, however, was less than prepregnancy levels. The decrease in consumption appeared related to adverse physiologic effects or to loss of desire to drink and was found only secondarily related to a concern for fetal welfare. Similarly, coffee drinking and cigarette smoking were found spontaneously to be reduced in quantity during pregnancy. Lee (1987), however, reported that although most drug-abusing women will decrease their use during this first trimester, they tend to increase their use through the second and then slightly lessen it in the third trimester.

There are several hypothesized reasons for the spontaneous decrease in drinking during pregnancy. Research evidence points to a fluctuation in alcohol use in relationship to estrogen and progesterone levels. Another possible explanation for the decreased alcohol consumption is the frequency of nausea during pregnancy, making alcohol consumption unpalatable. It has also been suggested that the reduction in alcohol intake spontaneously accompanying pregnancy is a fetoprotective mechanism guarding the fetus against noxious substances (Hook, 1976; Little, Schultz, & Mandell, 1976).

Maternal Alcohol Blood Levels: What is a Dangerous Dose?

Although there is no absolutely safe level of alcohol ingestion during pregnancy, when the mother drinks less than 1 oz alcohol daily, the risk of abnormalities appears low (Cooper, 1987). Twelve ounces of beer, 5 oz table wine, and a mixed drink with 1.5 oz 80-proof alcohol all contain approximately the same amount of absolute alcohol. A significant decrease in birth weight, however, has been observed in some pregnant women who ingest an average of 1 oz alcohol daily (Little, 1977). Spontaneous abortions have also occurred with such low intake twice a week (Harlap & Shiono, 1980; Kline, Shrout, Stein, Susser, & Warburton, 1980). Having three drinks a week in the first trimester and two drinks a week in the third trimester has been associated with attention deficits and slower reaction times among children at 13 months (Gusella & Fried, 1984).

Binge drinking—that is, when five or more drinks are consumed at a time—ranging from two times weekly to two to three times a month has been linked to structural brain abnormalities (Altman, 1979). Moderate drinking (two to four drinks daily) has also been associated with spontaneous abortions, decreased fetal weight gain, and neonatal behavioral decrements such as reduction in body activity, increase in tremors, and poor habituation. Heavy drinking (more than four drinks daily) increases the risk of stillbirth or spontaneous abortion in the first trimester and possibly the second trimester, affects infant sleep states, and has been related to poor muscle tone, jitteriness, and poor sucking responses. At very high maternal drinking levels, the infant is at serious risk for the development of classical FAS. These reported effects seem to be independent of other factors such as nutrition and smoking (Food and Drug Administration [FDA], 1981).

Thus, with an increased consumption of 1–2 oz daily, the risk of abnormalities may approach 10%. The odds increase to 19% when the mother drinks 2 oz or more daily (Cooper, 1987). A chronic alcoholic's risk of producing a clinically abnormal child may be 40% or more (Hanson et al., 1978). The exposure of the fetal nervous system to moderate to large concentrations of alcohol, causing repeated episodes of severe acidosis and hypoxia, may be important factors in the impairment of neurologic functioning (Fetal alcohol syndrome, 1978). Animal studies have also shown that bouts of drinking may damage the developing brain even at the end of pregnancy (Mukherjee & Hodgen, 1983).

Some of the damage assumed to have occurred during pregnancy, however, may be due to drinking while breast-feeding. During lactation, the amount of alcohol in the mother's bloodstream is transferred to her milk in the same amounts. Babies of mothers who consume alcohol may show pseudo-Cushing's syndrome characterized by high levels of the hormone cortisol and of glucose in the bloodstream; additionally, truncal obesity, purple abdominal striations, easy bruising, and a "moon" or "balloon" face have been observed. Evidence from animal studies indicates that drinking blocks the secretion of oxytocin, thereby preventing milk ejection; the consequence is a reduction in the amount of milk supplied to the infant (Altman, 1979).

Alcohol is also a direct testicular toxin, and heavy alcohol consumption (five or more drinks daily) is related to decreased spermatogenesis (Altman, 1979). Studies have not identified any effects of chronic paternal alcohol consumption on infant outcome (Bennett, Sorette, & Greenwood, 1982; Kuzma & Sokol, 1982; Randall, Burling, Lochry, & Sutker, 1982); however, women who drink heavily are often married to men who drink as heavily (Gomberg, 1975).

All of these reported increased risks with consumption of alcohol during pregnancy may, however, be overestimates. Reported studies of drinking have relied on self-reports, which are likely to be inexact especially for the heavy or dependent drinker (National Institute or Alcohol Abuse and Alcoholism, 1984). Rosett (1980) and Sokol (1980, 1982) question the correlation of increased risk with the so-called moderate drinker because of this. Nevertheless, in the absence of research establishing a safe drinking period or level, the U. S. Surgeon General advises pregnant women to abstain from drinking (National Clearinghouse for Alcohol Information, 1985). Only then can there be some assurance that a susceptible fetus will avoid alcohol's effects.

PREVENTION STRATEGIES

The National Healthy Mothers, Healthy Babies Coalition (see Appendix A) was founded in 1981 to promote preventive health habits for all pregnant women by developing education materials and networks to distribute them. Basic educational materials include topics such as smoking and pregnancy, alcohol and drug use, nutrition, and prenatal care. It has also coordinated efforts with the American Lung Association, the Office on Smoking and Health, March of Dimes, and National Cancer Institute (Wilner et al., 1987). This National Coalition serves as an extremely helpful resource when developing and delivering preventive health care services related to substance abuse for pregnant women.

Caffeine

Although information about caffeine's effects is still inadequate, enough is known to merit public education efforts for women of childbearing age. Toward this goal, the FDA is communicating through all Public Health Service programs serving pregnant women advice about caffeine use and is urging health professional organizations to notify their members of the latest scientific information about caffeine's effects. The message will also be spread through FDA professional and consumer publications. Many women, however, will be missed by these efforts and must be reached through community education programs.

Newly pregnant women must be cautioned about caffeine's effects, and their caffeine intake should be self-monitored. Although the effects of caffeine on the growing embryo and fetus do not appear to be as dramatic as the effects of smoking or drinking alcohol, caffeine nevertheless should be used cautiously.

Smoking

A 1980 Roper poll found that almost 50% of women do not know that smoking increases the risk of miscarriage and stillbirth (Ernster, 1987). This lack of awareness may change due to new warning labels that began to appear on cigarette packages and ads in October 1985. An example of one such label reads, ''Surgeon General's Warning: Smoking by pregnant women may result in fetal injury, premature birth, and low birth weight'' (Ernster, 1987, p. 22). These warnings, however, occupy only a small portion of an ad which often portrays women who smoke as healthy, appealing, and self-confident (Ernster, 1987).

Women *must* be educated about the damaging effects of smoking. They need to know that maternal smoking has been tied strongly to producing small babies, and that abortion, stillbirth, and neonatal complications occur more frequently when a pregnant woman smokes. Despite negative attitudes in the health education field toward scare tactics to achieve this goal, Sutton (1982) found that fear-arousal communication can be effective.

Health education efforts must be directed toward the childbearing population, especially high-risk groups, through mass media efforts, programs provided to school and community groups, and during health provider–client contacts. Counseling by a woman's primary care provider appears to be the most effective strategy (American Lung Association, 1982) and although group counseling, self-help materials, and mass media efforts are useful, they should not be used as the primary method of prevention. Social support is also an important adjunct to success. Unfortunately, a survey done as late as 1985 found that almost none of 1500 health care providers reported counseling pregnant women about the hazards of smoking. A ''Helping Smokers Quit Kit'' can be obtained by health care providers through the National Cancer Institute (Wilner et al., 1987).

Smoking must be recognized and dealt with as a true addiction. A pregnant woman's smoking behavior should be assessed when she calls for her first prenatal appointment; if necessary, an appointment scheduled solely for the purpose of discussing the possible effects of nicotine can be planned. Fielding and Yankauer (1978) suggest obtaining a carboxyhemoglobin or expired carbon monoxide level on every woman during the first prenatal visit and recommend subsequent testing during later prenatal visits for women who smoke.

Wilner, Blatt, and Naah (1985) developed a three-part system of intervention for smoking mothers who were also often low-income, teen-aged, and single parents. The three parts included provider training, a reminder system, and patient education materials. Providers followed four steps using the acronym STOP for Sympathize, Take a smoking history, Offer information, and Propose a quitting date (Wilner et al., 1987).

Authorities suggest weekly visits during the first trimester to reinforce smoking cessation advice (Lincoln, 1986). Each time the pregnant woman is seen, she should be asked about her smoking habits. Suggestions for altering smoking habits and referral to proven smoking cessation programs provide the pregnant woman with increased incentive to continue her efforts to stop smoking. The CDC has issued a monograph on the "Planning and Evaluation of Smoking Cessation Programs for Pregnant Women," which summarizes these programs (Wilner et al., 1987).

Health care providers must begin to advocate that government and commercial insurance programs cover the cost of approved smoking cessation activities. MacArthur and Knox (Giving up smoking, 1988) found an increase in birth weight when pregnant women stop smoking at any time up to 30 weeks' gestation, with the greatest effect seen when women stop before 16 weeks' gestation.

A 1985 report estimated that 20%–25% of women who smoke at the beginning of their pregnancy will quit on their own, and up to 30% could quit as a result of aggressive intervention programs (Institute of Medicine, 1985). Many believe that results of these programs are really about half this figure (Lincoln, 1986). For example, Windsor et al. (1985) found through a randomized trial of smoking cessation methods that even though a tailor-made program for pregnant women was more effective, only 14% actually stopped smoking. Sexton and Hebel (1984) showed greater reductions at 43% versus 20% in a control group with little variation explained by maternal characteristics (Hebel, Nowicki, & Sexton, 1985). Fifty percent of both groups exposed to some form of treatment, however, resumed smoking by 3 months after delivery. Forty percent of the remaining women were still not smoking after 3 years.

Relapse prevention must be done through continuous contact with these women after delivery. A British birth survey analyzed by Rush (Effects of maternal smoking, 1988) showed that children of women who smoked during pregnancy and after birth, as well as mothers who recently took up the habit, performed significantly lower in school than children of nonsmokers. Social covariants, however, accounted for about 75% of this effect.

Smoking among women must be considered a global public health problem. Public policy measures should include increasing cigarette taxes, cutting subsidies for growing tobacco with assistance for developing alternate crops, and prohibiting the sale of cigarettes through vending machines. Restrictions on smoking in the workplace are promising for encouraging smokers to quit and reduce the risks of passive smoking; however, employers could make special efforts toward their pregnant employees. Strategies to limit or ban cigarette marketing and advertising aimed at women must also be considered (Pinney, 1987).

Research is still needed, however, to ascertain whether smoking cessation during pregnancy is hazardous to the fetus (Sachs, 1985). It must also be pointed out that smoking cessation might not be a top priority for some pregnant women and that pregnancy, itself, is a time of many changes plus anxiety, which tends to increase the woman's vulnerability toward smoking at this time.

Alcohol

For prevention strategies to be effective in reducing the fetal effects of maternal alcohol ingestion, women must be reached *before* they become pregnant. Health providers have the responsibility to educate women who are contemplating pregnancy about the adverse effects drinking can have on pregnancy outcome. Young teenagers and women of all ages within the childbearing population must be provided with the facts about alcohol's effects on the growing baby. Visits to family planning clinics and gynecologic visits are ideal times to share this information with women and so is the first telephone contact a pregnant mother makes with her physician's or midwife's office.

Women must be educated as early in the pregnancy as possible about the importance of abstaining from drinking alcohol. For example, 90% of respondents in a recent survey (Little, Grathwohl, Streissguth, & McIntyre, 1981) knew that drinking while pregnant may be harmful; however, 75% of these individuals thought that an average of more than three drinks per day was safe.

Although education of the mother should be emphasized, it is important that this message be delivered without guilt, which may lead to even heavier drinking. Although possible teratogenic effects may have occurred already, any decrease in alcohol intake, even in the second to third trimester, may decrease the extent of fetal alcohol effects (Rosett, Ouellette, Weiner, & Owens, 1978).

Consumer pamphlets should be available in public areas such as libraries and markets. The NCALI (see Appendix A) is an excellent resource for obtaining lay publications. The DO IT NOW Foundation, the March of Dimes Birth Defects Foundation, the National Healthy Mothers, Healthy Babies Coalition, and the Pregnancy and Health Program at the University of Washington School of Medicine provide additional sources of information (see Appendix A).

A warning label law, as part of an Omnibus Drug Bill, was passed by Congress. As of November 1989, every bottle and can of alcohol sold must carry a label that states, "According to the Surgeon General, women should not drink alcoholic beverages during pregnancy because of the risk of birth defects. . ." (Eicher, 1988, p. C-1). Ultimately, the National Council on Alcoholism would like to see such warnings included in alcohol advertising.

Although knowledge of the adverse effects of alcohol during pregnancy is important and has increased appreciably, the proportion of women who drink at least 1 oz of absolute alcohol each day has remained constant (Streissguth, Darby, Barr, Smith, & Martin, 1983). The key to prevention of the teratogenic effects of alcohol lies not only in education efforts directed toward the lay public, but also toward health care professionals. In fact, education of health care providers to intervene with alcohol-abusing pregnant women may be the most rational and cost-effective approach to preventing fetal alcohol effects (National Institute on Alcohol Abuse and Alcoholism, 1984). Sokol and Miller (1980) suggest that clinicians do not identify these potentially high-risk cases three out of four times. Character traits, such as age, education, and the use of other drugs, are not reliable predictors in assessing the extent of a woman's drinking during pregnancy. Instead, a systematic drinking history is still the most practical for identifying women at such risk (Weiner, Rosett, Edelin, Alpert, & Zuckerman, 1983).

Sokol and Miller (1980) have detailed a protocol for evaluating alcohol intake during pregnancy. They recommend that assessment of alcohol use be an integral part of the obstetric history and should include the effects, if any, of alcohol on physical, social, family, economic, and psychologic functioning of the woman. Appropriate referral to an alcohol counselor, program, and support group such as Alcoholics Anonymous should be made when necessary. Lee (1987) believes that all such pregnant women who abuse drugs should be treated within an inpatient setting.

STREET DRUGS

Marihuana

Marihuana is one of the most widely used psychoactive substances, with about 25% of Americans aged 18–25 using it to some degree (U. S. Department of Health, Education, and Welfare, 1980). A considerable amount of marihuana use also occurs among women of childbearing age. According to Hingson et al. (1982), 10% of women of childbearing age in the United States smoke marihuana.

THC, delta-9-tetrahydrocannabinol, is the main psychoactive ingredient of cannabis. THC interacts with several neurotransmitters and affects the limbic system directly by causing slow-wave activity. Heath, Fitzjarrell, Garey, and Myers (1979) report ultrastructural synaptic alterations with clumping of synaptic vesicles and inclusion bodies among primates examined after long-term marihuana exposure. In humans, chronic use has been identified by a state of withdrawal, apathetic indifference, general mental and physical deterioration, and social stagnation (Nahas, 1986). Marihuana and THC have also been described as inducing immunologic impairment and malignant transformations in the lung. In animal studies, cannabis has been associated with disruptive effects among all phases of reproductive function by direct action on the hypothalamic-pituitary axis and gonads (Nahas, 1984).

The popular classification of marihuana as a "soft" drug is misleading in view of the acute and chronic adverse effects associated with its use (Nahas, 1986). It is only in recent years, however, that the potential effects of marihuana and its substances on human development have been scrutinized (Abel, 1983). Furthermore, studies of the potential effects of marihuana on the fetus and newborn have often been contradictory or inconclusive. Abel (1985) attributes this to many of these mothers being users of other drugs as well and the potential for drug-related undernutrition with cannabinoid compounds, which depress food and water consumption.

Charlebois and Fried (1980) identified the protective effects of a high-protein diet against animal fetal demise when exposed to marihuana.

Greenland, Staisch, Brown, and Gross (1982) and Fried (1980, 1982) in a preliminary report, however, identified no difference in birth weight, length, or head circumference among infants of marihuana users and nonusers. An alternate explanation was suggested by Tennes and coworkers (1985), who noted a decrease in marihuana use among women as their pregnancy progressed. This report also indicated that some protection from the potentially harmful effects of cannabis on fetal development may be due to the partial restriction of cannabis compounds by the placenta. Abel, Bush, Dintcheff, and Ernst (1981) also found that the most sensitive period for marihuana's effects on intrauterine growth retardation is the last trimester of pregnancy.

The CNS develops extensively during the postnatal period (Fried, 1985). Some studies (Fried, 1980, 1982) have identified altered neurobehavioral effects among children exposed to marihuana in utero. These effects include developmental differences, altered visual responses, changes in state regulation, increased tremors, and peculiar cry. Fried (1985) has further identified that the visual systems among these marihuana-exposed infants continue to be delayed at ages 3–6. Increases in myopia, strabismus, abnormal oculomotor function, and optic disks were identified. A decrease in mental development was also noted among those children with a decrease in visual response.

Other findings (Tennes et al., 1985), however, do not suggest that fetal or postnatal exposure to marihuana is associated with marked deficits in CNS functioning. This discrepancy may be due to the decreased maternal use described above or unknown differences among the subjects and methodologies used in the different studies.

There is some agreement, however, in that no increase in teratogenicity among the marihuana-exposed infants was identified in either of the studies described above. Abel (1985) substantiated this result by stating that prenatal exposure to cannabinoids did not produce gross malformations in humans and only did so in mice after high intraperitoneal doses. Linn et al. (1983) and Gibson, Baghurst, and Colley (1983) also reported that an increase in malformations among marihuana-exposed infants only occurred when potentially confounding variables were not controlled. For example, Hingson et al. (1982) and Qazi et al. (1982, 1983)

reported features similar to FAS among marihuana-exposed infants. Tennes et al. (1985), however, were unable to replicate this finding. Linn et al. (1983) were also unable to identify teratogenic effects among marihuana-exposed infants when specific maternal health, demographic, and drug histories were considered.

The teratogenic influence of cannabis may therefore be one of potentiation. For example, Nahas (1986) indicated that some of the consequences attributed to alcohol use may be partially caused by marihuana. Majewski (1981) also explained that FAS features tend to normalize with age and that findings may be transient (Fried, 1985). Rosett and coworkers (1983), however, identified an increase in congenital anomalies among women who drank heavily with no increase in risk with the use of cigarettes or marihuana.

Cocaine

It is now believed that 5 million Americans use cocaine regularly (Abelson & Miller, 1985) and that the use among pregnant women has paralleled this escalation (Chasnoff, Burns, Schnoll, & Burns, 1985). Unfortunately, the erroneous assumption that cocaine is not truly addictive or harmful to the fetus has remained throughout its escalation of use.

Cocaine readily crosses the placental barrier due to its high water and lipid solubility (Wilson, 1973). When absorbed, cocaine is a potent CNS stimulant that acts partially by preventing the reuptake of norepinephrine, causing vasoconstriction, hyperpyrexia, tachycardia, uterine contractions, and an acute rise in blood pressure. Furthermore, plasma cholinesterase, which helps to metabolize cocaine is lower in infants and during pregnancy (Bingol, Fuchs, Diaz, Stone, & Gromisch, 1987).

The use of cocaine during pregnancy has been associated with an increase in preterm labor and delivery and small-for-gestational age infants (LeBlanc, Parekh, Naso, & Glass, 1987; MacGregor et al., 1987), spontaneous abortions, and abruptio placenta (Bingol et al., 1987; Chasnoff et al., 1985). Cerebral infarction has also been noted with the newborn (Chasnoff, Bussey, Savich, & Stack, 1986). These adverse effects on the fetus can be attributed to vasoconstriction of the uteroplacental complex coupled with the direct and adverse hypoxia, hypertensive, anorexic, and uterine contractive effects of cocaine. The incidence of these fetal complications seems to be just as great when the mother uses cocaine during the first part of her pregnancy as when she uses the drug during her entire pregnancy (Chasnoff, 1987).

Possible teratogenic effects of cocaine on the developing fetus are just now being identified. For example, Bingol et al. (1987) concluded that cocaine abuse was associated with a higher malformation rate when compared to polydrug abusers and women who were drug free. These malformations involved heart and skull defects. It is speculated that the cocaine-induced vasoconstriction, sudden hypertension, or cardiac arrhythmias may interrupt fetal circulation causing disruption or deformation of morphogenesis. The role of hyperpyrexia must also be considered. Nine of 75 infants born to cocaine-using women in Chasnoff's (1988) study had malformations of the genitourinary tract, which included prune belly syndrome, pseudohermaphroditism, hypospadias, undescended testis, and hydronephrosis.

Unlike opiate-exposed infants, neonatal cocaine drug withdrawal is often mild to moderate. The normal triad of neurologic, gastrointestinal, and respiratory symptomatology seen in opiate-exposed newborns is often transient, mild, or not seen with cocaine-exposed infants (Madden, Payne, & Miller, 1986; Smith, 1988). Chasnoff and colleagues (1985), however, did observe a significant depression of interactive behavior and a poor organizational response to environmental stimuli among infants exposed to cocaine. In fact, Chasnoff (1988) classified cocaine-exposed infants as "...fragile infants with very low thresholds for overstimulation" (p. 99).

A decreased ventilatory response to carbon dioxide has also been identified among cocaine-exposed infants (Ward et al., 1986), thus placing them at a higher (15%) risk for sudden infant death syndrome (Chasnoff, 1987). The mean gestational age of these infants is reduced, and when prematurity is controlled for, these infants are also significantly lower in birth weight, length, and head circumference than infants born drug free. The reduced mean gestational age and weight-for-gestational age among these neonates are the two factors with the greatest implications for the long-term prognoses of these infants (Chasnoff, 1988).

Opiates

In the United States, the most commonly abused opioid is heroin. Maternal complications from the illegal use

of this drug include hepatitis, tetanus, pneumonia, bacteremia, cardiac disease (especially endocarditis), tuberculosis, and diabetes mellitus. Connaughton, Finnegan, Schut, and Emich (1975) identified, however, that morbidity in infants born to drug-dependent women was directly related to the amount of prenatal care received as well as to the type of narcotic dependence. Toxemia, for example, increased 15%–50% among heroin-dependent women when no prenatal care was given (Finnegan, 1978).

Infants born to opiate-dependent mothers are often lower in weight and Apgar scores. Postnatal problems besides withdrawal include jaundice, aspiration pneumonia, transient tachypnea, respiratory distress syndrome, and congenital malformations (Ostrea & Chavez, 1979). A decreased response to carbon dioxide and a five- to tenfold increase in risk of sudden infant death syndrome has also been identified among these infants (Ward et al., 1986).

Neonatal withdrawal from opiate abuse includes CNS hyperirritability, gastrointestinal dysfunction, respiratory distress, and vague autonomic symptoms (Finnegan, 1978). Studies have also shown that infants born to narcotic-addicted women, as well as those women maintained on methadone during pregnancy, were less able to interact than control infants born to drug-free women (Finnegan, 1985; Strauss, Lessen-Firestone, Starr, & Ostrea, 1975). Thus, the potential for disturbance in the mother-infant attachment process is present.

By 1975, 70,000-80,000 heroin addicts were in methadone maintenance programs with a significant portion being of childbearing age (Hutchings, 1985). The reports of methadone treatment during pregnancy, however, are conflicting. Although there is the advantage of improved intrauterine growth when mothers use methadone versus heroin, severe and prolonged withdrawal has been noted among neonates exposed to methadone in utero (Annunziato, 1971; Chasnoff, Hatcher, & Burns, 1982; Connaughton et al., 1975; Kandall et al., 1976; Zelson, Sook, & Casalino, 1973).

The rationale for weight gain among methadone-exposed versus heroin-exposed infants is also poorly understood. Arrested cell growth and multiplication have been identified among heroin-exposed fetuses (Naeye, Blanc, LeBlanc, & Khatamee, 1973), but not among those exposed to methadone. Reduction in head circumference, however, is consistent with both populations when compared to controls (Lifschitz, Wilson,

Smith, & Desmond, 1985). Methadone may alter levels of maternal steroids (Glass, Rajegowda, & Mukherjee, 1973) or produce hyperglycemia in the mother and fetus (Borison, Fishburn, Bhide, & McCarthy, 1962; Vassalle, 1961). The weight gain may also just reflect the better general health and nutrition of addicts in methadone programs (Doberczak, Thornton, Berstein, & Kandall, 1987).

As discussed above, methadone-exposed infants still remain smaller for gestational age with smaller head circumferences than controls. Neurologic and developmental testing also show significantly more abnormal reflexes and muscle tone, nystagmus, and delayed developmental milestones (Rosen & Johnson, 1985). Chavez, Ostrea, Stryker, and Strauss (1979) and Nelson, Ehrlich, Calhoun, Mattucci, and Finnegan (1987) also identified a higher incidence of strabismus, nystagmus, and ocular torticollis among infants of drug-dependent mothers maintained on higher doses of methadone. The ventilatory response of these infants has also been shown to be depressed for the first 2–4 weeks of life (Olsen & Lees, 1980).

As schoolchildren, these youngsters continue to do poorly with lower scores in receptive language, abnormal fine and gross motor coordination, decreased attention span, and increased incidence of behavior and academic problems. The comparison group used in this study, however, also began to show poor performance after some time. Differences between the two groups began to diminish. Thus, environmental effects must be considered (Rosen & Johnson, 1985). For example, as a group, methadone mothers require more assistance in parenting (Fiks, Johnson, & Rosen, 1985). This may be true of drug-dependent parents in general, however, and must always be considered as a major variable within any research measuring the effects of drug abuse on children. Only by using such a transactional model of analysis and intervention can the appropriate etiologic factors and results of maternal drug abuse be accurately assessed and prevented.

Prevention Strategies

Information about drug effects during the childbearing period is noticeably lacking. Warnings in the *Physicians' Desk Reference* are almost always the same: "Safe use in pregnancy, lactation, or in women of childbearing age has not been established. The use of the drug in pregnant women requires that its potential benefits be weighed against possible hazards to the patient as well as to the fetus." The same may be stated about nonprescription and street drugs. A step in the right direction is an FDA requirement that manufacturers show on the labels of prescription drugs all available information about the potential risks to the fetus. Five categories have been established for adverse effects of systemic drugs that may be taken in pregnancy. These categories range from the first category (*Category A*) comprised of drugs for which well-controlled studies have failed to show fetal risk to the fifth category (*Category X*) comprised of drugs contraindicated in pregnancy because they are associated with fetal abnormalities in either human or animal studies and whose potential risks "clearly outweigh the potential benefits" (FDA requires, 1979). Manufacturers of drugs with recognized utility during labor and delivery must provide information regarding the effects on both the mother and the infant—for example, indicating the possibility that forceps or some other intervention may be necessary or describing the effect of the drug on later growth. Information on drug excretion in human milk and its potential effect on the breast-fed infant must be noted on the label. Unfortunately these requirements have not been extended to nonprescription drugs.

Health providers also need to be alert to the possibility that a pregnant woman may be addicted to street drugs such as cocaine or heroin. As Chasnoff (Eleven percent, 1988) identified in his study, the majority of substance abuse cases among pregnant women are being missed because of the lack of thorough drug histories. Most medical school curricula do not offer detailed content or experience in dealing with patient substance abuse. Alcoholism and drug abuse content is also often absent or minimal in nursing curricula as well (Scavnicky-Mylant, 1987).

Many of these women complicate their pregnancies further by neglecting to seek early prenatal care. They may, in fact, "drop in" when birth is imminent, and the baby may be born suffering from the full effects of his mother's drug habits. Education, support, substance abuse treatment, and medical care must be available for these women with confidentiality assured so that pregnant addicts will seek out health services.

Substance abuse during the childbearing year is not always of maternal origin. Health professionals need to carefully evaluate their role in fostering unnecessary use of medication. The key is unnecessary use—the ultimate question being whether mother and fetus will benefit more from administering or withholding the medication. The American Academy of Pediatrics Committee on Drugs (1978) recommends that drugs known to produce significant changes in neurobehavior of the infant be avoided. The statement is not meant to suggest that women be denied reasonable pain relief during labor but rather that only the minimum effective dose of these agents be used.

If a serious inroad is to be made in curtailing abuse, nonessential use of drugs must be avoided by consumers and providers alike. There is *no* drug that has been proven safe for the developing baby. Remembering this and the serious potential dangers of prescription, OTC, and street drugs gives one pause to consider "Is this drug essential or are noninvasive and natural alternatives available?"

SUMMARY

A woman's habits during the childbearing year concerning drug use can have profound effects on the developing embryo and fetus. Although seemingly innocuous to many women, alcohol, nicotine, and caffeine—the so-called "soft drugs"—all have teratogenic potential in the developing embryo and fetus. Intake of these drugs during lactation may also result in undesirable effects on the newborn. Most soft drugs, including OTC medications, are self-prescribed; pregnant women generally are unaware that their use constitutes abuse because their consumption is considered socially acceptable by the larger drug-oriented culture in which they live.

The hard drugs—both "street" and prescription drugs—are less readily accessible, but also fairly common among pregnant and lactating women. Their teratogenic effects can be substantial and so can the problems occurring as a result of drug-induced pregnancy complications. Health providers must make a concentrated effort to become educated about the harmful effects and treatment of soft and hard drug abuse during pregnancy. No drug has yet been proven safe for the developing baby; therefore, nondrug alternatives should be used whenever possible, and if medication is needed, the minimum effective dose should be given.

REFERENCES

Abbott, P. J. (1986). Caffeine: a toxicological overview. *Medical Journal of Australia, 145,* 518–521.

Abel, E. L. (1985). Effects of prenatal exposure to cannabinoids. In T. Pinkert (Ed.), *Current research on the consequences of maternal drug abuse* (DHSS Publication No. ADM 85–1400). Washington, DC: U. S. Government Printing Office.

Abel, E. L. (1983). *Marijuana, tobacco, alcohol and reproduction.* Boca Raton, FL: CRC Press.

Abel, E. L. (1984). Prenatal effects of alcohol. *Drug and Alcohol Dependence, 14,* 1–10.

Abel, E. L., Bush, R., Dintcheff, B. A., & Ernst, C. A. S. (1981). Critical periods for marihuana-induced intrauterine growth retardation in the rat. *Neurobehavioral Toxicology and Teratology, 3,* 351–354.

Abel, E. L., & Dintcheff, B. (1978). Effects of prenatal alcohol exposure on growth and development in rats. *Journal of Pharmacology and Experimental Therapeutics, 207,* 916–921.

Abelson, H. I., & Miller, J. D. (1985). A decade of trends in cocaine use in the household population. In N. Kozel & E. Adams (Eds.), *Cocaine use in America: Epidemiologic and clinical perspective* (DHHS Publication No. ADM 85–1414). Washington, DC: U.S. Government Printing Office.

Altman, G. (1979). *Alcohol as a risk factor in pregnancy.* Seattle: University of Washington (Pregnancy and Health Program).

American Academy of Pediatrics, Committee on Drugs. (1978). Effect of medication during labor and delivery on infant outcome. *Pediatrics, 62,* 402–403.

American Lung Association. (1982). *Smoking and pregnancy: Handbook for health care providers.* New York: Author.

Andrews, J., & McGarry, J. M. (1972). A community study of smoking in pregnancy. *British Journal of Obstetrics and Gynecology, 79,* 1057–1073.

Annunziato, D. (1971). Neonatal addiction to methadone. *Pediatrics, 47,* 787.

Anton, A. H. (1979). Catecholamines during pregnancy and their effects on the fetus. *Pediatric Adolescent Endocrinology, 5,* 110–125.

Asmussen, I. (1978). Arterial changes in infants of smoking mothers. *Postgraduate Medical Journal, 54,* 200–205.

Barnes, D. E., & Walker, D. W. (1981). Prenatal ethanol exposure permanently reduces the number of pyramidal neurons in rat hippocampus. *Developmental Brain Research, 1,* 333–340.

Beaulac-Baillargeon, L., & Desrosiers, C. (1987). Caffeine-cigarette interaction on fetal growth. *American Journal of Obstetrics and Gynecology, 157,* 1236–1240.

Bennett, A. L., Sorette, M. P., & Greenwood, M. R. C. (1982). Effect of chronic paternal ethanol consumption on 19-day rat fetuses. *Federation Proceedings, 41,* 71.

Bills, B. (1980). Nursing considerations: Administering labor-suppressing medications. *American Journal of Maternal Child Nursing, 5,* 252–256.

Bingol, N., Fuchs, M., Diaz, V., Stone, R., & Gromisch, D. (1987). Teratogenicity of cocaine in humans. *Journal of Pediatrics, 110,* 93–96.

Borison, H., Fishburn, B., Bhide, N., & McCarthy, L. (1962). Morphine-induced hyperglycemia in the cat. *Journal of Pharmacology and Experimental Therapeutics, 138,* 229–235.

Brooten, D., Peters, M., Glatts, M., Gaffney, S., Knapp, M., Cohen, S., & Jordan, C. (1987). A survey of nutrition, caffeine, cigarette and alcohol intake in early pregnancy in an urban clinic population. *Journal of Nurse Midwifery, 32,* 85–90.

Charlebois, A., & Fried, P. (1980). The interactive effects of nutrition and cannabis upon rat perinatal development. *Developmental Psychobiology, 13,* 591–605.

Chasnoff, I. (1987). Perinatal effects of cocaine. *Contemporary OB/GYN, 29,* 163–179.

Chasnoff, I. J. (1988). Cocaine: Effects on pregnancy and the neonate. In I. J. Chasnoff (Ed.), *Drugs, alcohol, pregnancy, and parenting.* Boston: Kluwer Academic Publishers.

Chasnoff, I. J. (1990, February). *Substance abuse in pregnancy.* Paper presented at the Ninth Annual Research Conference sponsored by The University of South Florida College of Nursing and Sigma Theta Tau Delta Beta Chapter, Tampa.

Chasnoff, I., Burns, W., Schnoll, S., & Burns, K. (1985). Cocaine use in pregnancy. *New England Journal of Medicine, 313,* 666–669.

Chasnoff, I., Bussey, M., Savich, R., & Stack, C. (1986). Perinatal cerebral infarction and maternal cocaine use. *The Journal of Pediatrics, 108,* 456–459.

Chasnoff, I., Hatcher, R., & Burns, W. J. (1982). Polydrug and methadone-addicted newborns: A continuum of impairment? *Pediatrics, 70,* 210–213.

Chavez, C., Ostrea, E., Stryker, J., & Strauss, M. (1979). Ocular abnormalities in infants as sequalae of prenatal drug addiction. *Pediatric Research, 13,* 367.

Christianson, R. (1979). Gross differences observed in the placentas of smokers and nonsmokers. *American Journal of Epidemiology, 110,* 178–187.

Christoffell, D., & Salafsky, I. (1975). Fetal alcohol syndrome in dizygotic twins. *Journal of Pediatrics, 87,* 963–967.

Clarren, S., Alvord, E., Smith, D., Streissguth, A., & Sumi, S. (1978). Brain malformations related to prenatal exposure to ethanol. *Journal of Pediatrics, 92,* 64–67.

Clarren, S., & Smith, D. (1978). The fetal alcohol syndrome. *New England Journal of Medicine, 298,* 163–167.

Connaughton, J., Finnegan, L., Schut, J., & Emich, J. (1975). Current concepts in the management of the pregnant opiate addict. *Addictive Disorders, 2,* 21–35.

Cooper, S. (1978). Psychotropic drugs in pregnancy: Morphological and psychological adverse effects on offspring. *Journal of Biosocial Science, 10,* 321–334.

Cooper, S. (1987). The fetal alcohol syndrome. *Journal of Child Psychology and Psychiatry, 28,* 223–227.

Davies, D. L., & Smith, D. E. (1981). Effects of perinatally administered ethanol on hippocampal development (abstract). *Alcoholism: Clinical and Experimental Research, 5,* 147.

Davies, J., Latto, I., Jones, J., Veale, A., & Wardrop, C. (1979). Effects of stopping smoking for 48 hours on oxygen availability from the blood: A study on pregnant women. *British Medical Journal, 2,* 355–356.

Day, N., Wagener, D., & Taylor, P. (1985). Measurement of substance use during pregnancy: Methodologic issues. In T. Pinkert (Ed.), *Current research on the consequences of maternal drug abuse* (DHSS Publication No. ADM 85–1400). Washington, DC: U. S. Government Printing Office.

Doberczak, T., Thornton, J., Berstein, J., & Kandall, S. (1987). Impact of maternal drug dependency on birth weight and head circumference of offspring. *American Journal of Diseases of Children, 141,* 1163–1167.

Effects of maternal smoking during, after pregnancy. (1988, November 1–14). *Ob.Gyn. News,* p. 2.

Eicher, D. (1988, December). Liquor bottles to get hazard label. *The Denver Post,* pp. C–1, C–3.

Eleven percent of gravidas may use illicit drugs. (1988, November 1–14). *Ob.Gyn. News,* p. 3.

El-Guebaly, N., & Offord, D. (1977). The offspring of alcoholics: A critical review. *American Journal of Psychiatry, 134,* 357–365.

Erb, L., & Andresen, B. (1978). The fetal alcohol syndrome. *Clinical Pediatrics, 11,* 645–649.

Ericson, A., Kallen, B., & Westerholm, P. (1979). Cigarette smoking as an etiologic factor in cleft lip and palate. *American Journal of Obstetrics and Gynecology, 135,* 348–351.

Ernster, V. L. (1987). Advertising and marketing of cigarettes to women. In M. J. Rosenberg (Ed.), *Smoking and reproductive health* (pp. 16–23). Littleton, MA: PSG Publishing Company.

FDA requires teratogenicity information labels on drugs taken during pregnancy. (1979). *Ob. Gyn. News, 14,* p. 2.

Fetal alcohol syndrome linked to later communication disorders. (1988, November 15–30). *Ob.Gyn. News,* p. 61.

Fetal alcohol syndrome: New perspectives. (1978). *Alcohol Health and Research World, 2,* 2–12.

Fielding, J. & Yankauer, A. (1978). The pregnant drinker. *The American Journal of Public Health, 68,* 836–837.

Fiks, K., Johnson, H., & Rosen, T. (1985). Methadone-maintained mothers: 3-year follow-up of parental functioning. *International Journal of the Addictions, 20,* 651–660.

Find moderate alcohol in early pregnancy, birth defects not tied. (1988, November 1–14). *Ob.Gyn. News,* p. 32.

Finnegan, L. (1976). Clinical effects of pharmacologic agents on pregnancy, the fetus, and the neonate. *Annals of the New York Academy of Sciences, 281,* 74–89.

Finnegan, L. (Ed.). (1978). *Drug dependence in pregnancy: clinical management of mother and child* (DHEW Publication No. ADM 78–678). Washington, DC: U. S. Government Printing Office.

Finnegan, L. (1985). Effects of maternal opiate abuse on the newborn. *Federation Proceedings, 44,* 2314–2317.

Food and Drug Administration. (1981). Surgeon general's advisory on alcohol and pregnancy. *FDA Drug Bulletin, 11,* MS318.

Fried, P. A. (1982). Marihuana use by pregnant women and effects of offspring: An update. *Neurobehavioral Toxicology and Teratology, 4,* 451–454.

Fried, P. A. (1980). Marihuana use by pregnant women: Neurobehavioral effects in neonates. *Drug and Alcohol Dependency, 6,* 415–424.

Fried, P. A. (1985). Postnatal consequences of maternal marihuana use. In T. Pinkert (Ed.), *Current research on the consequences of maternal drug abuse* (DHHS Publication No. ADM 85–1400). Washington, DC: U. S. Government Printing Office.

Gibson, G. T., Baghurst, P. A., & Colley, D. P. (1983). Maternal alcohol, tobacco, and cannabis consumption and the outcome of pregnancy. *Australian and New Zealand Journal of Obstetrics and Gynecology, 23,* 15–19.

Giving up smoking even late in pregnancy said to be beneficial. (1988, November 1–14). *Ob.Gyn. News,* p. 23.

Glass, L., Rajegowda, B., & Mukherjee, T. (1973). Effects of heroin on corticosteroid production in pregnant addicts and their fetuses. *American Journal of Obstetrics and Gynecology, 117,* 416–418.

Gomberg, E. S. (1975). *Alcoholism and women: State of knowledge today.* New York: National Council on Alcoholism.

Graham, J. M., Phillips, E. L. R., Herman, C. S., & Little, R. E. (1982). *Manual for the assessment of fetal alcohol effects.* Seattle: University of Washington.

Greenland, S., Staisch, K., Brown, N., & Gross, S. (1982). The effects of marihuana use during pregnancy. 1. A preliminary epidemiologic study. *American Journal of Obstetrics and Gynecology, 143,* 408–413.

Gullekson, D., & Temple, A. (1978). Maternal drug use during the perinatal period. *Family and Community Health, 10,* 31–41.

Gusella, J. L., & Fried, P. A. (1984). Effects of maternal social drinking and smoking on offspring at thirteen months. *Neurobehavioral Toxicology and Teratology, 6,* 13–17.

Hanson, J., Smith, D., & Streissguth, A. (1978). The effects of moderate alcohol consumption during pregnancy on fetal growth and morphogenesis. *Journal of Pediatrics, 92,* 457–460.

Harlap, S., & Shiono, P. (1980). Alcohol, smoking, and the incidence of spontaneous abortions in first and second trimester. *Lancet, 2,* 173–176.

Haworth, J., Ellestad-Sayed, J., Dilling, L., & King, J. (1980). Fetal growth retardation in cigarette-smoking mothers is not due to decreased maternal food intake. *American Journal of Obstetrics and Gynecology, 137,* 719–723.

Heath, R. G., Fitzjarrell, A. T., Garey, R. E., & Myers, W. A. (1979). Chronic marihuana smoking: Its effects on function and structure of the primate brain. In G. Nahas & W. Paton (Eds.), *Marihuana: Biological effects. Analysis, metabolism, cellular responses, reproduction and brain* (pp. 713–730). Oxford: Pergamon Press.

Hebel, J., Nowicki, P., & Sexton, M. (1985). The effect of antismoking intervention during pregnancy and an assessment of interaction with maternal characteristics. *American Journal of Epidemiology, 122,* 135–148.

Henderson, G. I., Turner, D., Patwardhan, R. V., Lumeng, L., Hoyumpa, A. M., & Schenker, S. (1981). Inhibition of placental valine uptake after acute and chronic maternal ethanol consumption. *Journal of Pharmacology and Experimental Therapeutics, 216,* 465–472.

Hervada, A., Feit, E., & Sagraves, R. (1978). Drugs in breast milk. *Perinatal Care, 2,* 19–25.

Hill, R. M., Craig, J. P., Chaney, M. D., Tennyson, L. M., & McCulley, L. B. (1977). Utilization of over-the-counter drugs during pregnancy. *Clinical Obstetrical Gynecology, 20,* 381–394.

Hingson, R., Gould, J. B., Morelock, S., Kayne, H., Heeren, T., Alpert, J. J., Zuckerman, B., & Day, N. (1982). Maternal cigarette smoking psychoactive substance use, and infant Apgar scores. *Obstetrics and Gynecology, 144,* 259–266.

Hogue, C., & Sappenfield, W. (1987). Smoking and low birth weight: Current concepts. In M. J. Rosenberg (Ed.), *Smoking and reproductive health* (pp. 97–108). Littleton, MA: PSG Publishing Company.

Hook, E. (1976). Changes in tobacco smoking and ingestion of alcohol and caffeinated beverages during pregnancy: Are these consequences, in part, of feto-protective mechanisms diminishing maternal exposure to embryotoxins? In S. Kelly (Ed.), *Birth defects: Risks and consequences* (pp. 173–183). New York: Academic Press.

Horning, M., Butler, C., Hill, R., & Nowlin, J. (1975). Drug metabolism in the neonate. *Life Sciences, 16,* 651–672.

Horning, M., Stratton, C., Nowlin, J., Wilson, A., Horning, E., & Hill, R. (1973). Placental transfer of drugs. In L. O. Boreus (Ed.), *Fetal pharmacology* (pp. 355–373). New York: Raven Press.

Hutchings, D. E. (1985). Prenatal opioid exposure and the problem of causal inference. In T. Pinkert (Ed.), *Current research on the consequences of maternal drug abuse* (DHHS Publication No. ADM 85–1400). Washington, DC: U. S. Government Printing Office.

Institute of Medicine. (1985). *Preventing low birth-weight.* Washington, DC: National Academy Press.

Johnson, S., McCarter, R, & Ferencz, C. (1987). Changes in alcohol, cigarette, and recreational drug use during pregnancy: Implications for intervention. *American Journal of Epidemiology, 126,* 695–702.

Jones, K., Smith, D., Streissguth, A., & Ulleland, C. (1973). Pattern of malformation of offspring of chronic alcoholic mothers. *Lancet, 1,* 1267–1271.

Juchau, M. R. (1985). Biotransformation of drugs and foreign chemicals in the human fetal-placental unit. In C. Chiang & C. Lee (Eds.), *Prenatal drug exposure: Kinetics and dynamics* (DHHS Publication No. ADM 85–1413). Washington, DC: U. S. Government Printing Office.

Kandall, S., Albin, S., Lowenstein, J., Berle, B., Eidelman, A., & Gartner, L. (1976). Differential effects of maternal heroin and methadone use on birth weight. *Pediatrics, 58,* 681–685.

Kaplan, R. (1981). Caffeine: An update. *Drug and Chemical Toxicology, 4,* 311–329.

Khoury, M. J., Weinstein, A., Panny, S., Holtzman, N. A., Lindsay, P. K., Farrel, K., & Eisenberg, M. (1987). Maternal cigarette smoking and oral clefts: A population-based study. *American Journal of Public Health, 77,* 623–625.

Kline, J., Shrout, P., Stein, Z., Susser, M., & Warburton, D. (1980). Drinking during pregnancy and spontaneous abortion. *Lancet, 2,* 176–180.

Kline, J., Stein, Z., Susser, M., & Warburton, D. (1977). Smoking: A risk factor for spontaneous abortion. *New England Journal of Medicine, 297,* 793–795.

Knutti, R., Rothweiler, H., & Schlatter, C. (1982). The effect of pregnancy on the pharmacokinetics of caffeine. *Archives of Toxicology, 5,* 187–192.

Koop, C. E. (1986). Smoking and pregnancy. *American Pharmacy, NS26,* 34–35.

Kraemer, M. J., Richardson, M. A., Weiss, N. S., Furukawa, C. T., Shapiro, G. G., Pierson, W. E., & Bierman, C. W. (1983). Risk factors for persistent middle ear effusions: Otitis media, catarrh, cigarette smoke exposure, and atopy. *Journal of the American Medical Association, 249,* 1022–1025.

Kuhnert, P., Kuhnert, B., Erhard, P., Brashear, W., Groh-Wargo, S., & Webster, S. (1987). The effect of smoking on placental and fetal zinc status. *American Journal of Obstetrics and Gynecology, 157,* 1241–1246.

Kuzma, J. W., & Sokol, R. J. (1982). Maternal drinking behavior and decreased uterine growth. *Alcoholism: Clinical and Experimental Research, 6,* 396–402.

Laegreid, L., Olegard, R., Wahlstrom, J., & Conradi, N. (1987). Abnormalities in children exposed to benzodiazepines in utero. *Lancet,* January 10, 108–109.

Lauwers, J., & Woessner, C. (1983). *Counseling the nursing mother.* New Jersey: Avery Publishing Group, Inc.

LeBlanc, P., Parekh, A., Naso, B., & Glass, L. (1987). Effects of intrauterine exposure to alkaloidal cocaine ('crack'). *American Journal of Diseases of Children, 141,* 937–938.

Lee, M. I. (1987, November 15–30). Advises hospitalizing pregnant drug, alcohol abusers. *Ob.Gyn. News,* p. 16.

Lifschitz, M., Wilson, G., Smith, E., & Desmond, M. (1985). Factors affecting head growth and intellectual function in children of drug addicts. *Pediatrics, 75,* 269–274.

Lincoln, R. (1986). Smoking and reproduction. *Family Planning Perspectives, 18,* 79–84.

Linn, S., Schoenbaum, S. E., Monson, R. R., Rosner, R., Stubblefield, P. C., & Rayn, K. J. (1983). The association of marihuana with outcome of pregnancy. *American Public Health, 73,* 1161–1164.

Lipson, A. H., Yu, J. S., O'Halloran, M. T., & Williams, R. (1981). Alcohol and phenylketonuria. *Lancet, 1,* 717–718.

Little, R. (1977). Moderate alcohol use during pregnancy and decreased birth weight. *American Journal of Public Health, 67,* 1154–1156.

Little, R., Barr, H., Herman, C., & Streissguth, A. (1980). Decreased birth weight in infants of alcoholic women who abstained during pregnancy. *Journal of Pediatrics, 96,* 974–979.

Little, R., Grathwohl, H., Streissguth, A., & McIntyre, C. (1981). Public awareness and knowledge about the risks of drinking during pregnancy in Multnomah County, Oregon. *American Journal of Public Health, 71,* 312–314.

Little, R., Schultz, F., & Mandell, W. (1976). Drinking during pregnancy. *Journal of Studies on Alcohol, 37,* 375–379.

Little, R., & Streissguth, A. (1978). Drinking during pregnancy in alcoholic women. *Alcoholism: Clinical and Experimental Research, 2,* 179–183.

Little, R., & Streissguth, A. (1981). Effects of alcohol on the fetus: Impact and prevention. *Canadian Medical Association Journal, 125,* 159–164.

Luck, W., & Nau, H. (1985). Nicotine and cotinine concentrations in serum and urine of infants exposed via passive smoking or milk from smoking mothers. *Journal of Pediatrics, 107,* 816–820.

MacGregor, S., Keith, L., Chasnoff, I., Rosner, M., Chisum, G., Shaw, P., & Minogue, J. (1987). Cocaine use during pregnancy: Adverse perinatal outcome. *American Journal of Obstetrics and Gynecology, 157,* 686–690.

Madden, J., Payne, T., & Miller, S. (1986). Maternal cocaine abuse and effect on the newborn. *Pediatrics, 77,* 209–210.

Majewski, F. (1981). Alcohol embryopathy: Some facts and speculations about pathogenesis. *Neurobehavioral Toxicology and Teratology, 3,* 129–144.

Martinez, G., & Krieger, F. (1985). 1984 Milk-feeding patterns in the United States. *Pediatrics, 76,* 1004–1008.

Mirkin, B. L., & Singh, S. (1976). Placental transfer of pharmacologically active molecules. In B. Mirkin (Ed.), *Perinatal pharmacology and therapeutics* (pp. 1–69). New York: Academic Press.

Mukherjee, A., & Hodgen, G. (1983). Maternal ethanol exposure induces transient impairment of umbilical circulation and fetal hypoxia in monkeys. *Science, 218,* 700.

Mulvihill, J., & Yeager, A. (1976). Fetal alcohol syndrome. *Teratology, 13,* 345–348.

Naeye, R., Blanc, W., LeBlanc, W., & Khatamee, M. (1973). Fetal complications of maternal heroin addiction: Abnormal growth, infection, and episodes of stress. *Journal of Pediatrics, 83,* 1055–1061.

Nahas, G. (1986). Cannabis: Toxicological properties and epidemiological aspects. *The Medical Journal of Australia, 145,* 82–87.

Nahas, G. (1984). Toxicology and pharmacology. In G. Nahas (Ed.), *Marihuana in science and medicine* (pp. 109–246). New York: Raven Press.

National Center for Health Statistics. (1985). *Provisional data from the health promotion and disease prevention supplement to the national health interview survey: U.S., January-March 1985* (DHHS Publication No. PHS 86–1250). Washington, DC: U. S. Government Printing Office.

National Clearinghouse for Alcohol Information. (1985). *Fetal alcohol syndrome* (Alcohol Topics Fact Sheet, December). Rockville, MD: National Institute on Alcohol Abuse and Alcoholism.

National Institute on Alcohol Abuse and Alcoholism. (Fall, 1984). The effects of alcohol on pregnancy outcome. *Alcohol Health and Research World, 9,* 27–31, 67.

Nelson, L., Ehrlich, S., Calhoun, J., Mattucci, T., & Finnegan, L. (1987). Occurrence of strabismus in infants born to drug-dependent women. *American Journal of Diseases of Children, 141,* 175–178.

Nieburg, P., Marks, J., McLaren, N., & Remington, P. (1985). The fetal tobacco syndrome. *Journal of the American Medical Association, 253,* 2998–2999.

Niswander, K. R., & Gordon, M. (1972). *The women and their pregnancies. The collaborative perinatal study of the National Institute of Neurological Diseases and Stroke.* U. S. Department of Health, Education, and Welfare, Public Health Service. Philadelphia: W. B. Saunders.

O'Brien, T., & McManus, C. (1977). Drugs and the human fetus. *U. S. Pharmacist, 2,* 37–57.

Olsen, G., & Lees, M. (1980). Ventilatory response to carbon dioxide of infants following chronic prenatal methadone exposure. *Journal of Pediatrics, 96,* 983–989.

Ostrea, E., & Chavez, C. (1979). Perinatal problems (excluding neonatal withdrawal) in maternal drug addiction: A study of 830 cases. *Journal of Pediatrics, 94,* 292–295.

Ouellette, E., Rosett, H., Rosman, P., & Weiner, L. (1977). Adverse effects on offspring of maternal alcohol abuse during pregnancy. *New England Journal of Medicine, 297,* 528–530.

Palmer, R., Leightman, S., Ouellette, E., & Warner, L. (1974). Malformations in offspring of a chronic alcoholic mother. *Pediatrics, 53,* 490–494.

Persson, P., Grennert, L., Gennser, G., & Kullander, S. (1978). A study of smoking and pregnancy with special references to fetal growth. *Acta Obstetricia et Gynecologica Scandinavica, 78* (Supplement), 33–39.

Pinney, J. (1987). Public health and public policy issues. In M. J. Rosenberg (Ed.), *Smoking and reproductive health.* Littleton, MA: PSG Publishing Company.

Pirani, B. (1978). Smoking during pregnancy. *Obstetrical and Gynecological Survey, 33,* 1–13.

Qazi, Q., Mariano, E., Beller, E., Milman, D., & Crombleholme, W. (1982). Is marihuana smoking fetotoxic? *Pediatric Research, 16,* 272A.

Qazi, Q., Mariano, E., Beller, E., Milman, D., Crombleholme, W., & Buendia, M. (1983). Abnormalities in offspring associated with prenatal marihuana exposure. *Pediatric Research, 17,* 1534.

Qazi, Q., Masakawa, A., Milman, D., McGann, B., Chua, A., Haller, J. (1979). Renal anomalies in fetal alcohol syndrome. *Pediatrics, 63,* 886–889.

Quigley, M., Sheehan, K., Wilkes, M., & Yen, S. (1979). Effects of maternal smoking on circulating catecholamine levels and fetal heart rates. *American Journal of Obstetrics and Gynecology, 133,* 685–690.

Randall, C. L., Burling, T. A., Lochry, E. A., & Sutker, P. B. (1982). The effect of paternal alcohol consumption on fetal development in mice. *Drug and Alcohol Dependence, 9,* 89–95.

Ravenholt, R. T. (1987). Cell to organism: Tobacco's influence on development. In M. J. Rosenberg (Ed.), *Smoking and reproductive health.* Littleton, MA: PSG Publishing Company.

Rebond, P., Groulade, J., & Groslambert, P. (1963). The influence of normal pregnancy and the post partum state on plasma proteins and lipids. *American Journal of Obstetrics and Gynecology, 86,* 820–832.

Rosen, T., & Johnson, H. (1985). Long-term effects of prenatal methadone maintenance. In T. Pinkert (Ed.), *Current research on the consequences of maternal drug abuse* (DHHS Publication No. ADM 85–1400). Washington, DC: U. S. Government Printing Office.

Rosett, H. L. (1980). A clinical perspective on the fetal alcohol syndrome. *Alcoholism: Clinical and Experimental Research, 4,* 119–122.

Rosett, H. L., Ouellette, E. M., Weiner, L., & Owens, E. (1978). Therapy of heavy drinking during pregnancy. *American Journal of Obstetrics and Gynecology, 51,* 41–46.

Rosett, H., & Weiner, L. (1985). Alcohol and pregnancy: A clinical perspective. *Annual Review of Medicine, 36,* 73–80.

Rosett, H. L., Weiner, L., Lee, A., Zuckerman, B., Dooling, E., & Oppenheimer, E. (1983). Patterns of alcohol consumption and fetal development. *Obstetrics and Gynecology, 61,* 539–546.

Sachs, B. (1985, October). *A clinical perspective: A second opinion.* Paper presented at the International Conference on Smoking and Reproductive Health. San Francisco, CA.

Sachs, B. (1987). Sharing the cigarette: The effects of smoking in pregnancy. In M. J. Rosenberg (Ed.), *Smoking and reproductive health* (pp. 134–149). Littleton, MA: PSG Publishing Company.

Sameroff, A. J., & Chandler, M. J. (1975). Reproductive risk and the continuum of care-taking casuality. In F. D. Horowitz, M. Heatherington, S. Scarr-Salapatek, & G. Siegel (Eds.), *Review of child development research: Vol. 4* (pp. 187–244). Chicago: University of Chicago Press.

Sander, L., Gould, J., Lee, A., Ouellette, E., Rosett, H. L., & Snyder, P. (1977). Effects of alcohol intake during pregnancy on newborn state regulation: A progress report. *Alcoholism: Clinical and Experimental Research, 1,* 233–241.

Saxen, I. (1974). Cleft lip and palate in Finland: Parental histories, course of pregnancy and selected environmental factors. *International Journal of Epidemiology, 3,* 263–270.

Scavnicky-Mylant, M. (1987). Alcoholism nursing: Toward a policy perspective. *Journal of Nursing Education, 26,* 294–299.

Schnoll, S. H. (1986). Pharmacologic basis of perinatal addiction. In I. J. Chasnoff (Ed.), *Drug use in pregnancy: Mother and child* (pp. 7–16). Boston: MTP Press Limited.

Sexton, M., & Hebel, J. (1984). A clinical trial of change in maternal smoking and its effect on birth weight. *Journal of the American Medical Association, 251,* 911–915.

Shaywitz, S., Cohen, D., & Shaywitz, B. (1980). Behavior and learning difficulties in children of normal intelligence born to alcoholic mothers. *Journal of Pediatrics, 96,* 363–367.

Smith, J. (1988). The dangers of prenatal cocaine use. *The American Journal of Maternal Child Nursing, 13,* 174–179.

Sokol, R., & Miller, S. (1980). Identifying the alcohol-abusing obstetric/gynecologic patient: A practical approach. *Alcohol Health and Research World,* Summer, 36–40.

Sokol, R. J. (1980). Alcohol and spontaneous abortion. *Lancet, 2,* 1079.

Sokol, R. J. (1982). Alcohol and pregnancy: A clinical perspective for laboratory research. *Substance and Alcohol Actions/Misuse, 3,* 183–186.

Srisuphan, W., & Bracken, M. B. (1986). Caffeine consumption during pregnancy and association with late spontaneous abortion. *American Journal of Obstetrics and Gynecology, 154,* 14–20.

Strauss, M. E., Lessen-Firestone, J. K., Starr, R. H., & Ostrea, E. M. (1975). Behavior of narcotic addicted newborns. *Child Development, 46,* 887–893.

Streissguth, A. (1977). Maternal drinking and the outcome of pregnancy: Implications for child mental health. *American Journal of Orthopsychiatry, 47,* 422–431.

Streissguth, A. (1978). Fetal alcohol syndrome: An epidemiologic perspective. *American Journal of Epidemiology, 107,* 467–477.

Streissguth, A., Clarren, S., & Jones, K. (1985). Natural history of the fetal alcohol syndrome: A 10-year followup of eleven patients. *Lancet, 2,* 85–91.

Streissguth, A., Darby, B., Barr, H., Smith, J., & Martin, D. (1983). Comparison of drinking and smoking patterns during pregnancy over a six-year interval. *American Journal of Obstetrics and Gynecology, 145,* 716–724.

Streissguth, A., Landesman-Dwyer, S., Martin, J., & Smith, D. (1980). Teratogenic effects of alcohol in humans and laboratory animals. *Science, 209,* 353–361.

Sullivan, F. (1976). Effects of drugs on fetal development. In R. W. Beard & P. W. Natanielsz (Eds.), *Fetal physiology and medicine: The basis of perinatology* (pp. 43–58). Philadelphia: W. B. Saunders.

Sutton, S. R. (1982). Fear-arousal communications: A critical examination of theory and research. In J. R. Eiser (Ed.), *Social psychology and behavioral medicine* (pp.303–337). New York: John Wiley & Sons.

Suzuki, K., Adamson, K., Comas-Urrutia, A., Horiguchi, T., Morishima, H., & Mueller-Heuback, E. (1971). Pharmacologic effects of nicotine upon the fetus and mother in the rhesus monkey. *American Journal of Obstetrics and Gynecology, 111,* 1092–1101.

Suzuki, K., Adamson, K., Comas-Urrutia, A., Horiguchi, T., Morishima, H., & Mueller-Heuback, E. (1974). Placental transfer and distribution of nicotine in the pregnant rhesus monkey. *American Journal of Obstetrics and Gynecology, 119,* 253–262.

Suzuki, K., Johnson, E., & Minei, L. (1980). Effect of nicotine upon uterine blood flow in the pregnant monkey.

American Journal of Obstetrics and Gynecology, 136, 1009–1013.

Taylor, B., & Wadsworth, J. (1987). Maternal smoking during pregnancy and lower respiratory tract illnesses in early life. *Archives of Disease in Childhood, 62,* 786–791.

Tennes, K., Avitable, N., Blackard, C., Boyles, C., Hassoun, B., Holmes, L., & Kreye, M. (1985). Marijuana: Prenatal and postnatal exposure in the human. In T. Pinkert (Ed.), *Current research on the consequences of maternal drug abuse* (DHSS Publication No. ADM 85-1400). Washington, DC: U. S. Government Printing Office.

Toubas, P. L., Duke, J. C., McCaffree, M. A., Mattice, C. D., Bendell, D., & Orr, W. C. (1986). Effects of maternal smoking and caffeine habits on infantile apnea: A retrospective study. *Pediatrics, 78,* 159–163.

Tuchmann-Duplessis, H. (1980). Embryonic clinical pharmacology. In G. Avery (Ed.), *Drug treatment.* New York: Adis Press.

U. S. Department of Health and Human Services. (1982). *Cancer: A report of the surgeon general* (DHHS Publication No. PHS 82-50179). Washington, DC: U. S. Government Printing Office.

U. S. Department of Health, Education and Welfare. (1980). *Marijuana and health* (DHEW Publication No. ADM 80-945). Washington, DC: U. S. Government Printing Office.

Vassalle, M. (1961). Role of catecholamine release in morphine hyperglycemia. *American Journal of Physiology, 200,* 530–534.

Vorherr, H. (1974). Drug excretion in breast milk. *Postgraduate Medicine, 56,* 97–104.

Ward, S., Schuetz, S., Krishna, V., Bean, X., Wingert, W., Wachsman, L., & Keens, T. (1986). Abnormal sleeping ventilatory pattern in infants of substance-abusing mothers. *American Journal of Diseases of Children, 140,* 1015–1020.

Weathersbee, P., & Lodge, J. (1979). Alcohol, caffeine and nicotine as factors in pregnancy. *Postgraduate Medicine, 66,* 165–171.

Weathersbee, P., & Lodge, J. (1977). Caffeine: Its direct and indirect influence on reproduction. *Journal of Reproductive Medicine, 19,* 55–63.

Weathersbee, P., Olsen, L., & Lodge, J. (1977). Caffeine and pregnancy: A retrospective survey. *Postgraduate Medicine, 62,* 64–69.

Weiner, L., & Morse, B. (1988). FAS: Clinical perspectives and prevention. In I. J. Chasnoff (Ed.), *Drugs, alcohol, pregnancy, and parenting* (pp. 127–148). Boston: Kluwer Academic Publishers.

Weiner, L., Rosett, H., Edelin, K., Alpert, J., & Zuckerman, B. (1983). Alcohol consumption by pregnant women. *Obstetrics and Gynecology, 61,* 6–12.

West, J. R., Hodges, C. A., & Black, A. C. (1981). Prenatal exposure to ethanol alters the organization of hippocampal mossy fibers in rats. *Science, 211,* 957–959.

Wilner, S., Blatt, J., & Naah, S. (1985). *Quitting for you 2.* Boston, MA: Division of Maternal Child Health, The Massachusetts Department of Public Health Smoking Intervention Program.

Wilner, S., Secker-Walker, R., Flynn, B., Solomon, L., Collins-Burris, L., LePage, S., McPherson, B., Mead, P., Arkin, E., Monaco, K., & Burton, D. (1987). How to help the pregnant woman stop smoking. In M. J. Rosenberg (Ed.), *Smoking and reproductive health* (pp. 215–222). Littleton, MA: PSG Publishing Company, Inc.

Wilson, J. G. (1973). *Environment and birth defects.* New York: Academic Press.

Windsor, R. A., Cutter, G., Morris, J., Reese, Y., Manzella, B., Bartlett, E., Samuelson, C., & Spanos, D. (1985). The effectiveness of smoking cessation methods for smokers in public health maternity clinics: A randomized trial. *American Journal of Public Health, 75,* 1389–1392.

Yaffe, S. (1979). Drugs during pregnancy. *Professional Pharmacist, 6,* 2–3.

Zelson, C., Sook, J., & Casalino, M. (1973). Neonatal narcotic addiction: Comparative effects of maternal intake of heroin and methadone. *New England Journal of Medicine, 289,* 1216–1220.

Zervoudakis, I., Fuchs, F., & Krauss, A. (1980). Infants of mothers treated with ethanol for premature labor. *American Journal of Obstetrics and Gynecology, 137,* 713–718.

Zuckerman, B. (1985). Developmental consequences of maternal drug use during pregnancy. In T. Pinkert (Ed.), *Current research on the consequences of maternal drug abuse* (DHSS Publication No. ADM 85–1400) (pp. 96–106). Washington, DC: U. S. Government Printing Office.

CHAPTER 11

CHILDREN OF ALCOHOLICS

MaryLou Scavnicky-Mylant

An estimated 7 million youngsters' lives are centered around an alcoholic parent (Children of Alcoholics Foundation, 1985). Twenty-one million adults, bringing the total to one of every eight Americans, also may suffer from the long-term effects of living in such a family environment.

Children of alcoholics are becoming one of the fastest growing, yet treatable, populations in need of child health care services. As a group, they are twice as likely as children of nonalcoholics to develop alcohol-related problems, including alcoholism (Bosma, 1975; Goodwin, Schulsinger, Hermansen, Guze, & Winokur, 1973). Sons of alcoholic fathers are four times more likely and daughters of alcoholic mothers three times more likely than others to become alcoholics (Bohman, Sigvardsson, & Cloninger, 1981; Goodwin et al., 1973). Adolescent children of alcoholic fathers tend to try marihuana, hashish, speed, and cocaine more than adolescents of nonalcoholic or depressed fathers (Johnson, Leonard, & Jacob, 1986). Daughters of alcoholics are also more likely to marry alcoholic men and continue the cycle of family alcoholism (Nici, 1979). Black, Bucky, and Wilder-Padilla (1986) identified 20.7% of children of alcoholics versus 12.9% of children of nonalcoholics married alcoholics.

A higher incidence of mental, physical, and emotional problems has also been identified among this population (Russell, Henderson, & Blume, 1984). Sons of alcoholics, from preschool through adolescence, had 60% more injuries, were five times more likely to report emotional problems, and were two and one-half times more likely to be classified as severely ill or disabled. The daughters of alcoholics, on the other hand, were three to three and one-half times more likely to be hospitalized or attend a counseling session than daughters of nonalcoholics. Preschool children of alcoholics, both male and female, were 65% more likely to experience an illness than children whose parents were not alcoholic (Putnam, 1985).

Similar findings were noted in a study of 4- to 15-year-old children of alcoholics who had an 8% increase in medical visits, double the number of significant injuries, and five times more psychiatric examinations than children of nonalcoholics (Matajcek & Baueriva, 1981). Chafetz, Blane, and Hill (1977) also discovered more serious illnesses and accidents, perhaps due to neglect, in alcoholic versus nonalcoholic families. The only large-scale study of health problems of children of alcoholics, however, is just now being carried out by the Children of Alcoholics Foundation and the Philadelphia Health Management Corporation (Woodside, 1988a). This study of children of alcoholics through age 19 has found an increase in vulnerability to both general and specific health problems. Higher admission rates for hospital care and longer hospital stays have already been identified.

Former studies have identified specific problem areas which are more common among children of alcoholics. For example, fetal alcohol syndrome is the third most frequent cause of mental retardation (Shaywitz, Cohen, & Shaywitz, 1980), which often manifests subtle signs of neurologic dysfunction such as behavioral and learning difficulties that may not present until higher cognitive processes are required. During infancy more feeding problems, vomiting, and incessant crying have been identified (Nylander, 1960).

Younger children of alcoholics are also more likely to exhibit emotional problems such as headaches, abdominal pain, tiredness, tics, nausea, enuresis, sleep problems (Nylander, 1960) or nightmares (Moos & Billings, 1982), stuttering, fears, and temper tantrums (Haberman, 1966). Migraines, asthma, depression, anxiety (Moos & Billings, 1982; Schneiderman, 1975), hyperactivity, (Goodwin, Schulsinger, Hermansen, Guze, & Winokur, 1975; Morrison & Stewart, 1971), allergies, anemia, colds or coughs, and being overweight or underweight (Moos & Billings, 1982) are also associated with being a child of an alcoholic.

Among older schoolage and adolescent children of alcoholics, Fine, Yudin, Holmes, and Heinemann (1976) identified emotional detachment, dependency, social aggression, decreased attention span, fear, emotional liability, and a preoccupation with inner thoughts. Teachers of adolescent sons of alcoholics have also described them as less emotionally controlled, less mature, and less able to handle frustration, and more impulsive, depressed, and sensitive to criticism (Tarter, Alterman, & Edwards, 1985). Teachers of 7- to 9-year-old children of alcoholics described them as problem children and identified the same emotional instability and anxiety as the above study, as well as hyperactivity and difficulty concentrating (Nylander, 1960). Thus, cognitive and behavioral problems may not manifest themselves until the schoolage years.

Besides the emotional symptoms described earlier, Haberman (1966) identified that children of alcoholics fought with peers and were frequently in trouble within their neighborhoods and schools. A 20-year longitudinal study of multiproblem children also identified that only 45% of those children who were from alcoholic families finished high school (Miller & Jang, 1977). Another study found that older adolescent males of alcoholic fathers were less able to categorize, organize and plan, and more likely to repeat grades, attend more schools, need tutoring or special classes for dyslexia, and be referred to a school psychologist than children of nonalcoholics (Schulsinger, Goodwin, Knop, Pollock, & Mikkelsen, 1985). These older adolescents also showed more impulsivity, restlessness, and inconsistency in their school work, and less verbal proficiency than children of nonalcoholics (Knop, Teasdale, Schulsinger, & Goodwin, 1985). The majority of these children experienced some sort of difficulty during the schoolage period (Miller & Jang, 1977). Lower academic levels, math and abstract problem-solving skills, reading recognition, and comprehension were identified among this population as early as 4 years of age (Marcus, 1986; Tarter et al., 1985).

Jacob, Seilhamer, and Rushe's (1989) ongoing investigation of alcoholism and family interaction and the effects on schoolaged children stresses the importance of assessing intervening variables. The degree of child impairment among alcoholic families was within normal limits as a whole, but was associated with higher levels of fathers' alcohol-related problems and psychopathology in both parents among those children who were impaired. The mother's potential ability to mediate the negative effects of familial alcoholism on children has also been demonstrated by Obuchowska (1974) who identified positive social behavior and compensatory school achievement and affiliation among those children with an emotionally satisfying mother.

Children of alcoholics are often exposed to physical, emotional, and sexual abuse as well. Many studies have found that two-thirds of children referred for child abuse and neglect come from alcoholic homes (O'Gorman, 1985). Violence and aggression were frequently recurring themes in an inpatient therapy group for children of alcoholics (Owen, Rosenberg, & Barkley, 1985). Recent reports have related up to 50%–80% of battering and incest to alcohol abuse, with females being two times more likely to be sexually abused if raised in an alcoholic home (Black, 1985).

The emotional neglect and abuse which goes on in an alcoholic family is best understood when one considers that the primary focus of an alcoholic family is the alcoholic. The children often feel unwanted, unloved, unimportant, and invisible (Woodside, 1988a). The frequent mood swings experienced by the alcoholic parent often leave the children with a high tolerance for abnormal behavior, a hypervigilance and sensitivity toward predicting behavior, and being isolated from valuable social relationships.

Many children of alcoholics learn that it is not all right to experience certain feelings and that it doesn't help to feel. Any expression of feelings is either ignored or punished. Therefore, children of alcoholics often have difficulty expressing their feelings openly (Black, 1979a). The higher incidence of psychosomatic complaints (Nylander, 1960), excessive dependency (Richards, 1979), impaired self-concept and low self-esteem (Baraga, 1978; O'Gorman, 1976), suicidal behavior (Kearney & Taylor, 1969; Padula, 1975; Tishler & McKenry, 1982), role reversal (Clinebell, 1968), interpersonal difficulties (Ellwood, 1980; Miller & Jang, 1977), and social isolation (Cork, 1969) among these children may be the outcome of such abuse and neglect.

ADULT CHILDREN OF ALCOHOLICS (ACAs)

It is not surprising that as adults, children of alcoholics continue to have problems (Woodside, 1988b). Brown and Cermak (1980; Cermak & Brown, 1982), for example, have identified several characteristics of ACAs: the issue of control, avoidance of feelings, distrust of others, overresponsibility, and the tendency to ignore their own needs. In fact, these five issues have been found to differentiate children of alcoholics from other people with emotional difficulties (Brown cited by Policoff, 1985). Fear of being out of control is primary, since it often affects all of the other issues. The ACA often equates being out of control with strong feelings and an eruption of emotions if allowed to continue too far. There is also the fundamental belief that feelings are wrong, since they have often been unacknowledged or responded to with rejection and anger.

Children of alcoholics learn to minimize, deny and repress any feelings they may have (Brown & Cermak, 1980; Cermak & Brown, 1982). Feelings must be ignored since they are a direct or immediate cause of behavior versus a potential impetus. Gravitz and Bowden (1985) state that this belief, coupled with childhood self-centeredness and negative feelings or thoughts toward an alcoholic parent which may come true, often mark the beginning of an adult child's extreme difficulties with feelings and guilt.

Children of alcoholics often relieve emotional pain by discounting the importance of their own feelings, a person, or situation. They turn many negative feelings on themselves and then evaluate themselves as bad or crazy (Gravitz & Bowden, 1985). Children of alcoholics also believe they are responsible for other's emotions and actions, thus the issue of overresponsibility develops and feeds on the self-centeredness described earlier. The child of an alcoholic may feel responsible for an alcoholic parent's drinking as well as the parent's abandonment. This leads to a tendency to ignore personal needs, which if acknowledged would reflect vulnerability and create guilt. Prior experience has also proven the futility of being vulnerable. During childhood, one survived by being dependent only at certain times. Need recognition was separated from personal reality. Coupled with guilt, ACAs equate the expression of needs with being dependent and less capable or obligated. Thus, one's own needs should be avoided, ignored, or denied, since self-control must be maintained at all costs. Another result of this sense of overresponsibility for members of one's family of origin is the inability to form primary attachments to one's own present family and frequent problematic intimate relationships (Brown & Cermak, 1980; Cermak & Brown, 1982).

Other core issues of ACAs identified by Gravitz and Bowden (1984, 1985) include an ''all-or-none'' functioning, dissociation, and a crisis orientation. ACAs demonstrate an inability to function in terms of degree.

Everything is either black or white. This phenomenon, which seems to be a central issue pervading all others, inhibits the interpretation of the environment, ability to see things in part, and the understanding of feelings. Anger only leads to violence, relaxation means depression, intimacy means smothering, and spontaneity means irrationality. Children of alcoholics think in mutually exclusive terms. Things are either all right or all wrong. Trust is either present or absent, and either a person is all good or bad. This also prevents the breaking down of a problem into small workable parts, which may further lower one's self-esteem, because imperfection equals failure.

The ''all-or-none'' phenomena may create boundary issues for the adult child especially in regard to the alcoholic parent. Dissociation, described as an emotional anesthesia, functions as a protective mechanism. It helps to separate emotion from consciousness for a child of an alcoholic. These issues eventually lead to an extremely low self-esteem since distrust of one's self is the result of ignorance about one's own feelings. The ''all-or-none'' functioning discredits anything less than perfect. Disregard for one's own needs, overresponsibility, and the lack of a sense of personal rights results. Adult children feel they are the cause for any problem and are always apologizing. Expressing a need or desire creates an overwhelming sense of anxiety and immediate rationalization (Gravitz & Bowden, 1984, 1985).

Codependency

Characteritics of ACAs are also the characteristics of codependency (Cermak, 1985). Wegscheider (1985) describes five signs of codependency: delusions, low self-worth, compulsions, frozen feelings, and medical complications. The denial or delusion originates from love, believing that other people's happiness will lead to one's own. The realization that one cannot control the feelings and behavior of another, however, induces emotional paralysis. To recognize this relationship as pathologic would require the codependent to admit one's own dysfunction. Thus, the codependent does whatever possible to minimize and rationalize the situation. The low self-worth of the codependents, however, compels them to continue engaging in approval-seeking behavior feeling that they can never do enough to ensure love and approval. (Cermak, 1985; Cruse, 1988; Wegscheider, 1985; Wegschneider-Cruse, 1988).

Compulsive behaviors may also include pulling out of relationships and systems that exert stress or living in response to others' expectations. "Whenever you sense that you have no choice in how you behave, you are in the grips of a compulsion" (Cermak, 1985, p. 13). Major codependent compulsions may be to a substance (alcohol, drugs, nicotine, sugar) or to a behavior (workaholism, power, religiosity, overspending/gambling, compulsive eating, overexercising, sexual acting out). Often these compulsive behaviors lower one's self-esteem even further and are used to keep a lid on potentially immobilizing emotions, such as fear, guilt, anger, and loneliness (Cruse, 1988; Wegscheider-Cruse, 1988). Codependents deal with the uncertainty and possible uncontrollable nature of emotions by suppressing them and making them unavailable through many of the compulsions described above.

The chronic stress codependents are exposed to may also lead to the following medical complications, though not exclusively caused by the codependency: "hypochondria, anxiety, depression, insomnia, hypertension, anorexia nervosa, bulima, colitis, bowel problems, respiratory diseases such as bronchial asthma, and cardiac irregularities on a psychosomatic basis" (Wegscheider-Cruse, 1988, p. 7). For example, Nylander (1960) identified in an earlier study that adult sons of alcoholics used more surgical, ambulatory, and hospital services as well as made more visits to physicians for drug and alcohol abuse. The female adult offspring also made more visits to physicians for gynecologic services. Recent research on eating disorders indicates a relationship between parental alcoholism and bulimia (Pyle, Mitchell, & Eckert, 1981). These physical ailments are often dismissed, however, by the codependents through their denial and delusion (Cermak, 1985).

There has been a disparate amount of empirical research to support many of the previous descriptions of ACA characteristics, however. Cermak and Brown in 1982 cited virtually no research on adults from alcoholic households. In view of this, Seabaugh's (1983) grounded theory, Scavnicky-Mylant's (1988) qualitative study, and Cermak and Brown's (1982) and Gravitz and Bowden's (1985) descriptive approaches in examining the experiential data of ACAs have been appropriate levels for research in this new knowledge area. Seabaugh (1983), for example, theorized that ACAs have experienced certain developmental failures resulting in a vulnerable adult self.

Resiliency

It is important to remember, however, that not all children of alcoholics become alcoholic, nor do they experience the degree of mental, emotional, and physical problems just discussed. Thus, some children of alcoholics may be more resilient or "invulnerable" than others. The focus of more recent research has been to identify the levels of risks as well as protective factors within alcoholic families. In the past, only short-term negative effects of parental alcoholism were explored, and coping patterns, which may explain why some children are more or less affected, have been ignored. Many more longitudinal studies are needed to explain this dilemma (Woodside, 1988b).

One notable longitudinal study of resiliency among children of alcoholics from birth to 18 years of age has been conducted by Werner (1986). This study identified that male versus female offspring had more psychological problems, and children with alcoholic mothers were more vulnerable than children with alcoholic fathers. Over half of the 49 children, however, did not develop any serious problems by the age of 18 years. Characteristics which differentiated these seemingly invulnerable children included an affectionate temperament in infancy, average intelligence, adequate communication skills in reading and writing, an achievement orientation, a responsible attitude, positive self-concept, and a more internalized locus of control. Their home environments also indicated that they had received more attention and had not experienced any prolonged separation from their primary caretaker during their first year of life. No additional siblings were born, and parental conflict was absent during the first 2 years of their life.

The generalizability of Werner's (1986) findings may be limited, however, since the subjects were all Asian-Polynesian children born on the island of Kauai, Hawaii and reared in chronic poverty. Another study of resiliency using children of mixed socioeconomic status, however, supports the findings above since a more internalized locus of control and positive perception of the family were found among those children of alcoholics described as invulnerable (Keane, 1983).

Woodside (1988b) uses an alternative way to explore resiliency by examining factors which place children of alcoholics at higher risk. Lawson, Peterson, and Lawson (1983) identify these risk factors to be lower socioeconomic background with exposure to physical abuse, less than 6 years of age at the onset of parental alcoholism, and being the oldest or only child, and lack of a supportive family environment. To generalize these results is again questionable since studies have shown that children of alcoholics in treatment, from which this sample was drawn, are different from those who do not seek treatment and often reflect a wider range of difficult situations (Woodside, 1988b).

It is also questionable whether this behavioral outcome researchers are defining as resiliency is actually a ''protective factor'' or just a reflection of the super-coping strategies used by some children of alcoholics. Woodside (1988a) describes a child's hopeless quest for perfection as the result of the parents' blame for their alcoholic drinking pattern. Children do not know or believe that alcoholism is a disease, and they truly believe that if they receive good grades and behaved perfectly at home their parents wouldn't drink.

Role Behaviors

Black (1979a) applied Adler's birth order and family systems theory to identify specific role patterns or coping behaviors among children of alcoholics. The first of these role patterns is identified as the ''responsible one,'' which is an example of a super-coping strategy and is most typical for the oldest or only child who helps to maintain stability and develop self-worth in an inconsistent home. The ''adjustor'' is another role that can be combined with the first or assumed separately by a child. The child follows directions easily, is flexible, and able to adapt to social situations. The ''placater,'' or third role, acts to decrease any guilt feelings that may have caused their parent to drink. Children who take on this role are more likely to be sociable and helpers since their primary goal is to smooth over conflicts.

The work of Black has reflected much of Wegscheider's beliefs regarding chemically dependent families, and the role behaviors identified by each are very similar. Wegscheider (1979) collected materials over a 4-year period while working with several hundred chemically dependent persons and their families. Family systems theory explains the development of the roles, since every member adapts to the chemically dependent person by assuming a role that will create the least amount of stress. These roles are not static according to Wegscheider (1981), and family members will continuously switch roles to relate to the chemically dependent person.

The specific survival roles Wegscheider (1979) speaks of are the chief enabler, family hero, scapegoat, lost child, and mascot. The chemically dependent person relies most on the chief enabler, who represses all feelings to fulfill the dependent's responsibilities. The family hero also feels responsible for the entire family and tries to relieve the pain; however, due to the progression of the disease of alcoholism, this role leads to feelings of inadequacy. The family scapegoat realizes one is only rewarded for what one does and so withdraws, often destructively, from the family to achieve a sense of belonging elsewhere. The lost child never develops close ties within the family and suffers in silence, feeling very lonely. And finally, the family mascot brings fun into the family and uses charm and humor to survive.

The works of Black (1979a) and Wegscheider (1979, 1981) do meet criteria for scientific merit and replication; however, there have been few formal, scientific investigations to validate the typologies and those that have been done have failed to support the clinical findings (Woodside, 1988b). Manning, Balson, and Xenakis (1986), for example, did not find a prevalence of type A personalities, which they equate to Wegscheider's family hero role, among schoolage and adolescent children of alcoholics.

Rhodes and Blackham (1987) also attempted to assess role behaviors in children of alcoholics. This study evaluated whether differences existed in Black's role-prescribed behaviors among adolescents from alcoholic and nonalcoholic homes. Results indicated that only the acting-out role was significantly higher in adolescents from alcoholic homes. There was no main effect found for birth order. Scavnicky-Mylant's (1988) qualitative study of the process of coping among young adult children of alcoholics also failed to identify specific role behaviors. These findings may suggest the invalidity or current stage of development of Black's and Wegscheider's role behavior typology and assumption that they are affected by birth order.

Black's and Wegscheider's works, however, do seem to answer the demand for the study of ''invulnerable'' children of alcoholics. Their findings help to create a cautious approach in making such naive interpretations of resiliency among this population at risk, since it is the very positive external appearances of the role behaviors in which children of alcoholics engage that may cause one to perceive them as invulnerable or resilient (Scavnicky-Mylant, 1984). Defending against inner feelings of shame and inadequacy, these children achieve extraordinarily on the outside (Bingham & Bargar, 1985). Authorities suggest, however, "that some children of alcoholics will remain symptom-free until they encounter adult stresses that touch on latent areas of vulnerability" (Moos and Billings, 1982, p. 161).

INTERVENTION

In the past, little attention has been focused on children of alcoholics despite the high risk for potential physical, psychologic, and social problems. In the late 1970s, programs for children of alcoholics were few and this population could still be described as the forgotten children and hidden tragedy (Bosma, 1972; Cork, 1969). Although the number of programs have increased, the literature and research on treatment interventions for this population remain sparse (Owen et al., 1985). ACAs have also gone unrecognized or misdiagnosed due to coping styles that appear strong since they often include many approval-seeking and socially acceptable behaviors (Woititz, 1983). In part, this neglect has been due to ignorance of the detrimental effects parental alcoholism has on offspring and appropriate methods of intervention, fear of legal retributions regarding parental consent, lack of organized support, and the limited mobility of children (Services for Children of Alcoholics, 1981).

Required teaching hours devoted to alcoholism in medical schools remains below 1% (Pokorny & Solomon, 1983) and below 5 hours total in most nursing schools (Hoffman & Heinemann, 1987). This minimal amount of professional instruction seems incommensurate to one of our nation's primary health problems. It has also been demonstrated that only those nursing students who were exposed to a specialized program in alcoholism were able to improve their attitudes toward alcoholism (Gurel, 1976). Numerous studies in the past have also demonstrated that nurses have negative perceptions of alcoholics (Scavnicky-Mylant, 1987). Thus, a nontherapeutic relationship may develop, because the successful treatment of alcoholism largely depends on the rapport established between therapist and client (Poiner, 1967).

Professional attitudes may also create disinterest and denial, especially when dealing with a symptomless child of an alcoholic. This avoidance can be perpetuated by the thought of intervention being only a job for specialists and that giving one's attention to a child of an alcoholic is not a legitimate concern (Services for Children of Alcoholics, 1981). Transference issues may arise especially if the professional is a child of an alcoholic without treatment. Assuming the alcoholic's denial and guilt about the harm they have caused the family may prevent the professional from confronting parents about the need for intervention for their children (Owen et al., 1985). The professionals' denials of their own pain and need for treatment may prevent them from providing specific treatment after they identify the dysfunction among their clients caused by an alcoholic upbringing.

Limitations confronting professionals in carrying out interventions with a younger population also include the legality and difficulty in obtaining parental permission. McCabe (1977), however, describes the prospects of liability as minimal since a professional would have to clearly disrupt parental custody, and actions would have to cause an injury so exceptional and evident that money damages could be awarded. The Cambridge and Somerville Program of Alcoholism Rehabilitation (CASPAR) in Massachusetts is a school-based support system that requires parental permission to allow children to attend alcohol discussion groups (see Appendix A). After 5 years, no legal problems have been reported (Services for Children of Alcoholics, 1981). The Children of Alcoholics Foundation (see Appendix A) is also presently developing a medical education program (Woodside, 1988a). This foundation has developed a Health Education Packet to provide practitioners with information for identifying and assisting children of alcoholics.

Because of the limited mobility of young children, the treatment of children of alcoholics must be accessible and convenient. Authorities (Deutsch, 1982; DiCicco, 1981; Morehouse, 1979; Services for Children of Alcoholics, 1981) have suggested that the most logical place to provide these services is the school system. Morehouse (1979) states that, "Since the parents of most of these children do not attend alcoholism programs, the schools are the most logical place to provide help to these children" (p. 146). For instance, only 15% of the nation's alcoholics and alcohol abusers receive treatment every year (Archer, 1986). DiCicco (1981) also gives the rationale that Alateen and other alcoholism services reach only a few children because of the stigma and denial associated with alcoholism. Children learn about resources only in a limited fashion.

Questions about family alcoholism need to be asked routinely during screening of all children, adolescents, and adults. Three questions such as: Do you ever worry about your mom or dad's drinking or taking of medicine or drugs? Do you ever wish they would use less? Do you ever wish they wouldn't use at all? are very helpful. Since 25% of our population is affected by alcoholism and only 10% seek out help, health professionals need to be able to identify the children of alcoholics they are involved with and intervene appropriately.

Assessment

Unfortunately, many behaviors exhibited by children of alcoholics are subtle and similar to offspring from problematic families (Ackerman, 1983). All too often these symptoms have been the focus of treatment when the primary family disease is alcoholism. Thus, the first step in identification is educating the public, professionals, teachers, and school or community volunteers about alcohol so that it can be included in the general public's knowledge base, press, routine psychologic and physical assessments, and school curricula. Children of alcoholics could then come forward knowing their feelings and reactions are normal. Newlon and Furrow (1986) also suggest using teacher referrals and classroom guidance lessons on alcoholism and the family, followed by an invitation to join a small group which would deal with the subject more personally. An estimated 11 of a possible 16 young children of alcoholics were identified in this manner. The CASPAR Alcohol Education Program, the Children Are People (CAP), and Kids are Special projects all provide teacher training and group facilitation information and materials for school-based and community support groups for young and adolescent children of alcoholics (see Appendix A).

College-based support groups have also been instituted (Donovan, 1981; Downing & Walker, 1987; Klinefelter, 1983) for this high-risk population using self-referral through campus media publicity and fliers as well as counseling and student health referrals for recruitment. A psychoeducational versus intense group therapy approach has been recommended for the 18- to 22-year-old age group because this population often assumes the hero role and has not yet experienced the full psychologic impact of parental alcoholism (Downing & Walker, 1987). Downing and Walker (1987) describe a campus-based psychoeducational support group in detail. Klinefelter (1983), on the other hand, recommends

a cognitive plus experiential group counseling approach for university students. Cruse and Wegscheider-Cruse (1988) of Onsite's Living Centered Program also support experiential therapy as an important piece of codependency treatment, since "...one cannot heal what you cannot feel..." (p. 19). The age range of clients attending the Living Centered Programs has been between 20 to over 60 years with 75% of the clients being 30–50 years old.

Unfortunately, denial is inherent in the disease of alcoholism, and offspring often do not trust or were told not to discuss their parent's drinking with outsiders. Therefore, health care providers need to be knowledgeable about the general indicators (Ackerman, 1983; Deutsch, 1982; Scavnicky-Mylant, 1986, 1987; Triplett & Arneson, 1983) that a young child or adolescent may be living with parental alcoholism (see Table 11.1), the core issues of ACAs described earlier, and typical characteristics of ACAs (Cermak, 1985) or codependency (Wegscheider, 1985) (see Table 11.2) so appropriate

Table 11.1
General Indicators of Parental Alcoholism

Frequent absences or truancy, visits to the school nurse, or morning tardiness, especially Mondays

History of stress-related illnesses, psychosomatic complaints, accidents, chronic fatigue, sleep disturbances, injuries or bruises, and substance abuse

Inappropriate behavior (overly responsible, concerned with pleasing authority figures, passive or controlling, excessive use of humor or acting out)

Fluctuating or poor status of nutrition, grooming, hygiene, or clothing

Excessive or nonexistent peer contacts

Inappropriate school performance (exaggerated concern with achievement, erratic or poor performance without evidence of a learning disability)

Reports of excessive alcohol consumption (often being very negative toward alcohol use), inconsistent or violent discipline, and minimal shared interests among family members. These children also fear any contact between their parents and school personnel.

Emotional disturbances (absent or extreme emotional response, low self-esteem, feelings of being different or powerless)

Table 11.2
Characteristics of ACAs or Codependency

Fear of losing control

Attempts to control own and other's feelings and behavior

Inability and fear of identifying and expressing feelings

Fear of conflict, people in authority, angry people, or personal criticism

Overdeveloped sense of responsibility

Approval-seeking behavior

Perfectionism

Feelings of guilt especially when expressing own needs

Physical complaints or stress-related medical illnesses

Inability to relax, let go, have fun, or be spontaneous

Harsh, even fierce, self-criticism

Low self-worth

Denial or delusions

Difficulties with intimate relationships and sexuality

Victim stance

Compulsion to a substance or behavior

More comfortable with chaotic versus secure lifestyle

Confusion about love and pity

Fear of abandonment

Tendency to react rather than act

Black and white or all-or-none thinking, especially under pressure

Delayed grief reactions

Depression

Ability to survive

---

referral and treatment are instituted. For example, all professionals should assess for family alcoholism when a child or adolescent is referred for abuse or neglect, learning problems, physical complaints, school failures, or emotional concerns.

Core Issues for Young Children of Alcoholics

Although there are still a minimum number of treatment programs for children of alcoholics (Kern, Tippman, Fortgand, & Paul, 1977/78) despite their high-risk status, a few clinicians have documented both their

goals and interventions when working with this population. These goals and interventions are often based on the basic core issues children of alcoholics face. Even though treatment needs to be individualized, some primary problems differentiate children of alcoholics from others with emotional difficulties. Professionals must become familiar with these issues because most children of alcoholics will never talk about their family situation to anyone for reasons explained by the issues they face. Children, in general, also do not have the tools or experience to know why they feel the way they do or how things are different for them. The basic core issues of young children of alcoholics, many of which are similar to ACAs identified earlier, will be described.

First of all, children of alcoholics are often preoccupied with issues of self-control. They attempt to build their self-esteem through willpower and by controlling their own and others' feelings and behavior, which leads to failure and chronic stress (Cermak, 1984; Bogdaniak & Piercy, 1987). Children of alcoholics equate strong feelings with being out of control. This belief, coupled with normal childhood egocentrism and negative feelings toward the alcoholic and coalcoholic spouse, often creates extreme difficulty with the expression of feelings, which is the second major issue to be discussed. In fact, this need for control is so strong that it not only results in the denial of feelings, but also creates a sense of overresponsibility and mistrust or an ignoring of one's personal needs (Gravitz & Bowden, 1984), which are two additional issues faced by children of alcoholics.

Difficulty in identifying, differentiating, and expressing feelings occurs as a result of the child's and family's denial system, resulting in a distorted reality and family communication pattern (Wegscheider, 1981). Even those children who seem very well adjusted have learned that it is not okay to feel (Black, 1981). Discounting or disassociating from their feelings, which are often negative, or evaluating themselves as bad or crazy functions as a protective mechanism.

Children of alcoholics may also believe they are responsible for other's emotions and actions; thus, the issue of overresponsibility develops and feeds on the normal egocentrism a young child or adolescent is experiencing. Children of an alcoholic may feel responsible for an alcoholic parent's drinking or drug use as well as their parent's abandonment of them. Thus, to protect themselves from experiencing this sense of vulnerability and guilt, the children begin to ignore their own needs. Expressions of any need or want would mean that they cannot do it alone. Prior experience has proven this to be futile. Thus, their needs should be avoided, ignored, and denied since self-control must be maintained at all costs. This additional form of self-protection also eventually leads to self-isolation and the distrust of others.

To develop trust, one needs to believe in one's own sense of value from important people, such as parents. Needs must be met in a healthy and consistent way; however, alcoholic homes are often inconsistent and unpredictable. It is not safe to trust; promises are broken, and lies prevail. Bogdaniak and Piercy (1987) project that low self-esteem may result due to the self-identity issues which then occur. For example, the adolescent child of an alcoholic becomes overly dependent on peers because of the eventual rejection of adult role models (Woititz, 1983). The adolescent, who is really looking to compensate for the lack of nurturance, then becomes subject to many disappointments (Morehouse & Richards, 1983). To compensate for this unmet need, the child continues to deny personal needs and mistrusts others, resulting in more and more isolation (Bogdaniak & Piercy, 1987).

Treatment

Treatment goals of the various programs for children and adolescents of alcoholics, as well as for adults which will be described below, reflect many of the basic core issues identified above. First of all, a safe environment needs to be provided so that these children are able to share their feelings and family secret and improve their communication skills (Bingham & Bargar, 1985; Deckman & Downs, 1982; LePantois, 1986; Owen et al., 1985). Since the family secret may be being shared for the first time, group members must be given permission to not participate and be made aware of the intense feelings of guilt they may experience afterwards. Confidentiality must be maintained except for issues of harming one's self or others (Bogdaniak & Piercy, 1987). LePantois (1986) describes telling the parents of these children that the content of the children's group will not be shared and will remain confidential.

Children of alcoholics need to know that their feelings of guilt, shame, confusion, and anger toward their parents are normal responses and do not mean that there is something wrong or bad with them (Davis, Johnston, DiCicco, & Orenstein, 1985). Alternative methods of expression, such as through drawings, puppets, poetry, music, dance and play, must be made available since many of these children have trouble even identifying their feelings. Various workbooks (Black, 1979b) and manuals (Children Are People, 1989; Moe and Pohlman, 1988) are also available for this purpose.

Deckman and Downs (1982) identified that the most dominant emotional theme for their adolescent children of alcoholics group was identifying and appropriately expressing anger. Role playing and assertiveness techniques were used. The group process itself also allows for the identification of feelings and risk necessary to express one's feelings. The group process increases self-expression by allowing group members to identify with the problems of each other (Alibrandi, 1982). In fact, overcoming feelings of isolation has been described by adolescent children of alcoholics as the most helpful aspect of their group experience (Deckman & Downs, 1982). The social isolation children of alcoholics experience stems from the family secret of alcoholism and often prevents children from bringing friends home and experiencing normal socialization (Deutsch, 1982; LePantois, 1986; Wilson & Orford, 1978). Thus, group therapy is the treatment of choice for this population to facilitate healthy social interactions with both peers and adults (Bingham & Bargar, 1985). For example, one of Robinson's (1983) primary group goals is to develop peer socialization.

Group therapy also provides for the validation of one's feelings, perceptions, and judgments (Owen et al., 1985). It provides for a universality of one's experience and decreases the feeling of being unique or the only one this is happening to (Bingham & Bargar, 1985). Bogdaniak and Piercy (1987) believe that this helps release psychic energy, which was used to deny the family problem.

Children of alcoholics begin to identify and use the group as a form of support. They begin to see the group as a caring parent who is willing to listen and respond to them (Owen et al., 1985). A trusting relationship is established by demonstrating consistent behavior such as limit setting, being on time, and keeping promises to the group members (Edwards & Zander, 1985). This supportive environment also allows the child of an alcoholic to experience a wide range of roles (LePantois, 1986), since the alcoholic family commonly involves exposure to role reversal and poor role modeling (Deutsch, 1982; Nardi, 1981).

Alternative coping methods may also be explored (Owen et al., 1985; Scavnicky-Mylant, 1988). Scavnicky-Mylant's (1988) retrospective study of young adults identified that problem-solving, or confrontive, methods of coping did not develop until late young adulthood among children of alcoholics. Forms of reversed confrontive coping, or codependent and a rather unique style of coping in comparison to the general population, were more common among these individuals.

An individual's sense of control is increased when more styles of coping are available to choose from. A child's usual, although possibly rigid and ineffective, method of coping must never be stripped away, however. A choice of alternative coping styles can only be provided, since a child has neither the resources nor coping abilities of an adult. Furthermore, a child will usually not risk using a different method of coping unless it provides the same sense of relief that the original style of coping did. Many alcoholic families, whether active or recovering, may also not be flexible enough to absorb this type of change.

Children's sense of control may also be increased within an alcoholic family environment by helping them establish more realistic boundaries, especially between themselves and their parents' illness. Children of alcoholics need to be provided with alcoholism education. By giving them information on alcoholism being an illness which affects all members of the family and their methods of coping, realistic boundaries can be set between themselves and their parents and they can begin to feel less responsible for the illness (Owen et al., 1985). Alcoholism education confronts the taboo nature of the illness and provides a sense of objectivity and intellectual mastery or control for the child (Bingham & Bargar, 1985). Feelings of powerlessness and helplessness begin to diminish.

Moe (1988) stresses that the most important information one can give children of alcoholics is that they didn't cause their parent's alcoholism, they can't cure it, and they can't control it. Black (1979b) discusses that it is helpful to further explain such concepts as blackouts, personality changes, relapses, etc. The Decisions About Drinking alcohol curriculum stresses that alcoholism is not the alcoholic's fault and that alcoholics can and do recover (Deutsch, 1982). Gravitz and Bowden (1984) believe that it is the children who never realize the effect parental alcoholism has had on them that become more vulnerable to alcoholism or marrying an alcoholic.

Children of alcoholics need to know that they are at risk for alcoholism, but the goal of alcoholism education is to make alcohol less of an emotionally charged issue (Davis et al., 1985). They must begin to separate their own self from their parents and the alcoholism in the family so they may become responsible for their own behavior and happiness. Deutsch (1982) believes that a key idea which is stressed within the Decision About Drinking alcohol education curriculum is that the children of alcoholics need and deserve help themselves. By focusing on their own developmental needs, which can be met through the group and the positive peers and adults in their lives, an increase in self-esteem may evolve. Providing specific versus global statements of praise may also help increase each child's self-esteem (Edwards & Zander, 1985).

Adult Children of Alcoholics

The goals and interventions of ACA treatment programs are also based on core issues described earlier. In fact, according to Gravitz and Bowden (1984), these issues seem to enfold in a sequential manner during recovery and require different treatment strategies and services at each stage.

The current options available for ACA/codependency treatment include self-help groups, outpatient or inpatient, and retreat style programs. Self-help groups include ACOA (Adult Children of Alcoholics), CoDA (Codependents Anonymous), and Al-Anon. Outpatient services range from weekly 1–2-hour individual or group therapy visits to 4–6-hour daily visits for 5 days to 4 weeks followed by 3–12 months of weekly aftercare. Inpatient programs may also be of a short (3–5 days) or long (2–6 weeks) duration some of which are attached to inpatient chemical dependency programs (Cruse & Wegscheider-Cruse, 1988).

Recovery for the ACA occurs in predictable stages (Cermak, 1985). Gravitz and Bowden (1984) describe five stages of recovery for ACAs. The first stage is the *survivor stage,* although recover actually does not begin until stage two, since the ACA is still in denial at this point or using rationalization and projection to deal with those issues that cannot be denied. Unless some enlightening event, such as a media release or workshop, or an intervention perhaps by a concerned friend or professional takes place, the ACA remains in this survival stage.

Stage two of emergent awareness is the *coming out* or *identification stage* where ACAs begin to identify themselves as children of alcoholics. Breaking the denial is crucial during this phase and leads to the decrease of isolation and stigma, increased awareness with a release of psychic energy formerly used to control and suppress emotions. For the first time feelings are acknowledged, legitimized, and externalized (Gravitz & Bowden, 1984). This stage must also involve a realistic assessment of one's own distorted relationship to control issues and the admission of limited power, which often causes ACAs to get stuck halfway through this stage (Cermak, 1985). Thus, the use of support groups (ACOA, CoDa, Al-Anon), education classes, or workshops are the most appropriate therapeutic modality at this stage to facilitate the breakdown of denial.

Active exploration of how one's refusal to admit powerlessness and the fear of being out of control is affecting one's life describes stage three or the *core issues stage* (Cermak, 1985). Gravitz and Bowden (1984) believe that ACAs at this stage are ready to deal with the core issues affecting them as adults: control, trust, frozen feelings, overresponsibility, denial of one's own needs, all-or-none functioning, and dissociation. Gravitz and Bowden (1984) recommend continued use of support groups, as well as individual therapy, during this stage since these issues are so embedded. Cermak (1985) subsumes many of these issues under control, which are let go as delusions along with the continuous process of acknowledging one's realistic limits to willpower. Cermak (1985) equates this process to recovery that may be experienced as an emotional awakening and improved effectiveness in one's life.

Gravitz and Bowden (1984) agree with the improvement in functioning which takes place as these core issues are worked through and new behaviors and strategies are gained in stage four called *transformations.* Making connections between present behavior and past circumstances is identified as an important transformational agent. The major change agent, however, is a process of dividing each major core issue into small manageable tasks; an antidote to "all-or-none" functioning. Self-appreciation for each accomplished step becomes possible and qualitative changes, such as acknowledging one's own needs, rights, and feelings, begin to emerge. These changes are best facilitated by a continuation of individual psychotherapy and support groups, and the addition of an ACA psychotherapy group. Specific workshops regarding assertiveness, self-esteem, problem-solving, communication skills, and values clarification may also be helpful.

Recovery continues on to the *integration stage,* which begins when transformations instill even greater meaning into the ACA's life, and new belief systems become integrated. Thoughts, feelings, and behaviors emerge as an integrated experience. The primary task of this stage is to develop belief systems that legitimize self-acceptance. "A basic faith in honesty, for its own sake, becomes a part of daily life" (Cermak, 1985, p. 42). At this stage, control issues are resolved, trust and self-trust exist, and life becomes pleasurable and managed one day at a time (Gravitz & Bowden, 1984).

The final stage of recovery is called *Genesis,* which is less tangible and beyond the reclaiming of one's sensory experiences identified in the fifth stage of integration. Gravitz and Bowden (1984) describe it as ". . .a new and varied responsiveness to life. . .a synergistic relationship greater than the sum of those separate parts" (p. 36). Cermak (1985) sees the Genesis stage as the true beginning when ACAs begin to participate in the creation of their own world. Not all ACAs move into this stage, but those who do begin to trust in a process greater than themselves, and they are a part of this greater process. This stage may be facilitated, if the client is committed, by the twelve steps of Alcoholics Anonymous, coursework in philosophical or universal concerns, or a significant change in life-style (Gravitz & Bowden, 1984).

Evaluation

Few studies have been done to evaluate the success of these prevention and treatment programs for children of alcoholics, which have been largely recommended by the grass-roots children-of-alcoholics movement (Blane, 1988). Little, if any, information has been published on overall codependency treatment outcomes as well (Cruse & Wegscheider-Cruse, 1988).

Hughes (1977) did identify less negative emotional moods, low self-esteem, and poor social adjustment among children who attended Alateen. Robinson (1983) also did a 2-year follow-up of parents and children involved in a Preventative Youth Group Program. Of 20 children, 11 reported improvements in grade averages, 13 reported an increase in self-confidence, 17 fulfilled an expectation of not taking drugs but 11 consumed alcohol once or twice a year, 13 reported improved sibling and peer relationships, and 10 were getting along better with their parents. A significant increase in outside activities was also reported by 16 of the children.

A more recent study by Davis and coworkers (1985) noted that after a 10-week program, 49% more of the children had a better factual knowledge of alcohol. There was a 17% decrease in thinking that people who drink always drink too much. Twenty percent more of the children also recognized alcoholism as an illness and 15% fewer of the children believed that bad children make their parents drink.

These few evaluative research studies, however, are not highly controlled evaluations or strong generalizable assessments, which are sadly needed in the prevention area of treatment of children of alcoholics. Blane (1988) believes that prevention programs in this area have developed separately from the empirical research on children of alcoholics. The latter, in turn, has not been focused on the same outcomes as the grass-roots movement, which the majority of prevention programs are based on. Cruse and Wegscheider-Cruse's (1988) Living Center Program for the treatment of codependency, however, reports recovery rates (40%–100%) for the self-diagnosis of addictions and compulsions (primary characteristics of codependency) and 73%–93% improvement rates of some ACA core issues (quality of relationships, feeling feelings, liking self).

The Living Center Program focuses on some of the same outcomes as the grass-roots movement. The goals and outcomes of research and all forms of treatment must continue to be bridged if children of alcoholics are to be helped. Allowing these diverse efforts to continue down separate roads may only increase the risk status of this already vulnerable population.

SUMMARY

Children with an alcoholic parent are at risk for developing emotional or mental disorders, as well as physical problems due to genetic predisposition and adverse environmental influences. The deleterious effects of these risk factors on children tend to differ, however, according to the degree the risk factors are present as well as characteristics of the children themselves. Further study of resiliency among these high-risk youth may provide answers to problems of primary prevention.

Despite the high risk for potential physical, psychologic and social problems among children of alcoholics, literature and research on treatment interventions for this population remain sparse. This neglect is often due to ignorance, denial, or fear of legal retribution. The few treatment programs available for children of alcoholics are often based on core issues for this population: control; identifying, differentiating and expressing feelings; overresponsibility; and trust. Few studies have been conducted, however, to evaluate the success of these prevention and treatment programs, which have often developed separately from empirical research findings and may actually increase the vulnerability of this population.

REFERENCES

Ackerman, R. (1983). *A guidebook for educators, therapists, and parents*. Holmes Beach, FL: Learning Publications.

Alibrandi, L. (1982). The fellowship of Alcoholics Anonymous. In E. Pattison & E. Kaufman (Eds.), *Encyclopedic handbook of alcoholism* (pp. 979–986). New York: Gardner Press.

Archer, L. (1986). *Toward a national plan to combat alcohol abuse and alcoholism*. Rockville, MD: National Institute on Alcohol Abuse and Alcoholism, Department of Health and Human Services.

Baraga, D. J. (1978). Self conception in children of alcoholics. *Dissertation Abstracts International, 39*, 368B.

Bingham, A., & Bargar, J. (1985). Children of alcoholic families: A group treatment approach for latency age children. *Journal of Psychosocial Nursing, 23*, 13–15.

Black, C. (1985, February). *Adult children of alcoholics*. Paper presented at the Psychotherapeutic Associates' Advanced Winter Workshop on the Treatment and Rehabilitation of the Alcoholic, Colorado Springs, CO.

Black, C. (1979a). Children of alcoholics. *Alcohol Health and Research World*, Fall, 23–27.

Black, C. (1981). *It will never happen to me*. Denver: MAC Publishing.

Black, C. (1979b). *My dad loves me, my dad has a disease*. Denver: MAC Publishing.

Black, C., Bucky, S., & Wilder-Padilla, S. (1986). The interpersonal and emotional consequences of being an adult child of an alcoholic. *The International Journal of the Addictions, 21*, 213–231.

Blane, H. (1988). Prevention issues with children of alcoholics. *British Journal of Addiction, 87*, 793–798.

Bogdaniak, R., & Piercy, F. (1987). Therapeutic issues of adolescent children of alcoholics (AdCA) groups. *International Journal of Group Psychotherapy, 37*, 569–588..

Bohman, M., Sigvardsson, S., & Cloninger, C. (1981). Maternal inheritance of alcohol abuse: Crossfostering analysis of adopted women. *Archives of General Psychiatry, 38,* 965–969.

Bosma, W. (1975). Alcoholism and teenagers. *Maryland State Medical Journal, 24,* 62–68.

Bosma, W. (1972). Children of alcoholics—A hidden tragedy. *Maryland State Medical Journal, 21,* 32–36.

Brown, S., & Cermak, T. (1980). Group therapy with the adult children of alcoholics. *Newsletter from The California Society for the Treatment of Alcoholism and Other Drug Dependencies, 7,* 1–6.

Cermak, T. (1985). *A primer on adult children of alcoholics.* Pompano Beach, FL: Health Communications, Inc.

Cermak, T. (1984). Children of alcoholics and the case for a new diagnostic category of codependency. In R. Niven (Ed), *Children of alcoholics* (pp. 38–42). Rockville, MD: National Institute on Alcohol Abuse and Alcoholism.

Cermak, T., & Brown, S. (1982). Interactional group therapy with the adult children of alcoholics. *International Journal of Group Psychotherapy, 32,* 375–389.

Chavetz, M., Blane, H., & Hill, M. (1977). Children of alcoholics: Observations in a child guidance clinic. *Quarterly Journal on Studies of Alcoholism, 32,* 687–698.

Children Are People. (1989). *Children are people support group training manual.* (1989). St. Paul, MN: Children Are People, Inc.

Children of Alcoholics Foundation. (1985). *Report of the conference on research needs and opportunities for children of alcoholics.* New York: Children of Alcoholics Foundation.

Clinebell, H. J. (1968). *Understanding and counseling the alcoholic.* New York: Abingdon Press.

Cork, M. (1969). *The forgotten child.* Ontario: General Publishing.

Cruse, J. (1988). *Codependency as a disease.* Presented at the Onsite Institute on Co-Dependency and Adult Children Professional Training School, July, 1988.

Cruse, J., & Wegscheider-Cruse, S. (1988). Codependency: Uncovering the hidden disease. Clinical findings and treatment outcomes. *Focus,* June/July, 18–34.

Davis, R., Johnston, P., DiCicco, L., & Orenstein, A. (1985). Helping children of alcoholic parents: An elementary school program. *The School Counselor,* May, 357–363.

Deckman, J., & Downs, B. (1982). A group treatment approach for adolescent children of alcoholic parents. *Social Work With Groups, 5,* 73–77.

Deutsch, C. (1982). *Broken bottles broken dreams: Understanding and helping children of alcoholics.* New York: Teachers College Press.

DiCicco, L. (1981). Children of alcoholic parents: Issues in identification. In *Services for Children of Alcoholics* (DHHS Publication No. ADM 81–1007). Washington, DC: U. S. Government Printing Office.

Donovan, B. (1981). A collegiate group for the sons and daughters of alcoholics. *College Health, 30,* 83–86.

Downing, N., & Walker, M. (1987). A psychoeducational group for adult children of alcoholics. *Journal of Counseling and Development, 65,* 440–442.

Edwards, D., & Zander, T. (1985). Children of alcoholics: Background and strategies for the counselor. *Elementary School Guidance and Counseling,* December, 121–128.

Ellwood, L. C. (1980). Effects of alcoholism as a family illness on child behavior and development. *Military Medicine, 145,* 188–192.

Fine, E., Yudin, L., Holmes, J., & Heinemann, M. (1976). Behavioral disorders in children with parental alcoholism. *New York Academy of Sciences Annals, 273,* 507–517.

Goodwin, D., Schulsinger, F., Hermansen, L., Guze, S., & Winokur, G. (1975). Alcoholism and the hyperactive child syndrome. *Journal of Nervous and Mental Diseases, 160,* 349–353.

Goodwin, D. W., Schulsinger, F., Hermansen, L., Guze, S., & Winokur, G. (1973). Alcohol problems in adoptees raised apart from biological parents. *Archives of General Psychiatry, 28,* 238–243.

Gravitz, H., & Bowden, J. (1985). *Guide to recovery: A book for adult children of alcoholics.* Holmes Beach, FL: Learning Publications, Inc.

Gravitz, H., & Bowden, J. (1984). Therapeutic issues of adult children of alcoholics. *Alcohol Health and Research World,* Summer, 25–29, 36.

Gurel, M. (1976). An alcoholism training program: Its effect on trainees and faculty. *Nursing Research, 25,* 127–132.

Haberman, P. (1966). Childhood symptoms in children of alcoholics and comparison group parents. *Journal of Marriage and the Family, 28,* 152–154.

Hoffman, A. L., & Heinemann, M. E. (1987). Substance abuse education in schools of nursing: A national survey. *Journal of Nursing Education, 26,* 282–287.

Hughes, J. (1977). Adolescent children of alcoholic parents and the relationship of Alateen to these children. *Journal of Consulting and Clinical Psychology, 45,* 947.

Jacob, T., Seilhamer, R., & Rushe, R. (1989). Alcoholism and family interaction: An experimental paradigm. *American Journal of Drug and Alcohol Abuse, 15,* 73–91.

Johnson, S., Leonard, K., & Jacob, T. (1986, April). *Children of alcoholics: Drinking, drinking styles, and drug use.* Presented at the Research Society of America, San Francisco.

Keane, J. (1983, April). *Factors related to the psychological well-being of children of alcoholics.* Presented at the National Alcoholism Forum, Houston.

Kearney, T., & Taylor, C. (1969). Emotionally disturbed adolescents with alcoholic parents. *Acta Paedopsychiatrica (Basel), 36,* 215–221.

Kern, J., Tippman, J., Fortgand, J., & Paul, S. (1977/78). Treatment approach for children of alcoholics. *Journal of Drug Education,* 207–218.

Klinefelter, H. (1983). Cognitive and experiential group counseling for university students of alcoholic parentage (Doctoral dissertation, University of Florida, 1982). *Dissertation Abstracts International, 43,* 3218A.

Knop, J., Teasdale, T., Schulsinger, F., & Goodwin, D. (1985). A prospective study of young men at high risk for alcoholism: School behavior and achievement. *Journal of Studies on Alcohol, 46,* 273–278.

Lawson, G., Peterson, J., & Lawson, A. (1983). *Alcoholism and the family.* Rockville, MD: Aspen Systems Corp.

LePantois, J. (1986). Group therapy for children of substance abusers. *Social Work With Groups, 9,* 39–51.

Manning, D., Balson, P., & Xenakis, S. (1986). The prevalence of type A personality in the children of alcoholics. *Alcoholism: Clinical and Experimental Research, 10,* 184–189.

Marcus, A. (1986). Academic achievement in elementary school children of alcoholic mothers. *Journal of Clinical Psychology, 42,* 372–376.

Matajcek, Z., & Baueriva, N. (1981). Health status of children from families of alcoholics. *Czechoslovakian Pediatrics, 36,* 588–592.

McCabe, J. (1977). Children in need: Consent issues in treatment. *Alcohol Health and Research World,* Fall, 2–12.

Miller, D., & Jang, M. (1977). Children of alcoholics: A 20-year longitudinal study. *Social Work Research and Abstracts, 13,* 23–29.

Moe, J. (1988, April). *Implementing community programs for children of alcoholics.* Paper presented at the Governor's Sixth Annual Substance Abuse Conference, Cheyenne, WY.

Moe, J., & Pohlman, D. (1988). *Kids power: Healing games for children of alcoholics.* (Available from Kids Are Special, San Jose, CA).

Moos, R., & Billings, A. (1982). Children of alcoholics during the recovery process: Alcoholic and matched control families. *Addictive Behaviors, 7,* 155–163.

Morehouse, E. (1979). Working in the schools with children of alcoholic parents. *Health Social Work, 4,* 145–162.

Morehouse, E., & Richards, T. (1983). An examination of dysfunctional latency age children of alcoholic parents and problems in intervention. *Journal of Children in Contemporary Society, 15,* 21–33.

Morrison, J., & Stewart, M. (1971). A family study of the hyperactive child syndrome. *Biological Psychiatry, 3,* 189–195.

Nardi, P. (1981). Children of alcoholics: A role-theoretical perspective. *Journal of Social Psychology, 115,* 237–245.

Newlon, G., & Furrow, W. (1986). Using the classroom to identify children from alcoholic homes. *The School Counselor,* March, 286–291.

Nici, J. (1979). Wives of alcoholics as "repeaters." *Journal of Studies on Alcohol, 40,* 677–682.

Nylander, I. (1960). Children of alcoholic fathers. *Acta Paediatrica Scandinavica, 49* (Suppl. 121), 1–134.

Obuchowska, I. (1974). Emotional contact with the mother as a social compensatory factor in children of alcoholics. *International Mental Health Research Newsletter, 16,* 2, 4.

O'Gorman, P. (1976). Self-concept, locus of control, and perception of father in adolescents from homes with and without severe drinking problems. *Dissertation Abstracts International, 36,* (8–A), 5156.

O'Gorman, P. (1985). An historical look at children of alcoholics. *Focus on the Family, 8,* 5, 43.

Owen, S., Rosenberg, J., & Barkley, D. (1985). Bottled-up children: A group treatment approach for children of alcoholics. *Group, 9,* 31–42.

Padula, T. A. (1975). Suicide threats and attempts in latency-age children. *Smith College Studies in Social Work, 46,* 21–22.

Poiner, V. (1967). The role of the nurse in the treatment of alcoholics. *Journal of Psychosocial Nursing and Mental Health Services, 21,* 17–24.

Pokorny, A. D., & Solomon, J. (1983). A follow-up survey of drug abuse and alcoholism teaching in medical schools. *Journal of Medical Education, 58,* 316–321.

Policoff, S. P. (1985). Bottle babies. *New Age,* October, 54–60.

Putnam, S. (1985, November). *Are children of alcoholics sicker than other children? A study of illness experience and utilization behavior in a health maintenance organization.* Paper presented at the annual meeting of the American Public Health Association, Washington, DC.

Pyle, R. L., Mitchell, J. E., & Eckert, E. D. (1981). Bulimia: A report of 34 cases. *Journal of Clinical Psychiatry, 42,* 60–64.

Rhodes, J., & Blackham, G. J. (1987). Differences in character roles between adolescents from alcoholic and nonalcoholic homes. *American Journal of Drug and Alcohol Abuse, 13,* 145–155.

Richards, T. M. (1979). Working with children of an alcoholic mother. *Alcohol Health and Research World, 3,* 22–25.

Robinson, G. M. (1983). News and views: Children of alcoholics. *Social Casework: The Journal of Contemporary Social Work, 64,* 178–181.

Russell, M., Henderson, C., & Blume, S. (1984). *Children of alcoholics: A review of the literature.* New York: Children of Alcoholics Foundation.

Scavnicky-Mylant, M. (1984). Children of alcoholics: Children in need. *Family & Community Health, 7,* (2), 51–62.

Scavnicky-Mylant, M. L. (1986). The use of drawings in the assessment and treatment of children of alcoholics. *Journal of Pediatric Nursing, 1,* 178–192.

Scavnicky-Mylant, M. L. (1987). Alcoholism nursing: Toward a policy perspective. *Journal of Nursing Education, 26,* 294–299.

Scavnicky-Mylant, M. L. (1988). The process of coping and emotional development of young adult children of alcoholics: A nursing study. *Dissertation Abstracts International, 49,* page 2133B. (University Microfilms No. DA8816561).

Schneiderman, I. (1975). Family thinking in prevention of alcoholism. *Preventive Medicine, 4,* 296–309.

Schulsinger, F., Goodwin, D., Knop, J., Pollock, V., & Mikkelsen, U. (1985). Characteristics of young men at higher risk for alcoholism. In U. Rydberg (Ed.), *Alcohol and the developing brain* (pp. 193–205). New York: Raven Press.

Seabaugh, M. O. (1983). *The vulnerable self of the adult child of an alcoholic: A phenomenologically derived theory.* Unpublished doctoral dissertation, University of Southern California, Los Angeles.

Services for Children of Alcoholics. (1981). (DHHS Publication No. ADM 81–1007). Washington, DC: U. S. Government Printing Office.

Shaywitz, S. E., Cohen, D. J., & Shaywitz, B. A. (1980). Behavior and learning difficulties in children of normal intelligence born to alcoholic mothers. *Journal of Pediatrics, 96,* 978–982.

Tarter, R., Alterman, A., & Edwards, K. (1985). Vulnerability to alcoholism in men: A behavior-genetic perspective. *Journal of Studies on Alcohol, 404,* 329–356.

Tishler, C., & McKenry, P. (1982). Parental negative self and adolescent suicide attempts. *Journal of the American Academy of Child Psychiatry, 21,* 404–408.

Triplett, J., & Arneson, S. (1983). Working with children of alcoholics. *Pediatric Nursing, 9,* 317–320.

Wegscheider, S. (1979). *The family trap.* St. Paul, MN: Nurturing Networks.

Wegscheider, S. (1981). *Another chance.* Palo Alto, CA: Science and Behavior Books, Inc.

Wegscheider, S. (1985). *Codependency, ACA's and spirituality.* Palo Alto, CA: Science and Behavior Books, Inc.

Wegscheider-Cruse, S. (1988). *Onside institute on co-dependency and adult children manual.* Rapid City, SD: Onsite Training and Consulting, Inc.

Werner, E. (1986). Resilient offspring of alcoholics: A longitudinal study from birth to age 18. *Journal of Studies on Alcohol, 47,* 34–40.

Wilson, C., & Orford, J. (1978). Children of alcoholics, *Journal of Studies in Alcoholism, 39,* 121–142.

Woititz, J. G. (1983). *Adult children of alcoholics.* Hollywood, FL: Health Communications, Inc.

Woodside, M. (1988a). Children of alcoholics: Helping a vulnerable group. *Public Health Reports, 103,* 643–647.

Woodside, M (1988b). Research on children of alcoholics: Past and future. *British Journal of Addiction, 83*(7), 785–792.

12

Gerald Bennett

Substance abuse among the young constitutes a major health problem throughout the industrialized world. In the United States, the indicators of the problem are clear. Of the industrialized countries, the United States has the highest prevalence of illicit drug use among young people. Alcohol-related accidents are the leading cause of death for Americans 15–24 years of age. The National Council on Alcoholism estimates that as many as 3 million adolescents have serious drinking problems. Despite the near peak awareness in the society regarding the hazards of cigarette smoking, a substantial proportion of adolescents, particularly girls, report regular smoking.

In this climate, health professionals have a responsibility to be knowledgeable about youthful substance abuse and assist their communities in initiating viable prevention and intervention strategies. Specific aspects of the problem may be considered in the form of the following questions.

1. What is the historical background of contemporary youthful substance abuse?
2. What does research reveal about current patterns and recent trends in youthful substance abuse?
3. What is known about factors influencing substance abuse among the young?
4. What major approaches to prevention and intervention are being proposed and implemented for the young population?

Before proceeding to these questions, it is necessary to define key terms to be used throughout the chapter.

Definition of Terms

Youth. A broad term referring to the developmental stages of childhood and adolescence.

Childhood. This period in human development begins after infancy, or the first year of life, and ends at 12 years of age. According to Erikson's (1963) theory of development, three of the crucial psychosocial stages occur during the childhood period: *(1)* autonomy versus shame and doubt (1.5–3 years); *(2)* initiative versus guilt (3–5.5 years); and *(3)* industry versus inferiority (5.5–12 years).

Adolescence. For the purposes of our discussion, this developmental period begins at 12 years and ends at 17, although the outer limit will be extended at several points, particularly in relation to college students and young military personnel. Erikson's theory describes the adolescent period as the psychosocial stage of identity versus role confusion (Erikson, 1968). In large part the chapter focuses on adolescent substance abuse. Although the trend toward preteen problems deserves consideration, studies continue to confirm that the adolescent years are the focal point of substance abuse in the young population.

Substance Use. This term is used here in a scientific context; any consumption of a psychoactive drug, in any amount, however infrequent or frequent is referred to as substance use. Use is a quantifiable phenomenon either by observation, self-report, or physiologic measurement. Use, as a scientific term, does not imply normality or a socially acceptable pattern of consumption.

Substance Abuse. Substance abuse, as we are using the term in this book, refers to psychoactive drug use of any class or type, used alone or in combination, that poses significant hazards to health. Health is a concept now generally accepted by the health sciences to extend beyond physiologic well-being to include "psychological, interpersonal, and social aspects of living" (Orem, 1985, p. 174). This broad definition encompasses episodic drug use posing health hazards as well as substance dependence; a pattern of use characterized by compulsion, loss of control over when, where, and how much the substance is consumed, and continued use despite adverse consequences. With the exception of substance dependence, establishing widely accepted criteria for labeling a particular type or pattern of substance use in young people as posing significant hazards to health has been problematic. As stated by Johnston, O'Malley, and Bachman (1987), "While there is still no public consensus of what levels or patterns of use constitutes abuse, there is surely a consensus that higher levels of use are more likely to have detrimental effects for the user and society than are lower levels" (p. 3).

HISTORICAL BACKGROUND

Each successive historical period appears to bring its own patterns of youthful substance abuse (Bachman, Johnston, & O'Malley, 1981). The patterns of the 1960s and 1970s were particularly dramatic because American youth were exposed to a new range of drug choices. The emergence of the "new" drugs has led to a state of affairs in which "instead of simply smoking cigarettes and using alcohol, many of today's teenagers also use marijuana, and some use other illicit drugs" (Bachman et al., 1981, p. 67). On the other hand, there were some encouraging trends in the 1980s suggesting American youth were becoming increasingly aware of problems associated with all types of substance use. An exception to these trends is the growing crack epidemic in poor inner-city neighborhoods across the country. How did youthful substance abuse evolve in this fashion? A brief historical sketch will provide some insight into this question and be useful in placing subsequent discussion in perspective.

Smoking

Cigarette smoking is a product of the twentieth century. Approximately three-fourths of the male population born in the United States around the time of World War I (WWI), eventually became smokers, many beginning the habit at an early age (Horn, 1979). At that time it was thought to be quite normal for a young man to adopt what was generally viewed as a desirable accoutrement of civilization. Still, before World War II (WWII), smoking was forbidden in public schools. It was not until after WWII that some schools began to designate special areas for smoking on school property (Koop, 1986). Trying cigarettes and learning to smoke became entrenched as a predictable feature of adolescent life for many.

The scientific data linking cigarette smoking with risks to health were documented in the first federal report on smoking and health (Surgeon General, 1964). Twenty-five years later the full impact of the implications of the report are being felt. The social acceptability of smoking is being questioned on all fronts. Smokers are increasingly restricted in where and when they can smoke. Severe health warnings, naming specific diseases and conditions caused by smoking, are prominently displayed on cigarette packages and in cigarette advertising. With the goal of phasing out smoking in the United States during the same century in which it began, the Surgeon General, Dr. C. Everett Koop (1986), called for a smoke-free young America by the year 2000. Although this goal is undoubtedly idealistic, it is symbolic of an enormous change in the way Americans are viewing smoking and the cigarette industry.

Drinking

Rapid social change and the rise of a huge alcoholic beverage industry have shaped the cultural context of youthful drinking in America during this century (Bennett, 1986). Young people, most now growing up in urban areas, are increasingly exposed to a variety of alcoholic beverages. Some advertisements for alcoholic beverages in the mass media, particularly for beer and wine coolers, are targeted toward the young. It comes as no surprise that alcohol is the most commonly used and abused drug among American youth.

Until the 1920s, there were generally accepted norms on American college campuses prescribing when and how much to drink. These norms ignored prohibition but did reinforce moderation. Drunkenness was generally viewed as going beyond the bounds of social acceptability. In addition, since alcohol was the province of men during this period, it was not acceptable to drink in the presence of women. Many women actively reinforced this informal code. For example, drinking at dances and football games was not accepted because women were in attendance. In 1923, 2000 women students at the University of Wisconsin signed a pledge to boycott social gatherings of any type where there would be drinking (Fass, 1977).

By the late 1920s the "flaming youth" ushered in a new era in which drinking by men and women became a common feature of campus life. Factors cited as contributing to this change include the population shift from small towns to cities, rejection of traditional values following WWI, and the exposure of middle-class youth to European drinking customs through travel and literature (Room, 1984). Drinking became a rite of passage for many college students. Over the years similar attitudes toward alcohol became common among adolescents of high school age.

Following WWII, the baby boom and unprecedented affluence resulted in an American society in the 1960s in which the young, comprising a large proportion of the population, strongly influenced social institutions and the economy. In 1971 the voting age for all federal elections was dropped from 21 to 18. Soon after, many states lowered the drinking age to 18 or 19. Also in the early 1970s, the National Institute on Alcohol Abuse and Alcoholism (NIAAA) sponsored its first national survey on adolescent drinking.

Beginning in the 1980s, for the first time since Prohibition, a grass-roots movement developed to reduce drinking and alcohol-related problems among the young, focusing on drunk driving. In the United States, "No other single source of mortality approaches traffic accidents with a single known contributing factor—the interaction of beverage alcohol and a young driver's ability to control an automobile" (Douglass, 1983, p. 348). This is the only age group whose death rate increased rather than fell during the 1970s. In an effort to reverse this trend, the federal and state governments moved rapidly in recent years to return to a drinking age of 21.

Illicit Drugs

In the 1950s, Americans became aware that in at least two subgroups of the young population, psychoactive "street" drugs were being used. When the problem of juvenile delinquency came to the forefront as an issue in New York, Chicago, and other large cities, journalists found that in addition to drinking heavily from the age of 11 or 12, "street kids" were using a wide range of illicit substances. Marihuana, cocaine, and heroin were found to be available and used by teenagers of the "shook-up generation" (Salisbury, 1958).

The other subgroup of American youth to experiment with illicit drugs during the 1950s was the Beats; a small group of adolescents and young adults who generally came from middle-class or affluent backgrounds. Many were intellectuals and artists who rejected participation in modern society in the conventional roles they saw available to them. Goodman (1956) believed that

marihuana and other illicit drug use was one means of expressing creativity and their urge for an alternative sense of reality.

The dramatic changes that took place in American culture in the 1960s cannot be detailed here. Our primary interest is the emergence of a youthful "counterculture," promoting illicit drug experimentation as one of its primary features. For another discussion of the events during the 1960s that contributed to the increase in drug use, see Macdonald (1987).

Roszak (1969) wrote, in his analysis of the counterculture phenomenon, "At the bohemian fringe of our disaffected youth culture, all roads lead to psychedelia" (p. 155). He used the term psychedelics to refer to all illicit drugs used at the time to alter consciousness. He characterized the psychedelic experience as representative of a radical rejection of parental society.

As a supporter of many of the aims of the counterculture, Roszak (1969) viewed the increased use of drugs among younger and younger adolescents as a destructive force within the youth movement. He worried about what he described as a growing preoccupation with drugs and the commercialization of illicit drugs through paraphernalia shops and street dealing.

Yablonsky (1968), a sociologist, conducted a field study of hippie groups, using a participant observation technique. He reported widespread use of lysergic acid diethylamide (LSD) and claims by users that ultimate consciousness was available through this substance. His interpretation of this finding was that LSD and other drug experiences served as antidotes to the alienation toward modern society many of these young people felt. Yablonsky (1968) concluded that since disaffection with adult society was not uncommon among American youth, the impact of the hippie phenomenon on youth culture could become widespread. As it turned out, events related to the hippie phenomenon and drugs in the 1970s were much like those foreseen by Yablonsky (1968) and Roszak (1969). Much of the hippie experience was commercialized and influenced many aspects of life for young people. There was a growing preoccupation with drugs among the young as Roszak (1969) had feared, and the illicit drug market became a big business, with marihuana sales reaching $10 billion annually in the late 1970s (Novak, 1980).

With drug paraphernalia becoming available at the local shopping mall or corner store and with the increasing availability of illicit drugs to younger age groups, the late 1970s and early 1980s saw the rise of the concerned parent movement dedicated to reversing these trends (Lindblad, 1983). Initially the parent groups were strongest in the suburbs of major cities, such as Atlanta, Washington, DC, and New York (Brynner, 1980); at present the movement consists of as many as 4000 formal parent organizations throughout the country. One of their first political successes was a well-organized lobbying campaign to convince state legislatures to outlaw the sale of drug paraphernalia. In addition to political action, the parent groups hold neighborhood, regional, and national educational meetings on drug issues. Local activities include planning and supervising drug-free social events for young people. The "Just Say No" philosophy popularized by Nancy Reagan was born and nurtured in these groups. In recent years the parent groups are broadening their concern for the problem of alcohol abuse as well as illicit drugs (U. S. Department of Health and Human Services, 1984).

The most recent trends in substance use and abuse among the young to be discussed in the next section suggest that "middle-class young people seem to be getting the message about pot, pills and cocaine" (Miller, 1987, p. 33). However, there are reports that poor inner-city children and adolescents are succumbing in alarming numbers to crack addiction (Kolata, 1989). Crack is easily available on the streets in inner-city neighborhoods throughout the country. Young people in these neighborhoods are currently at the highest risk to develop drug problems.

The crack phenomenon in the 1980s can be traced to the growing popularity of cocaine smoking (see Chapter 4), a dramatic increase in the supply of cocaine, the resulting sharp drop in the price of the drug, and the importance of cocaine trafficking to the underground economy in inner-city areas. Crack, often sold in small quantities resembling slivers of soap, is inexpensive enough to attract young people with only marginal economic resources.

CURRENT TRENDS IN SUBSTANCE USE

The epidemiologic approach to studying drug abuse as a public health problem began less than 20 years ago (Kozel & Adams, 1986). By the early 1970s the waves of illicit drug use among the young population convinced public health officials and scientists of the need

for ongoing surveys of drug use in the general population. In 1975 the National Institute on Drug Abuse (NIDA) began sponsoring an ongoing national survey of drug use among high school seniors. The High School Senior Survey on drug use was developed as a component of the Monitoring the Future project conducted by the University of Michigan's Institute for Social Research (Johnston et al., 1987).

The annual High School Senior Survey provides the best available information on national trends in youthful drug use. Health professionals will find it worthwhile to become familiar with this study and follow it on an ongoing basis. The news media and professional journals typically provide annual updates on youthful drug use based on the most recent survey results. A representative sample of approximately 16,000 to 18,000 seniors, from about 130 public and private high schools throughout the coterminous United States, has been surveyed each Spring since 1975.

Because the study is relied on so extensively in this chapter and elsewhere, it is important to be aware of several issues related to the survey design. Kandel (1978) described the study as "groundbreaking" (p. 32). The study is designed to follow trends from each senior class to the next and to follow trends within each class after graduation. Data on the entire range of substance use are collected rather than narrowly focusing on smoking, alcohol use, or illicit drug use in isolation. This is an important strength of the design in that the results of comprehensive studies of this type provide a balanced perspective on substance use among adolescents (Schnoll, 1979).

Two inherent limitations in the design should be recognized. First, the study relies on a self-administered questionnaire, raising the question of the reliability and validity of self-reported drug use. Although some experts have expressed serious doubts on this question (Estes, Smith-DiJulio & Heinemann, 1980; Schnoll, 1979), others have concluded there is no reason to lack confidence in self-reports of drug use if questionnaires are carefully administered by experts (Lavenhar, 1980). Much consideration has been given to this issue by the researchers directing the High School Senior Survey (Johnston & O'Malley, 1985). Reliability was established by showing that respondents were highly consistent in their self-reports over several years (O'Malley, Bachman, & Johnston, 1983). Confidence in the validity of the reports has been strengthened by findings that self-reported drug use is related to a number of expected attitudes, behaviors, and beliefs (Johnston et al., 1987).

A second limitation of the design is that heavy substance users are almost certainly underrepresented in the sample. Heavy users are more likely to be dropouts or to be absent from school than abstainers or light users. Reports indicate that approximately 20% of those enrolled in school are absent from class each day (U. S. Department of Health and Human Services, 1981).

The possibility that some high school seniors are underreporting their drug use, and the likelihood that heavy users are underrepresented in the school population, leads to a reasonable conclusion that the estimates of drug use based on the High School Senior Survey are somewhat lower than actual use in the total population of older adolescents. However, because consistent procedures and methods are used each year, the degree of underestimation should be constant from one year to the

next. Thus, the trend curves over the years are considered to have a high degree of validity (Johnston et al., 1987).

Monitoring the Future: Selected Findings, 1975–1986

American youth are exposed to a wide variety of psychoactive substances before leaving high school. Alcohol, cigarettes, and marihuana are by far the substances most widely used by high school seniors. Figure 12.1 summarizes the prevalence and recency of substance use for the class of 1986. Although it is not surprising to find that alcohol is the most widely used drug, it is striking to see the extent to which the prohibition of alcohol for minors is ignored. This finding has

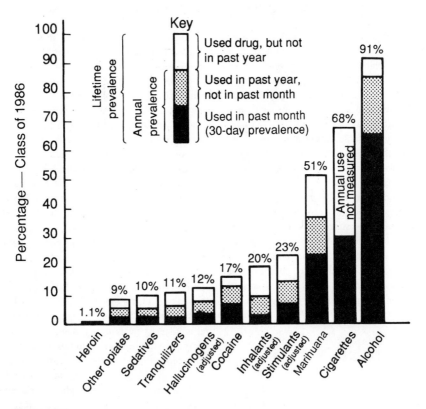

Figure 12.1
Prevalence and recency of use: Eleven types of drugs, class of 1986. From *National trends in drug use and related factors among American high school students and young adults, 1975–1986* (DHHS Publication No. ADM 87–1535), by L. D. Johnston, P. M. O'Malley, and J. G. Bachman. Washington, DC: U. S. Government Printing Office, 1987.

implications for alcohol education for young people, which will be discussed in a later section. Marihuana is the most widely used illicit drug with a majority reporting some use in their lifetime. Prevalence for the other illicit drugs is much lower but nearly four in every ten seniors (38%) report using an illicit drug other than marihuana at some time in their lives.

Prevalence comparisons for subgroups within the class of 1986 reveal some important differences. Variables significantly related to drug use include: gender, college plans, region of the country, and urbanicity.

Gender. Overall, significantly more males than females use illicit drugs. This distinction is most pronounced with daily use. The case of stimulants is an exception to the general pattern with females reporting slightly higher involvement than males. It is believed that this is explained by the popularity of "diet pills" among females.

College Plans. High school seniors with plans to complete 4 years of college use significantly fewer substances, at lower levels of involvement, than seniors without such plans. For example, annual marihuana use is reported by 43% of the noncollege-bound as compared to 36% of the college-bound seniors. Daily marihuana use is more than twice as high among the noncollege-bound (6.2%) as among those planning 4 years of college (2.3%).

Region of the Country. As for illicit drug use, the highest involvement is in the Northeast and the lowest rates are found in the South. Alcohol use tends to be higher in the Northeast and North Central part of the country than it is in the South and West. Large regional differences are found for regular cigarette smoking. Smoking half-a-pack or more a day is most common in the Northeast (16%), with the North Central region (12%), the South (10%), and the West (7%) reporting lower rates.

Urbanicity. The use of two illicit drugs is strongly related to urbanicity. Marihuana has an annual prevalence of 43% in large metropolitan areas as compared to 35% in nonmetropolitan areas. Cocaine is used twice as much in large cities (19%) as in nonmetropolitan areas (9%).

The Crack Epidemic

The crack epidemic is not fully reflected in the overall prevalence estimate for cocaine of 17%. For the first time, in 1986, those seniors reporting use of cocaine in the last year were asked if they had used the drug in crack form. Noncollege-bound seniors (5.2%) were more likely to have used crack than those bound for college (2.8%). Although the larger cities have a higher rate of crack use (5.9%) than small cities (3.5%) and nonurban areas (3.5%), the overall picture is one of a national problem. These figures accurately indicate the upward direction of crack use but because crack involvement is likely to be associated with poor school attendance, the estimates of prevalence are undoubtedly low.

Daily Use

The most serious pattern of substance abuse assessed in the High School Senior Survey is daily use. It is encouraging to note that less than 1% of high school seniors report daily use of illicit substances other than marihuana. A different state of affairs exists, however, for daily use of marihuana, alcohol, and cigarettes. Figure 12.2 illustrates trends for daily use of these substances for both males and females from 1975 through 1986. The trends indicate that a peak for youthful substance abuse was reached in the late 1970s with a gradual decrease since that time. Definite sex differences exist in the use of these drugs. Females are smoking cigarettes more than males. Contrary to some predictions that alcohol use patterns for males and females would converge (Demone & Wechsler, 1976), daily drinking is still disproportionately a pattern of males.

Availability of Drugs

Trends in the perceived availability of drugs are displayed in Figure 12.3. These data support the popular belief that law enforcement efforts to limit the drug supply have had little long-term impact on availability. Though it is encouraging that substance use is on a gradual downturn, the easy availability of illicit drugs is a reminder that drug education will continue to be a crucial element of health prevention for young people in the foreseeable future.

FACTORS POTENTIALLY INFLUENCING YOUTHFUL SUBSTANCE ABUSE

Numerous relationships have been proposed between various factors and youthful substance abuse. Some of these relationships have been supported by research and

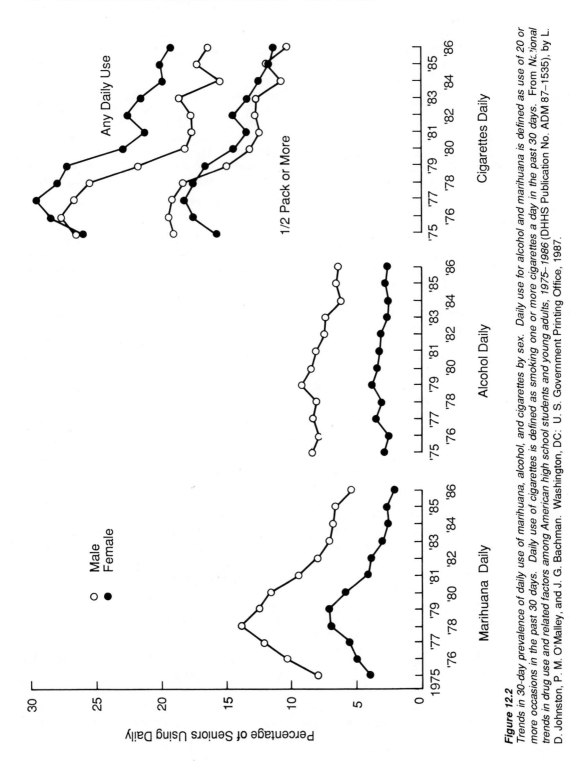

Figure 12.2
Trends in 30-day prevalence of daily use of marihuana, alcohol, and cigarettes by sex. Daily use for alcohol and marihuana is defined as use of 20 or more occasions in the past 30 days. Daily use of cigarettes is defined as smoking one or more cigarettes a day in the past 30 days. From National trends in drug use and related factors among American high school students and young adults, 1975–1986 (DHHS Publication No. ADM 87–1535), by L. D. Johnston, P. M. O'Malley, and J. G. Bachman. Washington, DC: U. S. Government Printing Office, 1987.

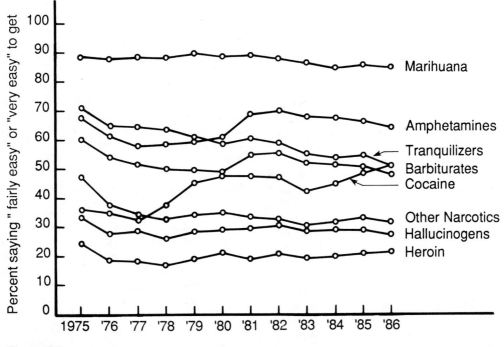

Figure 12.3
Trends in perceived availability of drugs. From *National trends in drug use and related factors among American high school students and young adults, 1975–1986* (DHHS Publication No. ADM 87–1535), by L. D. Johnston, P. M. O'Malley, and J. G. Bachman. Washington, DC: U. S. Government Printing Office, 1987.

some have not. Some relationships are linked to theory, whereas others stand as isolated propositions or hypotheses.

Biologic Factors

Although most factors considered influences on youthful substance abuse fall into the psychosocial realm, evidence has been presented in recent years supporting the significance of biologic factors in some patterns of substance abuse, particularly compulsive or addictive abuse. Studies of alcoholism in adoptees raised apart from their biologic alcoholic parents have been conducted in an attempt to separate genetic factors from rearing factors. Male children of alcoholic parents are more likely to become alcoholic (as adults) themselves than are children of nonalcoholic parents, even if not

reared in the alcoholic family environment (Winokur, 1976).

Furthermore, the concept of genetic predisposition may have implications for opioid and other substance abuse—perhaps even cigarette smoking (Jaffe & Kanzler, 1979). The thinking here is connected to the discovery of endogenous opioids (see Chapter 5) and the recognition that substance abuse may be related to disorders in the normal functioning of these opioids and their receptors. An example of this reasoning is the speculation that the opiate addict may have an inactive endogenous opioid system (Jaffe & Kanzler, 1979). Another example is the notion that, in some people, substance abuse may "trigger" a disorder of the endogenous opioid system. Schuckit and Rayses (1979) have shown in a small sample of subjects that acetaldehyde, the toxic metabolite of alcohol, is present, after the same dose of alcohol, at significantly higher levels in the blood of nonalcoholic men with a family history of alcoholism than in nonalcoholic men without such a history. These researchers reasoned that higher levels of acetaldehyde may stimulate the release of morphinelike alkaloids, thereby making alcoholic drinking more addictive for those genetically predisposed. Similarly, it has been suggested that cigarette smoking may indirectly stimulate the release of endogenous opioids. The possible relationships begin to multiply when one considers the fact that alcoholics and opiate addicts are often heavy smokers (Jaffe & Kanzler, 1979). This discussion is not meant to imply that there is a direct relationship between youthful substance abuse and adult dependence. However, clinicians often hear alcoholics, and others dependent on various substances, say that they knew from an early age that their "physical" reaction to alcohol or other drugs was not "normal."

In a quite different vein, Weil (1972) posits an innate human drive, on a par with libido and the hunger drive, to alter consciousness periodically. Psychoactive drugs are viewed as only one method of altering perception, but, as it turns out in modern society, drugs have become a ready source of consciousness alteration. Weil (1972) suggests that young children are responding to an inborn need to experience perceptual changes when they engage in spinning, turning, or hyperventilating to the point of dizziness. Meditation would be another example of drug-free consciousness alteration. Therefore, according to Weil's (1972) drive model, the youthful substance abuser is responding to an innate drive that is not being met through nondrug means.

Parental Influences

Cohen (1969) has commented, "One of the great myths of the day is that if a child goes wrong, becomes a drughead. . .this must be due to parental failure" (p. 115). Researchers have examined this proposition and have produced a complex array of findings. First, it is now known that parental influence is a multifaceted phenomenon. Actual substance use habits, attitudes toward use by children, agreement between parents on what constitutes proper use, degree of supervision exercised, and quality of parent–child relationships are all significant aspects of "parental influence."

As for cigarette smoking, the actual smoking behavior of parents is clearly most influential in comparison to the other aspects of parental influence identified (Evans, Henderson, Hill, & Raines, 1979). Poor parent–child relationships predicted initiation to marihuana and other illicit drugs in a study by Kandel (1978). Bachman and coworkers (1981) found that number of evenings out for recreation was positively correlated with all types of substance use. Studies of problem drinking among adolescents have shown that although heavy drinking by parents is a contributing factor in youthful alcohol abuse, nondrinking specific factors, such as social isolation, deprivation, cynicism, and antisocial behavior within the family system, are frequently present in the young abuser's home (Zucker, 1976).

Peer Group Influence

Research shows that substance use patterns and drug-related attitudes of peers are strong predictors of drug involvement (Kandel, 1978). For example, in the study by Johnston, Bachman, and O'Malley (1980) of the class of 1980, students reporting high marihuana use reported that their friends were also users. Such a finding does not support the notion of a uniform youth culture. Rather, there appear to be various subgroups in which a peer learning process operates to influence norms for a particular subgroup. Those students who become drug involved are usually participating in a peer group experience, with a significant influence on the maintenance of drug involvement.

Other Psychosocial Factors

Poor academic achievement, low levels of motivation for higher education, and involvement in delinquent activities often precede illicit substance abuse among young people. Personality characteristics common among adolescents involved in marihuana abuse include rebelliousness, independence, alienation, and low self-esteem (Kandel, 1978). The following Case Example of a young marihuana smoker (daily) illustrates these characteristics.

Case Example

T. J. is 17 years old and lives in a large city. He does not plan to attend college after graduation. His grades have been consistently below average, and he has cut classes more than most seniors. T. J. views himself as free from many of society's expectations and has little interest in religion. He does not like to stay home, spending much of his free time out with friends. He smokes cigarettes, drinks, and uses illicit drugs in addition to marihuana from time to time. He is not really sure what sort of job he would like. He would like to move away from home and to have more independence. This worries his parents since he has been in trouble with the law several times in the past year. The most serious arrest involved possession of a small amount of marihuana and driving while intoxicated.

Psychosocial Influences in Perspective

Jessor and Jessor (1977) have developed a theory of problem behavior, including marihuana smoking and problem drinking, that organizes psychosocial factors contributing to deviance in adolescence. Their theory recognizes three interaction systems: the *Personality System*, the *Perceived Environment System*, and the *Behavior System*. The Behavior System is considered the outcome of the interaction of personality and environment. In the Jessor and Jessor (1977) theory, it is the Perceived Environment that is significant, not the environment as defined by demographic variables. Briefly stated, problem behavior, and substance abuse as one aspect of problem behavior, is likely to occur when a Personality System characterized by low academic interest, independence, low religiosity, and tolerance of deviance interacts with a Perceived Environment System characterized by weak parental and peer controls, incongruence between peer and parent expectations, and a dominance of peer over parental influences. Monitoring the Future data support the generalization that those students who most avoid adult supervision at home, school, and church are "also most likely to be involved in all forms of substance use" (Bachman et al., 1981).

PREVENTION AND INTERVENTION

Prevention efforts for youth are directed toward a general population with goals of limiting or eliminating the exposure to a specific drug, or drugs in general. For example, several of the U. S. Public Health Service Healthy People 2000 alcohol and drug prevention objectives focus on youth (U.S. Department of Health and Human Services, 1990). These include:

- Increase by at least 1 year the average age of first use of cigarettes, alcohol, and marihuana by adolescents aged 12 through 17. (Baseline: 11.6 for cigarettes, age 13.1 for alcohol, and 13.4 for marihuana in 1988)
- Reduce the proportion of young people who have used alcohol, marihuana, and cocaine in the past month, as follows:

Substance/ Age	Baseline 1988	Target 2000
Alcohol/age 12–17	25.2%	12.6%
Alcohol/age 18–20	57.9%	29%
Marihuana/age 12–17	6.4%	3.2%
Marihuana/age 18–25	15.5%	7.8%
Cocaine/age 12–17	1.1%	0.6%
Cocaine/age 18–25	4.5%	2.3%

- Reduce the proportion of high school seniors and college students engaging in recent occasions of heavy drinking of alcoholic beverages to no more than 28 percent of high school seniors and 32 percent of college students. (Baseline: 33 percent of high school seniors and 41.7 percent of college students in 1989)
- Reduce alcohol consumption by people aged 14 and older to an annual average of no more than 2 gallons of ethanol per person. (Baseline: 2.54 gallons of ethanol in 1987)
- Increase the proportion of high school seniors who perceive social disapproval associated with the heavy use of alcohol, occasional use of marihuana, and experimentation with cocaine, as follows:

Behavior	Baseline 1989	Target 2000
Heavy use of alcohol	56.4%	70%
Occasional use of marihuana	71.1%	85%
Trying cocaine once or twice	88.9%	95%

- Increase the proportion of high school seniors who associate risk of physical or psychological harm with the heavy use of alcohol, regular use of marihuana, and experimentation with cocaine, as follows:

Behavior	Baseline 1989	Target 2000
Heavy use of alcohol	44%	70%
Regular use of marihuana	77.5%	90%
Trying cocaine once or twice	54.9%	80%

Major prevention strategies designed to reach these goals include: *(1)* public information and education programs, and *(2)* legislative and regulatory measures (Blane, 1986).

Intervention measures are aimed toward young people with substance abuse problems or those who are at high risk to become heavy users. Intervention goals include modifying or eliminating substance use, eliminating or minimizing high-risk behaviors, and linking individuals with continuing problems to appropriate treatment programs.

Public Information and Education

Mass Media Campaigns. Although research has not shown mass media campaigns to be effective in changing health behavior, it is believed that they can be instrumental in creating a context of knowledge, awareness, and attitudes supportive of behavior change (Rootman, 1985). The number and frequency of television antidrug messages and warnings regarding drunk driving have increased considerably in recent years. Less attention has been given to cigarette smoking. In an effort to counter the glamorous image often associated with cocaine use, celebrities with appeal to young audiences have been enlisted to present anticocaine messages. Peel (1981) cautioned against sensationalism in public information campaigns. He pointed out that "drug horror stories" in the media not only serve to damage credibility with young people, but may also attract youth in search of the incredible "high" or those who wish to take drugs involving the most risk to health.

School-Based Programs. School alcohol and drug education programs are usually designed to accomplish one or more of the following: *(1)* increased knowledge of drugs and stronger antidrug attitudes, *(2)* clarification of personal values and improved decision-making skills, and *(3)* increased social competency skills (adapted from U. S. Department of Health and Human Services, 1987). In addition, some programs are geared specifically to limit abuse of particular substances; this is especially the case in alcohol or cigarette education. However, there is a growing trend for programs to seek to prevent substance abuse in general (Swett, 1984).

Alcohol and drug education in the schools is fraught with thorny philosophical and theoretical issues as well as practical limitations. A philosophical debate continues regarding the ultimate purpose of alcohol and drug education (Milgram, 1987). Should the purpose be to help young people make informed decisions about substance use or should these programs simply discourage all use? Should the purpose be different for different substances? There is no consensus among experts on these questions. Although there has been a trend toward developing programs that address the full range of psychoactive substances, the underlying cultural attitudes regarding alcohol, illicit drugs, and tobacco pose serious contradictions. Whereas alcohol is accepted as a part of American society, illicit drugs are not. Tobacco is unique as a substance that is legal, marketed relentlessly in the popular print media, but rapidly losing its social acceptability.

A theoretical problem to be faced in school-based prevention programs is that the social and family variables associated with substance abuse among the young may be beyond the influence of classroom drug education (Lohrmann & Fors, 1986; Jessor, 1982). Practical limitations on school programs are also considerable. Time constraints, lack of adequate training for teachers, dependence on grants for funding, and the questionable value of guest speakers from outside the school system, are all problematic for school-based programs (Milgram, 1987).

Evaluation studies of school-based alcohol and drug education have shown mixed results. Even for those programs that show effects, the changes are not always in the desired direction. It is not unusual to find positive, negative, and neutral results for different subgroups of students (Goodstadt, 1980; Goodstadt, Sheppard, & Chan, 1982; Schaps, DiBartolo, Moskowitz, Palley, & Churgin, 1981). The role of teachers in substance abuse education is brought into question by the results of some studies. A review of 127 primary drug abuse prevention programs for young people concluded the most effective programs were delivered by parents or peers (Schaps et al., 1981).

Developmental considerations are important in planning prevention programs. For example, the "Here's Looking At You" demonstration project in Seattle was a successful alcohol education curriculum designed to be compatible with the cognitive and affective development of children by grade level (Prevention X three, 1980). A strategy that recognizes the importance of peer relationships during adolescence is using peer teachers and peer role models to present content or lead discussions.

The success of smoking prevention programs using the social influence approach has attracted much attention by those looking to the future of alcohol and drug education (DuPont, 1987; Flay, 1985; Polich, Reuter, & Kahan, 1984; U. S. Department of Health and Human Services, 1987). The social influence approach relies heavily on peer leadership and focuses on ''(a) teaching students about the social influences to smoke, (b) providing them with the behavioral skills with which to resist those influences, and (c) correcting their perception of social norms'' (Flay, 1985, p. 67). Older students who are confident nonsmokers are selected as peer leaders. They teach participants that contrary to popular beliefs, ''everyone'' does not smoke. In fact, it is emphasized repeatedly that smokers are a minority among youth. Finally, specific antismoking behavioral responses are taught and reinforced.

Peer Organizations. Peer organizations are active in alcohol and drug education throughout the country. Students Against Drunk Driving (SADD) has several hundred chapters in 22 states and is thought to reach as many as 3 million students. SADD promotes the parent–teenager contract to prevent drunk driving. The teenager pledges not to drink and drive—parents agree to respond without argument to a call for transportation. Parents also agree not to drink and drive themselves and to obtain alternative transportation rather than ride with someone who has been drinking. SADD and other peer organizations mount programs to prevent drunk driving on high school graduation and prom nights. On college campuses, BACCHUS (Boost Alcohol Consciousness Concerning the Health of the University) sponsors alcohol seminars, discourages drunk driving, and encourages the discussion of alcohol issues by appropriate student and faculty groups. Although the peer organizations mentioned here have an alcohol focus, other less well-known groups focus on preventing illicit drug involvement or smoking.

Legislative and Regulatory Measures

One of the most remarkable political developments of the 1980s was the emergence of a neoprohibition for the young. The return to the alcohol drinking age of 21 was the most visable change. Beginning in 1985, the military discontinued the practice of allowing young soldiers to drink on military bases regardless of age and began observing state drinking laws. Penalties have increased dramatically for those found guilty of violating laws regulating drinking and driving. Changes relative

to illicit drug use included a reversal of the trend toward decriminalization of marihuana and the outlawing of drug paraphernalia.

All indications are that the trend toward the increasing use of legislation and regulation to prevent substance abuse will continue in the next decade. William Bennett, the first Director of National Drug Control Policy, has outlined a plan to attack the drug problem that puts much emphasis on local law enforcement and establishing an atmosphere of ''zero tolerance'' for drug use in American society. For example, one recommendation specifically targeted to young people calls for local school districts to suspend or expel students who are caught using any illegal drug (Berke, 1989).

Intervention for Substance Abusers and High-Risk Youth

Problem behavior theory (Jessor & Jessor, 1977, 1980) and related research suggests that substance abuse is often linked to other adolescent problems such as poor school performance, truancy, sexual intercourse, fighting, or stealing. The extent to which young people are able to achieve success and personal satisfaction within the educational system, job market, and family is inversely related to the emergence of problem behavior.

An intervention approach which recognizes the linkages between problem behaviors is the Student Assistance Program (SAP). The SAP program model is based on the experience with employee assistance programs (EAPs) in industry (see Chapter 13). The SAP in the school system of Westchester County, New York, is considered a national model. It was developed for students with problems or those identified as at high risk (U. S. Department of Health and Human Services, 1987). Counseling was provided for newcomers, children of alcoholics, seniors, and students with various interpersonal problems. Alcohol problems and absenteeism were significantly decreased among program participants.

Another example of intervention programs targeting high-risk adolescents is a counseling program for delinquent youth in Denver, Colorado. The project involved intensive alcohol education for staff and peer education for clients. Outcomes of the program included an increase in alcohol awareness and a decrease in substance abuse problems among clients (U. S. Department of Health and Human Services, 1984).

SUMMARY

Experimenting with readily available psychoactive substances, including tobacco, alcohol, marihuana, and other illicit subtances, has become a part of growing up for many young people in the United States. Those young people who become heavily involved in substance abuse often have other problems as well, such as poor academic performance, truancy, and a tendency toward aggression. The popularity of the various substances has changed during different historical periods. The early and middle 1970s was a period of growing substance abuse of all types; however, the "new" illicit drugs were the object of most public concern. The downward drift in the age groups using drugs, particularly marihuana, became a cause for parents' action groups in the late 1970s and early 1980s. Data from the Monitoring the Future project indicate that the peak of youthful substance abuse, particularly daily use, has been reached, and a new trend of respect for health among young people is suggested by the drop in daily use of cigarettes, marihuana, and alcohol. On the other hand, the crack epidemic, especially in poor urban areas, poses a new threat to the health of youth. The 2000 Prevention Objectives for Alcohol and Drug Abuse highlight the need for prevention programs aimed at limiting substance abuse among the young. Intervention programs targeting youthful substance abusers and those at high risk for abuse are also important components of a comprehensive approach to addressing the problem.

REFERENCES

Bachman, J. G., Johnston, L. D., & O'Malley, P. M. (1981). Smoking, drinking, and drug use among American high school students: Correlates and trends, 1975–1979. *American Journal of Public Health, 71*(1), 59–69.

Bennett, G. (1986). Alcohol problems among the young. In N. J. Estes & M. E. Heinemann (Eds.), *Alcoholism: Development, consequences, and interventions* (3d ed.) (pp. 221–240). St. Louis: C. V. Mosby.

Berke, R. L. (1989, August 16). Bush endorses strategy outline for drug battle. *The New York Times,* p. 1.

Blane, H. T. (1986). Preventing alcohol problems. In N. J. Estes & M. E. Heinemann (Eds.), *Alcoholism: Development, consequences, and interventions* (3d ed.) (pp. 78–90). St. Louis: C. V. Mosby.

Brynner, E. C. (1980). New parental push against marijuana. *The New York Times Magazine,* pp. 36–38, 51–53.

Cohen, S. (1969). *The drug dilemma.* New York: McGraw-Hill.

Demone, H. W., & Wechsler, H. (1976). Changing drinking patterns of adolescents during the last decade. In M. Greenblatt & M. A. Schuckit (Eds.), *Alcoholism problems in women and children* (pp. 197–210). New York: Grune & Stratton.

Douglass, R. L. (1983). Youth, alcohol, and traffic accidents: Current status. In M. Galanter (Ed.), *Recent developments in alcoholism: Genetics, behavioral treatment, social mediators and prevention, current concepts in diagnosis* (pp. 347–366). New York: Plenum Press.

DuPont, R. L. (1987). Prevention of adolescent chemical dependency. *Pediatric Clinics of North America, 34*(2), 495–505.

Erikson, E. H. (1963). *Children and society.* New York: Norton.

Erikson, E. H. (1968). *Identity: Youth and crisis.* New York: Norton.

Estes, N. J., Smith-DiJulio, K., & Heinemann, M. E. (1980). *Nursing diagnosis of the alcoholic person.* St. Louis: C. V. Mosby.

Evans, R. I., Henderson, A., Hill, P., & Raines, B. (1979). Smoking in children and adolescents: Psychosocial determinants and prevention strategies. In N. Krasnegor (Ed.), *The behavioral aspects of smoking* (DHEW Publication No. ADM 79–882). Washington, DC: U. S. Government Printing Office.

Fass, P. S. (1977). *The damned and the beautiful: American youth in the 1920's.* New York: Oxford University Press.

Flay, B. (1985). What we know about the social influences approach to smoking prevention: Review and recommendations. In C. Bell & R. Battjes (Eds.), *Prevention research: Deterring drug abuse among children and adolescents* (NIDA Research Monograph Series No. 63. DHHS Publication No. ADM 85–1334). Washington, DC: U. S. Government Printing Office.

Goodman, P. (1956). *Growing up absurd.* New York: Random House.

Goodstadt, M. S. (1980). Drug education—a turn on or a turn off? *Journal of Drug Education, 10*(2), 89–99.

Goodstadt, M. S., Sheppard, M. A., & Chan, G. C. (1982). An evaluation of two school-based alcohol education programs. *Journal of Studies on Alcohol, 43,* 352–369.

Horn, D. (1979). Psychological analysis of establishment and maintenance of the smoking habit. In N. Krasnegor (Ed.), *Cigarette smoking as a dependence process* (DHEW Publication No. ADM 79–800). Washington, DC: U. S. Government Printing Office.

Jaffe, J. H., & Kanzler, M. (1979). Smoking as an addictive disorder. In N. Krasnegor (Ed.), *Cigarette smoking as a dependence process* (DHEW Publication No. ADM 79–800). Washington, DC: U. S. Government Printing Office.

Jessor, R. (1982). Problem behavior developmental transition in adolescence. *Journal of School Health, 52*(5), 295–300.

Jessor, R., & Jessor, S. L. (1977). *Problem behavior and psychosocial development: A longitudinal study of youth.* New York: Academic Press.

Jessor, R., & Jessor, S. L. (1980). Toward a social-psychological perspective on the prevention of alcohol abuse. In T. C. Harford, D. A. Parker, & L. Light (Eds.), *Normative approaches to the prevention of alcohol abuse and alcoholism* (DHEW Publication No. ADM 79–847). Washington, DC: U. S. Government Printing Office.

Johnston, L. D., Bachman, J. G., & O'Malley, P. M. (1980). *Highlights from student drug use in America 1975–1980* (DHHS Publication No. ADM 81–1066). Washington, DC: U. S. Government Printing Office.

Johnston, L. D., & O'Malley, P. M. (1985). Issues of validity and population coverage in student surveys of drug use. In B. A. Rouse, N. J. Kozel, & L. G. Richards (Eds.), *Self-report methods of estimating drug use: Meeting current challenges to validity* (NIDA Research Monograph No. 57; ADM 85–1402). Washington, DC: U. S. Government Printing Office.

Johnston, L. D., O'Malley, P. M., & Bachman, J. G. (1987). *National trends in drug use and related factors among American high school students and young adults, 1975–1986* (DHHS Publication No. ADM 87–1535). Washington, DC: U. S. Government Printing Office.

Kandel, D. B. (1978). Convergences in prospective longitudinal surveys of drug use in normal populations. In D. B. Kandel (Ed.), *Longitudinal research on drug use: Empirical findings and methodological issues* (pp. 3–38). Washington, DC: Hemisphere Publishing.

Kolata, G. (1989, August 11). In cities, poor families are dying of crack. *The New York Times,* p. 1.

Koop, C. E. (1986). The quest for a smoke-free young America by the year 2000. *Journal of School Health, 56*(1), 8–9.

Kozel, N. J., & Adams, E. H. (1986). Epidemiology of drug abuse: An overview. *Science, 234,* 970–974.

Lavenhar, M. A. (1980). Methodology in community research. In S. Einstein (Ed.), *The community's response to drug use.* New York: Pergamon Press.

Lindblad, R. A. (1983). Review of the concerned parent movement in the United States of America. *Bulletin on Narcotics, 35*(3), 41–52.

Lohrmann, D. K., & Fors, S. W. (1986). Can school-based educational programs really be expected to solve the adolescent drug abuse problem? *Journal of Drug Education, 16*(4), 327–339.

Macdonald, D. I. (1987). Patterns of alcohol and drug use among adolescents. *Pediatric Clinics of North America, 34*(2), 275–288.

Milgram, G. G. (1987). Alcohol and drug education programs. *Journal of Drug Education, 17*(1), 43–57.

Miller, M. (1987, November 23). Drug use: Down but not in the ghetto. *Newsweek,* p. 33.

Novak, W. (1980). *High culture: Marijuana in the lives of Americans.* New York: Alfred A. Knopf.

O'Malley, P. M., Bachman, J. G., & Johnston, L. D. (1983). Reliability and consistency in self-reports of drug use. *International Journal of the Addictions, 18,* 805–824.

Orem, D. E. (1985). *Nursing: Concepts of practice* (3d. ed.). New York: McGraw-Hill.

Peel, S. (1981). Scared witless. *The U. S. Journal of Drug and Alcohol Dependence, 5*(2), 9.

Polich, J. M., Reuter, P. L., & Kahan, J. P. (1984). *Strategies for controlling adolescent drug use.* Santa Monica, CA: Rand Corporation.

Prevention X three: Alcohol education for youth. (1980). National Clearinghouse for Alcohol Information, National Institute on Alcohol Abuse and Alcoholism. Rockville, MD.

Room, R. (1984). A "reverence for strong drink": The lost generation and the elevation of alcohol in American culture. *Journal of Studies on Alcohol, 45,* 540–546.

Rootman, I. (1985). Preventing alcohol problems: A challenge for health promotion. *Health Education, 24,* 2–7.

Roszak, T. (1969). *The making of a counter culture; Reflections on the technocratic society and its youthful opposition.* Garden City, NY: Anchor Book, Doubleday & Co.

Salisbury, H. (1958). *The shook-up generation*. New York: Harper & Row.

Schaps, E., DiBartolo, R., Moskowitz, J., Palley, C., & Churgin, S. (1981). A review of 127 drug-abuse prevention program evaluations. *Journal of Drug Issues, 11,* 17–43.

Schnoll, S. H. (1979). Alcohol and other substance abuse in adolescents. In E. L. Gottheil, A. T. McLellan, K. A. Druley, & A. I. Alterman (Eds.), *Addiction research and treatment: Converging trends* (pp. 40–45). New York: Pergamon Press.

Schuckit, M. A., & Rayses, V. (1979). Ethanol ingestion: Differences in blood acetaldehyde concentrations in relatives of alcoholics and controls. *Science, 203,* 54–55.

Surgeon General. (1964). *Smoking and health: Report of the advisory committee to the Surgeon General* (Public Health Service Publication No. 1103). Washington, DC: U. S. Government Printing Office.

Swett, W. E. (1984). Helping young people survive in a chemical world. *Family and Community Health, 7*(2), 63–73.

U. S. Department of Health and Human Services. (1981). *Fourth special report to the U. S. Congress on alcohol and health* (DHHS Publication No. ADM 81–1080). Washington, DC: U. S. Government Printing Office.

U. S. Department of Health and Human Services. (1984). *Fifth special report to the U. S. Congress on alcohol and health* (DHHS Publication No. ADM 84-1291). Washington, DC: U. S. Government Printing Office.

U. S. Department of Health and Human Services. (1987). *Sixth special report to the U. S. Congress on alcohol and health* (DHHS Publication No. ADM 87-1519). Washington, DC: U. S. Government Printing Office.

U. S. Department of Health and Human Services. (1990). *Healthy people 2000: National health promotion and disease prevention objectives.* Washington, DC: Author.

Weil, A. (1972). *The natural mind*. Boston: Houghton Mifflin.

Winokur, G. (1976). Alcoholism in adoptees raised apart from biological alcoholic parents. In M. Greenblatt & M. A. Schuckit (Eds.), *Alcoholism problems in women and children* (pp. 239–249). New York: Grune & Stratton.

Yablonsky, L. (1968). *The hippie trip*. New York: Western Publishing.

Zucker, R. (1976). Parental influences upon drinking patterns of their children. In M. Greenblatt & M. A. Schuckit (Eds.), *Alcoholism problems in women and children* (pp. 211–238). New York: Grune & Stratton.

CHAPTER 13

SUBSTANCE ABUSE IN ADULTHOOD

Janet H. Lee
Gerald Bennett

The previous chapter showed that the preadolescent and teenage years are times of psychoactive substance experimentation for a majority of young people in contemporary society. However, the group aged 18–25 has the highest prevalence of illicit drug use; it is also the time period when alcohol and cigarette use increases to a level about equal to the prevalence found in adults 26 and older (Miller & Cisin, 1980). Young adulthood brings greater opportunity to engage in substance use without interference from parents or other authority figures, and this use usually takes place in the context of peer relationships. In addition, during this time the use of alcohol becomes legal. With marihuana and other illicit drugs, the potential user is unlikely to go searching for an opportunity to begin use. The typical first experience with an illicit drug occurs after repeated opportunities to use the substance among acquaintances or friends (Somerville & Miller, 1980).

Most people are able to pass through this phase of heightened involvement with various substances without developing patterns of compulsive abuse; and, as adults, many are able to integrate some mix of controlled substance use into their lives without serious consequences. The self-reported consumption of alcohol is an example of this controlled substance use; an estimated one-third of the population are classed as abstainers, one-third as light drinkers, and one-third as moderate to heavy drinkers. The 10% of the drinking population who drink most heavily account for 50% of the alcohol consumed each year (U. S. Department of Health and Human Services, 1987).

There is no doubt that many social and recreational substance users believe their lives are enhanced by these habits. The linking of substance use with the "good life" is promoted and reinforced through advertising. The images of the attractive, successful smoker, the hearty beer drinker, and the sophisticated imbiber of wine and spirits cannot be avoided by any adult reading commercial magazines. Television reinforces this linkage through commercials portraying fun-filled evenings

drinking "lite" beer and amusing incidents encouraging consumers to drink wine coolers. In short, social substance use is promoted as desirable for adults, and it is accepted as such by many.

In addition to using drugs in recreational or social settings, many people use prescribed psychoactive drugs to relieve episodic symptoms of anxiety and stress associated with adult life, and this use is often appropriately guided and monitored by health professionals. Psychotherapeutic drugs accounted for 132 million prescriptions dispensed from retail pharmacies in 1986 (Drug utilization, 1988). Thus, controlled recreational and medical substance use in adulthood without a negative impact on health is "generally regarded as normal and appropriate" (American Psychiatric Association, 1987, p. 165).

Nevertheless, a substantial number of adults engage in clearly unhealthy patterns of substance abuse. This chapter looks at these patterns, focusing on the phenomenon of substance dependence. It concludes with a discussion of specific issues related to substance abuse in adulthood.

CHANGING CONCEPTS OF ADULT DEVELOPMENT

Developmental theory of adulthood has been substantially revised and expanded over the years. The 1970s and 1980s have seen an increased interest in the process of adult development in both the professional and lay literature. Books that describe the predictable changes in adulthood as well as those that suggest ways to cope with these changes and achieve a more fulfilling life have been best sellers. Traditional expectations about adult roles which emphasized marriage, child rearing, and occupation have been under fire from feminists, single parents, couples without children, homosexuals, and others seeking to legitimize diverse life-styles. Societal influences including the spiraling inflation of the late 1970s and early 1980s, expanding vocational opportunities for women, and increasing numbers of single parent families have resulted in more women entering and remaining in the job market. Clearly, role expectations for both men and women are being redefined.

Whether seeking adult success along traditional lines of occupational and family security or personal development through nontraditional life-styles, substance abusers are impaired in their ability to maintain healthy adjustment and adaptation. It is the phenomenon of substance dependence that is associated with the most serious role impairments and overall health consequences. The following case example provides a glimpse into these impairments and consequences as they occur in one person's life.

Case Example

S. J. is a 32-year-old white woman, divorced, with two children and no occupational skills. She began treatment in an outpatient alcoholism treatment program after a social worker had discovered a situation of child neglect during a home visit made pursuant to S. J.'s application for Aid to Families with Dependent Children (AFDC). The social worker found S. J. intoxicated, her apartment in disorder, the refrigerator empty except for beer and several containers of spoiled food, and the two children in a generally neglected state. On further evaluation, the social worker determined that S. J.'s parental rights depended on participation in an alcoholism treatment program, to which she agreed.

The history taken at the treatment center revealed a pattern of "sneak" drinking since S. J.'s early teens. Her family was never fully aware of her drinking until, at an older sister's wedding, S. J. became intoxicated. From that time, the older sister swore she would never forgive S. J., and her parents began a cycle of punishment, ambivalence, and hopelessness in an attempt to "talk some sense" into S. J. about her drinking.

S. J. escaped this situation when she married at the age of 23 and continued to drink secretly every day while fulfilling the role of housewife and mother for 8 years. S. J. found that drinking more and more was required to get the feeling of intoxication that she had enjoyed so much when she was younger. It became usual for her to drink a couple of bottles of wine and nearly a six-pack of beer a day. Each morning, S. J.'s head ached and her hands shook until she had several drinks. She knew by this time that she was an alcoholic but tried very hard to keep up appearances with her children and husband. In the eighth year of the marriage, when S. J. was 31, her husband left her and did not return.

For the first time, S. J. was thrown into the job market, with no skills, and ended up working for a maid service while her mother kept the children. This arrangement continued until 3 months before the time of treatment entry. At that time S. J. was fired for drinking on the job, and she was in such a debilitated condition that seeking further employment was impossible. Her mother helped to pay the rent and advised S. J. to apply for AFDC until she found another job. Her mother also told her to "stop drinking" and to do something about "how she looked."

The social worker soon called the mother to elicit information, and when she was finally requested to take charge of the children in the event that S. J. refused treatment, the mother agreed. Now S. J. has undergone detoxification for alcohol dependence, is beginning to talk about her past and present difficulties, and wonders what she will do next. Will she be able to stop drinking as the therapists say she must? Will she lose her children?

SUBSTANCE ABUSE AND DEPENDENCE

One of the long-standing difficulties both within and outside the substance abuse field is the lack of a consistently used, clearly defined nomenclature. This difficulty is compounded by the large variety of disciplines involved in the education, treatment, and research of substance abuse problems, each with its own terminology. The lack of precision causes difficulty in communication among professionals, hampers interpretation of research findings, and impedes the understanding and responses among those responsible for public policy decisions (Rinaldi, Steindler, Wilford, & Goodwin, 1988).

Throughout this text, the term substance abuse is used in a broad sense, which includes any number of consumption patterns or instances of use involving significant hazards to health. For example, both the nonalcoholic driving while intoxicated and the chronic alcoholic of 20 years experiencing withdrawal have substance abuse problems. However, only the latter person, based on the information provided, would clearly be alcohol dependent. This expansive concept of substance abuse allows discussion of a broad range of problems with ease and without undue specification. In exploring the concept of dependence in some depth in this chapter, it will be helpful to examine the American Psychiatric Association (APA) classification system.

APA Diagnostic System

APA's current diagnostic system (DSM-III-R) includes a category termed psychoactive substance use disorders (American Psychiatric Association, 1987). The official list of substance use disorders is presented in Appendix B. The diagnostic manual notes: "This diagnostic class deals with symptoms and maladaptive behavioral changes associated with more or less regular use of psychoactive substances that affect the central nervous system" (American Psychiatric Association, 1987, p. 165). The psychoactive substance use disorders are divided into two basic types: substance abuse and substance dependence.

Psychoactive substance abuse is distinguished from normal and appropriate substance use by three criteria. The first is a maladaptive pattern of substance use. This can be indicated either by substance use despite the knowledge of "social, occupational, psychological or physical" problems that it causes, or by continued use in situations which are "physically hazardous" (American Psychiatric Association, 1987, p. 169). The second criterion is that the pattern of behavior has continued for a month or has reappeared over a period of time. The third criterion for substance abuse is that the individual has never had symptoms severe enough to have been diagnosed with psychoactive substance dependence (American Psychiatric Association, 1987).

Psychoactive substance dependence is a "cluster of cognitive, behavioral, and physiologic symptoms" that indicate "impaired control of psychoactive substance use despite adverse consequences" (American Psychiatric Association, 1987, p. 166). There are nine criteria for this category, three of which must be met for an in-

dividual to be diagnosed as substance dependent. This pattern of behavior, like substance abuse, must have continued for a month or reappeared over time. The criteria include: tolerance, withdrawal, inability to control the quantity or duration of substance use, unsuccessful attempts at reducing substance use, spending much time in the pursuit of the substance use, inability to fulfill major role expectations at work, school or home, reduction or loss of important activities because of substance use, continued use despite perceived negative consequences, and the use of the substance to prevent withdrawal symptoms. Substance dependence may be further classified as mild, moderate, or severe, and in full or partial remission (American Psychiatric Association, 1987).

The current system of psychoactive substance use classification is substantially different from the previous APA criteria. No longer is substance dependence characterized solely by physiologic tolerance or withdrawal symptoms. The same basic criteria serve to distinguish abuse and dependence for each of the substance use classes, and a system for indicating the severity of the illness has been included. The impact of these changes was noted in one preliminary study that indicates an increase in the number of individuals meeting the new criteria for a substance use disorder. Also the new criteria may allow for diagnosis earlier in the course of the illness (Rounsaville, Kosten, Williams, & Spitzer, 1987).

Addiction

The reader has undoubtedly noticed the interchangeable use of the terms addiction and dependence in this text. This is because, despite the abandoning of the term "addiction" by APA, WHO and others, it continues in common usage and the professional literature. It is sometimes used to describe psychologic habituation, evidence of tolerance and withdrawal, or, more commonly, all of these conditions at once. In this book, addiction and dependence are used as synonymous terms.

THE NATURE AND EXTENT OF SUBSTANCE ABUSE PROBLEMS AMONG ADULTS

The focus of this section is on problems related to substances capable of producing a dependence syndrome as identified by APA: alcohol, amphetamines, cannabis, cocaine, nicotine, opioids, and sedatives, hypnotics, or anxiolytics. Problems associated with nondependent and dependent abuse of these substances are included with an emphasis on the latter. Hallucinogens, inhalants and phencyclidine (PCP), while classified by APA as drugs capable of producing dependence, will not be included in this section because of the relatively small numbers of regular adult users.

Alcohol Abuse and Dependence

Seixas (1986) stated: "For every drinker the first drink is a kind of initiation into an adult mode of living" (p. 67). According to the 1985 *National Household Survey on Drug Abuse*, 92.8% of adults ages 18–25, 93.2% of adults ages 26–34, and 88% of adults over age 34 have used alcohol. Of these, 33.5% of young adults, 33.6% of middle adults, and 29.2% of those over 34 report using alcohol once a week or more (National Institute on Drug Abuse [NIDA], 1987). While there is still much debate about which symptoms constitute a diagnosis of alcoholism, it is estimated that alcohol creates a problem for 18 million individuals over the age of 18 (U. S. Department of Health and Human Services [DHHS], 1987). This problem may relate to either abuse or dependence as defined by APA.

According to DSM-III-R there are three major patterns of chronic alcohol dependence: daily drinking of large amounts on a regular basis, weekend binging, and binges of heavy daily drinking between relatively long periods of sobriety. All three patterns can be associated with alcoholism. In addition, it is common for individuals who abuse alcohol to use or abuse other psychoactive drugs. This is particularly true in adults under age 30 (American Psychiatric Association, 1987).

The enormous impact of alcohol abuse and dependence on adults and society becomes evident on examination of the findings of recent studies. A summary of these findings was recently presented to the U. S. Congress in the *Sixth Special Report to the U. S. Congress on Alcohol and Health* (U. S. Department of Health and Human Services, 1987). Selected highlights from this report are presented below. Some points are included to further define the extent of drinking and drinking problems among adults.

Analysis of mortality data showed that death caused by excessive blood alcohol resulted in an average estimated loss of 29.1 years of potential life; death from alcohol abuse, 24.1 years; and death from alcohol dependence, 15 years.

Nearly half of the accidental deaths, suicides and homicides are alcohol related. Victims are intoxicated in about one-third of drownings, homicides, boating deaths, and aviation deaths, and in about one-fourth of suicides.

Nearly half of convicted jail inmates were under the influence of alcohol when they committed their offenses. More than half of the persons convicted of violent crimes had been drinking at the time of the offense.

Women drink significantly less heavily than men and have fewer drinking-related problems; however, the level of drinking in women ages 35–64 has increased.

Abstention from alcohol is more common among blacks. Black men are less likely to drink heavily than white men but the reverse is true for women.

Hispanic American men have a higher rate of alcohol use than the general population.

American Indians have alcohol-related illness and injury rates that are three times higher than the general population.

Homeless persons have a high rate of alcohol-related problems.

Approximately 7% of drinkers experienced moderate levels of dependence symptoms, and 10% experience moderate levels of tangible social or personal consequences.

The economic costs for alcoholism and problem drinking were estimated at $117 billion in 1983 (U. S. Department of Health and Human Services, 1987, pp. 6, 12, 21–23).

Although this compilation of facts and estimates may be overwhelming to the first-time reader, it is certainly not exhaustive in describing the tremendous cost of alcohol-related problems to society. A word of caution is in order, however. Remember that all estimates can be "turned around." For example, it is true that half of all accidental deaths are alcohol related. Notice, however, that when it is said that half of all accidental deaths are *not* alcohol related, one seems to come away with a more objective assessment of the situation. A prominent failing of the American temperance movement was the extremes to which societal evils were attributed to alcohol.

Amphetamine Abuse and Dependence

The 1985 *Household Survey* mentioned earlier found that 17.3% of young adults (18–25), 18.2% of middle adults (26–34) and 4.2% of older adults (35+) reported nonmedical experience with stimulants (excluding cocaine) at some time during their lives (National Institute on Drug Abuse, 1987). This compares to a 1982 rate in young adults of 18% and a 26+ age group rate of 6.2% (Miller et al., 1983). The increase in the 26–34 age group is likely the result of two factors. In 1985 there was a change in the reporting pattern for adult use from two divisions (18–25 and 26+) to three divisions (18–25, 26–34, and 35+). Additionally, the lifetime prevalence of stimulant use in the over 26 age group has consistently increased since reporting began in 1972. As each new cohort of persons enters this age group, they bring with them a background of psychoactive substance use from their youth.

The decline in the lifetime prevalence among the young adult group continues a trend that began in 1977. According to the University of Michigan survey of national trends in drug use among high school students and young adults, annual prevalence of stimulant use among young adults has declined dramatically since 1982, especially among college students. Along with this decline, however, is an increase in the use of over-the-counter stay-awake pills usually containing caffeine (Johnston, O'Malley, & Bachman, 1987).

There are generally two patterns of amphetamine abuse. The first is daily or almost daily use of the drug; the second is a binging pattern in which the drug is consumed in high doses for a relatively short period of time followed by one or more days of nonuse. A binge is frequently followed by a "crash" (American Psychiatric Association, 1987). Probably the most common severe disability following a pattern of compulsive amphetamine abuse is psychosis. The features of amphetamine psychosis are discussed in Chapter 4. Although for many years amphetamines were considered nonaddictive, it is now clear that tolerance may develop rapidly, and withdrawal, marked by emotional and physical depression, can radically disrupt normal adult life.

Cannabis Abuse and Dependence

Marihuana is the most popular illicit drug in the United States (American Psychiatric Association, 1987). Approximately 18 million Americans smoke it on a regular basis (Morganthau, 1988). In 1985, the lifetime prevalence rates of marihuana use were estimated at 60.5% of young adults (18–25), 58.5% of middle adults (26–34), and 15.9% of older adults (35+) with 21.7% of the young adults, 16.8% of the middle adults, and 2.2% of older adults having used the drug within the past month (National Institute on Drug Abuse, 1987).

In terms of lifetime prevalence and current use in the young adult group, the 1985 rate continues a downward trend that began in 1982. It appears that marihuana use in this age group peaked in the late 1970s. Yet, in 1982, approximately half the young men and one-third of the young women who had tried marihuana were current users. And, as shown in Table 13.1, substantial proportions of young adult marihuana smokers fell into the categories of using "100 or more times" and "daily" use. Also, the extent to which alcohol was used on the same occasion with marihuana is indicative of the polydrug abuse patterns in this population.

A comparison of the prevalence estimates from 1982 and 1985 reveals an important trend. As those who used marihuana in the 1970s move into the middle and older groups, they bring with them the experience of that era. Thus, current marihuana use among middle-aged adults is no longer a rarity (Miller et al., 1983).

Although there is a growing consensus that marihuana use is dangerous for children and adolescents, there is still much disagreement about adult use. There is no need to argue whether a dependence syndrome can develop (American Psychiatric Association, 1987). It is the question of abuse that is problematic—does regular cannabis use impair adult role performance?

In the past, much of the debate regarding marihuana use was centered around the concept of an amotivational syndrome. Ambition, competitiveness, and productivity are all cherished and rewarded in our society. The amotivational syndrome refers to a condition in which an individual, after establishing a pattern of regular cannabis use, loses interest in school or work and generally retreats from what society would regard as sustained and productive behavior. Jones (1977) reviewed a number of studies and uncontrolled clinical reports, which focused on the working habits of cannabis users, and did find evidence of impaired productivity. However, he was reluctant to use the term amotivational syndrome because low productivity may simply be due to chronic high-dose intoxication rather than to any larger syndrome existing between periods of use. Cohen (1982) summarized several studies dealing with

Table 13.1

Patterns of Use, Marihuana: Young Adults and Older Adults in 1982

	Young Adults Ages 18–25 (N=1283)	Older Adults Ages 26+ (N=2760)
Lifetime frequency of use		
1–2 times	9.5%	6.2%
3–10 times	12.6%	5.0%
11–99 times	17.4%	4.9%
100 or more times	24.0%	6.9%
Not sure how many times	0.6%	*
Never used	35.9%	77.0%
Alcohol use on the same occasion		
Usually	15.6%	5.3%
About half the time	8.1%	3.5%
Occasionally/rarely	27.3%	7.1%
Never	10.0%	5.9%
Not sure/skipped	3.0%	1.3%
Never used	35.9%	77.0%
"Daily" use		
Ever used on 20+ days in one month	21.1%	4.2%
All other users	42.9%	18.8%
Never used	35.9%	77.0%
Days used in past month		
20 or more	7.0%	1.1%
5–19	8.7%	2.1%
3–4	3.1%	1.2%
1–2	8.0%	2.2%
Not past month user	36.6%	16.4%
Not sure	0.6%	*
Never used	35.9%	77.0%

Source: Miller, J. D., Cisin, I. H., Gardner-Keaton, H., Harrell, A. V., Wirtz, P. N., Abelson, H. I., & Fishburne, P.M. (1983). *National Survey on Drug Abuse: Main Findings 1982* (DHHS Pub. No. ADM 83–1263). Washington, DC: U. S. Government Printing Office.

Note: Some categories do not add to 100% because of rounding.

*Less than 0.5%

amotivational syndrome and concluded that "frequently consumed marijuana appears to diminish drive states and goal direction" (p. 9). More recently, Jones (1987) reviewed numerous studies and concluded that there was evidence of impaired brain function for a few hours after each dose of marihuana, but it could not be determined if the amotivational syndrome was caused by drug use or if the drug use was a result of an amotivational state.

While the controversy over an amotivational effect from marihuana use continues, the current debate centers on impaired job performance. The 1987 Conrail-Amtrak collision focused national attention on the problem of marihuana use. Although marihuana impairment was cited as the cause of the accident, it is clear that many other factors were involved (Gieringer, 1988).

Evidence from simulations, laboratory experiments, and accident reports were reviewed by Gieringer (1988) and Jones (1987). They concluded that marihuana use appears to impair some but not all aspects of driving behavior. In addition, when marihuana use was involved in a fatal accident, it was almost always in combination with alcohol. Jones concluded that no currently available studies clearly demonstrate that workers using marihuana have more accidents or different work behavior than other employees. However, knowing that marihuana impairs brain functioning for a few hours after use and assuming that optimal brain functioning is necessary in the workplace, it seems likely that marihuana use on the job does effect performance (Jones, 1987).

Cocaine Abuse and Dependence

Although marihuana is the most popular illicit drug in the United States, it is clear that cocaine abuse and dependence was the major illicit drug problem for American society in the 1980s. Beginning in 1984 with the introduction of crack, a form of freebase cocaine, the sociologic problems of cocaine dependence increased dramatically. The availability of the drug combined with the low cost and intense "high" have created a shift in drug usage that affects all socioeconomic levels.

While current statistics on the use of cocaine are difficult to obtain, the *National Household Survey on Drug Abuse* estimates that, in 1985, 25.2% of adults ages 18–25 and 24.1% of adults ages 26–34 had tried cocaine, and 7.6% of young adults and 6.1% of middle adults had used it within the past month (National Institute on Drug Abuse, 1987). These estimates undoubtedly do not accurately reflect the full extent of crack use in recent years. It is currently estimated that 40% of young adults have used cocaine and 6.7% have tried crack (Adler, 1988; Johnston et al., 1987). Unlike other drugs of abuse, it appears that the number of adult cocaine users is increasing (Johnston et al., 1987). The at-risk population for crack use is estimated at 29 million individuals or 12% of the United States population (Morganthau & Miller, 1988).

Like other substances of abuse, cocaine use can be either a daily or an episodic pattern. Daily use may involve high or low doses of cocaine and may occur throughout the day or be restricted to specific time periods such as after working hours. Binging is common and generally ends when the user collapses from physical exhaustion or when the supply of cocaine is depleted. Binges are often followed by an extremely intense crash that is relieved by the use of alcohol, sedatives, hypnotics, or anxiolytic drugs (American Psychiatric Association, 1987).

Along with the increase in cocaine use is an increase in the numbers of individuals affected by the medical consequences of that use. According to the Drug Abuse Warning Network (DAWN) reports from hospital emergency departments in 1984, cocaine use was involved in 10.69% of the visits—up from 6.6% the previous year (National Institute on Drug Abuse, 1985; Weiss & Greenfield, 1986). Since 1983, the rate of cocaine overdoses in emergency departments around the country has increased 700% (Morganthau & Miller, 1988). The number of babies born to women who use crack also increased dramatically. In one study of 36 U. S. hospitals, 11% of pregnant women surveyed admitted to illicit drug use, with crack being the most common (Langone, 1988). Because crack use is attracting more females than other street drugs and because sexual services are traded directly for the drug, there has been an increase in the rate of sexually transmitted diseases in areas of increased cocaine use (Goldsmith, 1988).

The advent of crack has created enormous problems for the criminal justice system. The New York City arrest rate for crack rose from zero through June 1985 to 19,074 in the first 10 months of 1988 (Adler, 1988). Overall, the homicide rate has increased 18% in New York City, 44% in Houston, and 65% in Washington, DC with the percentage of drug-related homicides increasing from 25% in 1980 to 40% in 1988 (Slaughter, 1988).

These examples of the effects of cocaine abuse and dependence are only a few of many that could be given. From the low-income ghetto areas where adolescents earn $3000 a day dealing in drugs to well-known sports and entertainment personalities dying from cocaine use, from the war on crime in Washington, DC to the discovery of crack houses in rural areas, the impact of cocaine use on American society has been profound (Lamar, 1988).

Nicotine Dependence

In recent years there has been a growing concern about the addictive nature of tobacco use. One of the changes made by the APA with the publication of the DSM-III-R in 1987 was the broadening of the concept of nicotine dependence. The same diagnostic criteria are now used for nicotine dependence as for other psychoactive substance dependence disorders (American Psychiatric Association, 1987). The 1988 Surgeon General's report on smoking reaffirms the position of the APA and others and demonstrates conclusively that cigarette smoking and other forms of tobacco use are capable of causing dependence in the same sense as heroin or cocaine (Surgeon General, 1988).

Cigarette smoking is the leading cause of nicotine dependence. It is also the largest preventable cause of death in the United States, responsible for more than 300,000 deaths each year (Surgeon General, 1979b, 1988). Smoking is associated with heart and blood vessel diseases, chronic bronchitis and emphysema, cancers of the lung, larynx, pharynx, oral cavity, esophagus, pancreas, and urinary bladder, and other disorders ranging from minor respiratory infections to stomach ulcers. An estimated 10 million Americans suffer from smoking-related chronic diseases (Surgeon General, 1979b).

In 1985, approximately 76% of adults ages 18–25, 80.6% of those ages 26–34, and 80.4% of those over 34 had tried cigarette smoking (National Institute on Drug Abuse, 1987). This compares to a 1982 estimate of 76.9% for young adults, 85.4% of middle adults and 76.3% of older adults (Miller et al., 1983). Recognition of the hazards of smoking among adults has led to a decline in lifetime prevalence and regular use. From 1965 to 1985, the proportion of regular adult male smokers decreased from 52.1% to 32.7%. From 1965 to 1976, the proportion of regular adult women smokers, unlike men, remained nearly constant at 32%–33%. A slight decline to approximately 28% occurred from 1976 to

1979. In 1985, the estimate of adult female smoking prevalence was 28.3%. The overall smoking prevalence for adults of both sexes was 30.4% in 1985—the lowest recorded value in at least 50 years (Surgeon General, 1980, 1983, 1988). Of considerable concern, however, is the increase in female smokers in the young adult population (Johnston et al., 1987).

Opioid Abuse and Dependence

The lifetime prevalence for heroin use in the 1985 *Household Survey* was 1.2% for the 18–25 age group, 2.6% for the 26–34 age group, and 0.5% for the 35 and over age group (National Institute on Drug Abuse, 1987). This survey, in contrast to earlier reports, did not specify heroin use in either the past month or past year because of the low prevalence of use. The trends since 1972 have shown a steady decline in the lifetime prevalence rate among the young adult group, which leveled off in the early 1980s, and a steady but small increase in the 26–34 age group as those who used heroin earlier in life become older (Miller et al., 1983). Interestingly, the nonmedical use of analgesics has remained fairly constant in the young adult group since first measured in 1979. In 1985, the young adult prevalence rate was 11.4%, the middle adult rate was 13.2% , and the older adult rate was 2.9% (National Institute on Drug Abuse, 1987).

Opioid dependence is developed in one of two ways (American Psychiatric Association, 1987). The most common pattern involves adolescents and young adults who obtain opioids from illegal sources. These drugs may be used alone for their euphoric effect or in combination with other substances of abuse. In the second pattern, an individual legitimately obtains a prescription for an analgesic or cough suppressant but gradually increases the dosage and the frequency of use. The increase is justified by the individual as necessary to treat the original symptoms, but eventually the substance-seeking behavior takes control.

Perhaps nothing has done more to shake traditional notions of heroin addiction than the Vietnam War experience. Robbins (1974) found that over 90% of those veterans who had been addicted in Vietnam did not return to heroin dependence in the United States; there were also reports of recreational use of heroin without eventual development of a dependence syndrome. These findings were in direct opposition to the long-held belief that once a person tried heroin and experienced its euphoric powers, addiction was likely; and once addicted, there was no turning back. This belief is now referred to as the "irreversibility myth" (Johnson, 1977). The implications of exposing this myth have been numerous, including: *(1)* bringing heroin back into focus as another psychoactive drug, with addictive qualities, to be sure, but not a substance beyond human will to resist after experimental use; *(2)* support for the theory of a tendency in society toward controlled substance use, with only a minority of people going on to compulsive use after experimentation—indirectly suggesting that these people may be psychologically or constitutionally different from those who do not become addicted; and *(3)* realization that the deviant social adjustment of the addict appears to play a significant role in the dependence pattern that may outweigh the addictive properties of heroin itself.

The implications of heroin dependence for the health of young adults and the society have been summarized as follows:

> The toll from highly addicting heroin includes premature death and severe disability, family disruption, and crime committed to maintain the habit. The heroin user is at very high risk of overdose death, of hepatitis and other infections from contaminated equipment and impurities in the drug, and from chronic undernutrition because money is spent on heroin instead of food. Preventing consequences of overdose and infection in users is virtually impossible since there is no control over the strength and purity of the drug or the means of administration (Surgeon General, 1979a, p. 126).

Of particular concern with this population is the sharing of needles and syringes, which places the heroin user and others who inject illicit drugs at high risk for the development of acquired immune deficiency syndrome (AIDS).

Sedative, Hypnotic, or Anxiolytic Abuse and Dependence

Although statistical data from multiple sources can be misleading, it does appear that the use of sedatives, hypnotics, and anxiolytics is declining. Data based on prescription audits indicate that the use of anxiolytic drugs peaked in 1973. Prescriptions for benzodiazepines decreased from approximately 85 million in 1973 to 55.4 million in 1981 (Baum, Kennedy, Forbes, & Jones, 1983; Rickels, 1981).

It is the enormous legal production of sedatives, hypnotics, and anxiolytics for medical use that facilitates widespread availability of the substances, through pharmacies with a prescription, or through the black market (huge amounts of these substances are diverted from legal channels). In one national household survey of drug abuse, 11% of young adults (18–25) reported nonmedical experience with sedatives and 12.2% reported nonmedical use of tranquilizers at some time during their lives. In the same survey, 12.4% of middle adults (26–34) and 2.6% of older adults reported experience with nonmedical use of sedatives while 13.8% of middle adults and 4.7% of older adults reported nonmedical use of tranquilizers (National Institute on Drug Abuse, 1987). As with the other psychoactive substances mentioned in this chapter, these figures represent an apparent decline in the use of both sedatives and tranquilizers for nonmedical purposes among young adults and an increase in the nonmedical use of these drugs in middle adults. Populations such as those found in the military, prisons, hospitals, or skid row were not included since only households were surveyed, and therefore, the findings may underestimate overall population drug abuse prevalence.

The DSM-III-R (American Psychiatric Association, 1987) notes two patterns of sedative, hypnotic, and anxiolytic abuse and dependence. In the first pattern, an individual receives a prescription for a sedative, hypnotic, or anxiolytic drug in response to symptoms of anxiety or insomnia and gradually increases the prescribed dose without the physician's knowledge. To maintain an adequate supply, the individual may see several physicians, complaining of anxiety or difficulty sleeping, never revealing that multiple prescriptions are being issued. It is usually a matter of time, with increasing doses, before a full-fledged dependence problem develops, with the prospect of eventual withdrawal and the many problems related to maintaining a high-dose habit.

The second pattern usually involves teenagers or young adults and is characterized by periodic recreational intoxication. Here, the object is to become "high" during specific occasions, such as concerts, parties or, as the saying goes, any event can become an occasion for taking the drug as an abuse pattern becomes established. The hazards of this pattern are connected with the unreliable quality of drugs purchased on the black market; loss of behavioral control during intoxication associated with accidents; ever-present danger of overdose, particularly when the drug (or drugs) is used with alcohol or other depressants; and a tendency to rely on drugs for recreation, thereby setting the stage for possible dependence.

The decline in the medical use of this class of drugs in general and the benzodiazepines in particular was due, in large part, to the publicity surrounding one particular anxiolytic drug, Valium. Although Valium is not the only medication to receive widespread publicity, it is unique in the amount of attention received both in the media and the political arena (Medd, 1983). Introduced in 1963, Valium became the most frequently prescribed medication in the world (Cohen, 1983). The widespread acceptance of the drug is demonstrated in one movie when a psychiatrist attempts to deal with someone experiencing anxiety in a crowded department store. He turns to the group of onlookers and asks if anyone has a Valium—immediately an unbelievable commotion begins as nearly all of the bystanders reach into their pocketbooks or coats for the requested pill. By the mid-1970s, the problems of prolonged use and abuse of the drug began to surface. Magazine articles appeared emphasizing the adverse effects of the drug, and because Valium was so widely used, these articles along with "testimonies" of well-known individuals generated considerable public interest (Cohen, 1983). In 1979, the Senate Subcommittee on Health and Scientific Research held the so-called "Valium hearing" on the public health problem posed by the widespread use of this drug. By 1981, Valium had dropped to sixth in the list of frequently prescribed medications (Baum et al., 1983).

Finally, it is important to note that tranquilizers and sedatives are often used in suicide attempts. Cherubin (1980) is bold enough to admit in print that no one really knows the number of deaths due to drugs, sedatives, or otherwise. Moreover, it is difficult to know how many sedative deaths are intentional and how many are accidental.

SELECTED ISSUES IN ADULT SUBSTANCE ABUSE INTERVENTION

Employee Assistance Programs

Early intervention is an idea whose time has come and the focus is increasingly on the workplace. More than

60% of the Fortune 500 companies offer some kind of employee assistance program (EAP) (Dixon, 1988). These programs vary from those aimed primarily at alcohol and drug problems to those with a broader approach including identification, assessment, referral, and follow-up services for a wide variety of psychiatric and mental health problems (U. S. Department of Health and Human Services, 1987). Increasingly, the broad-based programs are gaining approval with many now offering preventive services such as risk appraisal, stress reduction training, and parenting classes (Dixon, 1988).

EAPs use employee performance as a basis for constructive confrontation. Supervisors are trained to identify and confront an employee with evidence of impaired performance or behavior problems and offer assistance in resolving the problems (U. S. Department of Health and Human Services, 1987).

The employment setting can be viewed as an ideal location for interventions aimed at preventing chronic substance abuse for several reasons. First, an intervention program based in an employment setting has frequent contact with the adult population. This logic is obvious and is similar to the rationale for placing primary prevention programs for young people in schools. Second, the desire to maintain a job can be a powerful motivator to seek help for a substance abuse problem when, otherwise, motivation for treatment does not exist. Third, as the practice of drug testing in the workplace becomes more widespread, a mechanism for confirming suspected intoxication or impairment as well as follow-up testing after treatment is in place (Moreland & McPhaul, 1988). Finally, ineffective job performance, tardiness and absenteeism, and increased accident rates have been attributed to drug use in the workplace (U. S. Department of Health and Human Services, 1987; Moreland & McPhaul, 1988). It makes economic sense for management to provide services which address these issues, thereby increasing productivity and lowering employee attrition.

Homeless Persons

The number of homeless people in the United States increased dramatically during the 1980s. National estimates of the homeless population have ranged from 250,000 to 350,000 (U. S. Department of Housing and Urban Development, 1984) to more than 2 million (Hombs & Snyder, 1982). Although studies by the U. S. Conference of Mayors (1986, 1987) show that the fastest growing group among the homeless are families, individual adults comprise the single largest group in the homeless population. With the notable exception of women who are homeless with their families, alcoholism is the most frequent health disorder diagnosed among homeless adults (Institute of Medicine, 1988). Ten percent of the clients of the Johnson-Pew clinics for homeless people were reported to have illicit drug problems (Wright & Weber, 1987). Other studies have reported higher prevalences of illicit drug use in homeless populations (Institute of Medicine, 1988). The risk for human immunodeficiency virus (HIV) infection is especially high for homeless intravenous drug users. Furthermore, substantial numbers of homeless people have multiple substance abuse and mental health problems as coexisting conditions.

An understanding of the problem of homelessness must begin with the recognition that "the cause of homelessness is lack of housing" (Kozol, 1988, p. 11). Thus, the fundamental solution to homelessness lies in substantially increasing the availability of affordable housing. However, for the homeless person with alcohol or other drug problems, substance abuse intervention is also needed. Beginning in 1988, the National Institute on Alcohol Abuse and Alcoholism (NIAAA) and the National Institute on Drug Abuse (NIDA) supported nine community demonstration projects for alcohol and drug abuse treatment of homeless individuals. See Argeriou & McCarty (1990) for a full description of these projects. A summary of the nine demonstration projects is presented in Table 13.2. Additional research demonstration projects will be funded by NIAAA and NIDA in the 1990s with an emphasis on rigorous evaluation of innovative interventions.

Changing Attitudes Toward Substance Abuse

There was a definite trend in the 1980s toward decreasing public acceptance of smoking, drinking, and illicit drug use. The Surgeon General's emphasis on a smoke-free workplace, limitations on smoking in public places, and a shift in attitudes to recognize the rights of nonsmokers created a climate which discouraged tobacco use. Groups such as Mothers Against Driving Drunk (MADD) increased public awareness and changed

Table 13.2
NIAAA Summary of Demonstration Grants

Project Name	Projected Estimate of Target Population to be Served	Treatment Settings	Kinds of Treatment	Related Services	Projected Number of Clients Served	Evaluation Methodology
Treating Homeless and Dual Diagnosis Substance Abusers Anchorage, AK	66% men 40% white 7% black 44% Alaskan native	Drop-in and detox center; supportive housing	Medical, diagnostic, alcohol, and mental health treatment services	Residential treatment opportunities; vocational education	3020	Psychosocial evaluation; follow-up study with a control group
Stabilization Services for Homeless Substance Abusers Boston, MA	90% men 66% white 25% black 9% Hispanic	Residential treatment centers; shelters	Intensive case management	Coordination of substance abuse rehabilitation services with other social services	960	Factorial design: program location (treatment agency vs. shelter) by case manager (present vs. absent)
Sober Transitional Housing and Employment Project Los Angeles, CA	80% men 44% white 40% black 26% Hispanic	Residential treatment center; supportive housing	Alcohol recovery; preemployment program	Vocational education; housing assistance	180	Retrospective study of program completers vs. noncompleters; comparison of outcomes; analysis of program implementation
Project Connect for Homeless Alcoholics and Drug Abusers Louisville, KY	100% men 60% white 40% black	Shelter/sobering-up station; job training center	Case management; alcohol/drug treatment	Work adjustment program; jail liaison	900	Longitudinal design; evaluation of program effects using causal modeling and ethnographic data
Community Treatment for the Chronic Public Inebriate Minneapolis, MN	100% men 43% native American	Community agencies	Intensive case management	Alcohol treatment; housing; financial support; employment	190	Controlled study of intensive vs. traditional case management comparing outcomes; documentation of client characteristics

Table 13.2 (continued)
NIAAA Summary of Demonstration Grants

Project Name	Projected Estimate of Target Population to be Served	Treatment Settings	Kinds of Treatment	Related Services	Projected Number of Clients Served	Evaluation Methodology
Outreach and Engagement for Homeless Alcoholic Women New York, NY	100% women and their children 95% black and Hispanic	Alcoholism clinic; comprehensive multi-service agency	Outreach-engagement teams; acupuncture clinic	Job and housing placement; child care; basic education/ literacy classes	1070 families	Time series analysis of significant service utilization patterns
Comprehensive Alcohol Recovery Services Oakland, CA	50% women 30% white 60% black 7% Hispanic 1% Asian	Alcohol crisis centers	Street and community outreach and education program	Drop-in center; alcohol inpatient services; sober housing	6370	Computer-based client tracking; structured interviews with program participants, providers and administrators; quantification of service activities
Comprehensive Services for Dual-Diagnosed Homeless Philadelphia, PA	90% men 30–35% white 55–60% black 15% Hispanic	Rehabilitation; supportive residential program	Intensive case management; outreach; individual service plans	Supportive living programs; boarding homes	210	Construction of a typology of dually diagnosed individuals; documentation of client activities and progress
Breaking the Cycle: The Addicted Homeless Mother Philadelphia, PA	100% women and their children 50% black	Supportive residential program	Outpatient alcohol/ drug treatment; housing	Rehabilitation and socialization services	200	Clients randomly assigned to residential and non-residential treatment settings; outcomes assessed at multiple points in time

Source: National Institute on Alcohol Abuse and Alcoholism. (1988, October). Synopses of Community Demonstration Grant Project for Alcohol and Drug Abuse Treatment of Homeless Individuals. Rockville, MD: Author.

attitudes and laws regarding drinking and driving. Some communities outlawed the "Happy Hour." Increased legal penalties for driving under the influence (DUI) of alcohol and other drugs and aggressive enforcement by law enforcement personnel sent the message that drinking and driving was no longer acceptable behavior in American society. For the first time in American history, a director of national drug control policy was appointed and began developing a comprehensive national anti-illicit drug effort. "Drug czar" William Bennett began placing high priority on making illicit drug use socially unacceptable.

SUMMARY

This chapter explored substance abuse in adulthood. Following a brief discussion of adult development, a case example of an adult substance abuser was presented. The APA diagnostic criteria were discussed as well as some of the difficulties with terminology. A summary of selected statistical data was given for the major substances of abuse. Patterns of abuse and dependence were identified for each drug class, and implications for adult health were described. A broad picture of substance abuse among adults has emerged with a special emphasis on problems with those drugs capable of producing a dependence syndrome. Finally, selected issues in adult substance abuse intervention were discussed.

REFERENCES

Adler, J. (1988, November 28). Hour by hour crack. *Newsweek*, pp. 64–67, 69–70, 75.

American Psychiatric Association. (1987). *Diagnostic and statistical manual of mental disorders* (3d ed. revised). Washington, DC: Author.

Argeriou, M., & McCarty, D. (Eds.) (1990). Treating alcoholism and drug abuse among homeless men and women: Nine community demonstration grants. *Alcoholism Treatment Quarterly, 7*(1).

Baum, C., Kennedy, D. L., Forbes, M. B., & Jones, J. K. (1983). Drug use in the United States in 1981. *Journal of the American Medical Association, 251*, 1293–1297.

Cherubin, C. E. (1980). Dying from drugs: Facts, mostly fantasies, and unknowns. In S. Einstein (Ed.), *Drugs in relation to the drug user: Critical drug issues* (pp. 173–191). New York: Pergamon Press.

Cohen, S. (1982). Cannabis effects upon adolescent motivation. In National Institute of Mental Health, *Marijuana and youth: Clinical observations on motivation and learning* (DHHS Pub. No. ADM 82–1186) (pp. 2–11). Washington, DC: U. S. Government Printing Office.

Cohen, S. (1983). Current attitudes about the benzodiazepines: Trial by media. *Journal of Psychoactive Drugs, 15*, 109–113.

Dixon, K. (1988). Employee assistance programs: A primer for buyer and seller. *Hospital and Community Psychiatry, 39*, 623–627.

Drug utilization review available. (1988, April). *FDA Drug Bulletin*, p. 10.

Gieringer, D. H. (1988). Marijuana, driving, and accident safety. *Journal of Psychoactive Drugs, 20*, 93–101.

Goldsmith, M. F. (1988). Sex tied to drugs = STD spread. *Journal of the American Medical Association, 260*, 2009.

Hombs, M. E., & Snyder, M. (1982). *Homelessness in America: Forced march to nowhere*. Washington, DC: Community for Creative Non-violence.

Institute of Medicine. (1988). *Homelessness, health, and human needs*. Washington, DC: National Academy Press.

Johnson, B. D. (1977). The race, class, and irreversibility hypotheses: Myths and research about heroin. In J. D. Ritterhouse (Ed.), *The epidemiology of heroin and other narcotics* (DHEW Pub. No. ADM 78–559). Washington, DC: U. S. Government Printing Office.

Johnston, L. D., O'Malley, P. M., & Bachman, J. G. (1987). *National trends in drug use and related factors among American high school students and young adults, 1975–1986* (DHHS Pub. No. ADM 87–1535). Washington, DC: U. S. Government Printing Office.

Jones, R. (1977). Human effects. In R. C. Petersen (Ed.), *Marihuana research findings: 1976* (DHEW Publication No. ADM 77–501). Washington, DC: U. S. Government Printing Office.

Jones, R. T. (1987). Drug of abuse profile: Cannabis. *Clinical Chemistry, 33*(11B), 72B–81B.

Kozol, J. (1988). *Rachel and her children: Homeless families in America*. New York: Crown.

Lamar, J. V. (1988, May 9). Kids who sell crack. *Time*, pp. 20–24, 27, 30, 33.

Langone, J. (1988, September 19). Crack comes to the nursery. *Time,* p. 85.

Medd, R. H. (1983). The benzodiazepines: Public health, social and regulatory issues: An industry perspective. *Journal of Psychoactive Drugs, 15,* 127–135.

Miller, J. D., & Cisin, I. H. (1980). *Highlights from the national survey on drug abuse: 1979* (DHHS Publication No. ADM 80–1032). Washington, DC: U. S. Government Printing Office.

Miller, J. D., Cisin, I. H., Gardner-Keaton, H., Harrell, A. V., Wirtz, P. W., Abelson, H. I., & Fishburne, P. M. (1983). *National survey on drug abuse: Main findings 1982* (DHHS Pub. No. ADM 83–1263). Washington, DC: U. S. Government Printing Office.

Moreland, R. F., & McPhaul, K. M. (1988). Drug testing: A preventive approach. *AAOHN Journal, 36,* 119–122.

Morganthau, T. (1988, March 28). The drug gang. *Newsweek,* pp. 20–25, 27.

Morganthau, T., & Miller, M. (1988, November 28). Getting tough on cocaine. *Newsweek,* pp. 76–77, 79.

National Institute on Drug Abuse. (1985). *Annual data 1984: Data from Drug Abuse Warning Network (DAWN)* (DHHS Pub. No. ADM 85–1407). Washington, DC: U. S. Government Printing Office.

National Institute on Drug Abuse. (1987). *National household survey on drug abuse: Population estimates 1985* (DHHS Pub. No. ADM 87–1539). Washington, DC: U. S Government Printing Office.

Rickels, K. (1981). Benzodiazepines: Clinical use patterns. In S. I. Szara & J. P. Ludford (Eds.), *Benzodiazepines: A review of research results, 1980* (DHHS Pub. No. ADM 81–1052) (pp. 43–60). Washington, DC: U. S. Government Printing Office.

Rinaldi, R. C., Steindler, E. M., Wilford, B. B., & Goodwin, D. (1988). Clarification and standardization of substance abuse terminology. *Journal of the American Medical Association, 259,* 555–557.

Robbins, L. N. (1974). *The Vietnam drug user returns* (Final Report, Special Action Office Monograph, Series A, No. 2). Washington, DC: U. S. Government Printing Office.

Rounsaville, B. J., Kosten, T. R., Williams, J. B. W., & Spitzer, R. L. (1987). A field trial of DSM-III-R psychoactive substance dependence disorders. *American Journal of Psychiatry, 144,* 351–355.

Seixas, F. (1986). The course of alcoholism. In N. J. Estes & M. E. Heinemann (Eds.), *Alcoholism: Development,* consequences, and interventions (3d ed.) (pp. 67–77). St. Louis: C. V. Mosby.

Slaughter in the streets. (1988, December). *Time,* p. 32.

Somerville, S. N., & Miller, J. D. (1980). Opportunity and decision: An analysis of drug use entry. In J. D. Rittenhouse (Ed.), *National survey on drug abuse during the seventies: A social analysis.* Washington, DC: U. S. Government Printing Office.

Surgeon General. (1979a). *Healthy people: Report on health promotion and disease prevention* (DHEW Pub. No. 79–55071). Washington, DC: U. S. Government Printing Office.

Surgeon General. (1979b). *Smoking and health* (DHEW Pub. No. PHS 79–50066). Washington, DC: U. S. Government Printing Office.

Surgeon General. (1980). *The health consequences of smoking for women.* Washington, DC: U. S. Government Printing Office.

Surgeon General. (1983). *Cardiovascular diseases* (DHHS Pub. No. PHS 84–50204). Washington, DC: U. S. Government Printing Office.

Surgeon General. (1988). *Nicotine addiction* (DHHS Pub. No. CDC 88–8406). Washington, DC: U. S. Government Printing Office.

U. S. Conference of Mayors. (1986). *The continued growth of hunger, homelessness, and poverty in America's cities: 1986. A 25-city survey.* Washington, DC: Author.

U. S. Conference of Mayors. (1987). *Status report on homeless families in America's cities: A 29-city survey.* Washington, DC: Author.

U. S. Department of Health and Human Services. (1987). *Sixth special report to the U. S. Congress on alcohol and health* (DHHS Pub. No. ADM 87–1519). Washington, DC: U. S. Government Printing Office.

U. S. Department of Housing and Urban Development. (1984). *A report to the secretary on the homeless and emergency shelters.* Washington, DC: Author.

Weiss, K. J., & Greenfield, D. P. (1986). Prescription drug abuse. *Psychiatric Clinics of North America, 9,* 475–490.

Wright, J. D., & Weber, E. (1987). *Homelessness and health.* New York: McGraw-Hill.

SUBSTANCE ABUSE IN THE AGING

Mary Boyd

For many people, becoming older is anticipated as an enjoyable time of life. With retirement there is more leisure time to spend with family and friends and to pursue activities and hobbies that were set aside during earlier years. For many others, however, the realities of aging are harsh. The many losses associated with aging, such as death of family and friends, loss of income, and decreased mobility, result in many elderly becoming isolated and lonely. The increase in physical disability produced by normal aging and chronic illness with the associated pain make daily living a trial for some.

These problems are only a few of the factors that combine to place the elderly at high risk for substance abuse. Until recently, substance abuse as a problem among the elderly has been largely unrecognized and ignored. It is the purpose of this chapter to discuss the scope of the problem, the patterns of use, the psychologic/social and physiologic risk factors, assessment, and prevention and intervention issues.

SCOPE OF THE PROBLEM

The actual extent of substance abuse in the aging is unknown. Although many studies have indicated that abstinence increases and the rate of heavy drinking decreases with age, substance abuse remains a significant problem for a large number of the elderly (Brody, 1982; Busby, Campbell, Borrie, & Spears, 1988; Williams, 1984).

According to the most recent surveys, at least 10% of the elderly population have alcohol-related problems (Bienenfeld, 1987). Atkinson (1984) reported the prevalence of problem drinking to be lower in women than in men with 5%–12% of men in their sixties being problem drinkers in comparison to 1%–2% of women in their sixties. Alcohol abuse rates were much higher in certain subpopulations. Problem drinkers have been found to constitute approximately 20% of nursing home residents and from 5% to as high as 60% of elderly men

admitted to acute medical wards (Atkinson, 1984; Bienenfeld, 1987). Higher rates of alcoholism have been found in widowers, single elderly, individuals who have been in difficulty with the police, and those living in disadvantaged areas (National Institute on Alcohol Abuse and Alcoholism, 1982).

In a study reported by Zimberg (1985), interviews of the staff of health, social service, and criminal justice agencies were conducted in three communities representing urban, rural, and mixed urban-rural populations to determine the extent of problem drinking among their elderly clients. Among those interviewed, 45% reported contact with an elderly problem drinker during that year. They also found that 30% of all calls received by the alcoholism information and referral service surveyed were for individuals over 55 years of age.

Because the elderly are the largest consumers of prescription drugs, they are especially susceptible to drug-induced illnesses. According to Finlayson (1984), the elderly consume 25% of all prescription drugs with cardiovascular agents, sedative-hypnotics, tranquilizers, and analgesics among the most frequently used. This heavy usage has been attributed to both chronic physical problems and the many psychologic difficulties associated with aging.

In addition to prescription drugs, over-the-counter (OTC) drugs are used more by the elderly than by younger age groups. Kofoed (1985) reported that 40% of persons over age 60 use OTC preparations every day, and this usage may account for two of every five drugs taken—a usage pattern he described as being seven times greater than that of younger age groups. Even more alarming was the discovery that 80% of these older OTC drug users also reported using alcohol, prescription drugs, or both.

In reviewing the literature, few studies were found which investigated illicit drug abuse in the elderly population. Schuckit (1977) reported an estimated 5% of methadone maintenance patients to be age 45 or older and 1% to be over age 60. The abuse of hallucinogens, illicit psychomotor stimulants, and marihuana was reported to be uncommon in old age, with usage almost exclusively by long-standing opioid users and aging criminals (Atkinson, 1984).

It is probable that substance abuse among the elderly will become more prevalent after the turn of the century when, as projected by Stern and Kastenbaum (1984), the elderly will comprise approximately 16% of the population in comparison to the approximate 11% at present. Several factors may contribute to the rise in substance abuse among the elderly of the future. Among these are: *(1)* the elderly will be less influenced by the Prohibition morality which may have reduced problem drinking for many; *(2)* societal attitudes toward female drinkers have greatly relaxed and may contribute to an increased number of women who will demonstrate alcohol-related problems in the future; and *(3)* we might expect that the present younger, heavier drinkers and drug abusers will continue their heavy usage into old age (Mishara & Kastenbaum, 1980; Stern & Kastenbaum, 1984).

PATTERNS OF USE

Alcohol

Among the researchers who have studied elderly alcoholics, several have divided this group into two subgroups with differing characteristics (Atkinson, Turner, Kofoed, & Tolson, 1985; Bienenfeld, 1987; Brody, 1982; Gomberg, 1982). The first group, early-onset alcoholics, began problem drinking before age 40. This group comprises the lifelong alcoholics who have managed to live into old age despite the many hardships caused by alcoholism.

The second group, late-onset alcoholics, reported no alcohol problems until late in life. A stress-reactive etiology for late-onset alcoholics has been suggested, with alcoholism developing in response to the stresses of aging, such as depression, bereavement, retirement, loneliness, marital stress, and physical illness (Atkinson et al., 1985; Zimberg, 1983). Approximately two-thirds of the elderly alcoholics are in the early-onset group and one-third comprise the recent-onset, reactive drinkers group (Brody, 1982).

According to Gomberg (1982), there may be a third, large group of elderly alcoholics who have demonstrated intermittent problem drinking. This group tends to alternate periods of problem drinking with periods of sobriety.

The early-onset and late-onset alcoholics differ in certain characteristics. Those in the early-onset group demonstrate personality characteristics more closely resembling those of younger alcoholics. This group is more likely to have experienced legal problems related to alcohol use, a history of familial alcoholism, greater current psychopathology as demonstrated on Minnesota Multiphasic Personality Inventory (MMPI) testing, and are more likely to use benzodiazepines (Atkinson et al., 1985). The early-onset group is also more likely to have severe medical problems resulting from long years of abusive drinking (Williams, 1984). Alcoholics in the late-onset group have generally had a more stable early adjustment, are more likely to be separated or divorced, and are prone to have dementia or a major health problem that existed prior to abusive drinking (Bienenfeld, 1987).

Brody (1982) and Zimberg (1983) have observed a change in drinking patterns as individuals get older. As they grow older, many individuals tend to drink less or to abstain altogether. Among the combination of factors proposed for this decrease in alcohol consumption are the cost of alcoholic beverages on a limited income, a decreased tolerance to alcohol and an increase in dysphoric effects, increased medical problems, and the impact of having grown up during Prohibition (Gomberg, 1982). The older alcoholic who continues to drink is more likely to consume smaller amounts on a daily basis than the younger alcoholic but is more prone to binge drinking (Gomberg, 1982; Schuckit & Pastor, 1978).

Prescription Drugs

The primary reasons for increased use of prescription drugs in the elderly are psychologic problems and chronic physical disorders such as cardiovascular disease and degenerative joint disease. The drug classes most frequently used are cardiovascular, sedative-hypnotic, tranquilizer, and analgesics (Finlayson, 1984). An elderly client with a variety of problems who does not have a primary care giver is at greater risk for prescription drug abuse. This type of client may see several physicians who prescribe medication without doing a complete assessment of drug usage (Caroselli-Karinja, 1985). Prescribing over the telephone, failure to take into account recent changes in the client's physical and mental status, and misunderstanding of instructions increase the potential for abuse (Abrahams & Alexopoulos, 1987).

Over-the-counter Medications

For various reasons, OTC drugs may be the drugs of choice for many elderly individuals. Those with reduced incomes and limited mobility are more likely to self-prescribe with OTC drugs than to see a physician. Many common age-related problems such as arthritis, sleep disturbances, and constipation are often treated with OTC drugs. The elderly are often the target for television advertising for these drugs, which may increase their appeal (Kofoed, 1985).

Analgesics, laxatives, and antacids are three frequently abused OTC drugs. The following is a summary of usage patterns and side effects of these drug categories as described by Kofoed (1985):

Analgesics. Ten percent of older men and 20% of older women use aspirin. Acetaminophen is used daily by 5% of the elderly. Important side effects may include gastrointestinal bleeding, acute metabolic or mental status abnormalities caused by overdosage, and renal disease.

Laxatives. Thirty percent of the elderly over 60 use laxatives on a regular basis. Side effects may include hypokalemia, hypocalcemia, diarrhea and malabsorption syndromes, and symptoms mimicking acute abdominal disorders.

Antacids. The frequency of usage was not reported. Based on their composition, antacids can produce psychiatric and physical symptoms. Neurologic symptoms and renal calculi may be caused by hypercalcemia. Nausea, vomiting, reduced reflexes, and central nervous system (CNS) depression are symptoms of hypermagnesemia. In patients with renal impairment, the chronic abuse of antacids containing aluminum may produce a dementialike toxicity.

Three basic patterns of misuse or abuse of drugs have been identified by Ellor and Kurz (1982). *Overuse* results in too high a level of medication. This pattern may result from lack of knowledge or may be intentional. An accidental overuse may occur when a person forgets taking a dose and repeats the medication. Another pattern is *underuse.* This usage pattern may result from forgetfulness or from "stretching" medications due to limited finances. The third pattern is that of *erratic use,* which may involve overuse and

underuse. Forgetting to take a dose of medication and making up for it by doubling the dosage the next time is an example of erratic use. Erratic use also occurs when a person uses medication only when symptomatic.

PSYCHOLOGIC/SOCIAL RISKS

People face many transitions throughout life—each with its own stressors. The move into old age is the one transition in which there is little formal or informal preparation, making this period of life even more stressful than it need be (Davis, 1986). The elderly face multiple stressors in all subsystems—social, psychologic, spiritual, and physiologic. As reported by Finney and Moos (1984), four of the ten events rated as most stressful on the Holmes and Rahe Social Readjustment Scale (death of spouse, death of close family member, personal illness or injury, and retirement) are associated with age. Due to the severity of the stressors associated with aging, many of the problems of the elderly have been attributed to the impact of these stressful life events.

Many authors have discussed stressors in aging as causative factors in substance abuse in the elderly (Brody, 1982; Gomberg, 1982; Schuckit, 1977; Stern & Kastenbaum, 1984; Williams, 1984). In addition to those stressors mentioned previously, these authors list lowered self-image and self-esteem, relocation, feelings of uselessness and dependency, loss of life structure, and a feeling of low status in society as significant contributors to the problem.

Another predisposing factor in substance abuse discussed by Caroselli-Karinja (1985) involves social learning theory. According to this theory, the elderly person who has received attention for illness and has achieved positive results such as relief or the secondary gains of sympathy would be at a higher risk for drug abuse.

Osgood (1987) discussed the connection of alcoholism to depression and suicide in late life. She related that more than one-third of all suicides in the United States are related to alcohol. She strongly suggested that the many losses faced by older persons result in a deep sense of emptiness and meaninglessness leading to depression. A sense of helplessness and hopelessness that results from an inability to control significant life events is also common in the elderly. Many elderly may turn to alcohol or drugs to relieve the feelings of depression, loneliness, and hopelessness. Osgood warned that alcohol is doubly dangerous in this situation. Due to its initial stimulating effects, it may reduce inhibitions and self-control and lead to suicide or due to its depressant effects, worsen the depression.

The use of the stress-reactive hypothesis as the only etiology of substance abuse among the elderly poses many problems. One difficulty is that all elderly people share the same stressors that are a part of aging, and yet relatively few develop problems with chemicals. Another problem with the use of this theory is that reduced consumption among aging, early-onset alcoholics has been attributed to the same age-related stressors (Atkinson, 1984). Schuckit (1977) noted that there are probably many geriatric abusers who never overtly experience these difficulties.

Finlayson (1984) reported that prescription drug abuse does not follow the stress-reactive pattern. He cited studies conducted at the Mayo Clinic that found that patterns of drug abuse by the elderly typically began before the crises of aging occur.

The weight of existing research suggests some relationship between stress and problem drinking. Finney and Moos (1984) and Moos and Finney (1984) are convinced that a much more complex process underlies this relationship.

These authors propose that life stressors are not a necessary or sufficient condition by themselves to produce problem drinking, but they are a component of a set of factors that must be considered. Among the factors that need to be identified are what these authors call moderators and mediators of the stress-drinking relationship. *Moderators* are described as those vulnerability factors which increase an individual's susceptibility to stressful life situations. The *mediators* are the causal mechanisms through which stressors produce alcohol abuse in these vulnerable individuals. Based on their belief that problem drinking is determined by a multitude of factors, they propose a conceptual framework that considers the relationship between stressful life circumstances and problem drinking to be affected by the following five broad factors:

1. *Sociodemographic factors* include social status, education and occupational level, sex, age, ethnicity, and religious affiliation. These variables indicate location in social structure and contribute to factors influencing chemical usage.

2. *Personal factors* that may help to explain methods chosen to channel the effects of stress include cognitive ability, problem-solving styles, self-esteem, anxiety, depression, and beliefs about the appropriate consumption of alcohol.

3. *Acute and chronic stressors* include three categories. Long-term strains exist when basic survival needs and personal security are chronically threatened. Stressful life events are changes in a person's ongoing life situation including illness, bereavement, retirement, and relocation. This is the group of stressors that the majority of current research has focused on. "Daily hassles" are those minor but frequent irritants and frustrations which come from both the physical and social environment. Examples in this category are noise, difficult stairways, and arguments with significant others. In one study cited, daily hassles were better predictors of depression than were major life events.

4. *Social resources* may include quantity, quality, and intimacy of relationships and meaningful community ties. Stressors may disrupt functioning by reducing social resources. On the other hand, higher levels of social support may protect an individual from adverse effects of life stressors.

5. *Appraisal and coping responses* affect how an individual adapts to stressful situations. Those individuals who possess a varied repertoire of coping responses seem to have the best defense against severe dysfunction. Those individuals who rely on emotion-focused as opposed to problem-focused coping responses were more likely to relapse following treatment.

PHYSIOLOGIC RISKS OF SUBSTANCE ABUSE IN RELATION TO AGING

The Nervous System

Although few studies report on the effects of drug abuse on the nervous system, much has been written on the effects of alcohol on the brain. Evidence indicates that prolonged, heavy consumption of alcohol adversely affects the brain. According to Grant (1987), neuropsychologic tests have demonstrated cognitive and perceptual deficits in alcoholics similar to those in patients with damage unrelated to alcohol. Alcoholics generally demonstrate impairments in abstract ability and in complex perceptual motor skills but retain verbal skills and psychometric intelligence.

Alcoholism also results in altered brain structure. Computerized tomographic studies indicate that chronic alcoholics are likely to have widened cortical sulci, ventricular dilation, and cerebellar atrophy (Grant, 1987).

Studies of cerebral blood flow, which indicate the degree of functional activity and level of metabolism in various parts of the brain, indicate lowered cerebral blood flow in alcoholics. This reduction is even greater in older alcoholics (Biomedical consequences, 1981).

Research reported by NIAAA (1981) indicated a continuum of alcohol-related effects on cognitive functioning ranging from no impairment in light social drinkers to the severe damage found in late-stage alcoholics. Larger amounts consumed on any one drinking occasion were associated with poorer results on neuropsychologic tests. Age and the amount of alcohol consumed seem to interact. The older social drinker who consumes larger amounts per drinking occasion performed at an even lower level.

Until recently, brain damage from chronic alcoholism has been thought to be irreversible. Recent research has indicated that at least some subgroups of abstinent alcoholics in recovery experience significant improvement in brain structure and function (Grant, 1987).

Due to the high incidence of dementia in the elderly population and its association with alcoholism, organic mental syndromes warrant special consideration. Hartford and Samorajski (1982) reported that, in a study done on more than 500 first hospital admissions of elderly patients, organic brain syndrome accounted for 87% of the total group when all types of organic brain disorders were considered. Of this group, 28% had severe alcohol abuse problems, and 20% were social drinkers.

Organic mental syndromes associated with psychoactive substances most likely used by the elderly include intoxication, withdrawal syndrome, dementia associated with alcoholism, and alcohol amnestic disorder.

Intoxication associated with alcohol, sedative-hypnotic, or anxiolytic use may be manifested by aggressiveness, impaired judgment, impaired attention, irritability, emotional liability, slurred speech, uncoordination, and unsteady gait (American Psychiatric Association, 1987). Any of these symptoms may be attrib-

uted to the aging process and a chemical etiology not explored.

The withdrawal syndrome associated with alcohol or other sedative drugs includes coarse tremors, nausea or vomiting, weakness, autonomic hyperactivity, insomnia, depression, possible transient hallucinations, and grand mal seizures (American Psychiatric Association, 1987). Again, any of these symptoms may be attributed to aging or an age-related medical problem.

The essential feature of dementia associated with alcoholism is impairment in short- and long-term memory associated with impairment in abstract thinking and impaired judgment (American Psychiatric Association, 1987). A careful assessment would need to be performed on the elderly client to determine if these symptoms are a result of aging or substance induced.

Alcohol amnestic disorder, or Wernicke-Korsakoff syndrome, is a severe form of cognitive impairment resulting from alcohol-induced brain damage. Wernicke's encephalopathy is manifested by confusion, ataxia, and eye movement disorders. If not treated early with large doses of thiamine, the full-blown Wernicke-Korsakoff syndrome develops. The most striking features of this disorder are severe amnesia, confabulation, and remarkable personality alterations. The memory disorder involves difficulty in learning new information and difficulty in recalling events from the recent past (American Psychiatric Association, 1987).

Sleep Disturbances

Sleep disturbances occur frequently among the elderly with as many as 50% of the people over age 50 complaining of insomnia (Bienenfeld, 1987). According to Hartford and Samorajski (1982), older individuals experience increased sleep latency and have shorter durations of rapid eye movement (REM) and stage 4 non-REM (NREM) sleep, with an increased number of awakenings during the night. Deprivation of REM sleep results in increased irritability and anxiety, difficulty in concentration, and an increase in depression. Many clients report using alcohol to help them sleep. Alcohol does decrease sleep latency but may reduce REM sleep and stages 3 and 4 of NREM sleep. These disturbances may lead to increased irritability and daytime lethargy. The combination of aging and regular use of alcohol may seriously impair the restful stages of sleep which could, in turn, lead to an escalation in drinking (Bienenfeld, 1987; Hartford & Samorajski, 1984).

Absorption

With aging, several changes in the gastrointestinal tract have significance for substances ingested by mouth. Esophageal clearance time in the elderly may be delayed because of weakened contractions of smooth muscle and failure of the lower esophageal sphincter to relax (Hayes, 1982). This physiologic change can result in oral medications being delayed in the esophagus for as long as 5 minutes or more, resulting in irritation, ulceration, or stricture (Lamy, 1985).

The volume of saliva produced diminishes with aging (Hayes, 1982). The resulting dry mouth can be especially problematic with drugs that potentiate this effect, such as anticholinergics, tricyclic antidepressants, and phenothiazines (Hayes, 1982).

Aging also produces slowed gastric muscular activity, decreased gastric emptying time, and a rise in pH of gastric juices. These changes may potentiate the irritating effects of certain medications such as aspirin or phentoin due to their extended time in the stomach (Hayes, 1982).

Alcohol is also irritating to the gastrointestinal system and can directly cause damage resulting in esophagitis and gastritis. Alcohol also influences nutrition by affecting the absorption, utilization, and storage of nutrients (Hoffman & Heinemann, 1986).

Chronic alcohol abuse causes serious damage to the liver and pancreas. Damage to the liver may produce fatty liver which is reversible; however, with prolonged, heavy consumption, permanent damage such as alcoholic hepatitis or cirrhosis may occur (Hoffman & Heinemann, 1986).

Distribution

Several changes resulting from aging can alter alcohol and drug distribution. An increase in body fat and decreases in body surface area and in body water content occur (Hartford & Samorajski, 1982). These changes alter the volume of distribution of drugs and alcohol. At a fixed dose of alcohol, blood alcohol levels are higher than in younger individuals; therefore, a smaller dose of alcohol in the elderly may lead to intoxication. As reported by Atkinson (1984), blood alcohol levels rose to a peak 20% higher in men over age 60 than in men under age 45.

The changes in lean body mass and total body water also result in a higher serum concentration of other water-soluble drugs and a lower one for lipid-soluble drugs (Baker, 1985). Drugs such as phenobarbital and diazepam, which are stored in fat deposits, would have a prolonged but less intense action (Hayes, 1982).

Metabolism

Normal aging produces a decrease in liver mass, a reduction in hepatic blood flow, impairment in microsomal enzymatic activity, and a reduction in plasma protein synthesis (Hayes, 1982). These changes may increase drug plasma blood levels and contribute to cumulative toxicity, especially with drugs taken over a long period of time (Baker, 1985). Drugs such as barbiturates, propranolol, and tricyclic antidepressants may have a prolonged effect on the elderly due to the decreased capacity of the liver to inactivate them (Hayes, 1982). As mentioned earlier, alcohol abuse may further impair liver functioning, compounding the problem.

Elimination

Aging produces both structural and functional changes in the kidney. These changes include a decrease in actual size, an approximate 30%–50% decrease in the number of nephrons, an approximate 46% reduction in the glomerular filtration rate, and a reduction in the functional capacity of the glomeruli and the tubular systems, leading to impaired excretory and reabsorbative capacities (Hayes, 1982). These changes can lead to impaired drug clearance and increased prevalence and severity of drug toxicities (Lamy, 1985).

The abuse of alcohol in combination with these changes can produce fluid and electrolyte imbalances. In normal individuals, rising blood alcohol levels cause diuresis, and stable or falling levels cause fluid retention. The elderly may have increased difficulties with these changes. Situations warranting special attention are withdrawal from alcohol, consumption of large quantities of beer, or the occurrence of vomiting or diarrhea (Hoffman & Heinemann, 1986).

ASSESSMENT

The prevalence of substance abuse in the elderly may be underestimated due to the many difficulties in assessment and diagnosis. The elderly substance abuser in many cases is hidden from public view, and many of the more visible impairments in social and occupational functioning generally associated with alcohol and drug abuse in younger people are not as obvious in older people. Loss of job, driver's license, and social supports, losses typically associated with consequences of substance abuse, are common experiences in normal aging and, therefore, may not call attention to substance abuse in this population (Abrahams & Alexopoulos, 1987; Williams, 1984).

Substance abuse in the elderly may be misdiagnosed by physicians because the symptoms are similar to those associated with aging. The elderly resemble younger populations in that they rarely seek help specifically for alcohol or drug problems (Bienenfeld, 1987). Symptoms of substance abuse are more subtle in the elderly and generally do not include the symptoms associated with dependence such as intoxication, withdrawal, increased tolerance, morning drinking, ensuring supply, and massive gastrointestinal bleeding (Zimberg, 1984). More typically, the elderly individual will seek medical attention for nonspecific complaints.

Among many nonspecific presentations of elderly alcoholics are malnutrition, falls, incontinence, mood swings, injuries, and unusual behavior (Bienenfeld, 1987). Wattis (1981) believes that alcohol abuse should be considered whenever an elderly client presents with repeated falls, confusion, and self-neglect.

Substance abuse and the withdrawal syndrome should also be considered when a client presents with fevers of unknown origin, transient arrhythmias, and brief shifts in mental status (Miller, Whitcup, Sacks, & Lynch, 1985).

Substance abuse in the elderly may produce effects on cognitive abilities that mimic changes normally associated with aging or organic brain syndromes. Smaller amounts of alcohol and alcohol combined with other medications may produce states out of proportion to the amount of alcohol consumed (Abrahams & Alexopoulos, 1987; Zimberg, 1984). Bienenfeld (1987) reported that 25%–65% of older alcoholics have a dementia syndrome. The majority of these have an alcohol-related dementia that resembles Alzheimer's disease but does not progress with abstinence. He noted further that at least 10% of clients presenting with dementia have alcohol-related brain disease with only a small proportion having the classic Wernicke's encephalopathy.

Another presentation that could be a warning for possible drug abuse is chronic pain. According to Finlayson (1984), chronic pain syndromes are a major cause of substance abuse, with the abuse itself being responsible for a great deal of the illness behavior. A useful clue to dependence is continued analgesic use in the absence of pain relief. He adds that a low level of psychosocial functioning may be the only clue to a problem.

Other symptoms, common to both aging and substance abuse, frequently reported in the literature are sleep disturbances, disturbances in sexual functioning, gastrointestinal disorders, and cardiovascular disease.

Tests which may be useful in identifying younger alcoholics or drug abusers may not be useful with elderly populations. Laboratory parameters were not helpful in identifying elderly alcohol-dependent patients. In a study conducted by Powers, Lichtenstein, and Spickard (1984), laboratory results were only abnormal in cases of pronounced chronic liver disease, with elevated liver enzymes the most common finding.

An unexpected reaction to medication may be an important indication of a substance abuse problem (Bienenfeld, 1987). According to Hartford and Samorajski (1982), alcohol interacts with more than 150 commonly prescribed medications. These authors reviewed the medications most frequently used by the elderly for their interaction with alcohol. They presented the following as being high risk:

1. Chloral hydrate in combination with alcohol is metabolized and excreted at a reduced rate. In addition, chloral hydrate competes with alcohol for the same enzymes for metabolism which prolong the effects of alcohol.
2. Barbiturate usage with alcohol is especially dangerous due to the mutually potentiating sedative effects. This combination has been implicated in many attempted suicides.
3. Tricyclic antidepressants exaggerate the effects of alcohol. Even the combination with a small amount of alcohol may markedly impair motor skills.
4. Antipsychotic drugs also potentiate the CNS depressant effects of alcohol and should be used with caution.

5. Aspirin and alcohol increase the risk of gastrointestinal bleeding.
6. Antihypertensive agents in combination with alcohol produce a greater risk of orthostatic hypotension.
7. Hypoglycemic agents and alcohol may produce severe hypoglycemia.
8. Antidiabetic oral medications are metabolized at a faster rate in the presence of alcohol.

Depression in the elderly may be an indicator of substance abuse. Here again, depression may also result from the many stresses and losses accompanying aging, requiring a careful assessment to determine the cause. Researchers debate whether depression causes alcoholism or whether alcohol use results in depression. Alcohol is a CNS depressant and may cause or worsen an existing depression. A small group of perhaps 10%–15% suffer from primary depression and may be using alcohol as a means to self-medicate or to self-destruct (Bienenfeld, 1987). Abstinence is the only way to assess if depression is primary or secondary to alcoholism. After several weeks of abstinence, depression secondary to alcoholism should greatly improve; primary depression will not have improved and will more than likely need specific treatment. As an important clue to substance abuse, depression may also be overlooked in the elderly because the symptoms may be difficult to distinguish from those of aging. According to Osgood (1987), depression in the elderly may manifest itself slightly differently than in younger age groups. The elderly consistently manifest more somatic symptoms of depression such as fatigue, insomnia, decreased or loss of libido, weight loss, increased heart rate, headaches, constipation, and preoccupation with bodily functions. Other common symptoms include anxiety, withdrawn or apathetic behavior, and functional slowness.

Attitudes of health care professionals may further contribute to the underidentification and treatment of elderly substance abusers. According to Zimberg (1974), physicians are often unwilling to recognize alcohol abuse in their patients. He reported that although house staff at an institution he surveyed admitted to recognizing drinking problems in the majority of their patients, they failed to translate their findings into diagnosis and treatment. Reasons for the unwillingness to recognize and treat elderly alcoholics are reluctance to separate the older individual from a remaining source of pleasure and the unfortunate widespread attitude that

treatment of the elderly is not worth the time and effort due to their limited life expectancy (Stern & Kastenbaum, 1984).

Dangerous situations can be created by health care providers who hold stereotypes of the elderly. A thorough assessment will not be performed by a professional who believes that illness and a general sense of not feeling well are normal for the aging (Smoyak, 1985).

Family members may enable the elderly substance abuser and prevent them from being diagnosed and treated. Family members may themselves be in denial of a substance abuse problem, but even if recognized, may be reluctant to refer a family member for treatment. Among factors which may contribute to this reluctance are shame, guilt, or the desire to control behavior to keep the elder comfortable with the use of alcohol or prescription drugs (Bienenfeld, 1987; Caroselli-Karinja, 1985; Williams, 1984).

Yet another problem with identification of elderly substance abusers concerns existing instrumentation. Graham (1986) reviewed the domains typically included in alcohol abuse questionnaires and discussed their applicability to the elderly. She identified problems in every domain. Among the problems described were inaccurate self-report due to impaired memory of past consumption and denial of abuse, lack of difficulty in the social and legal areas currently used as indicators of abuse in younger populations, absence of the classic symptoms of drunkenness or dependence due to consumption of smaller amounts, and difficulty in self-recognition of a problem due to living alone and having few obligations demanding sobriety.

In a more recent study, Willenbring, Christensen, Spring, and Rasmussen (1987) tested the validity of the Michigan Alcoholism Screening Test (MAST) on 52 hospitalized elderly male alcoholics and 33 nonalcoholic controls. They found the full 25-item MAST to have excellent sensitivity and specificity in these elderly men. They found the briefer versions, the Brief MAST (BMAST) and the Short MAST (SMAST), to be useful but with a significant increase in false positive results. Lowering the cutting scores increased the sensitivity and specificity. Their study did not address the use of these instruments in elderly women.

The Scale of Alcohol Abuse Severity develop by Zimberg (1983, 1984) has been reported to be useful in diagnosing alcoholism in the elderly based on level of severity. The Zimberg scale indicates that with greater frequency and quantity of alcohol consumption, there are likely to be greater associated social, health, and legal problems. This type of measurement is useful since the elderly generally show less of the classic medical problems associated with alcohol addiction.

With the unlimited number of obstacles making it difficult to identify the elderly substance abuser, how can the task be accomplished? Identifying the substance abuser requires a comprehensive physical, psychologic, and social multidisciplinary assessment with the inclusion of significant others whenever possible (Lasker, 1986). An alcohol and drug usage history should be routinely included in every assessment on elderly clients. In addition to the traditional questions on amount and frequency, the assessment should include attitudes toward alcohol, situations when drinking occurs, and the effects alcohol has on the client's overall behavior. Other important areas for investigation are the ratio of alcohol consumption to signs of personal neglect, weight loss, recurring episodes of memory impairment and confusion, legal difficulties, and an increase in social isolation (Lasker, 1986).

Physical complaints should be thoroughly assessed and not dismissed as part of the aging process. Questions should be asked regarding medications used to treat these physical complaints. According to Kofoed (1985), "Diagnosis of OTC misuse or abuse can only be made if clinicians have an index of suspicions, seek multiple sources of information, interview family members, obtain urine toxicologies, and critically analyze routine laboratory data" (p. 57). Many elderly people do not perceive OTC medications as drugs and fail to report their usage. A direct, focused interview including questions about treatment of pain, headaches, sleep, colds, constipation, diarrhea, and heartburn should be used (Ellor & Kurz, 1982).

Keeping in mind that increased physical complaints and concern over bodily functioning may indicate depression, a depression assessment is essential. Depression should be thoroughly assessed as to the precipitating factors—whether they be losses or other stresses occurring in aging or a result of substance abuse.

PREVENTION AND INTERVENTION ISSUES

Prevention and intervention with elderly substance abusers is a complex issue. The classic typology of pri-

mary, secondary, and tertiary prevention provides a workable approach in examining these issues in greater detail.

Primary Prevention

Primary prevention consists of lowering the incidence of disorders or reducing the rate at which new cases develop (Stuart & Sundeen, 1987). Primary prevention efforts may be focused on an entire population or certain high-risk groups. Determining who is at high risk for the development of substance abuse is essential.

According to Caroselli-Karinja (1985), the same emphasis that is placed on education and prevention with adolescents needs to be targeted toward the elderly population. Prevention efforts directed at the elderly who develop problems later in life may be the most useful. Brody (1982) suggested that education about the stressors of aging should be a major component of a prevention program. The essential topics he suggested include issues of retirement such as reduced income, a change in status and role, and increased leisure time. The issues around death such as grieving, loneliness, and physically living alone should be covered. Information should be presented on declining health with age and on the age-related illnesses that are inevitable risks. The essential message given throughout this education is that alcohol or drugs, although they might offer temporary relief, are likely to make matters worse.

Primary prevention also encompasses activities designed to identify and strengthen current coping mechanisms and support systems and to encourage activities that increase feelings of self-worth. Examples of such activities are volunteer or part-time work, community activism or consumerism, and attendance at self-help groups or other community-based activities (Williams, 1984).

Other efforts that are desperately needed and hold a promise for effective prevention include education of both professionals and the community. The pharmaceutical industry needs to educate health care professionals and the community about the nonabusive use of medication, side effects, risks of dependency, and dangers of extended use and use in combination with other drugs and alcohol (Caroselli-Karinja, 1985).

Professionals, in turn, need to educate their clients. The professional nurse, in the role of client advocate, is in an excellent position to accomplish this task. The following areas are essential for client education: the importance of adhering to a medication schedule, a system for remembering when to take medication, the reasons for a particular medication, the desired effects, possible side effects with recommendations as to the appropriate action to take, dangers of mixing drugs and self-medicating, and what action to take if a medication dose is missed (Caroselli-Karinja, 1985; Ellor & Kurz, 1982).

Secondary Prevention

Secondary prevention involves reducing the prevalence of a disorder through early case finding and prompt, effective treatment (Stuart & Sundeen, 1978). The overwhelming difficulties in identifying the elderly substance abuser demand that education in identifying these problems as different from those of normal aging be directed at all health care personnel. Gomberg (1982) specifically identified the following groups as target groups for more education: physicians, paramedical personnel, hospital emergency room personnel, police, home-visiting health agencies, and organizations designated for older persons such as senior centers.

Detoxification for elderly clients should be planned with caution. For a small percentage of elderly alcoholics, detoxification with medications may be indicated. Because of autonomic and cardiovascular instability of the elderly, detoxification is often safer if carried out in a hospital setting (Bienenfeld, 1987). According to Kofoed (1984), hospitalization is usually necessary for the drug-dependent elderly to manage withdrawal symptoms and regain medical stability. The protocol for detoxification follows the procedure for younger age groups and includes nutrition, hydration, and safe management of drug withdrawal. The withdrawal process may take longer in elderly clients, and medications generally used for detoxification such as the benzodiazepines should be used with caution. These medications may produce increased confusion and delirium in the elderly. Close observation is necessary and cautious treatment with benzodiazepines used if the symptoms of withdrawal are becoming more severe. Benzodiazepines with a short half-life, such as lorazepam, are recommended over the traditionally favored diazepam and chlordiazepoxide (Bienenfeld, 1987). Following detoxification, the remainder of treatment may follow that generally found in alcohol and drug treatment centers and consists of education, individual and group therapy, attendance at self-help

groups such as Alcoholics Anonymous (AA), and when possible, family counseling.

Tertiary Prevention

Tertiary prevention is aimed at reducing the severity of a disorder and the disability associated with it (Stuart & Sundeen, 1987). Tertiary prevention is generally focused on the chronic alcoholic. Reducing the disability resulting from the many medical problems associated with chronic alcoholism, such as cognitive impairment, malnutrition, vitamin deficiencies, liver disease, and chronic heart disease, is a major focus of tertiary prevention (Mishara, 1985). Another focus of tertiary prevention is to reduce the severe disruption in the life of the elderly substance abuser and support a better, chemically free life-style. Effective follow-up and aftercare programs are important in tertiary prevention. Components in aftercare may include involvement in AA, education to reinforce material learned in primary treatment, support in organizing leisure time and developing hobbies, individual, group, or family therapy, and involvement in an alumni group (Williams, 1984).

Primary prevention efforts seem to be the most promising level of intervention (Mishara, 1985). The tremendous cost of alcoholism or other drug abuse in terms of resources and social ramifications would be greatly reduced if substance abuse could be prevented before it begins.

TREATMENT

Just as the actual prevalence rate of substance abuse is unknown in the elderly, the effectiveness of treatment strategies is also unknown. Few outcome studies have compared the treatment of the elderly with that of younger age groups. The reported studies generally focus on alcohol problems and exclude abuse of other chemicals.

Several reasons can be given for the lack of knowledge regarding treatment of the elderly. One concerns the general attitude about any problem encountered by the elderly. It is often assumed that being old is a contraindication to treatment of any type. Mental and public health care givers many times have an aversion to caring for the elderly, and many geriatricians are reluctant to work with alcohol or drug-related problems (Mishara & Kastenbaum, 1980). Zimberg (1985) noted that elderly alcoholics carry the double stigma of being old as well as alcoholic.

The attitudes of the elderly themselves pose a problem. According to Williams (1984), the elderly also have a tendency to attribute most health problems to old age and to believe that little can be done to help.

Another possible reason for the lack of knowledge concerning treatment for the elderly is that the elderly make up a small percentage of individuals receiving formal treatment. The report from many treatment centers is that only about 10% of their population consists of individuals over 60 (National Institute on Alcoholic Abuse and Alcoholism, 1982). There is also the possibility that the small numbers of elderly who do seek treatment are not representative of the majority of elderly substance abusers. According to Brown and Chiang (1983), treatment centers seem to attract a disproportionate number of male and "younger" elderly abusers, a finding that could foster inaccurate information about older abusers. Among reasons noted throughout the literature for the smaller number of elderly being treated were that the elderly are more isolated and more able to hide their abuse; enabling by family members; dismissal of problems as being part of aging; and the fact that the elderly do have more physical problems and are more likely to be admitted to a general hospital.

Despite the negative attitudes held by many about treating the elderly, many other believe the elderly respond better to treatment than younger age groups (Abrahams & Alexopoulos, 1987; Mishara & Kastenbaum, 1980; Rosin & Glatt, 1971; Zimberg, 1983, 1984). The favorable prognosis is believed to be especially true for those whose substance problems developed in later life.

Mishara and Kastenbaum (1980) summarized the available data on treatment outcomes and found them to be encouraging. In a study conducted in two treatment centers in Ireland, one center reported the improvement rate for 11 clients over age 60 as being the same as for adults in the 30–49 age range and somewhat better than younger age groups. The second hospital reported a 77% improvement rate for a group of 15 elderly clients in comparison to a 36% improvement rate in their clients in the 20–29 age group. Other studies indicated that elderly patients may have a better prognosis because they are less likely to have severe psychopathology.

There is controversy over what constitutes the best measure of successful treatment for the elderly.

Abrahams and Alexopoulos (1987) suggested that abstinence may not be necessary for all elderly problem drinkers. Mishara and Kastenbaum (1980) suggested a broader range of criteria that focuses on a significant overall improvement in functioning with or without total abstinence. Their criteria take into consideration the belief of others that many who achieve and maintain abstinence do not always improve in other important areas of their lives.

Although various treatment alternatives exist, such as private inpatient and outpatient treatment centers, veterans' treatment programs, and state and public supported agencies, relatively few are available specifically for the elderly. Based on 20 years' experience at a major alcoholic treatment center, Snyder and Way (1979) suggested that there are no major drawbacks in integrating older problem drinkers into a treatment program with younger age groups. Their experience has been supported by a study done by Janik and Dunham (1983) to examine the need for specific alcoholism treatment programs for the elderly. Their study found little support for age segregation once the elderly alcoholic entered treatment. However, their study did not address age-related differences connected with entering treatment, and further research is indicated in this area.

On the other hand, others strongly advocate age-specific treatment for the elderly. Zimberg (1983, 1984, 1985) believes that the classification of elderly alcoholics into early- and late-onset is useful in treatment. Those in the early-onset group are more likely to have medical complications of alcoholism and require medical care, and the recognition of the factors contributing to the development of the problem in the late-onset group would make interventions more effective. In recognizing that social and psychologic factors associated with aging affect both groups, Zimberg (1984, 1985) proposes treatment based on psychosocial interventions.

The treatment techniques involved in Zimberg's approach consist of the use of group therapy. The group is not insight oriented or directive as far as alcoholism is concerned, but rather focuses on support and problem-solving. The group is heterogeneous and consists of clients with a variety of social, psychologic, organic, and physical problems, not just alcoholism. This heterogeneity maximizes opportunities for problem-solving by discussing many types of problems other than alcoholism. A socialization period is provided and usually involves activities, therapy, and trips or outings.

He describes the ideal staffing of these group programs as consisting of a psychiatrist who is knowledgeable about aging and alcoholism, a nurse, and paraprofessional workers who can provide various services for the clients, such as visiting the homes of clients who miss clinic appointments. Because many clients treated in these groups may be depressed, Zimberg advocates the judicious use of antidepressants. The location of these group programs is felt to be more appropriate in general geriatric health care facilities such as senior citizen day programs, outpatient geriatric, medical or psychiatric programs, nursing homes, and home care programs. Zimberg and others (Rosin & Glatt, 1971) have found little need to detoxify the older alcoholic, because they generally consume smaller quantities of alcohol.

SUMMARY

At least 10% of the elderly population have alcohol-related problems. In addition, the elderly are the largest consumers of prescription and OTC drugs. The combined usage of these substances places the elderly at high risk of drug-induced illnesses. With the elderly being one of the fastest growing populations in this country, problems with substance abuse among this population are likely to increase.

Assessment of substance abuse in the elderly is complicated by both the physical and psychologic problems associated with aging. The diagnostic indicators generally used to assess substance abuse such as depression, loss of job, economic problems, family changes, and physical deterioration often accompany normal aging. Unless health care providers perform a thorough assessment, including an alcohol and drug history, the symptoms of substance abuse presented by the elderly may be dismissed as problems caused by aging.

There is general agreement that treatment results are favorable for the elderly, especially for those whose problems are of later onset. However, the combined pessimistic attitude of health care workers and the elderly themselves may prevent treatment of many individuals.

Few treatment facilities are designed especially for the elderly. The hospital setting is the most common treatment setting, possibly due to the increased medical problems of the elderly and the stigma associated with alcoholism and drug treatment centers. Some research studies indicate that the best treatment approach for the elderly is a combination of socialization and group therapy delivered through community agencies serving the aging. Others believe that the elderly benefit as much from traditional treatment approaches as do younger age groups and believe that special programs are unwarranted.

Additional research on elderly substance abuse is needed. Health care providers need more education in assessment, treatment, and even more important, preventive measures. The pessimistic attitude that the aging cannot be treated must be replaced with the fact that aging is a normal process and many psychologic and physical problems occurring in old age can be diagnosed properly and treated successfully.

REFERENCES

Abrahams, R. C., & Alexopoulos, G. S. (1987). Substance abuse in the elderly: Alcohol and prescription drugs. *Hospital and Community Psychiatry, 38*,(12), 1285–1287,

American Psychiatric Association. (1987). *Diagnostic and statistical manual of mental disorders* (3d ed. revised). Washington, DC: Author.

Atkinson, R. M. (1984). Substance use and abuse in late life. In R. M. Atkinson (Ed.), *Alcohol and drug abuse in old age* (pp. 2–21). Washington, DC: American Psychiatric Press.

Atkinson, R. M., Turner, J. A., Kofoed, L. L., & Tolson, R. L. (1985). Early versus late onset alcoholism in older persons: Preliminary findings. *Alcoholism: Clinical and Experimental Research, 9*,(6), 513–515.

Baker, W. W. (1985). Psychopharmacology of aging: Use, misuse, and abuse of psychotropic drugs. In E. Gottheil, K. A. Droley, T. E. Skoloda, & H. M. Waxman (Eds.), *The combined problems of alcoholism, drug addiction and aging* (pp. 150–163). Springfield, IL: Charles C. Thomas.

Bienenfeld, D. (1987). Alcoholism in the elderly. *American Family Physician, 36*(2), 163–169.

Biomedical consequences of alcohol use and abuse. (1981). *Alcohol, Health and Research World, 5*(3), 10–23.

Brody, J. A. (1982). Aging and alcohol abuse. *Journal of the American Geriatrics Society, 30*(2), 123–126.

Brown, B. B., & Chiang, C. (1983). Drug and alcohol abuse among the elderly: Is being alone the key? *International Journal of Aging and Human Development, 18*(1), 1–11.

Busby, W. J., Campbell, A. J., Borrie, M. J., & Spears, G. F. S. (1988). Alcohol use in a community-based sample of subjects aged 70 years and older. *Journal of the American Geriatrics Society, 36*(4), 301–305.

Caroselli-Karinja, M. (1985). Drug abuse and the elderly. *Journal of Psychosocial Nursing, 23*(6), 25–29.

Davis, J. A. (1986). Growing old healthy: Meeting the emotional challenges of the senior years. In K. Dychtwald & J. MacLean (Eds.), *Wellness and health promotion for the elderly* (pp. 133–146). Aspen: Aspen Publishers.

Ellor, J. R., & Kurz, D. J. (1982). Misuse and abuse of prescription and nonprescription drugs by the elderly. *Nursing Clinics of North America, 17*(2), 319–325.

Finlayson, R. E. (1984). Prescription drug abuse in older persons. In R. M. Atkinson (Ed.), *Alcohol and drug abuse in old age* (pp. 62–70). Washington, DC: American Psychiatric Press.

Finney, J. W., & Moos, R. H. (1984). Life stressors and problem drinking among older adults. In M. Galanter (Ed.), *Recent developments in alcoholism* (Vol. 2) (pp. 267–288). New York: Plenum Press.

Gomberg, E. S. (1982). Alcohol use and alcohol problems among the elderly. (Alcohol and Health Monograph No. 4). Rockville, MD: Public Health Service, National Institute on Alcohol Abuse and Alcoholism.

Graham, K. (1986). Identifying and measuring alcohol abuse among the elderly: Serious problems with existing instrumentation. *Journal of Studies on Alcohol, 47*(4), 322–326.

Grant, I. (1987). Alcohol and the brain: Neuropsychological correlates. *Journal of Consulting and Clinical Psychology, 55*(3), 310–324.

Hartford, J. T., & Samorajski, T. (1982). Alcoholism in the geriatric population. *Journal of the American Geriatrics Society, 30*(1), 18–24.

Hayes, J. E. (1982). Normal changes in aging and nursing implications of drug therapy. *Nursing Clinics of North America, 17*(2), 253–262.

Hoffman, A. L., & Heinemann, M. E. (1986). Alcohol problems in elderly persons. In J. J. Estes & M. E. Heinemann (Eds.), *Alcoholism: Development, consequences, and interventions* (3d ed.) (pp. 257–272). St. Louis: C. V. Mosby.

Janik, S. W., & Dunham, R. G. (1983). A nationwide examination of the need for specific alcoholism and treatment programs for the elderly. *Journal of Studies on Alcohol, 44*(2), 307–317.

Kofoed, L. L. (1984). Abuse and misuse of over-the-counter drugs by the elderly. In R. M. Atkinson (Ed.), *Alcohol and drug abuse in old age* (pp. 50–59). Washington, DC: American Psychiatric Press.

Kofoed, L. (1985). OTC drug overuse in the elderly: What to watch for. *Geriatrics, 40* (10), 55–60.

Lasker, M. (1986). Aging alcoholics need nursing help. *Journal of Gerontological Nursing, 12*(1), 16–19.

Lamy, P. P. (1985). The aging: Drug use and misuse. In E. Gotthiel, K. A. Droley, T. E. Skoloda, & H. M. Waxman (Eds.), *The combined problems of alcoholism, drug addiction and aging* (pp. 130–149). Springfield, IL: Charles C. Thomas.

Miller, F., Whitcup, S., Sacks, M., & Lynch, P. (1985). Unrecognized drug dependence and withdrawal in the elderly. *Drug and Alcohol Dependence, 15,* 177–179.

Mishara, B. L. (1985). What we know, don't know, and need to know about older alcoholics and how to help them: Models of prevention and treatment. In E. Gottheil, K. A. Droley, T. E. Skoloda, & H. M. Waxman (Eds.), *The combined problems of alcoholism, drug addiction and aging* (pp. 243–261). Springfield, IL: Charles C. Thomas.

Mishara, B. L., & Kastenbaum, R. (1980). *Alcohol and old age.* New York: Grunne & Stratton.

Moos, R. H., & Finney, J. W. (1984). A systems perspective on problem drinking among older adults. (Reaction Paper) in National Institute on Alcohol Abuse and Alcoholism, *Nature and extent of alcohol problems among the elderly.* (Research Monograph No. 14). Washington, DC: U. S. Government Printing Office.

National Institute on Alcohol Abuse and Alcoholism. (1982). Alcohol and the elderly. *Alcohol Topics in Brief.* Rockville, MD: National Clearinghouse for Alcohol Information.

Osgood, N. J. (1987). The alcohol-suicide connection in late life. *Postgraduate Medicine, 81*(4), 379–384.

Powers, J. S., Lichenstein, M., & Spickard, A. (1984). Elderly alcoholics in a general medicine practice. *Journal of the Tennessee Medical Association, 77*(7), 397–400.

Rosin, A. J., & Glatt, M. M. (1971). Alcohol excess in the elderly. *Quarterly Journal of Studies on Alcohol, 32,* 53–59.

Schuckit, M. A. (1977). Geriatric alcoholism and drug abuse. *The Gerontologist, 17*(2), 168–174.

Schuckit, M. A., & Pastor, P. A. (1978). The elderly as a unique population: Alcoholism. *Alcoholism Clinical and Experimental Research, 2*(1), 31–37.

Smoyak, S. A. (1985). Old age. In D. L. Critchley & J. T. Maurin (Eds.), *The clinical specialist in psychiatric mental health nursing: Theory, research, and practice* (pp. 155–170). New York: John Wiley & Sons.

Snyder, P. K., & Way, A. (1979). Alcoholism and the elderly. In H. Cox (Ed.), *Aging* (4th ed.) (pp. 104–107). Guilford, CT: Dushkin Publishing Group.

Stern, D. S., & Kastenbaum, R. (1984). Alcohol use and abuse in old age. In J. P. Abrahams & V. Crooks (Eds.), *Geriatric mental health* (pp. 153–168). Orlando: Grunne & Stratton.

Stuart, G. W., & Sundeen, S. J. (1987). Principles and practice of psychiatric nursing. St. Louis: C. V. Mosby.

Wattis, J. P. (1981). Alcohol problems in the elderly. *Journal of the American Geriatrics Society, 29*(3), 131–134.

Willenbring, M. L., Christensen, K. J., Spring, W. D., & Rasmussen, R. (1987). Alcoholism screening in the elderly. *Journal of the American Geriatrics Society, 35*(9), 864–869.

Williams, M. (1984). Alcohol and the elderly. *Alcohol, Health and Research World, 8*(3). Rockville, MD: National Institute on Alcohol Abuse and Alcoholism, 4–9.

Zimberg, S. (1974). The elderly alcoholic. *The Gerontologist, 14*(3), 221–224.

Zimberg, S. (1983). Alcoholism in the elderly—A serious but solvable problem. *Postgraduate Medicine, 74*(1), 165–172.

Zimberg, S. (1984). Diagnosis and management of the elderly alcoholic. In R. M. Atkinson (Ed.), *Alcohol and drug abuse in old age* (pp. 24–33). Washington, DC: American Psychiatric Press.

Zimberg, S. (1985). Treatment of the elderly alcoholic. In E. Gottheil, K. A. Droley, T. E. Skoloda, & H. M. Waxman (Eds.), *The combined problems of alcoholism, drug addiction and aging* (pp. 284–299). Springfield, IL: Charles C. Thomas.

PART THREE

CLINICAL PRACTICE IN SUBSTANCE ABUSE TREATMENT

CHAPTER 15

SUBSTANCE ABUSE PROBLEMS ACROSS THE NURSING SPECIALTIES

Janet H. Lee

Substance abuse is clearly a significant health problem. Every day, in every area of practice, nurses interact with clients whose underlying problem is substance abuse. The statistics are startling. Alcohol-related deaths rank as the third leading cause of death in the United States (Smith, 1983). Nearly half of all accidental deaths, suicides, and homicides are alcohol related (U. S. Department of Health and Human Services, 1987). Two-thirds of the incidents of domestic violence and one-third of the cases of child abuse are related to substance abuse (West, Maxwell, Noble, & Solomon, 1984). Alcoholism and problem drinking cost an estimated $117 billion per year. Health care costs for alcoholism and its related complications account for approximately $15 billion of that amount (U. S. Department of Health and Human Services, 1987). Of the total amount spent nationally on hospital care, 20% is alcohol related (West et al., 1984).

Cigarette smoking is the largest preventable cause of death in the United States (Surgeon General, 1979). As of 1980, 37.9% of males and 29.8% of females in the United States were current regular smokers. Approximately 10% of all persons now alive will die prematurely of coronary heart disease if their current smoking behavior continues throughout their life (Surgeon General, 1983). The costs of medical care plus productivity losses attributable to smoking-induced disease in 1984 was estimated at $55–$60 billion per year (Loeb, Ernster, Warner, Abbotts, & Laszlo, 1984).

According to the 1985 *National Household Survey on Drug Abuse,* approximately 12% of individuals age 12 or over are current users of illicit drugs—that is, they have used illicit drugs within the 30 days prior to the survey (National Institute on Drug Abuse, 1987). Economic costs to society of drug abuse are estimated at $60 billion per year with health care costs accounting for approximately $2 billion of that amount (Harwood, Napolitano, Kristiansen, & Collins, 1984).

The statistics present only part of the problem. The 70-year-old grandmother admitted for a fractured hip, the 45-year-old business executive admitted for a peptic ulcer, and the 20-year-old college student admitted to coronary care for observation have something in common. They were admitted to an acute care setting as a direct result of their substance abuse. And, very likely, they will be discharged without that substance abuse ever being addressed!

Although it is difficult to determine the exact prevalence of alcoholism among clients in acute care settings, estimates range from 9% to 70%. Most studies conclude that 20%–33% of clients in the general hospital setting are there for alcohol-related problems (Mayou & Hawton, 1986; McIntosh, 1982; Moore, 1985; Smith, 1983; West et al., 1984). Smoking is the primary risk factor for a number of health problems ranging from coronary heart disease and chronic obstructive lung disease to some types of cancers. Data indicate that smokers are more likely to be hospitalized than nonsmokers (Surgeon General, 1979). Comparative data for drug abuse are not available (Anderson, 1986).

With so many clients in the general hospital setting affected by substance abuse, why is it that only one alcoholic in ten is appropriately identified and treated (Smith, 1983)? With so many health problems directly related to cigarette smoking, why is it that only one-third of nurses attempt to consistently counsel clients against smoking (Goldstein, Hellier, Fitzgerald, Stegall, & Fischer, 1987)? A number of barriers to effective intervention are found within the knowledge and belief systems of health care professionals. These include a lack of knowledge about substance abuse and its treatment, vagueness about the limits of heavy drinking, misgivings about one's own smoking, drinking and drug use patterns, previous unsatisfactory experiences with substance-abusing clients and family members, feelings of hopelessness, concern about prying into the client's personal habits, the belief that substance abuse is a sin or moral problem, and feelings of inadequacy in identification and intervention with substance-abusing clients (Bluhm, 1987; Estes & Heinemann, 1986; Jacobs & Stringer, 1987).

The purpose of this chapter is to examine the problem of substance abuse from a nursing perspective across the five specialty areas of adult, gerontologic, maternal/child, community health, and psychiatric nursing. The majority of the material will address the problem of alcoholism because it is more widespread than other forms of substance abuse. The National Nurses Society on Addictions (NNSA) position statement on the role of the nurse in alcoholism will be used as a framework for comments addressing all specialty areas. Following this, content specific to each specialty area will be discussed.

NNSA FRAMEWORK

In 1978, NNSA developed a position paper on the role of the nurse in alcoholism. This statement grew out of a perceived need to clearly define the role of the nurse in caring for alcoholic individuals and their families in all areas of practice. The five categories of nursing interventions described were identification of the problem with alcohol, communication about the problem, education regarding alcohol use, abuse and alcoholism, counseling the alcoholic individual, family, and significant others, and referral for treatment and aftercare (Bennett, Vourakis, & Woolf, 1983). This framework will be used to address general concerns related to substance abuse in all specialty areas.

Identification of the Problem with Substance Abuse

The identification of a problem with cigarette smoking presents little difficulty. Research clearly indicates that any amount of cigarette use is harmful. Additionally, 90% of smokers surveyed would quit if they could find an effective method of doing so (Surgeon General, 1983; Surgeon General, 1979). Because concern about health is a major motivating factor for individuals to quit smoking, the hospitalized client is a prime candidate for smoking cessation education (Bates, 1987; Goldstein et al., 1987; McMahon & Maibusch, 1988).

Of the five categories of intervention, it is in the area of identification of alcohol and drug abuse that health professionals seem to have the most difficulty (Moore & Malitz, 1986; Westermeyer, Doheny, & Stone, 1978; Whitfield, 1984). The initial question of what constitutes alcohol and drug abuse is critical to the process. The drinking of alcoholic beverages is both a legal and a socially acceptable way to relax, celebrate, and socialize; overindulgence occasionally is permissible. The recreational use of illicit drugs is acceptable in some segments of society. The point at which use becomes abuse or dependence can be difficult to determine. The definition of substance abuse presents a methodologic problem as well when interpreting research reports examining prevalence, diagnosis, and treatment (Moore, 1985).

Keeping in mind that the nurse's role is to identify the problem with alcohol and drug abuse, it would seem that the broadest possible working definition would encourage the highest degree of identification. The *Diagnostic and Statistical Manual* of the American Psychiatric Association defines substance abuse as a pattern of use characterized by either "continued use of the psychoactive substance despite knowledge of having a persistent or recurrent social, occupational, psychological, or physical problem that is caused or exacerbated by the use of the psychoactive substance or recurrent use in situations in which use is physically hazardous" (American Psychiatric Association, 1987, p. 169). Substance use becomes a problem when it interferes with the client's relationships, social or occupational functioning, or when use continues despite the possibility of physical harm.

How does the nurse identify alcohol and drug abuse? Table 15.1 presents examples of selected responses to a general nursing assessment using Gordon's Functional Health Patterns (Gordon, 1987). The behaviors, signs, and symptoms, listed are as indicative of substance abuse as they are of a variety of other problems. The list is not all inclusive nor is its purpose to provide a definitive profile of the substance abuser. Rather, it points out common responses to a routine nursing assessment that would raise the nurse's suspicion that substance abuse is part of the client's problem (Bluhm, 1987; Cohn, 1982; Estes & Heinemann, 1986; Zahourek, 1986).

In addition, several risk factors and medical conditions frequently are associated with alcoholism. Clients with any of the following factors are at an increased risk

Table 15.1
Nursing Assessment

Functional Health Pattern	*Responses That May Indicate Substance Abuse*
Health Perception– **Health Management**	1. Lack of compliance with medical/nursing regime especially failure to keep follow-up appointments 2. Leaving hospital against medical advice after 2 or 3 days 3. Frequent absences from work for various "sicknesses" 4. Frequent changing of physicians 5. Appearing older than stated age 6. Mentioning a desire to cut down on drinking, cigarette or drug use
Nutritional–Metabolic Pattern	1. Irregular or skipped meal schedule 2. Poor dental hygiene 3. Frequent complaints of heartburn, nausea 4. Malnutrition 5. Bruises or burns at different stages of healing 6. Skin problems
Elimination Pattern	1. Recurrent diarrhea
Activity–Exercise Pattern	1. Insufficient exercise 2. Lack of hobbies or recreational activities 3. Decrease in energy 4. Loss of interest in nondrinking activities 5. Poor hygiene 6. Smelling of alcohol 7. Heavy smoking
Sleep-Rest Pattern	1. Insomnia 2. Unusual reaction to sleeping or pain medication—achieving little effect from routine doses
Cognitive–Perceptual Pattern	1. Blackouts 2. Memory loss 3. Poor judgment 4. Poor reality testing 5. Hallucinations 6. Seizures

Table 15.1 (cont'd)
Nursing Assessment

Functional Health Pattern	*Responses That May Indicate Substance Abuse*

Self-perception–Self-concept Pattern
1. Defensive behavior
2. Rapid or careful responses when asked about substance use patterns
3. Frequent references to substance use; bragging about amount of use
4. Avoiding the subject if substance abuse is brought up
5. Low self-esteem
6. Denial
7. Guilt

Role-Relationship Pattern
1. Social life revolves around substance use
2. Frequent visitors who smell of alcohol
3. Irritable client who is much more agreeable after visitors have left
4. Loss of family relationships or family members who appear haggard
5. Lack of friends and other social relationships
6. Loneliness
7. Difficulty keeping job
8. Working at level below that for which client is educationally prepared
9. Increased incidence of job-related accidents or injuries
10. Arrest record including driving under the influence

Sexuality–Reproductive Pattern
1. Impotence

Coping–Stress Tolerance Pattern
1. Alcohol, tobacco, or drug use
2. Major changes in life
3. Loss or changes in support system
4. Irritability
5. Depression
6. Suicide attempts
7. Sudden mood changes without cause as length of stay increases
8. Frequent requests for mood altering substances
9. Frequent or chronic complaints of anxiety or stress
10. Recent decrease in alcohol tolerance after a long history of drinking

Value-Belief Pattern
1. Lack of philosophical or spiritual pursuits
2. Lack of realistic goals

for alcoholism: family history of either alcoholism or strong moral prohibitions against alcohol use, similar history in spouse's family, broken home with marital discord, youngest or almost youngest child, history of depression in more than one generation of females, and chronic pain (Bluhm, 1987; Estes, Smith-DiJulio, & Heinemann, 1980). Alcohol-related problems should be considered in clients with any of the following medical conditions: pneumonia, tuberculosis, cellulitis, gastritis, ulcers, pancreatitis, cirrhosis, seizure disorders, peripheral neuropathy, cardiomyopathy and other vascular diseases, uncontrolled diabetes, anemia, cerebellar degeneration, depression, suicide attempt, injuries from accidents or victimization, or malnutrition (Zahourek, 1986).

If there is any suspicion of alcohol abuse, a more detailed screening interview should be conducted. Several interview instruments are available for assessing alcohol abuse. The CAGE and the Michigan Alcoholic Screening Test (MAST) have been effective in identifying alcoholism in various populations (Bernadt, Taylor, Murray, Mumford, & Smith, 1982; Ewing, 1984; Mayfield, McLeod, & Hall, 1974; Selzer, 1971).

The CAGE is a brief assessment evaluating the individual's perception of his or her drinking behavior. Each positively answered item is given a score of one. A total score of two or three is indicative of alcoholism; a score of four is diagnostic. The MAST is longer but designed as a self-report questionnaire. A score of five or more is consistent with alcoholism; four is suggestive. Several authors have recommended that one of these instruments be included as part of every nursing assessment (Bernadt et al., 1982; Estes & Heinemann, 1986; U. S. Department of Health and Human Services, 1987).

THE CAGE QUESTIONNAIRE

Have you ever felt you should *Cut* down on your drinking?

Have people *Annoyed* you by criticizing your drinking?

Have you ever felt bad or *Guilty* about your drinking?

Have you ever had a drink first thing in the morning to steady your nerves or get rid of a hangover (*Eye*-opener)?

Source: Mayfield, D., McLeod, G., & Hall, P. (1974). The CAGE questionnaire: Validation of a new alcoholism screening instrument. *American Journal of Psychiatry, 131*, 1121–1123. Used with permission.

In conjunction with the assessment process, a more extensive history of substance use should be taken. The history can be prefaced with a statement such as:

To provide the best care possible, I need to know more about your drinking [and drug use] patterns. Drinking [and drug use] can influence a patient's response to many medications, including pain medication. Alcohol consumption [and drug use] can be related to numerous health problems. I have some questions to ask you, and the more able you are to answer, the better we will be able to help you (Zahourek, 1986, p. 5).

The history should include the following information:

1. Substance use patterns including onset of use, frequency, types and amounts, and circumstances of use. Questions should be asked related to the amount of drug required to feel high or intoxicated, periods without drug use, and reactions when drug use was discontinued.
2. Current use including the last episode, kind and amount, intake in the last 5 days, and current physical distress. Questions regarding shakiness, seizures, hallucinations and other withdrawal symptoms should be addressed.
3. Family history of substance abuse.
4. Legal problems with substance abuse.
5. Employment problems.
6. Medical and psychiatric history including prior treatment for substance abuse, depression and suicide attempts (Jacobs & Stringer, 1987).

If the client's status is such that the assessment cannot be completed, the information under current use should be obtained from family or friends. The possibility of alcohol or drug withdrawal should be evaluated.

Communication about the Problem with Substance Abuse

Once an alcohol or drug abuse problem is identified, the nurse has a responsibility to discuss the findings with the client, family, and appropriate members of the health care team. The family dynamics and methods of coping with the disease should be assessed (Fisk, 1986). Substance abuse affects all members of the family, and it is common to find other family members enabling the

MICHIGAN ALCOHOLISM SCREENING TEST (MAST)

Points		Yes	No
	0. Do you enjoy a drink now and then?		
(2)	1. Do you feel you are a normal drinker? (By normal we mean you drink less than or as much as most other people.)		
(2)	2. Have you ever awakened the morning after some drinking the night before and found that you could not remember a part of the evening?		
(1)	3. Does your wife, husband, parent, or other near relative ever worry or complain about your drinking?		
(2)	*4. Can you stop drinking without a struggle after one or two drinks?		
(1)	5. Do you ever feel guilty about your drinking?		
(2)	*6. Do friends or relatives think you are a normal drinker?		
(2)	*7. Are you able to stop drinking when you want to?		
(5)	8. Have you ever attended a meeting of Alcoholics Anonymous (AA)?		
(1)	9. Have you gotten into physical fights when drinking?		
(2)	10. Has your drinking ever created problems between you and your wife, husband, a parent, or other relative?		
(2)	11. Has your husband, wife, or another family member ever gone to anyone for help about your drinking?		
(2)	12. Have you ever lost friends because of your drinking?		
(2)	13. Have you ever gotten into trouble at work or school because of drinking?		
(2)	14. Have you ever lost a job because of drinking?		
(2)	15. Have you ever neglected your obligations, your family, or your work for 2 or more days in a row because you were drinking?		
(1)	16. Do you drink before noon fairly often?		
(2)	17. Have you ever been told you have liver trouble? Cirrhosis?		
(2)	18. After heavy drinking have you ever had delirium tremens (D.T.s) or severe shaking or heard voices or seen things that really weren't there?		
(5)	19. Have you ever gone to anyone for help about your drinking?		
(5)	20. Have you ever been in a hospital because of drinking?		
(2)	21. Have you ever been a patient in a psychiatric hospital or on a psychiatric ward of a general hospital where drinking was part of the problem that resulted in hospitalization?		
(2)	22. Have you ever been seen at a psychiatric or mental health clinic or gone to any doctor, social worker, or clergyman for help with any emotional problem, where drinking was part of the problem?		
(2)	23. Have you ever been arrested for drunk driving, driving while intoxicated, or driving under the influence of alcoholic beverages? (If yes, how many times? _____)		
(2)	24. Have you ever been arrested, or taken into custody, even for a few hours, because of other drunk behavior? (If yes, how many times? _____)		

*Alcoholic response is negative.

Five points for delirium tremens; two points for each arrest.

Source: Selzer, M. L. (1971). The Michigan alcoholism screening test: The quest for a new diagnostic instrument. *American Journal of Psychiatry, 127,* 1653–1658. Used with permission.

alcoholic or drug user to continue a pattern of abuse by denying the problem. The family members are frequently isolated from others in the community and have few sources of social support. They experience self-doubt, guilt, shame, and inadequacy (Whitfield, 1984). An open discussion of the substance abuse problem conducted in a caring and nonjudgmental manner by a nurse who has already established a relationship with the client and family members can have a significant effect on the course of the illness. Further, the nurse can encourage and support the family members to seek help for themselves through support groups such as Al-Anon, Alateen, and Adult Children of Alcoholics, and through individual and group therapy with a mental health professional.

The diagnosis of alcohol or drug abuse provides an excellent opportunity for the health care team to work together to confront the client and encourage admission to a treatment program. Open communication about substance abuse may be difficult (Gill, 1987; Westermeyer et al., 1978). The attitudes of health care workers mentioned previously, the reluctance to label the client as an "alcoholic" or "drug addict," and a general feeling of hopelessness regarding the treatment of addiction combine to enable the treatment of the medical problem but not the underlying cause (Bluhm, 1981; Galanter, Karasu & Wilder, 1976). Nonetheless, substance abuse should be discussed with the health care team as would any other chronic illness.

Education about Substance Use and Abuse

Just as the nurse would teach any chronically ill client about the disease, there is a responsibility to educate the substance abuser and the family. A combination of informal information giving and a formal teaching plan is appropriate. Teaching principles such as attention to timing, assessment of previous knowledge, utilization of a variety of approaches, involvement of the client in the teaching/learning process, and planning for reinforcement should be used with the substance abuser as with any other teaching endeavor.

Preparing audio or video cassettes for the client and family to use can save time and energy for the nurse and increase the effectiveness of the teaching program. Giving written literature about the addiction as well as the name, location, and phone numbers of treatment facilities, programs, and support groups can enhance an educational program. Many of the organizations listed in Appendix A will provide audio-visual aids, self-tests, brochures, and other literature at minimal or no cost. A checklist indicating all aspects of the teaching plan with space to record the client's response will be useful as well.

A teaching plan for the alcoholic would include:

Knowledge of the Disease

Signs and symptoms of alcoholism, effects of alcohol on the body, progression of the disease, physical problems associated with alcoholism, psychosocial effects of alcoholism, and ways in which the client's drinking affects the admission problem.

Treatment Options

General treatment options and types and locations of treatment facilities in community.

Emotional Help

Coping without alcohol and sources of support (Scherwerts, 1982).

The most effective smoking cessation programs are multidimensional and include: basic information on smoking and health, weight management, and exercise; stress management skills; specific and detailed plan to quit smoking; personal commitment; strong support system; and knowledge about the grieving process as it relates to cigarettes (Bates, 1987). It is useful to analyze a client's smoking behavior to determine the reasons an individual chooses to smoke. This enables the nurse to teach the client to recognize cues associated with the smoking behavior and to modify or avoid these cues. Techniques such as self-monitoring and contracting are most effective if combined with strong support from a spouse or significant other (Alexander, 1987).

It is difficult to separate the communication, teaching, and counseling interventions with all forms of substance abuse. Many clients know very little about the effects of substance abuse on their bodies or the process of addiction. Simply by offering the facts about the addiction, the nurse may begin to break down the client's or family's denial of the substance abuse problem.

Counseling the Individual, Family, and Significant Others about Substance Abuse

The overall goal of nursing intervention for the substance-abusing client is entrance into some type of treatment program. The manner in which the nurse relates to the client plays a critical role in determining the course of treatment. An open, empathetic and non-judgmental attitude will be most effective. Good communication techniques, privacy for discussions, and attention to nonverbal behaviors are important when counseling the substance-abusing client as with any other client. Because individuals who abuse alcohol and other drugs are generally masters at both manipulation and vague, indirect communication, a direct approach that encourages the client to give specific answers to questions will be most effective (Bluhm, 1987). Treating the client with respect and encouraging participation in the decision-making process are essential.

When approaching the client to discuss the substance abuse problem, the nurse should focus the conversation on that subject. Initially, it is not necessary to discuss "alcoholism" or "drug addiction." There will often be less denial and resistance when talking about "drinking patterns" or "problems with drug use" (Bluhm, 1981). The content should be specific, focusing on problems in everyday living caused by the abuse rather than on the substance use itself. The nurse should associate the reasons for hospitalization (i.e., accidents, falls, gastritis, emphysema, etc.) with the substance abuse. The client, particularly in the early stages of addiction, may not make that connection (Estes & Heinemann, 1986; Weist, Lindeman, & Newton, 1982).

Denial is a hallmark of the disease of addiction. It is used by substance-abusing clients and their families and is a major deterrent to recovery. In addition, substance-abusing clients project blame onto others, provide excuses for their behavior, and minimize the significance of both their abuse and its resulting problems. These defense mechanisms protect the client from being overwhelmed by intense feelings of guilt and shame (Zahourek, 1986). They also frustrate nurses, often leading to feelings of helplessness and anger. It is crucial for the nurse to effectively handle the client's defense mechanisms.

Countering defense mechanisms is accomplished over time. The nurse can feed back to the client the specific information given in the assessment (Zahourek, 1986). The negative consequences of the abuse must be tied to the substance use. For example, financial problems need to be connected to essential income being used for alcohol or drugs (Fisk, 1986). Arguing with the client serves no useful purpose. If the client becomes too defensive, the nurse can redirect the conversation or discuss the substance abuse at a later time (Zahourek, 1986).

Manipulation presents major difficulties particularly with the drug-abusing client. Violating rules and making unreasonable demands are examples of manipulation as are dismissing the nurse (e.g., "I'm sure you have more important things to do than staying with me") and staff splitting (e.g., "You are so helpful. I wish you could be my nurse all the time"). Manipulation is best handled through a team conference where information is shared and a care plan developed. This plan must be communicated to all personnel and shared with the client by both the primary physician and the nurse (Adams, 1988). Setting limits and calling the client's attention to the manipulation in a matter-of-fact manner may also be helpful (Zahourek, 1986).

If the client continues to deny the alcoholism or drug addiction, an "intervention" may be attempted. An intervention is a "therapeutic, planned strategy which challenges denial and is backed up with a plan for treatment and referral" (Bluhm, 1987, p. 127). It is an attempt to overcome the client's denial through the presentation of the facts of the addiction by significant others and members of the health care team. Intervention involves collecting as much specific data about the client's abuse as possible. The spouse, older children, coworkers, and health care team confront the client in a concerned manner, sharing specific incidences of ways in which the abuse has interfered with the family, social, employment, or health situation. The intervention is planned and rehearsed ahead of time. The goal is for the client to leave the hospital and enter a treatment program. In planning the intervention, it would be helpful to seek assistance from a psychiatric consultation/liaison nurse or a substance abuse specialist. These individuals are found on the staff of larger hospitals, local substance abuse treatment facilities, or local mental health centers.

The client who smokes cigarettes should be approached in a direct manner with emphasis placed on the positive benefits of quitting. The nurse should encourage persistent effort particularly with the client who has previously been unsuccessful in quitting. The message should be appropriate to the client's developmental stage. For example, when working with adolescents, stress the short-term effects of quitting rather than the long-term effects of continued use. Scare tactics, guilt, and negative directives should be avoided. Most important, every client who smokes should receive at least a brief, direct, and informative quit-smoking message (McMahon & Maibusch, 1988).

One additional point should be made. Substance-abusing clients sometimes refuse to discuss their abuse. In this case, the nurse should communicate concern openly and continue to intervene with the client's family. Written information about addiction can be given to the client, and the nurse can offer to be available if the client chooses to discuss the problem at a later date.

Referral for Further Treatment or Aftercare

Nurses practicing in any setting need to be aware of available community resources for substance-abusing clients and their families. Names, addresses, phone numbers, and contact people for various treatment programs and self-help groups should be kept at each nurse's station. Plans for referral should be personal, supportive, specific, and action oriented (Weist et al., 1982). Ideally, the nurse would discuss the various treatment options with the client and cooperatively develop a plan for treatment. However, the choice of treatment program is ultimately up to the client, and any method chosen should be encouraged. It is best if the client contacts the program while still in the hospital. Staff members from treatment facilities and members of Alcoholics Anonymous (AA) and Al-Anon are available to talk with clients and families. Smoking cessation programs are offered by support groups, church-affiliated groups, hospitals, individuals in private practice, and organizations such as the American Heart Association. At the very least, the client should leave the hospital with pamphlets on substance abuse and a list of treatment options (Bluhm, 1981).

ADULT NURSING

Although clients who abuse alcohol and other drugs are found in all acute care settings, they occur in greatest numbers on emergency, orthopedic, trauma, and gastroenterology units (Mayou & Hawton, 1986). According to Smith (1983), approximately 50% of home falls which result in a fracture are due to alcohol, and that figure increases to nearly 100% if the client delays seeking treatment for a day or two. Clients who smoke are found throughout the hospital. When compared to the nonsmoking population, they have a higher incidence of lung conditions such as chronic obstructive lung disease; cardiovascular problems such as coronary artery disease and peripheral vascular disease; cancer, particularly lung cancer and cancer of the larynx, kidneys, and pancreas; and peptic ulcer disease (Surgeon General, 1979).

The basic guidelines for the nursing care of the adult substance-abusing client were covered in the previous section. One of the most critical conditions related to substance abuse seen in adult nursing practice is alcohol withdrawal. This section will focus on the detection of the client who is in alcohol withdrawal and the associated nursing care.

The earliest signs of alcohol withdrawal syndrome (AWS) occur approximately 6–8 hours after the last drink. The client may experience nervousness or restlessness often described as a shaky feeling on the inside. The client may request "something to calm my nerves" (Kelly, 1986, p. 14). A tremor is always present. It may be mild or severe and is worse when the client's arms are outstretched or the client is physically active (Powell & Minick, 1988). Insomnia is common. A mild disorientation in time may be present during early withdrawal, but it is usually minimal. Even with the hallucinations characteristic of later withdrawal, orientation, memory, and sensorium remain clear. Disorientation to person, place, and time signals a progression of AWS into delirium tremens (DTs) (Butz, 1986).

About 24 hours after the last drink, behavioral cues to AWS become more apparent. Nausea and vomiting may be present. Confusion and misinterpretation of stimuli along with hallucinations are seen (Kelly, 1986; Powell & Minick, 1988). Clients may not acknowledge hallucinations or may refer to them as nightmares or vivid day dreams (Butz, 1986).

Seizure activity can occur 7–48 hours after the last drink. These grand mal seizures may last from several seconds to several minutes (Powell & Minick, 1988). Seizures precede DTs in about one-third of the clients, but once DTs is established, seizures subside (West et al., 1984). Seizure activity occurring 10–14 days after the last drink is indicative of withdrawal from other central nervous system (CNS) depressants (Butz, 1986).

DTs generally occur 3–5 days after the last drink, and is characterized by global confusion, agitation, delusions, and vivid hallucinations (Powell & Minick, 1988). The face is frequently flushed, and temperature, heart rate, and blood pressure are elevated. Diarrhea and diaphoresis combine with nausea and vomiting to cause fluid and electrolyte imbalance. The client may be belligerent and strike out both physically and verbally. The mortality rate in untreated DTs is 5%–15% (Kelly, 1986).

This is not to say that every client exhibiting anxiety, restlessness, and tremor is in alcohol or drug withdrawal. Medical conditions such as cerebral vascular accidents, intensive care psychosis, hypoxia, and sundown syndrome cause altered mental status and can be mistaken for AWS (Powell & Minick, 1988). However, with the large numbers of substance-abusing clients found in the general hospital setting, any client whose hospital course is not going as expected, or whose behavior is inappropriate should be evaluated for alcohol or drug withdrawal.

The nursing care of clients experiencing AWS includes routine nursing measures such as regular and frequent vital signs, intake and output, prevention of pneumonia, and nutritional support. The room should be kept quiet and dimly lit, and stimuli that could easily be misinterpreted should be removed. Side rails should be kept up with the bed in its lowest position. Restraints present a dilemma because, though they protect the client from falls, they increase distress, causing a further increase in pulse and blood pressure (Kelly, 1986). The nurse should reorient the client as necessary and encourage family members or friends to stay with the client (Powell & Minick, 1988). The client in early withdrawal is highly suggestible; statements such as "You are much calmer now" or "You certainly do look hungry" can be used to the client's advantage (Kelly, 1986, p. 17).

Clients experiencing DTs function in the "here and now." They are not able to relate the past or the future to the present. Consequently, they may not remember from one visit to the next what is required of them. The nurse may need to repeat requests frequently. It is useless to attempt to connect past drinking to current problems until the acute episode is past (Kelly, 1986).

The surgical client is of particular concern because withdrawal from alcohol or other drugs complicates the course of hospitalization. Any client taking a sedative-hypnotic or minor tranquilizer has the potential to become addicted even though the medication is given appropriately. The addiction is insidious, and the client is often not aware of the problem (Moore, 1983). The possibility of withdrawal should be included in the nursing care plan. It is important to note that if the client is receiving a narcotic for pain, AWS may be postponed until the narcotic is discontinued (Kelly, 1986). If the client is receiving a benzodiazepine, AWS may not be seen at all.

Case Example

Perry L., a 31-year-old male, was admitted to the orthopedic unit of the hospital for a fractured right femur following a skiing accident. He is in balanced traction receiving Tylenol for pain. Mr. L. states he "drinks about as much as everyone else." He has been divorced twice and states that his ex-wives were "always on my case about drinking with my buddies." Since his admission the previous day, Mr. L. has become increasingly restless. He slept little last night, has a mild tremor, and insists that he must "get out of this place."

Selected Nursing Diagnoses and Interventions

Potential for injury related to possible AWS as evidenced by tremor, restlessness, and difficulty related to alcohol use in the past.

1. Monitor vital signs and mental status frequently. If possible, have someone stay with the client.
2. Complete CAGE or MAST and in-depth history of alcohol and drug use, especially current use section.
3. Consult with physician regarding need for medication to control withdrawal symptoms.
4. Observe for further signs and symptoms of AWS.
5. Seizure precautions.

Anxiety related to possible AWS as evidenced by restlessness and verbalizations of need to leave hospital.

1. Monitor level of anxiety.
2. Maintain a calm, nonjudgmental manner.
3. Use simple, direct communications.
4. Provide safe, secure environment.
5. Decrease environmental stimuli.
6. Explain AWS and protocol to client.

GERONTOLOGIC NURSING

This section will discuss two issues related to substance abuse in elderly clients: alcoholism and prescription drug abuse. The general guidelines discussed in the first part of this chapter apply to this population although the assessment of alcohol and drug abuse is more difficult. Cigarette smoking continues to be a serious health risk. As clients become older, the effects of the chronic illnesses associated with smoking become more problematic.

Alcohol Abuse

A 30-year-old male with tremor, poor appetite, difficulty sleeping, and an unsteady gait would likely be assessed for alcohol abuse; a 70-year-old male with these same symptoms probably would not. Because alcoholism is not believed to be a significant problem in elderly clients, the index of suspicion among health care workers and the community at large is low. Yet alcoholism ranks as the second leading cause of admission to psychiatric facilities for elderly individuals, and it is a major factor in 15%–20% of nursing home admissions, 5%–15% of medical outpatient visits, and about 10% of hospital admissions (West et al., 1984). Family members tend to hide their elderly alcoholic members and rationalize their behavior. Many of the behavioral cues such as absenteeism from work, impaired job performance, or changes in financial status are not effective indicators of a problem with substance abuse in this population. General deterioration, malnutrition, mental deterioration, domestic quarrels, and social isolation are frequently attributed to the effects of aging or other degenerative diseases. In addition, because of the physiologic effects associated with aging, elderly alcoholics have less tolerance for alcohol and the amount consumed may not appear to be excessive (DiCicco-Bloom, Space, & Zahourek, 1986; Estes et al., 1980; West et al., 1984).

There are two distinct types of alcoholism in the elderly population. The early-onset type includes individuals whose problems with alcohol began early in life. This group demonstrates physical dependence, alcohol-related health problems, psychosocial and behavioral disturbances, and the physiologic consequences of long-term drinking (Hoffman & Heinemann, 1986). Drinking may have peaked at ages 40–50, and abuse may continue although the amount consumed may be less (DiCicco-Bloom et al., 1986). Late-onset alcoholics may have drunk normally or abstained during their younger years and consequently do not demonstrate the cognitive or somatic problems of the early-onset group. Their use is frequently related to coping with depression, bereavement, loneliness, retirement, marital stress, and health problems (DiCicco-Bloom et al., 1986; Estes et al., 1980; Hall, 1983; Hoffman & Heinemann, 1986; West et al., 1984).

The indicators of substance abuse in Table 15.1 apply to the elderly individual as well as to others in the population. In addition, suspicion of a problem with alcohol should be raised if the elderly client complains of changes in appetite, weight loss, abdominal distress, vomiting, or altered bowel habits. An increase in the incidence of accidents (especially falls) or infections (especially repeated pneumonias) could indicate alcohol abuse. Difficulties in cognitive-perceptual patterns may not be related to the aging process. Social isolation, particularly if it is combined with recent losses, may indicate a reliance on alcohol as a method of coping. The client who jokes about needing help with activities of daily living because of tremulousness may have a problem with alcohol (Estes et al., 1980; Lasker, 1986). When the elderly client exhibits symptoms consistent with AWS, the possibility of alcohol withdrawal should be evaluated.

In general, elderly late-onset type alcoholism has a favorable prognosis. Manipulation of the environment, provision of social support, and general improvement in physical health can assist in recovery (Estes et al., 1980). The psychosocial problems and developmental tasks of the elderly are different from those of younger adults; therefore, elderly individuals will benefit from a treatment setting with comprehensive program addressing these needs (Hoffman & Heinemann, 1986). In working with elderly clients, the nurse should emphasize strengths such as resiliency, coping strategies, and variety of life experiences. Clients should be encouraged to explore feelings about past and present losses. Alternative coping strategies (e.g., participation in congregate dining or senior citizen programs) should be discussed (Price & Andrews, 1982).

Prescription Drug Abuse

Elderly individuals are an at-risk group for intentional and unintentional drug abuse. Multiple physical problems combined with the emotional and developmental problems of old age increase the risk of drug abuse. The use of multiple physicians, multiple pharmacies, and the combining of prescription medications and over-the-counter (OTC) medications make unintentional drug abuse a real possibility (Caroselli-Karinja, 1985). The misuse of medications is a particularly critical problem of the elderly because they are more sensitive to the effects of various medications than their younger counterparts. Drugs are often absorbed at a slower rate and distributed in body tissues in a different pattern. Excretion takes place at a slower rate because of changes in the kidneys and gastrointestinal tract (Mullen & Granholm, 1981). Because of the physiologic effects of aging, many drugs produce ''altered or unexpected effects'' on the elderly individual (Mullen & Granholm, 1981, p. 108).

Drug abuse in elderly clients can be divided into three categories. *Overuse* is the intentional or accidental taking of medication in amounts greater than that prescribed. *Underuse* results when less medication is taken, for example, stretching medication because of an inability to pay for it. *Erratic use* contains elements of both of the above. An individual may forget to take a dose and then compensate by taking two doses (Ellor & Kurz, 1982).

Many factors contribute to this abuse. These include forgetfulness, cost of medication, subjective feelings of taking too many pills, hoarding drugs past expiration dates, sharing medications with friends, removing medications from their original containers, visual and hearing impairment, and taking as-needed medication too often (Caroselli-Karinja, 1985; Mullen & Granholm, 1981). Elderly individuals have a peer group which engages in substantial drug use (Caroselli-Karinja, 1985). In addition, the same stressors mentioned with late-onset alcoholism can cause an increase in the use of prescription medications as a method of coping.

Nursing intervention should begin with an assessment that includes identification of losses and coping mechanisms, significant events occurring in the past year, attitude toward the aging process, and the presence of significant others in addition to routine concerns regarding current medications. Because many people do not consider OTC preparations as medications, questions should be asked about the individual's treatment of pain, headaches, insomnia, common colds, constipation, diarrhea, and heartburn (Ellor & Kurz, 1982). After the assessment is completed, medication teaching can be done if needed. In addition to routine teaching, elderly individuals need to know what to do if a medication dose is missed. Family members or caretakers may need to be included in the teaching process. Day and night telephone numbers to call if a problem arises should be kept close to the telephone.

Labels on bottles should be in large type. A chart containing a list of all current medications, a short summary of their effects, and the dosage schedule may be helpful. A sample pill can be taped to the sheet for easy identification. A record should be kept of all physicians and pharmacies used by the client (Mullen & Granholm, 1981).

Case Example

Jeff S., a 73-year-old white male, lives alone in a small house. He suffers from arthritis and hypertension, and his eyesight has been failing for several years. His daughter became concerned about Mr. S. when he complained about tinnitus, dizziness, anxiety, and difficulty walking. He was admitted to a hospital medical unit after a fall. Mr. S. has difficulty remembering to take his medication. He states that he ''takes another one just to be sure.'' He also complains of difficulty sleeping and states he sometimes takes two aspirin ''just to relax.''

Selected Nursing Diagnoses and Interventions

Knowledge deficit related to memory loss as evidenced by tendency to take extra medication.

1. Assess client's use of OTC medications.
2. Teach necessary information related to client's prescription medication as well as any OTC medications frequently used.

Sensory-perceptual alteration: visual related to aging process as evidenced by client's complaints.

1. Consult with physician regarding an ophthalmology referral.
2. Consult with pharmacist regarding larger print on prescription labels.

Alteration in self-concept: self-esteem related to memory loss as evidenced by client's difficulty in remembering to take medication.

1. Provide large print chart listing each medication, schedule, and purpose. Tape a sample of each medication to the chart.
2. Teach daughter about client's medications.
3. Suggest a pill case that will hold a day's or a week's medication at one time.
4. Put all medications in one location.
5. Follow-up referral to community nursing service.

MATERNAL/CHILD NURSING

The assessment of both health risks and developmental accomplishments is an essential part of the practice of nurses in the maternal/child health setting. This orientation combined with a nurse–client relationship that continues over time can facilitate the identification of a substance abuse problem. This section will focus primarily on child/adolescent substance abuse followed by a brief discussion of cigarette smoking during pregnancy. Additional concerns during the prenatal period were discussed in Chapter 10.

The identification of a substance abuse problem in the child or adolescent population presents a challenge. The majority of adolescents have tried cigarette smoking and have used alcohol or other drugs at least on occasion (see Chapter 12). Because of the short history of use, neither the physical signs and symptoms nor the negative consequences of actions are readily apparent (Anglin, 1987). Adult criteria are not always effective in differentiating substance abuse in this age group. Many individuals identified in adolescence as problem drinkers do not go on to become young adults with a substance abuse problem (Zarek, Hawkins, & Rogers, 1987). It is highly unlikely that an adolescent will directly request help for a problem with smoking, alcohol, or drug use. It is also unlikely that the adolescent will appear for an office visit noticeably intoxicated (Anglin, 1987). Thus, all adolescents should be routinely screened for substance abuse problems.

Zarek, Hawkins, & Rogers (1987) compiled a summary of risk factors for adolescent substance abuse. In addition to a family history of alcoholism, the following factors may indicate an increased risk:

1. Family management problems such as unclear or inconsistent rules, poor monitoring of children's behavior, excessively severe discipline, and negative communication patterns
2. Early antisocial behavior
3. Academic underachievement especially in the mid to late elementary grades
4. Little commitment to education
5. Alienation, rebelliousness, and lack of social bonding to society
6. Antisocial behavior in early adolescence
7. Friends who use drugs
8. Favorable attitudes toward drug use
9. Early first use of drugs (pp. 489–490).

Physical symptoms such as poor appetite, insomnia, fatigue, recurrent abdominal pain, chest pain, coughs, sore throats, red eyes, or other upper respiratory complaints may indicate a substance abuse problem (Anglin, 1987; Macdonald, 1987; Morrison & Smith, 1987). Substance abuse should be suspected if the adolescent demonstrates a drop in grades, loss of interest in school and other activities, or a change in behavior (Macdonald, 1987). Frequent accidents or injuries may also indicate a problem with substance abuse.

Interviewing adolescents requires an increased sensitivity to their developmental needs. The interview should take place without parents present. As with other clients, attention to verbal and nonverbal cues and conveying empathy and respect are essential. General questions relating to overall assessment should be asked initially followed by questions relating to social and emotional development (i.e., school activities and peer relationships). Substance use questions should be prefaced as previously mentioned, with the nurse indicating that the majority of adolescents have tried cigarettes, alcohol, and other drugs. The issue of substance abuse can also be discussed when giving instructions for taking medications that interact with alcohol and other drugs. The specific drug interaction information should be given before asking questions relating to the adolescent's substance use (Anglin, 1987).

Trust is a key issue in the nurse–client relationship with the adolescent client. The pediatric office or clinic nurse who has proven to be trustworthy in the past can build on that relationship as the child moves into adolescence. Genuine interest in the client is essential as insincerity or disapproval on the part of the nurse is readily detected. One approach is to ask about smoking, drinking, and drug use in the school setting, inquiring about the amount of use at social gatherings and the methods of obtaining drugs at school. If the adolescent claims no smoking, alcohol, or drug use among students, trust is probably not established (Anglin, 1987). Anglin (1987) provides a more complete description of interview techniques with adolescents.

Substance abuse in adolescents can be conceptualized in four stages. These stages begin with experimentation, where the adolescent first experiences the pleasurable effects of the substance. In the second stage, the adolescent actively seeks these effects. An expertise is developed in the use of various substances to alter moods. Substance use increases and beginning changes in psychosocial functioning are seen. In stage three, a preoccupation with substance use becomes apparent with the adolescent losing control over the substance use. Tolerance is developed, and the main focus of life becomes the substance abuse. Psychosocial functioning deteriorates. In the last stage, a chronic brain syndrome may develop. At this point, the goal of substance abuse is to prevent negative feelings rather than to obtain pleasurable ones. The older adolescent or young adult is "no longer able to function productively in society" (Anglin, 1987, p. 394). This schema and others like it provide a mechanism for evaluating adolescent substance use and choosing appropriate referrals.

Communication, education, counseling, or referral for adolescents and their parents should be based on the assessment of the extent of the substance abuse problem. Chemical dependency programs designed especially for adolescents are the first choice for a treatment facility. These programs combine substance abuse treatment with development of the adolescent's self-esteem. School work is maintained during the course of treatment; programs for parents are frequently required.

Children who grow up in homes where one or both parents are alcoholic form a special high-risk group. In addition to being at greater risk for developing alcoholism, they are overrepresented in groups of children with problems such as stuttering, hyperactivity, eating disorders, learning disabilities, child physical and sexual abuse, school problems, suicide, and teenage pregnancy (Cermak, 1986; Wegscheider-Cruse, 1985). In other children, the effects are not so apparent. They adapt in socially acceptable ways often by becoming overly responsible. This behavior hides feelings of helplessness, anger, guilt, and fear. These children experience gaps in development related to issues of control, trust, dependency, and identification and expression of feelings that have a significant effect on their adult lives (Bingham & Bargar, 1985; Black, 1982). Whenever parental alcoholism is diagnosed, the children and adolescents in the family should receive education, counseling, and referral for further treatment.

Cigarette smoking is a major risk factor during pregnancy. Maternal smoking has a direct effect on infant birth weight; the more the mother smokes, the lower the baby's birth weight. Maternal smoking directly affects the fetal growth rate, resulting in a decrease in body length and head and chest circumference. In addition, maternal smoking increases the risk of abruptio placenta, placenta previa, antepartum hemorrhage, and prolonged rupture of membranes. Smoking during

pregnancy may affect physical growth, mental development, and behavioral characteristics of the child at least to the age of 11 (Alexander, 1987; Surgeon General, 1979). Because smoking is preventable, a major effort is needed to identify women who smoke early in pregnancy, and to provide counseling, education, and smoking cessation programs in the antepartal setting.

Case Example

Natalie P. is a 16-year-old black female who is in her fifth month of pregnancy. She is a high school junior and lives at home with her parents. This pregnancy was unplanned, and Natalie does not intend to marry the baby's father although she still dates him, and he accompanies her to prenatal clinic. Initially, Natalie denied drinking, smoking, or drug use, but during her second visit, she expressed concern for her baby stating "I want it to be normal." She stated that she had heard smoking was bad for the baby, and she admitted smoking about one pack per day.

Selected Nursing Diagnoses and Interventions

Potential for fetal distress related to maternal smoking as evidenced by smoking one pack per day.

1. Discuss the physiologic effects of smoking on fetal and infant development.
2. Provide written material regarding the dangers of smoking and the benefits of quitting.
3. Analyze smoking behavior and smoking cues.
4. Refer to smoking cessation program.
5. Continue to assess alcohol and drug use.

Anxiety related to pregnancy outcome as evidenced by client's concern for a normal baby.

1. Support client in her attempts to quit smoking.
2. Follow-up on referral to smoking cessation program.
3. Involve baby's father in supporting client's attempts to quit smoking.
4. Additional prenatal education regarding other aspects of pregnancy, labor, delivery, and infant care.

COMMUNITY HEALTH NURSING

Community health nurses have a unique role in the area of substance abuse. They have access to clients of various ages in a large variety of settings. They are familiar with the life-styles, cultures, and health statistics of the populations with whom they work. They have a working knowledge of community resources and health care systems. Their role has traditionally included health teaching for various community groups, counseling clients and families with chronic diseases, referrals to community resources, and coordination of health services for clients (Fortin, 1983).

The practice of community health nursing can be described in terms of primary, secondary, and tertiary prevention. Primary prevention "consists of activities directed toward decreasing the probability of specific illnesses or dysfunctions in individuals, families and communities" (Pender, 1987, p. 4). Secondary prevention "emphasizes early diagnosis and prompt intervention," and tertiary prevention is concerned with rehabilitation (Pender, 1987, p. 5). This section will discuss the nurse's role in substance abuse in these areas of prevention.

Primary Prevention

In the past, primary prevention in the area of substance abuse has consisted of media campaigns, school drug information programs, and affective educational programs. These activities were aimed at the "gateway" years—ages 12–20—because of evidence indicating that individuals who do not smoke or use alcohol or other drugs during adolescence or young adulthood will not begin this use later in life (DuPont, 1987). Media campaigns, popular in the late 1960s and early 1970s, emphasized the harmful effects of drug use. These effects were sometimes unrealistically exaggerated, creating a credibility gap. School drug programs, although varying in quality, generally improved the students' knowledge about drugs. Affective education programs focused on enhancing self-esteem, improving decision-making skills, and enriching personal and social development. As with the media campaigns and school drug programs, this generic approach seems to have had little or no effect on attitudes toward smoking or drugs or actual smoking or drug use (Blane, 1986; Botvin, 1986; Durell & Bukoski, 1984).

Currently, two approaches in primary prevention are being advocated. The first is the "macro" approach, so called because it focuses on the total environment. The goal of the program is to "create a community climate of nondrug use" (Durell & Bukoski, 1984, p. 28). This approach combines a public information campaign communicating straightforwardly the adverse effects of drug use with attempts to counter the drug-motivating factors present in society. Parents, schools, and community agencies work together to give negative drug messages to children and adolescents. Mothers Against Drunk Driving and the trend toward drug testing in the workplace are examples of "macro" programs aimed at adult populations (DuPont, 1987).

The second approach is exemplified by the "Just Say No" programs which utilize positive peer pressure and specific training to resist influences to use drugs. These programs have been effective in preventing students from beginning to smoke as well as in decreasing the frequency of alcohol and marihuana use (Botvin, 1986; Durell & Bukoski, 1984; McAlister, Perry, Killen, Slinkard, & Maccoby, 1980).

In addition to organizing and participating in "macro" and positive peer pressure programs, community health nurses can identify both individuals and groups at high risk for developing a substance abuse problem. This information can be communicated to other professionals in the community and available resources matched with those who need them. Nurses can be active in the legislative process to influence public policy and the financial commitment to prevent substance abuse.

Secondary Prevention

In the area of secondary prevention, community health nurses interact with clients in much the same way as their colleagues in acute care settings. They have the additional opportunity to assess the client's home environment, observing such things as empty beer cans, multiple prescription bottles, drug paraphernalia, and furnishings that are not consistent with others in the neighborhood (Fortin, 1983). They interact with family members and encounter neighbors and building managers that may share concerns regarding the client's substance abuse. If the nurse's suspicion is raised during the assessment process or at a later time, a more extensive evaluation for substance abuse should be completed and the NNSA framework used in planning the nursing care.

Tertiary Care

Generally, community health nurses will encounter individuals in recovery only when they are referred for other medical problems. In addition to the usual nursing assessment, the substance abuse history mentioned earlier should be obtained. Questions regarding the client's and family's past and present use of community resources and their methods of coping with the addiction should be included. The nurse should become familiar with the principles and practices of 12-step programs such as AA and Al-Anon. Attending open meetings will provide a first-hand knowledge to enable the nurse to match the client or family with the most appropriate group. Nurses should also have a working knowledge of the smoking cessation programs and the alcohol and drug treatment programs in the community and their follow-up services. If the client relapses, the community health nurse is available to support the family and guide the client into additional treatment programs.

Although community health referrals are generally not done on clients released from detoxification or treatment facilities, the community health nurse is in an ideal position to provide follow-up care. Continued education about the disease process, support, and health teaching as well as coordination and referral to existing services are part of the practice expertise of these nurses (Fortin, 1983). A collaborative relationship between the community health nurse and the personnel at the treatment facility would ease the transition for many alcohol and drug addicted clients and provide a new source of social support in the community.

Case Example

For some time, the administration at Mid-City High School had been aware of a drug problem at the school. In addition to the usual smoking and alcohol use at school functions, there was evidence of increased marihuana and cocaine use among students. When the third student in 2 weeks was caught smoking crack, the administration and the school nurse met to decide how to handle the situation.

Selected Interventions

Primary Prevention

1. Involve school board, parents, teachers, students and law enforcement personnel in activities.

2. Contact National Institute on Drug Abuse (NIDA) and local drug abuse professionals to develop a multiphase approach to drug use at school.
3. Develop positive peer pressure strategies to create a climate of nondrug use.
4. Encourage groups as Students Against Drunk Driving and Just Say No clubs.
5. Arrest students in school who possess or distribute illicit drugs on school grounds.

Secondary Prevention

1. Work with school board, parents, teachers and students in all activities.
2. Identify students at high risk and target intervention towards them.
3. Call 800-COCAINE for suggestions on diagnosis and treatment.
4. Contact parents of students involved in drug use to attempt to get them into a local treatment program.

Tertiary Prevention

1. Facilitate transfer of students between treatment programs and school.
2. Provide individual and group support for returning students.
3. Approach school board about holding A.A. and N.A. meetings on school grounds after school hours.

PSYCHIATRIC NURSING

Mental health/psychiatric nurses interact with substance-abusing clients in a wide variety of settings from the consultation/liaison nurse in the general hospital to the substance abuse specialist in the treatment facility. Smoking is widespread among psychiatric clients, with cigarettes used as rewards in many behavior modification programs. This section will address briefly the nursing care of the dual diagnosis client—the client diagnosed as having both a mental disorder and a problem with alcohol or drug abuse. In the past, the dual diagnosis client was directed into either the psychiatric or the substance abuse treatment system based on the primary diagnosis. Treatment in the psychiatric system focused on the psychiatric problem with little or no attention given to the substance abuse. Treatment in the substance abuse system was directed toward that one issue with underlying psychiatric problems not addressed. In recent years, it has become increasingly clear that treating either problem alone is not effective. The dual diagnosis client must be treated as a client with two enmeshed problems that mutually reinforce one another (McKelvy, Kane, & Kellison, 1987).

Substance use becomes a problem for the psychiatric client when it exacerbates symptoms and decreases the effectiveness of medication thus precipitating additional hospitalizations (McKelvy et al., 1987). A cyclical process occurs in which clients with minimal coping skills abuse a substance to relieve the discomfort caused by a psychological crisis. The substance abuse provides a temporary feeling of well-being followed by renewed discomfort both from the original issues and the substance abuse itself. This, in turn, leads to further substance abuse continuing the cycle (Bakdash, 1983). In one study, alcohol or drug use was a complicating factor in 60% of clients admitted to a state psychiatric hospital (McKelvy et al., 1987).

Nursing intervention with dual diagnosis clients is based on a holistic approach. The knowledge and skills used with the psychiatric problem are combined with those used to effect change in the substance-abusing client. Abstinence cannot be seen as a precondition to treatment nor can the client be expected to function without any drug use because psychotropic medications are often essential to recovery. The confrontational strategies and intense group therapy used with many substance-abusing clients may serve to precipitate acute psychotic episodes in the dual diagnosis client (McKelvy et al., 1987). A supportive, nonjudgmental approach is used initially and altered based on the client's behavior (Bakdash, 1983).

It is important to note that clients with either diagnosis, substance abuse or mental disorder, have a higher incidence of suicide and violent behavior, a high relapse rate and severely impaired social functioning. Having both diagnoses seems to increase the risks and the impairment (McKelvy et al., 1987). A thorough assessment combined with suicide precautions is warranted, particularly if the mental illness is an affective disorder.

Case Example

Cindy T., a 35-year-old white female, is admitted to a psychiatric unit with a diagnosis of depression. On admission, she expresses thoughts of "shooting" herself with a handgun she keeps for protection: She states that she "feels like I need to quit drinking," but denies that alcohol is a problem. She lost her job 3 weeks ago, the third job loss in 6 months. Cindy has a college degree in elementary education, but most recently worked as a waitress and sales clerk. She lives alone in a single room in a boarding house.

Selected Nursing Diagnoses and Interventions

Potential for self-injury related to depression as evidenced by verbalization of suicide ideation.

1. Evaluate suicide potential.
2. Observe frequently.
3. Restrict to psychiatric unit.
4. Encourage client to identify and verbalize feelings.
5. Contract with client to seek out staff member if thoughts of suicide occur.

Impaired social interaction related to depression as evidenced by current life-style.

1. Change room assignment if necessary to encourage friendships.
2. Seek client out for brief periods of conversation.
3. Encourage participation in informal social interactions.
4. Assess level of social skills.
5. Provide teaching plan for social interaction skills.
6. Provide positive reinforcement for appropriate socialization.
7. Involve in education and therapy groups.
8. Secure sponsor from AA.

Ineffective individual coping related to alcohol abuse as evidenced by frequent loss of job, working below educational preparation, and life-style.

1. Dispel myths about alcohol use and abuse.
2. Identify current problems in client's life and their relationship to alcohol abuse.
3. Confront client with alcohol abuse and its consequences.
4. Encourage abstinence.
5. Encourage client to attend AA group while in hospital.
6. Teach alternative methods of dealing with stress and conflict.
7. Transfer to alcoholism treatment unit when depression is under control.

SUMMARY

The role of the nurse in the care of the substance abusing client includes five categories of nursing interventions: identification, communication, education, counseling, and referral. Identification of the client with an alcohol or drug abuse problem seems to present the most difficulty. Interview instruments such as the CAGE or MAST can be used in combination with the nursing assessment. Once a substance abuse problem is identified, the nurse should discuss the findings with the client, family, and appropriate members of the health care team. The client and spouse should receive counseling and education. Denial, characteristic of the disease, should be considered in the process. The goal is referral to a treatment program.

Nurses in every specialty area interact with clients who abuse substances. The potential for withdrawal from alcohol and other drugs should be evaluated with every client. Substance abuse may be present in clients of all ages from adolescents to the elderly, although the identifying characteristics and treatment approaches may differ. Prevention of substance abuse should be addressed by nurses in all specialty areas.

REFERENCES

Adams, F. E. (1988). Drug dependency in hospital patients. *American Journal of Nursing, 88,* 477–481.

Alexander, L. L. (1987). The pregnant smoker: Nursing implications. *Journal of Obstetric, Gynecologic and Neonatal Nursing, 16,* 167–173.

American Psychiatric Association. (1987). *Diagnostic and statistical manual of mental disorders* (3d ed. revised). Washington, DC: Author.

Anderson, R. O. (1986). The physician as an enabler of the chemically dependent patient. *Postgraduate Medicine, 79*(8), 207–214.

Anglin, T. M. (1987). Interviewing guidelines for the clinical evaluation of adolescent substance abuse. *Pediatric Clinics of North America, 34,* 381–398.

Bakdash, D. P. (1983). Psychiatric-mental health nursing. In G. Bennett, C. Vourakis, & D. S. Woolf (Eds.), *Substance abuse: Pharmacologic, developmental and clinical perspectives* (pp. 223–239). New York: John Wiley & Sons.

Bates, R. C. (1987). Smoking and health implications for smoking cessation programs. *Health Education, 18*(3), 14–17.

Bennett, G., Vourakis, C., & Woolf, D. S. (Eds.). (1983). *Substance abuse: Pharmacologic, developmental and clinical perspectives.* New York: John Wiley & Sons.

Bernadt, M. W., Taylor, C., Murray, R. M., Mumford, J., & Smith, B. (1982). Comparison of questionnaire and laboratory test in the detection of excessive drinking and alcoholism. *Lancet, 1,* 325–328.

Bingham, A., & Bargar, J. (1985). Children of alcoholic families: A group treatment approach for latency age children. *Journal of Psychosocial Nursing, 23*(12), 13–15.

Black, C. (1982). *It will never happen to me!* Denver: MAC Publishing.

Blane, H. T. (1986). Preventing alcohol problems. In N. J. Estes & M. E. Heinemann(Eds.), *Alcoholism: Development, consequences, and interventions* (3d ed.) (pp. 78–90). St. Louis: C. V. Mosby.

Bluhm, J. (1981). When you face the alcoholic patient. *Nursing 81, 11*(2), 71–73.

Bluhm, J. (1987). *When you face the chemically dependent patient: A practical guide for nurses.* St. Louis: Ishiyaku EuroAmerica, Inc.

Botvin, G. J. (1986). Substance abuse prevention research: Recent developments and future directions. *Journal of School Health, 56,* 369–374.

Butz, R. H. (1986). Intoxication and withdrawal. In N. J. Estes & M. E. Heinemann (Eds.), *Alcoholism: Development, consequences, and interventions* (3d ed.) (pp. 103–109). St. Louis: C. V. Mosby.

Caroselli-Karinja, M. (1985). Drug abuse and the elderly. *Journal of Psychosocial Nursing, 23*(6), 25–30.

Cermak, T. L. (1986). *Diagnosing and treating co-dependence.* Minneapolis: Johnson Institute Books.

Cohn, L. (1982). The hidden diagnosis. *American Journal of Nursing, 82,* 1862–1864.

DiCicco-Bloom, B., Space, S., & Zahourek, R. P. (1986). The homebound alcoholic. *American Journal of Nursing, 86,* 167–169.

DuPont, R. L. (1987). Prevention of adolescent chemical dependency. *Pediatric Clinics of North America, 34,* 495–505.

Durell, J., & Bukoski, W. (1984). Preventing substance abuse: The state of the art. *Public Health Reports, 99,* 23–31.

Ellor, J. R., & Kurz, D. J. (1982). Misuse and abuse of prescription and nonprescription drugs by the elderly. *Nursing Clinics of North America, 17,* 319–330.

Estes, N. J., & Heinemann, M. E. (Eds.) (1986). *Alcoholism: Development, consequences, and interventions* (3d ed.). St. Louis: C. V. Mosby.

Estes, N. J., Smith-DiJulio, K., & Heinemann, M. E. (1980). *Nursing diagnosis of the alcoholic person.* St. Louis: C. V. Mosby.

Ewing, J. A. (1984). Detecting alcoholism: The CAGE questionnaire. *Journal of the American Medical Association, 252,* 1905–1907.

Fisk, N. B. (1986). Alcoholism: Ineffective family coping. *American Journal of Nursing, 86,* 586–587.

Fortin, M. L. (1983). Community health nursing. In G. Bennett, C. Vourakis, & D. S. Woolf (Eds.), *Substance abuse: Pharmacologic, developmental and clinical perspectives* (pp. 209–222). New York: John Wiley & Sons.

Galanter, M., Karasu, T. B., & Wilder, J. F. (1976). Alcohol and drug consultation in the general hospital: A systems approach. *American Journal of Psychiatry, 133,* 930–934.

Gill, D. J. (1987). Alcoholism and the consultation-liaison psychiatrist. *Psychiatric Clinics of North America, 10,* 129–139.

Goldstein, A. O., Hellier, A., Fitzgerald, S., Stegall, T. S., & Fischer, P. M. (1987). Hospital nurse counseling of patients who smoke. *American Journal of Public Health, 77,* 1333–1334.

Gordon, M. (1987). *Manual of nursing diagnosis 1986–1987.* New York: McGraw-Hill.

Hall, E. P. (1983). Substance abuse in the aging. In G. Bennett, C. Vourakis, & D. S. Woolf (Eds.). *Substance abuse: Pharmacologic, developmental and clinical perspectives* (pp. 192–205). New York: John Wiley & Sons.

Harwood, H. J., Napolitano, D. M., Kristiansen, P. L., & Collins, J. J. (1984). *Economic costs to society of alcohol and drug abuse and mental illness: 1980* (Pub. No. RTI/2734/00-0/FR). Research Triangle Park, NC: Research Triangle Institute.

Hoffman, A. L., & Heinemann, M. E. (1986). Alcohol problems in elderly persons. In N. J. Estes & M. E. Heinemann (Eds.), *Alcoholism: Development, consequences, and interventions* (3d ed.) (pp. 257–272). St. Louis: C. V. Mosby.

Jacobs, P., & Stringer, G. (1987). The person who abuses substances. In R. B. Murray & M. M. W. Huelskoetter (Eds.), *Psychiatric/mental health nursing: Giving emotional care* (pp. 403–447). Norwalk, CT: Appleton & Lange.

Kelly, F. M. (1986). Caring for the patient in acute alcohol withdrawal. *Critical Care Quarterly, 8*(4), 11–19.

Lasker, M. N. (1986). Aging alcoholics need nursing help. *Journal of Gerontological Nursing, 12*(1), 16–19.

Loeb, L. A., Ernster, V. L., Warner, K. E., Abbotts, J., & Laszlo, J. (1984). Smoking and lung cancer: An overview. *Cancer Research, 44,* 5940–5958.

Macdonald, D. I. (1987). Patterns of alcohol and drug use among adolescents. *Pediatric Clinics of North America, 34,* 275–288.

Mayfield, D., McLeod, G., & Hall, P. (1974). The CAGE questionnaire: Validation of a new alcoholism screening instrument. *American Journal of Psychiatry, 131,* 1121–1123.

Mayou, R., & Hawton, K. (1986). Psychiatric disorder in the general hospital. *British Journal of Psychiatry, 149,* 172–190.

McAlister, A., Perry, C., Killen, J., Slinkard, L. A., & Maccoby, N. (1980). Pilot study of smoking, alcohol and drug abuse prevention. *American Journal of Public Health, 70,* 719–721.

McIntosh, I. D. (1982). Alcohol-related disabilities in general hospital patients: A critical assessment of the evidence. *International Journal of the Addictions, 17,* 609–639.

McKelvy, M. J., Kane, J. S., & Kellison, K. (1987). Substance abuse and mental illness: Double trouble. *Journal of Psychosocial Nursing, 25*(1), 20–25.

McMahon, A., & Maibusch, R. M. (1988). How to send quit-smoking signals. *American Journal of Nursing, 88,* 1498–1499.

Moore, D. F. (1983). Detoxification. In G. Bennett, C. Vourakis, & D. S. Woolf (Eds.), *Substance abuse: Pharmocologic, developmental, and clinical perspectives* (pp. 328–340). New York: John Wiley & Sons.

Moore, R. A. (1985). The prevalence of alcoholism in medical and surgical patients. In M. A. Schuckit (Ed.), *Alcohol patterns and problems* (pp. 247–265). New Brunswick, NJ: Rutgers University Press.

Moore, R. D., & Malitz, F. E. (1986). Underdiagnosis of alcoholism by residents in an ambulatory medical practice. *Journal of Medical Education, 61,* 46–52.

Morrison, M. A., & Smith, Q. T. (1987). Psychiatric issues in adolescent chemical dependency. *Pediatric Clinics of North America, 34,* 461–479.

Mullen, E. M., & Granholm, M. (1981). Drugs and the elderly patient. *Journal of Gerontological Nursing, 7,* 108–113.

National Institute on Drug Abuse. (1987). *National household survey on drug abuse: 1985 population estimates* (DHHS Publication No. ADM 87–1539). Washington, DC: U. S. Department of Health and Human Services.

Pender, N. J. (1987). *Health promotion in nursing practice* (2d ed.). Norwalk, CT: Appleton & Lange.

Powell, A. H., & Minick, M. P. (1988). Alcohol withdrawal syndrome. *American Journal of Nursing, 88,* 312–315.

Price, J. H., & Andrews, P. (1982). Alcohol abuse in the elderly. *Journal of Gerontological Nursing, 8*(1), 16–19.

Scherwerts, P. (1982). An alcoholic treatment team. *American Journal of Nursing, 82,* 1878–1879.

Selzer, M. L. (1971). The Michigan Alcoholism Screening Test: The quest for a new diagnostic instrument. *American Journal of Psychiatry, 127,* 1653–1658.

Smith, J. W. (1983). Diagnosing alcoholism. *Hospital and Community Psychiatry, 34,* 1017–1021.

Surgeon General. (1979). *Smoking and health: A report of the Surgeon General* (DHEW Publication No. (PHS) 79–50066). Washington, DC: U. S. Government Printing Office.

Surgeon General. (1983). *The health consequences of smoking: Cardiovascular disease* (DHHS Publication No. (PHS) 84–50204). Washington, DC: U. S. Government Printing Office.

U. S. Department of Health and Human Services. (1987). *Sixth special report to the U. S. Congress on alcohol and health* (DHHS Publication No. ADM 87–1519). Washington, DC: Author.

Wegscheider-Cruse, S. (1985). *Choicemaking for co-dependents, adult children and spirituality seekers.* Pompano Beach, FL: Health Communications.

Weist, J. K., Lindeman, M. G., & Newton, M. (1982). Hospital dialogues. *American Journal of Nursing, 82,* 1874–1877.

West, L. J., Maxwell, D. S., Noble, E. P., & Solomon, D. H. (1984). U.C.L.A. conference: Alcoholism. *Annals of Internal Medicine, 100,* 405–416.

Westermeyer, J., Doheny, S., & Stone, B. (1978). An assessment of hospital care for the alcoholic patient. *Alcoholism: Clinical and Experimental Research, 2,* 53–57.

Whitfield, C. L. (1984). Co-alcoholism: Recognizing a treatable illness. *Family and Community Health, 7*(2), 16–27.

Zahourek, R. P. (1986). Identification of the alcoholic in the acute care setting. *Critical Care Quarterly, 8*(4), 1–10.

Zarek, D., Hawkins, J. D., & Rogers, P. D. (1987). Risk factors in adolescent substance abuse. *Pediatric Clinics of North America, 34,* 481–493.

16 | THE EMERGING SPECIALTY OF ADDICTIONS NURSING

Ann Solari-Twadell

Only since the 1940s has there been a sustained development of addiction specialties in the health professions. This development on the part of the nursing profession is even more recent in comparison with other professional groups (Toner, 1954). The 1970s was a crucial period of identity formation for nurses in the alcohol and drug abuse field. The 1980s saw a proliferation of professional associations representing the interests of the addictions nurse. The publication of a scope of practice statement (American Nurses Association, 1987), and soon after, the standards for addictions nursing practice (American Nurses Association, 1988), marked a momentous turning point in nursing's efforts to establish its particular contributions to the care of addicted clients and their families. Nursing education, with support from the National Institute on Alcohol Abuse and Alcoholism (NIAAA) and the National Institute on Drug Abuse (NIDA), is making some strides in incorporating addictions education in curricula. Within the context of a rapidly unfolding scene, this chapter will focus on the key elements which appear to be most related to the present and future development of addictions nursing as a specialty.

HISTORICAL PERSPECTIVES

The failure of Prohibition to resolve the nation's alcohol problems created a climate in the 1930s for the testing of new ideas regarding the nature of alcoholism (Levine, 1978). Dr. William Silkworth of the Charles B. Towns Hospital in New York City instructed his alcoholic patients on what he believed to be the essential features of their illness: an obsession of the mind leading to compulsive drinking and an allergy of the body resulting in madness or death. Bill W., a stockbroker, and a patient of Silkworth's, melded these ideas with the spiritual concepts and practices of the then popular Oxford Groups.

When Bill W. and Dr. Bob, a surgeon and an alcoholic, met in Akron, Ohio, in 1935 and made a commitment to take these ideas to other alcoholics, Alcoholics Anonymous (AA) was born (Alcoholics Anonymous, 1957). In the ensuing years the success of AA among growing numbers of recovering alcoholics, and the appeal of the disease concept of alcoholism for a small number of influential scientists and clinicians, led to the establishment of the National Council on Alcoholism (NCA) and the Yale Center for Alcohol Studies (Mann, 1973).

Attempting to trace nursing's contributions or involvement in these early years of the alcoholism treatment movement is difficult, but some evidence can be found (Bennett, 1983). For example, there were two articles published in the *American Journal of Nursing* during this period providing case studies of nursing care for chronic alcoholics (Callender, 1931; Parrish, 1934). Also, in the authorized history of AA (Alcoholics Anonymous, 1957), the work of pioneering nurses who supported AA during the early years is mentioned. The most detailed account is of Sister Ignatia and other Sisters of Charity of St. Augustine who were credited with providing excellent nursing care in the first hospital unit specifically for alcoholics wishing to enter the AA program. This unit was in the St. Thomas Hospital in Akron, Ohio.

The beginning of the Yale Center of Alcohol Studies Summer School in 1943 gave nurses the first opportunity to participate in university-based education on alcoholism. During the first 12 years of the school, 51 registered nurses attended. Although this was an important beginning for the profession, Golder (1956) commented on what she viewed as a missed opportunity. "Small as the number was, it could have been a nucleus for spreading the information among the profession. This did not happen because practically all these nurses returned to fields where they dealt exclusively with the problem of alcoholism" (p. 436).

In 1971, the National Institute on Alcohol Abuse and Alcoholism (NIAAA) began the federal government's initiative to support alcohol and drug abuse education for health professionals. Although most of the funds allotted went to medical education, the School of Nursing at the University of Washington in Seattle obtained grants to support alcohol and drug abuse education for undergraduate nursing students, graduate students, and visiting faculty from schools of nursing throughout the country (Heinemann & Estes, 1974). Some of the nurses who participated in these programs are today the leaders in advancing role development, working toward certification guidelines, and initiating new educational programs.

NIAAA funding was also instrumental in the development of curriculum guides for community health nursing (National Institute of Alcohol Abuse and Alcoholism, 1978) and nurse practitioner programs (Hasselblod, 1984). These materials made it possible for nonaddiction specialists in nursing to incorporate alcohol and drug abuse knowledge into their practices. After some recent years with no support available for nursing education, the NIAAA is now again awarding grant monies to schools of nursing for projects designed to integrate alcohol and drug abuse knowledge into undergraduate and graduate curricula.

In 1974, at an NCA annual forum in Milwaukee, Wisconsin, a small group of nurses met and developed the foundation for what is today the National Nurses Society on Addictions (NNSA). NNSA began as the National Nurses Society on Alcoholism, a component of the NCA. Initially, there was little formation to the assembly of nurses. A nurse from the group acted as a liaison with the NCA office. Within a few years a structure was put in place with the president of NNSA represented at the board meetings of the NCA. The nurses' component organization, along with a physicians' component and a researchers' component, continued with the NCA until 1981.

The first position paper published through the work of NNSA members was completed in 1979. The subject matter focused on the role of the nurse in alcoholism in direct service, education, management, and research (National Nurses Society on Alcoholism, 1979). Additional position papers on educating nurses, the impaired nurse and drug testing have been developed over the years (National Nurses Society on Addictions, 1981, 1983, 1988).

The NCA provided nurses the opportunity to have annual educational programs and meetings. This gave nurses an arena to present papers and discuss subjects common to their practice in addiction treatment. Papers were presented on topics such as patient classification systems (Zych, 1980), chemical dependency in women with infertility (Busch, 1982), nursing alcoholism educational programs (Estes, 1983), and various aspects of nurses' roles in alcoholism treatment. Nurses interested in the care of the alcohol- and drug-addicted patient had a place to meet, give and get support, and continue to develop the body of knowledge needed by nurses to care for addicted persons.

Treatment in the 1970s tended to be segregated by substance type. Alcoholics were treated in alcohol treatment centers, and drug addicts were treated in drug treatment agencies. This philosophy was reflected also at the federal level with the existence of the NIAAA and the National Institute on Drug Abuse (NIDA). Some nurses belonging to the then National Nurses Society on Alcoholism objected to the little attention given to drug addiction. This led to the development of the Drug and Alcohol Nurses Association (DANA) in 1979. By 1980 two specialty nursing organizations were organized focused on addiction.

In 1981 the National Nurses Society on Alcoholism separated their management from the NCA. This was done in agreement with the Council. Under the direction of President Etta Williams, the society was established as a separate organization. One of the organization's first decisions was to change the name to reflect the entire scope of the practice of the members. Consequently, the name became the National Nurses Society on Addictions (NNSA). There was hope that DANA would see this change as a way that the two organizations could become one. However, negotiations between the two organizations resulted in each organization continuing.

Today there are three national specialty nursing organizations focused on addiction. They are NNSA, DANA, and the National Consortium of Chemical Dependency Nurses. Each organization has interests in the role of the nurse, certification, and the impaired nurse issue.

PREPARATION FOR CERTIFICATION

Certification is a primary way for the nursing profession to implement self-regulation. Without the authority self-regulation provides, the collective could be identified as a trade group whose standards, codes, and beliefs are determined by others (Steel, 1985). McCorkle (1984) defines certification as a privately contracted method for guaranteeing to the public the quality of services of the professional group; it enables the public and employers to identify practitioners who have met a standard that is usually well above the minimum level required for licensure. Swift and Durkam (1985) describe the purposes and motivation for seeking certification as including: *(1)* increased respect from peers and colleagues; *(2)* improved self-image; *(3)* local, state, or national recognition; *(4)* evidence of superior knowledge and skill; and *(5)* increased material rewards or career advancement.

In 1983, the Division on Psychiatric and Mental Health Nursing Practice of the American Nurses Association (ANA) recommended that addictions nursing be recognized as a specialty area of nursing (American Nurses Association, 1987). The outcome of this was the development of a task force to outline the scope of practice and standards for this specialty area. This effort marked the first time that nurses with an expertise in this specialty came together with the intent to define the scope of their practice.

Murphy (1988) stated well that specialization constitutes a major advance in the discipline of nursing. It assumes a complexity of knowledge and clinical competence that can be known and practiced only by a segment of the nursing population who meet specific criteria. Identifying the scope of the specialty practice is one of the first steps toward clarifying the knowledge and skills inherent in that practice.

Addictions nursing challenged the writers of the scope statement from a variety of perspectives. First, it was necessary to clarify terminology and reach some common understanding regarding the essential nature of addictions nursing despite cultural/geographic differences in various parts of the country. It was also important to arrive at a scope of practice statement that was not only immediately applicable but also one that anticipated future developments.

The need to agree on the terminology to be used in the scope statement was cause for significant deliberation by the writers. It is very prevalent in addiction-related literature for terms such as alcoholism, chemical dependency, drug abuse, and addiction to be used without precise definitions given. Often the terms are used interchangeably. The writers of the scope statement were intentional about defining and being consistent in the terms used. One of the strengths of the final document was a clarification of these terms as they are applied to nursing theory and practice.

The cultural and geographic diversity of treatment philosophies and practices throughout the United States was represented by members of the task force. Preferences such as withdrawal regimen, terminology, length of stay, level of care, and adequate preparation of practitioners were discussed, considered, and debated with consensus the goal. This work was essential in establishing a strong foundation for this specialty's practice. The clarity of the scope document was an important contribution to the subsequent work done toward development of certification in addictions nursing.

The scope document identifies and clarifies the wide range of practice settings and roles in which the addictions nurse practices. It emphasizes the pivotal position nurses have in identifying patterns of abuse and addiction, not only in their clients, but also in their peers. The definition of addictions nursing in one sentence succinctly identifies the role of the nurse: "Addictions nursing is the diagnosis and treatment of human responses to patterns of abuse and addiction" (American Nurses Association, 1987). The precise definitions of abuse and addiction found in the nursing scope document clarify the intent of this statement.

The scope document categorizes the phenomena of concern to the specialty into human responses to abuse or addiction of an episodic or continuing nature. These human responses are separated into the psychosocial, biologic, cognitive/perceptual, and spiritual belief dimensions. This classification outlines the basis for nursing diagnoses with addicted clients and their families.

In December 1983 when the task force first met, the parameters of the scope focused exclusively on the use, abuse, and disease associated only with alcohol and drugs. The intent was to reflect the prevalent practice of that time. By 1985, the writers of the scope document, noting the apparent change in the practice of addictions nursing, altered the scope statement from an exclusive focus on alcoholism and drug addictions to include other addictions such as eating disorders, nicotine addiction, gambling, spending, and sexual addictions. By the 1987 publication date, the scope statement was pertinent to the current practice of most addictions nurses.

ESTABLISHING STANDARDS OF PRACTICE

Professional nursing associations have one function above all: to establish, maintain, and improve standards of practice (Follet, 1942). In 1986, the ANA invited representatives from the NNSA to participate on a task force for the writing of standards for addictions nursing.

The preliminary work on the standards was done by the NNSA certification committee. This was an advantage in that the first time the task force met a draft of standards was available. The work on the standards flowed from the foundation set in the scope of practice document (Nelson, 1989). The resulting *Standards of Addictions Nursing Practice with Selected Diagnoses and Criteria* (American Nurses Association, 1988) is a unique document because it is one of the few nursing standards statements that includes nursing diagnoses and criteria sets.

The first section of the Standards document follows the nursing process format with an emphasis on data collection, diagnosis, and planning. The intervention section covers six areas: therapeutic alliance, education, self-help groups, pharmacologic approaches, therapeutic environment, and counseling. Counseling is understood as both a role and a function. The remaining standards address evaluation, ethical care, quality assurance, continuing education, interdisciplinary collaboration, and use of community health systems and research. Each standard has a rationale which addresses the purpose, importance, and significance of the particular standard to the nurse practicing in addictions treatment. Following the rationale are the structure, process, and outcome criteria. These criteria are to be used in evaluating the quality of addictions nursing practice. At the same time, these criteria are outlining the administrative framework, actions of the nurse, and the intended result of the process. These standards are intended to be integrated into the clinical practice of nurses at the generalist level.

The second section of the Standards focuses on nursing diagnoses. The 26 nursing diagnoses presented were chosen from the North American Nursing Diagnosis Association (NANDA) list. The intention of the writers was not to be inclusive but rather to acquaint the readers with the process of utilizing nursing diagnoses in their clinical practice. As clinicians become knowledgeable in the use of nursing diagnoses, it is anticipated that additional diagnoses will also be used.

The document on standards and nursing diagnoses was instrumental in the development of a core curriculum for addictions nursing. A core curriculum for addictions nursing along with nursing care planning guides are available from NNSA.

CERTIFICATION

A process for recognizing nurses in chemical dependency was initiated by the California Association of Nurses in Substance Abuse in April 1986. Nurses completing the process were recognized with the designation CCDN (Certified Chemical Dependency Nurse). In January 1987, this designation was offered to nurses outside the State of California. In May 1987, a charter meeting of the National Consortium of Chemical Dependency Nurses was held in California. The consortium offers a certification program leading to the designation R.N.C.D. The content of these certification programs focuses primarily on alcoholism and drug addiction. The development of these certification programs predates the publication of the ANA scope of practice and standards documents.

NNSA administers a national certification process in collaboration with the National League for Nursing (NLN). The focus of the examination is broad, including problems related to alcohol, drugs, eating disorders, codependency, gambling, sexual, and spending addictions. The content of the examination is based on the ANA scope of practice and standard documents (American Nurses Association, 1987, 1988). The nurses who successfully complete the NNSA certification are designated as Certified Addictions Registered Nurses (CARN). The objectives of the certification exam are: *(1)* to determine the nurse's ability to apply knowledge from nursing and related disciplines in the care of persons with problems resulting from patterns of abuse, dependence, and addiction, and *(2)* to synthesize the nursing process in the care of persons with potential or actual problems resulting from patterns of abuse, dependence, and addiction. Registered nurses are eligible to take the certification exam if they: *(1)* hold a current, full and unrestricted license as a registered nurse in the United States, its possessions, or Canada; *(2)* have 3 years' experience practicing as a registered nurse; and *(3)* within the last 5 years prior to the application have had a minimum of 4000 hours or 2 years of addiction nursing experience as a registered nurse in a staff, administrative, teaching, consultant, private practice, counseling, or research capacity. The first examination was administered in December 1989.

ROLES FOR ADDICTIONS NURSES

Historically, the nurse's primary role in addiction treatment was one of caregiver, largely responding to the medical needs of the patient. As specialized addiction treatment became recognized and different levels of care for addicted persons were acknowledged, multiple roles for the nurse began to take shape (Solari-Twadell, 1982). Some nurses wishing to move beyond the traditional role moved into positions such as program manager or program director (Leck, 1981). These pioneers created opportunities and options previously not available to addictions nurses. Today, addictions nurses are functioning in a variety of roles and settings (American Nurses Association, 1987). They are employed in upper level management in large systems, as employee assistance program providers in corporate settings, as clinical specialists, managers of direct care, staff nurses, in their own business of private practice or consultation, and as researchers and educators.

One means for attaining credibility for the practice of addictions nursing is through the development of innovative models of practice (Murphy, 1988). These innovative models need to be communicated. It is only through active communication in publications and at professional meetings that other nurses will learn, be encouraged to take risks, and refine their practices. It is also very important that nurses leaving traditional roles for more innovative ones continue to identify themselves as nurses. The visible maintenance of the RN and advanced nursing credentials accentuates the advances being made in the specialty and profession.

Murphy (1988) suggests the complexity of caring for addicted clients is both a stimulus and detriment to the development of the specialty. Nursing's holistic view of the client promises to be a major asset in developing comprehensive approaches to care. The challenge will remain in effectively communicating, documenting, and substantiating through research those strategies and roles which are effective and contribute to the advancement of this specialty's practice.

CONTINUING ISSUES FOR THE SPECIALTY

Many issues are relevant to the continuing development of addictions nursing. On the current scene, five issues are of particular significance: *(1)* the challenge of increasing educational opportunities in the field of addictions for undergraduate and graduate nursing students, *(2)* the dearth of nursing research focusing on addictions, *(3)* the need for many more addictions nurses to

join and participate in professional organizations, *(4)* assuring the availability of adequate health insurance coverage for addiction treatment, and *(5)* responding to addictions among nurses themselves.

Education

Given the magnitude of the impact of addictions on the health of Americans, the attention given to addictions in curricula in most schools of nursing is disproportionately small (Hoffman & Heinemann, 1987). An ongoing challenge will be to significantly increase nursing students' access to the most recent advances in addictions knowledge. A recent program of the NIAAA and the NIDA was designed to address this serious problem. Three schools of nursing, the University of Connecticut, New York University, and Ohio State University, were awarded contracts to develop model curricula integrating alcohol and drug abuse content in undergraduate and graduate programs. In addition, NIAAA and NIDA support a grant program for nursing faculty with the goal of becoming teacher–clinicians in the specialty of addictions treatment. This kind of government emphasis and support is instrumental to the further advancement of this specialty.

Establishment and acceptance of certification at the generalist level will give impetus to development of cer.:fication in addictions nursing at the specialist level. A barrier to moving more quickly toward this stage is the limited availability of graduate education in addictios nursing. Currently, only a few universities offer master's in nursing programs with a concentration in addictions.

Research

The small number of graduate programs offering a concentration in addictions nursing points to the insufficient number of nurse educators prepared to teach addictions nursing at this level. A related problem is the small number of nursing research studies that focus on problems of addicted clients. A recent review of nursing journals from 1980 to 1988 found only six nurse-authored papers relating to addiction (Murphy, 1988). The scope of practice and standards documents (American Nursing Association, 1987, 1988) now provide some long-needed direction for practice and research. As clinicians and researchers work with these standards, it will be crucial that research questions are identified, studies designed and conducted, and results published. An ambitious effort is needed to educate nurse researchers committed to this area as well as to provide the funds to support their research.

Participation in Professional Organizations

Significant progress in addictions nursing being acknowledged as a specialty has come through the work of nurses participating in the specialty organizations for addictions nursing and the ANA. More nurses working in the addictions field need to contribute to the development of the specialty by joining professional nursing organizations. Nurses will grow professionally proportionate to the time, effort, and talent they contribute to their organizations. Leadership needs fostering. Nurses with leadership potential need the encouragement, support, and recognition only a professional organization can provide.

Collegial mentoring continues to be crucial in the career development of addictions nurses. Unless we know who the innovators are, what they are doing, how they are doing it, and what is working, all will struggle in isolation. The most effective means of fostering this communication and collegial dialogue is through participation in national educational programs sponsored by the professional organizations.

Health Insurance Coverage

As insurance companies increasingly attempt to manage the rising costs of health care, benefits for adequate coverage of addiction treatment services are at risk. As patient advocates, addictions nurses are concerned with the availability of adequate health care options for addicted clients. No other chronic progressive illness is plagued by the lack of adequate options for care through insurance coverage. The consumer needs to be educated and supported to pursue adequate health care for these illnesses. Addictions nurses are responsible for calling this crucial issue to the attention of the nursing profession, the public, and insurance companies. The importance of private and public funding for addiction treatment must be emphasized in nursing education programs.

The Impaired Nurse

Addictions nurses have a particular responsibility to their nursing colleagues. Nursing professionals need assistance in understanding addictions in relation to their own peer group. Since 1980 the nursing profession has made an impact in numerous states with the development of peer assistance programs and legislative changes. This work must continue. Through recognition of the impaired nurse issue, the imperative for prevention and health promotion is being identified as a priority for the profession.

The Nell Hodgson Woodruff School of Nursing, Emory University, under the guidance of Rose Dilday, began an annual symposium on the Impaired Nurse in 1982 (Haack & Hughes, 1988). The NNSA Impaired Nurse Committee headed by Patricia Green developed the Annual Nurse Impairment and Wellness Conference in 1988. This conference was repeated in 1989 and currently, NNSA incorporates a focus on the impaired nurse and wellness within its annual educational conference. Recent publications substantiate the work that has been done to address this issue (Haack & Hughes, 1988; Sullivan, Bissel, & Williams, 1987).

PROSPECTS FOR THE FUTURE

Numerous studies have shown that untreated alcoholics and their families use more health care services, sick days, and accident benefits than nonalcoholics (Niven, 1984). It has also been shown that this elevated demand for services and benefits can be reduced substantially by treatment for alcoholism. It is reasonable to generalize this statement to persons with other addictions. The imperative to identify the addicted person early in the disease process poses a special challenge to the nursing profession. Nurses assess patients on entry to physicians' offices, in the worksite, in schools, clinics, and hospitals. It is necessary that all nurses be educated on addiction if the task of identification of the addicted person is to be accomplished. A routine, detailed alcohol and drug history should be a part of every nurse's assessment of patients. Specialists in addictions nursing are needed to conduct further evaluations of those patients who appear to be having difficulties related to substance dependence or other addictions. Early identification, referral, and treatment of patients and families will continue to be a major goal of nursing in its efforts to make significant contributions to limiting the negative impact of addictions on the health of Americans. Nurses will continue to be the most versatile health care professionals in identification of addiction problems due to their roles in interacting with all patient populations in multiple settings.

It is through the efforts of addictions nurses working together that the specialty will advance. Given the current situation of having three organizations representing nurses in the field, differences will need to be artfully negotiated with an overriding concern for the welfare of the specialty as a whole. Splintering will only drain scarce resources, set up unnecessary competition, and send confusing messages to other professions and the public.

SUMMARY

Addictions nursing is embarked on an exciting period of development. Among the major challenges facing this embryonic specialty include increasing the number of addictions nurses participating in professional organizations, fostering a unity of purpose among the existing organizations, increasing educational opportunities and research, and continuing to effectively address the impaired nurse issue. It is also crucial that nurses be advocates for positive societal responses to the health problems associated with addictions. A social environment supportive of prevention, early intervention, and ongoing care for addicted clients and their families is one in which the specialty has the greatest opportunity to fulfill its highest potential.

REFERENCES

Alcoholics Anonymous. (1957). *Alcoholics Anonymous comes of age: A brief history of A. A.* New York: Alcoholics Anonymous World Services.

American Nurses Association. (1987). *The care of clients with addictions: Dimensions of nursing practice.* Kansas City, MO: Author.

American Nurses Association. (1988). *Standards of addictions nursing practice with selected diagnoses and criteria.* Kansas City, MO: Author.

Bennett, G. (1983). Nursing care for alcoholics in the United States since 1900: Exploring directions for historical research. *Proceedings of Nurse Educator Conference on Alcohol and Drug Abuse, 1982* (pp. 199–205). New York: National Council on Alcoholism.

Busch, D. (1982, April). *Chemical dependency in women with infertility and pain problems, nursing intervention.* Paper presented at the meeting of the National Council on Alcoholism Forum, Washington, DC.

Callender, E. (1931). Delirium tremens. *American Journal of Nursing, 31,* 177–178.

Estes, N. J. (1983, April). *Nursing and alcoholism: Living up to our promise.* Paper presented at the meeting of the National Council on Alcoholism Forum, Houston.

Follet, M. (1942). *Dynamic administration: The collective papers of Mary Follet.* New York: Harper and Beachess.

Golder, G. (1956). The nurse and the alcoholic patient. *American Journal of Nursing, 55,* 436–438.

Haack, M. R., & Hughes, T. L. (Eds.). (1988). *Addiction in the nursing profession.* New York: Springer.

Hasselblod, J. (1984). *Alcohol abuse curriculum guide for nurse practitioner faculty* (DHHS Publication No. ADM 84–1313). Washington, DC: U. S. Government Printing Office.

Heinemann, M. E., & Estes, N. J. (1974). A program in alcoholism nursing. *Nursing Outlook, 22* (9), 575–578.

Hoffman, A. L., & Heinemann, M. E. (1987). Substance abuse education in schools of nursing: A national survey. *Journal of Nursing Education, 26* (7), 282–287.

Leck, K. M. (1981). *Off with the caps--on with the program.* Paper presented at the International Council on Alcoholism and Addiction, Vienna, Austria.

Levine, H. G. (1978). The discovery of addiction: Changing conceptions of habitual drunkenness in America. *Journal of Studies on Alcohol, 39,* 143–174.

Mann, M. (1973). America's 150-year war: Alcohol vs. alcoholism. *Alcohol Health and Research World, 1* (1), 5–7.

McCorkle, R. (1984). What certification is all about. *Oncology Nursing Forum, 11* (6), 12–13.

Murphy, S. A. (1988). Addiction nursing: An agenda for the 1990's. *Issues in Mental Health Nursing, 9*(2), 115–126.

National Institute of Alcohol Abuse and Alcoholism. (1978). *The community health nurse and alcohol related problems.* Rockville, MD: Author.

National Nurses Society on Addictions. (1981). *Educating nurses on addiction.* Evanston, IL: Author.

National Nurses Society on Addictions. (1983). *The impaired nurse*. Evanston, IL: Author.

National Nurses Society on Addictions. (1988). *Drug testing*. Evanston, IL: Author.

National Nurses Society on Alcoholism. (1979). *The role of the nurse in alcoholism*. Evanston, IL: Author.

Nelson, N. (1989). The certification process: History and significance for addictions nursing practice. *Nursing Clinics of North America, 24*(1), 151–159.

Niven, R. G. (1984). Alcoholism—A problem in perspective. *Journal of the American Medical Association, 252*(14), 1912–1914.

Parrish, K. M. (1934). Case study in cirrhosis of the liver. *American Journal of Nursing, 34*, 1034–1041.

Solari-Twadell, P. A. (1982, April). *The multiple roles of a nurse in a comprehensive level of care system for alcoholic patients*. Paper presented at the meeting of the National Council on Alcoholism Forum, Washington, DC.

Steel, J. E. (1985). The impact of certification on specialty practice, *Rehabilitation Nursing*. March-April, 16–19.

Sullivan, E. J., Bissel, L., & Williams, E. (1987). *Chemical dependency in nursing: The deadly diversion*. Reading, MA: Addison-Wesley.

Swift, A. R. & Durkam, J. D. (1985). A career ladder step: You need certification (Develop your career potential!). *Nursing Success Today, 2*(6), 5–6.

Toner, M. T. (1954). *The role of the nurse in the treatment of alcoholism*. New York: National Council on Alcoholism. (Reprinted from the *Connecticut Review on Alcoholism), 5*(7), 2–13.

Zych, P. A. (1980, May). *Utilization of a patient classification system for a twenty bed medical alcoholism detoxification, evaluation and assessment unit*. Paper presented at the meeting of the National Council on Alcoholism Forum, Seattle.

CHAPTER 17 | DETOXIFICATION

Donna S. Woolf

Although symptoms of chemical dependence are seen almost every day by clinicians, few health care professionals have been trained to recognize the masquerade of symptoms presented by the dependent client. This lack of education coupled with the strong denial component of the disease of chemical dependency camouflages many clients needing treatment. Despite the known hazards of withdrawal, clients continue to be treated in a haphazard manner with little more than supportive care.

All health professionals must combine their knowledge of chemical dependency with a healthy dose of suspicion to uncover individuals needing treatment. Nurses are in excellent positions to screen for chemical dependency, because they play a primary role in monitoring physical and behavioral symptoms in most settings. This chapter provides the clinician in the substance abuse setting, as well as in general practice, with accepted methods of treatment for withdrawal syndromes and other physical and behavioral sequelae of drug abstinence.

NOMENCLATURE

The terms used to describe chemical abuse and dependency are frequently misunderstood and misused by both clients and clinicians. A clarification of the most commonly used terms is essential to an accurate description of the detoxification process and of drugs used to treat withdrawal.

Physical Dependency

The repeated administration of a drug may result in adaptation of the body's physiologic state referred to as *physical dependency*. Once physical dependence has developed, administration of the drug must continue to prevent withdrawal syndromes characteristic for that drug.

Many health professionals mistakenly believe that physical dependency and addiction are synonymous. Addicted people can routinely undergo detoxification so that their physical dependency no longer exists, but they relapse due to the behavioral component of their addiction. In an experimental setting almost anyone can be made physically dependent on a given drug, yet few, if any of them will develop the behavioral overlay that would allow for the diagnosis of addiction. Thus, to produce addiction, some unknown variables must exist. Whether these variables are behavioral or physiologic is not known.

The mechanisms by which drugs produce physical dependency are unclear. However, the net result appears to be that the body develops a form of counteradaptation in response to the presence of the drug so that its continued presence is required to avoid symptoms opposite those produced by the drug. The systems affected are said to have *rebound hyperexcitability* (Jaffe, 1985). For example, cocaine use produces mood elevation and alleviates fatigue; cocaine withdrawal is characterized by depression and lack of energy.

Withdrawal

The removal of a chemical from a person who is physically dependent on it produces symptoms characteristic for that drug. These symptoms, called *withdrawal,* are usually similar for drugs producing similar pharmacologic effects. The timing of the appearance of symptoms may vary somewhat according to the pharmacokinetic parameters of the individual drug used. The severity of the withdrawal syndrome depends on the particular drug used, how long it has been used, the dose used, and the rate at which the drug is eliminated from the body.

Cross-dependency

Cross-dependency is sometimes used to describe the condition in which one drug can be substituted for another to perpetuate the physical dependency or prevent the development of withdrawal. This is the basis for the use of a drug such as methadone to detoxify a client physically dependent on heroin. Chemicals may be either partially or completely cross-dependent. Whether complete or partial cross-dependency is shown depends more on similarities in how the drugs act than to chemical structure relationships.

Cross-addiction

Cross-addiction occurs when a person manifests the same behavioral sequelae of addiction when exposed to two different drugs. Examples of this are the chronic alcoholic switching to diazepam (Valium) or the methadone detoxification client increasing alcohol consumption as methadone is reduced (Green, Jaffe, Carlisi, & Zaks, 1978).

CENTRAL NERVOUS SYSTEM DEPRESSANTS

Of all the withdrawal reactions to various classes of drugs faced by the addicted client, the withdrawal from the central nervous system (CNS) depressant chemicals is the most dangerous. The severity of the withdrawal syndrome depends largely on the degree of physical dependence. As some clients are in the early stages of the development of physical dependence, nondrug treatments or drugs lacking cross-dependency attributes may appear effective as sole withdrawal regimens. In fact, studies have confirmed that many users will exhibit mild to moderate symptoms of withdrawal and will respond to nonpharmacologic treatments (Naranjo et al., 1983). Supportive nursing care as well as the judicious use of drugs have undoubtedly resulted in the low rate of delirium tremens (DTs) in this country. These treatments are of little consolation to the client who progresses to severe symptoms.

Although estimates of physical dependence may be made, physical dependence lies on a continuum ranging from mild to severe, and it is impossible to accurately predict which client will progress to major withdrawal symptoms. Research confirms that repeated episodes of alcohol withdrawal lead to progressively more severe syndromes, including seizures (Brown, Anton, Malcolm, & Ballenger, 1988). It is poorly understood why halting the progression of severe withdrawal patterns is so much more difficult than treating the pattern early in its development. This limitation requires that pharmacologic intervention of the withdrawal syndromes must begin before severe symptoms emerge. The potential adverse consequences of nondrug intervention outweigh the complications of the rational drug treatment of withdrawal.

Alcohol

Diagnosis. Isbell, Fraser, Wikler, Belleville, and Eisenman (1955) recognized that DTs resulted from the cessation of prolonged, heavy consumption of alcohol rather than being produced solely by vitamin deficiencies or psychologic dependence. The treatment of the alcohol withdrawal syndrome (AWS) depends on the recognition of such a disorder. When physical dependence is low, withdrawal symptoms of tremulousness, nausea, weakness, insomnia, and anxiety may last for only a few hours. Clients and clinicians alike may overlook or deny alcohol dependence as the etiology of mild forms of withdrawal. The AWS is described in detail in Chapter 2.

Treatment. The goal of the treatment of AWS is to halt or control the neuronal overactivity occurring in the dependent client when alcohol levels are reduced or alcohol is no longer present. This is accomplished by substituting and gradually tapering the dose of a pharmacologically similar drug. The alcohol intake is stopped, and the similar agent is started as the blood level falls. Withdrawal treatment therapy should not be started until alcohol levels are low enough to prevent a synergistic effect between the two depressants.

Since most sedative-hypnotic drugs are reasonably cross-dependent with each other and alcohol, how do we choose an appropriate alcohol detoxification regimen? The ideal agent needs to be pharmacologically similar to alcohol, be long-acting enough to afford a smooth tapering, cause low rates of respiratory depression at high doses, and possess some anticonvulsant properties. Since the benzodiazepine drugs (Valium, Librium, Tranxene, Ativan, and others) meet most of these requirements, they are the most commonly used alcohol withdrawal agents in the

Table 17.1
Drugs Used in Alcohol Withdrawal

Drug	Routes of Administration[a]	Common Dosage Range[b]
Chlordiazepoxide	PO	25–100 mg q4–6h
(Librium)	IM[c]	50–100 mg q4–6h
Diazepam	PO	5–20 mg q4–6 h
(Valium)	IV	2.5 mg/min
	IM[c]	5–10 mg q4–6h
Phenobarbital	PO	30–120 mg q4–6h
	IM	60–120 mg q4–6h
Paraldehyde[d]	PO	5–15 ml q4–6h
Clorazepate	PO	30 mg initially,
(Tranxene)		then 30–60 mg in divided doses/d
Lorazepam	PO	1–5 mg q6h
(Ativan)	IM	2 mg q6h

[a] PO = oral; IM = intramuscular; IV = intravenous
[b] Dosage for first day. Dosages may be lower in the elderly or clients with liver disease.
[c] IM absorption is erratic and not preferred.
[d] For reference only. Its use is not recommended.

United States (Schuckit, 1985). Commonly used dosages and routes of administration of several drugs used as substitutes in alcohol withdrawal are presented in Table 17.1. Probably the most widely used, nonmedically controlled withdrawal agent is alcohol itself (Jaffe & Ciraulo, 1985). Alcohol is a poor choice as a withdrawal agent since it has a short duration of action, resulting in fluctuations of the withdrawal pattern from intoxication to breakthrough symptoms such as seizures. Its continued use perpetuates the psychologic dependence and tissue damage produced by alcohol abuse.

It appears that both longer- and shorter-acting benzodiazepines can be used as withdrawal substitutes when dosages are adjusted for potency and duration of action. Longer-acting agents (Valium, Librium, Tranxene) accumulate and with proper dosing provide smooth withdrawal patterns. In clients with liver disease, accumulation of the longer-acting agents may be problematic, and the use of shorter-acting benzodiazepines may be advantageous to prevent benzodiazepine intoxication on repeated dosing (Schuckit, 1985). Shorter-acting agents may allow more breakthrough symptoms and require more frequent dosing intervals to keep drug levels high (Ritson & Chick, 1986).

Two approaches to the dosing of benzodiazepines in the treatment of alcohol withdrawal have been used. One approach involves initially using large doses of the benzodiazepine chlordiazepoxide (100–400 mg or more daily) or diazepam (20–100 mg or more daily) in divided doses. On a more or less scheduled fashion, the initial doses are decreased by 25% daily (Sellers & Kalant, 1976). Although many treatment programs use a "scheduled" dosage reduction, variability in the severity of each client's withdrawal and metabolism of the benzodiazepine demand some flexibility in regimens to optimize treatment. The duration of detoxification varies with the client, the drug used, and the preference of the physician. Most clients require 4–7 days for adequate detoxification from alcohol. One criticism of flexible scheduling in withdrawal is that with drug-seeking clients, it may be difficult to avoid struggles over necessary reductions and finally the discontinuance of the substitute.

The use of concrete rating scales, such as the Clinical Institute Withdrawal Assessment for Alcohol

(CIWA-A) scale, may offer a systematic method of dosing that can tailor drug prescribing to clinical symptoms. Variability in staff assessment of "improvement" is reduced by the use of such a tool. This 15-item scale weighs and rates the symptoms believed to measure withdrawal severity (Naranjo et al., 1983; Shaw, Kolesar, Sellers, Kaplan, & Sandor, 1981).

Another approach used with the longer-acting benzodiazepines, particularly diazepam, utilizes effectively its accumulation properties (Sellers & Naranjo, 1986). Diazepam is given in oral loading doses of 20 mg every 1–2 hours until the client shows a clinical improvement on the CIWA-A scale or becomes slightly sedated. It is recommended by Sellers and Naranjo (1986) that the loading dose of diazepam for moderate to severe withdrawal should be at least 60 mg to prevent the progression of the syndrome. Most of their clients responded within 7.6 hours and few required doses past 24 hours. Since the diazepam dose is relatively high and it is eliminated slowly, the loading dose tapers in the body at about the same time the withdrawal syndrome is resolved, eliminating the need for the administration of continued doses over the usual 4–7 days.

Some clients require massive doses of benzodiazepines to control withdrawal (Nolop & Natow, 1985; Woo & Greenblatt, 1979). Although adequate doses must be administered to stop the progression of the withdrawal syndrome, clients should be monitered closely for symptoms of toxicity, including ataxia and nystagmus. Oral administration is generally the preferred route in detoxification. Both chlordiazepoxide and diazepam are erratically absorbed by the intramuscular route. If the intramuscular route is necessary, lorazepam is preferred due to its rapid and reliable absorption (Greenblatt et al., 1979). The intravenous route is usually reserved for such emergencies as status epilepticus.

Various other CNS depressant drugs have been tried in the treatment of AWS. The use of two older drugs, chloral hydrate and paraldehyde, has dwindled due to undesirable properties of these drugs. Paraldehyde has an offensive odor, a short half-life which demands frequent dosing, chemical instability, hepatotoxicities, and the ability to irritate the gastrointestinal tract. Chloral hydrate produces results similar to paraldehyde. Considering the drawbacks with these drugs and the availability of newer products without their attending side effects, the use of these agents in detoxification will continue to wane. In countries other than the United States, clomethiazole and nitrous oxide are successfully used to treat alcohol withdrawal (Gillman & Lichtigfeld, 1986; Jaffe, 1985).

Since alcoholics sometimes presented with symptoms of hallucinosis and frequently presented with agitation, it was believed by some clinicians in past times that alcoholism was solely a psychiatric disorder. It is not surprising that antipsychotic drugs have been used to treat AWS. Antipsychotic drugs are not pharmacologically similar to alcohol, although they do cause sedation. Phenothiazine antipsychotics lower the seizure threshold, interfere with thermoregulatory mechanisms, produce hypotension, and produce extrapyramidal symptoms of dystonias, akathesia, akinesia, and tremors. All these potential complications are risks not encountered with currently used detoxification agents. The antipsychotic generally used as adjunctive therapy to standard detoxification agents is haloperidol (Haldol). When the risk of seizures has past, some clinicians use haloperidol to treat hallucinosis not controlled by the detoxification drug. The usual dose of haloperidol is 2.5–10 mg orally or intramuscularly every 1–2 hours until symptoms are controlled or five doses are given (Jaffe & Ciraulo, 1985).

Hydroxyzine (Vistaril) is an antihistaminic compound that has had prominence in the treatment of alcohol withdrawal. It is not pharmacologically similar to alcohol, does not possess anticonvulsant properties, and does not produce physical dependence. It has produced relief of mild withdrawal symptoms in some patients due to its mild sedative effects and antiemetic actions. Since many alcohol-dependent clients have not yet progressed to severe withdrawal, any agent giving symptomatic relief appears effective. It is hard to justify its general use alone as a detoxification agent when it is known that we cannot predict which client will progress to severe withdrawal states and when this progression may escalate.

Phenobarbital has been used to treat AWS (Jaffe, 1985; Young, Rores, Murphy, & Dailey, 1987). Although benzodiazepines are more widely used, phenobarbital fulfills most criteria for a "good" pharmacologic substitute in that it is long-acting enough to provide a smooth tapering, it is an anticonvulsant, and its actions are pharmacologically similar to alcohol. Critics of its use cite its ability to depress respiration when used in high doses. Phenobarbital is inexpensive and available in a reliable injectable form. It can be an excellent detoxification agent in the hands of a skilled clinician. The use of phenobarbital in the treatment of barbiturate abstinence syndrome is discussed in a later section.

Chronic alcohol abusers are distinct from abusers of other drugs by their frequent development of malnutrition and vitamin deficiencies, particularly the B vitamins (Thomson, Jeyasingham, Pratt, & Shaw, 1987). Other physical consequences of alcohol abuse may be the result of direct toxic effects and metabolic derangements. The treatment of vitamin deficiencies and infectious diseases is not a substitute for treatment of withdrawal syndromes, but ignoring their presence may complicate the withdrawal management.

Gastritis, vomiting, and diarrhea caused by alcohol intake and withdrawal may result in dehydration. Many clients are overhydrated (Eisenhofer, Whiteside, Lambie, & Johnson, 1982; Emsley et al., 1987), and fluid balance must be individually assessed. Intravenous glucose solutions use already limited thiamine levels and may precipitate Wernicke's encephalopathy (Korsten & Lieber, 1985) unless thiamine is concurrently administered. The practice of administering intravenous or oral fructose can increase the metabolism of alcohol, but the resultant development of lactic acidosis renders it of no utility in managing acute intoxication (Jaffe & Ciraulo, 1985). The replacement of potassium is indicated with hypokalemic symptoms or cardiac arrhythmias.

Alcohol abusers may have a total body deficit of magnesium and potassium (see Chapter 2). Magnesium deficiency may predispose a person to seizure activity (Flink, 1986). There is some debate as to the usefulness of magnesium sulfate in all withdrawing alcoholics. Wilson and Vulcano (1984) find no difference in withdrawal symptoms when magnesium sulfate is added to a detoxification regimen of chlordiazepoxide and recommend its use only when withdrawal is accompanied by cardiac arrhythmias. Replacement can be accomplished with parenteral magnesium sulfate at a dosage of 2 ml of a 50% solution intramuscularly every 3–4 hours for six to eight doses. Intramuscular administration of magnesium is painful, but oral administration for acute deficiencies is unpredictable, and controlled studies of oral forms are scant. The pain of injection can be reduced by premixing magnesium sulfate with lidocaine.

The best management of alcohol withdrawal seizures has been debated for several years. It is doubtful that routinely used anticonvulsants such as phenytoin (Dilantin) offer benefit in clients without a history of an underlying seizure disorder. If given orally, phenytoin requires 3–4 days to produce anticonvulsant blood levels. Since seizures secondary to alcohol withdrawal usually occur before that time, its use is questionable. Greenblatt and Shader (1975) have suggested that this be overcome by administering a loading dose of 10 mg/kg in 250–500 ml 5% dextrose in water infused over 1–4 hours. A loading dose may be administered orally by giving 600–1000 mg in divided portions over 8–12 hours (Rall & Schleifer, 1985). If phenytoin is used, it need not be continued past the withdrawal period except in clients with reliable histories of a preexisting seizure disorder. It is likely that most clients are adequately protected against seizures by the benzodiazepine used to stop the progression of the withdrawal. If seizures do occur, intravenous diazepam (Valium) or lorazepam (Ativan) is probably indicated. Since benzodiazepines and phenytoin may be used during detoxification, it should be noted that disulfiram (Antabuse) may inhibit the metabolism of these drugs (see Chapter 8) and concomitant use is not recommended.

Other strategies in alcohol withdrawal treatment are currently under investigation. Overactivity of the sympathetic nervous system is responsible for at least some of the symptoms of alcohol withdrawal (Linnoila, Mefford, Nutt, & Adinoff, 1987). For this reason the use of propranolol or atenolol, beta-adrenergic blocking drugs, has been suggested to reduce blood pressure, tremor, heart rate, and anxiety. Although beta-adrenergic drugs do decrease these symptoms, there is little evidence that they will prevent the progression of the withdrawal syndrome to more serious symptoms of hallucinations and seizures (Reed & Liskow, 1987). Jacob, Zilm, Macleod, and Sellers (1983) reported a high incidence of delirium and hallucinosis when propranolol was used alone as a detoxification agent. It may be undesirable to mask the early signs of alcohol withdrawal progression if these signs help the clinician gauge proper dosing of drugs, as the benzodiazepines, known to be effective in halting withdrawal. Beta-blocking drugs are contraindicated in clients with congestive heart failure, asthma, and diabetes. Clonidine, a centrally active alpha-adrenergic agonist drug, has also been tried in alcohol withdrawal to decrease the symptoms of overactivity of the sympathetic nervous system (Wilkins, Jenkins, & Steiner, 1983). Preliminary reports show some favorable results of clonidine over chlordiazepoxide in controlling blood pressure, pulse, and respiratory rate in alcohol withdrawal (Baumgartner, 1988; Glue & Nutt, 1987). It remains to be seen, however, if clonidine can prevent the progression of alcohol withdrawal to hallucinosis and seizures.

Only further research will define the role, if any, sympathetic nervous system blockers will assume in alcohol withdrawal treatment. Given their lack of anticonvulsant effects and seeming lack of the prevention of delirium, it is possible that these drugs will assume only an adjunctive role in most clients. It must be remembered that any drug *added* to a detoxification regimen will increase the possibility of an adverse drug reaction. Substantial clinical benefits of a two-drug regimen must be proven over an effective one-drug regimen before the risks of the additional drug are acceptable.

Barbiturates and Nonbarbiturate Sedatives

Diagnosis. The abuse of CNS depressants, both legitimately prescribed and illicitly obtained, represents a significant problem, in terms of overdosage and withdrawal severity. Depending on client population characteristics, benzodiazepine dependence may be seen as frequently as barbiturate dependence.

Anyone can be made physically dependent on a sedative-hypnotic drug. Low doses of these drugs may be taken sporadically without evidence of withdrawal. Since tolerance develops slowly, the increases in dosage necessary to obtain drug effects may be gradual and the development of physical dependency insidious.

Since the development of sedative-hypnotic dependence results in severe withdrawal, researchers and clinicians have tried to estimate dosages and durations of use beyond which physical dependence is expected. Secobarbital (Seconal) or pentobarbital (Nembutal) in doses of 900 mg to 2.2 g/d for longer than 30 days usually produces severe withdrawal symptoms (Fraser, Wikler, Essig, & Isbell, 1958). Although withdrawal should be suspected in anyone presenting with benzodiazepine, barbiturate, or other sedative-hypnotic drug intake, Perry and Alexander (1986) developed a conversion chart of sedative-hypnotics based on the work of Smith and Wesson (1983). This represents a predictive guide to withdrawal based on the likelihood of withdrawal reactions occurring in clients taking diazepam in doses greater than 60 mg/d or secobarbital, 600 mg/d, or the equivalent of these doses for several weeks to months. The use of the table involves converting the approximate doses of the drugs used to equivalents of diazepam or secobarbital and adding the results (see Table 17.2). Sums greater than 60 mg diazepam or 600 mg secobarbital would indicate the need for tolerance testing (Perry & Alexander, 1986) or use of a detoxification agent if tolerance testing is not utilized.

Table 17.2
Dose Conversions* for Sedative-Hypnotic Drugs Equivalent to 600 mg Secobarbital and 60 mg Diazepam

Drug	Dose (mg)
Benzodiazepines	
Alprazolam	6
Chlordiazepoxide	150
Clonazepam	24
Clorazepate	90
Flurazepam	90
Halazepam	240
Lorazepam	12
Oxazepam	60
Prazepam	60
Temazepam	90
Barbiturates	
Amobarbital	600
Butabarbital	600
Butalbital (in Fiorinal)	600
Pentobarbital	600
Secobarbital	600
Phenobarbital	180
Glycerol	
Meprobamate	2400
Piperidinedione	
Glutethimide	1500
Quinazolines	
Methaqualone	1800

*For patients receiving multiple drugs (e.g., flurazepam 30 mg/d, diazepam 30 mg/d, phenobarbital 150 mg/d), each drug should be converted to its diazepam or secobarbital equivalent. In the preceding example the patient is receiving the equivalent dose of diazepam 100 mg/d or secobarbital 1000 mg/d. Source: "Sedative/Hypnotic Dependence: Patient Stabilization, Tolerance Testing and Withdrawal," by P. J. Perry and B. Alexander, 1986, *Drug Intelligence and Clinical Pharmacy, 20,* p. 533. Copyright 1986 by Harvey Whitney Books. Reprinted by permission.

Tolerance testing involves using 20 mg diazepam or 200 mg pentobarbital in a client who is not either intoxicated or in withdrawal. This is best achieved by beginning the test early in the morning after either intoxication has cleared overnight or when the client has had diazepam doses necessary to prevent withdrawal the evening before. Diazepam, 20 mg, or 200 mg pentobarbital is given by mouth once and again in 2 hours. Signs of intoxication evaluated 2 hours after the dose indicates nontolerance. No detoxification would then be necessary. The requirement of more than two test doses to achieve intoxication indicates the need for substitute therapy during withdrawal. Diazepam is sometimes preferred over pentobarbital because pentobarbital cannot be given in doses over 1000 mg due to the risk of depressing respiration. Despite the safety of diazepam at higher doses, tolerance testing doses are usually limited to 100 mg. This testing procedure is then used to determine the starting point for tapering in detoxification. There is no experience in the use of tolerance testing in alcohol or mixed alcohol-CNS depressant-dependent users.

Treatment. When the diagnosis of physical dependency has been determined, appropriate detoxification is of vital importance. The potential for severe withdrawal symptoms makes close medical supervision necessary. The approach to treatment can be similar regardless of the depressant involved. As with alcohol detoxification, the drug used should be long-acting and gradually withdrawn.

The phenobarbital substitution method of detoxification from barbiturates and nonbarbiturate sedatives is preferred due to its safety (Martin, Kapur, Whiteside, & Sellers, 1979). Using the client's history or the pentobarbital tolerance test, the estimated daily dose of phenobarbital needed to suppress withdrawal is estimated; 30 mg phenobarbital can be substituted for 400 mg meprobamate, 10 mg diazepam, 25 mg chlordiazepoxide, and 100 mg pentobarbital. The estimated daily amount is then administered in three or four equally divided doses. The first day is a time for stabilization. If the client shows signs of toxicity such as nystagmus, ataxia, or slurred speech, the next one or two doses are withheld and the dosage recalculated. When stabilized, the dosage can be reduced at about 30 mg phenobarbital daily. If signs of withdrawal appear, the dosage could be increased by 25% and reduction again attempted. It has not been shown that the use of phenytoin has a place

in sedative withdrawal treatment; however, its use here is more appropriate than in alcohol withdrawal due to the intensity of neuronal overactivity and variable rates of excretion after abrupt withdrawal of these agents.

The increasing use of benzodiazepine drugs, both illicit and prescribed, has resulted in elucidation of the benzodiazepine withdrawal syndrome. Withdrawal severity would be expected to be more acute with shorter-acting agents than with longer-acting agents (Jaffe, 1985). In theory, longer-acting agents, as diazepam and chlordiazepoxide, should be self-tapering. In practice, even longer-acting agents appear to require prolonged tapering over a period of weeks, probably due to the emergence of a prolonged low-dose withdrawal syndrome (see Chapter 3). Although phenobarbital is frequently the detoxification agent used to treat withdrawal of barbiturates, benzodiazepines are commonly used where the abused chemical is a nonbarbiturate CNS depressant.

There has been some evidence that with alprazolam (Xanax) withdrawal management should be undertaken very slowly to prevent withdrawal symptoms such as seizures (Breier, Charney, & Nelson, 1984). Current recommendations for alprazolam withdrawal include tapering no faster than 0.5 mg every 3 days. In most cases, it is best to switch to a more long-acting benzodiazepine as a substitute for withdrawal. With the large doses of alprazolam used to treat panic disorders, some clinicians prefer to use tapering doses of alprazolam itself.

Since episodic cycles of low-dose benzodiazepine withdrawal syndromes include symptoms of neuronal overactivity such as increased blood pressure, tachycardia, and anxiety, Smith and Wesson (1983) have recommended the use of propranolol, 20 mg every 6 hours starting 5 days after withdrawal has begun and lasting for 2 weeks. "As needed" dosing only is continued after that to avoid problems of abrupt discontinuation of propranolol. Side effects of propranolol therapy do occur, including hypotension; advantages must be weighed against expected side effects. Propranolol is contraindicated in the presence of asthma, congestive heart failure, or diabetes.

Stimulants

Diagnosis. The rise in cocaine abuse has greatly affected how clinicians approach treatment for stimulant abuse. It has shaken our definitions of physical dependency and addiction. Cocaine dependency syndromes are not as distinct as those seen with alcohol, opioids, or barbiturates. In the past there was debate as to whether cocaine or amphetamines could induce physical dependency, as defined by the development of a withdrawal syndrome. It is now recognized that cocaine is one of the most reinforcing chemicals of abuse known to humans, particularly when used in newer abuse forms as freebase or crack. High brain levels achieved with smoking crack and freebase forms have contributed to the presentation for treatment of increasing numbers of clients experiencing intense withdrawal symptoms.

Acute intoxication effects of stimulants are especially prominent in high-dose abuse. These symptoms may include extreme agitation, impulsiveness, hypersexuality, and grandiosity. Cocaine psychosis, including hallucinations (cocaine bugs and snow lights) and paranoia, may be indistinguishable from nondrug induced psychosis. These similarities demand that in all but the very young and the very old, cocaine intoxication needs to be ruled out when clients appear with psychotic symptoms. A careful history, sometimes from significant others, and laboratory drug testing is important.

Abstinence following stimulant abuse usually involves a crash and withdrawal followed by an extinction period (Gawin & Ellinwood, 1988). Following a binge, a crash (a period of exhaustion) occurs. The crash has been compared to alcohol hangover in that the crash occurs in first-time users as well as chronic users (Kleber & Gawin, 1987). The client exhibits symptoms of depression (even to the point of suicidal behavior), anxiety, and the need for sleep. It is during this stage that many cocaine, as well as amphetamine, users ingest alcohol or other sedative-hypnotics. The withdrawal symptoms represent the opposite effects seen with intoxication. The client has no energy, very little interest in the surroundings, and seems to have little ability to experience pleasure. These symptoms appear to fluctuate in cycles, being the most intense during the first 3 days following the crash but continuing for 1–4 months. Craving, including cocaine dreams, are intense during this period. After the fatigue and dysphoria have abated, a long period of less intense episodic craving, called extinction, may occur. This period may last for months to years.

Treatment. Acute cocaine intoxication can present as a medical emergency. Drug treatment is mainly supportive, treating specific symptoms. Sbriglio and Millman (1987) present a brief review of these emergencies.

Treatment of cocaine psychosis usually begins with minor tranquilizers, such as benzodiazepines, and progresses to neuroleptics, usually haloperidol. Phenothiazines are generally avoided because they produce hypotension, add anticholinergic problems, and reduce seizure threshold. The use of any treatment agent should be short-lived, because the psychotic symptoms are usually self-limiting and will remit within a week.

After the need for detoxification from another concurrent drug has been ruled out, most drug treatment regimens are aimed at reducing craving or managing severe depression. Although causing discomfort, the withdrawal phase of stimulant abstinence does not result in the medical emergencies seen in alcohol or sedative-hypnotic withdrawal. Treatment is then aimed at peer group support, education, urine drug screens, and other types of group or individual therapies, helping the client deal with stimulant-specific symptoms such as the inability to feel pleasure, the lack of energy, and cocaine craving (Millman, 1988). Due to depression, clinicians should carefully monitor the need for intervention in suicidal ideations.

Since chronic stimulant abuse is thought to produce depletion of neuronal norepinephrine (NE) and dopamine (DA) and resultant postsynaptic receptor sensitivity, experimental pharmacotherapies have focused on reversing or compensating for these changes (Dackis & Gold, 1984). This is an effort to reduce craving and dysphoria while the client participates in other treatment modalities.

One experimental approach has been to provide the DA-depleted client with a DA agonist. Bromocriptine (Parlodel) in dosages of 0.625 mg two to four times daily reduces cocaine withdrawal symptoms, although higher doses may produce undesirable side effects of headaches, vertigo, or syncope (Giannini, Baumgartel, & DiMarzio, 1987; Tennant & Sagherian, 1987). Amantadine releases DA and NE from storage sites in the neurons, thereby increasing DA in the synapse. It also delays the reuptake of these transmitters into vesicles in the synapse. On this basis, it has been tried in the treatment of cocaine withdrawal with some success in dosages ranging from 100 mg two to four times daily (Handelsman, Chordia, Escovar, Marion, & Lowinson, 1988; Tennant & Sagheria, 1987). Side effects of dizziness and headache appear to be lower with amantadine than bromocriptine, although with wider use, fairly infrequent side effects of depression, congestive heart failure, orthostatic hypotension, psychosis, blurred vision, and urinary retention, as seen in individuals taking the drug for influenza prophylaxis, would be expected.

It has been suggested that tricyclic antidepressants may be useful in treating the withdrawal symptoms of cocaine by inducing adrenergic and dopaminergic receptor subsensitivity—reversing the supersensitivity of these receptors found in chronic cocaine abuse (Gawin & Kleber, 1984). Initial studies with desipramine indicate that it may increase abstinence rates and decrease craving (Giannini, Malone, Giannini, Price & Loiselle, 1986; Kosten, Schumann, Wright, Carney, & Gawin, 1987).

Since DA and NE appear to be depleted during chronic cocaine use, dietary precursors to these neurotransmitters have been suggested as treatments for cocaine withdrawal. Tyrosine and tryptophan, the precursors to serotonin, have been used in treatment regimens, mainly in addition to other therapies as bromocriptine, amantadine, or desipramine. Although these treatments offer few side effects, clinical trials of their roles, either as single agents or in combination, are scant. It is difficult to assess their efficacy at this time.

Other experimental therapies have included substitute stimulants such as methylphenidate and pemoline, other antidepressants, neuroleptic agents, and lithium. These therapies appear to offer little sustained success.

Pharmacotherapy for cocaine withdrawal symptoms is in its infancy. We have some ideas as to those agents that may show promise in reducing craving and anhedonia and increasing abstinence rates. We do not know how long therapy should be continued and at what dose. Controlled studies and time will be our judges.

Opiates

Withdrawal symptoms resulting from physical dependence on opioids is well recognized (see Chapter 5). Physical dependency can develop after therapeutic uses, without the behavioral components usually termed "addiction." How severe the withdrawal symptoms are depend on which particular drug was used, the drug's half-life, what dose was used, and how long it was used.

The traditional management of opiate withdrawal is accomplished by methadone substitution and detoxification. It is possible to detoxify the client with the drug of abuse, but generally a smoother withdrawal pattern can be achieved by using the longer-acting methadone.

Methadone substitution begins by giving enough methadone to suppress withdrawal symptoms. Reliance on client history is difficult. Initial dosages seldom exceed 15–20 mg. Additional dosages may be given after the first dose to establish and stabilize the client. Unless a history of tolerance to 40 mg methadone is established, the total daily dose rarely exceeds 40 mg. Stabilization and evaluation are goals for the first 24 hours. After stabilization, a tapering process begins. Dosages may be reduced at 5 mg/d or at a maximum of 15%–20% a day. Doses are given once or twice daily. Acute withdrawal can usually be achieved in 7–10 days, but the protracted withdrawal syndrome (see Chapter 5) may make final reductions of methadone difficult. The Food and Drug Administration (FDA) mandates that to be termed "detoxification" the tapering process must be complete in 21 days. Some clinicians argue that with high street doses of opiates, drug freedom is difficult to achieve in 21 days.

Since methadone detoxification can prove difficult and methadone maintenance represents continued dependency, researchers have searched for alternative, nonaddictive therapies effective in treating opioid withdrawal. Addicts, themselves, have used "cold turkey," or sudden abstinence and withdrawal without drug therapy, to decrease needed levels of opioids. Barbiturates and benzodiazepines used to treat alcohol and sedative-hypnotic dependency do not suppress opioid withdrawal. Propoxyphene (Darvon) has also been used in opiate detoxification without general success (Tennant, Russell, Casas, & Bleich, 1975).

Clonidine (Catapres), an alpha-agonist, suppresses certain, but not all, opiate withdrawal symptoms. It has been effectively used as a detoxification agent in doses of 10–25 µg/kg/d (Jaffe, 1985). Limitations of its use include the production of sedation and hypotension. Clonidine seems to more effectively suppress symptoms of adrenergic overactivity as gooseflesh, yawning, runny nose and watery eyes than those of diarrhea and anorexia. It has been suggested that diarrhea and anorexia symptoms are most noticed by the client, who may report clonidine as ineffective. The clinician who observes suppression of adrenergic overactivity may then report clonidine as an effective agent (Jasinski, Johnson, & Kocher, 1985).

One advantage to the use of clonidine in opiate withdrawal is its lack of similarity to the opiates. It is nonaddicting and can serve as a bridge to enable the client to stay opiate free long enough to initiate naltrexone (Trexan) therapy (see Chapter 5). This type of therapy is frequently used to terminate methadone maintenance, rapidly, with less discomfort. Dosages range from 0.1 mg to 0.2 mg three to four times daily, monitoring blood pressure and pulse for unacceptable decreases. Some clinicians report a decrease in effectiveness of clonidine after 2 weeks and suggest that rapid withdrawal of the methadone allows the most intense symptoms to be experienced while the clonidine is most effective. Tapering of doses is usually by 0.1–0.2 mg/d (Washton & Resnick, 1982).

Slow withdrawal of methadone causes a protracted discomfort, which is difficult for some clients to endure. These clients want to go rapidly through the last tapering of dosage to reach drug freedom. Naltrexone, a long-acting, oral opioid antagonist, displaces methadone from its binding sites and precipitates rapid withdrawal. Naltrexone is administered to the opioid-dependent client. Withdrawal is precipitated rapidly, and clonidine is given in initial doses of 5 μg/kg three times daily, titrating the dose to withdrawal symptom severity (Charney et al., 1982; Charney, Heninger, & Kleber, 1986). After symptoms have abated, naltrexone therapy may then be continued to prevent relapse. Most clients using rapid withdrawal regimens are taking methadone doses lower than 50 mg/d.

Propranolol (Inderal) has been tried in the treatment of opioid withdrawal. Although it is not successful alone as a detoxification agent, doses of 20 mg/d in divided doses have relieved residual restlessness and anxiety not relieved by clonidine regimens (Roehrich & Gold, 1987). The possibility of side effects with propranolol must be appreciated, however. Propranolol is contraindicated in clients with asthma, congestive heart failure, and diabetes.

HALLUCINOGENS

There are few standards for intervention in the management of adverse or toxic reactions to hallucinogens. Tapering of hallucinogen doses or substitute therapy with a detoxification agent is not required. Although reactions to marihuana and phencyclidine (PCP) could be addressed in separate sections, their treatment is closest to that of other hallucinogens included in this section.

LSD and Related Compounds

The treatment of the unpredictable "bad trip" or adverse reaction to lysergic acid diethylamide (LSD), psilocybin, mescaline, or dimethyltryptamine begins with supportive care in a quiet, nonstimulating environment by a reassuring friend or clinician. Most adverse reactions are time-limited, lasting up to 12 hours for LSD and 2–4 hours for mescaline and peyote (Schuckit, 1984).

If drug treatment is necessary to prevent harm to the client or others, antianxiety agents such as benzodiazepines or sleep induction with barbiturates are usually used. Antipsychotic drugs, as phenothiazines, are generally not needed, unless prolonged psychosis develops.

The existence of flashbacks and a prolonged psychosis may require treatment. LSD psychosis is indistinguishable from naturally occurring schizophrenia (Vardy & Kay, 1983). The psychosis should be approached as though it were a self-limiting condition. However, a psychiatric history as well as a family history of psychiatric disorders may help elucidate the propensity for a coexisting psychiatric disorder.

Marihuana

After high doses of marihuana are used for several weeks, symptoms of nervousness, tremor, restlessness, and insomnia may occur on discontinuance of use (Jaffe, 1985). Adverse reactions to high doses can range from psychosis with hallucinations and violent behavior to panic attacks. The most frequently observed adverse reactions to marihuana are anxiety, panic, and paranoid states, lasting 2-4 hours (Jones, 1983). Altered perception of time may make the affected user feel that this state will never end. Treatment consists of reassurance and support in a low-stimuli environment. The judicious use of benzodiazepines may be necessary.

Psychotic reactions may be managed with antipsychotics like haloperidol. Continuing psychosis indicates that the client should be evaluated for other drug use or the presence of a major psychiatric disorder. Stable schizophrenic clients can experience an exacerbation of symptoms when marihuana is used. Marihuana also can precipitate flashback in clients who previously used LSD. There is no proven drug treatment for the amotivational syndrome seen after chronic marihuana use.

Phencyclidine

PCP intoxication is difficult to diagnose because users exhibit a wide range of subjective effects. Its actions share properties with CNS stimulants, CNS depressants, hallucinogens, and opioids.

At low doses, the client looks "drunk," may stagger, and exhibits slurred speech—all symptoms common to alcohol intoxication. A blank stare and muscular rigidity similar to catatonia may occur. Behavior may range from apathy and drowsiness to hostility. High doses, toxic doses, or overdoses may be difficult for the clinician to manage. Initial overdosage symptoms, usually when doses over 25 mg are ingested, may include coma, hypertension, muscle rigidity, hyperthermia, and respiratory and cardiac failure. Since PCP is a basic chemical, it has been suggested that treatment should include gastric suction, acidification of urine, and the use of diuretics to speed elimination (Aronow & Done, 1978). In the presence of myoglobinuria and rhabdomyolysis, the increased risk of renal failure with this type of treatment must be weighed against its benefit.

The control of toxic symptoms of medical instability are supportive. Diazepam is usually administered for convulsions. Mechanical cooling may be necessary for hyperthermia. Several antihypertensives, including hydralazine, have been used to lower blood pressure.

As the client becomes conscious, management includes behavioral control and medical support. Isolation from external stimuli is extremely important. This can be a problem for a busy emergency room staff. Mechanical restraints may aggravate muscle damage from contractions. Drug treatment should be kept at a minimum; however, diazepam or haloperidol may be necessary to control violent or self-destructive behavior.

Toxic psychosis and prolonged psychotic episodes resembling schizophrenia may result from chronic or single PCP use. Toxic psychosis lasts 1–7 days or more. At this time some clients may move into a prolonged psychotic episode lasting for 30 days or longer. As with other drugs discussed in the section, clients with preexisting schizophrenia may experience an exacerbation of the psychosis after even single-dose PCP exposure (Smith, 1980). Clients with prolonged psychosis as well as those with exacerbation of existing schizophrenia may require longer-term antipsychotic maintenance.

PCP use may induce depression lasting for short periods or months. Follow-up after the clearing of psychosis is important to monitor clients for suicidal ideations.

POLYDRUG DETOXIFICATION

Not all clients take one chemical. In fact, the task of providing safe, effective drug regimens for detoxification would be much easier if they did. Alcoholic patients also abuse other CNS depressants, such as hypnotics and sedatives. Heroin-dependent clients supplement with alcohol. Amphetamine and cocaine users reduce their anxiety while high with "downers" and treat their insomnia with hypnotics.

Problems arise in treating mixed depressant-opiate withdrawal since substitute drugs effective in treating depressant withdrawal are not good substitutes for opiates and vice versa. Some controversy exists as to how to approach this type client. It is possible to simultaneously withdraw a client from both classes of drugs, but it is difficult to adjust dosages since both syndromes have some withdrawal symptoms in common. One approach is to stabilize the CNS dependency by giving enough of the detoxification substitute to produce mild intoxication. Using autonomic symptoms as a gauge, then administer an opioid, such as methadone, tapering doses until withdrawal is complete. The dosage of the CNS depressant substitute is then tapered (Jaffe, 1985). Another approach in mixed depressant-opiate withdrawal is to first treat the dangerous depressant withdrawal syndrome. The opiate dose may have to be kept constant during this time. After the depressant withdrawal is complete, then opiate withdrawal can be initiated. Either approach can be successful, but considering the frequent protracted opioid withdrawal syndrome, it may be easier to treat the shorter and more dangerous depressant withdrawal first.

When the dependency involves more than one depressant, treat the longer-acting chemical. The alcoholic also dependent on diazepam would be detoxified as though diazepam were the only drug to be considered (Schuckit, 1985).

SUMMARY

The design of effective detoxification regimens is based on a thorough understanding of the pharmacology of the abused substances and the general principles of physical dependency, withdrawal, and cross-addiction. Withdrawal patterns can range from the medical emergencies seen with withdrawal from CNS depressants, such as alcohol and other sedative-hypnotics, to stimulant withdrawal symptoms of suicidal behavior or psychologic emergencies. The emergence of abused drugs such as crack cocaine is changing our views on drug treatments of physical dependency. Some drug regimens are now aimed at reversing neuronal abnormalities induced by chronic drug use, thereby decreasing craving. In this way symptoms related to relapse may be treated, making other modes of therapy more successful.

The pharmacologic treatment of CNS depressant withdrawal symptoms is accomplished by the substitution and gradual tapering of a drug that is pharmacologically similar, as a benzodiazepine or phenobarbital. Opioid withdrawal, though not life-threatening, may have prolonged subtle phases requiring the search for detoxification agents and therapies that can be used for prolonged periods without the fear of cross-dependency development. Supportive reassurance from medical staff may be as important as drug treatment to those who suffer adverse reactions of toxic psychosis and panic following hallucinogen or related drug use.

Researchers are actively working in the area of the development of new, effective drug treatments in the complicated clinical picture of the withdrawing client. It is essential that the clinician and support staff have a workable knowledge of the abused drug effects as well as any agent used to alleviate withdrawal symptoms.

REFERENCES

Aronow, R., & Done, A. (1978). Phencyclidine overdose: An emerging concept of management. *Journal of American College of Emergency Physicians*, (2), 56–59.

Baumgartner, G. R. (1988). Clonidine versus chlordiazepoxide in acute alcohol withdrawal: A preliminary report. *Southern Medical Journal, 81*(1), 56–60.

Breier, A., Charney, D. S., & Nelson, J. C. (1984). Seizures induced by abrupt discontinuation of alprazolam. *American Journal of Psychiatry, 141*(12), 1606–1607.

Brown, M. E., Anton, R. F., Malcom, R., & Ballenger, J. C. (1988). Alcohol detoxification and withdrawal seizures: Clinical support for a kindling hypothesis. *Biological Psychiatry, 23*(5), 507–514.

Charney, D. S., Heninger, G. R., & Kleber, H. D. (1986). The combined use of clonidine and naltrexone as a rapid, safe, and effective treatment of abrupt withdrawal from methadone. *American Journal of Psychiatry, 143*(7), 831–837.

Charney, D. S., Riordan, C. E., Kleber, H. D., Murburg, M., Brauerman, P., Sternberg, D. E., Heninger, G. R., & Redmon, D. E. (1982). Clonidine and naltrexone: A safe, effective, and rapid treatment from methadone therapy. *Archives of General Psychiatry, 39*, 1327–1333.

Dackis, C. A., & Gold, M. S. (1984). New concepts in cocaine addiction: The dopamine depletion hypothesis. *Neuroscience and Biobehavioral Reviews, 9*, 469–477.

Eisenhofer, G., Whiteside, E., Lambie, D., & Johnson, R. (1982). Brain water during alcohol withdrawal. *The Lancet, 1* (8274), 50.

Emsley, R. A., Potgieter, A., Taljaard, J. J., Coetzee, D., Joubert, G., & Gledhill, R. F. (1987). Impaired water excretion and elevated plasma vasopressin in patients with alcohol-withdrawal symptoms. *Quarterly Journal of Medicine, 64*(244), 671–678.

Flink, E. B. (1986). Magnesium deficiency in alcoholism. *Alcoholism, 10*(6), 590–594.

Fraser, H. F., Wikler, A., Essig, C. F., & Isbell, H. E. (1958). Degree of physical dependency induced by secobarbital or pentobarbital. *Journal of the American Medical Association, 166*, 126–129.

Gawin, F. H., & Ellinwood, E. H. (1988). Cocaine and other stimulants: Actions, abuse, and treatment. *New England Journal of Medicine, 318*(18), 1173–1182.

Gawin, F. H., & Kleber, H. D. (1984). Cocaine abuse and treatment. *Archives of General Psychiatry, 41*, 903–909.

Giannini, A. J., Baumgartel, P., & DiMarzio, L. R. (1987). Bromocriptine therapy in cocaine withdrawal. *Journal of Clinical Pharmacology, 27*, 267–270.

Giannini, A. J., Malone, D. A., Giannini, M. C., Price, W. A., & Loiselle, R. H. (1986). Treatment of depression in chronic cocaine and phencyclidine abuse with desipramine. *Journal of Clinical Pharmacology, 26*, 211–214.

Gillman, M. A., & Lichtigfeld, F. J. (1986). Minimal sedation required with nitrous oxide–oxygen treatment of the alcohol withdrawal state. *British Journal of Psychiatry, 148*, 604–606.

Glue, P., & Nutt, D. (1987). Clonidine in alcohol withdrawal: A pilot study of differential symptom responses following i.v. clonidine. *Alcohol and Alcoholism, 22*(2), 161–166.

Green, J., Jaffe, J. H., Carlisi, J. A., & Zaks, A. (1978). Alcohol use in the opiate use cycle of the heroin addict. *International Journal of the Addictions, 13*(7), 1021–1033.

Greenblatt, D. J., & Shader, R. I. (1975). Treatment of the alcohol withdrawal syndrome. In D. J. Greenblatt & R. I. Shader (Eds.), *Manual of psychiatric therapeutics: Practical psychopharmacology and psychiatry* (pp. 211–235). Boston: Little, Brown.

Greenblatt, D. J., Shader, R. I., Franke, K., MacLaughlin, D. S., Harmatz, J. S., Allen, M. D., Werner, A., & Woo, E. (1979). Pharmacokinetics and bioavailability of intravenous, intramuscular, and oral lorazepam in humans. *Journal of Pharmaceutical Sciences, 68*(1), 57–63.

Handelsman, L., Chordia, P. L., Escovar, I. M., Marion, I. J., & Lowinson, J. H. (1988). Amantadine for treatment of cocaine dependence in methadone-maintained patients. *American Journal of Psychiatry, 145*(4), 533.

Isbell, H., Fraser, H. F., Wikler, A., Belleville, R. E., & Eisenman, A. J. (1955). An experimental study of the etiology of "rum fits" and delirium tremens. *Quarterly Journal of Studies on Alcohol, 16,* 1–33.

Jacob, M. S., Zilm, D. H., Macleod, S. M., & Sellers, E. M. (1983). Propranolol-associated confused states during alcohol withdrawal. *Journal of Clinical Psychopharmacology, 3*(3), 185–187.

Jaffe, J. H. (1985). Drug addiction and drug abuse. In A. G. Gilman, L. S. Goodman, T. W. Rall, & F. Murad (Eds.), *Goodman and Gilman's the pharmacological basis of therapeutics* (pp. 532–581). New York: Macmillan.

Jaffe, J. H., & Ciraulo, D. A. (1985). Drugs used in the treatment of alcoholism. In J. H. Mendelson & N. K. Mello (Eds.), *The diagnosis and treatment of alcoholism* (pp. 355–389). New York: McGraw-Hill.

Jasinski, D. R., Johnson, R. E., & Kocher, T. R. (1985). Clonidine in morphine withdrawal. *Archives of General Psychiatry, 42,* 1063–1066.

Jones, R. T. (1983). Cannabis and health. *Annual Review of Medicine, 34,* 247–258.

Kleber, H. G., & Gawin, F. H. (1987). Cocaine withdrawal (reply letter). *Archives of General Psychiatry, 44,* 298.

Korsten, M. A., & Lieber, C. S. (1985). Medical complications of alcoholism. In J. H. Mendelson & N. K. Mello (Eds.), *The diagnosis and treatment of alcoholism* (pp. 21–64). New York: McGraw-Hill.

Kosten, T. R., Schumann, B., Wright, D., Carney, M. K., & Gawin, F. H. (1987). A preliminary study of desipramine in the treatment of cocaine abuse in methadone maintenance patients. *Journal of Clinical Psychiatry, 48*(11), 442–444.

Linnoila, M., Mefford, I., Nutt, D., & Adinoff, B. (1987). NIH conference: Alcohol withdrawal and noradrenergic function. *Annals of Internal Medicine, 107*(6), 875–889.

Martin, P. R., Kapur, B. M., Whiteside, E. A., & Sellers, E. M. (1979). Intravenous phenobarbital therapy in barbiturate and other hypnosedative withdrawal reactions: A kinetic approach. *Clinical Pharmacology and Therapeutics, 26*(2), 256–263.

Millman, R. B. (1988). Evaluation and clinical management of cocaine abusers. *Journal of Clinical Psychiatry, 49*(2) (Supplement); 27–33.

Naranjo, C. A., Sellers, E. M., Chater, K., Iversen, P., Roach, C., & Sykorak, K. (1983). Non-pharmacologic interventions in the treatment of acute alcohol withdrawal. *Clinical Pharmacology and Therapeutics, 34*(2), 214–219.

Nolop, K., & Natow, A. (1985). Unprecedented sedative requirements during delirium tremens. *Critical Care Medicine, 13*(4), 246–247.

Perry, P. J., & Alexander, B. (1986). Sedative/hypnotic dependence: Patient stabilization, tolerance testing, and withdrawal. *Drug Intelligence and Clinical Pharmacy, 20,* 532–537.

Rall, T. W., & Schleifer, L. S. (1985). Drugs effective in the therapies of the epilepsies. In A. G. Gilman, L. S. Goodman, T. W. Rall, & F. Murad (Eds.), *Goodman and Gilman's the pharmacological basis of therapeutics* (pp. 446–472). New York: Macmillan.

Reed, J. S., & Liskow, B. I. (1987). Current medical treatment of alcohol withdrawal. *Rational Drug Therapy, 21*(2), 1–6.

Ritson, B., & Chick, J. (1986). Comparison of two benzodiazepines in the treatment of alcohol withdrawal: Effects on symptoms and cognitive recovery. *Drug and Alcohol Dependence, 18*(4), 329–334.

Roehrich, H., & Gold, M. S. (1987). Propranolol as adjunct to clonidine in opiate detoxification. *American Journal of Psychiatry, 144*(80, 1099–1100.

Sbriglio, R., & Millman, R. B. (1987). Emergency treatment of acute cocaine reactions. In A. M. Washton & M. S. Gold (Eds.), *Cocaine: A clinician's handbook* (pp. 87–95). New York: Guilford Press.

Schuckit, M. A. (1984). *Drug and alcohol abuse* (2d ed.). New York: Plenum Press.

Schuckit, M. A. (1985). Inpatient and residential approaches to the treatment of alcoholism. In J. H. Mendelson & N. K. Mello (Eds.), *The diagnosis and treatment of alcoholism* (pp. 325–354). New York: McGraw-Hill.

Sellers, E. M., & Kalant, H. (1976). Alcohol intoxication and withdrawal. *The New England Journal of Medicine, 294*(14), 757–762.

Sellers, E. M., & Naranjo, C. A. (1986). New strategies for the treatment of alcohol withdrawal. *Psychopharmacology Bulletin, 22*(1), 88–92.

Shaw, J. M., Kolesar, G. S., Sellers, E. M., Kaplan, H. L., & Sandor, P. (1981). Development of optimal treatment tactics for alcohol withdrawal. 1. Assessment and effectiveness of supportive care. *Journal of Clinical Psychopharmacology, 1,* 382–383.

Smith, D. E. (1980). A clinical approach to the treatment of phencyclidine (PCP) abuse. *Psychopharmacology Bulletin, 16*(4), 67–72.

Smith, D. E., & Wesson, D. R. (1983). Benzodiazepine dependency syndromes. *Journal of Psychoactive Drugs, 15,* 85–95.

Tennant, F. S., Russell, B. A., Casas, S. K., & Bleich, R. N. (1975). Heroin detoxification: A comparison of propoxyphene and methadone. *Journal of the American Medical Association, 232*(10), 1019–1022.

Tennant, F. S., & Sagherian, A. A. (1987). Double-blind comparison of amantadine and bromocriptine for ambulatory withdrawal from cocaine dependence. *Archives of Internal Medicine, 147,* 109–112.

Thomson, A. D., Jeyasingham, M. D., Pratt, D. E., & Shaw, G. K. (1987). Nutrition and alcoholic encephalopathies. *Acta Medica Scandinavica, 717,* 55–65.

Vardy, M. M., & Kay, S. R. (1983). LSD psychosis or LSD-induced schizophrenia? *Archives of General Psychiatry, 40,* 877–883.

Washton, A. M., & Resnick, R. B. (1982). Outpatient opiate detoxification with clonidine. *Journal of Clinical Psychiatry, 43*(6, sec. 2), 39–41.

Wilkins, A. J., Jenkins, W. J., & Steiner, J. A. (1983). Efficacy of clonidine in treatment of alcohol withdrawal state. *Psychopharmacology, 81,* 78–80.

Wilson, A., & Vulcano, B. (1984). A double-blind placebo-controlled trial of magnesium sulfate in the ethanol withdrawal syndrome. *Alcoholism: Clinical and Experimental Research, 8*(6), 542–545.

Woo, E., & Greenblatt, D. J. (1979). Massive benzodiazepine requirements during alcohol withdrawals. *American Journal of Psychiatry, 136*(6), 821–823.

Young, G. P., Rores, C., Murphy, C., & Dailey, R. H. (1987). Intravenous phenobarbital for alcohol withdrawal and convulsions. *Annals of Emergency Medicine, 16*(8), 847–850.

18

CURRENT APPROACHES TO SUBSTANCE ABUSE TREATMENT

Gerald Bennett and Donna S. Woolf

This chapter presents an overview of the diverse range of treatment settings and therapeutic modalities available for substance abusers seeking recovery. Treatment settings include community-based programs, hospital-based programs, freestanding residential facilities, and private offices of a variety of mental health or addiction treatment professionals. Therapeutic modalities may be broadly classified into four types: pharmacotherapies, psychotherapies, overt aversion therapies, and nonpharmacologic somatotherapies not involving aversive conditioning. These therapies are systematic attempts to alleviate the primary problem of substance abuse, or dependence, and usually do not begin in a serious fashion until the client has been stabilized through detoxification and other supportive interventions. Most of the therapies discussed may be carried out in a hospital or a community setting. In addition to describing current therapies, we discuss some of the issues determining an appropriate therapy selection for a particular client or set of clients.

Self-help approaches are not included in this chapter, but this exclusion should not be interpreted as a deemphasis of self-help as therapy (see Chapter 19). Rather, the purpose here is to focus on approaches, and their theoretical underpinnings, which health professionals use in their roles as therapists for the substance abuser. We will look at the pharmacotherapies, psychotherapies, overt aversion therapies, and nonpharmacologic somatotherapies separately, but, in practice, these approaches are often applied in combination.

Verbal aversion therapy (covert sensitization) relies mainly on the use of verbal instruction from a therapist and fantasy on the part of the client. For this reason, we will consider this approach as a type of psychotherapy. On the other hand, overt aversion therapy depends on a combination of psychologic conditioning and some overt aversive event or experience. Pairing of substance use with drug-induced nausea, an electric shock, or other aversive stimuli is the critical therapeutic factor in overt aversion approaches, and they are most accurately viewed outside the bounds of psychotherapy. Nonpharmacologic somatotherapies not involving aversive conditioning are not currently numerous in substance abuse treatment, but modalities such as acupuncture appear to hold promise.

TREATMENT SETTINGS*

Community-Based Programs

Two types of programs delivered in the community setting discussed here are alcohol and polydrug abstinence programs and smoking cessation programs. The role of the nurse in these programs is highlighted.

Alcohol and polydrug abstinence programs

It was not until 1948 that alcoholism treatment became part of a public program in the United States at the Virginia Department of Public Health (Chafetz & Demone, 1962). A study, encompassing the years 1959 to 1961, of eight unidentified outpatient alcoholism treatment centers, found psychiatric, medical, or social models in use but rarely a combination of the three in one program (Gerard & Saenger, 1966). Other conclusions of the study were that (a) social and psychiatric agencies were, in general, reluctant to work with alcoholics; (b) staff members in outpatient alcoholism treatment centers did not feel accepted in the larger health and welfare systems; and (c) conflicts between recovering alcoholics and professionals undermined morale and effectiveness of treatment. In general, the study found a climate of failure and insufficient community support for outpatient alcoholism treatment programs investigated.

*This section is in part adapted from a chapter in the first edition, "An Overview of Substance Abuse Treatment," written by Gerald Bennett, Jacquelin E. Graves, Martha T. Kavanaugh, and Christine Vourakis.

Now most communities throughout the United States operate public substance abuse treatment programs, many as components of the community mental health system. Community outpatient programs originally developed for alcoholism treatment now also typically treat the polydrug abuser as well. This broader scope of treatment has emerged for three basic reasons. First, it is becoming more typical in practice to find alcoholism complicated by other types of substance abuse. The "pure" alcoholic is becoming rare among younger alcoholic populations. Second, treatment professionals are increasingly viewing alcoholism as a type of drug abuse. Third, economic pressures on service programs make it difficult to offer specialized treatment for each type of substance abuse. Two substance abuse problems, heroin addiction and tobacco dependence, are not typically treated in alcohol and polydrug abuse abstinence programs and will be addressed separately.

The nurse's role in assessment is crucial in most community clinics. The essential data required to determine the appropriate disposition of the person applying for community treatment is summarized in Table 18.1. The clinician will undoubtedly wish to go beyond the essential data base presented here for assessment purposes. Several excellent sources are available for guidance in the detailed assessment of various substance abuse problems (Estes, Smith-DiJulio, & Heinemann, 1980; Smith, Wesson, & Linda, 1980; Wesson & Smith, 1979; Estes & Heinemann, 1986).

Table 18.1

Essential Data from Which to Base Initial Evaluation for Community Treatment

Alcohol and other drug history

1. Time and amount of last drink or use of drugs
2. Amount and type consumed and duration of present episode
3. History of severe withdrawal, including seizure history
4. Medical history, including:
   a. Recent trauma or illness requiring medical treatment and medication prescribed, including for client or spouse
   b. Previous and chronic conditions, e.g., cardiac disease, gastrointestinal disturbance, diabetes mellitus, liver disease
   c. Current medications and compliance with Rx
   d. Allergy history

Physical assessment

1. Vital signs
2. Stage of withdrawal
3. Nutritional status
4. Signs of recent trauma
5. Dehydration, lesions, rashes
6. Blood alcohol concentration, using analyzer

Psychologic assessment

1. Mental status to include orientation in all spheres, suicidal or homocidal ideation, signs of primary psychiatric disorder
2. Motivation for treatment

Social assessment

1. Living arrangements
2. Family support
3. Financial status
4. Potential for self-care

An excellent candidate for community treatment is the client who shows signs of mild to moderate withdrawal in early stages, has no immediate medical or psychiatric complications, does not report a history of severe withdrawal, is without recent trauma or debilitation, has support in the home, and has made prior successful attempts to undergo ambulatory detoxification. On the other hand, advanced stages of withdrawal, concomitant medical or psychiatric complications, history of severe withdrawal, recent trauma, extreme debilitation, absence of social support, and recent unsuccessful attempts at detoxification in an outpatient setting are all factors suggesting a possible need for hospitalization before community treatment.

We should point out here that many hospital-based programs refer their clients to community programs as a transition in treatment. In these cases, the assessment process within the community program is more like a "reception" than the critical decision-making required when a client is evaluated for initial and primary treatment in the outpatient center.

When ambulatory detoxification is one of the treatment components of an outpatient program, the nurse's responsibility in this procedure is primary, in that the physician is usually attached to the center part-time or "on call," with the use of protocols or "standing orders" for detoxification. In connection with the primary position of the nurse as health care provider in community programs is the responsibility for managing routine and urgent clinical situations. Tennant (1979) identified 13 emergency situations likely to occur in substance abuse treatment clinics and devised a set of protocols and procedures usually indicated. Among the critical incidents identified are stuporous or unconscious client suspected of narcotic overdose, convulsions, intoxicated client, acute psychotic reaction, alcohol consumption with disulfiram, and eight others. The nurse in this setting is often required to make judgments that are in the ill-defined border between nursing and medicine. Again, the importance of collegial relationships between team members, with planning for the roles each will assume in providing client care, is evident.

The recovering process for substance abusers is ongoing and depends on the client's assuming responsibility for self-care. Many clients may not have developed, before entering treatment, the skills and strengths necessary for active involvement in their care. Consequently, recovering implies not only abstinence and rehabilitation, but basic learning of skills necessary to accomplish self-care and productive living. In an outpatient treatment center, this process is instituted in the initial stage of treatment. The nurse establishes significant contact with the client in a supportive role during assessment, and if the client is receiving detoxification medications, the nursing relationship is reinforced. As the client is introduced to group therapy, the generally acknowledged therapy of choice in the treatment of substance abusers, the nurse is again encountered in the role of counselor and therapist. The nurse has a dual responsibility in the group process when a client is in the initial phase of recovery, that of monitoring overt physical progress, including response to the detoxification regime, as well as performing as a leader or coleader of the group.

It is desirable for a program to have a number of groups meeting throughout the day and evening, thus attempting to meet the diverse needs of the client population. First, clients should have a primary group, matching their level of progress. Levels may include orientation to treatment, or a "new" clients group; reorientation to treatment, or a "returning" clients group; and several groups for intermediate and advanced clients. The most advanced groups are best scheduled in the evening so that there is no interference with employment. In addition to primary group participation, groups planned for a particular population are helpful. For example, specific groups for adolescents, men, homosexuals, senior citizens, and specific ethnic populations are warranted in many programs. Of course, the ability to attain this high degree of specificity depends on adequate financial, client, and staff resources. Approaches to therapy in these various groups differ, according to the theoretical orientation of the leader or coleaders. Current approaches to substance abuse therapy are covered later in this chapter.

A well-integrated substance abuse program will coordinate the medical, psychologic, social, spiritual, and vocational components necessary to guide the client toward a recovery process. Every client benefits from a one-to-one relationship with an assigned staff member. Education about the health hazards of substance abuse, recreation, opportunities to learn stress reduction techniques, such as meditation or systematic relaxation, and expression of creative instincts through art or poetry therapy are important components of a contemporary treatment center. In this milieu, the role of the nurse as a health educator is accentuated.

The family component of a community program is vital. If there remains an intact family unit, the family system is more often than not as ravaged by the substance abuse problem as is the applicant for services. The nurse may become involved in family counseling with particular families or serve as a leader of a multiple-family group. Also, the nurse should be a referral source for the family seeking help beyond the treatment program, such as specialized medical and psychiatric diagnosis, marital counseling, family therapy (if not included in the program), sex therapy, or legal advice.

Client progress can be based on many variables: extensions of periods of drug-free living, limitations in periods of use, general improvements in physical and mental health, improved family conditions, elevated or stable economic and vocational status, and individual gains of any kind as subjectively defined by the client.

Smoking cessation programs

Since the early 1960s, smoking cessation programs have become rapidly established in communities throughout the United States. It is not known to what extent nurses are involved in providing care in these programs. Certainly, the nurse has a contribution to make in this area, and research focused on the potential role of nursing in smoking cessation treatment warrants attention in the near future. Also, the role of the nurse in general practice as a promoter of smoking cessation has received far less attention in the literature than has the role of the physician. It is often noted that nurses have high rates of smoking when compared to other health professionals and women in the general population. "Cessation of smoking by nurses is emphasized as necessary to enable nurses to serve as better role models of health for the public" (Schwartz, 1987, p. 58).

Programs in the community specifically designed to promote smoking cessation are numerous and diverse. We will consider one major program in each of two broad categories: nonprofit and commercial. The extensive review and evaluation of smoking cessation programs by Schwartz and Rider (1978) and Schwartz (1987) may be consulted for more information about these important community services.

Nonprofit programs. The most active nonprofit organization in the development of smoking cessation programs is the American Cancer Society (ACS). ACS "Quit Smoking Clinics" are offered through the 58 divisions and 3100 local units of the organization. Approximately 30,000–40,000 smokers attend these clinics each year (Schwartz, 1987). Basic elements of the program include participating in eight group sessions led by a *facilitator*, viewing a series of trigger films aimed at promoting group discussion, and practicing abstinence. Schwartz (1987) described the program in terms of three phases: "first, self-appraisal and insight development; second, practicing abstinence under controlled conditions; and third, a maintenance phase which varies according to the wishes of each participant" (p. 26).

Facilitators must have completed an ACS training program, may be professionals or nonprofessionals, and are all volunteers. Graduates of the clinic program are recruited for training and may become facilitators themselves. The ACS is working with a number of other organizations to place clinics throughout society. Through cooperation with the American Hospital Association, programs are being offered within hospitals to patients, outpatients, and interested people in the community. Cooperation with the military services has led to offering of these successful clinics and training facilitators. The U. S. Air Force is cooperating with ACS to train environmental health nurses to lead cessation programs as a part of a health maintenance program.

One evaluative study of the ACS clinics in the Los Angeles area between 1970 and 1973 found that abstinence continued for 30% of all participants after 6 months, 22% after 12 months, and 18% at 18 months (Schwartz, 1987). One study of enrollees in nine clinics using a format consistent with the ACS approach found a mean quit rate of 25% (Evans & Lane, 1980).

Commercial programs. SmokEnders is one of the largest commercial organizations providing smoking cessation services. An ex-smoker, Jacquelyn Rogers, and her husband, a dentist, organized SmokEnders in 1969 in New Jersey. Since that time, the program has spread throughout the United States and to a number of foreign countries. In 1983, the Comprehensive Care Corporation (CCC) began managing the programs.

The SmokEnders program emphasizes attitude change and positive reinforcement. A participant becomes involved in a 6-week seminar, meeting once a week. There is no attempt at quitting for the first 4 weeks. The end of the fourth seminar marks the beginning of abstinence, in an atmosphere of mutual group support. The program is described by SmokEnders' representatives as dealing with the total problem of smoking. The total problem is thought to include needs for oral gratification, poor nutritional habits, the use of smoking as a socializing tool, and other life-style factors. All seminar leaders are themselves graduates of the SmokEnders program. They receive special leadership training and are called *moderators*. The ability of the participant to identify with the moderator as an ex-smoker is considered essential to the program.

Evaluations of SmokEnders have yielded inconclusive results due to low response rates for graduates (Schwartz, 1987). Available data indicate that the program is at least as successful as the ACS program.

Hospital and Freestanding Residential Programs

There are programs for alcohol and other drug abusers in public and private general hospitals. Most state mental hospital systems have an alcohol and drug abuse unit or program. Throughout the country, there are many private, "freestanding" hospitals exclusively treating substance abusers. The Veterans Administration operates chemical dependency programs within its hospital system. Some hospitals can be highly selective in the type of abuser admitted for treatment, whereas other hospitals cannot. In the past 15 years, there has been an increase in the number of private facilities that, by virtue of their charges and the increased use of third-party payments, select whom they admit. In contrast, state mental hospital programs have little selection of the type of alcohol and drug abusers they admit because they serve community mental health centers who send them their young and old, their new and chronic, their indigent and paying, their voluntary and committed clientele. Thus, state mental hospitals typically serve a heterogenous group of clients, all of whom are initially in some physical, medical, social, or psychologic crisis. Private facilities tend to serve a more homogeneous group of middle- to upper-class clients.

In addition to the diversity of setting and the selectivity of clients for inpatient services, there is considerable difference in the operation of hospital-based programs, depending on the treatment philosophies and theories of substance abuse espoused by administration and staff. Most programs rely on verbal therapies, including individual and group, with a strong educational component for clients and families, with the goal of creating a drug-free life-style. These same modalities and goals are also used, with some innovations, for special populations, such as women, minorities, adolescents, and the elderly. A few programs use aversion-conditioning techniques to break the acute addictive pattern.

Moore (1985) prepared a national directory of over 500 private residential treatment facilities. The typical minimum duration of treatment in these centers is 28 days. Most programs are highly structured, providing comprehensive nursing, medical, psychologic, social, and spiritual care. Most programs also incorporate experiences with one or more of the major self-help groups. Treatment centers serve specific groups including adolescents, women, blacks, homosexuals, the hearing impaired, Hispanics, impaired health professionals, men, Native Americans, and older adults.

The role of the nurse in hospital-based and freestanding residential programs varies a great deal. Some programs rely extensively on alcohol and drug counselors, whereas others emphasize the contributions of the traditional health professions. Some nurses have become alcohol and drug counselors to become more involved in counseling roles (see Chapter 16 for a discussion of the evolution of the nursing role in these settings). Model programs incorporate the services of an interdisciplinary staff, including physicians, psychologists, registered nurses, social workers, pharmacists, and alcohol and drug counselors. According to the National Institute on Alcohol Abuse and Alcoholism (NIAAA), an essential characteristic for a facility to be classified as a "specialized alcoholism hospital" includes the availability of continuous nursing services under the direction of a full-time registered nurse. Nursing services are defined as rendering skilled nursing care, performing prescribed medical treatments, teaching treatment and health measures, and providing counseling and supportive care (Bast, 1984). The role of the nurse in alcoholism treatment as defined by the National Nurses Society on Addictions (NNSA) is presented in Appendix C.

The higher cost of residential treatment for alcoholism in contrast to less expensive community-based approaches has called into question whether residential care is more effective than outpatient treatment. A review of 26 controlled studies (using random assignment or matching) showed "no overall advantage for residential over nonresidential settings, for longer over shorter inpatient programs, or for more intensive over less intensive interventions in treating alcohol abuse" (Miller & Hester, 1986, p. 794). Furthermore, Miller and Hester (1986) concluded "the outcome of alcoholism treatment is more likely to be influenced by the content of interventions than by the settings in which they are offered" (p. 794). The need to contain rising health care costs in the United States and a growing commitment to science in the addictions treatment field is bringing to the forefront what is called "the matching issue": "which treatments and treatment settings are the most effective for which patients. . . ?" (Gordis, 1987, p. 583).

Private Practice

Although the number of mental health and addictions treatment professionals providing substance abuse therapy in their private offices is unknown, the number has certainly increased in recent years as more professionals have been educated in this area and the public has become aware of the need for professional assistance in managing substance abuse problems. Because of the nature of private therapy, probably the therapies selected and the approaches used vary greatly. Research is needed to explicate the extent to which addictions treatment services are being provided on an outpatient basis by private therapists, the therapies being used, and their relative effectiveness.

ISSUES IN THERAPY SELECTION

A major goal of the substance abuse field is to create a dynamic network of inpatient and outpatient services able to match therapeutic approaches to the specific needs and preferences of clients seeking or requiring help. Currently, efficacy of specific therapeutic combinations of setting and approach are not clearly delineated by research; the approaches utilized in any given setting depend a great deal on tradition, economy, and the model of addiction subscribed to by hospital or clinic administrations and therapists themselves. However, there is a growing dissatisfaction with this state of affairs (Gordis, 1987). Finney and Moos (1986) discussed at length the current enthusiasm for research that will provide a sound base of knowledge for "prescriptive treatment." They concluded that although the complexity of such research efforts is not yet fully appreciated, it is clear that questions surrounding the matching problem are likely to drive the clinical research agenda in the addictions field for some time.

There are some examples in the literature of what Finney and Moos (1986) called "naturalistic" matching, that is, prescriptive treatment based more on the judgment of clinicians rather than research findings. A process for therapy selection we are likely to see more of in the future is described by Levie, Claxton, and Barnes (1979).

These authors reported on the functioning of an interagency drug abuse intake and evaluation office in Omaha, Nebraska. This central intake office opened in 1975 to screen clients before making treatment assignments to specific programs and services within the metropolitan area. Intake workers in the office interviewed the client and scheduled a physical examination. An interdisciplinary intake committee, composed of intake workers, a consulting psychiatrist, and representatives from participating agencies, met each week to review current cases and make decisions and recommendations about which programs best suited a particular client's needs, given the resources available. Levie and coworkers (1979) believed that two chief advantages of this process were that the intake committee had the opportunity to "develop ideas about which clients work best in which programs," and "the committee has great flexibility in making decisions and treatment plans" (p. 485).

The following sections on the various therapies do not address setting up administrative policies and procedures facilitating appropriate therapy selection. However, we suggest the reader keep in mind the importance of structuring an agency or group of agencies so that there is flexibility and specificity in treatment planning. For the private practitioner, links to community resources and other substance abuse specialists ensure the client's access to a variety of therapy alternatives.

THE BIOPSYCHOSOCIAL MODEL

The biopsychosocial model of health, now widely applied in nursing, health psychology, medical sociology, and behavioral medicine, is emerging as the most useful overall conceptual perspective in research devoted to the treatment matching issue and naturalistic approaches to prescribing addiction therapies. The biopsychosocial model provides a "framework within which biological, psychological, and sociocultural approaches to health and illness can be integrated" (Donovan, 1988, p. 4). A cardinal assumption of the biopsychosocial model is that treatments should be based on specific problems uncovered by a thorough assessment of the client in terms of biologic, psychologic, and social functioning.

Use of the biopsychosocial model in assessment and treatment planning may be termed biopsychosocial eclecticism (Abroms, 1983). Although this term is perhaps more familiar in a traditional psychiatric context, it is also applicable to addictions treatment. Based on an analysis of the results of a multidimensional assessment of the addict, in light of research-based and clinical knowledge, treatments are selected by the clinician or treatment planning team, with appropriate participation by the client. In presenting an overview of the various therapeutic modalities in addictions treatment, the authors believe the biopsychosocial model provides a broad conceptual orientation from which to appreciate the importance of diverse approaches to a multidimensional phenomenon.

PHARMACOTHERAPIES

For years a variety of drugs have been administered to substance abusers to "cure" the problem. The following section will review a limited number of the drugs used as all or parts of a treatment plan for the substance abuser. Although some of these drug treatments have met with limited success, it must be recognized that giving an addicted person drugs may reinforce the behavior that says "a drug is the cure for my problem." Medications used to treat withdrawal are discussed in Chapter 17.

Disulfiram

Disulfiram (Antabuse) is a drug administered to alcohol abusers as a deterrent to drinking. Ingesting alcohol while disulfiram is in the body produces a well-recognized reaction involving "blurred vision, nausea, vertigo, anxiety, and cardiovascular effects, such as hypotension, palpitations, tachycardia, and flushing of the face and neck" (Kitson, 1977, p. 97). The symptoms begin within 15 minutes of the alcohol ingestion and may last for several hours. The severity of the reaction, which can range from mild discomfort to death, depends on how long the drug has been taken, how much alcohol was ingested, and how sensitive the individual client is (Ritchie, 1985).

This extremely unpleasant cluster of symptoms is thought to be caused by disulfiram's inhibition of acet-

aldehyde dehydrogenase—the enzyme necessary for the breakdown of acetaldehyde, a product of alcohol's metabolism (see Fig. 2.1 in Chapter 2). As acetaldehyde levels rise, the symptoms emerge. Many of the deaths reported in the literature occurred when clients were given high doses of disulfiram or were being given "test" doses of alcohol as a type of aversion therapy. Both the high doses of disulfiram and the test-dose procedure are rarely used today. Most clients are maintained on 250–500-mg doses. Clinical experience has shown that there are clients who "can drink" while taking 250 mg disulfiram daily. These clients may experience no symptoms or mild symptoms when drinking is resumed. Higher doses of disulfiram may be required for these clients. Some clinics administer disulfiram mixed with fruit punches or juice at the clinic to prevent clients from "cheeking" tablets or simply not taking them.

Disulfiram therapy should not be begun until at least 12 hours have elapsed since the last drink was taken, and many programs wait 24 hours since exacting histories are difficult to obtain from the withdrawing client. The disulfiram–alcohol reaction can occur for 6–12 days after the last disulfiram intake (Ritchie, 1985), although some clients may be able to drink within 4–5 days after the last dose.

Disulfiram, like any drug, has side effects. Drowsiness, or fatigue, a common complaint during the early phase of treatment, can be managed by giving the drug at bedtime (Kwentus & Major, 1979). Various stomach complaints and headaches are infrequent complaints. A garliclike breath occurs so frequently that it is sometimes used as an indicator of compliance. Allergy, manifested by a rash, may occur with this drug, as with any other. A rare, but important, reaction to disulfiram is disulfiram-induced encephalopathy or disulfiram psychosis. Symptoms of bizarre behavior, disorientation, ataxia, impaired memory, and hallucinations may develop a few days after disulfiram therapy has begun or may emerge over several weeks in some clients, necessitating the drug's discontinuance (Hotson & Langston, 1976; Knee & Razani, 1974). The most important drug–drug interaction of disulfiram is alcohol, but other important drug–drug interactions of disulfiram are discussed in Chapter 8. It should be noted that other alcohol-like drugs, such as paraldehyde, may give disulfiram–alcohol reactions.

To minimize the risks of a disulfiram–alcohol reaction, certain guidelines must be followed when a client is to be evaluated for disulfiram therapy. The client *must* understand fully what disulfiram is, how the disulfiram–alcohol reaction is triggered, and what symptoms might be expected if the client drinks while taking disulfiram. It is best to present these symptoms to the client in a clear, written form, express them verbally, and include a signed consent form in the client's chart. Clients who are confused, who cannot read or take the responsibility of avoiding "hidden" alcohol (as in medicines), or who have had previous hypersensitivities to disulfiram should not take the drug. A medical clearance for disulfiram therapy is also necessary. Severe cardiovascular disease, hepatic failure, or pregnancy are conditions under which clients may be excluded from disulfiram therapy, although the prospect of continued physical damage from alcohol use may make exclusion of some clients a difficult decision.

One issue of disulfiram therapy is the advisability of *requiring* that the client take disulfiram to participate in a treatment program. Some programs argue that many clients refuse to take disulfiram because they want and intend to drink. Requiring the client in the nonresidential program to take disulfiram gives some assurance that the client will not drink during the hours spent away from the treatment setting, particularly during the first few months of sobriety when relapse rates are high. There is some debate as to whether it can be statistically supported that disulfiram affects the length of abstinence achieved by the addict (Fuller et al., 1986; Mottin, 1973; Whyte & O'Brien, 1974).

Those health professionals opposed to disulfiram therapy argue that coercing a client into taking disulfiram achieves nothing and may provide the client with a reason to leave treatment. Some health professionals complain that giving disulfiram feeds the "a-drug-for-every-problem" mentality. These clinicians also question whether the side effects of disulfiram therapy justify its use in the debilitated alcoholic. Often, questions of client reliability in avoiding alcohol hidden in food and medicines play a part in the opposition to disulfiram therapy. Finally, the treatment program must have the medical facilities to evaluate and give clearance for clients to take disulfiram, a physician who is willing to prescribe the drug, and the ability to monitor the clients' use of the drug.

Disulfiram therapy has been a mainstay of sobriety for many clients. A strong psychologic component of disulfiram therapy exists for these people. Clients report that they "no longer have to worry—am I going to drink today?" and can, therefore, work more effectively on problems in psychotherapy. For these clients, disulfiram therapy may play a pivotal role in recovery.

Psychotropic Medications

Although some addicts suffer from the same psychiatric disorders as nonaddicted people and benefit from neuroleptic, antimanic, antidepressant, or antianxiety drugs, health professionals cannot consider the psychotropic drugs as cure-alls for problems of substance abusers. In fact, many clinicians are very cautious in prescribing psychotropics for substance abusers until clear psychopathology can be observed in the drug-free client. The antianxiety drugs; most of which have abuse and addiction potential, are best avoided entirely in the detoxified substance abuser. Clinicians often choose to treat the depression and anxiety, which are common in the newly detoxified abuser, with nondrug modes of therapy (Becker et al., 1975; Bissell, 1975; Overall, Brown, Williams, & Neill, 1973; Shaw, Donley, Morgan, & Robinson, 1975). When a substance abuser is diagnosed as having a dual problem of abuse and a psychiatric disorder, great care must be exercised to monitor the prescribed drug use. It must be remembered that the substance abuser has learned well the lesson that "if one pill makes me feel good, two will make me feel even better."

One area undergoing extensive research is the drug treatment of the stimulant, particularly cocaine, abuser. Studies focus on potential drug therapies to reduce craving in the immediate withdrawal period, as well as for continued therapy to prevent relapse. Some of these detoxification therapies are covered in Chapter 17. The reader is encouraged to continually review the literature, as new data involving the efficacy of certain pharmacologic agents used to treat drug craving or to block euphoria in various populations of cocaine abusers are emerging.

Since stimulant abuse appears to cause changes in norepinephrine (NE) and dopamine (DA) systems in the brain, drugs chosen as possible aids to reduce craving and block euphoria have been those known to increase NE and DA levels or availability by various mechanisms (Gawin & Kleber, 1986). Therapies currently under investigation include the use of antidepressant drugs as desipramine or imipramine to reduce beta-adrenergic receptor supersensitivity, tyrosine to increase the depleted dopamine levels by supplementing the dietary precursor, and the administration of amantadine or bromcriptine to increase DA release or stimulate DA receptors.

Methadone

Using methadone as a maintenance drug for opioid addicts is relatively simple (Cohen & Stimmel, 1978; Novick et al., 1988). Once the client has been accepted for treatment with methadone (that is, it has been determined that the client is physically dependent on an opioid drug), methadone is initiated at a low dose. This dose depends to some extent on the estimated daily street drug amount used. If there is no sedation or adverse reaction, the dosage of methadone will be slowly increased every 2–3 days until a level is reached that "blocks" the effects of heroin and does not allow the abstinence syndrome to occur. Debate occurs as to whether a high or a low dose should be used as a maintenance dosage. The side effects of methadone are discussed in Chapter 5.

A controversey exists concerning the use of methadone as a "maintenance" drug for opioid addicts (Bowden & Maddox, 1972; Nelkin, 1973; Newman, 1987). Advocates of the use of methadone maintenance emphasize the physical aspects of the drug: "It is a medicine." They point out that the client whose dose is properly adjusted has no heroin hunger, no euphoria, and no need to continue heroin-seeking behavior. This decreases the need to commit illegal acts to obtain heroin or to obtain money with which to buy drugs (Dole & Nyswander, 1965). Supporters contend that clients taking methadone have time to work on life problems without contending with the protracted opioid withdrawal syndrome (see Chapter 5). Economic factors play a role in the continuation of methadone programs, for these clinics require less money to operate than do many other types of treatment programs. People previously unable to work can return to work while on methadone maintenance programs, contributing to the economy and decreasing the numbers of addicts receiving federal assistance.

Opponents of maintaining clients on methadone argue that the methadone-dependent client is still an addict. They contend that giving a client a drug is a simplistic pharmacologic approach to a problem entailing complex social and psychologic factors. It is argued that police figures on arrests of addicts on methadone maintenance suggesting a lower rate of arrest than for addicts not using methadone therapy are inaccurate since the police will often forego arrest if the client is involved in a treatment program (Nelkin, 1973). Other critics contend that maintaining a client on methadone perpetuates the idea that a drug is the answer to the problem—an idea that the addict has had for some time. The client also retains the stigma of an "addict" and may have difficulty finding an employer willing to hire a person taking methadone.

It is clear that methadone maintenance is not a panacea for opioid dependence. However, until workable solutions are found, which decrease the crime involved in obtaining heroin, and until a better way is found to detoxify the opioid addict, allowing drug freedom to be maintained, the clinics will remain.

Naltrexone

Another therapy used as adjunctive therapy in the opioid dependent client is that of naltrexone. Naltrexone (Trexan) is an orally active, nonaddictive, long-acting competitive antagonist at the mu, kappa, sigma, and delta opioid receptors (see Chapter 5). When routinely taken, naltrexone blocks any ingested opioid from reaching the opioid receptor, preventing opioid action and euphoria. In theory, if no drug high can be achieved by the client, the opioid drug will not be taken and eventually the craving will disappear. Some researchers have suggested that proper dosing of clonidine for opioid withdrawal symptoms, in combination with naltrexone therapy, may reduce the length of opioid withdrawal syndromes (Charney, Heninger, & Kleber, 1986).

Naltrexone therapy is begun when the client has been withdrawn from opioids, generally by the use of clonidine regimens. Severe withdrawal symptoms will be induced by the administration of naltrexone to opioid-dependent clients. Frequently, negative opioid urine tests and the injectable challenge of the opioid antagonist, naloxone, are used to verify that the client is opioid free. If no withdrawal symptoms occur after 0.8-mg subcutaneous doses of naloxone, 25 mg naltrexone is administered. No withdrawal symptoms after 1 hour indicate that naltrexone maintenance may be initiated safely. Drug dosing is three times weekly and usually involves the oral administration of 100 mg naltrexone on Monday and Wednesday and 150 mg on Friday (Jaffe, 1985). Naltrexone cannot be used in methadone-dependent clients because it precipitates an abrupt withdrawal syndrome.

Naltrexone appears to cause subtle side effects often voiced by clients as fatigue or the loss of energy. Abdominal discomfort (heaviness and rarely cramps) is a complaint of some clients. This may be a sign of incomplete opioid withdrawal before the naltrexone therapy was initiated. It is possible that naltrexone is irritating to the gastrointestinal tract. Gastrointestinal complaints may be reduced by the administration of antacids or the administration of the drug with food (Volvaka, Resnick, Kestenbaum, & Freedman, 1976). It should be remembered that opioid drugs prescribed for medical needs will be blocked by naltrexone as well as illicit drugs. Opioids for anesthesia, severe pain, diarrhea, and coughs will not be effective while the client is taking naltrexone. It is possible to override naltrexone effects in the event of the emergency need for anesthesia, but large doses of the opioid must be used, and every effort should be made to avoid the use of naltrexone when opioid drugs are expected to be needed for medical reasons.

Naltrexone is too expensive for some patients to afford, although its use is generally cheaper than continued drug use. Tablets are usually administered by the clinic staff to ensure compliance and continued supportive treatment. Despite its drawbacks, naltrexone can be useful during the period immediately after opioid withdrawal, when relapse rates are high.

Drug Treatments for the Nicotine Abuser

Several pharmacologic approaches for achieving smoking cessation are available in the United States and Europe (Health & Public Policy Committee, 1986). None of these agents can offer no-fail results to the tobacco abuser.

Various smoking deterrents have been used in the past without substantiated success. Many of these products are available only in Europe. Most of these are in the form of mouthwashes or lozenges that irritate the oral mucosa, dry the mouth to decrease sensory drives, or leave an extremely unpleasant odor and taste in the mouth. More successful means of making smoking aversive are discussed in the later section on overt aversion therapy. Some of these products, such as silver-containing mouthwashes and lozenges, may have the risk of toxicity (Macintyre, Mclay, East, Williams, & Boddy, 1978).

With the exception of nicotine chewing gum, few pharmacologic agents have been proven effective, safe methods of withdrawing a client from nicotine. In this respect, nicotine is one area in which pharmacology neither offers a good drug solution for withdrawing the client from the drug nor for maintaining a tobacco-free client.

One approach to withdrawing a smoker is to substitute a drug as a nicotine replacement. To date, nicotine gum (Nicorette) has provided the most successful approach. Nicotine gum is available in the United States in 2-mg doses. European and Canadian gums are marketed in 4-mg doses.

Appropriate doses of Nicorette gum can be an effective aid to those persons attempting to stop smoking. As might be expected, this therapy appears most effective when combined with supportive group counseling and is more effective than placebo (Lam, Sacks, Sze, & Chalmers, 1987). The gum is chewed slowly, over 30 minutes, when the craving for tobacco products is felt, up to a maximum of 30 pieces a day. Side effects of nicotine gum therapy are generally mild. They include mouth blisters, sore mouth and tongue, indigestion, and hiccups. Rare palpitations can occur. The consistency of the gum may result in loosening of dental fillings. It is possible to become dependent on nicotine gum, and some estimate that 13%–38% of gum users continue to use the gum for longer than a year—even when advised to stop (Tonnesen et al., 1986).

Clonidine, an alpha$_2$-adrenergic agonist, is effective in the treatment of opioid withdrawal symptoms. It is believed to produce at least some of its actions through a connection between the adrenergic and opioid receptors in the locus coeruleus area of the brain. Since cigarette smokers seem to exhibit some symptoms seen in other withdrawal patterns, it has been used to treat nicotine withdrawal, as well, with some success (Glassman et al., 1988). Clonidine is said to reduce cigarette craving and other associated withdrawal symptoms as irritability and anxiety. The usual dosage is 0.15-0.3 mg/d in divided doses. Clonidine transdermal patches have also been used. Reported side effects include hypotension, dizziness, rashes, and lethargy.

Comparative studies need to be done on the short- and long-term efficacy of clonidine and nicotine gum therapies in the treatment of withdrawal from tobacco products. It is also noteworthy that none of the studies using these pharmacologic methods has shown much success without accompanying counseling and follow-up support.

PSYCHOTHERAPIES

Psychotherapy is not easily defined. We will not involve ourselves here with distinctions between various "levels" of therapy, such as problem-solving-focused (sometimes distinguished from psychotherapy altogether and termed *counseling*) and personality- or behavior-change-focused. Rather, we will adopt the following broad definition:

> Basically, psychotherapy consists of the interaction between two individuals, although more than two can be involved. One of the individuals, the client or patient, is the one who is seeking help for a problem that either he, some other individual or agency, or the therapist deems potentially helped by psychotherapeutic intervention. The other participant is obviously the person designated as the therapist, who supposedly has the training and personal resources to help the disturbed client. The interaction between the two participants is mediated primarily by verbal means, although bodily gestures, movements, and displays of affect enter in. Psychotherapy thus appears to be largely a verbal interaction between two people, a therapist and a client, by means of which the former somehow attempts to help the latter to overcome his difficulties. (Garfield, 1980, p. 9)

It is important to emphasize Garfield's (1980) statement that more than two people can be involved because group and family approaches are popular in substance abuse therapy.

At this point in our discussion, it would be satisfying to both the authors and the reader if the limitations of the pharmacotherapies in substance abuse treatment could be overcome in a dramatic way by the demonstrated effectiveness of the psychotherapies. Unfortunately, the psychotherapies have their share of limitations. However, recent years have seen impressive advances in psychotherapeutic approaches to substance abuse problems. Indeed, it is a great step forward that substance abuse disorders are now recognized as suitable for psychotherapeutic intervention. Even contemporary mental health professionals are likely to have had an educational background that casts the substance abuser as a poor candidate for psychotherapy. This view was fostered by a reluctance to tailor therapy to the problem of substance abuse. In particular, traditional psychotherapeutic approaches often failed because substance abuse was considered a symptom of another primary problem rather than a primary problem itself.

Theoretical Orientation of the Psychotherapist

As in other fields of psychotherapeutic endeavor, there is ongoing competition and dialogue among authorities of differing theoretical orientations toward therapy for the substance abuser. Yet, there seems to be a consensus in the literature that there can be no one approach to substance abuse problems. Most advocates of the various approaches, whether psychodynamic therapy (Wurmser, 1978), behavior therapy (Sobell & Sobell, 1978), or many others, view the techniques that they favor (and have worked hard to develop) as coexisting among alternative therapies that should be selectively available depending on the specific needs and preferences of individual clients. Ideally, as mentioned earlier, the match between therapy and client should be increasingly based on research findings if the notion of psychotherapy as an applied science is to have real meaning.

The theoretical orientation of a given psychotherapist can usually be described in one of three basic ways. First, there are certainly those therapists who claim *no theoretical orientation per se*. These therapists purport to work from intuition or experience, usually a combination of both. Such people are usually self-styled therapists and have minimal formal education, or, more rarely, have pursued a "gut-level" therapy after rejecting formal training. Of course, most trained therapists in this situation go on to develop their own theories or adopt the theories of authorities with whom they agree.

A second way to characterize the theoretical orientation of a psychotherapist is as *specific and fixed*. These therapists present themselves to the client and their colleagues as behavior therapists, gestalt therapists, psychoanalysts, or practitioners of some other specific therapeutic approach. Such people are likely to be well trained, although that is not necessarily so. They may have adopted their approach in a graduate school that emphasized one theoretical orientation to the exclusion of others. They may have attended an institute that taught the specific therapy, or they may have acquired their ideas and skills through personal study, perhaps supplemented by attendance at workshops.

A third way to describe the theoretical orientation of a psychotherapist is *eclectic*. Palmer (1980) has summarized the argument for an eclectic approach to theories of human behavior, mental health, and psychotherapy:

> Now that the science of human behavior is well over a century old, a student has the advantage of a variety of theories about the psychological functioning of the individual. It is my contention that the task of the current student of human behavior is not to choose among these theories but rather to be able to integrate the basic principles of each into a broad amalgam of theories. I call this selection of the essential features of the various theories about human behavior and their integration into a comprehensive theory eclecticism. (p. 6)

We agree with this position and propose that an eclectic theoretical framework for substance abuse psychotherapy provides the client with the best opportunity to receive help adequately considering the client's particular needs. Substance abuse is a complex phenomenon that is not adequately explained by any one theory. Westermeyer (1976) advocated an eclectic approach when he cautioned the therapist to avoid "(1) using only one model to understand all chemical dependency behavior and (2) employing only one model to all patients in lieu of collecting adequate clinical data and then applying models as clinically indicated" (p. 1).

Assessment is emphasized in the eclectic approach. Based on problems and dynamics presented by the client, a therapy plan is formulated by drawing on those theories and techniques that appear to constitute a good "fit" among the client's problem, the therapist's style of working, and the outcome sought. The therapist examines data collected during this crucial assessment phase and asks: *(a)* Which psychotherapeutic methods have been shown to be successful (in general) with this type of substance abuse problem (in general)? and *(b)* What modification should be made in these general methods in applying them to this particular client?

The eclectic therapist develops clinical techniques and decision-making skills through keeping abreast of research, participating in clinical conferences, and constantly seeking creative ways to maximize therapeutic effectiveness, given the resources and limitations of the specific practice situation. The eclectic professional feels free to learn from any discipline or "school" of therapy and purposely resists following leaders in the field who believe they have found the "one" way of working.

Some eclectic therapists choose to emphasize particular approaches, such as behavior therapy or transactional analysis; but according to Preisner (1980), it is not necessary to do so. Choosing an emphasis is one way to ensure that eclecticism does not become a superficial collection of diverse techniques applied on a "trial-and-error" basis. Some techniques are obviously contradictory and would lead to client confusion if applied together. The eclectic therapist is prepared to refer clients who have problems outside the therapist's expertise. As the education and experience of the therapist increase, the basis for effective eclectic practice becomes stronger.

Lazarus (1971) recommended that the eclectic therapist include, as relevant data to be considered in selecting the therapy, the client's directly or indirectly stated preferences for a particular type of therapy. Of course, the therapist should evaluate the degree to which a client's preferences indicate an accurate understanding of the problem of chemical dependency. It may be possible to help a client to see the advantages of therapeutic options that she or he has not considered. In any case, it is a good rule of thumb to present at least two alternatives for treatment to a client: whether these options are between approaches or settings for therapy may not be as important as the opportunity to participate in shaping the plan of care. Lazarus (1971) urged therapists not to fall into the trap of always pushing favorite techniques on clients no matter how resistant they may be.

Having completed our brief coverage of general issues in eclectic psychotherapy, we may now concentrate on specific approaches in substance abuse therapy. To consolidate the discussion, four major approaches to individual and group psychotherapy for substance abusers are identified—psychodynamic, cognitive-dynamic, behavioral, and humanistic (Belkin, 1980). Family approaches will be addressed separately as will social interventions, the disease concept, and crisis theory. In addition, we will briefly describe several of what Corsini (1981) has termed *innovative psychotherapies* and their potential application to substance abuse problems. The discussion provides an overview suitable for those interested in the therapies within or apart from the context of the eclectic approach. In either case, the discussion is not intended to be exhaustive but presents a general review of options in therapy.

Psychodynamic Approaches

Psychoanalysis is the classical psychodynamic approach. There are many adaptations of psychoanalysis that are psychodynamic in the sense that unconscious motivation is considered of prime importance in both symptom formation and therapy. There is a consensus among psychodynamic therapists concerned with alcoholism, opioid dependence, and polydrug dependence that the addict is fixated at the oral stage of psychosexual development (Adams, 1978; Forrest, 1983; Wurmser, 1978; Zimberg, 1985). Since the oral stage is the first stage of development in Freudian theory, chemical dependency is considered a "primitive" disturbance resulting in narcissistic tendencies. Narcissistic clients generally show an "overvaluation of the self or of others, a host of grandiose expectations, and an abysmal sense of frustration and letdown if these hopes are shattered" (Wurmser, 1978, p. 114). These intense affects are said to be narcissistic because their origin is traced to rejection or some other trauma occurring before clear boundaries between parent and child are established. Narcissistic clients are unable to differentiate accurately their emotions from those of others and have little capacity for meaningful empathy (Adams, 1978). The intense feelings of rage, guilt, anxiety, and depression, which cluster around the narcissistic conflict, call forth a number of defense mechanisms, including repression, denial, and compulsive substance abuse. In psychodynamic terms, substance abuse is often an effort to cope with extremely unpleasant and intense feelings. For example, cocaine addicts have been described as selecting their drugs of choice to find relief from "depression, self-esteem disturbances, impulsivity, acute and chronic dysphoria and cyclothymia" (Khantzian & Khantzian, 1984, p. 759).

Zimberg (1985) described a defense often seen in alcoholic clients, an intense need for grandiosity, called *reactive grandiosity,* which compensates for feelings of low self-worth and dependency. Alcoholism and reactive grandiosity are closely related because alcohol provides feelings of power and omnipotence. Denial plays a significant role in the association between alcoholism and reactive grandiosity. "Denial constitutes the main method by which alcoholics deal with life. They deny their feelings of inferiority, depression, lack of self-respect, and dependence on alcohol" (Chafetz, 1970, p. 10).

Most eclectic therapists recognize that unconscious motivation should be considered a factor in most severe substance abuse problems. This does not suggest that Freudian formulations are necessarily widely accepted. Whether unconscious material becomes a focus in therapy depends on several variables. The client's verbal ability and willingness to engage in insight-oriented therapy, the degree to which the history suggests early childhood trauma, and evidence of psychopathology continuing well beyond the withdrawal and detoxification period are some of the more important considerations. Of course, a clinician may proceed with therapy without a psychodynamic focus but still "pause" at times to help the client work through intense feelings in such a way that some insight is gained in terms of the destructive defenses involved in the substance abuse disorder. It is important to recognize there is danger in attempting to promote insight too quickly (Zimberg, 1985). Initial psychotherapeutic efforts should focus on shifting the client's energies toward constructive activities rather than deep introspection. Insight is best viewed as a long-term goal.

Most psychiatric nurses and other mental health professionals have a rather extensive background in psychodynamic theory, and many have learned that the addict is a poor candidate for psychodynamically focused therapy. Freud (1917/1972) described the "stone wall of narcissism" (p. 430), and Fenichel (1945) confirmed that people with character disorders, because of their ego-syntonic symptoms, are poor candidates for psychoanalysis. These ideas are changing slowly through the efforts of psychodynamic therapists who are experimenting with various new and classical techniques in their work with substance abusers.

Psychodynamic approaches are generally considered "intensive" and, in comparison to other therapies, are long-term (over a year), although brief psychodynamic therapies (less than a year) are becoming more acceptable to both clients and therapists. The one-to-one therapeutic experience is held in highest regard from a psychodynamic viewpoint, but some group and family applications are seen. In the treatment of addicts, the stereotype of the psychodynamic therapist as an uninvolved expert must be scrapped; the therapist should be warm, active, interested, questioning, available during crises—generally willing to show concern through action (Chafetz, 1970; Wurmser, 1978). Otherwise, the therapist will lose the client because needs for dependency and acceptance will not be met and because the addict tends to interpret distance as "not caring." Some therapists go so far as to say that the therapist must provide a substitute for alcohol or other drugs through support and involvement. Wurmser (1978) pointed out that too much involvement may constitute intrusion, so there is a need to exercise judgment in "getting involved."

A great deal of emphasis is placed on the transference and countertransference aspects of the relationship between client and therapist. The substance abuser will typically act out in the therapeutic relationship the full range of conflictual issues described earlier. The therapist can expect to be tested in several predictable ways. The client will be late for therapy or, at crucial times, not show up at all. She or he may come to therapy under the influence of psychoactive substances. There will be resistance to getting at significant problems and a tendency to discuss a flurry of superficial problems. At other times, especially during crises, the client will show marked dependence on the therapist.

The therapist can expect at times to have strong countertransference feelings of anger and frustration toward the client. It is necessary for the therapist to set limits, but a punitive response only confirms the substance abuser's feelings of inferiority and guilt. In the practice of psychodynamic therapy with alcoholics, an important step for the therapist in managing countertransference feelings is to recognize that she or he cannot have omnipotent control over the alcoholic's drinking (Zimberg, 1985). The same principle holds true for all kinds of substance abuse.

Psychodynamic therapists differ in the importance they place on abstinence as a prerequisite to therapy. Forrest (1983) and Zimberg (1985) contend that therapy for alcoholics is doomed to failure until drinking is terminated. Adams (1978) and Wurmser (1978), whose work has been primarily with clients having problems with drugs other than alcohol, do not place as great an emphasis on initial abstinence.

Adams (1978) described how therapists can use their feelings to encourage clients in the process of emotional growth. For instance, according to psychodynamic thinking (Spotnitz, 1969), if a therapist begins to have feelings of anger and irritation from an unidentified source, it may be worthwhile to explore the possibility that the client may have those feelings toward the thera-

pist but is communicating them in nonspecific ways. Bringing these feelings out in the open and handling them within the relationship is believed to be valuable in the psychodynamic therapy process.

Cognitive-Dynamic Approaches

Belkin (1980) identified three therapies under the rubric of cognitive-dynamic approaches: *reality therapy; rational-emotive therapy (RET);* and *transactional analysis (TA).* These psychotherapies share an attempt to assist "the individual's mobilization of logical faculties to overcome his or her emotional difficulties" (Belkin, 1980, p. 341).

Reality therapy is a sharp departure from traditional psychodynamic approaches. Therapy with a "reality" focus does not involve discussing the past, and the therapist is not looking for unconscious conflicts. Reality therapy, instead, emphasizes what is "right" or "wrong" for the client in the present and the possible consequences of actions in the near future. Substance abuse is not considered a mental illness but a set of behaviors having negative consequences for the client in the here and now. The addict is not viewed as helpless in his or her substance abuse; the reality therapy approach assumes the client is able to make choices and effect positive changes with the therapist's involvement (Bratter, 1976, Glasser, 1976).

RET relies extensively on what is called the *ABC hypothesis.* This hypothesis proposes that most dysfunctional human behavior and emotion may be traced to a basic cognitive process, described as follows. An activating event (A), for instance, criticism from a friend, is evaluated in relation to the person's belief system (B), which may include an irrational notion that criticism implies total rejection. The final step in this sequence is the emotional and behavioral consequences (C) to the interaction between A and B—perhaps for a person with alcoholic tendencies, it is to feel depressed and begin drinking (Ellis, 1979; 1985). RET helps the client evaluate and make appropriate changes in an irrational and self-destructive belief system.

TA has more links to psychodynamic theory than do reality therapy or RET. It is believed that within the TA framework, much can be gained in therapy by focusing on the basic unit of social interaction, the transaction. Each person responds in each transaction in one of three ego states: Parent, Adult, or Child. The Parent responds to a transaction from a position of authority and tradition, the Adult is rational and reality-bound, and the Child operates solely on the basis of feelings and impulse. A person's life is viewed as a series of transactions; sets of transactions with identifiable patterns are seen as "games"; and a life adjustment built around the playing of a particular game is termed a *script*. TA additionally describes interpersonal relationships in terms of the four possible life positions: I'm not O.K.—you're O.K.; I'm not O.K.—you're not O.K.; I'm O.K.—you're not O.K.; I'm O.K.—you're O.K. (Dusay & Dusay, 1979).

Steiner (1971, 1979) has applied TA to alcoholism and has identified three alcoholic games. In each of these games, the alcoholic transacts from the "I'm not O.K.—you're O.K." position. "Drunk and Proud" (D & P) is a game in which the alcoholic will frustrate anyone who tries to help. The drinker playing "Lush" is always looking for help. "Wino" is played by the addict who is choosing substance abuse as a means toward self-destruction and suicide. TA as therapy seeks to break up these alcoholic games.

The cognitive-dynamic approaches are effective in helping substance abusers understand their behavior in a straightforward fashion. These approaches appeal to American values of practicality, optimism, common sense, and freedom to choose. When an assessment indicates that a client is involved in a pattern of poor judgment associated with aversive consequences from school, work, or the legal system, reality therapy should be considered. For clients with irrational belief systems leading to depression or anxiety and involving substance abuse to ease resulting emotional pain, RET is an alternative to psychodynamic approaches.

TA is an approach that has been popularized by several bestsellers, and most clients will benefit from at least thinking about their "games" and the role of substance abuse in their social interactions. The everyday language of TA is extremely helpful to the therapist in discussing with a client issues of internal and interpersonal dynamics.

Bratter (1976) listed seven components of reality therapy: involvement, examination of current behavior, evaluation of behavior, planning responsible behavior, requiring a commitment in the form of a verbal or written contract, accepting no excuses, and no punishment under any circumstances. The goal is to foster a success identity for the client. Bratter (1976) proposed that group approaches are superior to one-to-one relationships in substance abuse because peers are able to

reinforce and support the therapist's work along the lines of the seven components listed. Groups are especially helpful in encouraging and reinforcing responsible behavior. The principles of reality therapy are particularly appropriate for psychotherapy with adolescent clients.

RET is essentially a didactic approach assisting the client in rejecting self-defeating beliefs through a process of cognitive self-analysis. Role playing can be used to identify irrational expectations that the client holds for him- or herself. The therapist may use humor to expose to the client the absurdity of these irrational beliefs. In addition, the therapeutic relationship demonstrates to the client that acceptance from others does not depend on living according to unrealistic and previously unquestioned self-expectations (Ellis, 1979, 1985). At the point in both reality therapy and RET at which the client is ready to change actual behavior, procedures from behavior therapy are often effective. Such a combination of approaches is often described as *cognitive-behavior therapy* (CBT) (Kendall, 1982; McCourt & Glantz, 1980; Persons, 1989). CBT is discussed in the following section on behavioral approaches.

In the application of TA in alcoholism psychotherapy, Steiner (1971) believes that "group treatment is a far more potent approach than individual, one-to-one therapy" (p. 103). However, the therapist should be willing to meet individually with a client during crises or when there is an indication that work can be done that cannot be accomplished in the group.

As in reality therapy, a contract is considered essential in TA to create leverage in the therapeutic relationship. Abstaining from alcohol is a necessary condition of the contract, although Steiner (1979) has found that some of his clients can begin moderate drinking after extended TA. He believes that alcoholism can be "healed" in the sense that alcoholics can, with the aid of TA, give up the alcoholic script. Disulfiram is reported to be helpful to clients who desire it in maintaining abstinence; however, Steiner (1979) stated that it should not be a forced condition of treatment. A clear benefit of the contract is that the client agrees to work in therapy and "Rescue" transactions are minimized. A "Rescue" plays into the alcoholic game by implying "I'm O.K.—you're not O.K.; therefore, I must save you." When a Rescue fails, as it inevitably does with the substance abuser, the therapist becomes angry and then takes the role of "Persecutor," confirming that the client is indeed "not O.K."

In the TA group, the therapist works with the alcoholic script, which "implies helping people to get rid of the injunctions, attributions, and destructive internal dialogues that originate within them, in their Enemy" (Steiner, 1979, p. 158). The "Enemy" is akin to the concept of the irrational and self-defeating belief system central to RET. The Enemy is usually a critical self-message on the order of "you're no good" or "you're stupid" and is closely allied to feelings of guilt, shame, fear, and low self-esteem. In TA, the Enemy is identified, attacked, and separated from the "true" self through the techniques of exposure, confrontation, and nurturing. See Steiner (1979) for a detailed explanation of these techniques in action. Alcoholics may have the injunction, "Don't have fun," from the Enemy; Fun therapy is a TA technique that may help to stimulate sources of joy in the client's life (Brockman, 1979).

Behavioral Approaches

Behavioral therapies are prescribed procedures designed to modify specific behaviors under certain environmental conditions. These procedures have their theoretical roots in experimental psychology and learning theory. They have been widely applied to substance abuse problems of all kinds and are much more diverse than the reinforcement procedures that most people think of in association with behavior modification. A major trend is the combination of several behavioral procedures and cognitive techniques in individual or group therapy—the so-called *broad-spectrum* approach.

Behavior therapists tend to view psychopathology in terms of behavioral deficits and excesses. Substance abusers obviously have a problem with excessive consumption of psychoactive drugs. However, deficits in coping behaviors, particularly problem-solving skills, are also common among substance abusers. The broad-spectrum approaches use some procedures to limit undesirable behavioral excesses and others to increase desirable behaviors that are lacking. Also, since anxiety is thought to trigger many substance abuse episodes, techniques that inhibit anxiety may be used, including relaxation and assertion. Behavior therapy along these lines depends on a comprehensive assessment of baseline behaviors, usually referred to as a *behavior analysis*. Once the baseline behaviors, including antecedents and consequences, have been documented, it is appropriate to discuss behavior change with the client and arrive at a contract for specific goals in therapy. In substance abuse treatment, the assessment focuses on substance use patterns, and the contract will specify procedures to assist in controlling or eliminating the problem behaviors.

Aversion procedures are usually designed to eliminate substance use behaviors. Overt aversion therapies are discussed later in a separate section. A type of aversion therapy depending only on psychotherapeutic intervention is *covert sensitization*. Cautela (1970) pioneered in this approach and described it as follows:

In the covert sensitization procedure, the client is instructed to imagine he is about to engage in the maladaptive behavior. Then he is instructed to imagine that he is receiving a noxious stimulus (usually the feeling of nausea and vomiting). The procedure is labeled covert sensitization because both the behavior to be modified and the noxious stimulus are presented in imagination. (p. 415)

In this procedure's treatment of smoking the client is asked to visualize smoking behavior paired with nausea and vomiting. This approach will only be effective with those clients who are able to produce through imagination a genuine feeling of revulsion. In addition, the client is instructed to imagine situations in which the unpleasant feelings are eliminated as soon as smoking behavior is stopped. Thus, the client learns to avoid smoking and experiences reinforcement while maintaining the avoidance response. A number of studies (reviewed in Cautela & Rosenstiel, 1975) have demonstrated that covert sensitization can be an effective technique for treating adolescent and adult clients with a variety of substance abuse problems. However, research examining the relative efficacy of covert sensitization and overt aversion (rapid smoking) found the overt procedure to achieve significantly superior results (Barbarin, 1978).

Behavioral approaches developed to assist clients in controlling their drinking, as opposed to abstaining from alcohol (Sobell & Sobell, 1978) have stirred a major and ongoing controversy in the alcoholism treatment field. O'Leary and Wilson (1987) give a fair and detailed account of this controversy from their perspective as behavior therapists. The controlled drinking versus abstinence debate began when Sobell and Sobell (1973) reported favorable results from an experiment designed to test the effectiveness of a controlled-drinking approach, *individualized behavior therapy (IBT)*, in comparison to a traditional approach. The controversy was heightened with the publication of a 10-year follow-up of the 20 IBT participants in Sobell and Sobell's (1978) experiment. The follow-up report (Pendery, Maltzman, & West, 1982) presented an extremely unfavorable picture of the long-term outcome for the IBT participants. Sobell and Sobell (1984) responded in part by pointing out that the long-term outcome for the abstinence-oriented comparison group had been no better, perhaps worse.

As for the future of controlled-drinking approaches, much depends on advances in assessment, which will clearly differentiate those clients who have manageable drinking problems from those who are alcoholic. It is now widely acknowledged that a goal of controlled drinking for alcoholics is not only unrealistic, it poses serious safety concerns and ethical issues.

One broad-spectrum behavioral approach developed specifically for nonindependent problem drinkers, *behavioral and self-control treatment (BSCT)* (Miller, 1983; Miller & Hester, 1980) shows much promise for broad application outside the context of treatment for alcoholism. The techniques used draw heavily on the approach pioneered by Sobell and Sobell (1978). O'Leary and Wilson (1987) described BSCT as including "self-monitoring of alcohol use, setting appropriate goals for drinking, self-reinforcement of safe drinking, and training in alternative coping skills to be used in situations which previously had triggered excessive drinking" (p. 307). A review of the research literature on the effectiveness of BSCT and similar approaches shows documented success in decreasing drinking among early-stage problem drinkers (O'Leary & Wilson, 1987).

A cognitive behavior therapy (CBT) approach that has broad application to alcoholics and those seeking help for other forms of substance abuse is a relapse management strategy developed by Marlatt (1978; Marlatt & Gordon, 1985). The approach is based on a cognitive-behavioral analysis of the relapse process and the "loss of control" phenomenon. According to this notion of relapse, rather than an actual inevitable urge to continue using the drug after a "slip," loss of control begins with the addict's sense of failure at the violation of abstinence. In other words, Marlatt (1978; Marlatt & Gordon, 1985) is challenging the idea that "one drink automatically means a drunk."

This approach includes a number of techniques specifically designed to help clients deal with high-risk situations and to manage a "slip" should it occur. Self-monitoring, problem-solving skills training, relaxation, stress management procedures to increase feelings of well-being and self-control, and learning strategies to cope with the negative feelings and "loss of control" experienced when and if abstinence is violated are all components of the approach. The client is provided a wallet-sized card to carry at all times in case of abstinence violation. The client is instructed by the card to stop after the first drink and to consider *(a)* a single slip is not an indication of failure; *(b)* the feelings of failure probably felt will pass—there is no need to give in to the feelings to take another drink; and *(c)* the slip at this early stage can be viewed as a learning experience—it can provide valuable information about what constitutes a high-risk situation and stimulate ideas for coping in the future. Finally, the client is urged to call the therapist (a backup number is also provided) if she or he is having difficulty resisting the urge to continue drinking (Marlatt, 1978; Marlatt & Gordon, 1985).

Assertiveness training is one of the behavior therapies designed to indirectly inhibit substance abuse behavior by helping clients learn new coping styles incompatible with substance abuse.

> We propose that by providing unassertive alcoholics with the social and interpersonal skills necessary to cope more effectively with their environment they will have less of a need to resort to self-anesthetization and escape from everyday life experiences. If alcoholics are taught alternative behavior to drinking as a vehicle for emotional expression, they might be able to decrease their drinking and lead a more comfortable and rewarding life. (Hirsch, von Rosenberg, Phelan, & Dudley, 1978)

Role playing is a primary feature of assertiveness training, in which clients have opportunities to observe the modeling of assertive behavior and practice it (Gareri, 1979). Assertiveness implies honest expression of both positive and negative feelings, including affection, praise, anger, and dissatisfaction, without excessive anxiety. The therapist helps the group learn ways of expressing these feelings within the bounds of what is socially acceptable and in a manner that communicates a respect for the rights of others.

Humanistic Approaches

Humanistic therapies view the client phenomenologically in the present, without attempts to reduce his or her problems to conflicts, games, or faulty social learning. Humanistic therapy is essentially a process of self-discovery, facilitated by an encounter or series of encounters between client and therapist. Above all, humanistic approaches urge the client to experience life, with its full potential for both joy and pain, and to accept responsibility for his or her choices.

Client-centered, or Rogerian therapy, developed by Carl Rogers (1942), has had an enormous impact on psychotherapy and counseling. Most of the basic principles of so-called "therapeutic interaction" learned by nursing students have their roots in Rogerian theory. Although this approach offers few specific applications in the treatment of substance abuse problems, the therapist's ability to demonstrate unconditional positive regard, empathy, and genuineness are generally recognized as essential in any helping relationship.

Gestalt therapy has been specifically applied to alcoholic clients in group work (Boylin, 1975). Dramatic techniques are used to encourage the client to experience him- or herself in the moment and to accept responsibility for drinking or not drinking. Perls (1947), originator of gestalt therapy, described the alcoholic as involved in a self-destructive pattern of "retroflection." In gestalt terms, this means that the alcoholic gives up all attempts to influence his or her life and prefers the risk-free position of victim. Thus, gestalt therapists challenge alcoholics when they blame others for their problem or speak fatalistically of their problems with alcohol. The group is a here-and-now encounter in which the clients are encouraged to experiment with new behavior and discover themselves as feeling people. "Why" questions are avoided in favor of "how" statements. For instance, to a client who poses the question, "Why did this have to happen to me?" the gestalt therapist would likely respond, "How are you feeling *now,* at this moment?" Boylin (1975) has found that alcoholics exhibit considerable fear when asked to engage in gestalt experiences, which involve expression of feelings. He described alcoholics as feeling phobic; "staying with a feeling" to the point of exaggeration is one method of desensitizing this fear.

Logotherapy is a humanistic approach originated by Frankl (1963) on the premise that the most important value in human experience is "meaning." It is considered an existential therapy because it, like gestalt therapy, emphasizes responsibility and also makes special efforts to acknowledge the spiritual and philosophic vacuum that many people experience in modern life. Holmes (1979), a logotherapist, referred to the alcoholic as "doubly sick," in the sense that she or he drinks because of an existential vacuum or spiritual sickness, and then experiences an outcome of also being physiologically sick. In short:

> Alcohol is a spurious answer to the religious quest, but the quest must be taken seriously. Hence the appropriateness of logotherapy—a psychotherapy which not only recognizes man's spirit, but actually starts from it. (Holmes, 1979, p. 244)

Similarly, Light (1986) stated that "spiritual isolation and impoverishment is probably the single most important factor in the genesis of alcoholism" (p. 109). Logotherapy seeks to affirm to the alcoholic that the human questions troubling him or her are indeed real but that alcohol is not the answer. There are four aspects of meaning that concern the alcoholic, as well as other people: *(1)* Is there a discernible pattern in life and how do I fit in? *(2)* Who am I? *(3)* What is the purpose of my life? *(4)* What should I do with my life? Logotherapy assists the client in responding to these questions and in discovering a new purpose in life, one that is incompatible with alcoholism. Participation in Alcoholics Anonymous (AA) is encouraged by logotherapists as one avenue toward finding "creative content" for the alcoholics' existential vacuum (Holmes, 1979).

Logotherapy has also been used with opioid addicts and polydrug abusers (Fraiser, 1979; Lukas, 1979). Lukas (1979) recognized that the search for meaning cannot go on during compulsive substance abuse and therefore believes that logotherapy should begin after more immediate approaches, such as behavioral procedures, have helped the client achieve abstinence. She also stated that the logotherapist strives to communicate a deep trust in the humanity of the client.

> From everything the therapist does must emanate a deep conviction that behind all that chemistry that can be treated, and all those psychological forces that can be manipulated, stands a human spirit that can be appealed to. (Lukas, 1979, p. 267)

This statement crystallizes the humanistic perspective in psychotherapy.

Family Approaches

Psychodynamic, cognitive-dynamic, behavioral, and humanistic principles and techniques are certainly applied in family therapy; however, there is a particular view toward the client that makes family approaches considerably different from anything discussed so far. That is, family therapists typically view the family unit as the client. The family as a system and a unit of study is elucidated in Chapter 20. Another perspective on family therapy in the treatment of alcoholism is provided by Brolsma (1986).

Family approaches are equally concerned with the impact of substance abuse on all family members—not just on the member who is the abuser. For example, Berenson (1976) stated that the "main leverage in a system where one spouse drinks excessively is the non-drinking spouse" (p. 292). Working with a cooperating family member to change the behavior of an uncooperative member has been termed unilateral family therapy (Thomas & Santa, 1982). Using Berenson's (1976) approach, the nondrinking spouse is helped to mobilize efforts away from controlling the alcoholic and toward becoming self-directed. This action leads the alcoholic to "hit bottom" and finally stop drinking. The second phase involves helping the family come closer together again but without the resumption of drinking. Abstinence leaves a void in the system until new patterns of functioning can be established. AA and Al-Anon may provide an effective complement to family therapy during this phase.

Bowen (1978) also emphasized the importance of focusing initial family therapy on the least impaired members:

> The therapy is directed at the family member, or members, with the most resourcefulness, who have the most potential for modifying his or her own functioning. When it is possible to modify the family relationship system, the alcoholic dysfunction is alleviated, even though the dysfunctional one may not have been part of the therapy. (p. 262)

When both spouses are alcoholics, the best approach is to work with either during "dry" periods (Berenson, 1976).

Family therapy approaches vary, depending on the theoretical orientation of the therapist (some are quite different from the "systems" approach just described). These variations cannot be elaborated here. A concise introduction to the field by Foley (1986) is highly recommended. Family approaches may include all the members of a family, spouses only, members from several different families in one group (multiple family therapy), or, as described, only one member of a family, who wishes to be an agent of change in the family in which the other members refuse to participate.

A national survey of drug abuse treatment agencies found that 93% of the 2012 respondents provided some kind of family therapy to clients (Coleman & Davis, 1978). Multiple substance abuse, including alcoholism, was reported as common in the families served. It was also found that opioid addicts received less family therapy than did clients with low-opioid involvement. The agencies surveyed were eager to have their staffs learn more about family approaches—the greatest need was in methadone clinics. Stanton and Todd (1982) reported success in increasing the number of drug-free days for heroin addicts with family therapy as compared to traditional treatment methods. They described the typical family structure for young heroin addicts to be composed of a very dependent mother-son (addict) dyad with a distant father. Effective family interventions focused on strengthening the parental system such that the father began to exercise parental authority in the relationship with his son. Keeping the parents working together was a major challenge in these families.

Social Interventions

Regardless of the psychotherapeutic approach chosen for a given client or group of clients, a sociologic perspective adds potency to substance abuse therapy. From the sociologic view, most chronic and serious substance abuse problems, particularly alcohol or opioid dependence syndromes, represent failures in normal socialization (Martindale & Martindale, 1971). In this sense, drug addiction has been described as a *deviant career* (Rubington, 1967).

Comprehensive treatment of the client includes recognizing the social significance of the deviant career and developing therapeutic strategies to promote normal socialization. In hospital treatment, the day-to-day interactions of staff and clients provide a setting in which problems in socialization can emerge and be improved. In the community, self-help groups and residential programs, such as halfway houses for alcoholics and therapeutic communities for opioid addicts, emphasize resocialization.

It is often unrealistic to expect the client to make changes in his or her social situation without the therapist's active intervention. For example, the therapist may be an advocate for the client in seeking vocational rehabilitation, finding employment opportunities, or locating a self-help group. The therapist may insist the family become involved in education about substance abuse, self-help groups for family members, family therapy, or a combination of these.

In focusing psychotherapy on the client's outside relationships, it is common to assign "homework." For instance, for a client who is ready to begin employment, the therapist may help the client rehearse approaching potential employers. An assignment may be given to engage in at least one job interview before the next therapy session. When such an assignment is given, it is of great importance to ask the client to share the outcome at the beginning of the next session. This will provide reinforcement for the desired behavior, communicate positive regard for the client, and show that the therapist is indeed serious about making links between the therapy relationship and resocialization.

The Disease Concept

The disease concept of alcoholism (Jellinek, 1960), now widely applied to addictions in general, has had a profound influence on the psychotherapies tailored to substance abuse problems. The belief that addiction is a progressive disease, with significant physiologic or genetic etiologic factors, is a guiding assumption for many treatment programs and psychotherapists. Thus, the disease concept becomes the background for several themes in psychotherapy. Clients are often told that they are unable to tolerate psychoactive substance use without eventual dependence. The defect in the chemically dependent person's biologic make-up is often described as analogous to diabetes—the diabetic must avoid sugars to stay well and the chemically dependent person must avoid psychoactive drug use to maintain health. Psychotherapy with this background of beliefs tends to generate discussion of frustration at being unable to use psychoactive substances in a society that is saturated with them. Emphasis is placed on finding alternatives to drug use for relaxation or socializing. Self-help group participation is consistent with this approach and assists the client in accepting the problem as chronic, without cure, and, eventually, as the basis for self-understanding and personal growth. Chapter 19 includes a discussion of how professional and self-help therapies may be integrated for the benefit of the client participating in both.

Crisis Theory

It is a rare occurrence when a substance abuser seeks help because of a vague existential despair or anxiety. These clients typically come to treatment following a crisis of some sort, usually involving a combination of incidents with dire implications for their physical and/or psychosocial well-being. This being the case, the early work of Lindemann (1944) and, later, the contributions of Caplan (1964) to crisis intervention and theory have not been missed by substance abuse therapists. Of particular interest has been the help-seeking behavior that people predictably demonstrate during a crisis and the potential for behavioral change inherent in the disorganization of crisis.

Studies of alcoholics have shown that by meeting the need for a helping relationship during a medical crisis, a favorable predisposition toward psychotherapy may be achieved (Chafetz et al., 1970a; Chafetz et al., 1970b). The success of many of the "street" clinics for young drug abusers during the 1960s and 1970s was due in large part to their crisis intervention approach.

Crisis intervention has been taken in an interesting direction by Johnson (1980) at the Johnson Institute in Minnesota. It was folk wisdom in the alcoholism field for many years that the alcoholic had to "hit bottom" before seeking treatment. Johnson's (1980) creative approach to "confrontation" and crisis creation has dramatically changed this notion. If the chemically dependent person still has significant others—family, employer, or close friends—their influence can be brought to bear in creating a crisis for therapeutic gain.

The first step in the creation of a crisis is forming a coalition between the therapist and at least three or four significant others. Family members and employers will usually have the most influence on the alcoholic or polydrug abuser. She or he is asked to meet at a certain place at an appointed time but is not given the reason for the meeting. Whether the employer or the family calls the meeting, the principles for intervention are essentially the same. The person of concern is asked to listen and to continue listening to what will be said even though it may be difficult to do so. At this point, each family member, or the supervisor if it is an employer confrontation, presents specific substance abuse-related behaviors that have caused problems and concern. The confronted person may offer protests, but it becomes difficult to maintain denial in the presence of support and an accounting of specific incidents. The influence of the family members or other meaningful people makes the confrontation an emotionally powerful experience. The goal is to show "deep concern" and exert some leverage on the potential client to seek treatment. A discussion of alternatives and plans for treatment should be thoroughly pursued before the meeting is terminated. Detailed examples of this kind of confrontation are included in Johnson's books (1980, 1988).

Innovative Approaches

An interesting book to appear on the psychotherapy scene is the *Handbook of Innovative Psychotherapies,* edited by Corsini (1981). Practitioners described 64 little-known and little-understood approaches, including meditation, poetry therapy, art therapy, actualizing therapy, natural high therapy, and rebirthing. It is worth noting that substance abuse treatment applications abound in this text. Evidence of the usefulness of innovative techniques as adjuncts to traditional substance abuse therapies has been reported in the literature. Mazza (1979) found poetry useful in stimulating discussion of feelings in group therapy with alcoholics. Responding to the lyrics of popular music may be helpful in establishing communication with adolescent clients (Santiago, 1969). Natural high therapy has been applied as a group and an individual approach in the treatment of opioid addiction (Croce, 1979).

There are three "levels" of intervention in natural high therapy: intrapersonal behavior (level 1); interpersonal behavior (level 2); and transcendental humanism (level 3). Natural highs are found through freeing the self of low self-esteem and the need to be perfect (level 1), developing positive mutual cooperation (level 2), and discovering the transcendent human experience through relaxation, meditation, or other nondrug methods (level 3). Natural high therapy recognizes the human "desire to achieve altered states of consciousness where one feels good about himself and others" (Croce, 1979, p. 20).

OVERT AVERSION THERAPIES

The overt aversion therapies involve pairing a noxious stimulus with substance abuse behavior, the goal being to decrease the behavior and eventually eliminate it altogether. In classical conditioning terms, the noxious stimulus is the *unconditioned stimulus* (UCS) because it will elicit an aversive reaction from the client without prior learning. The *conditioned stimulus* (CS) is represented by the substance of abuse. The repeated association of the UCS and the CS will result in an aversive reaction from the client when the CS is presented alone. Aversion therapy has been extensively used in the treatment of alcoholism and smoking, although not without considerable controversy. Rachman and Teasdale (1969) proposed a position on aversion therapy that we view as reasonable:

> Aversion therapy should only be offered if other treatment methods are inapplicable or unsuccessful *and* if the patient gives his permission after a consideration of all the information which his therapist can honestly supply. . . . The substitution of effective, but less unpleasant, alternative methods of treatment should be carried out as soon as this becomes feasible. (p. 174)

Chemical Aversion Therapy

Lemere and Voegtlin (1950) pioneered in the application of chemical aversion techniques in the treatment of chronic alcoholism at the Shadel Sanatorium in Seattle (currently Schick's Shadel Hospital). During a period of 15 years, in which they treated over 4000 alcoholics, a protocol for the treatment was developed through systematic follow-up studies. The current protocol for chemical aversion therapy at Schick's Shadel Hospital is described as follows:

> Briefly, the chemical method consists of five individual treatment sessions during which the sight, smell and taste of alcohol are paired with nausea induced in the patient by means of an intramuscular injection of emetine. After an intensive conditioning session of 20 to 30 minutes, the patient is returned to his room, whereupon he receives an oral dose of emetine in an alcohol solution which induces a slower-acting residual nausea lasting up to 3 hours. Thus, the patient

receiving chemical aversion therapy is conditioned for up to a total of 15 hours during the 10-day course of his initial treatment. (Jackson & Smith, 1978, p. 187)

To undergo this treatment, the client must be highly motivated and physically able to withstand repeated vomiting. Aversion therapy is the primary treatment modality at Schick's Shadel Hospital, but Pentothal interviews (psychiatric interviews while the client is under the influence of the drug), nursing care, medical services, psychiatric consultation, alcohol education, and access to counseling are also important aspects of the total program. Chemical aversion therapy is becoming increasingly available to middle- to upper-class alcoholics through the opening of Schick units in several cities and the adoption of the treatment by other private hospitals.

Bandura (1969) presented the results of ten outcome studies of clients who participated in chemical aversion therapy for alcoholism; six of the studies reported abstinence rates of higher than 50%. Another review of relevant research (Lemere & Voegtilin, 1950; Neubuerger, Hasha, Matarazzo, Schmitz, & Pratt, 1981; Wiens & Menustick, 1983; Wiens, Montague, Manaugh, & English, 1976) concluded that "patients who do well following chemical aversion therapy are married, socially stable, and of middle-class or higher socioeconomic status; they also have intact jobs and sufficient motivation to stay sober to expose themselves to an unpleasant treatment experience" (U. S. Department of Health and Human Services, 1987, p. 216).

Electric Aversion Therapy

Electric aversion procedures were ignored for many years in the United States because of the success reported from chemical methods. However, in the 1960s there was renewed interest in electric shock as an aversive stimulus because it is readily controlled by the therapist, less expensive than chemical methods, and is applicable to a broader group of alcoholics (clients with gastric problems or heart disease should not receive the chemical method). This method of treatment, electric shock paired with a variety of drinking behaviors, was adopted by many Veterans Administration hospitals (Sansweet, 1975). In 1970, Schick's Shadel Hospital adopted the electric technique as an alternative for those clients "physically unqualified for the rigorous chemi-

cal method" (Jackson & Smith, 1978, p. 187). However, research has not shown the electric method to be as effective as chemical aversion therapy (U. S. Department of Health and Human Services, 1987).

Rapid Smoking

Interest in electric aversion for smoking has been minimal because of the success of another aversive technique, *rapid smoking* (O'Leary & Wilson, 1987). In rapid smoking therapy, the client smokes the preferred brand of cigarette in a prescribed rapid fashion. Cigarettes are smoked at an average rate of one puff every 6 seconds until the client is unable to continue. The therapy environment is often saturated with cigarette advertisements and heaps of foul-smelling cigarette butts and ashes. Electric shocks may be administered during smoking but are not considered an essential part of rapid smoking treatment.

Although rapid smoking is consistently turning up in study after study as the most effective behavioral cessation treatment, there is concern about its health risks (Franks & Wilson, 1980). Rapid smoking leads to high blood levels of nicotine and carboxyhemoglobin, which is a basis for considering that the technique poses at least some risk to all but the young and healthy (Russell, Raw, Taylor, Feyerabend, & Saloojee, 1978). However, O'Leary and Wilson's (1987) review of the research literature on rapid smoking found no reports of serious consequences associated with the treatment. Most at risk are people with diagnosed coronary arterial disease and people over 35, particularly men, who may have an existing, undetected cardiac condition.

NONPHARMACOLOGIC SOMATOTHERAPIES

Westermeyer (1976) identified three nonpharmacologic somatotherapies: *biofeedback, electrosleep,* and *acupuncture.* These treatments have not as yet attracted much interest from clinicians. However, the potential effectiveness of those somatic approaches continues to be investigated from time to time.

Electrosleep and Acupuncture

Electrosleep involves the passage of low-voltage electric current through the head—this should not be confused with electroconvulsive therapy, which uses a high-voltage current. The client is asked to lie supine, with eyes closed, and is given instructions to relax or attempt to fall asleep. In some clients, the combination of low-voltage current and a restful environment with instructions to relax or sleep has the effect of producing a state of relaxation or sense of well-being. This therapeutic effect is often desirable for a client who is experiencing anxiety or insomnia during the early stages of recovery (Westermeyer, 1976).

Perhaps the reason for so little enthusiasm about the application of electrosleep to substance abuse treatment is that its effect does not appear to be any more dramatic in producing relaxation than the behavioral procedures mentioned earlier. A negative factor in electrosleep not present in behavioral relaxation procedures is the reliance on an external "gadget" to achieve a feeling that most people can reach on their own. This is of particular importance in treating substance abuse because looking for an external "fix" for anxiety is a major feature of the problem.

Acupuncture is a Chinese system of therapy that appears to have some application in substance abuse treatment (Jackson, 1988). Its primary use has been with opioid addicts in Asia and the United States to produce sedation during withdrawal and achieve relaxation during recovery. A recent study of recidivist alcoholics showed acupuncture to significantly decrease drinking episodes and admissions for detoxification as compared to a control group (Bullock, Culliton, & Orlander, 1989), and acupuncture has already been tried as a treatment for crack addiction (Kerr, 1988).

An expert trained in the acupuncture method (many states have formal credentialing mechanisms for determining the qualifications of a practitioner) places needles in prescribed body areas for sedation and relaxation (Westermeyer, 1976). It is difficult to predict the future application of acupuncture in substance abuse treatment in the United States because of incomplete research and cultural barriers to the technique.

In conclusion, electrosleep and acupuncture may provide some clients with needed relaxation and sedation during very early recovery when ability to learn behavioral techniques is impaired; however, in the long term, clinical experience and research findings have yet to show these therapies to be superior to behavioral relaxation procedures.

Biofeedback

"Biofeedback is a therapeutic method of forming information loops that allows the patient, the therapist, or both to observe and modify internal psychophysiological events while they are in process" (Forgione & Holmberg, 1981, p. 79). It is the use of technology to teach the substance abuser to "know himself or herself" psychophysiologically, rather than using technology as a psychophysiologic "fix," that makes biofeedback a promising somatotherapy. In fact, some health professionals would say biofeedback is essentially a psychotherapy for this reason, but we prefer to think of it as a somatotherapy because of the technology involved and its emphasis on the body.

One promising study of alcoholics who had participated in 10 hours of alpha biofeedback training found that trainees had significantly lower levels of anxiety than controls immediately after treatment (Passini, Watson, Dehnel, Herder, & Watkins, 1977) and 18 months later (Watson, Herder, & Passini, 1978). Also, in the follow-up study, there was some indication that alpha training may have been associated with reduction in alcohol consumption.

Electronic instrumentation in biofeedback allows a client to become aware of one or more of the following: tension or relaxation in muscles (electromyographic feedback); pulse rate and blood pressure (cardiovascular feedback); the amount of alpha waves as indicated by the electroencephalogram; and/or amount of perspiration on the skin (galvanic skin response). When relaxation is achieved, the instrumentation produces a stimulus, such as a specific tone, to provide the client his or her "feedback."

SUMMARY

This chapter discussed treatment settings and professionally administered therapies for substance abuse problems. A biopsychosocial perspective, relying on current research-based knowledge and clinical judgment, was recommended to guide assessment and treatment planning. The pharmacotherapies have clear limitations for clients whose primary problem is drug-focused; however, it is also counterproductive to withhold from clients drugs that have therapeutic potential because of an ideology to remain "chemical-free." In any case, the pharmacotherapies appear to be most effective if used in combination with psychotherapies. Psychotherapists may operate without a clear theoretical orientation to therapy, a specific and fixed orientation, or an eclectic orientation. The eclectic approach seems, in our view, most helpful to clients because we believe that no one approach is right for all clients (or therapists, for that matter). This approach was discussed, and descriptions of the use of various approaches in substance abuse psychotherapy were given. Aversion therapy, usually a combination of pharmacotherapy or electric shock and psychologic techniques, seems to be helpful to a limited population of substance abusers. Although nonpharmacologic somatotherapies are presently not widely applicable to substance abuse treatment, some research continues to be done in this area. In view of the many alternatives in substance abuse therapy discussed, treatment programs and clinicians in office practice are well advised to develop mechanisms in the assessment process that will help to effectively match clients and therapies.

REFERENCES

Abroms, E. M. (1983). Beyond eclecticism. *American Journal of Psychiatry, 140*(6), 740–745.

Adams, J. W. (1978). *Psychoanalysis of drug dependence: The understanding and treatment of a particular form of pathological narcissism.* New York: Grune & Stratton.

Bandura, A. (1969). *Principles of behavior modification.* New York: Holt.

Barbarin, O. A. (1978). Comparison of symbolic and overt aversion in the self-control of smoking. *Journal of Consulting and Clinical Psychology, 46,* 1569–1571.

Bast, R. J. (1984). *Classifications of alcoholism treatment settings* (DHHS Pub. No. ADM 84–1324). Rockville, MD: National Institute on Alcohol Abuse and Alcoholism.

Becker, C. E., Roe, R., Scott, R., Tong, T., Boerner, V., & Luce, J. (1975). Rational drug therapy of alcoholism with sedative hypnotic drugs! Is this possible? *Annals of the New York Academy of Sciences, 252,* 379–384.

Belkin, G. S. (1980). *Contemporary psychotherapies.* Chicago: Rand McNally.

Berenson, D. (1976). Alcohol and the family system. In P. J. Guerin (Ed.), *Family therapy: Theory and practice* (pp. 284–297). New York: Gardner Press.

Bissell, L. (1975). The treatment of alcoholism: What do we do about long-term sedatives? *Annals of the New York Academy of Sciences, 252,* 396–399.

Bowden, C. L., & Maddox, J. F. (1972). Methadone maintenance: Myth and reality. *American Journal of Psychiatry, 128,* 853–856.

Bowen, M. (1978). *Family therapy in clinical practice.* New York: Jason Aronson.

Boylin, E. R. (1975). Gestalt encounter in the treatment of hospitalized alcoholic patients. *American Journal of Psychotherapy, 29*(4), 524–534.

Bratter, T. E. (1976). A group approach with adolescent alcoholics. In A. Bassin, T. E. Bratter, & R. L. Rachin (Eds.), *The reality therapy reader* (pp. 296–312). New York: Harper & Row.

Brockman, J. (1979). Getting high in an alcohol treatment unit. *Transactional Analysis Journal, 9*(4), 305.

Brolsma, J. K. (1986). Family therapy in the treatment of alcoholism. In N. J. Estes & M. E. Heinemann (Eds.), *Alcoholism: Development, consequences, and interventions* (pp. 388–406). St. Louis: C. V. Mosby.

Bullock, M. L., Culliton, P. D., & Orlander, R. T. (1989). Controlled trial of acupuncture for severe recidivist alcoholism. *The Lancet, 1*(8652), 1435–1439.

Caplan, G. (1964). *Principles of preventive psychiatry.* New York: Basic Books.

Cautela, J. R. (1970). Treatment of smoking by covert sensitization. *Psychological Reports, 26,* 415–420.

Cautela, J. R., & Rosenstiel, A. K. (1975). The use of covert conditioning in the treatment of drug abuse. *International Journal of the Addictions, 10,* 277–303.

Chafetz, M. E. (1970). Practical and theoretical considerations in the psychotherapy of alcoholism. In M. E. Chafetz, H. T. Blane, & M. J. Hill (Eds.), *Frontiers of alcoholism* (pp. 6–15). New York: Science House.

Chafetz, M. E., Blane, H. T., Abram, H. S., Clark, E., Golner, J. H., Hastie, E. L., & McCourt, W. F. (1970a). Establishing treatment relations with alcoholics: A supplementary report. In M. E. Chafetz, H. T. Blane, & M. J. Hill (Eds.), *Frontiers of alcoholism* (pp. 60–64). New York: Science House.

Chafetz, M. E., Blane, H. T., Abram, H. S., Golner, J. H., Lacy, E., McCourt, W. F., Clark, E., & Meyers, W. (1970b). Establishing treatment relations with alcoholics. I. In M. E. Chafetz, H. T. Blane, & M. J. Hill (Eds.), *Frontiers of alcoholism* (pp. 42–60). New York: Science House.

Chafetz, M. E., & Demone, H. (1962). *Alcoholism and society*. New York: Oxford University Press.

Charney, D. S., Heninger, G. R., & Kleber, H. D. (1986). The use of clonidine and naltrexone as a rapid, safe and effective treatment of abrupt withdrawal from methadone. *American Journal of Psychiatry, 143*(7), 831–837.

Cohen, M., & Stimmel, B. (1978). The use of methadone in narcotic dependency. In A. Schecter (Ed.), *Treatment aspects of drug dependence* (pp. 2–31). West Palm Beach, FL: CRC Press.

Coleman, S. B., & Davis, D. I. (1978). Family therapy and drug abuse: A national survey. *Family Process, 17,* 2–29.

Corsini, R. J. (Ed.). (1981). *Handbook of innovative psychotherapies*. New York: John Wiley & Sons.

Croce, V. M. (1979). Natural high therapy: Innovative approach to drug dependency. *Journal of Psychiatric Nursing, 17*(5), 20–22.

Dole, V. P., & Nyswander, M. A. (1965). Medical treatment for diacetyl morphine (heroin) addiction. *Journal of the American Medical Association, 193,* 645–656.

Donovan, D. M. (1988). Assessment of addictive behaviors: Implications of an emerging biopsychosocial model. In D. M. Donovan & G. A. Marlatt (Eds.), *Assessment of addictive behaviors* (pp. 3–48). New York: Guilford Press.

Dusay, J., & Dusay, K. M. (1989). Transactional analysis. In R. J. Corsini & D. Wedding (Eds.), *Current psychotherapies* (4th ed.). Itasca, IL: Peacock.

Ellis, A. (1985). *Overcoming resistance: Rational-emotive therapy with difficult clients*. New York: Springer.

Ellis, A. (1989). Rational-emotive therapy. In R. J. Corsini & D. Wedding (Eds.), *Current psychotherapies* (4th ed.). Itasca, IL: Peacock.

Estes, N. J., & Heinemann, M. E. (1986). *Alcoholism:: Development, consequences, and interventions* (3d ed.). St. Louis: C. V. Mosby.

Estes, N. J., Smith-DiJulio, K., & Heinemann, M. E. (1980). *Nursing diagnosis of the alcoholic person*. St. Louis: C. V. Mosby.

Evans, D., & Lane, D. S. (1980). Long-term outcome of smoking cessation workshops. *American Journal of Public Health, 70,* 725–727.

Fenichel, O. (1945). *The psychoanalytic theory of neurosis*. New York: W. W. Norton.

Finney, J. W., & Moos, R. H. (1986). Matching patients with treatments: Conceptual and methodological issues. *Journal of Studies on Alcohol, 47*(2), 123–134.

Foley, V. D. (1986). *An introduction to family therapy* (2d ed.). Orlando: Grune & Stratton.

Forgione, A. G., & Holmberg, R. (1981). Biofeedback therapy. In R. J. Corsini (Ed.), *Handbook of innovative psychotherapies* (pp. 79–94). New York: John Wiley & Sons.

Forrest, G. G. (1983). *Alcoholism, narcissism, and psychopathology*. Springfield, IL: Charles C. Thomas.

Fraiser, A. R. (1979). Narcotics. In J. B. Fabry, R. P. Bulka, & W. S. Sahakian (Eds.), *Logotherapy in action* (pp. 253–261). New York: Jason Aronson.

Frankl, V. E. (1963). *Man's search for meaning* (revised ed.). New York: Washington Square Press.

Franks, C. M., & Wilson, G. T. (1980). *Annual review of behavior therapy, theory and practice, 1979*. New York: Brunner/Mazel.

Freud, S. (1972). *A general introduction to psychoanalysis*. New York: Pocket Books. (Originally published, 1917).

Fuller, R. K., Branchey, L., Brightwell, D. R., Derman, R. M., Emrick, C. D., Iber, F. L., James, K. E., Lacoursiere, R. B., Lee, K. K., Lowenstam, I., Manny, I., Neiderhiser, P., Nocks, J. J., & Shaw, S. (1986). Disulfiram treatment of alcoholism: A veterans administration cooperative study. *Journal of the American Medical Association, 256*(11), 1449–1455.

Gareri, E. A. (1979). Assertiveness training for alcoholics. *Journal of Psychiatric Nursing, 17*(1), 31–36.

Garfield, S. L. (1980). *Psychotherapy: An eclectic approach*. New York: John Wiley & Sons.

Gawin, F., & Kleber, H. (1986). Pharmacologic treatments of cocaine abuse. *Psychiatric Clinics of North America, 9*(3), 573–583.

Gerard, D. L., & Saenger, G. (1966). *Outpatient treatment of alcoholism*. Toronto: University of Toronto Press.

Glasser, W. (1976). Notes on reality therapy. In A. Bassin, T. E. Bratter, & R. L. Rachin (Eds.), *The reality therapy reader* (pp. 92–109). New York: Harper & Row.

Glassman, D. H., Stetner, F., Walsh, B. T., Raizman, P. S., Fleiss, J. L., Cooper, T. B., & Covey, L. S. (1988). Heavy smokers, smoking cessation and clonidine: Results of a double-blind randomized trial. *Journal of the American Medical Association, 259,* 2863–2866.

Gordis, E. (1987). Accessible and affordable health care for alcoholism and related problems: Strategy for cost containment. *Journal of Studies on Alcohol, 48*(6), 579–585.

Health and Public Policy Committee, American College of Physicians. (1986). Methods for stopping cigarette smoking. *Annals of Internal Medicine, 105,* 281–291.

Hirsch, S. M., von Rosenberg, R., Phelan, C., & Dudley, H. E. (1978). Effectiveness of assertiveness training with alcoholics. *Journal of Studies on Alcohol, 39*(1), 89–97.

Holmes, R. M. (1979). Alcoholics. In J. B. Fabry, R. P. Bulka, & W. S. Sahakian (Eds.), *Logotherapy in action* (pp. 243–252). New York: Jason Aronson.

Hotson, J. R., & Langston, J. W. (1976). Disulfiram-induced encephalopathy. *Archives of Neurology, 33,* 141–142.

Jackson, L. (1988). Acupuncture: An important treatment option. *Nurse Practitioner, 13*(9), 55–66.

Jackson, T. R., & Smith, J. W. (1978). A comparison of two aversion treatment methods for alcoholism. *Journal of Studies on Alcohol, 39*(1), 187–191.

Jaffe, J. H. (1985). In A. G. Gilman, L. S. Goodman, T. W. Rall, & F. Murad (Eds.), *Goodman and Gilman's the pharmacological basis of therapeutics* (pp. 532–581). New York: Macmillan.

Jellinek, E. M. (1960). *The disease concept of alcoholism.* Highland Park, NJ: Hillhouse Press.

Johnson, V. E. (1980). *I'll quit tomorrow* (revised ed.). New York: Harper & Row.

Johnson, V. E. (1988). Intervention: How to help someone who doesn't want help. New York: New American Library.

Kendall, P. C. (1982). *Advances in cognitive-behavioral research and therapy* (Vol. 1). New York: Academic Press.

Kerr, P. (1988, Sept. 30). Acupuncture experiment in New York is said to ease addiction to crack. *New York Times,* p. 9.

Khantzian, E. J., & Khantzian, N. J. (1984). Cocaine addiction: Is there a psychological predisposition? *Psychiatric Annals, 14,* 753–759.

Kitson, T. M. (1977). The disulfiram-ethanol reaction. *Journal of Studies on Alcohol, 38*(1), 96–113.

Knee, S. T., & Razani, J. (1974). Disulfiram and acute organic brain syndrome. *American Journal of Psychiatry, 131*(11), 1281–1282.

Kwentus, J., & Major, L. F. (1979). Disulfiram in the treatment of alcoholism: A review. *Journal of Studies on Alcohol, 40*(5), 428–446.

Lam, W., Sacks, H. S., Sze, P. C., & Chalmers, T. C. (1987). Meta-analysis of randomized controlled trials of nicotine chewing gum. *The Lancet, 2*(8561), 27–30.

Lazarus, A. A. (1971). *Behavior therapy and beyond.* New York: McGraw-Hill.

Lemere, F., & Voegtlin, W. (1950). An evaluation of the aversion treatment of alcoholism. *Quarterly Journal of Studies on Alcohol, 11,* 199–204.

Levie, C. A., Claxton, F., & Barnes, J. (1979). Using a central intake office to serve drug abuse clients from several agencies. *Hospital and Community Psychiatry, 30*(7), 484–485.

Light, W. J. (1986). *Psychodynamics of alcoholism: A current synthesis.* Springfield, IL: Charles C. Thomas.

Lindemann, E. (1944). Symptomatology and management of acute grief. *American Journal of Psychiatry, 101,* 141–148.

Lukas, E. (1979). A supplementary form of therapy for addicts. In J. B. Fabry, R. P. Bulka, & W. S. Sahakian (Eds.), *Logotherapy in action* (pp. 265–267). New York: Jason Aronson.

Macintyre, D., Mclay, A. L. C., East, B. W., Williams, E. D., & Boddy, K. (1978). Silver poisoning associated with antismoking lozenge. *British Medical Journal, 2*(6154), 1749–1750.

Marlatt, G. A. (1978). Craving for alcohol, loss of control, and relapse: A cognitive-behavioral analysis. In P. E. Nathan, G. A. Marlatt, & T. Loberg (Eds.), *Alcoholism: New directions in behavioral research and treatment* (pp. 271–314). New York: Plenum Press.

Marlatt, G. A., & Gordon, J. (1985). *Relapse prevention: Maintenance strategies in addictive behavior change.* New York: Guilford Press.

Martindale, D., & Martindale, E. (1971). *The social dimensions of mental illness, alcoholism, and drug dependence.* Westport, CT: Greenwood.

Mazza, N. (1979). Poetry: A therapeutic tool in the early stages of alcoholism treatment. *Journal of Studies on Alcohol, 48*(1), 123–128.

McCourt, W., & Glantz, M. (1980). Cognitive behavior therapy in groups for alcoholics. *Journal of Studies on Alcohol, 41*(3), 338–346.

Miller, W. R. (1983). Controlled drinking. *Journal of Studies on Alcohol, 44,* 68–83.

Miller, W. R., & Hester, R. K. (1980). Treating the problem drinkers: Modern approaches. In W. R. Miller (Ed.), *The addictive behaviors: Treatment of alcoholism, drug abuse, smoking and obesity* (pp. 11–141). Oxford: Pergamon Press.

Miller, W. R., & Hester, R. K. (1986). Inpatient alcoholism treatment: Who benefits? *American Psychologist, 41*(7), 794–805.

Moore, J. (1985). *Roads to recovery: A national directory of alcohol and drug addiction treatment centers.* New York: Macmillan.

Mottin, J. L. (1973). Drug-induced attenuation of alcohol consumption. *Quarterly Journal of Studies on Alcohol, 34,* 444–472.

Nelkin, D. (1973). *Methadone maintenance: A technological fix.* New York: George Braziller.

Neuberger, O. W., Hasha, N., Matarazzo, J. D., Schmitz, R. E., & Pratt, H. H. (1981). Behavioral-chemical treatment of alcoholism: An outcome replication. *Journal of Studies on Alcohol, 42,* 806–810.

Newman, R. G. (1987). Methadone treatment: Defining and evaluating success. *New England Journal of Medicine, 317*(7), 447–450.

Novick, D. M., Pascarelli, E. F., Joseph, H., Salsitz, E. A., Richman, B. L., Des Jarlais, D. C., Anderson, M., Dole, V. P., Nyswander, M. E. (1988). Methadone maintenance patients in general medical practice. *Journal of the American Medical Association, 259*(22), 3299–3302.

O'Leary, K. D., & Wilson, G. T. (1987). *Behavior therapy: Application and outcome* (2d ed.). Englewood Cliffs, NJ: Prentice-Hall.

Overall, J. E., Brown, D., Williams, J. D., & Neill, L. T. (1973). Drug treatment of anxiety and depression in detoxified alcoholic patients. *Archives of General Psychiatry, 29,* 218–221.

Palmer, J. O. (1980). *A primer of eclectic psychotherapy.* Belmont, CA: Wadsworth.

Passini, F. T., Watson, C. G., Dehnel, L., Herder, J., & Watkins, B. (1977). Alpha wave biofeedback training therapy in alcoholics. *Journal of Clinical Psychology, 33,* 292–299.

Pendery, M., Maltzman, I., & West, L. J. (1982). Controlled drinking by alcoholics? New findings and a reevaluation of a major affirmative study. *Science, 217,* 169–174.

Perls, F. (1947). *Ego, hunger, and aggression.* New York: Random House.

Persons, J. B. (1989). *Cognitive therapy in practice.* New York: W. W. Norton.

Preisner, J. M. (1980). A proposed model for the nurse therapist. In J. P. Riehl & C. Roy (Eds.), *Conceptual models for nursing practice* (2d ed.). New York: Appleton-Century-Crofts.

Rachman, S., & Teasdale, J. (1969). *Aversion therapy and behavior disorders: An analysis.* Coral Gables, FL: University of Miami Press.

Ritchie, J. M. (1985). The aliphatic alcohols. In A. G. Gilman, L. S. Goodman, T. W. Rall, & F. Murad (Eds.), *Goodman and Gillman's the pharmacological basis of therapeutics,* (pp. 382–383).

Rogers, C. R. (1942). *Counseling and psychotherapy: Newer concepts in practice.* Boston: Houghton Mifflin.

Rubington, E. (1967). Drug addiction as a deviant career. *International Journal of Addictions, 2*(1), 3–20.

Russell, M. A. H., Raw, M., Taylor, C., Feyerabend, C., & Saloojee, Y. (1978). Blood nicotine and carboxyhemoglobin levels after rapid-smoking aversion therapy. *Journal of Consulting and Clinical Psychology, 46,* 1423–1431.

Sansweet, S. J. (1975). *The punishment cure.* New York: Mason/Charter.

Santiago, P. R. (1969). The lyrical expression of adolescent conflict in the Beatles songs. *Adolescence, 4,* 199–210.

Schwartz, J. L. (1987). *Review and evaluation of smoking cessation methods: The United States and Canada, 1978–1985* (NIH Pub. No. 87–2940). Washington, DC: U. S. Government Printing Office.

Schwartz, J. L., & Rider, G. (1978). *Review and evaluation of smoking control methods: The United States and Canada, 1969–1977* (DHEW Pub. No. CDC 79–8369). Washington, DC: U. S. Government Printing Office.

Shaw, J. A., Donley, P., Morgan, D. W., & Robinson, J. A. (1975). Treatment of depression in alcoholics. *American Journal of Pschiatry, 132*(6), 641–644.

Smith, D. E., Wesson, D. R., & Linda, L. K. (1980). Clinical approaches to acute and chronic intervention in the sedative-hypnotic abuser. In S. Einstein (Ed.), *Drugs in relation to the drug user* (pp. 192–243). New York: Pergamon Press.

Sobell, M. B., & Sobell, L. C. (1984). The aftermath of heresy: A response to Pendery et al.'s (1982) critique of "Individualized Behavior Therapy for Alcoholics." *Behaviour Research and Therapy, 22,* 413–440.

Sobell, M. B., & Sobell, L. C. (1978). *Behavioral treatment of alcohol problems.* New York: Plenum Press.

Sobell, M. B., & Sobell, L. C. (1973). Individualized behavior therapy for alcoholics. *Behavior Therapy, 4,* 49–72.

Spotnitz, H. (1969). *Modern psychoanalysis of the schizophrenic patient.* New York: Grune & Stratton.

Stanton, M. D., & Todd, T. C. (1982). *The family therapy of drug abuse and addiction.* New York: Guilford Press.

Steiner, C. (1971). *Games alcoholics play: The analysis of life scripts.* New York: Grove Press.

Steiner, C. M. (1979). *Healing alcoholism.* New York: Grove Press.

Tennant, F. S. (1979). Physician extender protocols for urgent situations in drug and alcohol clinics. *Journal of Psychedelic Drugs, 11*(3), 211–215.

Thomas, E. J., & Santa, C. A. (1982). Unilateral family therapy for alcohol abuse: A working conception. *American Journal of Family Therapy, 10,* 49–58.

Tonnesen, P., Fryd, V., Hansen, M., Helsted, J., Gunnersen, A., Forchanner, H., & Stockner, M. (1986). Effect of nicotine chewing gum in combination with group counseling on the cessation of smoking. *New England Journal of Medicine, 318,* 15–18.

U. S. Department of Health and Human Services. (1987, January). *Sixth special report to the U.S. Congress on alcohol and health* (DHHS Pub. No. ADM 87–1519). Washington, DC: U. S. Government Printing Office.

Volvaka, J., Resnick, R. B., Kestenbaum, R. S., & Freedman, A. M. (1976). Short-term effects of naltrexone in 55 heroin ex-addicts. *Biological Psychiatry, 11,* 679–685.

Watson, C. G., Herder, J., & Passini, F. T. (1978). Alpha biofeedback therapy in alcoholics: An 18-month follow-up. *Journal of Clinical Psychology, 34*(3), 765–769.

Wesson, D. R., & Smith, D. E. (1979). A clinical approach to diagnosis and treatment of amphetamine abuse. In D. E. Smith (Ed.), *Amphetamine use, misuse, and abuse* (pp. 260–274). Boston: G. K. Hall.

Westermeyer, J. (1976). *A primer on chemical dependency: A clinical guide to alcohol and drug problems.* Baltimore: Williams & Wilkins.

Whyte, C. R., & O'Brien, P. M. (1974). Disulfiram implant: A controlled trial. *British Journal of Psychiatry, 124,* 42–44.

Wiens, A., & Menustik, C. (1983). Treatment outcome and patient characteristics in an aversion therapy program for alcoholism. *American Psychologist, 38,* 1089–1096.

Wiens, A. N., Montague, J. R., Manaugh, T. S., & English, C. J. (1976). Pharmacological aversive counterconditioning to alcohol in a private hospital: One year follow-up. *Journal of Studies on Alcohol, 37,* 1320–1324.

Wurmser, L. (1978). *The hidden dimension: Psychodynamics in compulsive drug use.* New York: Jason Aronson.

Zimberg, S. (1985). Principles of alcoholism psychotherapy. In S. Zimberg, J. Wallace, & S. B. Blume (Eds.), *Practical approaches to alcoholism psychotherapy* (2d ed.) (pp. 3–22). New York: Plenum Press.

SELF-HELP GROUPS

19

Gerald Bennett
Janet H. Lee

The novice professional in the addiction treatment field soon discovers the enormous impact of self-help groups. These groups, beginning with Alcoholics Anonymous (AA) in 1935, were the earliest, most effective, continuing organizations directed toward recovery from addiction. Originally developed in response to a perceived lack of professional services, the self-help movement has continued to grow in membership and influence even as the availability of professional treatment services has increased tremendously in recent years. All indications are that the influence of these groups will continue. A theoretical and practical understanding of self-help groups and how they "work" is essential for professionals who strive to offer their clients the full range of resources for recovery. This chapter presents an introduction to self-help groups including characteristics of such groups and an underlying theoretical framework. AA, Al-Anon Family Groups, and Adult Children of Alcoholics (ACOA) groups are introduced with an emphasis on their therapeutic factors. Issues related to the interface of professional treatment and self-help group involvement are also presented.

ORGANIZATIONAL CHARACTERISTICS

Five organizational characteristics have been identified by Levy (1976) as essential to defining a group as a self-help organization. These elements are listed in Table 19.1. Many self-help organizations focus on recovery from addictions with the basic elements described by Levy. Table 19.2 is a selected list of these groups, with their target populations identified.

The purpose of addiction self-help groups is to assist participants in stopping a particular addictive pattern, such as alcoholism, smoking, overeating, or cocaine dependence, or to assist family members to recover from the consequences of living with an addicted spouse or parent. Although many of the organizations hold meetings in professional treatment settings and are incorporated into professional treatment programs, the self-help groups are independent and self-supporting. Membership in these groups is a self-selection process. Individuals who believe they have the specific problem addressed by the group may attend as many or as few of

Table 19.1
Five Organizational Characteristics of Self-Help Groups

1. *Purpose.* Its express, primary purpose is to provide help and support for its members in dealing with their problems and improving their psychological functioning and effectiveness.
2. *Origin and Sanction.* Its origin and sanction for existence rest with the members of the group themselves, rather than with some external agency or authority.
3. *Source of Help.* It relies upon its own members' efforts, skills, knowledge, and concern as its primary source of help, with the structure of the relationship between members being one of peers, so far as help-giving and support are concerned.
4. *Composition.* It is generally composed of members who share a common core of life experience and problems.
5. *Control.* Its structure and mode of operation are under the control of members although they may, in turn, draw upon professional guidance and various theoretical and philosophical frameworks.*

*Reproduced with permission from *The Journal of Applied Behavioral Science*, Self-help groups: Types and psychological processes, by Leon H. Levy, (1976) pp. 310–322, (12), 3, NTL Institute.

the group meetings as they choose. No dues are charged; financial support comes from members on a voluntary basis. Quite unlike professional therapy, help is offered and received within the context of peer relationships with an emphasis on common experiences with a shared problem.

SELF-HELP GROUPS AND SOCIAL SUPPORT

Borkman (1984) presents an intriguing theoretical framework for self-help groups in which the group is seen as providing a special element of support in the social support network of the self-help group member. She hypothesizes that the families, friends, and other members of the individual's network are "selectively unsupportive with respect to the focal problem of the self-help group" and that the self-help group is oriented toward "offsetting" that unsupportiveness (p. 206).

Self-help groups use an experiential problem-solving method—that is, knowledge based on first-hand experience. This is distinctly different from both folk knowledge, ideas passed down through the generations, and lay information, ideas taken from science or the mass media by the general public. Self-help group members have found that neither folk nor lay nor professional knowledge is adequate to resolve their problems.

Each self-help group has its own experiential problem-solving paradigm. The focus of this paradigm is very narrowly limited to the particular problem for which the self-help group was founded. But the problem-solving approach is holistic, viewing the focused problem in terms of the whole person, and acausal, emphasizing effective problem-solving rather than insight into causes of the problem (Borkman, 1984). AA, with its focus on the problem of alcoholism and its holistic approach to everyday living given in the Twelve Steps, certainly exemplifies Borkman's description.

The social network is seen as unsupportive of the individual in four ways. The first is stigmatization in which the family members accept the folk knowledge that this problem is a stigmatizing condition and react by ignoring the problem, manipulating the situations to protect the individual, reacting to the individual in a stereotypical manner, or showing embarrassment or discomfort during interactions. In addition to being problematic in themselves, these interactions create "distance in the relationship" (Borkman, 1984, p. 210). The second has to do with what Borkman calls the "emotionscape" of the problem. As a landscape shows a small scene in its entirety, the emotionscape "refers to the meanings and feelings about the troublesome features in living with a given focal problem" (Borkman, 1984, p. 210). Members of self-help groups frequently feel alone or misunderstood because their significant others do not understand the emotionscape of the problem. The third manner in which significant others are seen as unsupportive has to do with role relationships. The focal problem frequently limits or destroys the individual's ability to fulfill the responsibilities of family and work relationships. Over a period of time,

Table 19.2

Self-Help Groups Focusing on Substance Abuse Problems

Group	Target Population
Alcoholics Anonymous	Alcoholics
Al-Anon Family Groups	Families of alcoholics
Alateen	Teen-aged children of alcoholics
Women for Sobriety	Female alcoholics
Narcotics Anonymous	Narcotics addicts
Nar-Anon	Families of narcotics addicts
Cocaine Anonymous	Cocaine addicts
Potsmokers Anonymous	Marihuana smokers
Families Anonymous	Parents with children who have substance abuse problems
Overeaters Anonymous	Food addicts

Note: Addresses of the national offices for these groups are provided in Appendix A.

the social network pulls away. The last way in which unsupportiveness occurs is with regard to the focal problem itself. To the extent that network members are bothered by the problem, their capacity to support the individual is reduced (Borkman, 1984).

According to Borkman, the self-help group intervenes to strengthen the support network in three ways. The first of these is simply by participation in the group itself. The experiential approach to solving the problem is practiced and reinforced. Through the giving and receiving of help, the individual feels cared about, understood, and useful. Consequently, the amount and kind of support required from the existing personal network is reduced.

Second, participation in the self-help group transforms the individual's perspective on the personal network. Expectations for support are lowered, folk and lay ideas are seen as indications of a lack of knowledge rather than unsupportive or stigmatizing, and responsibility is taken for one's own actions and not for the reactions of others in the network.

Third, the self-help group supports that individual in restructuring the personal network. Continuing relationships are modified, and problematic relationships are replaced with more supportive ones.

In one study examining the relationship between social support and self-esteem in young alcoholics in recovery, participation in AA was seen as a major source of social support (Bennett, 1988). It was common for subjects to list fellow self-help group members as very important members of their social network. All measures of social support also had a significant moderate positive relationship to self-esteem.

THERAPEUTIC FACTORS

Involvement in a self-help group is a holistic experience that has been described as no less than discovering "a new social world" (Denzin, 1987, p. 91). Three aspects of the self-help group experience believed to have particular therapeutic significance are *(a)* accepting group beliefs; *(b)* engaging in group processes; and *(c)* entering into sponsor relationships. We will examine these factors in some detail in an analysis of the prototypical self-help group in the substance abuse field, AA.

Alcoholics Anonymous

The development of AA was an outcome of changing conceptions about alcoholism in the United States, inadequate professional services for alcoholics, and the enduring commitment of the early founders. The temperance movement promoted a view of alcoholism that stressed the addictive potential of alcohol on anyone using the substance. With repeal of Prohibition in 1933, the view that alcohol should be considered a dangerous drug, even in small amounts (as heroin is viewed today), began to lose ground in America. A new view emerged in the late 1930s and early 1940s, which considered alcohol a danger only to those people with the disease of alcoholism. Alcoholism became a phenomenon within people rather than inherent in the substance itself (Levine, 1978). This new conception of alcoholism set the stage for, and in large part was promoted by, AA. The Yale Center for Alcohol Studies, primarily through Jellinek's (1952) leadership in the description of the disease concept and process in the 1950s, gave scientific support to the new orientation.

Nevertheless, there was a gap of at least 20 years between the emergence of the disease concept and its acceptance by the mainstream health delivery system (Chafetz & Demone, 1962). This professional void further stimulated the growth of AA as the only group with a consistent and reliable response toward alcoholism. During the 1950s and 1960s, the emergency departments of most hospitals were not prepared to treat the alcoholic. The disposition of a client not requiring hospitalization, but seriously impaired by acute intoxication, was determined in varying ways by hospital policies, the attending nurses and physicians, and other staff members. The response was usually to request assistance from the police, which often resulted in either a ride home (or away from the immediate area) or a trip to a local "drunk tank." The utilization of AA members available to do rescue work was neither advocated by the hospital nor AA but gratefully discovered by some health professionals to be a more satisfactory alternative than calling the police (Bennett, Graves, Kavanaugh, & Vourakis, 1983).

The emerging conception of alcoholism as a disease and the lack of adequate professional services for alcoholics created the environment for AA growth. Two men with serious alcoholic histories, Bill Wilson and Dr. Bob Smith, founders of AA, provided leadership and commitment that sustained the organization through the early years.

Wilson and Smith met in 1935 in Akron, Ohio, and discovered that they could help one another stay sober through mutual peer support and guidance. They had both had experience with a spiritual movement known as the Oxford Group, which advocated group confession of problems as a means to a better life. Wilson and Smith began to apply the "changed life" principles of the Oxford Group to peer treatment of alcoholism, much to the dismay of Oxford Group leaders. They wanted no part of a movement that would bring them into association with alcoholics (Hurvitz, 1976).

Left to their own resources, Wilson and Smith began to gather a small group of members and develop a unique identity. This identity retained many spiritual aspects but also embraced the disease concept of alcoholism and abstinence as the only means of recovery for the alcoholic.

Membership of AA

Beginning in 1968, AA has surveyed its membership on a triennial basis to provide information on the characteristics of members in the United States and Canada. The most recent survey of the AA membership was conducted by the General Service Office of Alcoholics Anonymous (1990) in 1989. Several trends are apparent since 1968. AA is attracting more women and more people 30 years old or younger, and an increasing proportion of the membership are addicted to other drugs in addition to alcohol.

The number of women members continues to increase from 22% in 1968, to 29% in 1977, to 34% in 1986, and 35% in 1989. Twenty-two percent of the members were 30 years old or younger in 1989, as compared to only 7% in this age group in 1968. Forty-six percent of the membership reported addiction to at least one other drug in addition to alcohol in 1989, a substantial increase from 18% in 1977.

Beliefs

Self-help groups have been described as "fixed communities of belief" (Antze, 1976, p. 325). AA's ideology is set forth in "The Big Book" (Alcoholics Anonymous, 1939) and further elaborated in the *Twelve Steps and Twelve Traditions* (Alcoholics Anonymous, 1953). The steps and traditions are presented in Tables 19.3 and 19.4. It should be emphasized that the steps and traditions are fixed as an ideal for the group but are not forced on individual members.

Table 19.3
The Twelve Steps of Alcoholics Anonymous

1. We admitted we were powerless over alcohol —that our lives have become unmanageable.
2. Came to believe that a Power greater than ourselves could restore us to sanity.
3. Made a decision to turn our will and our lives over to the care of God *as we understood Him.*
4. Made a searching and fearless moral inventory of ourselves.
5. Admitted to God, to ourselves, and to another human being the exact nature of our wrongs.
6. Were entirely ready to have God remove all these defects of character.
7. Humbly asked Him to remove our shortcomings.
8. Made a list of all persons we had harmed and became willing to make amends to them all.
9. Made direct amends to such people whenever possible except when to do so would injure them or others.
10. Continued to take personal inventory and when we were wrong promptly admitted it.
11. Sought through prayer and meditation to improve our conscious contact with God *as we understood Him,* praying only for knowledge of His will for us and the power to carry that out.
12. Having a spiritual awakening as the result of these steps, we tried to carry this message to alcoholics and to practice these principles in all our affairs.

Source: From Alcoholics Anonymous, *The Twelve Steps and Twelve Traditions,* copyright 1939, by Alcoholics Anonymous World Services, Inc. Reprinted by permission of Alcoholics Anonymous World Services, Inc.

The beliefs summarized in the *Twelve Steps and Twelve Traditions* have therapeutic value in their "persuasive function" (Antze, 1976, p. 324). Antze (1976) reviewed studies of the personality traits of alcoholics and concluded that they tend to exaggerate their "authorship in the events" of life and find themselves at "center stage" (p. 331). According to Antze's analysis, AA teachings encourage a realistic sense of individual power and acceptance of limitations. The "Higher Power"

Table 19.4
The Twelve Traditions of Alcoholics Anonymous

1. Our common welfare should come first; personal recovery depends upon A.A. unity.

2. For our group purpose there is but one ultimate authority—a loving God as He may express Himself in our group conscience. Our leaders are but trusted servants; they do not govern.

3. The only requirement for A.A. membership is a desire to stop drinking.

4. Each group should be autonomous except in matters affecting other groups or A.A. as a whole.

5. Each group has but one primary purpose—to carry its message to the alcoholic who still suffers.

6. An A.A. group ought never endorse, finance, or lend the A.A. name to any related facility or outside enterprise, lest problems of money, property, and prestige divert us from our primary purpose.

7. Every A.A. group ought to be fully self-supporting, declining outside contributions.

8. Alcoholics Anonymous should remain forever nonprofessional, but our service centers may employ special workers.

9. A.A., as such, ought never be organized; but we may create service boards of committees directly responsible to those they serve.

10. Alcoholics Anonymous has no opinion on outside issues; hence, the A.A. name ought never be drawn into public controversy.

11. Our public relations policy is based on attraction rather than promotion; we need always maintain personal anonymity at the level of press, radio, and films.

12. Anonymity is the spiritual foundation of all our traditions, ever reminding us to place principles before personalities.

Source: From Alcoholics Anonymous, *The Twelve Steps and Twelve Traditions,* copyright 1939, by Alcoholics Anonymous World Services, Inc. Reprinted by permission of Alcoholics Anonymous World Services, Inc.

provides relief from anxiety and isolation while taking the place of the exaggerated sense of personal will. The belief system also includes a focus on helping alcoholics over all concerns, maintaining the independence of the organization, the significance of anonymity, and an open-door policy to anyone wishing to stop drinking.

Group Processes

The "group meeting" is the central experience of self-help group participation. It is in the group dialogue that the troubled person realizes others are coping with the same or similar problems. AA has grown at such a rapid pace that meetings are now held in almost every community in the country, and many groups have age, ethnic, and socioeconomic specificity, which further enhances the process of identification. The format for AA meetings and other self-help groups is predictable, even ritualistic in some cases, which provides a clear set of ground rules for participants. The typical AA meeting begins with a recognition of visitors, if the meeting is open, and an introduction to a proposed theme for discussion offered by the chosen leader for the particular meeting. Soon the members begin to seek recognition from the leader to offer comments related to the theme. Members always introduce themselves by first names, adding, "I'm an alcoholic," and the group responds in unison with a rousing "hello." The theme is explored in a context of the members' personal experiences and often related to the group ideology. The leader brings the meeting to a close with an attempt to summarize the meaning of the thoughts, feelings, and actions discussed. A prayer ends the formal meeting, and a time for social interaction begins. This period is often marked by exchange of telephone numbers with new members and the planning of small-group social activities.

In a study of members' perspectives of self-help groups, including members of AA, Knight, Wollert, Levery, Frame, and Padgett (1980) found that members believe that the social involvement, or fellowship, provided by the group is the most helpful aspect of participation.

The Sponsor Relationship

Self-help groups not only depend on an ideology and frequent group meetings for their success, but formal and informal "sponsor" relationships between members and newcomers are also important. Alibrandi (1985) has termed the sponsor–newcomer relationship in AA *folk psychotherapy,* with therapeutic outcomes for both sponsors and newcomers. The sponsor reaches out to the alcoholic with the AA message and personal experience. This reaching out is called *twelfth-stepping* (see step 12 in Table 19.3) and is considered an essential task in the sponsor's program of recovery because it is through active contact with the suffering alcoholic that the sponsor maintains a true perspective on the illness.

The newcomer benefits from the sponsor's experience and the expression of concern and positive regard, which are often withheld by others who have no significant knowledge about alcoholism. Alibrandi (1985) studied the sponsor–newcomer relationship from the standpoint of five stages of recovery, classified in progressive degrees of sobriety, beginning with a day to a week and ending with a year or more. He found that sponsors emphasize different aspects of the AA message, depending on the length of sobriety.

> Most pertinent to the newcomer is surrender and powerlessness, participation in the fellowship, and specific prescriptions for sobriety. As the length of sobriety increases, there is a shift from specific advice and morale-building to self-change, spirituality, and the action steps. (Alibrandi, 1985, p. 254)

Thus, the sponsor relationship is a significant part of self-help group participation and becomes more intensive as recovery advances.

Case Example

John W. is 32 years old and has 2 years of sobriety in AA. He attended his first AA meeting at age 28 when he entered an alcoholism treatment program following a serious automobile accident for which he was held responsible and charged with driving under the influence. At that time, John drank daily, and he could not predict how much he would drink on a particular day. He was having trouble remembering what he had done during periods of heavy drinking. He was very upset by the accident and realized he needed to "cut down" and agreed to go for treatment. During his first AA meetings, John had the most difficulty with introducing himself as an "alcoholic" because he didn't feel that he was. He

didn't contact other members outside the group or ask for a sponsor. But he enjoyed talking about himself and the problems he had been having because everyone seemed to know exactly what he was talking about.

He now looks back on this experience as an unwillingness to take the first of The Twelve Steps, "We admitted we were powerless over alcohol—that our lives have become unmanageable." After another automobile accident, a divorce, and losing his job, he went back to AA 2 years ago with no doubts about the fact that he was an alcoholic. After taking the First Step, he found that working the other Steps with the help of his sponsor changed his life. He attends at least three meetings a week, more during stressful times in his new job. He remarried recently and hopes his wife will attend Al-Anon. He often leads meetings for his home group and is particularly effective in discussing the importance of the First Step.

Al-Anon Family Groups

The Al-Anon Family Groups include Al-Anon, Alateen, and Al-Anon affiliated Adult Children of Alcoholics (ACOAs). Al-Anon is a fellowship for spouses, parents, other relatives, and close friends of alcoholics. Alateen is for adolescent children of alcoholics. Al-Anon affiliated ACOAs is the newest family program, organized for adult children graduating from Alateen and those coming to Al-Anon for the first time as adults.

Although Al-Anon programs are independent of AA, the traditions and therapeutic processes are very similar. Family groups focus on changing maladaptive behaviors that have been developed in response to substance abuse and have often had the effect of reinforcing substance abuse. The Al-Anon philosophy holds that alcoholism is a disease with serious consequences for the family, family members cannot take responsibility for the alcoholic's drinking or sobriety, and recovery for family members does not depend on recovery of the alcoholic.

Jackson's (1954) classic study was the first to elucidate stages of behavioral dysfunction in spouses of alcoholics. She interviewed wives attending Al-Anon meetings and found evidence of a typical response pattern of the wives to their husbands' drinking. Early responses included denial, attempts to control the drinking, and social isolation. Eventually most wives would face what they felt to be a hopeless situation by assuming total responsibility for the family. This stage often led to separation from the husband.

Two cardinal concepts useful in understanding how alcoholism becomes a family illness are *enabling* and *codependency*. Robertson (1988) wrote a vivid description of enabling:

> In the end, almost everything the family does is a reaction to what the alcoholic does. They become fixated on his disease. They become enablers. . .An enabler pays the alcoholic's overdue bills, cleans up his messes, calls the boss on Monday morning to say he has the flu, hides his liquor, pours it down the sink, assures him he wasn't a clod the night before when he made a pass at his best friend's wife. An enabler lies for the alcoholic, protects and rescues him. An enabler, without realizing it, makes it possible for the alcoholic to continue drinking. (pp. 156–157)

While enabling allows the addict to become increasingly dependent on the substance of abuse, the enabler becomes socially and emotionally isolated from normal interpersonal relationships and dependent on the addict for a sense of well-being and worth. In other words, the enabler becomes a codependent in the illness of addiction.

Wegscheider-Cruse (1985) defines codependency as "a specific condition that is characterized by preoccupation and extreme dependence (emotionally, socially, and sometimes physically) on a person or object. Eventually, this dependence on another person becomes a pathological condition that affects the co-dependent in all other relationships" (p. 2). Recovery from codependency is the goal of the family groups.

The need for the Al-Anon program was recognized in the 1940s by spouses and relatives of AA members, and by the early 1950s about 50 groups were active (Ablon, 1986). Today there are over 29,000 groups meeting in countries throughout the world. Ablon (1986) identified three enduring operational principles responsible for the organization's widespread success. These are "loving detachment" from the alcoholic, reestablishment of self-esteem and independence, and reliance on a higher power. The book *Al-Anon's Twelve Steps and Twelve Traditions* (Al-Anon, 1981)

and other Conference-Approved Literature (CAL) provide a comprehensive program for implementing the operational principles on a daily basis.

Case Example

Susan M. is 38 years old and a member of Al-Anon. Her husband, Jack, has a long history of alcoholism. He has been in treatment many times and has been successful in staying sober for as long as 16 months at a time but is especially prone to relapse during December and January. He is an infrequent participant in AA and has a close friend who has 8 years' sobriety in AA. Every Christmas season since Susan and Jack were married 14 years ago has been particularly difficult for Susan. Along with the usual pressures of the holiday season, she put a great deal of energy into trying to keep Jack from drinking. Over the years, Susan engaged their two children in the familiar family project—keeping Dad sober. Two Christmases ago Jack returned home from shopping intoxicated. After an argument with Susan and the children, Jack left in a rage, not saying where he was going or when he would return. He did not come home that night and, in a panic, Susan called Jack's friend in AA to ask for his help in finding Jack and sobering him up. The friend said he would do what he could and said he might know where to find Jack. He also said his wife, a member of Al-Anon, would come over to visit Susan while he went out to look for Jack. Jack did return home and apologize for his behavior. The friend's wife, Deborah, visited, listened to Susan's story, and suggested that they go to an Al-Anon meeting together the following night. At Al-Anon Susan learned to accept that she had no control over Jack's drinking and recognized how unmanageable her life had become. Now her happiness during the holidays is not linked to whether or not Jack drinks. She is focusing on what is positive in her own life, a day at a time.

Adult Children of Alcoholics

There are 22 million adult children of alcoholics (ACA) in the United States (Woodside, 1988). The 1980s will likely be remembered in the addiction field as the decade of the ACA. In 1981, there were only 14 Adult Children groups formally affiliated with Al-Anon. By 1987 there were 1100 ACOA groups registered with Al-Anon headquarters (Robertson, 1988). An unknown

Table 19.5
**Common Characteristics of
Adult Children of Alcoholics**

1. Adult children of alcoholics guess at what normal behavior is.
2. Adult children of alcoholics have difficulty following a project through from beginning to end.
3. Adult children of alcoholics lie when it would be just as easy to tell the truth.
4. Adult children of alcoholics judge themselves without mercy.
5. Adult children of alcoholics have difficulty having fun.
6. Adult children of alcoholics take themselves very seriously.
7. Adult children of alcoholics have difficulty with intimate relationships.
8. Adult children of alcoholics overreact to changes over which they have no control.
9. Adult children of alcoholics constantly seek approval and affirmation.
10. Adult children of alcoholics usually feel that they are different from other people.
11. Adult children of alcoholics are super responsible or super irresponsible.
12. Adult children of alcoholics are extremely loyal even in the face of evidence that the loyalty is undeserved.
13. Adult children of alcoholics are impulsive. They tend to lock themselves into a course of action without giving serious consideration to alternative behaviors or possible consequences. This impulsivity leads to confusion, self-loathing, and loss of control over their environment. In addition, they spend an excessive amount of energy cleaning up the mess.

Source: Woititz, J. G. (1983). *Adult Children of Alcoholics.* Pompano, FL: Health Communications. Reprinted with permission.

number of ACOA groups meet independently of Al-Anon and two new organizations have been formed in recent years to support the movement, the National Association for Children of Alcoholics (NACOA) and the Children of Alcoholics Foundation. Self-help books for ACAs occupy more than a few shelves in most bookstores. ACAs even have a national magazine devoted to topics of special interest to them. Much of this literature focuses on the dynamics of alcoholism as a family illness, the roles children adopt to survive in the alcoholic family, the resulting problems and characteristics children of alcoholics experience in adulthood, and the concepts of codependency and recovery.

Black (1981) described how adapting to alcoholism in one way or another is the formative experience in the young lives of children growing up in an alcoholic home. She identified three role types adopted by children to cope with their situation: the *responsible one,* the *adjuster,* and the *placater.* Some children show a blending of these roles. Each of the roles has serious implications for adult interpersonal functioning. The responsible child is often extremely controlling as an adult and is unable to enjoy play and relaxation. The adjuster withdraws as a child, learning to survive through detachment. As an adult the adjuster has difficulty engaging in intimate relationships. The placater learns as a child to survive by meeting the needs of others and may continue this pattern in adulthood. Based on her experience with ACOA groups, Woititz (1983) identified some common characteristics of adult children. These characteristics, presented in Table 19.5, have become accepted common ground for ACOA group discussions.

Case Example

Mary M. is 55 years old and has recently been divorced after 30 years of marriage to a man she describes as a "workaholic." She has been in an ACOA support group for a year. Mary learned about the group from her therapist. Beginning therapy when she became depressed and anxious following her divorce, she found it difficult to talk about her father and his alcoholism. For the first several ACOA meetings Mary introduced herself as an "adult child of an alcoholic," but was unable to share much because she would start crying, unable to quiet herself enough to speak. Gradually she was able to describe her painful childhood and share her feelings with tears, but in a more controlled way. She said she was the "lost child" in her family, the quiet one who stayed in her room, read books, and fantasized. Her father was a violent man who swore, threw things, and beat her mother, herself, and her sister when he was drunk. The day she was able to say at an ACOA meeting that she felt hatred and rage for her father was a breakthrough for Mary. She realized that denial of her own feelings for so long had limited her ability to have meaningful relationships with her husband and children. Mary recognized that she had many of the characteristics of ACOAs that were read at the beginning of each ACOA meeting. With the help of a sponsor she began to work the Twelve Steps for ACOAs. After a year of weekly meetings, Mary feels closer to her children than ever before. She is developing true intimacy in her relationships for the first time in her life. She is learning who she is and what she wants independent of her family. She understands now that her father was ill and is working on forgiveness.

PSYCHOTHERAPY AND SELF-HELP GROUP INVOLVEMENT

Brown's (1985) developmental model of recovery from alcoholism explicates four stages: drinking, transition, early recovery, and ongoing recovery. The model encompasses the developmental process of self-concept change from a self-definition of "I am not an alcoholic—I can control my drinking" to one of "I am an alcoholic—I cannot control my drinking." Derived from an exploratory study of 80 (40 men and 40 women) abstinent alcoholics participating in AA, the clinical application of the model involves a triadic therapeutic relationship between the recovering alcoholic, AA, and the psychotherapist. This concept of a triadic relationship may be quite applicable to psychotherapy with clients participating in groups other than AA.

According to Brown (1985), the effective therapist recognizes the primary importance of AA participation for the recovering alcoholic, particularly during the transition and early recovery stages. As the client's

self-concept begins to change, the therapist's role is to promote discussion of the meaning of this change and continue to reinforce the value of AA participation. This approach reserves intensive psychotherapy for clients in the stage of ongoing recovery. From this perspective, many of the unsatisfactory experiences with psychotherapy reported by therapists and alcoholics alike are due to a limited appreciation for the stages of recovery and the importance to timing.

INTERFACE OF THE PROFESSIONAL WITH THE SELF-HELP GROUP

Self-help groups have been uniquely successful in their approach to treating individuals with substance abuse problems. Attendance at AA meetings, for example, is an integral part of many alcoholism treatment programs. Yet not all clients seem to benefit from attendance at self-help group meetings and often clients do not follow through with referrals made to such groups. What can the professional do to increase the likelihood of an effective referral to a self-help group?

Initially, it is important to have a clear understanding of 12-step and other self-help group programs. The professional needs to know something about the self-help group process and the basic philosophical tenents on which the group is founded. It is significant to consider that many self-help groups were founded to fill a void in the substance abuse treatment field. When evaluating the benefits and risks for a particular client, this traditionally adversarial relationship should be kept in mind (Powell, 1975). Concrete information such as requirements for membership and individuals for whom the group is not appropriate should be obtained. The referral to the self-help group should be an integral part of the overall plan of care.

The professional should be familiar with the self-help groups that operate in the community. The best way to gather data is to visit open meetings of the various groups. The social service agencies or other private groups as the United Way sometimes publish directories of community assistance groups including self-help groups. Community health nurses and professionals associated with substance abuse treatment facilities are also potential sources of information. It is suggested that this task be divided among several individuals who pool their information. An index card file could be maintained in each agency including the following information about each self-help group (Newton, 1984): *(1)* name of group, *(2)* criteria for membership, *(3)* day and time of meeting, *(4)* location of meeting—including directions and accessibility by bus or car, *(5)* name and phone number of contact person, *(6)* demographic characteristics of group (age, sex, socioeconomic information), and *(7)* individuals for whom the group would not be suitable. The goal is to make an effective match in which the client feels comfortable with individuals who share similar values (Powell, 1975).

The client and family should be assessed for their willingness to participate in a self-help group. Factors such as the social acceptability of attending such groups, individual motivation, and compatibility in views of the substance abuse problem should be evaluated (Newton, 1984). Self-help groups may be more acceptable and accessible to clients in the community than to those in inpatient substance abuse units. For the significant others, self-help groups may be the preferred treatment.

The client who decides to try participation in a self-help group should be prepared for the experience ahead of time. The professional should share information about a typical meeting, the expectations for participation and commitment, and some general characteristics of others who will be attending. Arranging for a meeting with a current group member prior to attending the first group meeting can be helpful. The professional should follow-up on the initial referral and provide ongoing support for the client's participation in the self-help group.

SUMMARY

The self-help movement is a major force influencing addiction treatment in North America and increasingly its impact is being felt throughout the world. Knowledge of the various self-help groups is essential for the professional to be effective in working with addicted clients and their families. AA, Al-Anon family groups, and ACOA support groups often are viewed as models. Self-help groups focusing on recovery from addictions other than alcoholism have their unique characteristics and are worth further investigation by the reader. The National Self-Help Clearinghouse (see Appendix A) is an excellent resource for the professional in learning about the full range of groups in existence in various parts of the country.

REFERENCES

Ablon, J. (1986). Perspectives on Al-Anon family groups. In N. J. Estes & M. E. Heinemann (Eds.), *Alcoholism: Development, consequences, and interventions* (pp. 415–425). St. Louis: C. V. Mosby.

Al-Anon. (1981). *Al-Anon's twelve steps and twelve traditions.* New York: Al-Anon Family Group Headquarters, Inc.

Alcoholics Anonymous. (1939). *Alcoholics Anonymous.* New York: Alcoholics Anonymous World Services.

Alcoholics Anonymous. (1990). *Analysis of the 1989 Survey of the Membership of AA.* New York: Alcoholics Anonymous World Services.

Alcoholics Anonymous. (1953). *Twelve steps and twelve traditions.* New York: Alcoholics Anonymous World Services.

Alibrandi, L. A. (1985). The folk psychotherapy of Alcoholics Anonymous. In S. Zimburg, J. Wallace, & S. Blume (Eds.), *Practical approaches to alcoholism psychotherapy* (2d ed.) (pp. 239–256). New York: Plenum Press.

Antze, P. (1976). The role of ideologies in peer psychotherapy organizations: Some theoretical considerations and three case studies. *Journal of Applied Behavioral Science, 12*(3), 310–322.

Bennett, G. (1988). Stress, social support, and self-esteem of young alcoholics in recovery. *Issues in Mental Health Nursing, 9*(2), 151–167.

Bennett, G., Graves, J., Kavanaugh, M. & Vourakis, C. (1983). An overview of substance abuse treatment. In G. Bennett, C. Vourakis & D. Woolf (Eds.) *Substance Abuse: Pharmacologic, developmental, and clinical perspectives.* New York: John Wiley & Sons.

Black, C. (1981). Innocent bystanders at risk: The children of alcoholics. *Alcoholism, 1*(3), 22–26.

Borkman, T. (1984). Mutual self-help groups: Strengthening the selectively unsupportive personal and community networks of their members. In A. Gardner & F. Riessman (Eds.), *The self-help revolution* (pp. 205–215). New York: Human Sciences Press.

Brown, S. (1985). *Treating the alcoholic.* New York: John Wiley & Sons.

Chafetz, M. E., & Demone, H. (1962). *Alcoholism and society.* New York: Oxford University Press.

Denzin, N. K. (1987). *The recovering alcoholic.* Newberry Park, CA: Sage.

Hurvitz, N. (1976). The origins of the peer self-help psychotherapy movement. *Journal of Applied Behavioral Science, 12*(3), 283–294.

Jackson, J. (1954). The adjustment of the family to the crisis of alcoholism. *Quarterly Journal of Studies on Alcohol, 15,* 562–586.

Jellinek, E. M. (1952). Phases of alcohol addiction. *Quarterly Journal of Studies on Alcohol, 13,* 673–684.

Knight, B., Wollert, R. W., Levy, L. H., Frame, C. L., & Padgett, V. P. (1980). Self-help groups: The members' perspectives. *American Journal of Community Psychology, 8,* 53–65.

Levine, H. G. (1978). The discovery of addiction: Changing conceptions of habitual drunkenness in America. *Journal of Studies on Alcohol, 39,* 143–174.

Levy, L. H. (1976). Self-help groups: Types and psychological processes. *Journal of Applied Behavioral Science, 12*(3), 310–322.

Newton, G. (1984). Self-help groups: Can they help? *Journal of Psychosocial Nursing, 22*(7), 27–31.

Powell, T. J. (1975). The use of self-help groups as supportive reference communities. *American Journal of Orthopsychiatry, 45,* 756–764.

Robertson, N. (1988). *Getting better: Inside Alcoholics Anonymous.* New York: William Morrow.

Wegscheider–Cruse, S. (1985). *Choicemaking for co-dependents, adult children and spirituality seekers.* Pompano Beach, FL: Health Communications.

Woititz, J. G. (1983). *Adult children of alcoholics.* Pompano Beach, FL: Health Communications, Inc.

Woodside, M. (1988). Research on children of alcoholics: Past and future. *British Journal of Addiction, 83,* 785–792.

CHAPTER 20 | FAMILY THERAPY

Mary Ann Walsh Eells

Those of us from substance-abusing families, in which rehabilitation for alcoholism and drug addiction has occurred, look upon today's scene with mixed feelings. On the one hand, the scientific advances and more widely available clinical treatment have brought a new peace and serenity into our lives; but also, we see our communities rapidly being penetrated everywhere with ever more damaging, addictive drugs that go hand in hand with disorganization and devastation in great numbers of American families.

Even we in recovery are not safe. Too often people who are clean and sober in self-help programs live under a cloud of continuing, severe family problems that can lead to relapse. Frequently, an unwanted burden of addiction and associated family problems are passed down to future generations. There is no escape from worry, but the problem is often maneuvered to a plateau where, displaced from attention and denied, it can be managed. Unfortunately, self-help and rehabilitation programs encourage this denial because they cannot address the complex family dynamics substantively while focusing on the addicted individual. Something additional is needed. I have said before (Eells, 1986) that effective treatment of the family dysfunction is a necessary condition to the long-term recovery of the alcoholic, and this should be broadened to include the recovery of nuclear and extended family members.

How widespread is this problem of family dysfunction? There was a time when most thought about 10% of the population in the United States suffered from alcoholism, that figure being raised a few points if drug addiction were added. The true magnitude of the problem was demonstrated by a study conducted by the National Institute of Mental Health, the purpose of which was to estimate the prevalence of psychiatric disorders in three communities (New Haven, Baltimore, and St. Louis). Six-month prevalence estimates, the proportion of the population experiencing mental disorders in the 6

months prior to the study, showed that alcoholism was the most common disorder among men of all age groups (Myers et al., 1984). Although the most common diagnoses for women were depression and phobias, women 18–24 years old reported drug abuse and drug dependence next in frequency after phobias. For men 18–24 years old, drug abuse and drug dependence were ranked second in frequency after alcoholism. These estimates and others indicate that substance abuse involves a substantial number of families in the United States.

Readers of this chapter should gain a sense of how to identify substance-abusing families at high risk, what is important to know, and how this knowledge can augment practice. Specifically, there is a focus on how to discern dysfunctional family patterns and use them to formulate interventions. Preexisting factors in families that lead to failures in treatment are also discussed.

AT WHAT STAGE DOES A FAMILY NEED TREATMENT?

By definition, all families with substance-abusing family members can find treatment useful; the question is what kind of interventions are most useful. One way of deciding this is to look at the level of symptomatology in those being treated. For alcoholics alone (and this also could apply to those addicted to drugs) there appears to be an interesting learning curve associated with recovery. For a long time, people in self-help groups have discussed the different stages they experience in sobriety, the first being surrender to the program, than a "pink cloud" stage, followed by a stage of grappling with real life problems during sobriety, success being marked by longer and longer periods of serenity and fewer and fewer periods of emotional upset. There have been efforts to explore such stages with psychiatric symptom rating instruments such as the Symptom

Check-List (SCL-90-R) (Derogatis, 1977). The findings of a recent study (DeSoto, O'Donnell, Allred, & Lopes, 1985) are particularly germane to this discussion.

DeSoto and his colleagues (1985) assessed the level of emotional symptoms in 312 alcoholics in Maryland who were from a few months to 15 years abstinent in Alcoholics Anonymous (AA). As in Figure 20.1, the 163 men and 149 women studied revealed very high levels of emotional symptoms in the early months of abstinence, almost as high a level as psychiatric outpatients presenting themselves for initial interviews. Their scores were much higher than the normative population's average, only approaching the average when sober for many years. This cross-sectional study showed those in early abstinence, the first year, experienced a substantial decline in symptoms, and another decline by 3 years. The scores are much higher than some would expect, reflecting emotional symptoms of, in order of severity: depression, interpersonal sensitivity, obsessive-compulsive emotions including persisting guilt, anxiety, psychosis, paranoid ideation, somatization, phobic anxiety, and hostility. Females more rapidly improved during the first 3 years, though scores

for both genders were comparable over time. The researchers thought the symptoms depicted a long-term process of recovery from alcoholism, consistent with what is now called a protracted withdrawal syndrome, a partially reversible brain syndrome, and a general psychosocial dysfunction and demoralization following the period of active alcoholism. Several items for cognition were utilized as a cognitive deficit subscore (O'Donnell, DeSoto, & Reynolds, 1984) and the high scores on this were thought to represent a residual cognitive dysfunction.

The implications of the DeSoto et al. (1985) study are many. Some think that only the healthier individuals affected by alcoholism come to AA, so this study population may represent the healthiest alcoholics. AA maintains that its members represent only 1 of 37 alcoholics, the others presumably ill and dying from their addiction, jailed because of crimes associated with it, or in mental hospitals. Until there is a validating, well-designed, longitudinal study, on the basis of these results we have to conclude that rather high levels of emotional symptoms are only the proverbial tip of the iceberg with respect to the true magnitude of the

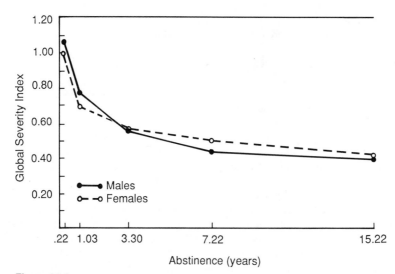

Figure 20.1
Severity of symptoms (mean scores on the Global Severity Index of the SCL-90-R) for subjects grouped by sex and length of abstinence. From DeSoto, C., O'Donnell, W., Allred, L., & Lopes, E., Alcoholism: Clinical and Experimental Research, 9 (6), 506, 1985. Copyright 1985 by Research Society on Alcoholism. Reprinted with permission.

problems of emotional disorders among *all* alcoholics, and that many more alcoholics have dual diagnoses —alcoholism plus a mental health disorder—than is generally thought.

Another implication of the study findings is the question of how resources are deployed for treating alcoholics. Presently, most funding is funneled into 28-day rehabilitation programs; the DeSoto et al. (1985) results indicate that there is an obvious need for continued treatment, probably of a different type than the present treatment facilities are equipped to handle. Reconfiguring the family dynamics that accompany alcoholism may be just that type of needed treatment, and this raises questions as to what type of personnel are needed. Twenty-eight-day rehabilitation programs are often staffed with alcoholics who themselves are recovering, and the value of this approach is incalculable. However, it should be pointed out that staff persons are themselves undergoing a prolonged and problematic recovery and consequently are not the best persons to provide family treatment, though they could be educated to do this once they themselves have undergone it.

Turning now to Figure 20.2, a theoretical recovery curve for family members is displayed alongside that of the recovering alcoholic, assuming they too enter treatment and/or self-help groups based on 12-step programs (Al-Anon, AA, Nar-Anon, Alateen, Adult Children of Alcoholics [ACOA], Codependents, etc.). There is also a theoretical comparison made to psychiatric outpatients and the normal population. Few data directly support such a curve for family members; however, numerous studies show a high incidence of affective disorders generally among spouses of alcoholics, and recent studies of children of alcoholics show similar outcomes. Clinical observations of many who work with this population support this view that emotional symptoms

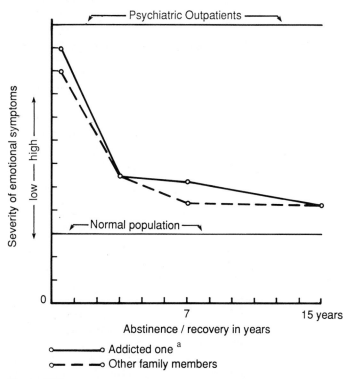

Figure 20.2
Theoretical recovery curve for family members as compared to alcoholics, psychiatric outpatients, and the normal population.
[a]Adapted from DeSoto et al., 1985.

run high, that all family members have certain mental health problems in common (e.g., low self-esteem), and that all benefit from treatment approaches such as the 12-step programs. Wegscheider's (1981) classic work demonstrates the similarities of family members' roles. Individual family members were different on the outside, with all family members having a shell of outer defenses. However, there was a common inner set of walled-off emotions for all family members. The myth that the alcoholic has the problem, and that the family will return to normal when his abstinence is established, is slowly being put to rest. All family members have problems, apparently many of them emotional ones.

Some of the similarities in cognitive and emotional dysfunction in alcoholics and their adult children are introduced in Table 20.1. Both groups have a need to learn the disease concept of alcoholism, not only to understand it but also to reduce the blame being directed toward the alcoholic, which actually prevents the

rehabilitation of the family member doing the blaming. Both groups have cognitive problems, symptoms of the alcoholics surely aggravated by lingering brain damage, that are related to the processing of information. In addition, they all suffer from what could broadly be categorized as ego deficits including low self-esteem, inabilities to modulate and express emotions, and problems in relationships. The weak ego is associated with an overblown self-centeredness that must be surrendered, as Tiebout (1949, 1954) long ago pointed out.

The remarkable parallels occurring in all family members, having to do with relationships, raise important questions as to methods of treatment. Assuming all family members have available to them membership in a self-help group, and the addicted one has an inpatient 28-day treatment minimally, treatment for all of them should include a focus on interpersonal relationships and ways in which to process emotional information. Particular deficits for any of the family members could be identified with an intake interview by a qualified

Table 20.1
Similarities in Cognitive and Emotional Dysfunction in Alcoholics and Their Children

	Alcoholics	*Children of Alcoholics*
Cognitive	Trouble remembering things Difficulty in making decisions Trouble concentrating Your mind going blank Feeling blocked in getting things done Repeated unpleasant thought that will not leave your mind (DeSoto et al., 1985)	Lacks in information, experience, cognitive processing and a widely recognized need for resolution of emotional problems on a cognitive level first, teaching how to translate information into productive behavior (Woititz, 1976, 1983)
	Need to learn the disease concept of alcoholism	Need to learn the disease concept of alcoholism
Emotional	The wish to maintain a sense of personal control Denial of dependency needs Striving to look independent Unable to ask for help Problems with intimate relationships Emotions viewed as dangerous Unable to put impulses into words Intense guilt, anger, and powerlessness under a facade of control (Levinson, 1985)	The wish to maintain a sense of personal control Denial of dependency needs Striving to look independent Unable to ask for help Problems with intimate relationships Emotions viewed as dangerous Unable to put impulses into words Intense guilt, anger, and powerlessness under a facade of control (Levinson, 1985)

professional or assessment by means of a wide range of instruments available. The instrument used in the DeSoto study could be utilized, the Symptom Check-List (SCL-90-R) devised by Derogatis (1977), along with the O'Donnell subscale, (O'Donnell et al., 1984) to measure cognitive deficits.

Thus far, an underlying assumption is that the mental health and other life problems with addiction exist mostly in the psyches or behaviors of the individual, secondarily in the relationships the individual has with others. Conventional treatments often utilized for such problems include the psychoanalytic, the behavioral, and the psychodynamic. Each, however, in its own way is flawed. The psychoanalytic falls short because it is expensive and time-consuming. Not only is the cost prohibitive, but also during the process, the addicted family member may not become clean of drugs and sober, because this is not a focus of the therapy. The behavioral approach, effective for reducing stress and somatization, has a continuing effect only so long as the positive reinforcement of therapy continues. The psychodynamic approach focuses on the needs related to ego deficits and the self; however, it does not focus enough on context, and gains made can disappear when family situations are overwhelming.

The problems associated with substance abuse arise and take shape in the family, are reinforced, sustained by, and intertwined with the family dynamics. Consequently, it is in the family that critical and incisive interventions must be made. And, since the problem is one of multigenerational transmission of addiction from generation to generation, family patterns occurring over at least three generations must be addressed. A family focus is needed, even if the individual seems to have no family, for the client is a carrier of family patterns and must understand them to overcome the illness. The same thing is true whether family ties are close, conflictual, or alienated since the interpersonal relationships support the addiction and its associated problems. Finally, a family focus will be needed, no matter what is found in the future about the genetic control of addiction (Bower, 1988), because the family dynamics of relating turn such genes on and off.

FAMILY THERAPY INTERVENTIONS

By the time any member of a family—but not likely the addicted member—seeks treatment, a certain fixed des-

peration and hopelessness has set in. Most likely the one seeking treatment is a very responsible, competent, and overfunctioning individual. The facade presented to the outside world covers deep anxieties, fears, guilt, interpersonal sensitivities, intense and unmet dependency needs, and poor self-esteem. These hidden flaws periodically emerge, and become internally felt and externally visible, during episodes of crisis at work, in intimate relationships with others, or in family matters concerning the nuclear or extended family. Treatment is then sought.

The first objective is to restore hope, to communicate that the family situation can improve and that perhaps, given time, the addicted family member can be brought into treatment. These reassurances restore hope but they depend on the cooperation and willingness of the client to try new behavioral strategies. Interestingly, hope also emerges with the major intervention of the drawing of a family genogram.

The Family Genogram

A sample family with addiction is portrayed in Figure 20.3, though the genogram may extend well beyond this three-generational drawing to include progeny, ancestors, and other relevant information (Bowen, 1978; McGoldrick & Gerson, 1985). The first questions generally asked to construct the genogram include birth dates, death dates, and marriage dates for all family members, though these are not represented in Figure 20.3. Other early and helpful information includes occupations, birthplaces, present location, and what each person is (or was) like. Illnesses of the various family members are noted, including alcohol or drug addiction and causes of death as appropriate. During this initial effort, extremely valuable nonverbal and verbal facts emerge in the discussion. For example, the family "black sheep" commonly is mentioned, a role associated with scapegoating in the family.

As the genogram is drawn, and added to over time, family members make important personal gains, demonstrating the genogram is in itself an important intervention. Positive and calm feelings return, a new self-confidence appears, hope is renewed, and a resolve takes shape to change the dysfunctional patterns to prevent passing them on to yet another generation. Perhaps these occur as awareness grows that there was a historical pattern of survival, despite the family problems. Doing the genogram is also an aid in learning

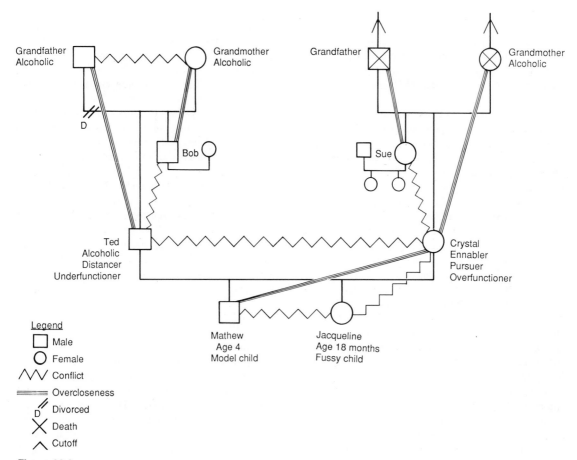

Figure 20.3
Typical patterns found in a family with addictions.

from the mistakes and achievements of others. It engenders pride in family. Certainly a most important outcome in a reframing—from intense concern with the present and its problems—to include the family's past, a base from which future and new goals can emerge.

A holistic view of a system requires addressing the interdependencies and interactions among the different components, in this case, the relationships among the various family members. At the level of the family, this is where the interventions must occur. It is of great importance to identify what those interpersonal patterns are and, as in Figure 20.3, the typical family patterns associated with addiction are illustrated.

Crystal, married to Ted who is an alcoholic, is the one to seek treatment in this case. In doing so, she has crossed the boundary from the usually very closed family that hides the secret of addiction to the outside world. She has opened up the family system to a source of external influence, an act eventually and inevitably changing the system, with consequences for all family members. She has done this largely because exhaustion set in after many, many years of overfunctioning, of taking on more family responsibilities, as Ted's functioning declined and his alcoholism progressed. Though she is told undertaking intervention involves change, which is not always easy, she feels she must pursue it.

That alcoholism exists at the grandparent level comes to light while drawing the genogram, and Crystal is told of the strong genetic control for this disease.

This relieves a burden of guilt, since she has believed she could be responsible for her husband's alcoholism. As patterns of relationship are explored, she becomes aware that marital conflict also existed in previous generations, that she and Ted learned this pattern in childhood, and they acquired few healthy relationship skills due to lack of exposure. She learns that unresolved conflict has created bitterness in both her and Ted, constituting what Guerin, Fay, Burden, and Kautto (1987) call a "bitter bank." This information clarifies what she is learning in Al-Anon meetings, with respect to resentments. Marital conflicts also meant the lack of a strong spousal and parental platform with which the spouses could have expressed their common beliefs in child rearing, monitored their relationships with in-laws, created intimacy, and identified mutual goals to pursue.

An invisible, but crucially important boundary between parents and children would have existed and Crystal's closest relationship would have been with Ted, not with her alcoholic mother and oldest child, as shown in Figure 20.3. Such a boundary would have prevented the sharing of inappropriate information with her mother and child. Without this boundary, Crystal's complaints about her husband and his drinking were shared with especially Mathew who, though only 4 years old, already feels superior to and critical of his father and equal to his mother. Mathew has become a parentified child, too caught up in the triangle of his parents to attend wholly to his own developmental tasks. Life's central goal for him is to grow up quickly, achieve at whatever he undertakes to absolve his father's underfunctioning, and through his overachieving rescue his mother from her fate. Later 18-month-old Jacqueline will develop a similar role, meanwhile discounting her mother with whom she already is in conflict, and being overly close to a father she will attempt to redeem either through overfunctioning or acting out to distract the family from its real problems.

In Figure 20.3, we can see that children in all generations, notably Crystal and Ted, lived in similar triangles constituting coalitions that set one parent and child against the other parent and child. An implication of this pattern is that children cannot be close to their siblings, thereby drawing strength out of these associations over a lifetime; instead, they are doomed to mutual alienation and conflict. The learning is at a deep level, and later it will mean problems in relating to others at a peer level, at work and in marriages, as the pattern of conflict is replicated.

Other Family Interventions

The previously mentioned boundary between generational levels and the natural hierarchy of generations are marked off continually or weakened through the relationships as people interact. It is necessary to identify the sequence of acts by individuals as they move toward or away from each other, to examine their closeness and distance patterns which, when viewed in this way, assume more importance than is generally believed by the family members. In Family Systems Theory, one type of reciprocal pattern is labeled *pursuing* and another type, *distancing* (Bowen, 1978). Retreating from personal interactions by ingesting quantities of alcohol and becoming relatively unavailable to others is distancing behavior. Monitoring the alcohol intake, pleading with the alcoholic to stop drinking, and hoping and wishing the alcoholic will change are all pursuing behaviors. Distancing and pursuing are complementary behaviors, that is, left to their own devices, pursuers and distancers seek each other and trigger each other's behavior. A corollary to this is that each is forever disappointed in the other's behavior, constantly seeking to change it as in Figure 20.4. The behaviors can be modified and those usually changed first are pursuing behaviors, because the pursuer often seeks treatment for assistance in changing the alcoholic. The pursuer must be taught what seems to be a law of human behavior: pursuit always results in distance, as the pursued one moves away from relationship; however, if pursuing is modified, the distancer eventually will approach the pursuer. Pursuers have trouble waiting it out, however, and make the mistake of reactivating pursuit when the distancer shows any sign of approach. Fogarty (1983) has elaborated on this pattern at some length.

One of the best remedies for pursuing behavior is strongly encouraging the pursuer's work on the genogram. It gives the pursuer another direction to move in, thus decreasing the pursuing toward the spouse distancer. As genogram work proceeds, the pursuer works on differentiating a self by working on relationships in the family of origin, and eventually becomes involved in new personal goals and a higher level of functioning. The distancer, most often the addicted family member, comes to dread the possibility that the pursuer might leave the relationship. If the pursuer can persevere and solidify gains, the distancer will enter treatment. In the meantime, the pursuer has attended Al-Anon meetings and also AA meetings to gain

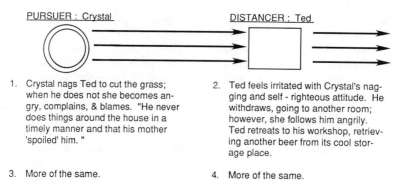

PURSUER : Crystal   DISTANCER : Ted

1. Crystal nags Ted to cut the grass; when he does not she becomes angry, complains, & blames. "He never does things around the house in a timely manner and that his mother 'spoiled' him. "

2. Ted feels irritated with Crystal's nagging and self - righteous attitude. He withdraws, going to another room; however, she follows him angrily. Ted retreats to his workshop, retrieving another beer from its cool storage place.

3. More of the same.

4. More of the same.

Figure 20.4
A pursuer and distancer sequence of mutually causative behaviors.

some understanding of addiction, explored the treatment facilities available, become less overwhelmed by emotions and clearer about stating positions for the sake of personal growth and development, and has prepared for the eventual scenario should the distancer enter and complete treatment. As these developments occur, for a time it looks as if the pursuer is ready to leave the distancing alcoholic, because being ready to do so is imperative for the pursuer's health. It is necessary that the nonalcoholic partner develop this mind set. It is a powerful means of leverage for treatment of the addiction. It is also necessary to maintain it during the early stages of recovery, otherwise relapses occur in response to a too forgiving attitude in the pursuer. Unfortunately, when the nonalcoholic partner does not receive needed support during this period, the relationship ends. Then, it is inevitable that the two will seek out yet other partners and repeat the very same pattern.

Similar patterns exist with respect to the level of energies the partners expend on family responsibilities. In this case Crystal was the overfunctioner. She had assumed on more tasks involved with family life including complete care of the children, housecleaning, yard work, arrangements for house maintenance, making plans for the family's limited social life, and tending to medical care needs that arose. Her increased overfunctioning had been met by reciprocal underfunctioning in Ted who had neglected tasks by drinking more alcohol. In Al-Anon terms, Crystal had become an enabler and made it easier for Ted to drink to excess and avoid the consequences of his alcoholism. It is understandable, once the addiction is established, a person like Crystal carries out many adult tasks in the household; but earlier there were opportunities to prevent this from happening by coaching Crystal to confine her efforts to her own responsibilities and not worry about Ted's. Early in the relationship clearly assigned roles or deliberate underfunctioning on Crystal's part would have prompted a higher level of functioning in Ted. Gains can be made now by helping Crystal reconfigure her patterns of relating to people in her family of origin, and this will change how she relates to Ted. Substantial gains are made when the two patterns, at the marital level and the level of her original family, are linked as she thinks through the sequence of interactions with Ted and identifies where the same overfunctioner pattern existed in her family of origin.

For Crystal, situations in her family of origin had a characteristic pattern of overcloseness to her mother and distance from her father. Usually this primary triangle is very central to how one differentiates a self from the family of origin. Even if the father is nonexistent or separated from the family, there is relationship to the absent one and attitudes about him in the family. Crystal's overcloseness to her mother gave her a special place, a position above her father. She was also above her mother, since the alcoholic mother needed Crystal's care and concern. The family history was incorporated into her psyche, and Crystal left the family deriving most of her self-esteem from the caretaking of others, overfunctioning, and denigrating the value of the male parent and older sister. This pattern became replicated in the family she and Ted established, then Mathew experienced a triangle similar to the one Crystal lived in as a child.

So long as relationships are skewed in the family of origin, there is less opportunity to differentiate a self at a high level. To help Crystal remedy this, she was encouraged to move toward the distant parent, her father. He is no longer living and, during his lifetime, was alienated from his family of origin, making this task difficult but not impossible. Nonliving relatives live on in the memories of families and neighbors, in public and private records and memorabilia of various types, and in the cemeteries of communities in which they lived. Making trips to places, exploring histories and cemeteries, talking with other relatives who knew the father when he was living, in short, reconstructing the past can be of great benefit to Crystal. Such adventures help elaborate fully the different aspects of personalities that before were only partly visible.

As the father's personality, his family of origin, and his roles in life became clearer, Crystal began to appreciate the full dimensions of the man; a man who was an easily discounted alcoholic, but also a person who had youth and dreams and good intentions. As she liked her father more, she appreciated her mother somewhat less, which was not bad because previously she had put her on a pedestal. She became more real and human, thus easier emulated, now that she was less saintlike. Other beneficial effects came about as Crystal worked to form a one-to-one relationship with each individual in her family.

The distraction of working on her family of origin gave her new confidence and other ways in which to view her children and her husband. She became interested in Ted's family, able to observe their patterns with a new objectivity, and able to see how those patterns were projected to her marriage and children. She began moving closer to her daughter Jacqueline in an understanding way. She stopped complaining about her husband's drinking to her children. Her new respect for her husband did not mean approval of his alcoholism, but she blamed him less and respected his position of authority in the family more, even though he could not live up to it. The changes occurred over a lengthy period of time, about a year.

At some point Crystal began to make plans as it became clear that Ted was caught in the grip of his addiction, perhaps always would be, but that she and the children had to go on with their lives. This is a very difficult decision to make, and she needed much support over a period of time to get clear about this. Ted could discern this and volunteered to come into treatment. Finding Crystal disbelieving and rather cynical about the outcome, and further, finding she was making plans to leave, Ted made two telephone calls, one to AA and one to a nearby treatment center. He had interpreted her lack of pursuing, the fact she ceased taking responsibility for his addiction, the lessening of their marital conflict, and her new and renewed relationships with her family members, as signals she had forsaken him and was changing her life to one not including him. He became frightened for himself and was gripped by panic. Blindly he realized he had to do something to help himself or he would lose his wife and children. He knew his life was on the line.

What other methods can be used in family therapy to ensure a positive outcome? Strong patterns of behavior are associated with addiction, and one pattern is resistance to treatment by the addicted family member. But also the nonaddicted spouse, or codependent to use the popular term, also exhibits strong resistance to change through persistent and powerful blame toward the substance abuser. Also, there is resistance toward exploring the root of the problem back in the families of origin. Those seeking help may be puzzled by an emphasis on family work, when to them the real problem is the alcoholism and the blameworthy alcoholic or addict. At first they cannot see that their own direct efforts have failed and that professional efforts to do more of the same are doomed to failure too, until or unless some leverage can be gained that is more powerful than the addiction. In the hands of an experienced professional, the family system, already more powerful than the addiction though at present actually sustaining it, can be shifted to overcome the addiction and the long-standing family patterns. This does not mean, of course, that interventions for necessary medical care, hospitalization, or even incarceration are not undertaken; it does mean that, long-term, the interventions having the most powerful effects are family ones.

With strong resistance, the choice intervention almost always is to go along with the resistance, substantially supporting the client's point of view even more fully than the client himself. If the alcoholic resists discontinuing his alcohol intake, he should be encouraged to try to drink more, perhaps he will feel better if he does. There is seldom any danger in using this approach, since he will drink anyway, no matter what is said or done, and he will drink the amount required to maintain the blood alcohol level his addiction demands. He is so invested in his resisting whatever someone else suggests, on the other hand, he will heroically stop drinking just to prove he can, thinking the person encouraging him to drink more must think he is an alcoholic who needs the alcohol. A similar approach works with nonalcoholic spouses. When nothing is being accomplished in moving forward with the family work, they can be encouraged to try pursuing harder, that perhaps they are just not trying enough. Overfunctioning too can be encouraged by saying that there is, after all, only one responsible adult in the household and, if things aren't working, it may be a question of not trying hard enough. This method, called the use of reversal, usually results in the client indignantly refusing to do what is suggested and what she has done in the past. Then productive family work can resume.

Other suggested techniques include dividing the session in half, partly for family work and partly for immediate problems (which can then be tied to the family of origin); homework assignments to identify sequences in behavior, for example, over- and underfunctioning; reading about family patterns and roles in alcoholic or addicted families; attending self-help meetings; engaging in self-care activities such as proper medical care and attending to needs for socialization; and identifying closely held values and beliefs. Over the course of work with a given individual and family, all of the above-mentioned methods will be useful at some time or other. One family member may engage in this work while the partner comes in later. In any case, the guiding principle is to work with the family members who are willing, always with multigenerational focus. Being mindful of the interactions and interdependencies prevailing in family life, working with just one member induces change in the other family members and in the entire family system.

FAMILY SYSTEMS CHANGE

It is often said, when extended families have undergone change the family never again will be quite the same. This truism makes it no less fearsome for family members to undertake changes that are needed. If their energies to contain the family problem are distracted to other purposes or activities that involve change, they fear the problem could get out of hand. Things get worse before they can get better; clients know this at some level, and this should be mentioned at the outset. The apparent worsening is due to the inherent nature of

change. A dysfunctional family system with addiction usually undergoes a predictable changing cycle, lots of activity, but without real change occurring. For example, a building tension occurs between spouses who pursue and distance, this escalates to a certain level, the drinking bout occurs again, and the family system settles down until the cycle is repeated. No real change occurs this way, though energies are spent. The dysfunctional patterns are repetitive.

When true change does occur with family treatment, new information triggers the system, and it is thrown into disequilibrium, during which time events and behaviors become unpredictable and sometimes chaotic (Eells, 1989a, 1989b). The surprises are not always welcome. As new behaviors are tried out these conflict with older, entrenched behaviors of other family members who represent the conservative family faction. Ultimately, the entire system is shaken, but after a long enough period of time of experimentation and conflict, the system appears to close down with a plateau stage, during which the system appears to do not much of anything. However, during the plateau period internal reordering occurs and then ends suddenly with a restructuring of the entire system. A new, higher level behavior appears, and along with it there is an "aha experience" that comes with new learning. The system is reenergized, whereas before, there was only disorder and energy depletion. Crucial to the entire change process was an influx of new and better information than the system previously possessed. This model of change, Prigogine's discovery for which he won the Nobel prize, is more fully described in his work (Prigogine and Stengers, 1984) and was applied previously to families by this author (Eells, 1985, 1989a, 1989b; Eells & Horensky, 1985). The absorbing rhythmic effects, the irresistible and catastrophic power of major change, when it is overtaking a system, is a true vortex, and family members feel caught up in it. The interventions suggested will lead the addicted family down just such a pathway resulting in improvement. Just such a momentous, dramatic change empowers the family and halts the addiction. Perhaps even for generations to come, the family will never again be quite the same, although fine tuning smaller changes will continue.

FAILURES IN FAMILY THERAPY

As with all types of treatment for alcoholism and drug addiction, family therapy has its share of failures, and it is well to mention a cautionary note. Although there are no data on treatment failures involving family approaches in the substance abuse field, there is information about therapy failures with families in general. Coleman (1985) edited a book on the subject, analyzing antecedent factors existing in the families, therapist variables, and the context within which failures in therapy occurred.

Family Variables

In Coleman's (1985) book, families who were treatment failures possessed certain characteristics: *(a)* existence of the same symptoms over a lengthy history of 3 or more years; *(b)* previous experiences with the therapy (for example, previous therapy for an individual or family may lead them to have certain expectations about how therapy should be done); *(c)* limitations of family members imposed by physical health, poor medical histories, poor socioeconomic conditions, and general inadequacies in overall functional level socially and ocupationally; and *(d)* the existence of certain diagnoses, such as psychoses (schizophrenia, manic depressive illness) limiting contacts with reality or severe personality disturbances (sociopathic, borderline), widely known as very difficult to treat successfully.

Coleman's (1985) antecedent characteristics of treatment failures also included alcoholism and drug addictions. We could assume from the abundant, first-hand clinical observations presented that such addictive symptoms had been present for a significant number of years. Also mentioned was the family's life-cycle stage of development; almost all failures were in families in which the dominant issue was growing up and leaving home, a family stage often marked by abusive experimentation with mood-altering substances, if not outright addiction. Other characteristics of many of the families with substance abuse, for example the lack of intact family systems, result in therapy failures according to Coleman's (1985) analysis.

Therapist Variables

Factors regarding the therapist or person rendering treatment were also critical. For some time those in the field of psychotherapy have recognized that therapists with considerable training, wide experience relevant to the presenting problem, and having an empathic connection are successful with patients. The therapist's

own family history and current personal life situation are also central. Given this, in the field of substance abuse, we could expect that those working with families with addiction should have wide knowledge and experience in the field, and should have addressed successfully their own family's problems with alcoholism and drug addiction, as well as their own problems. We could expect that current difficulties in the therapist's life or family of origin could undermine effectiveness. Perhaps the ideal person to do therapy with families who have substance abuse is someone who has had academic training and supervised therapy with such client families. The therapist's enthusiasm and interest in the case may very well depend on having a deep personal interest.

Contextual Variables

Other factors surround the therapy; some of these can be controlled more than others, and some of the factors may augment and some may undermine efforts with family therapy. If other therapists are involved, particularly a cotherapist, both persons should be qualified as mentioned above, and their alliance should be free of substantial struggle or competition that would be distracting to client families and diminishing of potential outcomes.

Coleman (1985) also mentions the possible destructiveness of ongoing collisions with other professional systems. The client family may be involved with other social systems (e.g., schools, courts, other social agencies) which work at cross purposes to family therapy. The author's personal experience in graduate school comes to mind, when a client family was involved with 27 different agencies in a city that prided itself on its social services. The single, head of the household could hardly keep her appointments straight with the people representing these agencies who came into her home each week, let alone sort out the different pieces of advice she received. The situation was resolved by a meeting attended by professionals from each of the 27 agencies. One person was selected to work with the family and act as liaison to the other agencies. This worked well. Current examples from the field of substances abuse abound. Perhaps this problem is at its worst in rehabilitation facilities where several different therapies exist for the inpatient (including individual therapy, group therapy, alcoholism counseling, AA or other 12-step, self-help programs, education about substance abuse, and family education as a very introductory form of family work). Anyone who has attempted family therapy with such families in rehabilitation facilities will readily recognize the difficulties involved, most of which emanate from the different professionals involved who insist on the rectitude and priority of their different, conflicting approach in the client's recovery.

Another limiting factor is the referral circumstances, whether referral is family-motivated, whether the family is involved as only one part of the required treatment by an agency, and who in the family is seeking treatment. When family therapy is family-motivated, family members are seeking a goal they intrinsically want. When reluctant family members come to therapy, the professional must enlist them by listening for and helping to draw out personal and closely held goals of the individuals, parents, and children. Often all family members can agree they want growth and development for all, and parents usually can identify with a common goal of not wanting to transmit to yet another generation an unwanted burden of family dysfunction and addiction. Goals associated with only abstinence from the addictive drug, as desirable as these are, focus the attention on the addicted member, when the family members need and deserve treatment in their own right, independent of the addict.

Coleman (1985) mentions that inadequate or inaccurate assessment of the family to begin with leads to failure, and this is intertwined with the lack of an adequate conceptual framework. In the author's experience with families with addiction, successful treatment must include at least a three-generational perspective to identify the power distribution and boundaries in the family, important cross-generational coalitions among family members, and the process with which the dynamics involving addiction are transmitted from generation to generation. Without this knowledge, family therapy predictably ends in failure or results in a short-lived, only partial success.

SUMMARY

It is a maxim in general systems theory that, when dysfunction is found at one system level, change in that system can be brought about by enlarging the focus to include the next higher system level. In this chapter, data were presented to illustrate just how complex the problem of alcoholism and drug addiction is, in that many individuals are affected, but the family members of those addicted are also involved so deeply that only curing the addict and sending him back to the family will not cure the problem. The focus of treatment must be enlarged to include the nuclear family and the extended family and the true length of time in recovery —a protracted one—must be addressed.

The holistic view of the family as the focus includes the interactions, interdependencies, and intergenerational and interpersonal boundaries among the various family members, all of which constitute distinctive family patterns. In families with addiction, these patterns are often rigid, inflexible, too pronounced or almost entirely absent, and the work of family therapy is to bring such patterns into balance. Patterns of pursuing and distancing, over- and underfunctioning, and triangles are easily taught and eagerly learned by dysfunctional families, particularly by the spouse of the alcoholic or drug abuser, usually the first one to seek treatment. However, the most important intervention may well be the drawing of the family genogram and a refocusing of this spouse's attention to include the families of origin. Moving the focus up to include the senior generational hierarchies makes significant change possible, by uncovering sources of stress and introducing other alternatives.

The Prigogine model of systems change has proven efficacy with families of addiction, and its stages of change give those who would intervene some notion of the likely scenarios and what can work at different times.

Finally, common antecedents of failures in family therapy were presented in this chapter as a reminder that certain strains and forces may preclude therapeutic improvement, or at least tremendously complicate the treatment undertaken. Particularly with this group of families, it is well to keep in mind the therapist should be a coach who helps the family to uncover and remove obstacles, so the family's basic tendencies toward health may find expression. Keeping expectations low, while continuing to link dysfunctional patterns back to similar patterns in the families of origin, together with a multi-generational focus, is an effective, and in the long run, a cost- and time-saving approach.

REFERENCES

Bowen, M. (1978). *Family therapy in clinical practice*. New York: Jason Aronson.

Bower, B. (1988). Alcoholism's elusive genes. *Science News, 134,* 74–75, 79.

Coleman, S. B. (1985). *Failures in family therapy.* New York: Guilford Press.

Derogatis, L. R. (1977). *SCL-90-R: Administration, scoring and procedures manual.* Baltimore, MD: Johns Hopkins University School of Medicine, Psychometrics Research Unit.

DeSoto, C., O'Donnell, W., Allred, L., & Lopes, E. (1985). Symptomatology in alcoholics in various stages of abstinence. *Alcoholism: Clinical and Experimental Research, 9*(6), 505–512.

Eells, M. A. W. (1985). The alcoholic client and family. In D. L. Critchely & J. T. Maurin (Eds.), *The clinical specialist in psychiatric and mental health nursing.* New York: John Wiley & Sons.

Eells, M. A. W. (1986). Interventions with alcoholics and their families. *Nursing Clinics of North America, 21*(3), 493–504.

Eells, M. A. W., & Horensky, J. (1985). Temporal perceptions as self-regulating structures in two populations: Individuals and family members. In B. H. Benathy (Ed.), *Proceedings of the Society for General Systems Research,* International Conference, Los Angeles, May 26–31, 1985.

Eells, M. A. (1989a). *Case studies in home health: Problem families, problem agencies.* Baltimore: Williams & Wilkins.

Eells, M. A. W. (1989b). The Prigogine model of change for family systems: Stages, emergent properties, and generational hierarchies. International Society for Systems Science 33rd Annual Conference, University of Edinburgh, Scotland, July 2–7, 1989.

Fogarty, T. (1983). The distancer and the pursuer. In *The family,* New Rochelle, NY: The Center and Family Learning.

Guerin, P. J., Fay, L. F., Burden, S. L., & Kautto, J. G. (1987). *The evaluation and treatment of marital conflict.* New York: Basic Books, Inc.

Levinson, V. R. (1985). The compatibility of the disease concept with a psychodynamic approach in the treatment of alcoholism. Psychosocial issues in the treatment of alcoholism. *Alcoholism Treatment Quarterly, 2*(1), 7–24.

McGoldrick, M., & Gerson, R. (1985). *Genograms in family assessment.* New York: W. W. Norton.

Myers, J. K., Weissman, M. M., Tischler, G. L., Holzer, C. E., Leaf, P. J., Orvaschel, H., Anthony, J. C., Boyd, J. H., Burke, J. D., Kramer, M., & Stoltzman, R. (1984). Six-month prevalence of psychiatric disorders in three communities: 1980 to 1982. *Archives of General Psychiatry, 41,* 959–967.

O'Donnell, W. E., DeSoto, C. B., & Reynolds, D. M. (1984). A cognitive deficit subscale of the SCL-90-R. *Journal of Clinical Psychology, 40,* 241–246.

Prigogine, I., & Stengers, I. (1984). *Order out of chaos.* New York: Bantam Books.

Tiebout, H. M. (1949). The act of surrender in the therapeutic process. With special reference to alcoholism. *Quarterly Journal of Studies on Alcoholism, 10,* 48–58.

Tiebout, H. (1954). Ego factors in surrender to alcoholism. *Quarterly Journal of Studies on Alcoholism, 15,* 610–621.

Wegscheider, S. (1981). *Another chance.* Palo Alto, CA: Science & Behavior Books.

Woititz, J. G. (1976). A study of self-esteem in children of alcoholics. *Dissertation Abstract International, 37,* 12-A, 7554-A.

Woititz, J. G. (1983). *Adult children of alcoholics.* Pompano Beach, FL: Health Communications, Inc.

CHAPTER 21

WOMEN IN RECOVERY

Ann D. Sumners

World wide, women represent half of the population, about one-third of the official labor force, and do nearly two-thirds of all the work (Smith, 1987). Furthermore, it is estimated that one-third of all households in the world are headed by a woman. Yet, women are concentrated in the lower paid and most menial occupations (Smith, 1987).

The woman of today faces economic pressures to work outside the home, has limited career options, has child care responsibility, and experiences stress from single-parenting and divorce. Twenty-five years ago women's roles in the family and society were clear and well-defined. For example, when an aging parent required care, the daughter would assume that responsibility. Today women are caught between the role expectations of the past and the demands of present. Unfortunately, when many women attempt to meet past role expectations they find they are no longer afforded the protection and assistance from the family that once existed; rather, these roles are simply added to her already burgeoning demands. Each aspect of her multiple roles, with its concomitant expectations, strains her existing coping skills. It is at this point that many women seek relief and solace by using drugs and alcohol. Although women have received more attention from researchers since the 1970s empirical data related to prevention and treatment remains minimal. Women remain somewhat neglected in the field of research.

Whether or not women are in treatment or recovery, they are not a uniform and simplistic group. They share a common gender but are diverse in other aspects of their persons and lives. Understanding their diversity is essential prior to any discussion of their use of drugs, alcohol, or other substances and most emphatically with treatment and recovery. Each addicted patient cannot be treated as if she were a random draw from an essentially homogeneous population (MacAndrew, 1988).

We live in a drug using society. From corporate executives who use liquor, nicotine, and prescription drugs, to the young who use crack, pot, and heroin, drugs offer instant gratification. Yet, the issue of women's substance use cannot be understood independently of the position of women in society (Marsh, Colten, & Tucker, 1982). Early in Colonial America, a scarlet D was placed on the clothing of a drunken woman to mark her evilness (Sandmaier, 1980). Regrettably, the social stigma continues to exist for the woman who abuses substances (Beckman & Amaro, 1986; Efinger, 1983; Marsh et al., 1982). Although some research indicates that the social stigma has lessened (Nathan & Skinstad, 1987), the reactions to alcohol and drug abuse in women remains harsh, which promotes hiding the problem (National Institute on Alcohol Abuse and Alcoholism, 1981).

Orford (1985) supports the view that only when a substance or behavior threatens the young or the caretakers of the young do we see a surge of social interest to limit or prohibit its use. The fact that women share the general problems of alcohol and drug abuse is commonly accepted. It is sad that the focus on neonatal addiction and fetal alcohol syndrome has been used as evidence of impairment in the caretaker role and as reason to further reject a group of women who need help so badly (Gomberg, 1982).

A new understanding of women and substance abuse in our society is required to dispel the myths and misperceptions. Genetics, psychosocial variables, circumstances, and biologic differences interact in each woman to produce a unique and complex individual. This chapter will include a discussion of assessment, risk factors, and characteristics of women in treatment for substance abuse. Research findings will be incorporated in the discussion to clarify some of the issues unique to women as well as to substantiate treatment concerns and prevention efforts.

The major focus of this chapter is women's treatment and recovery from alcohol and drug abuse, but coexisting problems cannot be ignored. Depression, a history of family violence, and substance abuse may be present in the same person so that the study of any one of these problems to the exclusion of the other limits our understanding of the person and the problems (McBride, 1987).

MAJOR THEMES

The major themes that dominate the literature on women's substance use and abuse include: *(a)* changing social mores (McCormack, 1985); *(b)* a tendency to treat women as a homogeneous entity rather than as a social group whose substance use and abuse varies by circumstances (McCormack, 1985); *(c)* viewing alcoholism or drug abuse as dependent variables making gender insignificant; *(d)* sex-role conflict (Gomberg, 1977; Wilsnack, 1973a); *(e)* stress and coping; and *(f)* role conflict or role burden (Marsh, 1982; McBride, 1987). These themes recur in terms of explanations for, antecedents to, and consequences of women's substance involvement.

A social factor that has been implicated as an explanation for women's substance abuse is her relationships. When the significant other is a heavy drinker, either parent or spouse, the woman is more likely to abuse substances (Harrison & Belille, 1987; Wanberg & Horn, 1970). However, it is a common misconception that only alcoholic women have alcohol problems. Women can have a wide range of problems associated with alcohol, including job difficulties, problems with friends and family, accidents, arrests, and health and emotional problems (National Institute of Alcohol Abuse and Alcoholism, 1981). Many of the problems result from being in a relationship with an actively chemically dependent person. Indeed, codependency issues may be the reason some women begin the long process of recovery. One self-help organization that offers support for the woman trapped in a chemically dysfunctional relationship is Al-Anon.

Case Example

Jane has been married to Phillip for 15 years. They have two boys age 14 and 12. Phillip, who was always a drinker, is getting drunk on a frequent basis and has started leaving work early to have a few with his buddies. After his evening of drinking, he becomes abusive to Jane and the boys. For the past 6 months the marital conflicts plus the financial problems have made life almost unbearable for Jane. She believes Phillip when he tells her it is her nagging and the boys' bad behavior that makes him drink so much. She has tried everything she knows to keep Phillip happy so he will not drink so much, but all efforts have failed. She now feels helpless, hopeless, angry, and resentful, and is contemplating a separation. A counselor recommends that she attend an Al-Anon meeting.

Jane resists the idea because she knows it is her husband who is sick, but she does go. The support of the group helps her begin to talk about what it is like to live with an alcoholic and to see that she must let go of the caretaking role with him.

Substance abuse is more common in men than women, yet it is a significant health problem for women (Fillmore, 1987; Hilton, 1987; Vannicelli, 1984). Alcohol is the most frequently abused substance in women (Bry, 1983); however, benzodiazepines are almost equally threatening to women (Marsh et al., 1982; Ogur, 1986). Women receive two-thirds of the prescriptions (Ogur, 1986) for these drugs, which are written by nonpsychiatrists for anxiety or as a sleeping aid with little clinical follow-up provided (Kulberg, 1986). Although benzodiazepines offer a wide safety margin in dosage, they are potentially deadly when combined with alcohol or other central nervous system depressants.

Several explanations have been offered for the paucity of information on women's substance abuse. First, a majority of studies were conducted in treatment settings where women are not available in large numbers (Gomberg, 1986; Harrison & Belille, 1987; Vannicelli, 1984). Second, research reports frequently combine the genders when reporting findings making it impossible to glean information about women. In addition, researchers assumed that there were minimal differences between genders in terms of addiction; therefore, what worked for males would work equally well for females (Babcock & Conner, 1981; Beckman, 1975; Beckman & Amaro, 1986). The research studies which address substance abuse in women are primarily concerned with patterns and frequency of alcohol consumption (Fillmore, 1987; John, 1987; Wilsnack, Wilsnack, & Klassen, 1984). These studies show that women are predominantly abstainers or light drinkers.

INCIDENCE AND PREVALENCE

Any mood-altering substance has the potential to be abused. However, alcohol has the unique distinction of being socially acceptable even when used to produce self-intoxication. Some assert that alcoholism is the third most serious health problem in the United States (Helzer, 1987), with women accounting for at least 20%–25% of the 12 million identified alcoholics (Beckman & Kocel, 1982). Other sources place the range of women thought to be alcoholic at 20%–50%, yet only 20% of the alcoholics now in treatment are women (Efinger, 1983). A paradox is evident in that cultural mores protect women's use and abuse of substances and simultaneously reject the addicted woman (National Institute on Alcohol Abuse and Alcoholism, 1981).

The scope of the problem of substance abuse in women is difficult to ascertain. In the majority of studies, women are compared to men in terms of prevalence of use. Most national surveys have focused on trends and patterns of alcohol consumption in both sexes (Fillmore, 1987; Hilton, 1987; Wilsnack et al., 1986). The reported data are consistent in that men consume more alcohol more frequently than women (Gomberg, 1982; Hilton, 1987). Women are identified more frequently as abstainers (Celentano & McQueen, 1984; Helzer, 1987; Hilton, 1987). However, an estimated 60% of the women in the United States drink and at least 2 million can be classified as alcoholics (Gomberg, 1982; McCormack, 1985). The ratio of male to female addiction in the general population remains questionable (Bissell & Skorina, 1987) due in part to the variable estimates of prevalence provided by population surveys (Celentano & McQueen, 1984). The lack of consistent definitions and measurements yields variable estimates of the scope of the problem (Celentano & McQueen, 1984). For instance, Ferrence and Whitehead (1980) found evidence that the number of women with alcohol problems was increasing. On the other hand, Wilsnack and colleagues (1984) found there was no major increase in women's consumption in general, but there was an increase in the consumption among middle-aged women.

According to Fillmore (1987), the percentage of American women who drink varies with age and generation. Younger women show a relatively high percentage of drinkers and those over age 50 a relatively low percentage (Fillmore, 1987; Gomberg, 1982). In the case of problem drinking, the thirties seem to be crucial years. Because the thirties are also the childbearing years, the woman may be at risk for problem pregnancy or rejection from family and friends if her mothering role seems lacking.

Another critical area of concern in relation to women's drinking patterns is the tendency to combine alcohol with at least one other mood-altering substance (Harrison & Belille, 1987; Marsh et al., 1982). Frequently, a prescription psychoactive drug is used to soothe the irritability, depression, or sleeplessness experienced from drinking.

Indeed, women use more minor tranquilizers, stimulants, hypnotics, antidepressants, and over-the-counter (OTC) sleeping medications and tranquilizers than men (Chambers, Inciardi, & Siegal, 1975). Baum, Kennedy, Formes, and Jones (1984) found codeine-containing products to be the second most commonly prescribed drug. Furthermore, Harrison and Belille (1987) found that, though alcohol was the substance of choice, women over age 30 frequently combined it with minor tranquilizers, whereas those under age 30 combined it with marihuana, cocaine, or stimulants.

The number of addicted women is growing and legal sanctions, which are commonly found in the male addict, are not so for the female (Bissell & Skorina, 1987). Although no rationale is given for the differences found in legal complications for the genders, a possible explanation may lie in the paradoxical way society views a woman's substance abuse. On the one hand, the community protects the woman's use of substances and, on the other, she is stigmatized for having a problem with substance abuse.

Addictions have been described as impulse control disorders, excessive appetites, and sensation-seeking behaviors (Orford, 1985; MacAndrew, 1988). Probably as many reasons for addictions exist as do addicts.

Explanations for Drug/Alcohol Use

Explanations for substance abuse among women have focused on psychopathology, coping-stress, social roles, and medicinal uses as causes of addiction (Beckman,

1975; MacAndrew, 1987; Tucker, 1982). The medical model, along with several others, has been used to examine the problem in women (Marsh et al., 1982). The necessity for the different models indicates that a unitary explanation is yet to be found.

Psychologic factors that motivate women to seek solace from alcohol and drugs have been examined by Beckman (1980). She found that women alcoholics believed that drinking frequently made them feel more adequate, self-confident, less anxious, worried, and lonely, and increased power and control. In other words, women drank to escape unpleasant feelings and to gain positive psychologic effects.

Women reportedly use substances to increase positive affect and to obliterate negative feelings of powerlessness and inadequacy (Beckman & Amaro, 1986). Chemicals used in this way are for the purpose of escape (National Institute on Alcohol Abuse and Alcoholism, 1981). Alcohol or drugs are used to cope with loneliness, boredom, depression, marital problems, and menopause (Marsh et al., 1982). Many stressful circumstances are derived from the traditional female role and constraints such as middle-age identity crisis (Marsh et al., 1982).

The changes that have occurred in feminine roles warrant special discussion. Role conflict and role burden come to the forefront when women move into the work force (McBride, 1987). Social drinking is more prevalent in housewives, yet the proportion of heavy drinkers is greater for women who are employed outside the home (Gomberg, 1982). Traditional work roles for women, such as teacher, nurse, and social worker, are no longer the major career choices for women. Women now enter professional fields that were previously reserved for men and, therefore, they are seen by others and themselves as not fulfilling the traditional female role. Women living in out-of-role life-styles, employed, unmarried, and possibly single-parenting, have heavier drinking patterns (Gomberg, 1982). Full-time employment contradicts traditional expectations of femininity (Meisenhelder, 1986), and attempting to simultaneously fulfill both sets of expectations produces massive stress and role burden. Researchers have been prompted by multiple role expectations and the emerging conflict to investigate coping skills and stress. Women reportedly are likely to use discussion as a coping strategy when available, but tend to use nonsocial or dysfunctional strategies to deal with depression and anger (Tucker, 1982). The dysfunctional strategies for women include withdrawal and substance abuse. Drugs and alcohol are used in situation-specific instances to deal with unpleasant emotional stress (Tucker, 1982).

Many women report that they began to use alcohol or drugs or both in response to gynecologic or obstetric problems (Busch, McBride, & Benaventura, 1986). Problems which were identified by Busch and coworkers (1986) include pelvic pain due to menstruation or other conditions, stress and emotional pain associated with infertility, and other reproductive problems. In an earlier study (Wilsnack, 1973b), 78% of the alcoholic women studied had experienced gynecologic disorders as compared to 35% of the control subjects. One-fourth of the married alcoholic women reported having infertility problems, whereas only 4% of the controls experienced infertility. Although the women in these studies report having begun to use alcohol or drugs in response to problems with the reproductive system, it is also known that these substances can produce similar problems in the same system.

The findings from these two studies become more meaningful when one considers that, during stages of the menstrual cycle, it is socially acceptable for women to turn to drugs (i.e., analgesics, diuretics, or tranquilizers). The idea that medication offers relief from physical discomfort and illness can easily be transferred to emotional discomfort such as malaise, lack of energy, and other discomforts such as unhappiness and feelings of depression (Gomberg, 1982). Women use drugs medicinally; they make more nonillness-related office visits to physicians, and physicians tend to prescribe more readily to women patients (Cooperstock, 1971; Gomberg, 1982; Ogur, 1986). The implicit message is that medicine offers relief, and it is okay for women to use it, but that same message is not true for alcohol (Gomberg, 1982).

Much of the writing about substance-abusing women concerns stress and coping. Stress associated with reproductive disorders was addressed by Busch and colleagues (1986), and stress from other situational circumstances has been offered as a primary motivation for women to use and abuse drugs and alcohol (Cooke & Allan, 1984; Wilsnack, 1973a). Tucker (1982) purported that drug-abusing women are either subjected to more stressful situations than others or that they perceive themselves to be. And, indeed, when listening to women in recovery talk about their past lives, the divorces, emotional and physical abuse, the shame and self-doubt that engulfed them, one is inclined to agree.

Some authors point out that current research methods may fail to reflect some stressful experiences common to women. Weissman and Klerman (1977) suggested that life events research may be a gender, class, and age-biased form of measurement of life stress because it is geared toward acute changes such as loss of job, loved one, or relocation. Furthermore, sources of chronic stress such as poverty, poor health, childrearing responsibility, fear of assault and violence, and low status, which are common to women, are ignored or not considered as important.

Areas thought to be stress producing and leading to substance abuse for women include conflict in roles (Douglas & Nutter, 1986; McBride, 1987); divorce, separation, and single-parenting (John, 1987; Lester, 1982; McBride, 1987); negative circumstances, such as pain, anxiety, guilt, and shame (Bry, 1983; Celentano & McQueen, 1984; Mello, 1980); and major life crisis (Curlee, 1970). Schuckit and Morrissey (1979) report that the closest relationship between potentially stressful events and the onset of alcohol problems occurred among those who were already heavy drinkers. The question that occurs is: Which came first, the drinking or the problems? Cooke and Allan (1984) reported no evidence that women increase their alcohol consumption in relation to life events.

Wilsnack (1973a) suggested a relationship between feminine identification disturbances and alcoholism in women. Since drinking and drugging are considered behaviors more appropriate for men, the woman who indulges is seen as more deviant. Chomak and Collins (1987) examined the relationship between drinking and sex-role identification and found support for the hypothesis that a feminine sex-role orientation is associated with lighter alcohol consumption. They reasoned that drinking may be used as a way to reject the traditional role and embrace the more liberated role.

Another factor that has been implicated in the explanations for women's substance abuse is family of origin. When a parent has a substance abuse problem, the woman is more likely to abuse substances (Harrison & Belille, 1987; Wanberg & Horn, 1970). In regard to parental alcoholism, Schuckit (1987) reports sons and daughters of alcoholics are three to four times as likely to develop alcoholism. This finding is supported by Parker and Harford (1987), who found children of alcoholics were at elevated risk for the development of alcoholism.

Women at Risk

Women who abuse substances come from all segments of society. The substances used vary with age, social class, living conditions, cultural backgrounds, and stage of addiction. Although there is no true profile of the addicted woman, certain women seem to be at high risk for developing substance abuse. Most research on women has been conducted on those already in treatment for substance abuse. Attempts have been made to categorize subgroups of women to understand the disease. Labels such as the invisible alcoholic (Sandmaier, 1980), and reactive, primary, and secondary alcoholism have been used to describe the women (Schuckit, 1972).

Predictor variables most commonly identified in research are age, marital status, vulnerability, stress, and poor physical health (Timmer, Veroff, & Colten, 1985). Among the risk factors that increase a woman's predisposition for substance abuse are: (a) a history of early traumatic life events such as physical or sexual abuse (National Institute on Alcohol Abuse and Alcoholism, 1981); (b) family history of alcoholism or drug abuse or both (Parker & Harford, 1987; Peele, 1986); and (c) early emotional deprivation due to loss of one or both parents (Joyce & Hazelton, 1982). Furthermore, she frequently has a low sense of self-esteem or confusion about her role in life (National Institute on Alcohol Abuse and Alcoholism, 1981; Weathers & Billingsley, 1982), uses drugs or alcohol to escape from painful feeling states, and has a substance abusing spouse or significant other (Beckman & Amaro, 1986; National Institute on Alcohol Abuse and Alcoholism, 1981).

Serious substance abuse problems may be precipitated in the woman who has any of these risk factors when she experiences a life crisis or a traumatic loss. The loss may occur through divorce, death of a loved one, or children leaving home. Women who are experiencing marital instability, recently divorced or separated, or whose lives have changed rapidly may turn to a chemical substance to assuage the loneliness, emptiness, and feelings of failure (Bissell & Skorina, 1987; Celentano & McQueen, 1984).

Younger employed women have higher self-esteem than older employed women (Meisenhelder, 1986). Younger women no longer match the stereotyped female substance abuser who is still depicted as the homemaker secluded with her bottle and Valium prescription (Harrison & Belille, 1987). The younger woman is frequently single, unemployed, and dependent on welfare, and will combine alcohol with other drugs.

Young women, under age 30, have reported additional emotional and psychologic problems. They complain of restlessness, lack of energy, weight, or sexual problems during the year preceding treatment (Harrison & Belille, 1987). These problems, along with the marital instability, other alcoholics in the family, particularly the spouse, often bring the woman into contact with helping professionals (Bissell & Skorina, 1987). It is at this point that many women are introduced to prescription drugs because the disease is not recognized (Kennedy, 1985). See Chapter 13 for further discussion of alcoholism and other drug problems in adults.

Women aged 55 and older are at risk for alcoholism, medication use and abuse, and depression (McBride, 1987). Problems with the elderly are discussed in a separate chapter; therefore, they are only mentioned as being at risk in this discussion. See Chapter 14 for discussion of substance abuse in older women.

Characteristics of Women in Treatment

The empirical data available on addicted women have been primarily collected in treatment settings. Although no prototypical profile of the substance-abusing woman emerges, general characteristics and potential risk factors can be extrapolated. Two variables, age and socioeconomic status, have been found to be highly significant predictors of problems. McBride (1987) and Harrison and Belille (1987) indicate that there is a relationship between these two variables and the multiple societal changes that have occurred in relation to women's roles. Younger women with employment difficulties are increasingly involved in substance abuse.

Marsh and Simpson (1986) describe women opiate addicts as tending to somaticize, feel anxious, worried, and upset. They often need more financial assistance and would benefit from job training and counseling. Furthermore, there are fewer reported positive benefits for stopping drug use for women.

Although controversy occurs in the descriptions provided, it is essential to remember that addiction problems are multifaceted, and different people experience different problems for different reasons at different times. For each woman, choices about drug or alcohol use emerge from a complex mixture of religious beliefs, values, background, the availability and accessibility of

the substance, and a host of other variables. Understanding why some women will make the choice to use substances and risk becoming abusers while others do not remains elusive. Coping theorists and drug use researchers recognize that under certain circumstances many individuals in our society will use substances to cope with stress (Marlatt, 1985; Pearlin & Radabough, 1976).

Characteristics of women substance abusers who come for treatment are primarily based on studies of women with alcoholism. It is important to remember that the majority of women combine two or more substances (Marsh et al., 1982).

Demographic descriptions of the female alcoholic provide some interesting insights. In a study conducted over a 6-month period of women entering driver alcohol education programs, McCormack (1985) found that the average person was likely to be under age 30, divorced or separated, and living alone with children. The importance of the marital status as a variable is consistently considered significant (Beckman & Kocel, 1982; Celentano & McQueen, 1984; Harrison & Belille, 1987; Schulte & Blume, 1979).

The woman is typically unmarried, begins to use alcohol or other substances early (18–24 years of age), and increases her use until she abuses (ages 28–39 years). The increased quantity of alcohol consumed causes rapid progression of her alcoholism (Fillmore, 1987; Lester, 1982) with a telescoping of biomedical effects (Beckman & Amaro, 1986). Research findings show that the average age of the woman seeking treatment is between 40 and 50 (National Institute on Alcohol Abuse and Alcoholism, 1982/1983), but it appears that female problem drinkers are entering treatment at a younger age (Harrison & Belille, 1987; John, 1987). Heavily drinking women are more likely to develop liver cirrhosis and die from it than heavily drinking men (Booth, 1987; National Institute on Alcohol Abuse and Alcoholism, 1981). Furthermore, women suffer significant memory loss and accelerated rates of deterioration (Beckman & Kocel, 1982). It is the woman herself that suffers the negative consequences of substance abuse primarily in her health and welfare.

Frequently, she relates the onset of her heavy drinking to a specific incident or life event (Curlee, 1970; Wilsnack, 1973a). Schuckit and Morrissey (1979) question this linkage and postulate that the event may be a consequence of the drinking rather than the antecedent. The woman may be attempting to justify her alcoholic drinking and to shift the responsibility to an external source (Corrigan, 1980).

Women substance abusers present with feelings of guilt, shame, anxiety, depression, and low self-esteem as the predominant feeling states (Bissell & Skorina, 1987; Boyd & Mast, 1983; Gomberg, 1977). Chronic alcohol use increases irritability, depression, anxiety, and is associated with increased aggression (Mello, 1980). In view of this, it is not surprising that the women are more likely to suffer physical or sexual abuse (Beckman & Amaro, 1986). Much research effort has gone into the study of depression in the female substance abuser (Colten, 1979; MacAndrew, 1986; Rounsaville, Dolinsky, Babor, & Meyer, 1987; Schuckit, 1972). Rounsaville and coworkers (1987) report that 58% of the women studied had their first depressive episode after the onset of alcoholism or drug abuse.

The woman is ashamed of her drinking (Caroselli-Karinja & Zboray, 1986), has very low self-esteem, deteriorated defenses, social isolation (Butterfield & LeClair, 1988), and marital or family instability (Bissell & Skorina, 1987; Lester, 1982; Schulte & Blume, 1979). In turn, the community is concerned and views her negatively because of myths and misconceptions of the drinking woman and the poor job performance in her nurturing, caretaker role. She is aware that she faces the negative attitudes of the community and that there is less tolerance for female addicts/alcoholics (Gomberg, 1982). The combination of her negative self-view, community reaction, the depression associated with the drinking problem, and instability in support system contributes to the high incidence of suicide ideation and attempts (Bissell & Skorina, 1987).

The poor self-image that characterizes the woman alcoholic may reflect unsuccessful struggles with sex-role conflict, a basic lack of self-confidence and self-worth, or some other factors. However, the manifestation of social isolation and alienation (Butterfield & LeClair, 1988), feelings of inadequacy (Andersen, 1980), dependency (Boyd & Mast, 1983; Caroselli-Karinja & Zboray, 1986), and low self-esteem is common in women in treatment. They view themselves as less effective in goal achievement, less socially competent, and more anxious than other women (National Institute on Alcohol Abuse and Alcoholism, 1982/1983).

Employment has been linked to both a cause of heavy drinking and drug use and a predictor of a favorable prognosis (Harrison & Belille, 1987; Markowitz, 1984; Schuckit & Morrisey, 1979). Celentano and McQueen (1984) report that women employed outside the home had a greater proportion of moderate and heavy drinkers. The heaviest drinking was found in women in professional, clerical, and service jobs. Markowitz (1984) related the use of alcohol as a coping strategy to the person's perception of powerlessness in her occupation. On the other hand, Bateman and Petersen (1972) found that employed women had a higher rate of abstinence after treatment than those who were not employed. An issue of concern is the identification of drug and alcohol problems in women in the workplace and the referral of these employees. (Trice, 1979).

Barriers to Treatment

With the overwhelming negative emotions and feelings, physical illness, societal rejection, and family disruptions occurring, one would think the woman would race for treatment. However, this is not the case for the majority of women. Multiple barriers exist which prevent women from seeking treatment (Beckman, 1975; Beckman & Kocel, 1982; Efinger, 1983). The most frequently discussed barrier is the social stigma associated with female addiction.

Those closest to the woman, her family and friends, are reluctant to admit that a problem exists (Beckman & Amaro, 1986), which enables the woman to postpone seeking treatment. The family's reluctance is based on shame, fear of violence, and the fact that they feel powerless. Even after problems occur, the denial continues, which increases the danger for the woman (Robins & Smith, 1980). She also denies the problem and is not motivated to seek help.

Other barriers to treatment are directly or indirectly related to socioeconomic issues. Financial problems, small children at home (Andersen, 1980; John, 1987), and social costs involving relations with significant others contribute to the problem of getting the woman into treatment (Beckman & Amaro, 1986). Relatively few men seem willing to involve themselves in family treatment programs when the wife is the patient (Bissell & Skorina, 1987); in fact, parents and children are more likely to support treatment for women (Beckman & Amaro, 1986). An area of great concern to women who need treatment is having small children at home with no one to care for them (Andersen, 1980).

Attitudes of health care professionals toward the addicted woman and the woman's attitudes toward health care professionals are thought to present barriers to treatment. Often the attitudes are negative on both parts (Babcock & Conner, 1981; Beckman & Amaro, 1986). Kennedy (1985) reported that physicians are reluctant to diagnose alcoholism and prefer to make another diagnosis. Rosser (1981) found that physicians were more likely to prescribe antidepressants to women than men. The woman who is seeking help and receives these prescriptions is set up for multiple drug dependencies.

In addition, many treatment programs are designed for men and do not meet the special needs of women. Alcoholic women are undertreated, understudied, and represent less than 2% of the subjects in treatment outcome studies (Emrick, 1980; Vannicelli, 1984). Consequently, reliable information about the benefits of treatment are not available to the prospective client. These barriers to treatment often impede the early identification and treatment of the woman.

Treatment Needs

An examination of the barriers to treatment for women helps to understand why 85% of all chemically dependent people receive no treatment for their disease (Kennedy, 1985). The picture developed from clinical studies depicts the woman as feeling overwhelmed by difficult family situations, isolated from others (Butterfield & LeClair, 1988; Wanberg & Horn, 1970), divorced or living alone (Beckman & Amaro, 1986), and having low self-esteem, feelings of inadequacy, poor self-concept, and extreme guilt (National Institute on Alcohol Abuse and Alcoholism, 1982/1983). The needs of the woman demand a multifaceted approach to treatment (Beckman & Amaro, 1986; Lester, 1982; Marsh et al., 1982).

Women come to treatment in various ways, usually after some years of substance abuse (John, 1987) and after problems have developed (Robins & Smith, 1980). The literature paints a picture of the female addict as one who has more psychopathology than the male addict (Jones & Jones, 1976; MacAndrew, 1986; Rounsaville et al., 1987), a poorer prognosis after treatment (Nathan & Skinstad, 1987; Vannicelli, 1984), suffering with low self-esteem, and heightened feelings of guilt (Babcock & Connor, 1981; Beckman & Kocel, 1982). Women's initiation, continuation, and cessation of drug use is much more influenced by intimates, usually male,

than are men (Suffet & Brotman, 1976; Tucker, 1982). Nathan and Skinstad (1987) found support for the belief that men and women benefit from treatment at comparable rates overall, but women benefit less because they enter and remain in treatment in significantly lower rates than men.

Treatment facilities offer several levels of care designed to meet the specific needs of the client. Specialty hospital care for the seriously impaired, ambulatory inpatient care in a freestanding facility and outpatient facilities are available for initial and ongoing treatment. The combination of high levels of psychologic distress, family dysfunctions, and impaired psychosocial functioning poses a challenge to connecting the woman with the appropriate care and to the treatment systems (Harrison & Belille, 1987).

Considerable attention has been paid to the gynecologic problem in the alcoholic woman. Women who abuse substances suffer the additional biologic consequences of reproductive disorders, poor pregnancy outcomes, amenorrhea, and dysmenorrhea (Bry, 1983; Jones & Jones, 1976). While controversy continues regarding these problems as antecedents or consequences, they are found in high proportion in treatment populations and warrant attention.

Treatment programs designed for women recognize that there are identifiable gender needs which must be addressed in treatment and recovery. Therefore, these programs provide services designed to alleviate or ameliorate the problems of drug-abusing women (Marsh, 1982). Services which have been found to be valuable to women are: *(a)* provision for child care (Beckman & Kocel, 1982; Marsh, 1982); *(b)* medical services, such as pregnancy testing and prenatal and postnatal care (Marsh, 1982); *(c)* assertiveness training and strategies to deal with anger constructively (Beckman & Amaro, 1986; Beckman & Kocel, 1982; Boyd & Mast, 1983; Marsh et al., 1982); *(d)* strategies to build self-esteem (Boyd & Mast, 1983); *(e)* educational counseling (Beckman & Amaro, 1986); and *(f)* a rehabilitation program offering family therapy, support groups, and individual therapy (Lester, 1982). Programs should provide psychologic counseling, job training, behavioral therapy, and education on women's roles in society (Ogur, 1986). Social skills training, self-control strategies, cognitive restructuring, and modeling are some of the methods used to develop coping skills and bolster self-efficacy for both genders (Wilson, 1987).

Role modeling is viewed as an extremely important factor in women's treatment (Beckman & Amaro, 1986; Bissell & Skorina, 1987). Women need a single-sex therapy group and a predominance of female staff (Beckman & Amaro, 1986; Schulte & Blume, 1982). Bissell and Skorina (1987) point out that most treatment should be with other women if possible, along with supplementary groups to discuss the woman's particular concerns.

Females, particularly adolescents, often must deal with complex issues regarding sexuality. McBride (1987) states that one in three women have been sexually abused at some point in childhood and that incest is more prevalent than ever thought. Therefore, women need an opportunity to discuss these issues in an open and nonjudgmental climate. Interaction and identification with healthy sex-role models assist women to see themselves as separate, autonomous individuals, and should help with the sex-role conflicts they have experienced (Beckman & Amaro, 1986; Beckman & Kocel, 1982; Tucker, 1982). The female staff members demonstrate how one can be independent, strong, successful, loving, and gentle without losing sight of who and what they are. Addicted clients need help to overcome the stresses and limitations of present day sex roles (Douglas & Nutter, 1986).

Alcoholic women coming into treatment prefer one-to-one relationships; however, they do very well when introduced to group therapy as a modality (National Institute on Alcohol Abuse and Alcoholism, 1982/ 1983). Because relationships are so important to women, treatment must include all significant people in her life. Support of a critical tie in the form of a spouse or opposite sex partner is an important factor in successful treatment, and therapy must address this relationship (Tucker, 1982). Without entering the debate about the absence of social support and coping as an antecedent or consequence of alcohol and drug abuse, it is a consideration that must be addressed in treatment. Women who are successful in recovery, according to Bry (1983), are those who are still living with their families and have succeeded in modifying the family structure so they can play a more satisfying role within it. Support groups, such as Alcoholics Anonymous, Narcotics Anonymous, and Cocaine Anonymous can also provide external social support for the recovering female and should be introduced during treatment.

This section has attempted to discuss some of the special needs of the alcohol and drug abusing female in treatment. However, because women's addictions are often hidden, early intervention and primary prevention strategies must be developed (National Institute on Alcohol Abuse and Alcoholism, 1982/1983).

Prevention

Primary prevention efforts must be directed at women who have not yet experienced problems but who are at risk for developing them (National Institute on Alcohol Abuse and Alcoholism, 1982/1983). Most prevention programs for women place stress on developing cognitive and behavioral skills. Included in these are coping skills, decision-making skills, enhancing self-esteem, and increasing their options. Education about the physical and psychologic effects of alcohol and drugs is essential. The challenge is to discover who comes into contact with the women and what types of strategies are most needed by them (National Institute on Alcohol Abuse and Alcoholism, 1981, 1982/1983).

Since the literature indicates women with alcoholism in their family of origin are susceptible to development of the disease, the self-help group, Adult Children of Alcoholics (ACOA), may offer a primary prevention for the woman. The characteristics of adult children which have been identified portray a likeness to the description of the female addict in that they both have overwhelmingly low self-esteem; have often experienced emotional, psychologic, or physical abuse; feel isolated and alienated; frequently fear intimate relationships; and have a need to be "perfect." Having grown up in a chaotic, inconsistent family dynamic, adult children do not trust what others tell them nor what they see themselves. They feel unique in their experience and have a tendency to see situations and people in terms of either/or and black or white, called the all-or-none perception. A case example will be used to exemplify.

Case Example

Jennifer is a 28-year-old single parent employed in a local hospital as a nurse. She came to the first ACOA meeting after being referred by a therapist who felt her issues were with codependency. When she described her past experiences with an alcoholic father, substance-abusing brother and boyfriends, she was tearful. She consistently sees her mother, now deceased, as "having given her life for this worthless man" and being a saint. Furthermore, in talking about other relationships it is clear that she uses anger to keep distance. She reports many short-term relationships with men along with an overpowering need to have a man in her life. She rejects them when they don't live up to her expectations of calling her every day and being constantly available when she wants to see them.

After approximately a year in the group she begins to discuss her mother's role in keeping the family together. She vacillates between the mother being a saint and questioning why she would subject them to the destructive things that happened in the family. Her relationships with her coworkers have improved. She currently does not have a significant male in her life and states she does not want that at this time. Her relationship with her child has improved and she plans activities for the two of them.

While Jennifer has much more work to do in recovery, she has begun to relinquish some of her need to control other people and to take a broader perspective in evaluating situations. A major issue at this point will be to gain a balance of perspective when examining the relationship with her mother.

Future research efforts should be directed toward the study of single-parent coping, social support, stress and coping, role conflict, and role burden in women. The prevalence of alcoholism and drug abuse in older women is an issue that needs to be investigated. A comparison of women that do not use drugs or alcohol to cope with family and work pressures to those that do would provide helpful descriptive information and possible preventive measures. Furthermore, factors that influence the recovery process in women must be investigated to provide additional information for treatment and early intervention strategies.

SUMMARY

This chapter has dealt with the special needs of the woman in treatment and recovery from alcohol and drug abuse. Particular attention was focused on the risk factors and characteristics as they are presented in the literature. A great deal of research is accumulating on the drinking and drug use patterns in women along with descriptors of the person who abuses substances. Yet, in most of the studies, females continue to be compared to males and, consequently, are said to be sicker, have more psychopathology, and be less willing to be treated than males. Drug and alcohol use among women is linked to gender roles, power, ambivalence, anger, and fear (Gomberg, 1982). The rates for chemical substance abuse among women are increasing yearly (Mulligan, 1983). Stress associated with employment produces the same health risks and consequences for women as for men, but women appear to be less healthy overall.

In many ways the literature can be interpreted to say that alcohol and drugs are the solution to problems long before they cause problems. Treatment programs are attempting to meet the needs of female clients, but they continue to be fewer in number than males. By and large, there is much work to be done understand the woman who uses and abuses substances and her subsequent treatment needs.

REFERENCES

Anderson, M. D. (1980). Personalized nursing: An intervention model for drug dependent women in an emergency room. *Journal of Addictions and Health, 1*, 217–226.

Babcok, M. L., & Conner, B. (1981). Sexism and treatment of the female alcoholic: A review. *Social Work, 46*(3), 233–238.

Bateman, N. I., & Petersen, D. M. (1972). Factors related to outcome of treatment for hospitalized white male and female alcoholics. *Journal of Drug Issues, 2*, 66–74.

Baum, C., Kennedy, D., Forbes, M., & Jones, J. (1984). Drug use in the United States in 1981. *Journal of the American Medical Association, 251*, 1293–1297.

Beckman, L. (1975). Women alcoholics: A review of social and psychological studies. *Journal of Studies on Alcohol, 36*, 797–824.

Beckman, L. J. (1980). Perceived antecedents and effects of alcohol consumption in women. *Journal of Studies on Alcohol, 41*, 518–530.

Beckman, L. J., & Amaro, H. (1986). Personal and social difficulties faced by women and men entering treatment. *Journal of Studies on Alcohol, 47*, 135–145.

Beckman, L. J., & Kocel, K. M. (1982). The treatment-delivery system and alcohol abuse in women: Social policy implications. *Journal of Social Studies, 38,* 139–151.

Bissell, L., & Skorina, J. (1987). One hundred alcoholic women in medicine: An interview study. *Journal of the American Medical Association, 257,* 2939–2944.

Booth, P. G. (1987). Managing alcohol and drug abuse in the nursing profession. *Journal of Advanced Nursing, 12,* 625–630.

Boyd, C., & Mast, D. (1983). Addicted women and their relationships with men. *Journal of Psychosocial Nursing and Mental Health Services, 21*(2), 10–13.

Bry, B. H. (1983). Substance abuse in women: Etiology and prevention. *Issues in Mental Health, 30,* 253–272.

Busch, D., McBride, A. B., & Benaventura, L. M. (1986). Chemical dependency in women the link to OB/GYN problems. *Journal of Psychosocial Nursing and Mental Health Services, 24*(4), 26–30.

Butterfield, P. S., & LeClair, S. (1988). Cognitive characteristics of bulimic and drug-abusing women. *Addictive Behaviors, 13,* 131–138.

Caroselli-Karinja, M. F., & Zboray, S. D. (1986). The impaired nurse. *Journal of Psychosocial Nursing, 24*(6), 14–19.

Celentano, D. D., & McQueen, D. V. (1984). Alcohol consumption patterns among women in Baltimore. *Journal of Studies on Alcohol, 45,* 355–358.

Chambers, C. D., Inciardi, J. A., & Siegal, H. A. (1975). *Chemical coping: A report on legal drug use in the United States.* New York: Spectrum Publications.

Chomak, S., & Collins, R. L. (1987). Relationship between sex-role behaviors and alcohol consumption in undergraduate men and women. *Journal of Studies on Alcohol, 48,* 194–201.

Colten, M. E. (1979). A descriptive and comparative analysis of self-perceptions and attitudes of heroin-addicted women. *Addicted women: Family dynamics, self-perceptions, and support systems* (NIDA Services Research Monograph Series, DHEW Pub. No. ADM 80–762). Washington, DC: U. S. Government Printing Office.

Cooke, D. J., & Allan, C. A. (1984). Stressful life events and alcohol abuse in women: A general population study. *British Journal of Addiction, 79,* 425–430.

Cooperstock, R. (1971). Sex differences in the use of mood-modifying drugs: An explanatory model. *Journal of Health and Social Behavior, 12,* 238–244.

Corrigan, E. M. (1980). *Alcoholic women in treatment.* New York: Oxford University Press.

Curlee, J. A. (1970). A comparison of male and female patients at an alcoholism treatment center. *Journal of Psychology, 74,* 239–247.

Douglas, J. J., & Nutter, C. P. (1986). Treatment-related change in sex roles of addicted men and women. *Journal of Studies on Alcohol, 47,* 201–206.

Efinger, J. M. (1983). Women and alcoholism. *Topics in Clinical Nursing, 4*(4), 10–19.

Emrick, C. D. (1980). *Alcoholism and alcohol abuse among women: Research issues* (Research Monograph No. 1, p. 150). Washington, DC: National Institute on Alcohol Abuse and Alcoholism.

Ferrance, R. G., & Whitehead, P. C. (1980). Sex differences in psychoactive drug use: Recent epidemiology. In O. J. Kalant (Ed.), *Alcohol and drug problems in women* (pp. 125–201). New York: Plenum Press.

Fillmore, K. M. (1987). Women's drinking across the adult life course as compared to men's. *British Journal of Addiction, 82,* 801–811.

Gomberg, E. S. L. (1977). Historical work and alcohol: A disturbing trend. *Supervisory Management, 22,* 16–20.

Gomberg, E. S. L. (1982). Historical and political perspective: Women and drug use. *Journal of Social Issues, 38,* 9–23.

Gomberg, E. S. L. (1986). Women with alcohol problems. N. J. Estes, M. E. Heinemann (Eds.) *Alcoholism: Development, Consequences and Interventions* (pp. 241–256). St. Louis, Moseby, S. 1986.

Harrison, P. A., & Belille, C. A. (1987). Women in treatment: Beyond the stereotype. *Journal of Studies on Alcohol, 48,* 574–578.

Helzer, J. E. (1987). Epidemiology of alcoholism. *Journal of Consulting and Clinical Psychology, 55,* 284–292.

Hilton, M. E. (1987). Drinking patterns and drinking problems in 1984: Results from a general population survey. *Alcoholism: Clinical and Experimental Research, 11*(2), 167–175.

John, U. (1987). Alcohol-dependent men and women in detoxifications: Some comparisons. *Alcoholism: Clinical and Experimental Research, 11,* 155–157.

Jones, B., & Jones, M. (1976). Women and alcohol: Intoxication, metabolism, and the menstrual cycle. In M.

Greenblatt & M. Schuckit (Eds.), *Alcohol problems in women and children* (pp. 103–136). New York: Grune & Stratton.

Joyce, C., & Hazelton, P. (1982). Women in groups: A pregroup experience for women in recovery from alcoholism and other addictions. *Social Work With Groups, 5,* 57–63.

Kennedy, W. J. (1985, February). Chemical dependency: A treatable disease. *Ohio State Medical Journal,* 77–79.

Kulberg, A. (1986). Substance abuse: Clinical identification and management. *Pediatric Clinics of North America, 33*(2), 325–361.

Lester, L. (1982). The special needs of the female alcoholic. *The Journal of Contemporary Social Work,* 451–456.

MacAndrew, C. (1986). Similarities in self-depictions of female alcoholics and psychiatric outpatients: Examination of Eysenck's dimension of emotionality in women. *Journal of Studies on Alcohol, 47,* 478–484.

MacAndrew, C. (1988). Differences in the self-depictions of female alcoholics and psychiatric outpatients: Towards a depiction of the modal female alcoholic. *Journal of Studies on Alcohol, 49,* 71–77.

Markowitz, M. (1984). Alcohol misuse as a response to perceived powerlessness in the organization. *Journal of Studies on Alcohol, 45,* 225–227.

Marlatt, G. A. (1985). Cognitive factors in the relapse process. In G. A. Marlatt & J. Gordon (Eds.), *Relapse prevention* (pp. 128–200). New York: Guilford Press.

Marsh, J. C., Colten, M. E., & Tucker, M. B. (1982). Women's use of drugs and alcohol: New perspectives. *Journal of Social Issues, 38,* 1–8.

Marsh, J. C. (1982). Public issues and private problems: Women and drug use. *Journal of Social Issues, 38,* 153–165.

Marsh, K. L., & Simpson, D. D. (1986). Sex differences in opioid careers. *American Journal of Drug and Alcohol Abuse, 12,* 309–329.

McBride, A. B. (1987). Developing a women's mental health research agenda. *IMAGE: Journal of Nursing Scholarship, 19*(1), 4–8.

McCormack, A. (1985). Risk for alcohol-related accidents in divorced and separated women. *Journal of Studies on Alcohol, 46,* 240–243.

Meisenhelder, J. B. (1986). Self-esteem in women: The influence of employment and perception of husband's appraisals. *IMAGE: Journal of Nursing Scholarship, 18*(1), 8–14.

Mello, N. K. (1980). Some behavioral and biological aspects of alcohol problems in women. In O. J. Kalant (Ed.), *Alcohol and drug problems in women* (pp. 263–298). New York: Plenum Press.

Mulligan, J. E. (1983). Some effects of the women's health movement. *Topics in Clinical Nursing, 4*(4), 1–7.

Nathan, P. E., & Skinstad, A. H. (1987). Outcomes of treatment for alcohol problems: Current methods, problems, and results. *Journal of Consulting and Clinical Psychology, 55,* 332–340.

National Institute on Alcohol Abuse and Alcoholism. (1981). *Spectrum: Alcohol problem prevention for women by women.* (DHHS Pub. No. ADM 81–1036, 1–10). Washington, DC: U. S. Government Printing Office.

National Institute on Alcohol Abuse and Alcoholism. (1982/1983). How women recover. *Alcohol Health and Research World, 7*(2), 28–40. Washington, DC: U. S. Government Printing Office.

Ogur, B. (1986). Long day's journey into night: Women and prescription drug abuse. *Women and Health Review, 11,* 99–115.

Orford, J. (1985). *Excessive appetites: A psychological view of addictions.* New York: John Wiley & Sons.

Parker, D. A., & Harford, T. C. (1987). Alcohol related problems of children of heavy drinking parents. *Journal of Studies on Alcohol, 48,* 265–268.

Pearlin, L. I., & Radabaugh, C. W. (1976). Economic strains and the coping of alcohol. *American Journal of Sociology, 82,* 652-663.

Peele, S. (1986). The implications and limitations of genetic models of alcoholism and other addictions. *Journal of Studies on Alcohol, 47,* 63–73.

Robins, L. N., & Smith, E. M. (1980). Longitudinal studies of alcohol and drug problems: Sex differences. In O. J. Kalant (Ed.), *Alcohol and drug problems in women* (pp. 203–232). New York: Plenum Press.

Rosser, W. W. (1981). Influence of physicians gender in amitriptyline prescribing. *Canadian Family Physicians, 27,* 1094–1097.

Rounsaville, B. J., Dolinsky, Z. S., Barbor, T. F., & Meyer, R. E. (1987). Psychopathology as a predictor of treatment outcomes in alcoholics. *Archives of General Psychiatry, 44,* 505–513.

Sandmaier, M. (1980). *The invisible alcoholics: Women and alcohol abuse in America*. New York: McGraw-Hill.

Schuckit, M. (1972). The alcoholic woman: A literature review. *Psychiatry in Medicine, 3*, 37–43.

Schuckit, M. (1987). Biological vulnerability to alcoholism. *Journal of Consulting and Clinical Psychology, 55*, 301–309.

Schuckit, M. A., & Morrissey, E. R. (1979). Psychiatric problems in women at alcoholic detoxification. *American Journal of Psychiatry, 136*, 611–617.

Schulte, K., & Blume, S. B. (1979). A day treatment center for alcoholic women. *Health and Social Work, 4*, 222–233.

Smith, J. P. (1987). Women's lot in society. *Journal of Advanced Nursing, 12*, 543–544.

Suffet, F., & Brotman, R. (1976). Female drug use: Some observations. *The International Journal of Addictions, 11*, 19–33.

Timmer, S. G., Veroff, J., & Colten, M. E. (1985). Life stress, helplessness, and the use of alcohol and drugs to cope: An analysis of national survey data. In S. Shiffman & T. A. Wills (Eds.), *Coping and substance abuse* (pp. 171–197). New York: Academic Press.

Trice, H. M. (1979). Women employees and job-based alcoholism programs. *Journal of Drug Issues, 9*(3), 371–385.

Tucker, M. B. (1982). Social support and coping: Applications for the study of female drug use. *Journal of Social Issues, 38*, 117–137.

Vannicelli, M. (1984). Treatment outcomes of alcoholic women: The state of the art. *Current issues in alcohol and drug abuse nursing: Research, education, and clinical practice*. New York: National Council on Alcoholism.

Wanberg, K. W., & Horn, J. L. (1970). Alcoholism symptom patterns of men and women. *Quarterly Journal of Studies on Alcohol, 31*, 40–61.

Weathers, C., & Billingsley, O. (1982). Body image and sex-role stereotype as features of addiction in women. *International Journal of Addictions, 17*, 343–347.

Weissman, M. M., & Klerman, G. L. (1977). Sex differences and the epidemiology of depression. *Archives of General Psychiatry, 34*, 98–111.

Wilsnack, S. C. (1973a). Femininity by the bottle. *Addictions, 20*(2), 2–19.

Wilsnack, S. C. (1973b). The effects of social drinking on women's fantasy. *Journal of Abnormal Psychology, 82*, 44–63.

Wilsnack, S. C., Wilsnack, R. W., & Klassen, A. D. (1986). Epidemiological research on women's drinking, 1978–1984. *Women and alcohol: Related Issues*. (NIAAA Research Monograph No. 16, DHSS Pub. No. ADM 86–1139, 1–68). Washington, DC: U. S. Government Printing Office.

Wilson, G. T. (1987). Cognitive studies in alcoholism. *Journal of Consulting and Clinical Psychology, 55*, 325–331.

CHAPTER 22 | IMPAIRED HEALTH CARE PROFESSIONALS

Eleanor J. Sullivan

Increasing attention is being paid to substance abuse today. Public figures announce their treatment for alcoholism or drug dependency. Railroad and plane accidents are followed by testing of engineers or pilots for drug use. Public debate continues on drug testing—when, where, who, and why. Courts are becoming increasingly harsh with penalties for drunk driving, and organizations have sprung up to stop it (Mothers Against Drunk Driving [MADD] and Students Against Drunk Driving [SADD]). Attention to the problem among health care professionals is also increasing. Professional organizations and the public are becoming more concerned as reports of physicians' or nurses' addictions surface.

Addiction in health care professionals (and others who have an impact on public safety) is more serious because of the potential consequences to vulnerable people in their care. When a physician or a nurse, whose professional capabilities are impaired by alcohol or drug use, is caring for patients, those patients are put at risk. Both acts of commission and omission are possible. At the very least, the clinician is not working at his or her best, alert to subtle signs and symptoms of problems, able to make critical decisions, or respond quickly in an emergency.

PREVALENCE

The prevalence of substance abuse problems in health professionals has not been adequately determined. What is known, however, is that the majority of disciplinary cases that come to the attention of regulatory boards are related to use or misuse of controlled substances (Chesney, 1988; National Council of State Boards of Nursing, 1980–1981). Studies of physi-

cians and nurses who are recovering from addictions, however, indicate that few were identified or sanctioned by their respective regulatory boards (Bissell & Haberman, 1984; Bissell & Jones, 1981; Sullivan, 1987a).

Some limited studies have been conducted on the prevalence of addictive disorders in health care professionals. Drug use by physicians and medical students was reported (McAuliffe et al., 1986) as well as that by pharmacists and pharmacy students (McAuliffe et al., 1987). Engs and Hanson (1985) and Haack and Harford (1984) studied students' drinking patterns and consequences of drinking. Sullivan (1987b) surveyed over 500 registered nurses for indications of problem drinking or drug use. Table 22.1 illustrates the percentage in each study who indicated an alcohol or drug abuse problem.

Health care professionals and students reported similar percentages of problems related to alcohol or drug use, whereas college students, in general, reported a higher prevalence of problems. It is interesting to note that the prevalence of diagnosed substance abuse in physicians and nurses was identical in these samples.

The prevalence of alcoholism and drug addiction in the general population is known, and these data indicate the extent of the problem among health care professionals. According to the National Institute on Alcohol Abuse and Alcoholism (NIAAA), approximately 10% of the population has an alcohol abuse problem. Drug abuse occurs in approximately 2% of the population according to the National Institute on Drug Abuse (NIDA). Using these figures as a guide and assuming that health care professionals experience substance abuse with similar frequency, a large number of practicing health care clinicians are at risk for substance abuse. The number of patients that each clinician affects magnifies the impact of the problem.

Table 22.1
Studies of Professionals' and Students' Substance Use Problems

Author	Year	Profession	N	% with Substance Use Problems[a]
McAuliffe et al.	1986	Physicians	337	4[b]
McAuliffe et al.	1986	Medical students	381	16
McAuliffe et al.	1987	Pharmacists	312	18
Engs & Hanson	1985	College students	6115	20
Haack & Harford	1984	Nursing students	103	13
Sullivan	1987	Nurses	552	18 (4% reported diagnosed substance abuse)

[a] Includes reports of heavy alcohol/drug use and/or negative consequences to such use.
[b] Only diagnosed substance abuse is reported.

ARE HEALTH CARE PROFESSIONALS DIFFERENT?

There are many questions about how health care professionals may or may not differ from the general population on: *(a)* the effect (if any) of the profession or the health care environment on substance use or abuse; *(b)* selection of the drug(s) of abuse; *(c)* the likelihood of someone prone to substance abuse choosing a helping profession; and, *(d)* the influence of health care education on alcohol or drug use.

The Health Care Environment

It has been suggested that the health care environment, with the stressors of clinical work and the easy access to highly addictive drugs, makes physicians, nurses, pharmacists, and dentists more prone to developing addiction problems than others in the general population. Despite the large number of health care professionals and students who report problem drinking or drug taking shown in Table 22.1, a higher than average incidence of addiction has not been documented. The choice of addictive substances used by this population, however, does indicate differences. Among follow-up studies of physicians sanctioned by medical boards, approximately one-fourth reported alcohol abuse only with the remainder using drugs or a combination of alcohol and drugs (Gualtieri, Cosentino, & Becker, 1983; Shore, 1987). In a study of 139 nurses recovering from addiction (but not necessarily identified or sanctioned

by state boards of nursing), 43% reported only alcohol abuse. Since alcohol use is legal and even drunkenness is considered only poor judgment, larger percentages of nurses and other health care professionals may be at risk for alcohol problems than these figures would suggest. We could suspect, though, that if a health care professional does become addicted to a mood-altering substance, that substance may be a legal or illegal drug as well as alcohol.

The stress of the clinical work is often suggested as contributing to substance abuse, but documentation for this has not been found. In fact, if this were true, one could surmise that anyone in a stressful situation (e.g., mothers of young children, families of dying patients, bus drivers) would be at risk for substance abuse. In short, everyone living in today's fast-paced, stressful world would become addicted. We know that is not true. Reports from people recovering from addiction suggest, however, that experiencing stress made them more likely to reach for a drink or a pill to relax and ease their pain. So, although initial use (a necessary but not sufficient precursor to addiction) may be more likely in a stressful environment, continued use, abuse, and ultimately, addiction may be no more likely for physicians, nurses, pharmacists, or dentists than anyone else.

Another aspect of clinical work, however, may encourage substance use among practitioners. This phenomena is called "pharmaceutical coping"—the tendency to use a chemical substance to cure, care, and fix whatever problem develops. Physicians and nurses see their patients recover, have less pain, and sleep better with medication. "A pill for every ill" or "better living through chemistry" are common slogans, albeit subconsciously. One may then automatically reach for a pill, capsule, or injection for one's own pain or need for sleep. Added to the long hours, shift work, and physically demanding (and sometimes painful) aspects of clinical work, it may be that nurses and physicians are even more likely to "need" some relief. Along with access, this phenomenon may explain the higher than average percentage of health care professionals who report using drugs other than alcohol.

The Choice of a Helping Profession

There has also been speculation that people who choose helping professions (health care, social work, psychology) are more likely to have substance abuse problems in their family of origin (Black, 1981). The theory suggests that in a family disrupted by substance abuse, children learn caretaking roles, giving them some rewards although not providing for their own needs. The need to be needed carries over into adulthood where they seek a career whose primary function is the care of others.

The research data are confusing regarding whether this theory is acceptable. Bissell and Haberman (1984) found that approximately one-third of the addicted professionals they studied reported an alcoholic family member. In Sullivan's comparison of addicted and nonaddicted nurses, 61% of the addicted nurses reported alcoholism or drug addiction in their family of origin, whereas only 37% of the nondependent sample reported substance abuse in their family (Sullivan, 1987b). Additionally, 48% of the addicted nurses reported they assumed parental roles in childhood in response to family dysfunction; only 22% of the nonaddicted nurses did so. It is possible that nonaddicted respondents may not be aware or knowledgeable enough about substance abuse or family dysfunction to recognize it in family members, and they may be in denial, as well, about people close to them having such a problem. Despite this, the difference between the two groups is statistically significant and is enough to suspect actual differences.

Research evidence is accumulating to support the genetic predisposition of alcohol and drug addiction (Beglieter, Porjesz, Bihari, & Kissin, 1984). Results with health care professionals concur. People with a family history of addiction are more likely to develop substance abuse problems than those whose families do not have addiction problems. We do not know if people who choose helping professions are more or less likely to have a family history of addiction.

Education about Substance Abuse

Another aspect of working in health care suggested as contributing to substance abuse problems is education regarding addictive illnesses. Although schools of medicine, dentistry, pharmacy, and nursing generally include information on physiologic actions of alcohol and drugs, they seldom provide information on substance abuse or progression of abuse to dependence (Polorny & Solomon, 1983). Hoffman and Heinemann (1987) found that only 57% of schools of nursing (N=336) reported teaching substance abuse content in the curriculum and, of these schools, the required instruction was 5 hours or less in 72% of them. Because of what health care professionals do learn about physiologic and chemical actions of addictive substances, they are likely to believe they are knowledgeable about alcohol and drugs. Thus, they believe that their education prevents addiction from occurring. In a similar fashion, diabetic education does not preclude one from developing diabetes, but, once educated about the disease, a person does know what to do to treat it. Unfortunately, education about addictions in the health care professions has not kept up with education about diabetes.

Stigma

One other factor related to nurses' use of addictive substances, in general, and controlled substances, in particular, should be noted. For both females and males, a certain amount of stigma is associated with alcohol or drug abuse. Despite the fact that the American Medical Association designated alcoholism as a disease in the late 1950s, many still believe that substance abuse disorders are a matter of willpower and self-control rather than addiction. Today, the American Psychiatric Association's designation of psychoactive substance abuse and dependence clearly identifies these disorders as primary diseases requiring treatment (American Psychiatric Association, 1987). Nurses, who are primarily female (97%), experience the added stigma associated with addiction in women. Although only about half the number of females are alcoholic compared to males, it is not known if the actual incidence is less or if the stigma of addiction is so great that both females and their families are successful at hiding the addiction problem from themselves and others. Thus, nurses who become addicted are more likely to feel shame and experience guilt over their use than others in predominantly male professions (physicians, dentists, pharmacists). (This may be changing, however, as medical, dental and pharmacy schools report increasingly larger percentages of female students.)

Legality

Nurses have another problem. If they become addicted to controlled substances, they often obtain the drugs illegally. Physicians and dentists can simply write their own prescriptions and, although their rationale for use is questionable, their legal right to order the drug is not. Nurses and pharmacists cannot write prescriptions so they may take drugs from hospital supplies. Nurses may take medications ordered for patients, especially if their addiction progresses to the point where the drug is needed to prevent withdrawal. Having violated their own ethical principles only adds to the shame and guilt.

WHAT IS BEING DONE TO HELP?

National organizations in all the health care professions have recognized the problem of addiction among their practitioners. In nursing, the American Nurses' Association (ANA) passed a resolution at the 1982 House of Delegates meeting recognizing substance abuse as a disease and resolving that nurses should be offered treatment for it before losing their jobs or their licenses. (A similar resolution had failed 2 years previously.) Shortly thereafter, the ANA Board of Directors appointed a committee consisting of ANA members and representatives from the National Nurses Society on Addictions (NNSA) and the Drug and Alcohol Nursing Association (DANA). This committee was charged with developing guidelines to assist state nurses' associations in establishing peer assistance programs. The result of the committee's work was the publication of a monograph titled, *Addictions and Psychological Dysfunctions in Nursing: The Profession's Response to the Problem* (American Nurses' Association, 1984).

Concurrently with activity at the national level, a number of state associations began developing mechanisms to assist their colleagues impaired by

substance abuse. Only a few assistance programs existed in the early 1980s. Today, almost all states either have a program or are planning one. Although the type of services offered and the service arrangements differ, the philosophy of helping impaired colleagues is consistent from state to state.

A State Nurses' Association Peer Assistance Program

The state nurses' associations with established peer assistance programs generally offer a support and referral service, monitor recovery, and offer education to the state nursing and health care community. Figure 22.1 illustrates how a peer assistance program works.

As a support and referral service, trained members answer calls from impaired nurses, their families, friends, or employers. The members assist with getting a nurse to treatment for evaluation of substance abuse problems by referring the nurse to the appropriate service or by confronting the nurse after a report from others. If the nurse accepts a recommendation for treatment, the peer assistant (volunteer nurse) will continue to monitor the nurse's recovery for a period of time (1–2 years). The peer assistant may also serve as the nurse's advocate by helping the nurse approach an employer or the board of nursing, providing information or testifying on the nurse's behalf. In most states, volunteers provide intervention, monitoring, and educational services, although a few of the larger states have salaried staff assigned to peer assistance as well. Peer assistance programs, for the most part, do not provide treatment for substance abuse but refer nurses to treatment facilities.

Developing a program in the state, establishing policies and procedures, convincing the membership to accept such a program, training volunteers to intervene with vulnerable people (nurses) in sensitive situations, and monitoring the recovery of impaired nurses is time-consuming and emotionally taxing for the participants. Therefore, different mechanisms for offering services to nurses have evolved.

State Regulated Assistance

With increasing awareness of the risk to the public and the expanding need for services to nurses, some states have passed legislation regulating assistance to nurses. To date, California, Texas, Florida, New Mexico, and Kansas have passed legislation providing a mechanism

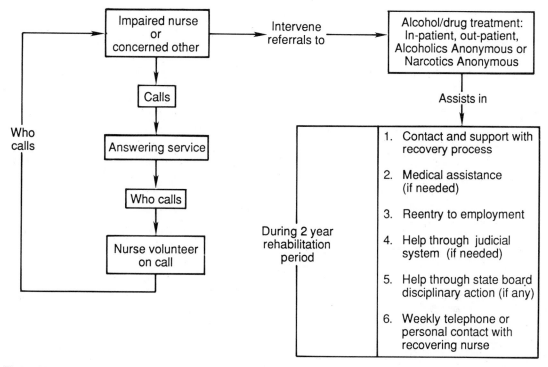

Figure 22.1

Model peer assistance program. From Sullivan, E., Bissell, L., & Williams, E. (1988). *Chemical dependency in nursing.* Menlo Park, CA: Addison-Wesley. Copyright 1988 by Addison-Wesley, California. Reprinted by permission.

for nurses to receive treatment of substance abuse in lieu of disciplinary action. When a nurse satisfactorily completes an extended program of recovery, no disciplinary action is taken against the nursing license.

Because assistance is mandated by state law, it is then funded by the state. This offers considerable advantage over the volunteer staffed assistance programs by use of a paid staff with legal parameters clearly established. The state controls the preparation and credentials of the staff who are, in turn, accountable to the state. These probrams are all recently established and evaluation data are not yet available so it is too soon to know if they are effective in identifying impaired nurses earlier in the addiction process and in assisting them into recovery.

Other Support Services

In an effort to help their impaired colleagues, recovering addicted nurses have formed local support groups.

Often, these groups are called AA (Alcoholics Anonymous) groups for nurses or, simply, support groups for nurses. In either case, they are usually fashioned after the AA model requiring anonymity and confidentiality. These groups provide a safe, supportive environment for a newly recovering nurse to talk freely about addiction experiences and the special problems of returning to work in the profession. Nurses have found that they are sometimes unable to talk about drug-taking behaviors in other AA groups because most of the members used alcohol almost exclusively. In addition, other AA members are often distressed to hear that a nurse was using drugs while caring for patients and even more disturbed to hear a nurse describe using medications meant for patients. However, if the nurse is to resolve issues around the impaired practice, accept the past, and make restitution, it is necessary to be able to share past experiences freely, just as others do in AA meetings. Thus, a group of only recovering addicted nurses offers this kind of support. Most nurses also attend regular AA meetings.

Nurses' support groups offer another benefit. If nurses are facing a disciplinary hearing with the state board of nursing or facing criminal charges in connection with drug use, they can benefit from other nurses' experiences with these legal problems. Names of attorneys are shared, and strategies to protect the nurses' rights while safeguarding the public are discussed.

The disadvantage to a support group just for nurses is that negative experiences may be reinforced. Disciplinary hearings with the state board occur when the board believes patient safety has been jeopardized. It is not easy for nurses to hear their behavior described and then to be given a punishment (licensure restrictions). Even with the most considerate attention to the nurse's feelings, it is difficult for this to be a positive experience. So, when nurses get together to share their experiences, the negative perspective often prevails. Reinforcement for what has been done *to* one rather than accepting responsibility for the consequences of one's action can occur and is not helpful to the nurse's recovery. One way to combat this outcome is to encourage members to remain in the group past their initial recovery to serve as role models to newer members. It is also helpful to have members who did not experience legal consequences to help the group focus on positive recovery issues.

It is difficult to know just how many groups exist because even their presence is often anonymous. Anecdotal accounts from nurses in larger cities suggest that many groups exist. Some are formed by active members of state peer assistance programs. Some treatment centers have initiated such groups and, in other areas, a few nurses who knew each other just began meeting and inviting others. Members may or may not do intervention. In either case, intervention is usually more informal, consisting of members sharing their experiences with a nurse who is showing signs of substance abuse.

One activity that these support groups usually do not do is monitoring. Since its inception several years ago, one nurses' AA group in Minneapolis has maintained the position that monitoring is the responsibility of the state board (or other designated organization) and that adequate support for an impaired nurse precludes that group from reporting to any other agency. That is, the members have stated that if the nurse knew that what he or she said in the meeting would be reported to an employer or the state board, that nurse would be reluctant to share anything except positive behavior. On the other hand, if the nurse is to resolve problems when they occur (including using alcohol or drugs), he or she must feel free to come to the group with any subject and report both positive and negative behavior.

Nurses are also being helped through institutional employee assistance programs (EAPS). Hospitals were slow to establish EAPs for their employees although industry experience had shown the cost benefit of rehabilitating, rather than firing, a valuable employee (Sullivan, 1986). Because of the threat of licensure sanction in addition to the job threat, nurses have been somewhat reluctant to share their addiction problem with anyone associated with their institution. This is especially true if they use drugs on the job or stole them from the workplace. Even with such assurances, professional staff used EAPs only occasionally.

Some hospitals are establishing, either formally or informally, internal assistance programs for nursing staff. One example of such a program is in operation at the Jewish Hospital in St. Louis where the Vice President for Nursing conducts all interventions and, in cooperation with the hospital's EAP counselor, monitors recovering nurses. An agreement between the nurse and the institution is made, clearly stating the nurse's responsibilities, how the nurse's behavior will be documented, and the consequences if the contract is not kept. This type of agreement is commonly called a "return to work" contract (see Fig. 22.2).

HOW TO HELP AN IMPAIRED NURSE

There are three steps in assisting a nurse, whose professional functioning is impaired by alcohol or other drug use, into recovery: identification, intervention, and reentry.

Identification

Identifying an impaired nurse is difficult for many reasons. One is the belief many people have that "it can't happen to someone I know/love/like/trust." Another is the mistaken belief health care professionals have that they and their colleagues are immune (or at least unlikely) to develop addiction problems because they are so well informed about alcohol and drugs. A third reason is that drugs are so commonly used in health care that their danger and potential for addiction are often ignored, especially in self-treatment. And, finally, health care professionals may still be under the false

_____ HOSPITAL

Employee Assistance Program

AGREEMENT BETWEEN EMPLOYEE AND

_____ HOSPITAL

I, _____, agree to the following conditions upon my continuing employment at _____ Hospital. These conditions will apply for a period of two years, beginning on _____ and ending on _____.

1. If it should be determined that I am using any mood-altering chemicals (except with the agreement of my therapist and under the direction of a physician who will keep the Employee Assistance Program informed as to reason and specific period of time), I will be immediately terminated and reported to the State Board of Nursing.

2. I agree to cooperate in any random urine check requested by _____ Hospital. The results will be sent to the Employee Assistance Program. If at any time mood-altering substances are found, my employment will be terminated immediately and I will be reported to the State Board of Nursing.

3. I agree to follow the prescribed program of aftercare, including attendance in AA. I will be responsible for providing documentation of attendance to the Employee Assistance Program and if I do not comply either in attendance and/or documentation, my employment will be terminated immediately and I will be reported to the State Board of Nursing.

4. If I should voluntarily terminate from _____ Hospital, I agree to keep the Employee Assistance Program informed as to my compliance with prescribed program of aftercare, my address and place of employment. I further agree to inform my new employer of my condition and request my new employer to keep the Employee Assistance Program at _____ Hospital informed of my progress. Unless other arrangements are made which are mutually agreeable to the new employer and the Employee Assistance Program at _____ Hospital, and if the above conditions are not met I will be reported to the State Board of Nursing.

These four conditions have been read and agreed upon by:

_____   _____
(Employee signature)   (Date)

In the presence of:

_____   _____
(Director of Nursing--_____ Hospital)   (Date)

_____   _____
(EAP Coordinator-- _____ Hospital)   (Date)

Figure 22.2
Return to Work Contract. From the Jewish Hospital of St. Louis. Reprinted with permission.

impression that alcoholics are "skid row bums" (actually only about 5% of alcoholics can be classified in this way), thus precluding anyone like themselves.

When a nurse is developing a substance abuse problem, many signs and symptoms appear. Not any one is diagnostic of substance abuse or dependence but, rather, it is the pattern of signs and symptoms, in combination and over time, that indicates a possible abuse problem. Diagnosis, in fact, can only be done by professionals in the addiction field. Others (physicians, nurses, administrators) can recognize the pattern and assist the nurse into being evaluated for substance abuse. Indicators of substance abuse include behavioral signs, physical symptoms, and worksite environmental factors.

Some behavioral signs may indicate the potential risk for substance abuse. These include: *(a)* increasing isolation from colleagues, friends, and family; *(b)* frequent complaints of marital and family problems; *(c)* frequent reports of illness, minor accidents and emergencies; *(d)* complaints from others about the person's alcohol/drug use or poor work performance; *(e)* evidence of blackouts (memory losses while conscious); *(f)* mood swings, irritability, depression or threats or attempts at suicide (which may be caused by accidental overdose); *(g)* strong interest in patients' pain control, the narcotics' cabinet, and use of pain control medications; *(h)* unexplained brief absences from the unit or frequent trips to the bathroom, often taking purse; *(i)* request for night shift; *(j)* little socializing with staff, eating alone, increasing isolation; *(k)* elaborate or inadequate excuses for being late or missing work (such as taking long lunch hours or sick leave immediately after days off); *(l)* difficulty meeting schedules and deadlines; and *(m)* illogical or sloppy charting.

Physical symptoms include: *(a)* shakiness, hand tremors; *(b)* slurred speech; *(c)* watery eyes, dilated or constricted pupils; *(d)* diaphoresis; *(e)* unsteady gait; *(f)* runny nose; *(g)* nausea, vomiting, diarrhea; *(h)* weight loss or gain; and *(i)* increasing carelessness about personal appearance (later symptom).

In addition to the above signs and symptoms, the nurse abusing narcotic drugs may: *(a)* show rapid mood change from irritation to depression to euphoria; *(b)* wear long-sleeved clothing continuously, even in warm weather; *(c)* come to work early or stay late, or come in on days off; *(d)* request assignment that increases access to drugs; and *(e)* wait until alone to open the narcotics' cabinet, going into restroom immediately afterward.

At the worksite, other indicators should alert a nursing manager or other nursing staff that a person(s) on the unit may be diverting and using controlled substances. These include: *(a)* frequently incorrect narcotic counts; *(b)* apparent alteration of narcotic vials; *(c)* increasing number of reports from patients that pain medications are not effective; *(d)* discrepancy between patient reports, for example, patient saying he only takes pain medication during the day, but the record showing nighttime administration as well); *(f)* large amount of narcotics wasted or many corrections noted on records; *(g)* erratic patterns of narcotic discrepancies (these may be timed with the addicted nurse's work schedule); *(h)* marked variation in quantity of drugs required on a unit (reflecting who is on duty for that particular shift). Usually combined with these indicators of diverted drugs is a pattern of "enabling" a particular nurse who seems to be having problems, such as frequent illness or family problems. Other staff think they are helping a colleague in need but, in fact, are allowing the dependency to continue. By the time this pattern is recognized, staff may have become resentful of the recurring problems and the extra work. Morale may already have slipped.

When a pattern of worksite indicators is examined with the behavioral signs and physical symptoms of a specific nurse, it is usually easy to identify the nurse with a substance abuse problem. The first step is to document this information regarding job performance impairment. Once the nurse has been identified, intervention must be planned.

Intervention

The goal of intervention is to enable the nurse to be evaluated for a possible substance abuse problem. Professionals in addiction are found in institutions or units specializing in substance abuse treatment. These institutions/units are usually called chemical dependency treatment centers. Chemical dependency refers to dependency on any mood-altering chemical—alcohol, marihuana, cocaine, narcotics, tranquilizers, barbituates, or others.

Intervening with a nurse who has (or may have) a substance abuse problem requires skill and sensitivity. It may be done by concerned colleagues, family members, friends, or the supervisor. Regardless of who the person is, he or she should be familiar with substance abuse problems and their manifestation so that the intervenor is prepared for any response on the nurse's part. The intervenor must have several resources available to provide the nurse with help. Finally, the intervenor and any others involved in the intervention must carefully examine their own attitudes toward substance abuse in nurses, especially if the nurse diverted drugs from the patient or the hospital. (It is difficult to accept that addiction can be so powerful as to allow a person to violate one's own ethical principles or commit illegal acts.)

Prior to intervening, the involved parties should contact experts in the chemical abuse field for assistance in planning the intervention. This expertise may be available if the institution has an EAP or from a local chemical dependency treatment unit. These professionals in addiction problems are expert in helping plan for various outcomes. If the nurse agrees to an evaluation for substance abuse, specific plans for follow-up to the evaluation must be made. If the evaluation reveals a diagnosis of substance dependence and the recommendation is for treatment of the dependence, it is expected that the recommendation will be followed. Plans will be made for reentry to the workplace and actions to be taken in case recovery is not maintained.

If the nurse refuses to be evaluated, intervenors must be prepared to carry out actions that will prevent the nurse from continuing addiction while caring for patients. For example, if a nursing manager has identified that a nurse has been diverting narcotics and the nurse refuses to go for an evaluation, the manager should follow through with responsibility to patients, the public, and the nurse by terminating employment and reporting the nurse to the state board of nursing.

Reentry

After treatment, the goals of reentry are to return the nurse to productive employment and to support the recovery process. This requires careful individual planning with each returning nurse. It requires an assessment of the nurse's readiness to return to work, a review of the precursors that led to the nurse's referral to treatment, and identification of worksite factors that may inhibit recovery.

Nurses, like other recovering people, require extended aftercare treatment (usually 1–2 years) and ongoing attendance at self-help groups such as AA, Narcotics Anonymous (NA), Cocaine Anonymous (CA), or a nurses' support group. Most attend meetings two or more times a week, especially during the early recovery period. Schedules must be adjusted for regular attendance at these meetings and treatment sessions.

An alcohol-abusing nurse may be able to return to work shortly after inpatient treatment (or may be successfully treated in outpatient therapy), whereas a drug-dependent nurse may need to avoid contact with the drug of addiction for an extended period of time (6 months to 2 years). Others may be moved to units or jobs with less stress for a period of time. Almost all returning nurses need to work regular hours because shifts interfere with attendance at self-help group meetings and aftercare therapy as well as interfere with sleep cycles which may have been disrupted by the alcohol or drug use.

Plans must also be made for monitoring the nurse's recovery. This may include regular reports from the treatment counselor, documentation of attendance at AA or NA, and, if possible, random urine screens for drugs. A "return to work" contract, described earlier, is used to delineate the nurse's responsibilities and the consequences if the agreement is violated (firing, reporting to the state board). Thus, the institution can assist the nurse and know, with some amount of reasonable assurance, that the nurse is indeed continuing recovery and, thus, patients are protected. The nurse is also assured that recovery is documented, thus obviating the need for continual observation or suspicion.

Strict confidentiality must be maintained when dealing with an impaired nurse. Whether or not to tell coworkers and what to tell them must be the nurse's decision. Some nurses simply say they had personal problems, others tell the whole story, and still others tell a few close friends. The decision about what to reveal is the nurse's.

If the staff's attempts to help the nurse failed and resentments followed, the supervisor will need to help everyone deal with feelings of anger and resentment toward the nurse. If the nurse agrees to disclosure, the best approach is straightforward. The nurse has a chronic, but treatable, disease but, because the disease is now "in remission," that behavior is no longer expected, nor will it be allowed. Furthermore, staff should be told that management will be responsible for supervision of the abuse recovery, and no one will be expected to "watch" the nurse.

Plans must also be made in case the nurse relapses and returns to alcohol or drug use. Most programs specify what constitutes a "relapse." Criteria for relapse usually include a period of use, such as daily use for several days or a full blown "binge." Seldom is one or two drinks a criterion but is cause for assessment of the person's potential for extended relapse. The institution should enlist the nurse's treatment counselor in making such an assessment.

A return to work contract clearly specifies the institution's response to relapse. This usually includes reporting to the state board of nursing and termination. *Consequences must be adhered to regardless of the circumstances.* It would be impossible to justify why the nurse had to keep his or her end of the bargain if the hospital bent the rules. More importantly, allowing the nurse to remain on the job or unreported could put the institution at risk, ethically as well as legally, should a patient be harmed because the nurse's clinical skills were impaired. As long as a careful assessment of the alcohol or drug use is made and the nurse is referred for increased assistance (e.g., return to treatment, more frequent counseling), the institution has met its obligation to the nurse, its patients, and the public.

RECOVERY RATES OF HEALTH CARE PROFESSIONALS

How well nurses, physicians, and the general public recover from alcoholism or drug dependency is a matter of much speculation and debate. Adding to the controversy is the debate whether abstinence is the sole criterion on which recovery is determined. This position has been maintained by the clinical treatment community, whereas researchers suggest there are indications that social drinking is possible for certain alcoholics. (This latter stance is more common in the United Kingdom than in the United States.) Neither clinicians nor researchers advocate illegal drug use no matter how "recreational" the use.

Studies of physicians' recovery from addictive illness indicate, in general, a higher than expected rate of recovery. Morse, Martin, Swenson, and Niven (1984) found 83% of the 73 physicians treated were abstinent at a 2-year follow-up compared to only 62% of the general population group. The authors suggest that the threat of licensure sanction is a strong motivator for continued recovery of this population when compared to others whose profession might not be denied to them due to their abuse problem. Shore (1987) reported an 8-year follow-up of physicians disciplined by the Oregon Board of Medical Examiners with 75% of the 63 sanc-

tioned physicians in recovery (as determined by stable employment and family relationships). However, Vogtsberger (1984) reviewed studies from 1950 to 1982 of treatment outcomes of substance-abusing physicians and found considerable differences in the reported recovery rates ranging from 27% to 97%. Variations in outcome criteria as well as methodology make it impossible to reach conclusions on these findings.

Studies on nurses' recovery rates have not been reported in the literature. There are some indications that relapse occurrence is minimal, however. Sullivan (1987a) found 67% of the 139 nurses had not relapsed since they began recovery. All reported abstinence at the time of data collection with 85% reporting a year or more of abstinence. Longitudinal studies of nurses in recovery are essential to determine if the possible high rate of recovery reported in physicians is also true for nurses.

POLICY IMPLICATIONS

Health care practice is controlled by both ethical principles and legal guidelines. Ethically, the ANA Code for Nurses guides the nurse in making practice decisions. Principle #3 of the Code states, "The nurse acts to safeguard the client and the public when health care and safety are affected by the incompetent, unethical, or illegal practice of any person." This statement clearly indicates that all nurses are responsible for protecting the public from potentially unsafe care provided by a health care professional whose practice is impaired due to alcohol or drug use. Ethical principles are operationalized into legal mandates when the consequences for not following the ethical guidelines are recognized by the public. Unsafe nursing practice is such a consequence of substance abuse.

Legally, the practice of nursing (and other professions) is regulated by the state's nurse practice act and administered by the state board of nursing. Recently, state boards of nursing have established mechanisms of support (reported earlier) based on the assumption that early intervention is more likely with assistance used as the primary response to addiction rather than discipline. Earlier identification and subsequent treatment is greater protection for the public.

Some states have become more stringent in requiring reporting of an impaired professional. These laws mandate that another nurse is responsible for reporting the impaired health care professional under threat of losing his or her *own* license if the nurse knows about the impaired practice, and if the nurse is indeed practicing while impaired. Obviously, such laws are difficult to prosecute but there has been one case in Minnesota of a physician who was disciplined because he did not report his physician son who was using cocaine (Eelkema & Schlueter, 1988). Despite the unlikely prosecution, in the states where this legislation has been enacted, reporting has increased (Chesney, 1988).

In additon to state responsibility, institutions also face risks in monitoring impaired practice. The tension between providing safe care for patients and protecting the rights of employees makes employment decisions difficult. It is obvious that a hospital cannot allow a nurse to care for patients while under the influence of alcohol or drugs but knowing when that is occurring is difficult. The nurse may have many years of practicing "under the influence" before his or her actions make use apparent. Firing all nurses who are found to be using addictive substances does not prevent unsafe practice; it only allows the nurse to go elsewhere. Furthermore, it does not intervene in the disease process so that recovery is possible.

Once a nurse has been identified as addicted, he or she is protected in employment-related actions by federal law for handicapped persons. Thus, employment decisions must be based on job-related criteria, not on the person's handicap. Also, employers must be careful to follow regular disciplinary procedures in firing an employee for problems related to substance abuse, or they may be faced with a wrongful termination case. Because of the complexity of protecting both patients and employees, some institutions are recognizing the value of EAPs. These programs will probably become more prevalent in the future.

Regardless of the legal issues surrounding substance abuse among nurses, humane concern for one's employees and colleagues mandates that health care institutions intervene in a person's illness and offer support during recovery. If the employee had another chronic disease, for example, diabetes or hypertension, and needed treatment for it, the employer would be willing to provide medical leave and adjust the work setting for the nurse to return. Responsible policies and procedures for handling this difficult situation can assure the employer that the nurse's practice is safe. Such actions protect both patients and nurses.

In addition to institutional assistance, state boards of nursing and state nurses' associations must continue to work to develop ongoing intervention and assistance for nurses. Schools of nursing must develop curricular offerings to educate future nurses, as well as practicing nurses, about substance abuse problems in themselves and in their colleagues. Only by education and early intervention can the practice of impaired health care professionals be influenced.

For more information about the problem of substance abuse in nursing and how to assist nurses, the reader is referred to *Chemical Dependency in Nursing: The Deadly Diversion* by Sullivan, Bissell and Williams, published by Addison-Wesley (1988).

SUMMARY

Substance abuse affects health care professionals as well as their clients. There are no clear data on the prevalence of substance abuse in nurses, but nurses and physicians appear to abuse alcohol more often than other drugs. There are no clear indicators that the stress of the health care environment encourages substance abuse; however, the belief in "pharmaceutical coping" may encourage use. Many substance abusing health professionals have a family history of substance abuse.

There is a serious need for substance abuse education in professional schools. State Peer Assistance Programs for nurses are being developed. These programs refer potentially abusing nurses for treatment, monitor recovery, and provide education. Posttreatment resources for recovering nurses include support groups for nurses, employee assistance programs and return-to-work policies in hospitals. Substance abusing nurses can be assisted through problem identification, formal or informal intervention, and assistance in reentering nursing practice.

REFERENCES

American Nurses' Association. (1984). *Addiction and psychological dysfunction in nursing: The profession's response to the problem.* Kansas City, MO: Author.

American Psychiatric Association. (1987). *Diagnostic and statistical manual of mental disorders* (3d ed. revised). Washington, DC: Author.

Begleiter, H., Porjesz, B., Bihari, B., & Kissin, B. (1984). Event-related potentials in boys at risk for alcoholism. *Science, 211,* 1064–1066.

Bissell, L., & Haberman, P. W. (1984). *Alcoholism in the professions*. New York: Oxford University Press.

Bissell, L., & Jones, R. W. (1981). The alcoholic nurse. *Nursing Outlook, 29*(2), 96–100.

Black, C. (1981). *It can never happen to me*. Denver: MAC Publishing.

Chesney, A. (1988). State board of nursing licensure violations and actions—1985. In E. Sullivan, L. Bissell, & E. Williams (Eds.), *Chemical dependency in nursing*, (170–174). Menlo Park, CA: Addison-Wesley.

Eelkema, R. & Schlueter, A. L. (1988). Minnesota's Physician Reporting Law: When am I My Brother's Keeper? *Minnesota Medicine, 71*, 551–553.

Engs, R. C., & Hanson, D. J. (1985). The drinking patterns and problems of college students: 1983. *Journal of Alcohol and Drug Education, 31*, 65–83.

Gualtieri, A. C., Cosentino, J. P., & Becker, J. S. (1983). The California experience with a diversion program for impaired physicians. *Journal of the American Medical Association, 249*(2), 226–229.

Haack, M. R., & Harford, T. C. (1984). Drinking patterns among student nurses. *International Journal of the Addictions, 19*(5), 577–583.

Hoffman, A. L., & Heinemann, M. E. (1987). Substance abuse education in schools of nursing: A national survey. *Journal of Nursing Education, 26*(7), 282–287.

McAuliffe, W. E., Rohman, M., Santangelo, S. L., Feldman, B., Magnuson, E., Sobol, A., & Weissman, J. (1986). Psychoactive drug use among practicing physicians and medical students. *New England Journal of Medicine, 315*(13), 805–810.

McAuliffe, W. E., Santangelo, S. L., Gengias, J., Rohman, M., Sobol, A., & Magnuson, E. (1987). Use and abuse of controlled substances by pharmacists and pharmacy students. *American Journal of Hospital Pharmacy, 44*(2), 311–317.

Morse, R. M., Martin, M. A., Swenson, W. M. & Niven, R. G. (1984). Prognosis of physicians treated for alcoholism and drug dependence. *Journal of the American Medical Association, 251*, 6, 743–346.

National Council of State Boards of Nursing. (1980–1981). *Preliminary sample of board actions*. Unpublished data.

Polorny, A. D. & Solomon, J. (1983). Follow-up survey of drug abuse and alcoholism teaching in medical schools. *Journal of Medical Education, 58*, 316–326.

Shore, J. H. (1987). The Oregon experience with impaired physicians on probation. *Journal of the American Medical Association, 257*(21), 2931–2934.

Sullivan, E. J. (1986). Cost savings of retaining chemically dependent nurses. *Nursing Economics, 4*(4), 179–182, 200.

Sullivan, E. J. (1987a). A descriptive study of nurses recovering from chemical dependency. *Archives of Psychiatric Nursing, 1*(3), 194–200.

Sullivan, E. J. (1987b). Comparison of chemically dependent and non-dependent nurses on familial, personal, and professional characteristics. *Journal of Studies on Alcohol, 48*(6).

Sullivan, E. J., Bissell, L., & Williams, E. (1988). *Chemical dependency in nursing: The deadly diversion*. Menlo Park, CA: Addison-Wesley.

Vogtsberger, K. N. (1984). Treatment outcomes of substance-abusing physicians. *American Journal of Drug and Alcohol Abuse, 10*(1), 23–27.

TREATING ADDICTIVE EATING PATTERNS

Claudia Crenshaw

Curiosity about problem eating patterns, attempts to address this difficulty in substance abuse populations, and new programs treating eating disorders with an addiction model have brought eating disorders to the attention of the substance abuse field. This chapter will present a rationale for reframing the eating disorders as another substance abuse syndrome with cross-addiction potential. The treatment of eating disorders within an addiction model as developed and implemented at the Decatur Hospital, in Decatur, Georgia, will be described. It will be shown that eating disorders can be viewed as an addiction, and addiction-oriented therapy can be used effectively to address this problem. Like alcoholism and other drug addictions, eating disorders are primary, chronic, and progressive with definite signs and symptoms. Furthermore, many clients with eating disorders are from substance-abusing families.

EATING DISORDERS

According to the revised *Diagnostic and Statistical Manual of Mental Disorders,* (DSM-III-R) (American Psychiatric Association, 1987) the eating disorders are characterized by gross disturbances in eating behavior. They include anorexia nervosa, bulimia nervosa, pica, and rumination disorders of infancy. Pica and rumination disorders of infancy are disorders of young children and appear unrelated to anorexia nervosa and bulimia nervosa. Simple obesity is not included within DSM-III-R, but a particular case of obesity may fit the criteria for bulimia nervosa. Anorexia nervosa and bulimia nervosa will be the eating disorders discussed in this chapter.

Anorexia Nervosa

Anorexia nervosa is characterized by the refusal to maintain body weight to a point that appears psychoticlike in the strength of the denial on clinical interview. Victims have an intense fear of gaining weight and of becoming fat, even while emaciated. The DSM-III-R diagnostic criteria included a 15% loss of ideal body weight (revised from 25%) and absence of three consecutive menstrual cycles. The onset of the illness is often after an effort to diet in mildly overweight females. Studies have reported a prevalence of 1 in 800 to as many as 1 in 100 females aged 12–18 (American Psychiatric Association, 1987).

Bulimia Nervosa

The essential feature of bulimia nervosa is recurrent episodes of binge eating. Clients describe eating from several thousand to 30,000 calories at one time. There is an overwhelming feeling of lack of control during the binges. The individual engages in activities to then purge the food, including self-induced vomiting, laxative or diuretic abuse, strict dieting or fasting, or vigorous exercise. The binging must average at least two episodes a week for 3 months to meet diagnostic criteria. There is an associated overconcern with body image and weight. Controversy exists regarding the actual incidence and prevalence of bulimia nervosa. After reviewing the literature on this topic, Johnson and Conners (1987) estimated approximately 8% of females and 1% of males would meet the criteria for bulimia.

Bulimia Nervosa and Obesity

Most clients with bulimia nervosa are normal or slightly above normal body weight. The question is raised whether obese people are bulimic. The obese population who fit the criteria for bulimia are binge eaters who have failed in their attempts to purge their overeating. Obese bulimics will describe alternate periods of binging and strict dieting or fasting resulting in weight gains and losses of 50–100 pounds in the course of the disease. As the bulimia progresses, the ability to fast and diet appears to decrease. In fact, this is also seen frequently with anorexia nervosa. The ability to starve appears to lessen over the years, resulting in binges and purges similar to the bulimic. Weight may not be an important factor in the dynamics of eating disorders or response to treatment. Many individuals caught in the obsession and compulsion of the food disorders have ranged in size from anorexic to obese during the course of the illness.

MODELS OF TREATMENT

Psychoanalytic Model

The premise of the psychoanalytic model and psychodynamic approaches to eating disorders is that an underlying conflict or personality structure is present and must be treated to affect the eating disorder. Traditional interpretative psychoanalysis has evolved from the classical biologically determined approach to those of ego psychology, object relations, and self-psychology (Bruch, 1985). Goodsitt (1985) described the self-psychology approach to the treatment of anorexia nervosa which was developed by Bruch. Given the "self-deficits" of the client, the therapist must take an active stance differing from the traditional interpretative psychoanalytic role. The therapist actively reaches out, teaches, coaches, encourages, and may even take over, if necessary, if the symptoms become life-threatening.

Cognitive-Behavioral Model

Thoughts and behaviors must change during the treatment of anorexia nervosa and bulimia nervosa. A cognitive-behavioral approach focuses on changing thoughts and behaviors directly with techniques to effect these changes. Interestingly, Garner and Bemis (1985) pointed out that Bruch utilized common clinical strategies to effect change in her clients although coming from a different theoretical approach. The major distinction of a cognitive approach is a reliance on conscious and preconscious experience with cognitions (thoughts) as a mediating variable for feelings. Halmi (1985) pointed out that almost all treatment programs use a behavioral component to some extent.

Family Systems Model

The client suffering from an eating disorder is treated within the context of the family system. Techniques from family systems theory and other treatment models are used to effect change toward family health. As much of the family as can be engaged is used. The eating disorder may be viewed as a problem of family organization and functioning (Sargent, Liebman, & Silver, 1985). Adolescents must be treated within the context of the whole family and may respond well to this kind of approach.

Addiction Model

The addiction model was first used to treat alcoholism. Based on the disease concept, alcoholism was viewed and treated as a primary illness, not a symptom of mental illness or lack of moral character (Jellinek, 1960). As translated to the treatment of eating disorders at Decatur Hospital, the eating disorder is viewed as a primary, chronic, and progressive illness. It is not treated as a symptom of another psychiatric disorder although psychiatric and personality disorders may coexist with an eating disorder.

The client is assisted to obtain physical, psychologic, and spiritual recovery through individual, family, and group psychotherapy and utilization of principles of the 12-step program of Overeaters Anonymous. Techniques from psychodynamic, family systems, and cognitive-behavioral approaches are used during treatment. According to the addiction model, abstinence from the problematic behavior is essential to initiate effective treatment. Just as the chemically dependent client is required to abstain from all nonprescribed, mood-altering drugs, the client with an eating disorder is required to abstain from all nonprescribed eating. Peer support and pressure are integral to accomplish abstinence. The self-help groups of the anonymous programs provide long-term support.

EVOLUTION OF THE ADDICTION MODEL

Historical Context

The prevalence of anorexia nervosa and bulimia nervosa has increased dramatically in the 1980s. Bruch (1985) pointed out that anorexia nervosa was first described a little more than 100 years ago. Anorexia nervosa was rare until the late 1950s. Bruch (1985) wrote her first paper in 1961 on observations of 12 anorexic patients, then a relatively large number. Symptoms of bulimia were initially described within the context of anorexia nervosa. During the late 1970s and early 1980s an epidemic of binge eating in nonemaciated individuals generated an abundance of reports, research, and theorizing seeking to better describe and explain the nature of eating disorders. *The Diagnostic and Statistical Manual of Mental Disorders* (DSM-III) (American Psychiatric Association, 1980) for the first time described bulimia as a diagnostic category separate from anorexia nervosa. The major diagnostic criteria differentiating it from anorexia nervosa was the lack of 25% loss of ideal body weight. The 1987 Manual (American Psychiatric Association, 1987) revised the diagnosis of anorexia nervosa to require only 15% loss of ideal body weight and changed "bulimia" to "bulimia nervosa" to reflect the strong relationship to anorexia nervosa.

Why are we seeing so many women with eating disorders now? Johnson and Connors (1987) hypothesized that rapid changes in role expectations for women and the cultural preoccupation with thinness since the 1960s have contributed to a marked increase in eating disorders. Women have had unrealistic expectations of what they should look like. Many clients have reported beginning their eating disorder with early efforts at dieting. Dieting mimics starvation. Binging is a natural biologic consequence of physiologic starvation. For those susceptible to the development of an eating disorder, this may be the trigger into the disease process—either the self-imposed starvation of anorexia nervosa or the binge–purge cycle of bulimia nervosa.

Recent reports in the popular press suggest that men are increasingly developing eating disorders. Dunn (1987) reported that men are underpresented in the reporting of anorexia nervosa and bulimia. The prevalence in males may be much higher than currently believed. It is hypothesized that men may hesitate to ask for help, embarrassed to find themselves suffering from what is perceived as a women's disorder.

Treating eating disorders as an addiction with an addiction model is an innovative approach to this problem. The addiction model, as developed at Decatur Hospital, incorporates techniques from psychoanalytic, cognitive-behavioral, and family systems models. The key difference in a treatment program guided by the addiction model from other approaches is the belief that the eating disorder is a primary illness and must be treated with an approach to the primary nature of the illness. Abstinence from the destructive food behaviors is required before treatment can proceed. Peer support and pressure are necessary to accomplish this during treatment; they then continue in the self-help groups of the anonymous programs. The client is assisted in obtaining physical, psychologic, and spiritual recovery through individual, family, and group psychotherapy and the 12-step program of Overeaters Anonymous, which is discussed in this chapter.

Eating Disorders as An Addiction

Several authors suggest a correlation between psychoactive substance abuse and eating disorders. Jonas, Gold, Sweeney, and Pottash (1987) found that 32% of 259 cocaine abusers surveyed on the National Cocaine Hotline meet DSM-III criteria for either anorexia nervosa, bulimia, or both disorders. Brisman and Siegel (1984) hypothesized that the actual substance abused in alcoholism and bulimia is not as important as the role the substance serves. The behavior of some clients suggests support for this hypothesis. After treatment of their alcohol or drug dependency, clients may then develop an eating disorder.

Mansfield (1984) reviewed the family system dynamics of eating disorders and addiction. The parallels in behavior of the eating disorder clients and their families with alcoholics and their families are described. Families become caught in the disease process of the eating disorder and begin enacting roles of enabling, persecution, and overdependency on the person and the eating disorder.

Clients with eating disorders have described whole lives absorbed in food. One obese bulimic recalled spending 3 of his 8 hours a day on the job looking for food, hiding food, or eating food. A young anorexic described blackouts from brain starvation, inability to concentrate or read, and an intense preoccupation with food but forgetting to eat or hiding food for others to think it was eaten. A bulimic's mother reported a reduction in the household food bill of $500 a month when her daughter was hospitalized. A bulimic woman told of taking a week off from work to repeatedly binge and purge in isolation. One bulimic was so obsessed with binging that staff had to remove the handles from the water faucet in her room to prevent her from binging on water.

Repeatedly, these clients' lives were out of control. A basic principle in treating eating disorders as an addiction is that the obsession and compulsion involved with anorexia nervosa and bulimia nervosa parallel the obsession and compulsion of alcoholism and chemical dependency. The anorexic, bulimic, alcoholic, and chemically dependent all progressively build a life around the addiction. They lie, steal, and manipulate to get and use their substance. The substance means more than the trouble it causes. For the anorexic, not eating is a paradoxical nonuse of food; however, the anorexic suffers nonetheless from an obsession and compulsion about food. Addiction may be viewed as not a dependence to the actual substance, but to the feelings the use or nonuse creates.

Wooley and Wooley (1981) identified two marked differences of the food abuser from the other substance abusers: no access to a subculture of users and a unique interplay of cultural, psychologic, and physiologic processes.

No access to a subculture of users. Wooley and Wooley (1981) described the secretness and isolation of those with eating disorders. Many of these clients do not know what is wrong with them and rarely seek help until they have read about eating disorders in a magazine or through other media exposure. Unlike the alcoholic who can share drinking at the bar or the cocaine addict who can share a freebase pipe, the anorexic and bulimic have no subculture of users. Clients often seek treatment or tell their families of their problem after a television program or newspaper article on eating disorders. This sense of isolation carries over into treatment. Initially clients with eating disorders have trouble eating together and are competitive in comparing their lives and eating habits.

Unique interplay of cultural, psychologic, and physiologic processes. Unlike any other abuse, food abuse is unique, in that eating is biologically necessary yet used in a self-destructive manner. Because eating must be managed every day, abstinence from food abuse is very difficult. Abstinence is defined as three meals a day, no more or no less. Clients have explained that this makes abstinence difficult, liking it to the alcoholic who would be told to just drink a half a shot of whiskey three times a day. Because food is biologically required but alcohol and drugs are not, the eating disorder clients cannot just stop using their substance of choice.

Addiction Model and 12-Step Approach

Mack (1981) described how the addiction model and treatment based on the 12-step program of Alcoholics Anonymous (AA) (1952) helps people recover from alcoholism. Over the years, there has been remarkable growth in 12-step recovery programs offering a method of living that can be used by anyone whose life has become unmanageable. Many of the principles such as "One day at a time" or "Let go and let God" offer solutions to the pressures of today. See Chapter 19 for a detailed discussion on AA and similar programs.

Where the 12-step approach differs from traditional psychologic or psychiatric approaches is that the destructive substance abuse must cease before other problems are addressed. Therefore, the key requirement with the addiction approach advocated here is the adherence to a strict abstinence model. For the eating disorder client, this is eating the prescribed three meals a day, no more or no less. This framework for recovery affords great relief to most clients. Many have had other hospitalizations or therapies but not the requirement of abstinence from their self-destructive food behaviors. For these clients their food behaviors have reached the point that their lives are unmanageable. The clients find the eating disorder has taken on a life of its own as an "addiction" and has to be addressed before other problems can be resolved.

The second difference with the 12-step approach from traditional approaches is the emphasis on spirituality. The eating disorder client is classically empty, eating to fill some void. Bulimia comes from Latin, meaning "ox hunger"; however, these people are not hungry in the traditional sense. The clients are looking for answers for themselves. Many individuals with eating disorders suffer from a range of narcisstic and borderline tendencies with their own inherent emptiness (Johnson & Connors, 1987). The spiritual component of recovery is addressed in working the 12 steps and gives these patients relief from their internal emptiness.

The third difference with the 12-step addiction approach is the focus on physical recovery. Like the alcohol and drug dependencies, eating disorders have severe physical complications and sequelae. Anorexia nervosa is the most lethal psychiatric illness with a mortality rate of 6%–18% (Rockwell, 1986). The chronic progression of anorexia and bulimia affects all body systems. The psychoeducational approach in learning about the physical complications of the eating disorders assists the clients in following the recommended treatment plan. Abstinence from the destructive food behaviors and adherence to the food plan is the first step in physical recovery. Clients actually go through a physical stabilization phase that is similar to alcohol and drug detoxification.

Overeaters Anonymous (1980) has been active since 1960 in offering help to those suffering from an eating disorder. Overeaters Anonymous is the self-help group based on the principles of AA and uses the 12 steps as applied to food. Overeaters Anonymous is an adjunct utilized with the rehabilitation program to offer clients a group with which to identify and a method to continue their recovery after treatment.

Besides finding that abstinence, spirituality, physical recovery, and self-help groups are as essential in the treatment of eating disorders as with alcohol and drugs, there are other important reasons the addiction model is helpful. A large number of people with eating disorders come from alcoholic or drug-dependent families. With the addiction approach they are able to get a new perspective on their roles and responses within their family of origin and their own families.

In addition, many food abusers have a coexisting alcohol and drug dependency. A thorough assessment of alcohol and drug history is indicated for all clients with eating disorders. Conversely, all clients with alcohol and drug problems should be screened for the presence of an eating disorder. If coexisting disorders are identified early in the treatment process, both disorders may be addressed under an addictions framework. Clients may relapse on alcohol or drugs due to an untreated eating disorder. Clients may develop a clinical eating disorder after recovery from alcohol and drug dependency.

DEVELOPMENT OF A COMBINED ADDICTION TREATMENT PROGRAM

Eating disorder clients were first admitted to the substance abuse treatment program at Decatur Hospital in 1982 through the influence of Judith Knight Earley, Ph.D. and Charles Allard, M.D. They wanted to see if selected eating disorder clients could benefit from a hospitalization addressing their food difficulties as an addiction. Their intention was to set up a separate program for the eating disorders if the treatment worked.

However, admitting and treating the eating disorder clients with the alcohol and drug clients generated new ideas. The early clients identified the alcohol and drug addiction in their own families and their own coaddiction to alcohol and drugs. Because of the impact of this on the course of treatment for the eating disorder, the staff became committed to treating the eating disorder clients integrated within the alcohol and drug program.

The mixing of eating disorder clients with alcohol and drug clients benefits both groups. Because the majority of clients with eating disorders are women and the majority of alcoholic and drug addicts in treatment are men, it normalizes the male-to-female ratio on the unit. Also, the alcohol and drug clients are able to explore their own food issues. Thus, Decatur Hospital is uniquely set up to treat the individual with an alcohol, drug, and eating disorder. Decatur Hospital serves as a tertiary referral resource for this population.

Staff members have seen benefit from the mix of clients. Those who have worked with a purely eating disorder population are pleased with how the alcoholics and drug addicts facilitate reaching those with eating disorders. The paradigm of alcohol and drug addiction as presented by the other clients reframes for the eating disorder clients their difficulties in a way that emphasizes the seriousness of their disease. The emphasis is not on cure, but on coping with and recovering from a severe, chronic, and progressive disorder.

Inpatient and Outpatient Treatment Program

The treatment program now offers a 4–6-week inpatient or outpatient rehabilitation program. The outpatient program is a partial hospitalization model and treatment equivalent to the inpatient program. The outpatient program meets 20 hours a week for 4 to 6 weeks. The core components of both programs include assessment, medical stabilization, nutritional consultation, group, individual and family counseling, education, family treatment, step work, continuing care, integration into the 12-step anonymous group, and membership in the client alumni association.

Assessment

Each client is evaluated by clinical interview by the intake worker and medical director. A psychiatric and medical history is taken, focusing on addiction and eating disorders. The eating disorder history includes presenting symptoms and age of onset. Weight history and food intake are obtained. Binging, dieting, purging, and exercise must be asked about directly.

Depending on the severity of symptoms, the psychiatric, addiction, and medical history, and support systems still in place, the client will be admitted to the outpatient or inpatient program. Both programs accept adults 18 years and older on a voluntary basis. Those requiring intensive medical stabilization are admitted to a separate medical stabilization unit.

Nursing Management

In reframing the eating disorders as an addiction, Orem's (1985) self-care philosophy of nursing is used. Staff members care for the patients in the manner clients would care for themselves if they were healthy enough to do so. The addiction model holds the client responsible for recovery. Staff initially set ground rules on abstinence, facilitate treatment, break through denial, and assist the client in identifying with the 12-step self-help groups. The clients become more and more self-directive in their treatment and bring this to the newer patients. Staff members take a secondary role as quickly as possible. This approach is consistent with Orem's philosophy of nursing and with traditional alcohol and drug rehabilitation. To do more for clients than what they cannot do for themselves would be "enabling" to the addiction or the eating disorder. Eating disorder clients respond to this kind of rehabilitation model.

Clients admitted to the medical stabilization unit require 24-hour monitoring for medical complications. Cardiac arrhythmias or severe malnutrition and dehydration, with resulting fluid and electrolyte imbalance, may require cardiac monitoring, intravenous rehydration, hyperalimentation, or nasogastric feeding. Less than 5% of admissions require such intensive intervention. These clients are in medical crisis and are treated in an intensive nursing setting with supportive care. Emotional support, education, and guidance are also provided by the nursing staff.

The majority of clients enter immediately into the inpatient or outpatient rehabilitation programs. The medical complications and psychologic aspects of eating disorders are so intertwined that the nurse is in a unique position to provide the continuum of nursing care from physical assessment to psychologic counseling. The opportunity for creativity in working with these clients is enormous. Nurses provide education, lead therapy groups, and function as treatment plan coordinators. They assess and care for physical complications requiring nursing intervention. The physical complications of anorexia nervosa result largely from starvation. Bulimics develop medical and dental consequences of binging and purging. The medical complications of anorexia and bulimia addressed by the nurse include malnutrition, brain starvation syndrome, fluid and electrolyte imbalance, endocrine deficiency, gastrointestinal distress, salivary gland swelling, and dental caries and enamel erosion. The treatment of choice for all complications once the patient is out of medical crisis is simple: *restabilization on an adequate food plan*. This restabilization period is similar to the detoxification phase of alcohol and drug treatment.

Malnutrition is a consequence of all of the eating disorders. Anorexia nervosa may progress to catabolism of muscle mass to stay alive. Bulimics ingest enough calories to maintain weight or even obesity but starve for certain nutrients. Anemia and osteoporosis may be consequences of the malnutrition. Cardiac changes secondary to starvation in the anorexic may include thinning of the left ventricle and decreased chamber size (Herzog & Copeland, 1985). Arrhythmias are exacerbated by the presence of electrolyte imbalance. The mental status of clients with eating disorders is affected by the brain starvation suffered from malnutrition. Keys, Brozek, Henschel, Mickelsen, and Taylor (1950) studied the effects of starvation on normal subjects. In the extreme, the brain-starved clients presented with flat affect, thought blocking, and denial of the reality of their situation. In even milder forms, poor concentration, obsessionality, and concrete thinking diminished the clients' ability to benefit from psychotherapy. These clients are much easier to work with once they stabilize physiologically on their meal plan.

Fluid and electrolyte imbalance results from the starving, vomiting, diuretic use, and laxative abuse in anorexia and bulimia. Dehydration may result in orthostatic hypotension. Electrolyte abnormalities include elevated bicarbonate, hypochloremia, hypokalemia, and hyponatremia (Mitchell, Seim, Colon, & Pomeroy, 1987). Vomiting reduces hydrogen and chloride ions. Volume depletion results in the generation of aldosterone, promoting potassium loss through the kidneys. Metabolic alkalosis shifts hydrogen out of the cells with potassium shifting into the cells. Cardiac arrhythmias and death may result from hypokalemia. Low serum bicarbonate levels (metabolic acidosis) can be seen in the laxative abusers secondary to the loss of bicarbonate in the diarrhea. Restabilization of fluids and electrolytes may result in a fluid rebound even with gradual refeeding that clients experience as distressing because of the temporary weight gain.

Endocrine deficiency may result in estrogen deficiency (or testosterone deficiency in men), menstrual irregularities, and amenorrhea. This is most pronounced in the anorexic. The DSM-III-R (American Psychiatric Association, 1987) included amenorrhea as a diagnostic criteria for anorexia nervosa. Thyroid function is compromised in the anorexic. Bradycardia, cold intolerance, dry skin and hair, slowed relaxation of reflexes, and hypercarotenemia are clinical manifestations (Herzog & Copeland, 1985). Elevated growth hormone and elevated cortisol levels are common for the anorexic.

The dental complications and salivary gland swelling are seen in the self-induced vomiters (Dalin, 1986). The poor dental health is due to the acid in the vomitus wearing on the teeth. The salivary gland swelling (parotid enlargement) is a hallmark symptom of bulimia, creating a transitory mumps or chipmunk appearance. This is due to the vomitus irritating the salivary glands and is reversible when the vomiting stops.

Gastrointestinal complaints are the most common complaints during refeeding of the eating disorders. Stomach cramps, bloating, feeling too full, and constipation are common. The gastrointestinal tract must adjust to a normal diet. Clients are prescribed a bulk laxative for constipation initially. The laxative and enema abusers have the most difficult time. Ironically, laxative abuse has been found to be probably ineffective in decreasing caloric absorption (Herzog & Copeland, 1985). Most complaints subside in 10 days to 3 weeks. Gastrointestinal diagnostic studies must be done to rule out an organic disorder when an underlying disorder is suspected.

The role of the nurse in managing the medical complications during stabilization is paramount. Eating disorder clients have symptomatic complaints that must be assessed. Many of the complaints revolve around the fear of eating and getting fat, focusing on gastrointestinal distress. These complaints arise at meal time. The nurse's role is to reassure the clients that they can eat the meal plan as prescribed and that the gastrointestinal difficulties will get better. The fluid rebound during refeeding also generates fear about being able to eat normally and not gain tremendous amounts of weight.

The nurse also translates to the clients the seriousness of the medical complications. Some clients report chronic emergency room visits for heart palpitations and receive potassium supplements without revealing the underlying binge–purge behavior. One 18-year-old anorexic was on cardiac medication for cardiac damage due to anorexia nervosa. Despite this, her refusal to change her anorexic behavior remained the core issue of treatment. One bulimic had $3000 worth of dental work due to caries and enamel erosion. Because many of the eating disorder patients are young women in the childbearing years, counseling concerning replenishing body nutrients in preparation for pregnancy is necessary. Clients may suffer from a reversible osteoporosis due to estrogen and calcium deficiency. Two recovering anorexics broke their legs after treatment because the bone tissue regeneration is slow, once reversed. All these issues must be discussed during treatment to help clients understand their illness and break through the denial of its consequences.

The Use of Medication

At Decatur Hospital we have found the eating disorder clients have a high addiction potential to alcohol and mood-altering drugs. Brisman and Siegel (1984) found that a significant number of bulimics reported the abuse of alcohol and drugs. Medication is prescribed only when specifically indicated. Clients do have an initial vitamin regimen, and a bulk laxative is used for constipation. Clients frequently request other medication for symptoms that will be alleviated as they progress with refeeding. These medications are usually not provided unless there is a clear medical indication beyond refeeding issues.

Psychotropic medication is prescribed when indicated for specific symptoms. Pope and Hudson (1984) and Herzog (1986) presented arguments for an antidepressant trial, particularly for bulimics. However, both agree that the nature of the relationship between eating disorders and affective disorders remains controversial as does the efficacy of antidepressant treatment. Mitchell's (1988) review of literature on the pharmacologic management of bulimia nervosa also concluded that the question of efficacy of antidepressant medication remains unresolved. Antidepressants are prescribed only when depressive symptoms do not respond to the primary treatment for the eating disorder.

Nutritional Consultation

The role of the nutritionist or registered dietician is paradoxical. The eating disorder is not about food, but about the addictive obsessions and compulsions that are acted out self-destructively around food. The dietician is the first person the eating disorder patient wants to see. Typically these clients have read many nutrition and diet books. They want to tell the dietician how their situation with food is different. Nutritional consultation is sought, then discounted as the clients let the dietician know they are unique and will not be able to eat normally.

The dietician works with the clients throughout treatment and then in continuing care. Normalizing the eating pattern is the first requirement of abstinence so that physiologic and psychologic recovery can begin. The dietician works closely with the physician on the physiology of refeeding, and refers to others on the team to address the psychologic and physical complaints that arise through the refeeding.

The eating disorder guidelines for abstinence and refeeding are straightforward. Patients are prescribed a meal plan of three meals a day, no more and no less, that they are expected to eat. The meal plan is balanced from the basic four food groups. Initially patients drink water, juice, or milk with meals and only water between meals. All "diet" products are eliminated including artificial sweeteners and diet soda. These clients frequently consume large quantities of these products compulsively. The artificial sweeteners can precipitate the compulsion for sweets and similarily, desserts are eliminated because they are low in nutritional content and may trigger the desire for more sweets. Caffeine is initially eliminated, because it is also compulsively abused. Alcohol is not included in food plans because it lowers the patient's inhibition and ability to follow a meal plan. This client group is also at risk for cross-addiction to alcohol and mood-altering drugs. Religious preferences of foods and vegetarianism are explored. At times these choices are part of the eating disorder.

The focus of the refeeding is not on the client's weight, but on reestablishing a healthy enough food intake to maintain psychologic and physical health. Clients are not told their weights, and weight goals are not used. The obsession about weight is often a part of the eating disorder. Anorexics are refed gradually, 800–1000 calories a day, and may initially require a liquid supplement. As noted earlier, very infrequently do they require invasive procedures to begin refeeding. Bulimics initially begin with 1200–1400 calories a day to allow an adjustment in retaining that amount of food physiologically and psychologically. Obese bulimics are refed in the 1600–1800-calorie range, because they need a meal plan that can maintain health with a slow and consistent weight loss.

When clients start on a normalized meal plan, whether anorexic, bulimic, or obese bulimic, they do not want to eat. The anorexics have an intense fear of getting fat. The bulimics have tried eating normally before and found the weight gain from fluid rebound proof they cannot eat a normal diet. The obese bulimics have either been binging or dieting, never eating normally. They often believe dieting is their solution and want to eat less than prescribed to have a rapid weight loss.

Given the excessive patterns of all types that these clients bring to treatment, one may question how such a structured program is maintained. Initially, peer support and peer pressure allow the program to work. Clients eat together as a group on the unit until they progress to selecting food themselves in the cafeteria. Not eating, eating that is not prescribed, purging, and compulsively exercising are labeled as "using" on the unit, the same as drinking beer or snorting cocaine. The pressure to comply with the meal plan is substantial. With the addiction model, the consequence of *nonabstinence* is administrative discharge. The clients struggle with trying to bend the abstinence requirement, including developing many physical complaints. However, as the clients remain abstinent on the meal plan, the physical complaints disappear and the psychologic clearing and improvement of mental status allow the necessary psychotherapy to begin.

It is remarkable how difficult interpreting three meals a day as prescribed can be for the nursing staff. Clients will ask pleadingly to trade an apple for an orange. A meal time crisis can be generated around a refusal to eat spinach. Clients do get to state three food dislikes, but even the refusal to eat a certain food is usually based on some therapeutic issue. Once, beets were sent at lunch and dinner, an unusual and certainly questionable occurrence. However, helping the patients stick to the meal plan, including the beets, generated the most productive psychotherapy for the week. For the eating disorders client, food is not food as it is for the normal population. The emotional crises over food subside with treatment. The goal is to help the patients allow food to become just food again, and not the center of their lives.

Physical Modifications of the Unit

Several modifications were made on the unit to accommodate the eating disorder patients. The clients eat in a room that can be viewed from the nursing station. All food is kept in a locked kitchen that is monitored when it is opened for the alcohol and drug patients. Several rooms have locked bathrooms for initial admission of binge purgers. The locked bathroom helps the client regain control of the vomiting initially and is unlocked by staff when the client needs to toilet or shower. Clients are not allowed to weigh themselves. The scale on the unit has a digital read out that faces the nurse, not the client.

Group, Individual, and Family Counseling

Each client is assigned to a treatment group headed by a masters' prepared counselor. The clients in the group include those with eating disorders, alcoholics, and drug addicts. This group meets daily for group psychotherapy. Here the differences among the addictions fade away, and common problems of living, relating, and recovering are discussed. All individual and family work is focused back to the psychotherapy group. The peer treatment and support of the group is the crux of the addiction program. Clients work individually with staff on completing steps 1–5 of the 12–step anonymous programs. Family counseling is focused on resolving the immediate crisis of the hospitalization for treatment of the eating disorder and beginning plans for recovery on discharge from the hospital or outpatient program. Referral is made for those families requiring structured family therapy to address underlying family issues. In the outpatient program family members attend the 20 hours of treatment with the client for the full 4–6 weeks.

Another important group for the clients is the twice weekly eating disorder focus group. This group is led by the registered dietician and a recovering eating disorder counselor. It consists of all the eating disorder patients meeting to discuss addiction issues particular to food. Additionally, many of the education groups address particular food issues and recovery processes for those with eating disorders.

Role of Education

Daily educational presentations address the many facets of eating disorders, including physical and psychologic complications, relationship to alcohol and drugs, the addictive process, relapse prevention, and recovery tools. In managing the eating disorder clients on an addiction unit, education is important for the alcohol and drug clients to understand the nature and seriousness of the eating disorders. Like the general population, the alcohol and drug clients will otherwise minimize the eating disorders or try to give these clients food or soda.

Family Treatment

The family members of those with eating disorders have a difficult time accepting the addictive nature of the disease. Many have tried to get the clients to eat or stop binging and purging without success. These families need support and education in understanding the disease and accepting that willpower has not worked as a solution.

It is very painful for families to see a son, daughter, husband, or wife become emaciated by anorexia nervosa and still beg to be thinner. Family members need help understanding the rewards of starving and the binge–purge cycle for those with eating disorders.

The feedback from families in the outpatient program about their own recovery has helped us begin a family week for the inpatient eating disorder families. The families come for a week of education and therapy during their family member's hospitalization. During the course of their family member's treatment they meet with the family member and individual counselor on a weekly basis. Families then come to 16 weeks of continuing care and attend Al-Anon and O-Anon.

The 12-Step Anonymous Programs

Overeaters Anonymous, AA, Cocaine Anonymous, and Narcotics Anonymous use space at the hospital for meetings, which are attended by the clients regardless of their substance of choice. Families attend Al-Anon and O-Anon, 12-step programs for family members. O-Anon is the anonymous group for those with a family member suffering an eating disorder. The eating disorder clients also attend Overeaters Anonymous meetings outside the hospital and are asked to find a home group and sponsors while in treatment.

The Interdisciplinary Team

Eating disorder clients are multifaceted, requiring the consultation and care of many disciplines. Each staff member has a unique perspective that is shared with the treatment team. The medical director, psychiatrist, psychologist, program director and coordinator, team leaders, nurses, nutritionist, and technicians meet weekly to discuss the treatment plan for each individual client. It is easy for the staff to disagree because of the complexity of the eating disorder problems. The weekly meeting gives everyone a chance to share information and opinions, reaching a consensus on the best care for the patients. Nurses have a unique perspective because they are with the patients 24 hours a day and at meal times. Despite each individual's discipline and training, clinical decisions have to be reframed into the addiction model by the team as a whole.

Inpatient Community

The client community on the inpatient unit plays an important role in recovery. The community meets daily with the direct care staff to resolve the small miscommunications that can become negative on the unit. The client community supports recovery of all its members and is influential when clients get stuck in treatment, want to leave, or are having a hard time. The community treatment milieu places pressure on the individual not to use binging, purging, or not eating. It is this milieu that ensures food is not abused during treatment. Abuse of food is subject to administrative discharge, the same as using alcohol or drugs while in treatment. The community goes to the YMCA daily as a group and is the first to observe if an eating disorder client begins to compulsively exercise to purge food. Eating disorder clients do negotiate an exercise contract if purging by exercise is a part of their problem.

Continuing Care

On discharge from the primary inpatient or outpatient program, the eating disorder clients attend a weekly continuing care group with the alcohol and drug clients for 16 weeks. The group utilizes a psychoeducational model to support recovery. During this period the clients recontract not to use, whether their substance is alcohol, drugs, or food. They also attend 90 recovery anonymous meetings in 90 days and develop a comprehensive continuing care plan for themselves.

Client Alumni Association

In 1987 the patient alumni of the treatment programs incorporated as a private nonprofit group. The Decatur Hospital Alumni Association is open to patients on completion of continuing care. The mission of the group is to support recovery of the treatment program alumni while providing support back to the hospital for those just beginning treatment. This unique aspect of the program gives clients hope that they too will be able to finish treatment and enjoy a recovery program and new life-style.

Transference Issues

Clinicians who undertake the treatment of eating disorder clients must look at their own food issues and pay attention that they do not interfere with treatment (Johnson & Connors, 1987). The clinician's own size and weight often become a therapeutic issue. Shortly after the birth of the author's second child a client burst into tears in the office saying she wanted help but could not see how she could get it if people this size were going to treat her. A sense of humor is helpful in working with these clients as they grapple with their recovery.

Overdiagnosis

As these disorders become more recognized, there is the danger of overreaction and overdiagnosis of the eating disorders by both the public and treatment providers. Adolescent girls who were slightly overweight or underweight but not obsessed with food have been brought in by their parents. A 70-year-old woman with no history of an eating disorder presented wondering if the 10 pounds she was overweight were due to an eating disorder. Again, the core disorder is not related to weight, but to the obsession and compulsion around food and body image.

SUMMARY

Addictive eating patterns (the eating disorders) are serious problems that respond well to the addiction model approach. The key components of that approach are abstinence, peer support and pressure, spirituality, and psychologic and physical recovery. Those working in addiction settings must recognize and diagnose these difficulties early so clients can work on them at the same time as their alcohol and drug dependency. Those working with eating disorder clients in traditional treatment settings must consider if another approach would work if the patient is still starving, binging and purging, or overeating. Overeaters Anonymous is a self-help group that has helped thousands and is available to everyone. In addition, primary prevention for the recovering alcohol and drug client is necessary to avoid switching to food to handle the obsessive compulsive urge underlying every addiction.

This chapter proposes that we keep an open mind within the field of addiction to consider food as a substance of abuse. In addition, we must be open to the possibility of other substances and addictions as the sociocultural pressures change away from the current focus on thinness and food.

Nurses have a unique position on the interdisciplinary team in addressing and helping those suffering from eating disorders. Nurses' preparation to consider the total wellness of a client makes them able to sort out the complex physical and psychologic complications of these disorders.

REFERENCES

Alcoholics Anonymous. (1952). *Twelve steps and twelve traditions.* New York: Alcoholics Anonymous World Services.

American Psychiatric Association. (1980). *Diagnostic and statistical manual of mental disorders* (3d ed.). Washington, DC: Author.

American Psychiatric Association. (1987). *Diagnostic and statistical manual of mental disorders* (3d ed. revised). Washington, DC: Author.

Brisman, J., & Siegel, M. (1984). Bulimia and alcoholism: Two sides of the same coin? *Journal of Substance Abuse Treatment, 1,* 113–118.

Bruch, H. (1985). Four decades of eating disorders. In D. M. Garner & P. E. Garfinkel (Eds.), *Handbook of psychotherapy for anorexia nervosa and bulimia* (pp. 7–18). New York: Guilford Press.

Dalin, J. B. (1986). Oral manifestations of eating disorders. In F. E. F. Larocca (Ed.), *Eating disorders: Effective care and treatment* (pp. 71–82). St. Louis: Ishiyaku EuroAmerica, Inc.

Dunn, M. (1987, July 13). Men fight eating disorders: Support groups give special help. *The Atlanta Constitution,* pp. 1, 3.

Garner, D. M., & Bemis, K. M. (1985). Cognitive therapy for anorexia nervosa. In D. M. Garner & P. E. Garfinkel (Eds.), *Handbook of psychotherapy for anorexia nervosa and bulimia* (pp. 107–146). New York: Guilford Press.

Goodsitt, A. (1985). Self psychology and the treatment of anorexia nervosa. In D. M. Garner & P. E. Garfinkel (Eds.), *Handbook of psychotherapy for anorexia nervosa and bulimia* (pp. 55–82). New York: Guilford Press.

Halmi, K. A. (1985). Behavioral management for anorexia nervosa. In D. M. Garner & P. E. Garfinkle (Eds.), *Handbook of psychotherapy for anorexia nervosa and bulimia* (pp. 147–159). New York: Guilford Press.

Herzog, D. B. (1986). Antidepressant use in eating disorders. *Psychosomatics, 27* (Suppl. 11), 17–23.

Herzog, D. B., & Copeland, P. M. (1985). Eating disorders. *The New England Journal of Medicine, 313* (5), 295–303.

Jellinek, E. M. (1960). *The disease concept of alcoholism.* New Haven: Yale Center of Alcohol Studies.

Johnson, C., & Connors, M. E. (1987). *The etiology and treatment of bulimia nervosa.* New York: Basic Books.

Jonas, J. M., Gold, M. S., Sweeney, D., & Pottash, A. L. C. (1987). Eating disorders and cocaine abuse: A survey of 259 cocaine abusers. *Journal of Clinical Psychiatry, 48* (2), 47–50.

Keys, A., Brozek, J., Henschel, A., Mickelsen, O., & Taylor, H. L. (1950). *The biology of human starvation.* Minneapolis: University of Minnesota Press.

Mack, J. E. (1981). Alcoholism, A. A. and the governance of the self. In M. H. Bean & N. E. Zinberg (Eds.), *Dynamic approaches to the understanding and treatment of alcoholism* (pp. 128–162). New York: Free Press.

Mansfield, E. (1984, July–August). Eating disorders and alcoholism: Linking family system dynamics. *Focus on the family,* pp. 22, 27–28, 31.

Mitchell, J. E., Seim, H. C., Colon, E., & Pomeroy, C. (1987). Medical complications and medical management of bulimia. *Annals of Internal Medicine, 107,* 71–77.

Mitchell, P. B. (1988). The pharmacological management of bulimia nervosa: A critical review. *International Journal of Eating Disorders, 7*(1), 29–41.

Orem, D. E. (1985). *Nursing: Concepts of practice* (3d ed.). New York: McGraw-Hill.

Overeaters Anonymous. (1980). *Overeaters Anonymous*. Torrance, CA: Author.

Pope, H. G., & Hudson, J. I. (1984). *New hope for binge eaters: Advances in the understanding and treatment of bulimia*. New York: Harper & Row.

Rockwell, W. J. K. (1986). A critique of treatment methods for anorexia nervosa. In F. E. F. Larocca (Ed.), *Eating disorders: Effective care and treatment* (pp. 11–24). St. Louis: Ishiyaku EuroAmerica, Inc.

Sargent, J., Liebman, R., Silver, M. (1985). In D. M. Garner & P. E. Garfinkel (Eds.), *Handbook of psychotherapy for anorexia nervosa and bulimia* (pp. 257–279). New York: Guilford Press.

Wooley, S. C., & Wooley, O. W. (1981). Overeating as substance abuse. In Mello, N. K. (Ed.). *Advances in substance abuse behavioral and biological research, 2,* (pp. 41–67). Greenwich, CT: JAI Press.

AIDS AND HUMAN IMMUNODEFICIENCY VIRUS INFECTIONS IN DRUG ABUSERS

James R. Allen

The acquired immune deficiency syndrome (AIDS) was recognized as a unique medical condition in 1981, although unrecognized cases of the illness undoubtedly occurred in the United States and other countries during the 1970s and perhaps earlier. The disease was characterized clinically by opportunistic infections such as *Pneumocystis carinii* pneumonia or cryptosporidial enteritis and unusual malignancies such as Kaposi's sarcoma or primary lymphoma of the central nervous system (CNS). Immunologically, persons with AIDS had a profound deficit of cellular immunity, particularly characterized by a loss of T4 helper lymphocytes.

Epidemiologically, the first cases of the new disease—later to be called AIDS—were associated with young homosexual men. Within a few months, as additional cases of the new disease were identified and reported, it became apparent that persons who abused drugs intravenously also had the same clinical and immunologic conditions. By mid-1982 cases were described in men with hemophilia who had received clotting factor concentrates, and by the end of that year cases were recognized in persons who had been transfused, in the heterosexual partners of persons with AIDS, and in children.

Laboratory investigations of the new condition kept pace with the rapid development of epidemiologic, clinical, and immunologic information, so that by 1984 not only had the basic patterns of transmission and disease expression been defined clearly, but a new cytopathic human retrovirus called human immunodeficiency virus (HIV) had been isolated and identified as the probable cause of AIDS.

Retroviruses were first described in animals early in this century, but were not identified in humans until the isolation of human T-lymphotropic virus type I (HTLV-I) in the late 1970s. HTLV-I, which also establishes a chronic infection in the target human cells, is a trans-forming retrovirus that is not closely related to HIV. This virus also has been associated with human disease —adult T cell leukemia, tropical spastic paraparesis, and myelopathy—in a small percentage of infected persons, and the prevalence of infection with it has been increasing in intravenous (IV) drug users in the United States during recent years.

Because of the intense interest and concern about AIDS, this chapter will focus only on the epidemiology and clinical aspects of HIV infection and AIDS, particularly on infection and disease in IV drug abusers, and conclude with a discussion of prevention efforts to curtail further spread of HIV in this population.

ETIOLOGY OF AIDS: HUMAN IMMUNODEFICIENCY VIRUS (HIV)

The virus that causes AIDS, HIV, was first isolated in France and the United States in 1983 and 1984. It is one of a small number of human retroviruses that share the characteristic of having an RNA genome and the enzyme reverse transcriptase that is essential for establishing infection in cells.

Infection with HIV

HIV infects human cells that have an appropriate receptor site on the cell surface; the primary receptor identified has been the CD4 molecule. The major cell type infected by HIV, therefore, is the T4 helper lymphocyte, although monocytes, macrophages, and probably selected cells of the CNS also can be infected.

Once HIV binds to the receptor molecule, the virus envelope fuses to the cell membrane, and the viral core enters the cell. After being internalized, the RNA genome is transcribed to DNA by the reverse transcriptase enzymes; this proviral DNA can then be integrated into the human host chromosomal DNA using other enzymes produced by the virus. The integrated proviral DNA thereby establishes a chronic viral infection of the host cell.

HIV has a complex genetic structure for a virus. The primary structural genes—named *env, gag,* and *pol*—code, respectively, for the envelope and core proteins and for the enzymes required for the various viral functions. In addition, HIV has a number of other genes, at least some of which serve a regulatory function to increase or inhibit replication of virus in the host cell. These regulatory genes are believed to have an important function in determining the pathogenicity of the infection.

The infected host cell with the integrated proviral DNA may remain in a latent phase for months or years until an event triggers activation of the cell and stimulates production of viral components with assembly of new virions that bud from the surface of the infected cell.

Pathogenesis of HIV Infection

The pathogenesis of HIV infection in humans is primarily through destruction of the immune system, although evidence is also accumulating which suggests that a number of the clinical findings may result from a primary response of the host to the infection.

The T4 lymphocyte, the primary cell infected with HIV, has a central role in regulating the human immune system, primarily by inducing the function of virtually all of the multiple components of the immune response. Activation of a T4 lymphocyte latently infected with HIV, therefore, may result in destruction of the cell (cytotoxicity) by one of a number of mechanisms that have been postulated. The percentage of susceptible cells infected with HIV is estimated to be low, suggesting that the depletion of T4 cells that is a hallmark of HIV infection may occur by mechanisms other than direct cytotoxicity of infected cells. One mechanism, for example, is believed to be fusion of the cell membrane of HIV-infected cells with those of other uninfected cells to form multinucleated giant cells, or syncytia, which result in death of all the involved cells. Autoimmune phenomena also are believed to play a role in cytotoxicity of T4 cells.

In addition to the quantitative depletion of T4 lymphocytes, HIV infection results in significant functional abnormalities of the cells. Because T4 lymphocytes play a central inducer role in the immune system function, the combined quantitative and qualitative deficits in the T4 cells associated with HIV infection result in significant functional abnormalities in other components of the immune system. For example, B cell function is abnormal, characterized by inadequate antibody response to antigens and a nonspecific polyclonal hyperactivity resulting in hypergammaglobulinemia; monocyte functions such as chemotaxis are impaired; and natural killer cell function is decreased.

An important component of HIV infection is the fact that the virus can establish a latent (no active virus production) or chronic (low-grade) infection of cells—probably both lymphocytes and monocytes—without inducing either significant immunologic or clinical abnormalities for years after infection has been established. The role of infected monocytes in this process is not yet fully established, but because of the relative immunity of these cells to HIV-induced cytotoxicity, it is possible that these cells may be the primary reservoir of HIV infection in the human body, at least under some circumstances. In addition, it has been postulated that monocytes are the primary source and reservoir of HIV infection of the brain.

The cell activators and stimulators of HIV production in latently infected cells have been termed "cofactors," although the range of cofactors and the way in which they function has not been fully defined. Evidence continues to accumulate that selected other viruses—for example, Epstein-Barr virus (EBV), cytomegalovirus (CMV), herpes simplex virus (HSV), or hepatitis B virus—may function as cofactors, although this area still requires extensive work.

AIDS: CLINICAL AND IMMUNOLOGIC FEATURES

Clinical Features of AIDS

Clinically, AIDS is the end stage of infection with HIV. The first diseases associated with AIDS were pneumonia caused by *P. carinii* and a previously rare skin cancer, Kaposi's sarcoma. Subsequently, an acute syndrome associated with HIV infection was recognized, and the extremely broad range of clinical conditions associated with HIV infection is much better appreciated (Yarchoan & Pluda, 1988).

Before the cause of AIDS was known, the definition of AIDS for surveillance purposes was narrow, tightly defined, and strictly clinical. It was revised in 1985 and again in 1987 by the Centers for Disease Control (CDC) to reflect the increased knowledge of clinical conditions associated with HIV infection and to incorporate the increase in sensitivity and specificity that could be obtained by including data from HIV antibody testing (Centers for Disease Control, 1987c).

The acute syndrome caused by HIV infection occurs in a variable proportion of clients. Onset of this acute illness is usually 3–6 weeks after the infection is believed to have occurred, and duration of illness ranges from a few days to approximately 2 weeks. Clinically, it is a transient mononucleosislike illness characterized by sudden onset of fever, malaise, headache, myalgia and arthralgia, lymphadenopathy, sore throat, skin rash, and occasionally gastrointestinal symptoms and weight loss. Some clients also have been described with viral meningitis or other neurologic symptoms, and rarely even with an opportunistic infection. Recovery is spontaneous. The nonspecific nature of the illness and variety of clinical manifestations make a correct diagnosis difficult unless a careful history suggests that exposure to HIV is possible. Specific diagnosis is based on seroconversion to HIV in the weeks or months following the illness.

Following acute infection, whether symptomatic or asymptomatic, the person usually enters a phase of infection characterized by absence of overt symptoms. In some persons, the first clinical manifestations of AIDS may be lymphadenopathy or nonspecific signs or symptoms of illness, or they may be specific opportunistic infections, neurologic conditions, or malignancies (including Kaposi's sarcoma). Ultimately, in some way, HIV has the potential for affecting virtually every organ system of the human body (Bartlett, Laughon, & Quinn, 1988; Brew, Rosenblum, & Price, 1988; Kovacs & Masur, 1988; Krigel & Friedman-Kien, 1988; Levine, 1988).

The natural histories of AIDS and HIV infection are still being described, so the relative frequency, time of onset, and duration of many clinical characteristics are not yet fully known. Generalized lymphadenopathy is a frequent finding, however, if it is carefully elicited on physical examination. Some combination of nonspecific signs and symptoms including fever, unintentional weight loss, chronic diarrhea, fatigue, and malaise, also are relatively frequent. These symptoms may not be readily recognized by the patient initially, and they can be attributed to a variety of causes other than HIV. In particular, in IV drug abusers who may have suboptimal nutrition and are subject to a variety of other infections and medical conditions, correctly attributing the clinical findings to a specific diagnosis may be difficult. These conditions by themselves usually are not life-threatening, but severe diarrhea and other clinical problems resulting in malnutrition and wasting can be fatal.

The combination of clinical findings in HIV-infected persons that do not satisfy the definition for AIDS often are subsumed by the terms AIDS-related complex (ARC), lesser AIDS, or pre-AIDS. These terms are themselves nonspecific and have created confusion in the literature. To try to avoid these problems, a classification scheme emphasizing the continuum of the spectrum of HIV infection has been developed (Centers for Disease Control, 1986a), but it has not been widely adopted.

Opportunistic infections secondary to waning cell-mediated immunity are the most prominent clinical hallmarks of HIV infection and AIDS. The infections range from those that are not usually life-threatening—such as oral candidiasis, herpes simplex, herpes zoster, or parasitic and protozoal gastrointestinal infections—to those such as *P. carinii* pneumonia that often are fatal (Kovacs & Masur, 1988). Significant opportunistic infections include those caused by protozoa, fungi, bacteria, and viruses. Examples include encephalitic or disseminated toxoplasmosis; candida esophagitis; crytococcosis, either meningitis or disseminated infection; atypical mycobacterial infections, particularly caused by *Mycobacterium avium-intracellulare;* salmonellosis; and CMV retinochoroiditis, pneumonia, or encephalitis. In HIV-infected IV drug abusers, bacterial pneumonias appear to be more frequent than in other HIV-infected adults (Selwyn et al., 1988).

Tuberculosis has been identified as an extremely important problem in persons with HIV infection and AIDS, particularly IV drug abusers (Centers for Disease Control, 1987d). In one cohort of IV drug abusers in New York City, 12 of 279 who had AIDS or were HIV-infected developed tuberculosis, compared with none of 240 persons who were not HIV-infected. In another unpublished study from New York City, 31 (53%) of 58 males hospitalized for suspected tuberculosis were positive for HIV-antibody. Increases in tuberculosis cases linked to AIDS and HIV infection have occurred in multiple areas, including New York, New Jersey,

Connecticut, and Florida. Although the exact reason for the interaction of these two infections is not known, it is probable that the declining cellular immunity of HIV-infected persons places them at high risk for clinical activation of a previously acquired latent tubercular infection. Diagnosis of tuberculosis may be difficult since persons with AIDS and HIV infection may have unusual clinical presentations of the disease, including infection at multiple sites and extrapulmonary involvement, loss of tuberculin skin reactivity, and absence of cavities even with extensive pulmonary disease. Because of the close interaction between HIV infection and tuberculosis, diagnosis of one infection should prompt a search for the other.

Neurologic conditions, including both CNS and peripheral nervous system conditions and dementia, are recognized as important complications of HIV infection (Brew et al., 1988). These conditions may occur early in infection, but they become increasingly common with progression of infection. They contribute significantly to the disability associated with HIV infection and to the difficulty in managing the client. The pathogenesis of these conditions includes not only direct HIV infection of the CNS, but also autoimmune disorders, opportunistic infections (e.g., cytomegaloviral or toxoplasma encephalitis), and space-occupying lesions (e.g., lymphoma involving the CNS).

Treatment of Clients with AIDS and HIV Infection

Treatment of clients with AIDS and HIV infection can be viewed on two levels: specific treatment for the HIV infection and specific treatment for the opportunistic infections and other diseases that occur in these persons.

At present, the most widely used and effective pharmacologic agent against HIV is a nucleoside analogue, 3'-azido-2',3'-dideoxythymidine (AZT or Zidovudine) (Yarchoan & Broder, 1988). It enhances life expectancy in persons with AIDS, and it is currently being evaluated in persons with HIV infection at various stages. The mechanism of action is to inhibit replication of HIV by acting at the level of the HIV DNA polymerase (reverse transcriptase). Other antiviral pharmacologic agents are being evaluated that similarly inhibit viral replication at various stages in the cycle. Since HIV establishes a chronic infection in human cells, with integration of proviral genome into the human chromosome, AZT and similar agents will at best inhibit replication of the virus during the time they are taken. They will not cure the viral infection. In addition, AZT and most of the other pharmacologic agents being developed have significant toxicity or side effects, and their use must be carefully monitored.

Other types of treatments for HIV infection being evaluated include those to stimulate the immune system. None of these has proved particularly promising yet.

Because AIDS is a fatal condition, many persons have argued strongly for more ready availability for persons with AIDS to new therapies that appear in laboratory testing or early clinical trials to have benefit, even though they have not been tested thoroughly for safety and efficacy. Many of these agents are available in other countries or can be obtained in the black market, with the result that persons with AIDS may try a variety of unproven or marginal drugs, most of which have not been studied for their interaction with other pharmacologic agents that may be prescribed for them.

Survival of AIDS clients also depends on early diagnosis of opportunistic infections and other complicating conditions and aggressive treatment of these conditions. Often the clinical response to treatment is less satisfactory than in clients with normal immune function, requiring that the treatments be continued for longer than usual or that the antimicrobial agents be delivered in higher doses. For HIV-infected clients with tuberculosis, a more aggressive treatment approach has been recommended because of higher treatment failure rates; clients should be carefully monitored for compliance and for adverse drug reactions (American Thoracic Society & Centers for Disease Control, 1987; Centers for Disease Control, 1986b).

Prophylactic treatments are also being evaluated to try to prevent selected opportunistic infections in persons with AIDS or who are significantly immunosuppressed secondary to their HIV infection—for example, aerosol pentamidine on a monthly basis is now recommended prophylaxis against *P. carinii* pneumonia. In HIV-infected infants and young children, some physicians use intravenous immune globulin to try to prevent opportunistic infections, and in adult patients, the issue of whether to consider preventive immunization with polysaccharide vaccines against *Streptococcus pneumoniae* and *Hemophilus influenzae* is being discussed since these bacteria are associated with pneumonia in many of these patients.

EPIDEMIOLOGY OF AIDS AND HIV INFECTION

AIDS Cases: Descriptive Epidemiology

Between June 1981, when the first cases were reported, and June 1989, almost 100,000 AIDS cases had been reported in the United States; more than 33,600 (34%) cases were reported in the last 12 months. Although mortality associated with AIDS is not completely reported to health departments, more than 58,000 (58%) deaths have been reported. Projections of the future trend of the epidemic made in May 1988 suggest that approximately 365,000 cumulative cases will be diagnosed and 263,000 deaths will have occurred in the United States by the end of 1992.

AIDS cases have been reported from all 50 states, Washington, DC, Puerto Rico, and several other territories. The most heavily affected states have been New York and California, with almost 43,000 cases between them; other heavily affected states have been Florida, New Jersey, and Texas (almost 7000 or more cases each), and Illinois, Pennsylvania, Puerto Rico, Georgia, Massachusetts, the District of Columbia, Maryland, Ohio, Louisiana, Washington, Connecticut, Michigan, Colorado, and Virginia (1000–3000 cases each). Most cases have occurred in urban areas. The incidence rate nationally during the 12 months ending June 1989 was 13.0/100,000 population, with rates in large, heavily affected metropolitan areas ranging as high as 47.5 (Miami), 53.6 (Newark), 64.5 (New York), 73.5 (Jersey City), 78.6 (San Juan), and 108.3 (San Francisco).

Transmission of HIV

HIV has been documented in multiple epidemiologic studies over the years to be transmitted by only three primary routes: sexual intercourse, whether male homosexual or heterosexual; parenteral infusion or inoculation of infectious blood, primarily through sharing of injection equipment by IV drug abusers; and congenital or perinatal transmission from an infected woman to her fetus or perhaps her infant at birth. The virus is not transmitted by person-to-person contact other than sexual intercourse and is not transmitted by insects, food, water, inanimate objects, or casual contact in families, schools, or the workplace.

Risk to Health Care Professionals and Family Members

More than 3500 persons who have worked in a health care setting have been reported with AIDS, but almost all have reported a high-risk behavior as the source of infection rather than occupational exposure. Prospective studies of the risk of infection to health professionals after direct accidental exposure to potentially infectious fluids or tissues from a person with AIDS or HIV infection in a health care setting have consistently documented the rate of transmission to be less than 0.5% (Marcus & the CDC Needlestick Surveillance Group, 1988). The exposures typical for health care workers included needlestick injuries (80%), cuts with sharp objects (8%), open wound contamination (7%), and mucous membrane exposure (5%). More than one-third of the exposures were judged to have been preventable if the worker had adhered to recommended infection control precautions (Centers for Disease Control, 1987b, 1988). It is important to emphasize that health professionals have not become infected with HIV from contact with patients while performing routine nursing and medical care or therapies.

Similarly, the defined ways in which HIV can be transmitted from one person to another mean that the probability of transmission of HIV in a household or family setting is immeasurably small except between sexual partners or persons sharing equipment for intravenous injection. Prospective studies that have followed family members living with or taking care of a person with HIV infection or AIDS have not found any evidence for transmission of the virus through routine family interactions or activities.

Natural History of HIV Infection

Although much remains to be learned about the natural history of HIV infection, a great deal already has been learned even though the epidemic was first recognized less than a decade ago. As indicated previously, HIV establishes a chronic infection in which immunologic and clinical manifestations often first appear years after the infection is established. Longitudinal studies of cohorts of people for whom a time of HIV infection can be determined suggest that few adults will develop AIDS during the first 2 years after infection. About 4% will have been diagnosed with AIDS 3 years after infection, and this increases to 15% after 5 years, 34%

after 7 years, and 50% or more after 10 years. Many of the persons who do not have AIDS at this point, however, do have other manifestations of HIV-related illness, including impaired immunologic function and clinical conditions such as lymphadenopathy or recurrent infections. Since HIV infection and AIDS are relatively new phenomena, it is impossible to know what the long-term effect of HIV infection will be in persons who have not been diagnosed with AIDS and appear to be healthy years after infection. Statistical projections from the available data, however, suggest that the majority will develop AIDS at some point.

Few studies of progression to AIDS have been conducted in cohorts of IV drug abusers because of problems with prospective follow-up of a cohort and missed diagnoses (a death attributed to a drug overdose, for example, may have been caused by AIDS that had not been diagnosed). Although the 5-year cumulative incidence of AIDS among a cohort of infected drug abusers in one study was 17%, the total mortality in the group was almost 50%, which was four times the mortality rate in drug abusers who were not infected with HIV (Goedert & Blattner, 1988). The excess mortality in the HIV-infected group quite possibly was related to HIV infection.

During the first years of the epidemic, median survival after a diagnosis of AIDS was no more than a year; fewer than 5% of patients survived as long as 4 years. With earlier and more accurate diagnoses of the complicating infections, the improvements in medical care that have occurred, and the availability of specific therapies, survival time after diagnosis of AIDS has improved, but is still less than 2 years for most persons.

EPIDEMIOLOGIC FEATURES OF AIDS IN IV DRUG ABUSERS

Demographic Features of AIDS Cases

As of the end of March 1989, a total of 24,267 AIDS cases had been reported in persons who gave a history of having injected drugs (Table 24.1); 17,898 (73.8%) cases were in heterosexual men and women and 6369 (26.2%) were in homosexual men. In this latter group, it is impossible to state with certainty what source of infection was of greater significance, although careful analysis of the data clearly suggests that patterns differ. For example, in San Francisco where the proportion of

AIDS cases in heterosexual IV drug abusers has been extremely low during the early years of the epidemic, the demographic features of the cases in male homosexual IV drug abusers have been similar to those in homosexual men with no history of drug abuse. In contrast, in New York City where the proportion of all cases that have a drug abuse history is high, the demographic features of male homosexual IV drug abusers have been much more similar to cases in male heterosexual IV drug abusers. Because of uncertainty about the source of infection in male homosexual IV drug abusers, the data about them are presented separately from cases in heterosexual men and women.

Of the heterosexual IV drug abusers with AIDS, 14.3% also have a second potential risk factor for HIV infection listed on the case report form. In only 2% of the cases was the other exposure judged to be of as high a risk as the history of drug abuse—for example, a history of receiving antihemophilic clotting factor—and in 81% the exposure was judged to be of moderate risk compared with the history of drug abuse, that is, a history of sexual contact with a heterosexual partner who was at risk of infection. For the male homosexual IV drug abuser with AIDS, 9.3% also had a history of a third (or more) potential exposure to HIV, the vast majority of which were not significant in comparison with the primary risk factors listed.

The proportion of AIDS cases in male homosexual IV drug abusers has decreased since the early years of the epidemic (Table 24.1). Among cases diagnosed before 1985, an average of 9.1% were in male homosexual IV drug abusers, but this group has accounted for only 6.5% of cases diagnosed and reported to date in 1987–1989. In contrast, the proportion of cases in heterosexual IV drug abusers has increased from only 12.1% of cases diagnosed before 1982 to 17.9% of cases diagnosed from 1982 through 1986, and 22.8% of cases diagnosed and reported in 1987–1989. This proportion is increasing for both men and women. These cumulative figures for heterosexual men and women obscure the important point that for women with AIDS, IV drug abuse is the primary risk factor for 52.1% of cases.

The age distribution of IV drug abusers with AIDS shows that only 0.3% are less than 19 at diagnosis, more than half (56.5%) are in their thirties, and only 4.3% are 50 years of age or older (Table 24.2). The age distribution for homosexual male IV drug abusers and for female IV drug abusers is similar and shows a shift toward a younger age at diagnosis than for heterosexual

Table 24.1
AIDS Cases Associated with IV Drug Abuse by Year of Diagnosis[a]

Year of Diagnosis	Total AIDS Cases	IV Drug Abuse-Associated AIDS Cases								
		Homosexual Men		Heterosexual Men		Heterosexual Women		Total	
		Number	Percent[b]	Number	Percent	Number	Percent	Number	Percent
Pre-1981	76	7	9.2	6	7.9	0	0.0	13	17.1
1981	279	17	6.1	26	9.3	11	3.9	54	19.4
1982	976	92	9.4	141	14.4	35	3.6	268	27.5
1983	2,842	276	9.7	402	14.0	115	4.0	793	27.9
1984	5,766	513	8.9	790	13.7	202	3.5	1,505	26.1
1985	10,653	788	7.4	1,513	14.2	405	3.8	2,706	25.4
1986	17,113	1,318	7.7	2,413	14.1	667	3.9	4,398	25.7
1987	24,230	1,623	6.7	3,731	15.4	1,139	4.7	6,493	26.8
1988	24,964	1,604	6.4	4,452	17.8	1,347	5.4	7,403	29.7
1989	2,086	131	6.3	386	18.5	117	5.6	634	30.4
TOTAL	88,985	6,369	7.2	13,860	15.6	4,038	4.5	24,267	27.3

[a] Cases diagnosed and reported through March 1989.
[b] Percent of total AIDS cases diagnosed that year.

male IV drug abusers. IV drug abusers are diagnosed with AIDS at a younger age on average than persons in most other transmission categories. The younger age at diagnosis for women is particularly puzzling since they would not generally be expected to start injecting drugs at a younger age than would men; it may indicate different patterns of drug use or a different susceptibility to infection or to disease once infected.

In contrast to the race and ethnic group distribution of all AIDS cases in adults, the distribution of cases in

Table 24.2
AIDS Cases Associated with IV Drug Abuse by Age at Diagnosis[a]

Age at Diagnosis	IV Drug Abuse-Associated AIDS Cases							
	Homosexual Men		Heterosexual Men		Heterosexual Women		Total	
	Number	Percent[b]	Number	Percent	Number	Percent	Number	Percent
13–19	21	0.3	21	0.2	20	0.5	62	0.3
20–29	1,730	27.2	2,189	15.8	1,115	27.6	5,034	20.7
30–39	3,400	53.4	7,997	57.7	2,323	57.5	13,720	56.5
40–49	1,007	15.8	2,905	21.0	496	12.3	4,408	18.2
> 50	211	3.3	748	5.4	84	2.1	1,043	4.3
TOTAL	6,369	100.0	13,860	100.0	4,038	100.0	24,267	100.0

[a] Cases diagnosed and reported through March 1989.
[b] Percent of total AIDS cases diagnosed that year.

Table 24.3
AIDS Cases Associated with IV Drug Abuse by Race/Ethnic Groups[a]

Racial or Ethnic Group	All AIDS Cases		IV Drug Abuse-Associated AIDS Cases					
			Homosexual Men		Heterosexual Men		Heterosexual Women	
	Number	Percent	Number	Percent	Number	Percent	Number	Percent
White	51,344	57.7	3,805	59.8	2,699	19.5	870	21.5
Black	23,403	26.3	1,608	25.2	6,628	47.8	2,324	57.6
Hispanic	13,392	15.1	925	14.5	4,481	32.3	815	20.2
Asian	525	0.6	8	0.1	11	0.1	9	0.2
Native American	107	0.1	14	0.2	7	0.1	10	0.2
Unknown	214	0.2	9	0.1	34	0.3	10	0.2
TOTAL	88,985	100.0	6,369	100.0	13,860	100.0	4,038	100.0

[a] Cases diagnosed and reported through March 1989.

heterosexual men and women who abuse drugs intravenously is markedly skewed—79.6% of the cases—toward black and Hispanic populations (Table 24.3). This is particularly dramatic in comparison with the distribution of the population in the 1980 census: 11.5% of the population was black and 6.4% of the population was Hispanic.

The geographic distribution of AIDS cases in IV drug abusers is equally dramatic, with five states—New York, New Jersey, California, Florida, and Texas—and Puerto Rico accounting for 77.4% of cases (Table 24.4). Puerto Rico has the highest percentage of total cases that are IV drug abuse associated (69.1%), but a large number of states in the northeastern United States and along the Atlantic coast also have a high proportion of cases that are in IV drug abusers. California and Texas have a relatively high percentage of cases in male homosexual IV drug abusers (9.9% and 10.1%, respectively), but in contrast have only a low proportion of cases among IV drug-abusing heterosexuals (3.8% and 4.8%, respectively). As discussed previously, this may indicate the relatively low probability that the male homosexual IV drug abusers in these states were infected with HIV through drug abuse. Although the distribution of AIDS cases in IV drug abusers shows a high degree of clustering, no area should be complacent since the vast majority of states have reported at least a few cases in IV drug abusers. This broad distribution of reported cases suggests that in all these areas many

more persons are HIV infected who will become ill in the future, and these persons are capable of transmitting infection to others if effective prevention programs are not implemented.

AIDS Cases in Sex Partners and Children

AIDS cases associated with IV drug abuse also occur in two other groups—heterosexual partners of IV drug abusers and children of couples in which one or both parents are IV drug abusers. Although only 2.2% of AIDS cases in adults are reported to be heterosexual persons who were infected through sexual contact with an IV drug abuser, this route accounts for 18.3% of cases in women. Even more unsettling is the fact that of the heterosexually transmitted AIDS cases among persons born in the United States, more than 73% of the cases in men and 71% of those in women were infected through sexual contact with an IV drug abuser. Studies of the heterosexual partners of men and women infected with HIV through IV drug abuse also demonstrate transmission of the virus from the infected person; the rate of transmission is variable, with reported prevalence rates ranging about 50% in steady sexual partners in some studies (Allen, 1988). The parameters that influence transmission of HIV among heterosexual persons have not been fully described.

Table 24.4
AIDS Cases Associated with IV Drug Abuse by Selected States/Territories of Residence[a]

State/ Territory	Total AIDS Cases	IV Drug Abuse-Associated AIDS Cases							
		Homosexual Men		Heterosexual Men		Heterosexual Women		Total	
		Number	Percent	Number	Percent	Number	Percent	Number	Percent
New York	21,041	964	4.6	6,162	29.3	1,629	7.7	8,755	41.6
New Jersey	6,031	281	4.7	2,433	40.3	790	13.1	3,504	58.1
California	18,037	1,786	9.9	541	3.0	146	0.8	2,473	13.7
Florida	6,965	450	6.5	864	12.4	377	5.4	1,691	24.3
Puerto Rico	2,067	253	12.2	980	47.4	196	9.5	1,429	69.1
Texas	6,187	623	10.1	240	3.9	59	1.0	922	14.9
Connecticut	1,091	72	6.6	286	26.2	131	12.0	489	44.8
Massachusetts	1,915	78	4.1	258	13.5	88	4.6	424	22.1
Illinois	2,542	117	4.6	225	8.9	49	1.9	391	15.4
Maryland	1,577	79	5.0	214	13.6	86	5.4	379	24.0
Pennsylvania	2,348	173	7.4	256	10.9	59	2.5	488	20.8
Georgia	2,152	187	8.7	148	6.9	34	1.6	369	17.1
Michigan	1,024	65	6.3	176	17.2	54	5.3	295	28.8
Washington, DC	1,574	97	6.2	96	6.1	40	2.5	233	14.8
North Carolina	754	57	7.6	104	13.8	35	4.6	196	26.0
Virginia	1,056	49	4.6	89	8.4	24	2.3	162	15.3
All other states	12,624	1,038	8.2	788	6.2	241	1.9	2,067	16.4
TOTAL	88,985	6,369	7.2	13,860	15.6	4,038	4.5	24,267	27.3

[a] Cases diagnosed and reported through March 1989; states and territories included that have reported >100 cases of IV drug abuse-associated AIDS among heterosexual men and women.

Of the pediatric AIDS cases reported in the United States, the source of infection in approximately 79% has been congenital or perinatal transmission. Of these children, about 52% have been born to an IV drug abuser mother and 20% have been born to a mother whose sex partner was an IV drug abuser. Because of the geographic, racial, and ethnic group distribution of AIDS cases in adults, most of these children have been clustered in the inner cities of the large urban areas of the northeastern United States, and a high proportion have been black or Hispanic.

Prevalence of HIV Infection in IV Drug Abusers

HIV infection is diagnosed in a person primarily through use of serologic tests for antibody against HIV. Data about the frequency of HIV infection among IV drug abusers are obtained by state and local health and drug abuse agencies and by agencies of the Public Health Service such as the National Institute on Drug Abuse of the Alcohol, Drug Abuse, and Mental Health Administration and the CDC. These seroprevalence surveys are limited in scope to persons who present to a drug abuse treatment facility or some other clinic or facility (e.g., hospital, sexually transmitted disease clinic, prison clinic) in which HIV antibody testing is performed and the risk factors recorded. Consequently, the seroprevalence data, although highly useful, are biased and only approximate the true situation.

Seroprevalence studies during the late 1980s suggest an extremely high rate of HIV infection among IV drug abusers in New York City (50%–60%), with the rate declining with distance from New York City. Selected studies in urban areas of northern New Jersey, Connecticut, Rhode Island, Massachusetts, Maryland, the District of

Columbia, and Puerto Rico all show rates of infection of approximately 10%–40%. Infection rates in IV drug abusers in other cities around the country in which both AIDS and IV drug abuse are common—including San Francisco, Los Angeles, Denver, Atlanta, Detroit, and Miami—are 5%–10%. Most other cities in which seroprevalence studies have been done show rates of HIV infection of 2% or less in the IV drug abuser populations studied. The reasons for the differences in the infection rates compared with those in homosexual and bisexual men probably include the timing of the introduction of HIV into the drug-using population and the patterns of use of drugs and sharing of injection equipment.

The best method of determining the incidence of new HIV infections is through longitudinal studies in a cohort of people. These studies have been difficult to do in IV drug abusers, and, as a surrogate, an increasing prevalence of HIV infection from a steady population sample has suggested an increasing incidence of infections. The incidence of HIV infection among IV drug abusers in the most heavily affected urban areas is still significant in contrast to the almost zero incidence among homosexual men reported in several studies done during the late 1980s.

Unsuspected HIV Infection in IV Drug Abusers

The impact of HIV infection in IV drug abusers in some areas of the United States and the association of HIV infection with other clinical conditions such as tuberculosis may be significantly greater than is commonly appreciated. In New York City, the number of unexpected deaths of young adult drug abusers has increased dramatically during the 1980s (Stoneburner et al., 1988). The causes of death have included nonspecific pneumonia, endocarditis, and tuberculosis, often in association with clinical or serologic evidence of HIV infection or AIDS-related conditions. Since these cases did not satisfy the clinical definition of AIDS used for surveillance and reporting to the health department, they were never reported. Health Department personnel in New York City estimate that from 1982 through 1986, approximately 2500 IV drug abusers in the city who were never reported as having AIDS died of HIV-related illness (Joseph, 1988). Including these deaths in the AIDS mortality statistics would have increased the proportion of IV drug abuse-related deaths in the city from 31% of the AIDS-related deaths to 53% during that time period.

As noted previously, CDC has revised the AIDS case definition used for surveillance purposes to broaden the clinical illnesses that are used to diagnose AIDS and has included a reporting classification for presumptively diagnosed cases where the diagnosis is strongly suspected but has not been determined definitively. The impact of the revised case definition, particularly for IV drug abusers with AIDS, is reflected in the fact that 29% of the AIDS cases reported since the revised definition was implemented satisfy only the broadened definition. HIV antibody test results are a critical component of the broadened case definition, however, and persons with clinical conditions compatible with HIV-related disease are not reported if HIV antibody testing is not done.

Sociology of HIV Transmission Among IV Drug Abusers

Transmission of HIV among IV drug abusers and their sexual partners is inextricably tied to the sociology of drug abuse. The person who abuses drugs by injection must have not only the drugs but also access to injection equipment. In many states it is illegal not only to purchase and use drugs such as heroin and cocaine, it is illegal to purchase or own needles and syringes except with a physician's prescription; thus the entire process of drug usage must be clandestine. This contributes to a climate in which equipment is shared among a circle of friends or acquaintances or in which equipment ("house works") is rented for a small fee at a "shooting gallery" or from the dealer (Des Jarlais & Friedman, 1988; Feldman & Biernacki, 1988). The pattern of behavior in which sharing of equipment is the norm is reinforced by both the social relationships of IV drug abuse and the biologic response of an addict who needs the next drug dose to avoid or counter withdrawal symptoms (Des Jarlais & Friedman, 1988).

Sexual behavior is the second important social aspect of HIV infection in IV drug abusers. In the United States, about three-fourths of IV drug abusers are males, which means that the majority primarily will have non-drug users as their steady sexual partners (Des Jarlais & Friedman, 1988). In addition, many drug abusers, both men and women, will trade sexual services for drugs or cash to buy drugs. A phenomenon of the late 1980s in the United States is the frequent use of sexual services by women in trade for crack cocaine, placing them at risk of HIV infection through sexual contact even though the drug of abuse is not injected.

PREVENTING HIV INFECTION IN DRUG ABUSERS

Preventing HIV infection among persons injecting drugs of abuse is an urgent and difficult task. Drug abusers function in a subculture that is distrustful of and often mutually hostile with the predominant society in which they live. The illegal status of the activity serves to highlight the problems of accessibility to those involved and difficulty of trying to deal with them in an open environment. This is compounded by the addictive nature of the drugs taken and the psychologic and social dependence on them even in the absence of physical addiction.

Although the common belief is that drug abusers are unaware of much that happens around them and do not care about their own personal health, studies of drug abusers suggest that the majority are well aware of and concerned about the AIDS epidemic and would like to be able to reduce their own personal risk (Feldman & Biernacki, 1988; Selwyn, Feiner, Cox, Lipshutz, & Cohen, 1987). Although many have taken steps to reduce their risk of HIV infection through their injection of drugs—even though the steps taken often are ineffective—they are much less likely to have taken steps to reduce risk of transmission to their sexual partners.

Outreach, Treatment Programs, and HIV Risk Reduction

The potential for HIV infection through IV drug abuse depends on the circulation of the virus among drug abusers in the community and on the frequency of drug injection and the pattern of sharing injection equipment. The most certain way to avoid infection is to stop using drugs, or if this is not possible, then to avoid sharing injection equipment. To accomplish these ends requires a sustained effort on the part of society in general, and drug abuse treatment programs, in particular, because it is not likely that most persons regularly abusing drugs will be able to achieve these by themselves.

The first problem, therefore, is getting the drug abuser to a treatment program. New Jersey and other areas have pioneered the use of outreach programs using specially trained ex-addicts to find drug abusers and give them basic information about AIDS and the dangers of drug abuse, and to try to convince them to come for treatment (they also provide information about disinfection of equipment and safer injection practices for those who will not come for treatment). These outreach education and recruitment programs have been effective at getting drug abusers to come for treatment.

The second problem is the availability of drug abuse treatment positions for those seeking treatment. While the National Institute on Drug Abuse estimates that there are about 1.1–1.3 million IV drug abusers in the United States, the number of positions in drug treatment programs was only about 148,000 in 1988. Efforts are under way in many areas to increase the number of available treatment positions, but demands for treatment generally exceed available positions, and waiting lists for entry into treatment may be months long (Des Jarlais & Friedman, 1988). The expansion of drug abuse treatment programs requires not only funding for the programs (at an estimated cost of almost $5000 per treatment position per year), it also requires the availability of health professionals for the new programs and community support to allow the development of the programs. All of these requirements make it unlikely that sufficient treatment positions to manage the need will become available in the near future.

The third problem is the quality and effectiveness of the treatment offered in the programs. Because of declining funds for drug treatment programs during the 1980s, services were frequently cut and sufficient well-trained personnel were not available, resulting in a decline in the quality of the programs and the effectiveness of treatment. While methadone maintenance programs for opiate abusers have been proved effective at reducing the frequency of drug use and needle-sharing among those who remain in the treatment program, the majority of persons who left treatment before being discharged relapsed to drug abuse (Ball, Lange, Myers, & Friedman, 1988). Unfortunately, similar types of specific pharmacotherapy for persons who are abusers of amphetamines and cocaine are not yet available, and further research is needed urgently in this area. For both opiate and nonopiate abusers, treatment for longer than a year often is necessary to achieve maximum effectiveness.

Because of the social and medical problems often associated with drug abuse (particularly if compounded by HIV infection), it is highly desirable to have drug abuse treatment centers that provide a range of medical and social services or that are affiliated with hospitals and clinics where these services are readily available to facilitate the coordination of care.

HIV Antibody Counseling and Testing for IV Drug Abusers

The public health community has placed major emphasis on the use of early diagnosis of HIV infection through the use of HIV antibody testing programs because this information, when coupled with counseling and education programs, can be used by an individual to reduce his or her own personal risk of infection if uninfected or to protect others if infected. In addition, the diagnosis of HIV infection can be used as an opportunity to plan medical care for that person and to refer sexual and needle-sharing partners for counseling and testing (Centers for Disease Control, 1987a).

Only a few studies have been done to evaluate the validity of these concepts in IV drug abusers. In general, persons who were infected modified their risk behavior more than did those who were negative (Des Jarlais & Friedman, 1988). While these results tend to support the utility of counseling and testing programs, it should be cautioned that the studies were performed in treatment settings in a highly supportive environment with many protections for the individual client. HIV antibody testing under other circumstances, particularly in the absence of counseling and without proper precautions to protect the confidentiality of the results could be detrimental.

The Public Health Service recommendation is that health professionals in all health care settings, including prison clinics, should seek a history of IV drug abuse from clients. All persons who have a history of or who are seeking treatment for IV drug abuse should be routinely counseled about AIDS and HIV infection and offered testing for HIV antibody (Centers for Disease Control, 1987a). Because of the profound implications of HIV infection for an individual, specific consent should be obtained before testing. A prerequisite for HIV antibody testing is counseling about the test and its implications before seeking permission to do the test, discussion about the significance of the test results after testing, and education about how to avoid acquiring or transmitting HIV infection. Persons who are found to be HIV infected should be instructed in how to notify their sexual and needle-sharing partners and to refer

them for counseling and testing; if they are unwilling to notify their partners or if it cannot be assured that their partners will seek counseling, health department personnel should be requested to assist with notification using confidential procedures (Centers for Disease Control, 1987a).

Needle Disinfection and Exchange Programs

Studies of IV drug abusers during recent years clearly indicate that many persons who continue to inject drugs have modified injection practices because of concern about AIDS. The most frequently reported changes in behavior have been attempts to obtain clean needles, to disinfect those available, and to reduce sharing of injection equipment. Unfortunately, however, methods to disinfect equipment by rinsing too often are not likely to be effective, and providers of "clean" needles often repackage previously used equipment and resell them as new.

Outreach and education programs in areas such as New York City, New Jersey, Baltimore, Washington, DC, Chicago, and San Francisco have attempted to educate drug abusers who do not wish to seek treatment about safer ways to inject drugs, including boiling equipment or rinsing it with hypochlorite (bleach) solutions. These methods obviously are effective only if used correctly and consistently and without any sharing of equipment among friends or partners. Even in areas where these practices have been strongly advocated, it is not clear what the impact has been on the transmission of HIV infection among drug abusers.

In a few areas of the United States—and more widely in Europe—drug treatment programs have attempted to reduce transmission of HIV among IV drug abusers by making sterile needles and syringes available through a distribution or exchange program. Although these programs have been in existence in some areas for a number of years, the way in which they operate has made it extremely difficult to obtain unequivocal evidence of their efficacy. These programs have remained extremely controversial because public health and political leaders are reluctant to endorse any program that appears to encourage or even condone the continued use of drugs. In addition, there is concern among drug treatment advocates that reliance on less expensive methods of HIV infection prevention, such as needle exchange, would reduce the urgency for creation of more treatment program positions and the education of additional workers for these programs.

Avoiding HIV Infection: Precautions for Health Professionals

HIV is extremely unlikely to be transmitted from infected persons to health care workers providing routine care. Because personnel who have contact with blood or other body fluids or tissues containing visible blood are at risk of infection with HIV, hepatitis B virus, and other bloodborne pathogens, infection control efforts for these pathogens should focus on preventing exposures to blood (and on immunization against hepatitis B to prevent infection with this virus).

The basic element of infection control against these exposures is appropriate barrier precautions, referred to as Universal Blood and Body Fluid Precautions (or simply as Universal Precautions) (Centers for Disease Control, 1987b, 1988). Universal precautions are intended to supplement rather than replace recommendations for routine infection control, such as routine handwashing. Examples of barriers that are used are gloves, gowns, masks, and protective eyewear. Gloves should reduce the incidence of contamination of the hands, but they cannot prevent penetrating injuries due to needles or other sharp objects. These barriers should be used when it is anticipated that the worker will be exposed to blood or other body fluids or tissues that are likely to be contaminated with blood. Gowns would be used only for procedures in which it is likely that clothing will be soiled with blood, and masks and protective eyewear are recommended only for procedures in which it is likely that blood will be splashed or splattered.

Standard sterilization and disinfection procedures for patient care equipment and environmental surfaces are adequate for those items and surfaces contaminated with blood or other body fluids from persons infected with bloodborne pathogens, including HIV (Centers for Disease Control, 1987b). Studies have shown that HIV is rapidly inactivated after being exposed to commonly used chemical germicides at concentrations that are much lower than used in practice. In addition to commercially available chemical germicides, a solution of sodium hypochlorite (household bleach) prepared daily is an inexpensive and effective germicide against HIV for use on environmental surfaces. Dilutions ranging from 1:10 to 1:100 are effective depending on the amount of organic material (e.g., blood, mucus) present on the surface to be cleaned and disinfected. Commercially available chemical germicides may be more compatible with certain medical devices that might be corroded by repeated exposure to sodium hypochlorite.

SUMMARY

The recognition that IV drug abusers and sexual partners of IV drug abusers are at high risk for contracting AIDS has dramatically affected many aspects of the treatment of substance abusers. The etiology, clinical features, and epidemiologic and sociological considerations of HIV infection and AIDS in IV drug abusers are explored. Basic understanding of the transmission of HIV and infection control is necessary to allay the fears of health professionals and clients alike.

Health professionals in treatment settings must use these facts to facilitate appropriate testing and counseling with clients. The serious nature of opportunistic infections, such as tuberculosis and bacterial pneumonias, in AIDS clients who depend on substances of abuse requires the cooperation of the entire health team. The treatment of life-threatening illnesses and the need to address attendant issues of grief and death, compound the commonly encountered treatment issues surrounding achieving and maintaining sobriety. Health professionals in all treatment settings must use Universal Precautions to minimize risk to themselves. Reduction of the risk of HIV infection in substance abusers depends on outreach education, recruitment programs, and the availability of effective treatment programs.

REFERENCES

Allen, J. R. (1988). Heterosexual transmission of human immunodeficiency virus (HIV) in the United States. *Bulletin of the New York Academy of Medicine, 64,* 464–479.

American Thoracic Society & Centers for Disease Control (1987). Mycobacterioses and the acquired immunodeficiency syndrome. *American Review of Respiratory Diseases, 136,* 492–496.

Ball, J. C., Lange, W. R., Myers, C. P., & Friedman, S. R. (1988). Reducing the risk of AIDS through methadone maintenance treatment. *Journal of Health and Social Behavior, 29,* 214–226.

Bartlett, J. G., Laughon, B., & Quinn, T. C. (1988). Gastrointestinal complications of AIDS. In V. T. DeVita, Jr., S. Hellman, & S. A. Rosenberg (Eds.), *AIDS—Etiology, Diagnosis, Treatment, and Prevention* (2d ed.), (pp. 227–244). Philadelphia: J. B. Lippincott.

Brew, B., Rosenblum, M., & Price, R. W. (1988). Central and peripheral nervous system complications of HIV infection and AIDS. In V. T. DeVita, Jr., S. Hellman, & S. A. Rosenberg (Eds.), *AIDS—Etiology, Diagnosis, Treatment, and Prevention* (2d ed.), (pp. 185–198). Philadelphia: J. B. Lippincott.

Centers for Disease Control (1986a). Classification system for human T-lymphotropic virus type III/lymphadenopathy-associated virus infections. *Morbidity and Mortality Weekly Report, 35,* 334–339.

Centers for Disease Control (1986b). Diagnosis and management of mycobacterial infection and disease in persons with human T-lymphotropic virus type III/lymphadenopathy-associated virus infection. *Morbidity and Mortality Weekly Report, 35,* 448–452.

Centers for Disease Control (1987a). Public Health Service guidelines for counseling and antibody testing to prevent HIV infection and AIDS. *Morbidity and Mortality Weekly Report, 36,* 509–515.

Centers for Disease Control (1987b). Recommendations for prevention of HIV transmission in health-care settings. *Morbidity and Mortality Weekly Report, 36* (Suppl. 2S), 1–16.

Centers for Disease Control (1987c). Revision of the CDC surveillance case definition for acquired immunodeficiency syndrome. *Morbidity and Mortality Weekly Report, 36* (Suppl. 1S), 1S–15S.

Centers for Disease Control (1987d). Tuberculosis and acquired immunodeficiency syndrome—New York. *Morbidity and Mortality Weekly Report, 36,* 785–790, 795.

Centers for Disease Control (1988). Update: Universal precautions for prevention of transmission of human immunodeficiency virus, hepatitis B virus, and other blood-borne pathogens in health-care settings. *Morbidity and Mortality Weekly Report, 37,* 377–382, 387–388.

Des Jarlais, D. C., & Friedman, S. R. (1988). Transmission of human immunodeficiency virus among intravenous drug users. In V. T. DeVita, Jr., S. Hellman, & S. A. Rosenberg (Eds.), *AIDS—Etiology, Diagnosis, Treatment, and Prevention* (2d ed.), (pp. 385–395). Philadelphia: J. B. Lippincott.

Feldman, H. W., & Biernacki, P. (1988). The ethnography of needle sharing among intravenous drug users and implications for public policies and intervention strategies. In R. J. Battjes & R. W. Pickens (Eds.), *Needle Sharing Among Intravenous Drug Abusers: National and International Perspectives* (NIDA Research Monograph 80, pp. 28–39). Washington, DC: U. S. Government Printing Office.

Goedert, J. J., & Blattner, W. A. (1988). The epidemiology and natural history of human immunodeficiency. In V. T. DeVita, Jr., S. Hellman, & S. A. Rosenberg (Eds.), *AIDS—Etiology, Diagnosis, Treatment, and Prevention* (2d ed.) (pp. 33–60). Philadelphia: J. B. Lippincott.

Joseph, S. C. (1988). Political and social issues surrounding AIDS. *Bulletin of the New York Academy of Medicine, 64,* 506–512.

Kovacs, J. A., & Masur, H. (1988). Opportunistic infections. In V. T. DeVita, Jr., S. Hellman, & S. A. Rosenberg (Eds.), *AIDS—Etiology, Diagnosis, Treatment, and Prevention* (2d ed.), (pp. 199–226). Philadelphia: J. B. Lippincott.

Krigel, R. L., & Friedman-Kien, A. E. (1988). Kaposi's sarcoma in AIDS: Diagnosis and treatment. In V. T. DeVita, Jr., S. Hellman, & S. A. Rosenberg (Eds.), *AIDS—Etiology, Diagnosis, Treatment, and Prevention* (2d ed.), (pp. 245–262). Philadelphia: J. B. Lippincott.

Levine, A. M. (1988). Reactive and neoplastic lymphoproliferative disorders and other miscellaneous cancers associated with HIV infection. In V. T. DeVita, Jr., S. Hellman, & S. A. Rosenberg (Eds.), *AIDS—Etiology, Diagnosis, Treatment, and Prevention* (2d ed.), (pp. 263–276). Philadelphia: J. B. Lippincott.

Marcus, R. & the CDC Cooperative Needlestick Surveillance Group (1988). Surveillance of health care workers exposed to blood from patients infected with human immunodeficiency virus. *New England Journal of Medicine, 319,* 1118–1123.

Selwyn, P. A., Feiner, C., Cox, C. P., Lipshutz, C., & Cohen, R. L. (1987). Knowledge about AIDS and high-risk behavior among intravenous drug users in New York City. *AIDS, 1,* 247–254.

Selwyn, P. A., Feingold, A. R., Hartel, D., Schoenbaum, E. E., Alderman, M. H., Klein, R. S., & Friedland, G. H. (1988). Increased risk of bacterial pneumonia in HIV-infected intravenous drug users without AIDS. *AIDS, 2,* 267–272.

Stoneburner, R. L., Des Jarlais, D. C., Benezra, D., Gorelkin, L., Sotheran, J. L., Friedman, S. R., Schultz, S., Marmor, M., Mildvan, D., & Maslansky, R. (1988). A larger spectrum of severe HIV-1-related disease in intravenous drug users in New York City. *Science, 242,* 916–919.

Yarchoan, R., & Broder, S. (1988). Pharmacologic treatment of HIV infection. In V. T. DeVita, Jr., S. Hellman, & S. A. Rosenberg (Eds.), *AIDS—Etiology, Diagnosis, Treatment, and Prevention* (2d ed.), (pp. 277–294). Philadelphia: J. B. Lippincott.

Yarchoan, R., & Pluda, J. M. (1988). Clinical aspects of infection with AIDS retrovirus: Acute HIV infection, persistent generalized lymphadenopathy, and AIDS-related complex. In V. T. DeVita, Jr., S. Hellman, & S. A. Rosenberg (Eds.), *AIDS—Etiology, Diagnosis, Treatment, and Prevention* (2d ed.), (pp. 107–120). Philadelphia: J. B. Lippincott.

APPENDIX A | RESOURCES

Addiction Research Foundation
33 Russell Street
Toronto, Ontario, Canada M5S2S1

Al-Anon Family Group Headquarters
P.O. Box 182
Madison Square Station
New York, NY 10010

Alcohol and Drug Abuse Nursing Program
Department of Psychosocial Nursing, SC-76
University of Washington
Seattle, WA 98195

Alcoholics Anonymous
General Service Office
P.O. Box 459
Grand Central Station
New York, NY 10164-0371

American Cancer Society
1599 Clifton Road, N.E.
Atlanta, GA 30329

American Lung Association
1740 Broadway
New York, NY 10019-4374

Cambridge and Sommerville Program for Alcoholism
    Rehabilitation (CASPAR)
Alcohol Education Program
226 Highland Avenue
Sommerville, MA 02143

Children Are People, Inc.
Chemical Abuse Prevention Programs
493 Selby Avenue
St. Paul, MN 55102

Children of Alcoholics Foundation
200 Park Avenue, 31st Floor
New York, NY 10166

Cocaine Anonymous
P.O. Box 1367
Culver City, CA 90232

Comp Care Publishers
Box 2415
Annapolis Lane
Minneapolis, MN 55441

Delancey Street Foundation
2563 Divisadero Street
San Francisco, CA 94115

Families Anonymous
P.O. Box 528
Van Nuys, CA 91408

Gay International Advisory Council
P.O. Box 492
Village Station
New York, NY 10614

Healthy Mothers, Healthy Babies National Coalition
600 Maryland Avenue, S.W.
Suite 300-E
Washington, DC 20024-2588

Kids Are Special
525 Race Street
San Jose, CA 95126

March of Dimes Birth Defects Foundation
1275 Mamaroneck Avenue
White Plains, NY 10606

Nar-Anon Family Headquarters
P.O. Box 2562
Palos Verdes Peninsula, CA 90274

Narcotics Anonymous
World Service Office
16155 Wyandotte Street
Van Nuys, CA 91406

National Cancer Institute
9000 Rockville Pike
Bethesda, MD 20892

National Clearinghouse for Alcohol and
    Drug Information
P.O. Box 2345
6000 Executive Blvd., Suite 402
Rockville, MD 20852

National Council on Alcoholism
12 West 21st Street
New York, NY 10010

National Institute on Alcohol Abuse and Alcoholism
U.S. Department of Health and Human Services
5600 Fishers Lane
Rockville, MD 20857

National Institute on Drug Abuse
U.S. Department of Health and Human Services
5600 Fishers Lane
Rockville, MD 20857

National Nurses Society on Addictions
2506 Gross Point Road
Evanston, IL 60201

National Self-Help Clearing House
Graduate School and University Center
City University of New York
33 West 42nd Street
New York, NY 10036

Office on Smoking and Health
Center for Disease
Park Building, Room 1-10
5600 Fishers Lane
Rockville, MD 20857

Overeaters Anonymous
4025 Spencer Street, #203
Torrance, CA 90504

Pacific Institute for Research and Evaluation
7101 Wisconsin Avenue, Suite 805
Bethesda, MD 20814

Pills Anonymous
184 East 76th Street
New York, NY 10021

Potsmokers Anonymous
316 East 3rd Street
New York, NY 10009

Rutgers Center of Alcohol Studies
Rutgers University
Smithers Hall
Busch Campus
Piscataway, NJ 08855-0969

SmokEnders
18551 Von Carmen Avenue
Irvine, CA 92715

Vista Hill Foundation
Drug Abuse and Alcoholism Newsletter
Suite 100
3420 Camino del Rio North
San Diego, CA 92108

Women for Sobriety, Inc.
Box 618
Quakertown, PA 18951

B | PSYCHOACTIVE SUBSTANCE USE DISORDERS: APA DIAGNOSTIC AND STATISTICAL MANUAL OF MENTAL DISORDERS, THIRD EDITION-REVISED (DSM-III-R)

303.90	Alcohol dependence
305.00	Alcohol abuse
304.40	Amphetamine or similarly acting sympathomimetic dependence
305.70	Amphetamine or similarly acting sympathomimetic abuse
304.30	Cannabis dependence
305.20	Cannabis abuse
304.20	Cocaine dependence
305.60	Cocaine abuse
304.50	Hallucinogen dependence
305.30	Hallucinogen abuse
304.60	Inhalant dependence
305.90	Inhalant abuse
305.10	Nicotine dependence
304.00	Opioid dependence
305.50	Opioid abuse
304.50	Phencyclidine (PCP) or similarly acting arylcyclohexylamine dependence
305.90	Phencyclidine (PCP) or similarly acting arylcyclohexylamine abuse
304.10	Sedative, hypnotic, or anxiolytic dependence
305.40	Sedative, hypnotic, or anxiolytic abuse
304.90	Polysubstance dependence
304.90	Psychoactive substance dependence not otherwise specified
305.90	Psychoactive substance abuse not otherwise specified

C NATIONAL NURSES SOCIETY ON ADDICTIONS POSITION STATEMENT ON THE ROLE OF THE NURSE IN ALCOHOLISM

The National Nurses Society on Addictions (NNSA) affirms its belief that alcoholism is a primary disease. NNSA also stresses the fact that nursing in alcoholism transcends the traditional dividing lines of clinical nursing specialties; that nursing care of alcoholic individuals and families is encompassed in every nursing specialty and not exclusively Psychiatric-Mental Health Nursing.

At its Annual Meeting in April, 1978, NNSA developed a statement of beliefs concerning the definitive role of nursing in caring for alcoholic individuals, families, and significant others. This statement grew out of questions raised at previous annual meetings and the perceived need of many members for a clear delineation of functions by which to conduct their day-to-day nursing practice. It seemed appropriate that NNSA, as the official nursing component of the National Council on Alcoholism*, should establish a position which would stand as a baseline in guiding nursing actions in the field of alcoholism as well as in all areas where nurses encounter the disease of alcoholism in their practice. From this baseline, further analysis and evaluation can be made which would result in further development and refinement of the position paper.

Four areas of nursing practice were examined: Direct Service, Education, Management, and Research. The area of Direct Service was further subdivided into Direct Service—General Setting and Direct Service—Alcoholism-specific Setting in order to highlight the potential distinctions in nursing functions. The following general categories of nursing intervention were then examined within each of the (now) five areas:

*NNSA is now an independent organization (see Chapter 16).

Note. Reprinted by permission of the National Nurses Society on Addictions.

1. *Identifying the Problem with Alcohol.* In all five areas of nursing practice, NNSA holds that it is indeed appropriately the role of the nurse to systematically assess each patient in any setting for problems related to alcohol abuse and alcoholism. Each nurse should further identify the stage of progression of alcoholism based on the physical and psychosocial data which she has obtained in her nursing assessment. Procedures and policies of both alcohol-specific and general-care facilities should provide for such client assessment in cooperation with the interdisciplinary health team. It is the responsibility of Nursing Education at all levels to provide theoretical content and learning experiences which enable the learner to identify alcohol abuse and alcoholism in their patients. At present, nursing research is needed to determine the extent to which the preceding are being implemented in actual practice. Later, the effectiveness of such nursing assessment should be measured. Clinical nursing research might also identify specific nursing criteria for assessing the existence and severity of the alcohol problem.

2. *Communicating about the Problem with Alcohol.* NNSA believes it is appropriate nursing intervention to open communication about the problem with alcohol with the patient, with the family or significant others, and with appropriate members of the interdisciplinary health team. Communication concerning the problem should be based on a body of knowledge and a philosophy which are conducive to recovery and approached in a consistent, nonjudgmental manner. Nurses in a general care setting may require the guidance of a clinical specialist in alcoholism in order to acquire the necessary knowledge and skills for communicating directly about the problem. A

future goal would be that all nurses would obtain the necessary knowledge and skills in their basic nursing education with which to open communication about alcohol problems and alcoholism. Nursing education, management, and research must provide for the appropriate knowledge, methods, and tools to reach this goal.

3. *Educating about Alcohol Use, Abuse, and Alcoholism.* NNSA firmly believes that every nurse is responsible for educating patients, families, and significant others concerning alcohol use, abuse, and alcoholism. Additionally, nurses with special knowledge and skills in alcoholism should educate other members of the interdisciplinary health team as well as community groups. As the natural and logical health educator, the nurse is able to teach in both informal and formal settings and is able to use systematic and individualized approaches according to the needs of the learners. Nursing education and management must provide for the necessary knowledge, skills, and resources to ensure that the teaching role will be implemented. Nursing research must be aimed at devising improved measurements of teaching effectiveness and thus improved teaching methods and materials.

4. *Counseling the Alcoholic Individual, Family, and Significant Others about Alcoholism and Its Resulting Problems.* It is NNSA's position that nurses in all settings should have a basic level of knowledge and skill to provide some alcoholism counseling. The use of the defense mechanism of denial by alcoholic individuals, families, and significant others is a major deterrent to recovery. Recognizing that inadvertent reinforcement of that denial by the nurse can be detrimental, it is crucial that nurses intervene to identify and confront it. In alcohol-specific settings, it is appropriate that nurses additionally have direct counseling functions, including individual and group therapy, and that they be active members of the treatment team. Nursing management should ensure that the counseling functions of the nurse are included in job descriptions and in nursing care plans for alcoholic patients. Evaluation of the fulfill-

ment of these functions should be an integral part of nursing supervision. Nursing educators must accept the responsibility of incorporating basic alcoholism counseling skills in all levels of nursing education. Nursing research might demonstrate the effectiveness of nurses as counselors as well as the comparative effectiveness of counseling approaches by nurses.

5. *Referring for Further Definitive Alcoholism Treatment and/or After-Care.* NNSA believes that all nurses in any setting should be sufficiently knowledgeable about available resources to initiate an appropriate treatment referral when the alcoholic patient and/or significant others express readiness for help. The importance of timing in such a referral cannot be overemphasized. Nurses who practice in alcohol-specific settings should acquire additional knowledge of resources in order to individually match the agent/agency to the needs of the patient, family, and/or significant other. Successful recovery may depend upon the appropriateness of the treatment or after-care referral. Continuity of care and follow-up are essential nursing responsibilities in all settings. Nursing management should provide procedural information and directories which assist nurses in discharge planning and in the referral process. Faculty of schools of nursing should be knowledgeable about national and regional as well as local resources in order to teach and encourage students to make appropriate referrals for alcoholism treatment and after-care. Nursing research should evaluate the appropriateness of nursing referrals and their effectiveness in providing continuity and quality of care.

NNSA has herein addressed only those functions of the nurse which directly and specifically define the role of the nurse in relation to the problem with alcohol. Comprehensive nursing care in alcoholism does encompass a wide range of nursing functions and responsibilities which are not necessarily unique to alcoholism per se. For the sake of clarity and brevity, nursing functions which are common in the care of all or many other categories of patients have been intentionally omitted.

INDEX